THE YOUNG TURKS IN OPPOSITION

STUDIES IN MIDDLE EASTERN HISTORY

Bernard Lewis, Itamar Rabinovich, and Roger Savory, *General Editors*

OTHER VOLUMES ARE IN PREPARATION

THE YOUNG TURKS
IN OPPOSITION

M. ŞÜKRÜ HANIOĞLU

NEW YORK   OXFORD
OXFORD UNIVERSITY PRESS
1995

Oxford University Press

Oxford   New York
Athens   Auckland   Bangkok   Bombay
Calcutta   Cape Town   Dar es Salaam   Delhi
Florence   Hong Kong   Istanbul   Karachi
Kuala Lumpur   Madras   Madrid   Melbourne
Mexico City   Nairobi   Paris   Singapore
Taipei   Tokyo   Toronto

and associated companies in
Berlin   Ibadan

Library of Congress Cataloging-in-Publication Data
Hanioğlu, M. Şükrü.
The Young Turks in opposition / M. Şükrü Hanioğlu.
p. cm.   Includes bibliographical references and index.
ISBN 0-19-509115-9
1. Ittihat ve Terakki Cemiyeti
2. Turkey—Politics and government—1878–1909.
3. Turkey—Politics and government—1909–1918.
I. Title.   DR572.5.H37   1995   320.9561—dc20
94-18606

2 4 6 8 9 7 5 3 1

Printed in the United States of America
on acid-free paper

Acknowledgments

I owe a debt of gratitude to Professors Abraham L. Udovitch and Bernard Lewis, who approached me about presenting my research on the Young Turks before the English-speaking public. Professor Michael Cook has given invaluable assistance by his most able guidance throughout the preparation of this text. I also wish to thank Ms. Dalia Geffen, Professors Magda al-Nowaihi, Gökhan Çetinsaya, Richard L. Chambers, François Georgeon, Dimitri Gondicas, Norman Itzkowitz, Hasan Kayalı, Rashid Khalidi, Heath Lowry, Hossein Modarrisi, Hasan Ünal, Erik J. Zürcher; and also Mr. Benjamin Fortna, Ms. Nilüfer Hatemi, Mr. Ronen Raz, and Mr. Mehmet Ulucan, who contributed to this study in various ways.

Princeton   M.Ş.H.
June 1994

Contents

Note on Transliteration

The sources and names in Ottoman Turkish are rendered in modern Turkish usage without transliteration, as is normally done in modern Turkish writing. The Arabic and Persian sources and names are transliterated according to the transliteration system of the International Journal of Middle East Studies (IJMES). The Greek sources and journal names are given in Greek script. Slavic sources are transliterated according to the modified Library of Congress transliteration system. There was no standard use for Albanian in Latin chararacters at the turn of the twentieth century, and the original usage found in the sources is preserved and is not converted into modern Albanian usage. Since the Ottoman intellectuals wrote their names differently when they published articles or works in languages written in Latin characters, one might find a single person's name written in two or more different ways. In this book, the original usage is preserved. Therefore, we have Abdullah Djevdet and Ahmed Riza when they wrote in French, but Abdullah Cevdet and Ahmed Rıza when they wrote in Turkish.

THE YOUNG TURKS IN OPPOSITION

1

Introduction

This book is about the Young Turk opposition movement against the regime of Abdülhamid II, with particular emphasis on the Committee of Union and Progress (CUP). It begins by examining the inception of the original CUP nucleus in 1889 and continues to expose in detail the internal workings of the movement until 1902. I chose to write about this phase of the CUP because it is seminal and because a clear demarcation can be made in 1902, at which time the network collapsed, leading to the formation of drastically different organizations. I believe that such an in-depth study is long overdue, not least because the Young Turks had a formative and lasting impact on the modern Turkish state.

The CUP, an outgrowth of the Young Turk movement, constituted the major ruling power in the Ottoman Empire between 1908 and 1918 except for a brief interlude; the founders of modern Turkey, including the first three presidents, serving from 1923 to 1960, were former CUP members.[1] Further, although the period 1889–1908 has been viewed as remote by some political scientists, the official ideology of modern Turkey as shaped during this period by the early Young Turks has continued to exert its influence even today on Turkey's intellectual and political life. Clarification of this period is thus both fundamental and essential to serious studies of events since 1889.

Too many scholars have overlooked the movement prior to the revolution of 1908, preferring to concentrate their efforts on the aftermath— the Young Turks in power. Moreover, the body of scholarship on events prior to 1908 is marked by four major methodological flaws.

3

First, there has been very little scholarship based on the private papers of the CUP. The CUP was an underground organization from the formation of its first nucleus in 1889 until the revolution of 1908. This fact makes a meticulous examination of the private papers of the CUP essential to any serious study of its agenda and/or ideology. In virtually every domain, one can find evidence to show that whatever was claimed in the official organs of the movement was contradicted by decisions taken by its executive branches. For instance, while its official organs were promoting an Ottomanist policy, the central committee was shifting to Turkish nationalism. Also, Turkish journals published by the CUP and official organs published abroad in other languages for European public consumption consistently promoted divergent themes.[2]

The presumption of a monolithic political organization is a second methodological problem. Thus far researchers have acknowledged only the struggle for leadership, especially that between Murad Bey and Ahmed Rıza. Abundant material reveals the fallacy of this presumption. The CUP was an umbrella organization until 1902 and was overflowing with member groups whose only common agenda was the dethronement of Abdülhamid II. Nor did the CUP maintain a constant identity, for it passed through ongoing transformations involving its ideology, its leadership, the ethnic origins of its leaders, and its membership; it is even plausible to speak of at least three different organizations having the name CUP in common. Therefore the CUP of 1889–1902 bore little resemblance to the CUP of 1906–1908 except that a scattering of individual members remained from the earlier period.

Third, the vague and inaccurate use of the term *Young Turk,* especially in the writings of non-Turkish scholars, has created confusion, because many activities have been falsely attributed to the Young Turks. There were many independent groups working in the Ottoman Empire against the regime of Abdülhamid II, and only some of these had dealings with the Young Turks.

The fourth methodological failure found in every study to date is that each examined the CUP as if it were a single-faceted phenomenon. But this subject presents at least three essential and interrelating aspects for historical analysis. It is a topic of Ottoman political history; it was an affair in the diplomatic history of Europe; and it was a watershed in Ottoman intellectual history.

Regarding work by various scholars, we may observe that for many years Turkish scholars approached this topic from the mind-set of the "new history thesis" prevalent in early modern Turkey, according to which all late Ottoman events were analyzed starting from a single critical question: Why did the members of certain movements fail to accomplish missions that were later successfully realized by the current regime? This theme prompted excellent research into the Tanzimat movement by various scholars even within these constraints.[3] Although virtually every political leader in Turkey during the late 1920s had belonged to the CUP, it became incumbent upon them to repudiate allegiance to it and to distance themselves from any current association with that society. During the War for Turkish National Independence in 1919–1922, CUP leaders attempted to dominate the nationalist movement, which deepened the estrangement between the existing CUP and the new republican leaders, although all had once been members. In 1926 active CUP members openly opposed the new regime in Turkey and were repulsed, and at this point the emerging negative approach to the CUP was firmly locked into place.

Hikmet Bayur, assigned to write the history of the Turkish revolution, used the fact that he was a grandson of Kâmil Pasha, the most outstanding opponent of the CUP after 1908, to lend authority to his heavily censorious examination of the movement.[4] Ahmed Bedevî Kuran, a prerevolutionary member of the CUP, published four books between 1945 and 1960 that included many documents of vital importance to scholars.[5] However, his study lacked analytical method, and his former membership in the faction led by Sabahaddin Bey detracted from some valid questions that he raised. Also his criticisms of the followers of Ahmed Rıza and of the activist-nationalist faction were excessive and heavy-handed.

All the works by Turkish scholars paid scant attention to the Young Turk *Weltanschauung* and viewed the CUP as a mere political organization. With the exception of a single article by Tunaya,[6] the ideas of the Young Turks have been examined only by Mardin, who accurately scrutinized their convictions as expressed in the official organs of the CUP.[7] His comments are extremely well constructed, and his work serves well as a political theory analysis; it was never intended to be a full historical account of the movement and the CUP.

As for works by non-Turkish scholars, the greatest obstacle seems to have been the material. Even Ramsaur's classic work contains few original sources, those being letters written to him by various former CUP members in response to his own questions.[8] However, none of those members had played a significant role in the movement, and few had participated in the movement before the reorganization of the CUP in 1906. Because Ramsaur based his examination of the Young Turks and the CUP on European sources and did not even look into the official organs of the movement, his conclusions reflect only European public opinion about the Young Turks.

Later the topic was subjected to analyses made within more theoretical contexts through the application of various theories. The first such study to be published was by the Soviet historical writer Petrosian, who endeavored to prove that the Young Turk revolution was a bourgeois uprising.[9] Relying on "Marxist classics," he went to great lengths to form a consistent theory and in the process overinterpreted public statements made by Young Turks. Other than bringing to light a few hitherto-unknown Russian documents, this study contributed nothing to the field. Even less may be said for articles written by Quataert, who analyzed the movement and the revolution by focusing on economic conditions.[10] His and other essays claiming to analyze this subject within a theoretical context tell us nothing about the movement and fail to support their theories.

My examination of the early phase of this movement is intended to fulfill four objectives, while relying heavily upon the private papers of the CUP.

First, the dissection of the organizational framework, with special focus on internal factions within the CUP network, is a necessary preliminary to a systematic definition of the movement.

Second, in distinguishing the CUP from other opposition movements and studying relations with them when relations existed, I uncover some of the other existing opposition forces while further defining the CUP and the Young Turk movement.

Third, I examine the European diplomatic affair with the Young Turk movement within the larger context of Ottoman and European diplomatic histories.

Fourth, since the Young Turk *Weltanschauung* propelled the CUP and continued to wield a profound influence even in much later periods, I have attempted to uncover this ideological phenomenon and trace its roots and development. This was the underpinning and the single relatively constant element in this secret society. It is essential to scholars for that reason, as well as for its enduring impact on Turkish culture and intellectual life.

2

Ideological Roots
of the Young Turks

Westernization as an Instrument of Change

Works written about the Young Turk movement, whether by its members[1] or their contemporaries,[2] all confirm a particular point: the movement was a link in the historical chain of Ottoman westernization and bureaucratic modernization and represented the modernist wing of the Ottoman intelligentsia and bureaucracy. However, it is difficult to find any evidence of these connections in relevant scholarly studies published since 1945. Nevertheless, the Young Turk and westernization movements were indisputably intertwined, and the latter, starting as early as the late eighteenth century, played an undeniable role in shaping the Young Turk *Weltanschauung*.

In a book written nearly fifty years after the onset of the Ottoman westernization movement, the following question was posed: "Was the gravitation toward western ways precipitated by spontaneous attraction, or was it the fruit of wise counsel and foresight by Ottoman statesmen?"[3] Undeniably both elements propelled westernization, and although it was initially a spontaneous development, it soon became the policy of Ottoman statesmen.

After the Ottomans' humiliating defeats by western powers, self-doubt and questioning became the order of the day. Initially, Ottoman intellectuals promoted their conclusion that Ottomans had been overcome by "infidels" who had mastered the "new technology."[4] Later their praises of the Russian example of westernization and their enjoinder to Ottomans to imitate their eastern neighbor were uttered everywhere.[5] According to Mehmed Behic, "the Muscovite nation of inconsiderate animals has in thirty years reached a point that poses a danger to states of five hundred or a thousand years," and "because not only the civilized Ottoman but even the ordinary Muslim peasant who resides within the borders of the Sublime State [Ottoman Empire] is more competent than the cleverest European," westernization will be an easy mission for Ottomans to accomplish.[6] Subsequently, European works, most of which dealt with military science, came to be regarded as avenues to understanding a new world by exploring the new technology.[7] Two salient characteristics emerged from this new approach: modernization was to be stitched into an Islamic jacket,[8] and the only purpose of westernization became the attainment of superiority over the West through the adoption of western technology.[9] Thus interaction with western Europe was initially undertaken solely as a means for importing superior technology.

However, contacts with Europe and sallies into modernization in the form of imitating the West produced unexpected results in the mid-nineteenth century. A consequence of intellectual borrowing from Europe was the emergence of a distinguished group of intellectuals who envisaged an ideal society antithetical to the one they inhabited. For Ottoman statesmen this was an awful as well as unlooked-for outcome.

To acquire western knowledge, the Ottoman government sent students to Paris to study the latest scientific advances, renting mansions so as to house them outside the city. The students were required to speak only Turkish and Arabic among themselves and were instructed by the most capable French professors so that "they might not be unduly influenced by the detrimental values of a foreign culture."[10] Ottoman statesmen were deeply disturbed by the revolutions in Europe, starting with the French Revolution of 1789 and continuing with the revolutions of 1830 and 1848, and warned against acquiring anything other than superior technology from Europe.[11] Nevertheless, the mental transformation of Ottoman intellectuals exposed to western thinking was catalytic to ensuing social change.

As soon as Ottoman intellectuals became exposed to western life and culture, they perceived profound differences between these and their own civilization.[12] They felt constricted by their own intellectual framework and, with a sense of inferiority,[13] extolled what they saw in the West:

> Clearly a large part of the natural and industrial wealth of Europe has been entirely a result of the patriotic and rational endeavors of the Europeans themselves. In brief, although Europe was the smallest continent, it became, with scientific advances, the hub of modern power. In other words, nations all around the world were obliged to depend upon the science of Europe. The Europeans are even struggling to rule the air as they had once mastered the sea. . . . In short, it is obvious that they, in addition to multiplying the branches

of knowledge and science, will also succeed in inventing new sciences as well as maintaining the old ones.[14]

These intellectuals faced an irrefutable challenge and believed that their only choice was to adopt western systems. Many memoranda given to the Ottoman sultans during this transition period were prefaced by such phrases as "Although it can be called improper for the Muslims to imitate unbelievers [*kefere*];" following this, they would underscore the necessity of such imitation due to "special circumstances."[15] Also, admiration replaced the sense of inadequacy that the Ottoman elite felt vis-à-vis the non-Ottoman and non-Islamic traditions and values of the western powers.[16] Concerning the power of the Ottoman state, realistic, gloomy, and never-before-mentioned expressions such as "the Sublime State has insufficient power and strength to adopt a policy of neutrality" began to find their way into parlance.[17]

"Geographically small but foremost in civilization and prosperity": this was the perception of visitors to Europe, who romanticized what they saw[18] and reached the conclusion that the only avenue before them was to be educated by Europeans. As one Ottoman officer declared in a fictitious dialogue: "Although I have spent my life on battlefields, the skill of Christians in producing weapons of war and superior stratagems is beyond my comprehension."[19] And in his respectful prefatory remarks to a translated work, an Ottoman mathematician who had been sent to Vienna confessed that western supremacy had attained indisputable proportions.[20] Similarly, an Ottoman statesman visiting Cambridge University acknowledged, after comparing the university with Ottoman *medreses*, that the best thing the Ottomans could do would be to install an identical educational system throughout the Empire.[21] His desire to imitate the West was aptly symbolized in his drawings depicting the modern balloons he had seen for the first time in Great Britain, with this simple alteration—they were bearing Ottoman flags.[22]

Here we demarcate a turning point in Ottoman intellectual history. Until then Ottoman political writers had analyzed every situation relative only to their own political system, and their proposed solutions were consistent with the boundaries of the status quo. A pamphlet set forth the question "Why has the world fallen into anarchy from its formerly tranquil state?" The "world" here refers to the Ottoman lands.[23] Another characteristic of this genre of political writing is that the qualifications requisite for an administrator are enumerated and evaluated,[24] with each analysis ending on a moralistic note.[25] Most of these analyses were based on the presumption of an ideal state of affairs in a bygone era[26]—perhaps the age of the Prophet (*asr-ı saadet*) or the heyday of the Ottoman state—and current woes were contrasted with that paradigm. Solutions were drawn from the examples of that earlier time.[27]

As E. J. W. Gibb so brilliantly expounded, "The new culture is spoken of by the Turks as 'gharbí' that is 'western' or 'occidental' and is contrasted with the 'sharqí' that is the 'eastern' and 'oriental,' " and

> . . . the Fatherland, the Nation, Liberty—these three words are the legend on the banner of Young Turkey and the ideas they represent form the very core of the true and living faith of the regenerated people. . . . Aided by the general spread of education among both sexes and all classes, it [Islam] has relegated to the background the old dogmatic Muhammedanism, just as in Western Europe the old dogmatic Christianity has been rudely shaken by the popular-isation of science and the wide diffusion of knowledge.[28]

Although some Ottoman statesmen who encountered the West claimed to despise it,[29] even Halet Efendi, a prime example, attests to how profoundly he was influenced by Europe.[30] The *Weltanschauung* of the Ottoman intelligentsia was dissociated in every way from the traditional world view, and this ushered in a new era in the intellectual history of the Empire and the dawn of drastic developments.

The question might be raised why—given that the initial response of Egyptian intellectuals such as Ḥasan 'Aṭṭār, al-Jabartī, and Rifā'ah Rāfi' al-Ṭahṭāwī to western culture was identical to that of Ottoman intellectuals in the capital—no similar transformation should have been realized in Egyptian culture.

The answer is threefold. First, superwesternization in the Ottoman capital was led by non-Muslim inhabitants and followed by Muslims. Second, in contrast to Egypt, Ottoman statesmen held their empire to be geographically European and believed that their destiny lay with Europe. Third and most important, the Turkish ulema, due to their close adherence to the establishment, seemed unable to produce ideologies that challenged the westernization movement, leaving fervent popular feeling against west-ernization with no strong guiding ideology. The Islamic revivalist move-ments, such as the modernism of al-Afghānī and 'Abduh, and the Salafi-yyah movement, which emerged in Egypt and Syria, had little influence on the Turkish intelligentsia of the Empire until 1908. Even the Islamic modernism movement of 1908 to 1918, represented by the journal *Sırat el-Mustakim* (later *Sebil'ür-Reşad*), was relatively weak in comparison with parallel movements in the Arab provinces.

Contemporary Science and Its Impact on Ottoman Thinking

Clearly the enormous changes in the mental life of Ottoman intellectuals that accompanied their embrace of western social and cultural values pre-cipitated far-ranging results. One oft-used word, *science,* was credited for this perceived western supremacy. Ottoman statesmen proffered various explanations, such as "philosophy," to explain western supremacy[31]; how-ever, when it came to comparisons between the Ottoman Empire and the West, science was invariably designated as the cause.[32] "Science," wrote an admirer of western culture, "is the reason Europeans can travel from one pole to another, while peoples on the other continents cannot even leave their own land."[33] A prominent figure in the westernization movement presented "science" and "the application of modern civilization" as essential in the successful maintenance of a state. After comparing an "uneducated" individual with an "intelligent" one, he commented that a similar comparison might be drawn between a state that "applied modern civilization" and one that "refused to apply it." He wrote:

> Around twenty or thirty thousand Europeans traveled a long way for many months and easily defeated the Chinese state, one unique in size of population and land, and upon entering its capital they compelled China to accept their terms. At that time, of course, the Chinese emperor became aggrieved because his military was ignorant of new technological warfare. Had not the Chinese stubbornly insisted on preserving their imperfect civilization, would they have been subjected to humiliation by a few thousand foreigners?[34]

During the early 1850s, the concept of "modern science" began to usurp the authority of religious constructs in traditional Ottoman thought. Scholarly discourse now studied questions from a "scientific" viewpoint rather than invoking religious proofs. Here is a typical argument comparing geology and history as tools for acquiring knowledge:

> Just as it is unacceptable for man to be ignorant of his origins, whether physical or moral, it is shameful for him to neglect the study of geology. By means of the study of history, the lives and customs of previous peoples may be understood, but the science of geology uncovers thousands of centuries of natural history. History consists of reports and stories passed down through generations by man, but the science of geology cannot be influenced by the changing conditions of communication.[35]

Because geology relies more heavily on science, it was deemed the superior tool. Similarly, the effective administration and continued prosperity of the Empire began to be reexamined in relation to science:

> The progress of a nation results from increase in its population, agriculture, art, capital, and commerce, as well as from the endeavors of its people, and this progress depends upon science and reason and requires the acquisition of greater knowledge.[36]

It was also necessary for public administration to be in the hands of men who understood science:

> Those who govern in this century must be fully acquainted with various subjects, especially government administration and international relations. In our time the administration of governmental affairs may not reside in the hands of ignorant men as formerly.[37]

For Ottoman intellectuals science attained the status of religion, and faith in science usurped the position of religious belief; thus "science" became endowed with a transcendent meaning. Since *religion* and *science* had been synonyms in Ottoman terminology for centuries—the term *ilm* referred to both—[38] this transition initially was smooth, but eventually the inevitable clash between the new "scientific religion" and Islam occurred. For example, in one of his texts, Sadık Rıfat Pasha enumerated the evils of fanaticism and the virtues of science:

> However praiseworthy integrity in and fidelity to religion may be, fanaticism is unacceptable. For in addition to the unworthy nature of hypocrisy and fanaticism, the great harm they cause to all is obvious. . . . If science be equated with knowledge, and learning be the most praiseworthy human activity, all should strive to learn that which they do not know.[39]

This attitude may be compared with a cold-blooded strain in European thought, beginning with Machiavelli, which did not employ moral values in analysis.[40] In one journal, suicide was examined without mentioning ethics or referring to religion.[41] Discussions on the conflict between science and religion abounded, while in many "scientific" books science appeared as the authority destined to replace religion and to ensure sounder guidance for mankind.[42] Strong criticism, disguised as refutations of "superstitions," was leveled against religion.[43] The comparison between geology and history was not made by happenstance and immediately calls to mind Sir Charles Lyell's work on geology and the Christian clergy's denunciations. All traditional knowledge was fiercely denigrated and called useless by the defenders of contemporary science among the Ottoman intelligentsia,[44] and chemistry ascended to paramount importance. Popular journals began to publish "chemistry lessons,"[45] and it grew fashionable to explain everything by way of chemistry.[46] Science reigned supreme:

> Today an educated man needs to know nothing other than science and technology. Today science has reached such a level that all things are knowable. Just as men were once distinguished by caste in olden times in India and Egypt, today we see all men divided into three classes: Scientists, technicians, and workers.[47]

Besides the glowing tribute paid to contemporary science, the notion of progress became a cornerstone of Ottoman thought, and the phrase "new progress" (*terakkiyat-ı cedide*) became a watchword in every field.[48] This was also due to the fact that in traditional Ottoman thought, progress had always been held in high esteem, but this time it carried a distinctly different meaning,[49] for in this new usage the term concurred precisely with the meaning Turgot and Condorcet had assigned to it.[50]

The impact of contemporary science on Ottoman intellectuals was so profound that many became convinced that in such a "century of progress" every aspect of life would be regulated according to science. Thus science became a "consummatory value," as defined by David Apter in the political modernization literature.[51]

Since the science that so deeply impressed Ottoman intellectuals was biological-materialist and Darwinist, and the aimed-for "progress" had a materialistic meaning, the Empire was soon flooded with a plethora of popular materialist literature, to the utter amazement of visiting foreign scholars.[52] Typical of the manner of teaching political theory, ancient materialist thinkers and their philosophies were widely discussed in the popular journals of the 1860s,[53] and praises for Spinoza began to appear.[54] But traditional Ottoman intellectuals who intended to demonstrate the evils of materialism translated only critiques of Spinoza.[55] Darwinism[56] and the theory of evolution[57] also became major subjects of discussion in popular journals.

In the field of political discourse, which had fallen by the wayside when it was deemed not a "truly scientific" one, attention was paid to Jean Jacques Rousseau and Voltaire, who were held in esteem by many Ottoman statesmen.[58] Voltaire, especially, was respected for his views on religion,[59] and Rousseau, although presented as a great anticlerical thinker,[60] was disparaged for his skepticism toward science.[61]

The popularity of contemporary science among the Ottoman elite was prodigious, and when the first significant journal in this field came off the press, its list of subscribers included many cabinet ministers, ambassadors, and high-ranking civil and military officials.[62] Later, scientific articles began to appear even in conservative journals.[63] Although they employed the term *science,* thereby reconciling it with Islam,[64] these two uses of the term were as unrelated as the uses of the term *liberty* by Marxists and liberals. The employment of the word by members of the new Ottoman elite undoubtedly allowed them to claim superiority, since their opponents were ill prepared to challenge their efforts at reconciliation. In one of his works, Mardin, citing characters from novels, has shown how a superwesternized Ottoman elite emerged in the capital during the late nineteenth century.[65] Its members were living an extravagantly European lifestyle and were doing their utmost to become ever more European. Their *Weltanschauung* can be summarized in two words: *science* and *progress.*

The Tug of War between Conservatives and Modernists

The emergence and rise of this popular scientific ideology drove Ottoman intellectuals to align themselves in three camps. Those advocating modern western ideologies and wishing to apply them to various aspects of life composed the largest and most dominant group. Soon after, a reactionary group emerged, claiming the preeminence of the Ottoman ulema[66] and accusing the modernist group of alienating itself from its own culture and values. They took a firm stance in opposition to the materialist element in Ottoman thought. Although this second group survived until the end of the Empire, it had no impact on the modernist group and was regarded by them as reactionary and ignorant. An example of this is a book written in refutation of the ideas of Ludwig Büchner. The author, himself ignorant of western languages, asked a friend to summarize the French translation of Büchner's famous work *Kraft und Stoff* and then wrote an elaborate critique of the theories of the German thinker, exploring many Islamic texts, including quotations from the Holy Quran, and adding an outdated understanding of physics.[67] This criticism made no impact on the numerous admirers of Büchner, who judged it unworthy of refutation.

Somewhere between these two rather extreme factions another group emerged. It was accused of being politically liberal and religiously conservative[68] and attempted to capitalize on the Ottoman intellectuals' disgust for the new, superwesternized elite. Mardin presents this disgust as a pillar of the Young Ottoman movement.[69] Nevertheless, one may say that, except for their frequent appropriation of Islamic symbols, the Young Ottomans gravitated toward the modernist and prowestern Ottoman elite. Even Şinasi can be considered as a representative of this group,[70] and Ziya Pasha, another prominent figure in the Young Ottoman movement, underscored the inevitability of imitating the West.[71] Similarly, Namık Kemal concluded one of his articles with this interesting couplet, a lament over the government's failure to provide jobs for those returning from Europe after successfully receiving education and training there: "He is called unfortunate who acquired perfection of skills/ In order to die of grief in the hands of the ignorant."[72] Furthermore, the Young Ottomans' organ claimed that "as an individual's health and safety rely upon rationality, so a nation's maintenance and happiness are bound to science."[73] Similar slogans appeared in the Young Ottoman publication in Istanbul: "Our position in comparison with France is like that of an uneducated child beside an accomplished scholar."[74] What they objected to was the superwesternization and the annihilation of domestic culture, as thus described:

> In order to advance our civilization we shall try to obtain scientific and industrial progress from Europe. We do not want their street dances, amorality, and satanic afflictions, such as callousness toward people who are starving to death, or to view fairness and tenderness of heart as outlandish notions.[75]

This vision of westernization is remarkably congruent with the post–Balkan Wars program of the moderate wing of the 1908–1918 westernization movement, which embarked on a campaign to prevent wholesale westernization while promoting a single-minded westernization policy: The development of whatever technology was needed to defeat the West. The leader of this wing, however, cannot be accused of being a reactionary.[76]

It should be further remarked that the approach of the Young Ottomans, as will become clearer when we study the Young Turk movement, would have been better received in a predominantly Muslim society. As Namık Kemal described in a letter, this gave prominence to their policy toward westernization:

> It was written previously in *İbret* that we will accept every kind of progress achieved by Europeans, however we must never become Europeans, for God's sake! The insistence by the Muslims on not becoming Europeanized is a hundred times more apparent than it has ever been. Today if we show people a Latin character, we face more opposition than would have been manifested were we formerly to have shown them a frock-coat and pants. Because every-

one eschews Europeanization, we shall face unending opposition and troubles.[77]

There were also more sincere advocates of reconciliation, such as Hayreddin (Khayr al-Dīn) Pasha,[78] who warned of problems due to "ulema ignorant of progress" and "politicians ignorant of Islam."[79]

However, those trying to employ Islam as a modernizing tool and those who genuinely believed in a reconciliation between Islam and western civilization were vehemently denounced by modernists, who dominated intellectual life in the Ottoman Empire, even under Abdülhamid II. A prominent figure of the movement wrote:

> Some of our intellectuals, in order to avoid fanatical reactions, have attempted to make European culture more acceptable and so to insinuate modern culture into Islamic lands. They even claimed that European culture had Islamic origins. In newspapers, in their books, and in other writings, they have maintained that European science and technology derived from Muslim discoveries. This is a worthy effort. But although there is much truth in what they assert, there is also great exaggeration, and they have spawned new problems. However diligently we might renew our study of the medicine of Avicenna, the physics of Averroës, and the chemistry of Jahiz, translate their books, publish them, and found schools for these purposes, we must likewise obtain the best scientific works of our century. For just as we cannot cure malaria with the medicine of Avicenna, so we cannot build a railroad, a ship, or use the telegraph with the chemistry or physics of Jahiz. If we wish to modernize ourselves we must do so by borrowing from contemporary science and technology. . . . Even in Europe there appeared some intellectuals who tried to reconcile religious texts with modern science and to extinguish fanaticism by appeasing it. However, since fanaticism is not a monster that can be seduced through gentleness, it has brutally destroyed those who have attempted to appease it. Finally the intellectuals gathered together, hand in hand, and waged a war against fanaticism, using axes and powder to demolish it, and only then did progress in civilization begin. In our society, too, in order to achieve progress in civilization and save the Muslims from the ignorance that is precipitating their annihilation, a war must be declared against fanaticism to forcibly crush it and thus open the road to civilization.[80]

According to advocates of modernization, "a new philosophy called *philosophie positive* had emerged which relied on science and rationality, and this superseded all other, now out-dated philosophies."[81] Conservatives responded by claiming that Islam could be reconciled with modern science[82]; however, this had no influence on modernists.

The modernist-materialist intellectual, further, considered domestic culture old-fashioned and unresponsive to the problems of the day. When a modernist journal invited its readers to contribute books toward the establishment of a library, some high-ranking Muslim statesmen and intellectuals donated their entire libraries; among the 126 volumes collected, including works by Bacon, La Fontaine, Helvétius, Montesquieu, Shakespeare, and Adam Smith, only two were Oriental—the *Mukaddimah* of Ibn Khaldūn and a single volume of Ottoman legal codes.[83] Soon after, the libraries of Ottoman intellectuals were found to contain either originals or translations of Büchner, Draper, Isnard, and Schopenhauer. Even Ahmed Midhat, a critic of materialism,[84] had a serious enough interest in Schopenhauer's philosophy to write a pamphlet about it.[85]

Later a translation of John William Draper's *Conflict Between Religion and Science* appeared.[86] Draper's main contention was that an ongoing war between science and religion had been waged throughout history. Although Ahmed Midhat wrote a critical preface to the translation, two important questions may be raised.[87] First, why did this issue become the salient topic of discussion for Ottoman intellectuals? Second, why was there almost no criticism and an overwhelming acceptance of Draper's ideas within Ottoman society, while religious and conservative groups in other countries vehemently denounced his book?[88]

It is remarkable that Beşir Fuad, described as a "pure materialist,"[89] held views typical among the Ottoman intelligentsia. While no other member of this new intelligentsia committed suicide and took notes up to the point of losing consciousness in order to prove that life is merely a materialistic event, as did Beşir Fuad,[90] it is certain that his ideas attained wide acceptance.[91]

As Ahmed Midhat mentioned in one of his works, during the second half of the nineteenth century the concept "alla franca" gained enormous popularity and was a subject of wide discussion.[92] This construct was often associated with the catchwords "the century of progress," "contemporary science," and "civilization."[93] Undoubtedly modernization was a pillar in the ideology of the new materialist intelligentsia and was presented as a scientific necessity.

The Young Turks and Modernization

With the onset of the Ottoman modernization and westernization movements, Ottoman bureaucrats were polarized into two groups according to the stand they took. Further, all bureaucratic advocates of the reform and westernization movements perceived themselves as members of a distinct group, even though they had no significant organizational framework such as that of a political party. This was true for the reforming pashas of Selim III,[94] the leading statesmen of the Tanzimat,[95] and Midhat Pasha with his reforming compatriots, all of whom were depicted as members of the Young Turkey party by foreign diplomats and the press, even though no such party existed.[96] The Young Turks also claimed to be the successors of the Parti de la Jeune Turquie of the Ottoman bureaucracy and heirs to the struggle against the Parti Conservateur.[97] They stated that their ideology galvanized all pro-modernists, regardless of political affiliation.[98] On many occasions CUP leaders represented themselves as directors not only of a distinct political organization but also of a much larger ideological movement. The official organs of the CUP claimed to be both "the central organ of the CUP" and "the organ of the *Jeune Turquie*." In response,

Abdülhamid II issued an imperial decree: "Some scoundrels going by the name of Young Turks have attempted to differentiate themselves from other [classes of the nation] as a distinct group, and hereby [he] will curse anyone who uses the term 'Young Turk' instead of 'agitator.' "[99] A CUP member later called the Young Turk movement a link in the long chain of struggle against conservative groups, and said that "those who were not officially members of the CUP were supporters at heart."[100] Many members of the CUP later confessed that while involved in the movement they only vaguely comprehended the ideas of the committee but had been influenced by Ahmed Rıza, whom they depicted as a modernist undertaking political opposition against the sultan and smuggling pamphlets throughout the empire; yet they admitted ignorance of the content of these publications.[101] At some point they realized that they were working in a group "fighting the absolutist regime."[102] The government's severe measures against those lacking affiliation with a political organization but "propagating liberal ideas"[103] helped the Young Turks to convert many members of a generation educated at western-type institutions in the Empire. A prime expression of the way the Young Turks viewed themselves can be seen in a couplet published as a requiem for a deceased friend: "Although one member dies, a thousand others are born to the cause of enlightenment/ The class of liberals is immortal."[104]

Epitomized in another much-quoted couplet by Namık Kemal is this vision of the Young Turks as an intellectual group, aware of social reality and therefore not suppressible by absolutism: "It is impossible to eliminate liberty by oppression and cruelty/ Try to annihilate understanding from humanity if you can."[105]

This attitude may be analogous to that of Marxists, who deprecate other ideologies based on their allegiance to a construct of social reality.

In short, the Young Turk movement was unquestionably a link in the chain of the Ottoman modernization movement as well as representing the modernist wing of the Ottoman bureaucracy. In their periodicals, the Young Turks praised Mahmud II's reforms,[106] the Tanzimat movement,[107] Mustafa Reşid Pasha,[108] Mustafa Fâzıl Pasha,[109] the Young Ottomans,[110] and Midhat Pasha.[111] Members of the Young Turk movement, most of whom were low-ranking bureaucrats and students at royal colleges, regarded themselves as the natural heirs of the reform movement. They frequently demanded that the Ottoman state install western institutions. In the words of Abdullah Cevdet, a founder of the first nucleus of the CUP in the Royal Medical Academy in 1889 who later led the westernization movement of 1908–1918: "There is only one civilization, and that is European civilization. Therefore, we must borrow western civilization with both its rose and its thorn."[112] Another Young Turk leader, Sabahaddin Bey, wrote: "Since we established relations with western civilization, an intellectual renaissance has occurred; prior to this relationship our society lacked any intellectual life."[113] *Osmanlı*, the official organ of the CUP, contrasted a European and an easterner as follows: "Europeans always walk through the streets with their heads up, whereas easterners walk with their heads under the heavy pressure of absolutism, bent to the ground and nearly dragging."[114]

Letters penned by CUP members to Istanbul newspapers about European life bear a striking resemblance to reports written by the first Ottoman ambassadors describing their marvelous experiences and observations of western civilization.[115]

It should be noted that the phrase "imitating the West" may cause confusion when the policies of Abdülhamid II are examined. On numerous occasions phrases such as "as it is in Europe" were used by the sultan's loyal bureaucrats.[116] However, in the Young Turk terminology, European civilization was essentially synonymous with "contemporary science," and the Ottoman state was enjoined to adopt it.[117] The Young Turks' commitment to modernist and western ideas was undeniably a bone of contention with Abdülhamid II, who wished to appropriate only western technology and abhorred "western civilization."[118]

How Contemporary Science Colored Young Turk Thinking

There is abundant evidence that "popular science and materialism" were mainstays of the Young Turks. The birthplace of the CUP, the Royal Medical Academy, as well as the high number of the members who were medical doctors and students, testifies to this.

In comparison with prior intellectual movements, likewise influenced by contemporary science and popular materialism, the Young Turk movement was avant-garde. Except for articles written for propaganda purposes,[119] the Young Turks gave no credit to efforts to reconcile western civilization and science with Islam and traditional values. Even the ideas of Namık Kemal seemed useless to them, and their reaction echoed the denigration of Thomas Moore's *Utopia* in England by the generation succeeding him—the ideas might be well put and interesting, but they were devoid of any practical value.

Two of the four founders of the CUP at the Royal Medical Academy, Abdullah Cevdet and İbrahim Temo, wrote for popular scientific journals. Abdullah Cevdet, as he so proudly mentioned in his autobiography covering the years 1889 to 1903,[120] had translated portions of Ludwig Büchner's works into Turkish[121] and had published "Lessons in Chemistry for Everyone,"[122] as well as scientific articles in popular journals, before being banished to Tripoli of Barbary.[123] İbrahim Temo for his part wrote an early essay for a popular scientific journal in defense of Şerafeddin Mağmumî, another CUP member,[124] who had been critical of poets and the poetic mentality, proclaiming that "poets committed a crime against science by attributing the functions of the brain to the heart in their poems."[125] There are strange passages in the prison letters of the Young Turks, such as "The body is composed of many cells, i.e., small animals. Just as we wish to be healthy, so they desire their own health and work toward that end. Therefore illness, occurring in spite of the efforts of so many animals working for our health, results from our own carelessness."[126] Another writing by Şerafeddin Mağmumî about the poetic mentality yields insights into the ideas of the first members of the CUP:

> What about chemistry! What about chemistry! Is there anything similar to occasion so deep a feeling as that caused by the formation of various materials having many characteristics, by the mixing of two uncolored liquids, or by the appearance of a stronger poison from the combination of two other poisons, or by observing water becoming frozen and the appearance of flames in it? Can a more exquisite poetic panorama be imagined than these scientific wonders and chemical transactions? . . . It is impossible to examine meticulously the poetry left by ancient poets and reach any clear concept. . . . If we wish to state something about ancient and modern poetry, from a conceptional point of view, besides their stylistic flavor, we can say nothing beyond calling it amateurish. Look at the *divans*, uselessly occupying the shelves in the libraries. Other than a few eulogies and elegies, all others are about love. . . . Now, why does this idea delight us? Which aspect of it accords with reason and science? The only path for becoming a poet relies upon writing in rhymes and meters and lies. What an absurd idea! . . . An average poet watches nature and novelties with amazement. He describes the elegance of the sunrise in a vineyard or a garden or the sunset on a farm accompanying the return of the animals. Everybody likes it. However, let's consider the occurrence of an illness in that garden or among those animals. O reader! Read the description by our poet at the patient's bedside. Can you make any improvement? . . . However, a serious medical doctor, a real poet, gratifies himself not by watching those vineyards, animals, novelties, and universe with amazement, and writing a description full of lies but rather by acquiring a thorough knowledge he leaves a precious text of four sentences which we may decry as spiritless. If due to an action performed according to those four sentences, during a time of epidemic, the vineyards and animals would be saved from illness. . . . Ancient and modern poetry, i.e., average poetry, can make neither bread nor clothing for man. . . . The true poets, i.e., scientists, invented ships and the telegram.[127]

These strange claims are unintelligible without an appreciation of the relationship of "science" to their way of thinking. For instance, when for the first time in history a Young Turk questioned the value of the Ottoman Royal House in a journal article, he was basing his opinion on Théodule Armand Ribot's theory of heredity. According to this article, Ottoman princes were the children of concubines, and therefore, "since experiments on animals had proved that offspring born to imprisoned animals cannot inherit the racial characteristics of their fathers," the Ottoman Royal House ought to be deposed.[128]

One might conclude that Şerafeddin Mağmumî and Abdullah Cevdet were representing extreme materialist sentiments, influenced by contemporary science. However, the popular journals of the time were filled with such "scientific" articles,[129] and this viewpoint was evident even in works presented to the sultan. One of these claimed that "The philosophies of Socrates, Plato, and Aristotle, all emanating from empty imaginings, never promoted scientific progress and hence the progress of civilization."[130]

Later, Abdullah Cevdet published "scientific" poems dealing with chemistry, biology, and physiology,[131] and launched a new trend in Ottoman poetry which has remained unexamined until now.

As suggested in his book about life at the Royal Medical Academy, a one-time member of the CUP, who became a vocal opponent after the revolution of 1908, wrote about discussions by students likening a unification of their forces to the combination of elements in chemical experiments.[132] Another prominent member described the founders of the CUP as "freethinkers" and claimed that their single goal was "to replace religion with science, in the way [François-Vincent] Raspail had prophesied decades before."[133] The placard held aloft by Royal Medical Academy students during the celebrations of the 1908 revolution, reading "le salut de la nation c'est la science," was not raised lightheartedly and expressed their deepest feelings.[134]

The role the Royal Medical Academy played through the socialization of its students is noteworthy. This institution had been a spawning ground for materialist and antireligious ideas for decades when the Young Turk movement emerged there.[135] Senior fellows required pious students to read chapters from Darwin's works in order to unseat their convictions.[136] Most of these students were astonished "when they perceived the difference between nature and religion," and soon after they usually converted to "scientific" materialism.[137] İbrahim Temo informed Karl Süssheim that Shiite works were also used to convert pious students.[138] Temo also speaks of a popular antireligious book employed usefully to this end.[139] At secret meetings held in the seniors' rooms, belief in God was harshly criticized and religion was presented as a human crutch during the premodern era.[140] The best example of a conversion by this process was Abdullah Cevdet, who entered the academy as an extremely pious fellow, devoutly observant and the author of numerous religious poems and even a *na't-i şerif* (a eulogy of the Prophet Muḥammad).[141] However, after his first year, Abdullah Cevdet became an ardent devotee of "scientific" materialist ideas and later published the first journal in the Ottoman Empire openly to criticize Islam.

The founders of the CUP, who were greatly influenced by the "scientific" materialist theories of their time, had four examples to follow. One was Raspail, whose prophecy was a bylaw for CUP members. However, they did not share Raspail's concern for public health, and they had no intention of participating in politics to that end. They undoubtedly admired Raspail but had no desire to emulate his political career.[142]

Claude Bernard is the second example of someone who impressed the Young Turks. One of the professors at the Royal Medical Academy during the onset of the Young Turk movement, Şakir Pasha, had worked beside Bernard during the years 1872 to 1876.[143] His work entitled *Dürûs-i Hayat-ı Beşeriye* in many ways expressed views similar to those of Bernard's *Introduction à l'étude de la médecine expérimentale*.[144] Through Şakir Pasha, Bernard deeply impressed the first members of the CUP nucleus at the academy. Undoubtedly the Young Turks shared the ideas of Bernard on a "méthode scientifique" free from the "joug philosophique et théologique."[145] However, Bernard's rejection of all philosophical systems, including positivism, even though it had greatly influenced him,[146] rendered his theories richly illuminating but impractical for Young Turks wishing to transform their society. The critical viewpoint of Bernard toward Darwinism, which the Young Turks deeply revered but which he considered the generalized notions of a naturalist and not pure science because it omitted experiment,[147] may have contributed to the fact that the Young Turks did not choose him as a model, even though they admired him.

A third example was Ludwig Büchner, whose many works were excerpted and translated into Turkish. Büchner, like his fellow thinkers Carl Vogt and Jakob Moleschott, developed a popular *naturwissenschaftlich orientierten Materialismus,* and was adamantly opposed to religion, which he considered a major obstacle to human progress. As Marx, Engels, and Lenin termed this movement *Vulgärmaterialusmus* in their works,[148] Büchner and his fellow thinkers deprecated Marxist materialism and despised such politics.[149] They underscored the material foundations of life, and even though they wrote about such matters as republican or monarchic regimes,[150] their primary focus was "science," from which religion should be eliminated. For instance, Vogt espoused the view that social institutions and the social contract are rooted in biology.[151]

The simplicity of his theory and his refusal to use a sophisticated, philosophical language,[152] along with his praise of Darwinism, established Büchner's major work, *Kraft und Stoff,* as a cornerstone for Young Turk thought.[153] This popular theory instilled in the Young Turks the belief that they had found a "scientific" theory with which to transform their antiquated society. Their efforts to this end were supported by their undaunted belief that the history and progress of mankind had been a tug of war between science and religion.[154] The most prominent Turkish book on "religion and science throughout history" was written in 1944 by a former Young Turk who, in his preface, described the days when he read Büchner's "*Force et Matière* . . . as the time when his mind knew its deepest peace."[155] Likewise when the Bosnian Muslims sent letters to Young Turk journals complaining that Catholic priests were forcing them to convert,[156] Young Turks advised them to diminish the power of Catholicism in the way the French had done—by opening schools similar to the Sorbonne.[157]

The Ottoman administration of Abdülhamid II perceived the Young Turks as a group of atheists. Ahmed Rıza was described as "a person who denies the existence of God and is an atheist."[158] Lûtfullah Bey too was portrayed as an atheist in a communiqué.[159] Certainly the Young Turks disparaged religion and God in their private correspondence,[160] and probably they rejoiced in these epithets.

Besides reflecting their striving to become oriental Büchners, the thinking of most early members of the CUP bore the deep stamp of the

theory of social Darwinism, which the Young Turks saw as a tool for understanding reality. They drew heavily on these theories in their early writings,[161] and later it became popular in Young Turk circles to apply these
constructs to social life. Ahmed Rıza explained the evolution of language
by using a Darwinist methodology,[162] the Egyptian branch of the CUP
claimed that its decision to establish a new committee was taken because
"the previous committee had been rendered out-of-date by the law of
evolution,"[163] and finally Sabahaddin Bey drew the line more clearly by
saying, "The law of evolution as it applies to the natural phenomenon
relates to the social phenomenon and secures progress by bestowing life
on those who best succeed in their environment." Sabahaddin Bey further
claimed that since it was impossible to change the laws of nature, the only
thing for the Young Turks to do was to understand and apply these laws
to the social events in which they participated.[164]

The Young Turks' commitment to Büchner's battle against religion
was, along with their employment of Darwinist theories, a mainstay for
the Young Turk ideology at the outset of the movement. However,
although they held these theories as their ultimate aim, the Young Turks
soon came to realize that these tenets lacked any revolutionary praxis.
Their ideas about new science and the ensuing transformation of their
society could undoubtedly play a significant role in their movement, just
as the ideas of French revolutionaries on science had figured in their revolution.[165] A "scientifically" founded political theory was nevertheless
needed, but ignorance of contemporary political movements, due to
Abdülhamid II's rigid censorship, left them with only the populist rhetoric
of the Young Ottomans of the 1860s. A step toward a more concrete
political ideology was taken when Hüseyinzâde Ali enrolled in the Royal
Medical Academy. An Azeri educated at the University of St. Petersburg
before he entered the academy, he became the fifth member to join the
first nucleus of the CUP. Having observed the Narodnik movement in St.
Petersburg, he now expounded Narodnik ideas to the Young Turks. What
he had to say greatly impressed his fellows, who regarded him as a "distinguished prophet."[166] Had there been social bases for a populist ideology
in the Ottoman Empire, the Young Turks would probably have become
Narodniks, like their counterparts in Russia, who were also under the influence of Büchner's writings.[167] For a brief period the Young Turks tried to
be Narodniks while advocating "scientific" materialist theories; then they
hit upon an elitist theory—undoubtedly a more suitable device to explain
peculiar social structure of the Ottoman Empire—and with this they
expected to resolve every social dilemma. This was the *psychologie des foules*
of Gustave Le Bon. Hachtmann was correct in saying that this book, which
bore as its title the name of Le Bon's theory, "ist in der Türkei geradezu
zur soziologischen Bibel geworden und vielfach übersetzt."[168] Le Bon was
indeed the fourth materialist icon of the Young Turks.

The Young Turks discovered Le Bon's ideas in Şakir Pasha's *Dürûs-i
Hayat-ı Beşeriye*, at the Royal Medical Academy.[169] Le Bon had already

achieved popularity for his work on Arab civilization,[170] thus enabling his theories to become fashionable with the Ottoman intelligentsia.[171] However, his enormous attraction and popularity came in response to his researches in phrenology, in which he classified all elements of society according to a hierarchy of physiological superiority.[172] Le Bon's research in millinery shops in Paris, with which he claimed to have proved that intellectuals have larger cranial capacities than do peasants and servants, was translated into Turkish and presented as a key to the understanding social problems.[173] Abdullah Cevdet, who shared Le Bon's idea that scholarly work can increase the size of a person's brain, construed the ferocious headaches he had experienced in his first two years of military high school as proof that his brain had been expanding.[174] Also according to Abdullah Cevdet, "The existence in a society of many individuals with brains of heavier than average weight is a natural and suitable force to secure progress for that society."[175] He again underscored the value of an "intellectual aristocracy":

> According to a recent philosopher, progress is always achieved by an (intellectual aristocracy). . . . The British philosopher S[tuart] Mill is adamant about this fact, and he is prominent among those who advocate this. I am also considering the particular theory which asserts that a nation's progress springs from the efforts of a few geniuses, but that the appearance of genius does not result from overall national progress.[176]

Due to their alleged scientific nature, Le Bon's elitist theories became the political component of the Young Turk ideology and, along with the sociological discourse of Charles Letourneau, which also depended on race theories and phrenology, shaped the political aspect of the Young Turk ideology; thus a "scientific," antireligious, and elitist ideology was born.[177]

Bureaucracy Challenged: Loyalty versus Merit

A potent feature of the Young Turk program was the aspiration to replace the sultan's neopatrimonial administrative system with a modern bureaucracy. To the Young Turks, this undoubtedly seemed a step toward modernization with the mandate of "science." The Tanzimat era, a watershed in Ottoman history, saw the rationalization movement propelled more dynamically onward than it had ever been before, and the reorganized Sublime Porte began to exert a vital influence on the administration. But by the Hamidian era the concept of loyalty, deemed by antimodernist statesmen to be the sole underlying tenet of the state,[178] had been reinstituted as a principle fundamental to Ottoman administration.

It is not entirely accurate, however, to describe this reorganization as a reinstatement of patrimonialism, nor was it a wholehearted return to the pre-Tanzimat era. The regime's patrimonial façade was misleading. Arbitrary decisions were issued only by the sultan. Abdülhamid II did not wish to reestablish a totally patrimonial system such as that of the pre-Tanzimat era. In other words, he did not wish to be only the uppermost patron in a patrimonial chain but rather the single patrimonial leader, ruling with the help of a rational bureaucracy. Although the sultan was guiding the country whimsically with imperial decrees, all bureaucrats' actions, including those of the grand vizier, were constrained by laws. The sultan always based his decrees on "imperial will" (*arzu-yu şâhâne*), and he took special care never to refer to any particular law.

A comparison of the official correspondence of the Hamidian era with that of the Tanzimat period reveals a remarkable increase in the use of special phrases for denoting loyalty to the sultan. After the proclamation of the Tanzimat, and especially before 1871, an impersonal style of address had become standard. Although the term *bende*, "your subject," was used in front of the title and signature of the officer, no other special terms were employed to connote personal loyalty to the sultan. By the end of the Tanzimat era and early in the absolutist reign of Sultan Abdülaziz, this standard form of address had been transformed, and despite the activities of recalcitrant modernized bureaucrats, such as the dethronement of Sultan Abdülaziz, the special relationship between ruler and officers continued into the reign of Abdülhamid II. We find various descriptions of personal loyalty replacing the term *bende*, which had its equivalents in other modern bureaucracies. For instance, the bureaucrats of the Hamidian regime most frequently described themselves as "slaves who would not accept liberation." This attitude was apparent in a memorandum by Memduh Pasha, the minister of the interior, which was presented to the sultan:

> Despite neither having the ability nor worthiness to be your slave, due to your kindness am I a slave who has grown happy through service as the Minister of the Interior. . . . I dare, impelled by devotion and loyalty, to present my humble thoughts before your exalted throne.[179]

In another memorandum, he addressed the sultan in the following manner:

> I confess it is beyond my power to say [anything in response to] your loyal slave's being so honored by [His Imperial Majesty] saying "he became my faithful servant": [It is] an example of the kindness of His Majesty, the protector of the Caliphate, which gives your slave endless, incalculable joy. Since every slave of the state is nourished by blessings, his commitment to the creation of good works for the administrative branches of the state accords with patriotism and loyalty.[180]

Before appointing high-ranking officials, the sultan spoke to them directly, emphasizing that they owed their appointments to his kindness and that they were responsible only to their imperial sovereign. Tahsin Pasha has given us details of the sultan's words immediately prior to his appointment:

> I heard about your excellent conduct and chose you, myself, to become first chamberlain. I hope you will serve properly. . . . You are indebted to no person

for recommendation or protection, nor did any post provide information or petition toward your acquiring this job. You derive this favor solely from me. Therefore you should regard no authority as superior to me and have no aim but obedience to my orders.[181]

Another example of the very personal relations between the sultan and his officials is the fact that they frequently petitioned him for extremely lucrative favors.[182]

The sultan's determination to rule the Empire with the aid of loyal officials responsible only to himself sheds light on the ubiquitous spying practiced during his reign. Turkish historiography commonly describes the increase in spying as a form of mass hysteria; however, it is impossible to attribute the millions of spy reports, sent mostly to the palace, to hysteria. Unfortunately, only a few such reports remain extant. Observing that nearly all civil and military officials, including the eventual heroes of the Young Turk revolution of 1908, had filed such reports, a special commission assigned after the revolution to examine these papers consigned them to destruction. But remarkably those that still exist contain no practical information; rather, their purpose in most cases was to express loyalty to the sultan. It was also fashionable to express loyalty by sending letters to the monarch depicting him as seen in a grandiose dream.[183] The testimony of a prominent Young Turk describes the prevailing mood of the period:

> To insist on publishing all the spy reports will not produce pleasant results, because a person who presented a spy report during the inauspicious regime of Hamid was not necessarily an absolute traitor, nor a traitor to the fatherland. Among them was a large number of people who did not know what they were doing. It was as if they were keeping up with the fashion. Those lower-ranking officials who had to submit spy reports did so in order to [protect] their positions. Had they not behaved like that, it would have been impossible for them to retain their posts. In addition, the probability of being exiled or banished would have been ninety-nine percent.[184]

The palace regarded these activities as the regular duties of civil and military officials. When the Ministry of the Navy took measures against an official who had been dispatching spy reports to the palace about the internal affairs of the ministry, the sultan took action against those who treated the official as a spy and told them that secretly informing the ruler was every official's duty.[185]

Meanwhile Abdülhamid II began to institute western-style education throughout the Empire, and significant inroads were made in educational and bureaucratic modernization. These advances were announced in the European media in articles written at the sultan's behest in order to promote his administration in the eyes of Europeans.[186] He frequently extolled the value of well-educated modern bureaucrats.[187]

Because he promoted western technology and education, "modern" bureaucrats emerged throughout the Empire, and this new group, known as the Young Turks, found that they were unable to rise within the bureaucratic ranks because of the sultan's neopatrimonial regime. Neoteric bureaucrats were subject to the authority of reliable and loyal old-fashioned bureaucrats, named the Old Turkey party by Europeans, and sophisticated military personnel were likewise placed under unschooled but politically reliable officers.

A major theme throughout the Young Turks' critical writings was their opposition to a system that required loyalty only to the sultan—never to the fatherland or the state. The student bodies in the imperial colleges concurred with this opinion, and on several occasions the students of the Royal Medical Academy refused to shout "Long live the sultan!"[188] After Zeki Pasha, one of the sultan's close confidants, was appointed to the Ministry of Military Schools, he visited the Royal Medical Academy and told the students that "what His Majesty the sultan and His Imperial government really care about is not the scientific ability of the students, but the loyalty that they express toward the Imperial sovereign."[189] On a mission to investigate antiabsolutist slogans scribbled on the walls of the same academy, İsmail Pasha commented similarly: "This displays ingratitude toward the benefactor, who owes nothing to anyone, and it is ungrateful toward the very bread he has bestowed."[190] The Young Turks vehemently opposed appointments on the basis of loyalty rather than merit:

> As is known in our country, what is sought [in granting] appointments is loyalty, not merit. . . . If someone does not accept [the principle of loyalty to an individual], then it is impossible for him to receive a post even were he to possess the ability of Reşid Pasha.[191]

When an author from the opposition inquired of the Young Turk leaders Ahmed Rıza and Murad Bey as to their primary demands of the government, they responded that their main request was that all state jobs be rendered universally accessible.[192] Similar demands were advanced on behalf of military officers in CUP journals by means of fictitious dialogues between loyal high-ranking commanders and more capable, well-educated, but low-ranking officers.[193] The Young Turk journals also revealed a deep hatred toward a regime that relied on loyalty to the sultan,[194] and Ottoman customs and traditions, which rewarded obedience, were calumniated.[195] Foreign statesmen, who had allegedly joined opposition forces in their own countries, were extolled and hailed as examples to their Ottoman counterparts.[196] It must be pointed out, however, that this was the attitude of only those Young Turks who had received a modern education. As for groups of local Young Turks formed in the provinces, no action could be further from their imagination than to dethrone the sultan and transfer their loyalty to a new and liberal one. In contrast to the Young Turks' main organs, loyalty was praised in the journals of the provincial opposition groups.[197]

Under pressure from low-ranking officials and officers, who believed a merit system would throw open the doors to the bureaucratic ranks,[198] the Sublime Porte[199] and the Imperial War Office[200] petitioned the sultan to stop awarding ranks, decorations, and extra salaries without their approval, and warned all officials against making direct applications to the palace, thus bypassing the ministries and the Sublime Porte. All these efforts, however, came to nought.

When Abdülhamid II noted the new spirit among westernized intellectuals and students, he attempted to appease it by promoting curricular reform and new institutional measures.[201] The contradictory aspirations of Abdülhamid II became a major impetus for the expansion of the opposition movement against him—on the one hand he desired to be the single patrimonial figure in the empire, and on the other he intended to govern efficiently with the help of a modern bureaucracy and military.

The data most useful in discerning differences between Abdülhamid II and the Young Turks regarding the political character of his neopatrimonial administration were a series of articles written by a confidant at the sultan's behest describing his type of regime; a debate ensued between this confidant and the Young Turks in the European press.

Ahmed Midhat, a famous writer and a confidant of the sultan, penned a series of articles in 1878 to defend the regime of Abdülhamid II; two of them are remarkable. The first, titled *"İstibdad"* ("Absolutism"), tries to distinguish autocracy from absolutism. It claimed that absolutism was synonymous with lawlessness, and thus that for a ruler to adopt such a course was irrational. An absolutist government would ensue, due to corrupt bureaucrats and political leaders, just as when leaders of the French Revolution tried to manipulate laws for their own ends.[202] The second article, entitled *"Hürriyet-i Kanuniye"* ("Legal Freedom"), defines "law" as representative of general customs, and the ruler upholding them as an *âdil* (just) one. Those obedient to this just ruler constitute free people. This system is antithetical to absolutism, and the only way to shift to an absolutist regime is for a selfish group of bureaucrats to misuse the freedoms for their self-interest.[203] In this vein, after an in-depth discussion in 1906, the Ferid Pasha cabinet described itself as not a "constitutional government," but a "just government [*hükümet-i âdile*]."[204]

In 1896 a foreign journalist made strikingly similar claims by characterizing the sultan as "an autocrat" but not a "despot," and calumniating the Young Turks[205]; a Young Turk, most probably Murad Bey, countered him, saying, "Autocratie et despotisme, ne sont ce pas là deux termes qui presque toujours sont indissolublement liés l'un à l'autre?"[206] Ahmed Midhat responded immediately, making a sharp distinction between absolutism and autocracy, and insisting that the sultan's rule was entirely true to Islam. He commented further: "Ces plaintes de la Jeune Turquie me rappelent les plaintes des Jésuites lors de la laïcisation des écoles de France."[207] Two Young Turks replied with a denial stating that the sultan's rule was not in any sense an Islamic one, and that there was no real difference between absolutism and autocracy; they seized the opportunity to denounce the sultan's regime for its reliance on loyalty.[208] Other than this lengthy controversy with Ahmed Midhat, there were few articles and works in which the Young Turks engaged in polemical discussion on the specifics of the sultan's regime from a political perspective. Nevertheless, the real concern of the Young Turks was not whether there was a sharp distinction between an absolutist regime and a benevolent autocracy but that a loyalist administration had emerged and replaced the rational Tanzimat bureaucracy. When the Young Turks seized power in 1908, they reorganized and reduced the size of civil and military officialdom, and because they issued laws rescinding ranks awarded by the sultan,[209] many bystanders believed they were motivated by vengefulness against supporters of the former regime. Actually these actions reveal their values—their dream of an ideal society relying on merit instead of loyalty to an individual.

Constitutionalism, "Parliament," and the Young Turks

As a rule, historians have defined Young Turk activities as a "constitutional movement." The reason for this is that the Young Turk revolution proclaimed the restoration of the Ottoman Constitution of 1876. However, the notion of a constitution, based on the constitutional history of the European and North American governments, had little affinity with the direction that Ottoman bureaucrats took while drafting their 1876 constitution or with the thinking of the Young Turk intellectuals of the succeeding generation.

In Europe constitutional episodes were invariably promoted by social groups, pressing to gain more representation from absolute monarchies. Clearly no such entities had yet emerged in the Ottoman Empire. Eight prominent men—statesmen and intellectuals—framed the document, and it is noteworthy that not one of them was well schooled in constitutional theory. The entire Ottoman Constitution was taken directly from the contemporary Belgian and French constitutions, and the resulting document, as its architects intended, in no respect represented the Ottoman people. The framers omitted the right to establish political parties or to peacefully assemble. Seen from a viewpoint informed by constitutional law, it is clear that this constitution provided no foundation for a parliamentary system because ministers and cabinets bore no responsibility to the parliament.

Ottoman intellectuals envisaged a distinct use for a constitution. Raymond Aron touched the heart of the matter when he observed that at the time when Ottoman statesmen and intellectuals were carrying out their reform program, "la modernisation de la politique était symbolisée par un parlement."[210] Ottoman intellectuals struggling to reform government bureaucracy since the late eighteenth century perceived constitutional regimes as the builders of the most sophisticated, streamlined, and scientific civil systems. Ziya Pasha wrote:

> Please take a look at the states on the European continent. Is there any absolutist government there except the Russian state? Isn't even it trying to imitate

gradually the existing regulations in other European states? Are the power and greatness of the French and Austrian emperors, the Italian and Prussian kings, and the British queen less than that of the Russian [czar]? Since European public opinion is flooding as a tidal wave in that direction, and the Sublime State is being regarded as a European State, it will be impossible for us to survive if we set ourselves against the entire [western] world.[211]

Ottoman bureaucratic reformers—the proreform wing of Sublime Porte statesmen—used the new constitution as a wild card in their game to undermine the hegemony of the sovereign and to install their reforms. Said Halim Pasha wrote:

This Constitution of '93 [1876] was in fact an undertaking by the very bureaucrats of the despotic regime, intending to curtail the absolute dominance of the sultan and to establish a balancing and countering jurisdiction to match this authority. . . . Our reformers of that time envisaged the forging of a new element—nationhood—neglected and considered tame until that time, which was now to join in their business [of administration] to effect, change, and alter the deplorable administrative system; in other words, [they] promulgated and instituted a constitution parroting Western customs. However, because these reforming ministers and high-ranking officials knew their country well, they realized that people would be unable, in the foreseeable future, to fulfill the duties and privileges granted to them. . . . Thus, the *raison d'être* of the policy adopted by the reformers of '93 [1876] may have been that, due to the inability of the Ottoman people to exercise their authority and rights in the near future, these rights and liberties could be abrogated by Ottoman statesmen for many years to come. Therefore, the liberalism exhibited by representatives of absolutism meant in fact simply that a new title—advocates for the nation—had been added to their former title—state representatives, and that now they could use the "nation" as a weapon against the sultan. By forcing the sultan to grant a constitution to his nation they pretended to depend upon both the sultan and the nation, thereby dispensing with the sultan's absolutism and executing their reform program by exploiting the people's ignorance and lack of awareness.[212]

Although Said Halim Pasha correctly identified the motives of the commission members who prepared the constitution, he was mistaken in presenting the constitution as the first instance of this kind of reform ploy. The Tanzimat was a salient example of this tactic. When the *Hatt of Gülhane* pledged to guarantee "life and the protection of chastity, honor and property," one might erroneously conclude that a society of *lupus homo homini* had existed for all Ottomans prior to the Tanzimat era; in fact, such a life was a reality only for statesmen. Prior to 1839 confiscations and *siyaseten katl* had never been applied to ordinary Ottoman peasants but only to officials, grand viziers, and governors.

Said Halim Pasha also entirely neglected the most salient motive for an Ottoman constitution. Considering the firm objection by Âli Pasha to a representative regime, which he deemed harmful to a multinational and multireligious empire,[213] let us pose this question: Why did Ahmed Midhat Pasha suddenly shift from promoting bureaucratic modernization to espousing representative constitutionalism? The point that he and his bureaucrat friends so shrewdly made was that equalization of ethnic and religious groups under a constitution in 1876 would benefit the Muslims. When the Great Powers intervened in Ottoman politics following the *Hatt of Gülhane*, they forced the Ottoman government to institute reforms favoring Christians and endowing them with privileges, and thereby occasioned a hue and cry among Muslims, who supposed that these rights were being conferred at their own expense. In this regard the Ottoman constitution of 1876 was an unsuccessful device for turning the tables on the Great Powers by guaranteeing equality to all Ottomans, thereby blocking special reforms in favor of particular ethnic and religious groups.[214]

The proclamation of the Ottoman constitution of 1876 occurred during the Istanbul (Tersane) Conference, when the Great Powers were imposing unacceptable reform proposals on European Turkey. Even Ahmed Midhat Pasha, described as "beyond question the most energetic and liberal of the Turkish statesmen [and who] always wished to follow English advice,"[215] told Lord Salisbury, the British representative at the conference, that "he was resigned to the will of God . . . but no Turk would yield any one of the nine points [reform measures for European Turkey]."[216] Safvet Pasha's attempt to end the conference by announcing to the delegates that all Ottoman citizens had become equal under a constitutional regime apparently made no impression on representatives of the Great Powers, who were seeking a new administrative system more favorable to Christians in the Empire. At this point Ahmed Midhat Pasha played his card of the new constitution for the last time, calling on the Great Powers to put the Ottoman Constitution under their collective protection.[217] When Lord Derby refused to consider this, Ahmed Midhat Pasha and his confreres curtailed any further plans to use the Ottoman constitution to divert the Great Powers.

The first Ottoman parliament duly convened in Istanbul, but it was closed by Abdülhamid II on June 28, 1877, after sitting only fifty times; the sultan gradually reinstated his neopatrimonial regime. Nominally, the Ottoman Constitution was still in force, but even mention of the word *constitution* had become a ground for exile during the period 1878–1908. The following document—a summary of a spy report—and the accompanying imperial decree provide firsthand examples of the sultan's views on a parliamentary regime:

Summary:

There is a large, artistically fashioned painting at the gate of Ragıb Bey's Rumeli Hotel in Beyoğlu. The painting depicts the meeting of a European Parliament, and people are watching it with their hands raised, ready to applaud; [this painting] has been viewed with awe by many people.

Decision:

An imperial decree has been issued that the above-mentioned painting be removed from that place, and it be ascertained, by questioning Ragıb Bey, how it came to be hung there.[218]

Again, according to Ahmed Midhat, who as we have mentioned had been paid by the sultan to refute his opponents' ideas, constitutionalism, with its inevitable result, a parliament, was hazardous in a multireligious and multinational state:

In the event a parliament would be allowed to issue laws which would, if adopted, violate the ability of the people and their necessities, and because such laws could never be implemented, the executive branch of the state would be obliged to cancel them. Furthermore, [parliaments] violate public peace because they promote conflict among various religious sects. It is remarkable that this [often] occurs [in western countries] among religious sects which, although founded on common Christian values, exhibit divergence in their practices. In the case of a country [such as ours], consisting of various ethnic groups, a parliament would be irrelevant to Islam, and the problems it might cause are obvious even to the simplest mind.[219]

Identical assertions were made by the ministers of Abdülhamid II when discussing the Young Turk movement.[220]

For the Young Turks the idea of a constitution became a romantic symbol of western modernity—the main object of their so-called constitutionalism. Also a strong faction within the Young Turk movement—Ahmed Rıza and his followers—still considered the constitution a useful tool in fending off the intervention of the Great Powers in Ottoman politics. Articles 23 and 61 of the Berlin Congress of 1878 had granted its signatories the right of such intervention in favor of the Christians of Macedonia and the Armenians living in the six eastern provinces of the Empire. Whenever the Armenians or Macedonian Christians suggested intervention, Ahmed Rıza and his supporters exhorted them to turn their efforts toward the restoration of the Ottoman constitution of 1876 and not simply to seek special reforms for themselves. As the Albanian opponents of Ahmed Rıza pointed out, by using the constitution in this way, he and his friends intended to solve all the ethnic problems of the empire:

L'idée fixe d'Ahmed Rıza c'est de se croire "philosophe" et de le répéter sans cesse. Le système philosophique de ce Turc se réduit à cette phrase: "Le souverain bien, c'est la Constitution." Si la Turquie a une Constitution, plus de question arménienne, albanaise etc. La prospérité, le bonheur, la tranquillité partout. La Constitution, c'est la panacée même. . . .

A[h]med Riza s'imagine que la Constitution suffira-telle une baguette magique—à changer l'état d'esprit turc.[221]

Except for its value as a "modern" symbol and a mechanism for preventing the Great Powers' intervention, "parliament," as well as "representative government," meant little to the Young Turks. Their stalwart adherence to Le Bon's theories shaped their attitude toward parliament as an institution. In Le Bon's compelling concept of group psychology, which made so profound an impact on Freud,[222] the French sociologist defined the *foule* as a dangerous body. According to Le Bon, assemblies are a type of mob that could be hazardous to any society.[223] For this reason constitutionalism and representative government seemed valueless to the Young Turks—parliament itself was nothing more than a heterogeneous crowd. Nothing is more telling than the fact that even Doctor Nâzım, a central committee member between 1895 and 1908 and one of the 1906 reorganizers of the CUP, was wholly ignorant of the content of the Ottoman Constitution. Later, during an interview he confessed:

> At that time we wanted the reproclamation of the Constitution of Midhat Pasha. . . . What were the main lines of that Constitution? . . . For God's sake, I have never seen that Constitution and never learned what was in it. But when we were young, that is to say, working in Paris, we believed that Ahmed Rıza Bey had seen and read it.[224]

The Young Turk ideology was originally "scientific," materialist, social Darwinist, elitist, and vehemently antireligious; it did not favor representative government. However, in a short period members of the intelligentsia came to understand how difficult it was to achieve the changes needed to establish their ideal "scientific" administration. They readily recognized the necessity of allying themselves with various groups opposed to the regime of Abdülhamid II. By achieving this, the Young Turk movement transformed itself from a mere "amusement of Medical Academy children," according to Murad Bey's characterization,[225] into a serious political opposition movement. However, the original Young Turk *Weltanschauung* lost its purity during this process.

3

The CUP, Other Opposition Forces, and the Sultan

Historians of the age of Abdülhamid II have tended to lump together all opposition to the Hamidian state under the rubric of Young Turk opposition. This usage, however, has created confusion. The CUP, which initiated the era of Young Turk rule in 1908, was by no means the sole opposition to Sultan Abdülhamid II between 1876 and 1908. A careful examination of the evidence shows that the CUP did not become a prominent actor until 1894–1895, and its prior activities were quite insignificant. More important in these first phases were the Freemasons and such lesser-known organizations as Le Parti Constitutionnel en Turquie, Le Comité Turco-Syrien, and the Cemiyet-i İlmiye, the society of the ulema. Also deserving of mention are the activities of high-ranking government officials, governors, and palace officials.

Relations between the Freemasons, the Young Turks, and the CUP

In the late Ottoman Empire, during the period 1876–1908, the Freemasons were undoubtedly among the most active opposition organizations. Although this group has been the subject of several articles and has been discussed at length in a book, none of these works has paid much attention to its activities before 1902.[1] Instead, the focus has been on its relations with the Osmanlı Hürriyet Cemiyeti (The Ottoman Freedom Society founded in 1906) and its impact on the political life of the Ottoman Empire after the Young Turk Revolution of 1908. It is noteworthy that during the trial of the assassins of Mahmud Şevket Pasha (murdered on June 11, 1913), the conspirators claimed that their aim was to recapture power that had too long been in the hands of the Freemasons.[2] This statement attests to the fact that the activism of the Freemasons antedates the foundation of the Ottoman Freedom Society. Indeed, it can be traced to the 1870s.

It is well established that a number of prominent Tanzimat statesmen and dignitaries played crucial roles in bringing Sultan Murad V to the throne for a brief period in 1876.[3] A key figure in this process was Cléanthi Scalieri. An Istanbul Greek by birth, Scalieri was inducted in 1865 into the ranks of the French Masonic lodge of the Ottoman capital, L'Union d'Orient. Ten years later, he had already attained a position of authority in the union's Paris center.[4] Drawing upon his close friendship with Murad Efendi, the heir apparent, and perceiving the fanciful political aspirations of eastern Masonry, Scalieri devoted himself to the establishment of a new Byzantine state.[5] He envisioned a state that would unite Turks and Greeks beneath the shadow of an enlightened Ottoman sultan. Here is a contemporary Greek account of Scalieri's role in these events:

> The cooperation and friendship of these two nations and the realization of a new Byzantine state required immense efforts and a candidate to embody this ideal. To this end, there was none more suitable than Murad Efendi. He possessed a noble temperament, was favorably disposed to the idea of freedom, was capable of hard work, and was ready to bestow freedom upon his people through a constitution. In addition to this, Murad had the attribute of being a Freemason. It was therefore not difficult for Scalieri to prepare the Prince for his ideas. Having obtained the authorization of the French Obedience, Scalieri convened the notables of the lodge of Proodos of which he was the president, and inducted Murad on October 20, 1872. Later he introduced Prince Nureddin and other dignitaries of Turkish society to this lodge. Earlier, on May 14, 1872, Scalieri obtained the permission of the French Obedience of Proodos for the publication of a Turkish pamphlet—a complement to two Greek ones—which made clear his aims. Then, following a coup d'état Murad Efendi, the nephew of Sultan Abdülâziz, ascended the throne on May 18 [30], 1876. Upon his accession, he took steps to enact the constitution and other related reforms. The preliminary measures in the implementation of these policies were undertaken by Scalieri, who was assisted by our brother Francis L. Aimable, then a lawyer in Istanbul and later mayor of Paris, by our brother A. Holinsk, a former diplomat, by the former Grand Vizier Midhat Pasha, by S. G. Elliot, then British ambassador in Istanbul, and by our brother Malcom, Persian ambassador. Furthermore, we had to contend with the reaction of the populace. For this reason, it was necessary to teach the basics [of our program] to a group that had influence over the population. But we also had to win more adherents. With this in mind, Scalieri established under the auspices of the French Obedience the Envâr-ı Şarkiye [The Lights of the East]; the lodge became famous by virtue of its membership, which included several distinguished politicians and high-ranking religious officials. From this nucleus the faction of the Young Turks was born.[6]

Other sources indirectly attest to the veracity of this account. Thus we learn that "first the Young Turks entertained good relations with some Greek notables; but then they began to apply their own program."[7] Such statements indicate that Scalieri's leadership defined some of the early elements of the Young Turks and the liberal movement.[8]

Scalieri's letters corroborate this and give further details of his efforts on behalf of Murad V and of the role of the ulema and the *softas* (theological students) in the early phases of the opposition.[9]

The activities of Scalieri and the Freemasons continued after the accession of Murad V on May 30, 1876. The committee Scalieri created did its utmost to save him from being ousted, but it soon became clear that Murad V could not deal with the complex pressures of palace and street politics. On August 31, 1876, he was declared mentally unfit to rule and was deposed.[10] After the failure of the so-called Scalieri-Aziz Bey Committee to reenthrone Murad V, Scalieri fled Istanbul.[11] He was sped away from the turmoil of the capital to the Piraeus.[12] In his trial in Greece, Scalieri revealed that the beleaguered Murad had tried to convince him to return to Istanbul and that he had refused. The court record also shows that while in Istanbul, Scalieri had maintained contact with a certain Ahmed Es'ad, a colonel who had once overseen the publication of the journal *Teşvik (Encouragement)* in Greece. Es'ad was not a reliable supporter, however; and in Murad and Scalieri's hour of need he did not come through.[13]

For the next fifteen years Scalieri directed his efforts toward winning the support of the Great Powers, especially Great Britain, for the reinstatement of Murad V and his liberal program.[14] To this end he relayed personal messages to British officials through Masonic channels in Istanbul.[15] His work bore no fruit, however, and he died in 1891.

Subsequently other Masonic groups tried their hand at Ottoman politics; and some of them shared Scalieri's aspirations. One of these was led by Stefanos Skulidis, who concurred with Scalieri's agenda for a new Byzantine state but believed that it was equally important to oppose Slavic imperialism.[16] Skulidis never developed a network of contacts comparable to Scalieri's, partly because of the suspicions of the Hamidian regime, which kept a careful eye on all Masonic activities and took harsh measures to curb them.[17] The Freemasons were singled out for repression when Abdülhamid II got wind of their efforts in Europe on behalf of Murad V. Eventually, the government branded the Freemasons "a habitual source of sedition."[18]

Government repression and scrutiny notwithstanding, in the mid-1890s Greek Freemasons in Istanbul resumed their activities.[19] Again, let us turn to a Greek account of these events:

At the beginning of 1894, after receiving special instruction, the son of Scalieri and [others, notably] Iglesis, Kefallineos, and Spanopulos established an informally organized lodge. Again they took up the idea of founding an Eastern state. Other members of the lodge, Olimpios, Stamelos, Sulidis, and Gakkos, embarked on a plan in conjunction with the Greek ambassador, Mavrokordato, the French ambassador, Paul Cambon, and the British ambassador, Philip Currie.

In Istanbul through the agency of this informally organized lodge, a reaction against the regime was coordinated. It entailed reviving the older Ottoman constitution. The intervention of this lodge saved the life of [deposed] Sultan Murad V when the threat of execution hung over him and it further encouraged the nascent Committee of Union and Progress.[20]

Although this lodge may have been founded as early as 1894, Freemason activities resumed in the late 1890s, with a surge of new publications condemning Sultan Abdülhamid II.

The earliest example available is a brief correspondence in the *Daily News* of London: "The Turkish revolutionary party have [has] issued a stirring manifesto to the Mohammedan subjects of the Sultan."[21] When the Ottoman Foreign Ministry instructed the London embassy to trace this telegram to its source, it was discovered that no such telegram had been sent.[22] In fact, this document was an initiative of the Freemasons, since there was no active "Turkish revolutionary party" at the time and identical themes were expounded by the Freemasons in their subsequent appeals and pamphlets.

A more significant initiative came before the public a year later with the publication of *La Turquie Libre*, which appeared in London with little fanfare.[23] The editor of this newspaper was Justin Marengo, who had angered the Ottoman government and provoked a flurry of investigations.[24] Marengo had been based in Paris but was expelled by the French government for engaging in activities that endangered public order.[25] He insisted, however, that he had been deported at the behest of the sultan.[26] Marengo remains an elusive character. Little is known of his background and affiliations other than what is indicated on the masthead of *La Turquie Libre*, which describes the periodical as the organ of Le Parti Constitutionnel Ottoman. Yet within the pages of this journal are a number of interesting declarations on behalf of an organization called Le Comité Libéral Ottoman[27]—none other than the cover name used by Freemasons in their political endeavors in Turkey.

Particularly striking in the pages of Marengo's periodical is the plethora of articles supporting the former sultan Murad V.[28] Further, barely a year after beginning publication, *La Turquie Libre* published texts of speeches, delivered at a Masonic gathering of the Grand Orient, in praise of the ex-sultan.[29] The texts were accompanied by the names of the speakers and their Masonic ranks. For reasons unknown, *La Turquie Libre* ceased publication soon afterward.

Late in 1893, on the heels of the demise of *La Turquie Libre*, a curious pamphlet appeared. Entitled *The Armenians and the Turks under Sultan Abdul Hamid*, the work proclaimed on its title page that it had been printed in Istanbul at the presses of the Committee of the Young Turks.[30]

The Ottoman Foreign Ministry instructed several Ottoman embassies to trace the publisher, because it deemed it impossible for such a pamphlet to have originated in Istanbul.[31] The pamphlet proved to have been published in Great Britain and sent through the British post.[32] Soon after, a new pamphlet appeared, entitled *La Turquie sous Abd-ul-Hamid*, making a similar claim as to its origin.[33] This was a loose translation into French of *The Armenians and the Turks under Sultan Abdul Hamid* with minor discrepancies; it was similarly investigated by the Ottoman government,[34] in part because of the notoriety the text gained in Europe, where the press had expatiated on "this interesting work by the Committee of the Young Turks in Constantinople."[35] The "Young Turk press" credited in both pamphlets had no ties to the CUP,[36] and neither did the "envoy of the Young Turkey [party]" to a Freemason conference held in Paris in 1892.[37] In each case the term *Young Turk* referred to the political wing of the Freemasons. Of particular note is the difference in style between these pamphlets and the later publications of the CUP, especially the more lenient attitude displayed in the pamphlet toward the Christian populations of the Empire.[38]

In tandem with these events, a number of declarations were issued by Le Comité Libéral Ottoman. At this time no official CUP books or periodicals were published,[39] and the declarations of the Comité appeared in foreign-language papers with a reputation for being "activist."

Two years later, on November 25, 1895, in the midst of political turmoil and unrest in Istanbul, a declaration was posted throughout the capital. This action, which the European press attributed to the Young Turks,[40] was in fact the first overt propaganda ploy undertaken in the capital by Le Comité Libéral Ottoman, or the Osmanlı Hürriyetperverân Cemiyeti, as it came to be known in Turkish.[41]

Still, the Comité acted as if it were a separate organization from the Freemasons, and it continued to pursue its reform program and to disseminate literature against government policies that curbed freedom.[42] More significantly, it printed a number of provocative declarations.[43]

Until about 1895, Masonic lodges operated in a largely clandestine fashion, avoiding any direct link with Young Turk groups. Ali Şefkatî—a member of the lodge overseen by Scalieri and editor of the newspaper *İstikbâl*, which he founded in Naples—forged the first link in 1881.[44] Ali Şefkatî's paper soon aroused apprehensions at the palace,[45] and the sultan's agents attempted first to intimidate Şefkatî and then to mend relations with him.[46] But Ali Şefkatî's contacts in Europe were all wool and a yard wide, and he always found a way to escape the net cast by the palace as he kept up his activities in various European cities.[47] His great mobility may be further explained by the fact that he was subsidized by Ismāʿīl, the former khedive of Egypt.[48]

It is striking that Ali Şefkatî's paper never mentioned its editor's links with the Freemasons. Indeed, when Şefkatî moved to London[49] and the paper resumed publication in June 1895 after a failed reconciliation with the palace, it continued to remain silent about those connections.[50] With the exception of *Hürriyet (Liberty)*, it enjoyed being the only journal of the opposition. Ali Şefkati's importance for the Freemasons is confirmed by his relations with CUP leader Ahmed Rıza. He met the latter in London shortly before Ahmed Rıza's paper, *Meşveret (Consultation)*, commenced publication in Paris as the principal organ of the CUP.[51] The friendship was short-lived because Ali Şefkati succumbed soon after, thereby closing the bridge between the CUP and the Freemasons.[52]

There is no evidence supporting the frequent assertion first made by Ramsaur that İbrahim Temo, the founder of İttihad-i Osmanî Cemiyeti (Ottoman Union Society), made contact with the Freemasons in Italy in 1888.[53] The evidence suggests that the Freemasons continued to operate their own independent political organizations until 1902. This is supported by Ahmed Rıza's refusal to accept an invitation to join a Masonic lodge in 1892, on the grounds that the Freemasons' beliefs conflicted with his well-known positivist tendencies.[54]

Until the Congress of Ottoman Opposition, which was held in Paris in 1902, Le Comité Libéral Ottoman continued to interest the European press, largely owing to several high-level efforts to enlist the help of the European powers.[55] In particular, in 1901 it petitioned King Edward VII, a long-standing Freemason, on behalf of the former sultan Murad V, who was imprisoned in the Çırağan Palace.[56] Then it lodged a formal protest with La Ligue des Droits de l'Homme.[57] And finally, it addressed a letter to the French government.[58] The Ligue's response was disappointing.[59] Meanwhile, the Ottoman government reacted swiftly to these appeals and advised the king against any reply.[60] The king complied with the request of the Porte, and this most daring action of Le Comité Libéral Ottoman came to an end.[61] The style of these appeals was entirely different from that of one sent to the kings and presidents of Europe in favor of former Sultan Murad V by the CUP.[62] Some prominent CUP leaders had difficulty identifying the organization that had sent the appeals, and when they understood that this was an initiative of the Freemasons, they denounced it.[63]

After the Congress of Ottoman Opposition, the overt political activities of the Freemasons appeared to end. No doubt this was a relief for the beleaguered regime of Abdülhamid II; but a closer examination shows that these activities did not in fact cease. Instead, a new and subtler liaison was forged, and ultimately much more dangerous connections followed—a new coalition fashioned in Paris by Sabahaddin Bey and his Albanian ally, İsmail Kemal. They took over the principal organ of the CUP, the journal *Osmanlı (Ottoman)*, and declared themselves a separate organization of Turks and Greeks whose intent was to seize power by a coup d'état. It was no coincidence that this group adopted the name Osmanlı Hürriyetperverân Cemiyeti (Ottoman Freedom Lovers' Committee).[64] For official purposes, they adopted the French name Le Comité Central de la Ligue Ottomane,[65] but later, in their dealings with French police, they called themselves Le Comité Libéral Ottoman.[66] They announced their intention of carrying out a coup d'état, and the support they enjoyed among a number of Greek notables and in British government circles leads one to suspect that Freemasons had infiltrated Sabahaddin Bey's organization. The evidence for this is scanty, however, and the only direct proof is a few vague references in a speech Sabahaddin Bey gave several years later, in 1908, at the Greek Masonic lodge of Isiodos, in which "he praised the Masonic contributions to the constitutionalist movement."[67] But since Sabahaddin Bey's ambitions for a coup d'état and the creation of a loosely federated empire were ill conceived, it was not long before the CUP reasserted itself and established its grip over the Young Turk movement. The name Le Comité Libéral Ottoman was quickly forgotten. Ahmed Rıza's faction was still the most important group and bore a name similar to the CUP, only with an apparent reversal of priorities: the Committee of Progress and Union.

At a moment that they judged favorable, the Freemasons once again made an overture to Ahmed Rıza. In 1903 the French Masonic journal *L'Acacia* published an article that hinted at these contacts:

> Not willing to allow Constantinople to succumb and not wishing to take it herself, it is in the interest of France to maintain the status quo, that is, the preservation of the Ottoman Empire. This is also in the interest of England and Germany. Furthermore, this excludes the creation of rival independent states from the majority of Christian provinces of European Turkey that will be dominated by Russia. But how is one to reconcile the disappearance of the outrageously tyrannical government of a sultan—after Abdul Hamid there could well be one no better—with the preservation of the Ottoman Empire? There seems to be a contradiction.
>
> There is no contradiction, says Mr. Ahmed Riza, head of the *Jeune Turquie* movement, who has taken refuge in a paper called *Mechveret*. In his opinion and that of the members of his faction who are all prominent men, Christian and Muslim, Turkey can become, without undue disruption, an honestly governed country, ruled by just laws established by a national parliament of Christians and Muslims.[68]

Upon learning that Armenian organizations had also approached Masonic groups to solicit their help,[69] Ahmed Rıza asserted the following:

> Since these secret societies have lost their *raison d'être* in the free countries [of Europe], a number of Masonic organizations have taken it upon themselves to intervene in political affairs abroad. They have mobilized their energy to fight despotism and repression all over the world. Abdülhamid understands the importance of these Masonic groups and the respect that they have for the suppressed sultan Murad V. For this reason he commissioned secret agents to make inquiries about the policies and the ideas of these organizations. But the Masonic groups were well aware of Abdülhamid's spying endeavors, and I trust that they will take the necessary precautions to bring their undertakings to a satisfactory conclusion.[70]

In another article he commented: "L'action maçonnique peut avoir un effet salutaire pour notre cause."[71] It is impossible to maintain that a man like Ahmed Rıza, who held a special position among the Young Turks and who had always staunchly defended his positivist ideas, would suddenly abandon them to don the ideology of the Freemasons. Nevertheless, the Young Turk circle around Ahmed Rıza included numerous prominent Freemasons. Chief among these was Prince Muḥammad 'Alī Ḥalīm, the leader of the Freemasons of Egypt,[72] which had been suspect in the eyes of the sultan since the mid-1890s.[73] The prince had been in contact with Ahmed Rıza for some time, and during the 1906 "reorganization" of the Young Turks was given important duties. Also in this group was Talât Bey, who had maintained correspondence with Ahmed Rıza since 1903. In July 1903 he joined the lodge Macedonia Risorta.[74]

Throughout this period, Masonic organizations continued to support the Young Turks in their publications. The significance of this for the palace is illustrated in an incident of 1905. A Russian citizen tried to enter the country with a copy of the banned newspaper Σκρίπ, which contained a comment about the plans of the Young Turks.[75] Despite being banned in the Ottoman Empire, Σκρίπ did not change its editorial stance. This comes as no surprise, since the editor was the younger Scalieri, who had joined the Young Turks[76] and was still striving to draw the Freemasons together to create a coherent political program.[77] By 1906 palace intelligence channels had noted the increase in the number of Freemasons traveling to Istanbul from Athens.[78] In response to this flurry of activity, the palace maintained constant contact with the inspectorship of Rumelia to learn about Freemason activities in Salonica.[79] The palace's suspicions were fueled by the fact that the Osmanlı Hürriyet Cemiyeti (later the Internal Headquarters of the Committee of Progress and Union) had been based in two important Masonic lodges.

At this point the Freemasons began to supply the Young Turks with safe houses where they could take refuge from government agents.[80] Although we have evidence that the Freemasons from Turkey participated in international Freemason congresses during the Young Turk revolution,[81] we do not know whether they offered any support for the revolution. It was also claimed that "Ce n'est que lorsque les jeunes turcs mirent fin à l'absolutisme en 1908 et proclamèrent une Constitution 'pour la Turquie nouvelle,' qu'un Suprême Conseil put se mettre au travail, après que la Conférence de Bruxelles des Conseils Suprêmes du Rite Ancien et Accepté (1907) eut approuvé son institution."[82] However, the Young Turks did not comment on this event.

Major differences still separated the Freemasons from the Young Turks. This issue was raised in August 1908, when, in an interview, a Young Turk named Refik Bey commented: "Il est vrai que nous avons eu l'appui moral de la franc-maçonnerie surtout de la franc-maçonnerie Italienne."[83] He tried to dissociate the Young Turks from the Greek Freemasons on the grounds that the nationalism of the former was irreconcilable with what he perceived to be the nationalist aims of the latter. The Freemasons seized the opportunity to declare themselves the main force behind the July 1908 revolution,[84] and the Greek Freemasons compelled Refik Bey to retract his comments.[85] In spite of these differences, the Freemasons supported the Young Turks and were more than satisfied with the reinstatement of the constitution[86]; Freemasonry thrived after the downfall of Abdülhamid II.[87] It was clear to the Freemasons that the bulk of the populace, now fired by emerging Turkish nationalism, would be unmoved by any idea of reviving a Byzantine state[88] or by the prospect of resolving tensions among nationalist groups in the Empire. They understood that their alliance with the Young Turks had been based on mutual interest and that the Young Turks had made similar alliances with Armenian, Macedonian, and Albanian committees in 1907–1908. In spite of the cooperation between them, the depiction of the Young Turk revolution as a Freemason conspiracy—a notion popular between the world wars[89]—is erroneous. The inescapable reality was that these movements were following divergent paths.

Le Parti Constitutionnel en Turquie and Its Relations with the CUP

Although the Freemasons were an effective opposition group in the reign of Abdülhamid II, theirs was not the only network working against the regime. Even before the CUP's overt activities in the Ottoman capital and the inception of its official organ in Paris, a group called Le Parti Constitutionnel en Turquie had begun intriguing against the regime.

The leader of this party was Salīm Fāris, an Ottoman of Arab descent. His father Aḥmad Fāris al-Shidyāq was the editor of the well-known journal *al-Jawā'ib*, published in Istanbul under the auspices of Sultan Abdülhamid II with a pro-British and anti-French line.[90]

Salīm Fāris followed his father's example; he fled the Empire for England and published essays to promote the role of the British in the Near East.[91] He also published articles and pamphlets criticizing the rule of Abdülhamid II[92] and inveighing against his regime from an Islamic point of view.[93] In so doing, Fāris had two underlying objectives: To create an Arabist movement, dependent on British involvement in Near Eastern affairs, and to reconstruct an opposition faction among the high-ranking officials in the Ottoman bureaucracy.

When Fāris's activities gained impetus, the Ottoman government ordered its London embassy to put him under surveillance.[94] The embassy then warned the palace that Fāris was maneuvering to form an opposition committee.[95] Indeed, Fāris had established the Cemiyet-i Cedide-i Osmaniye (New Association for Ottomans)[96]; but his attempts to organize the opponents of the Ottoman regime and to attract leaders of the opposition residing in Europe met with little success,[97] though they were not altogether in vain. They attracted high-ranking statesmen hoping to return power to the Sublime Porte through a constitutional coup d'état. Following Gladstone's election victory in 1892, members of this Ottoman Reform party, as it was called by the European press, desperately searched around for an opposition group abroad whose cooperation they might enlist in engineering a British-led intervention in Ottoman politics.[98] In addition, Fāris's supporters in Istanbul distributed copies of the Ottoman constitution.[99] In February 1894, after the ground had been prepared, Fāris began publishing a journal in London called *Hürriyet (Liberty)*.[100] The leading article for the maiden issue delineated the administrative problems of the Ottoman Empire but gave no hint regarding the organization behind the publication.[101] Another article in an early issue, however, expressed the aspirations of those seeking a coup d'état similar to that which had taken place in 1876.[102]

The journal also attended closely to Syrian affairs,[103] an interest Fāris tried to reconcile with the official ideology of Ottomanism in the first issues. The journal's editors apparently felt compelled to explain its use of specifically Arabic autography, which was different from that used in Turkish papers, claiming that this resulted not from an anti-Turkish tendency but from technical necessity.[104]

In its twelfth issue, the journal announced its affiliation with an association called Le Parti Constitutionnel en Turquie, though it made no other mention of it in that issue. This was probably because Le Parti Constitutionnel was nothing more than a rallying point for the opponents of the regime. One of those who wrote for Fāris's journal claimed that "he shared none of Fāris's ideas, but contributed to his journal in order to express his sincere and patriotic feelings"[105]; he described the movement of that time as an unorganized one and a continuation of the Young Ottoman movement.[106] This was the main reason that Fāris made sure to send his journal to the high-ranking bureaucrats.[107] Thus he wrote an appeal on behalf of the "Partisans of the Constitutional Regime in Istanbul,"[108] and distributed it both abroad[109] and within the Empire through British post offices.[110] This appeal focused on themes used by the Young Ottomans.

Following these events, the Ottoman government launched a campaign against Fāris and his so-called organization, implemented tough measures to obstruct distribution of his journal,[111] and warned the British that the continuance of the publication might damage Ottoman-British relations.[112] In addition, the Ottoman embassy in London tried to buy off the director of the publishing house that produced the journal[113] and finally filed a lawsuit in London against Fāris and his periodical.[114] When the Ottoman authorities learned that the journal was being sent to the Ottoman Empire inside copies of the *Times* of London, they banned the distribution of that newspaper within the Empire.[115] Although the praise accorded to *Hürriyet* by the British press[116] and Armenian journals[117] published abroad irritated the Ottoman authorities, the real reason behind these strict measures was fear in the palace of Fāris's relations with high-ranking officials. The sultan was terrified of a palace coup d'état, and this fear spread among palace and government officials.[118] They offered to pay Fāris to cease publication, but he refused.[119]

In January 1895, Fāris's organization published an appeal to the sultan under the name Comité du Parti Constitutionnel Ottoman à Constantinople,[120] again expressing the discontent of high-ranking bureaucrats. It also published a series of appeals under the names Hürriyetperverân Fırkası (Freedom Lovers' party) and Islahatperverân-ı Osmaniye Fırkası (Ottoman Reformers' party) and distributed them in Istanbul.[121] These petitions adopted a more religious tone than the request circulated in January 1895, indicating that Fāris was now appealing to the ulema.

However, the Ottoman intelligence service now began to arrest Fāris's supporters in the capital.[122] In May 1895, Muṣṭafā Zakī, an Egyptian, who translated Arabic articles into Turkish, was arrested.[123] At the peak of the Armenian crisis, the lawyer İzzet Bey, nicknamed "Persian İzzet," was also apprehended. He had written and disseminated a manifesto inviting Armenians to join in common action,[124] which the Armenians had welcomed.[125] He then sent a letter to Lord Salisbury calling for his intervention in the crisis.[126] But Celâleddin Bey, İzzet Bey's secretary, informed the authorities about his activities and his organization,[127] denouncing them as attempting to establish a republican regime.[128] The police apprehended more than fifty members and sympathizers of the enterprise and exiled them at once.[129] On his way to exile in Tripoli of Barbary, İzzet Bey complained of the weak organizational framework of their society to a member of the CUP, who was likewise being exiled to Tripoli of Barbary.[130]

Although *Hürriyet* continued to publish letters sent by members of Le Parti Constitutionnel in Istanbul, this was merely an attempt to delude its readers.[131] In 1896, the Ottoman embassy in London bought off two important authors who wrote for *Hürriyet*.[132] Eight months later, when they were still writing for the journal, it required each to swear "not to write for the journal *Hürriyet* and to become loyal subjects of the sultan" if they wanted to receive the sums the government offered.[133] This had a disastrous effect on the journal. After the Ottoman victory over the Greeks in 1897, when the Ottoman government asked its opponents to come to terms with it, Fāris started negotiating with the representatives of the sultan to terminate publication.[134] In return for this concession, he obtained the privilege of controlling the distribution of drinking water in Beirut,[135] which was described by a European diplomat as an expensive payoff to an opponent of the regime.[136] In addition, Fāris promised to become a loyal subject of the sultan and to withdraw from the opposition. Despite this bargain, Fāris later tried to organize an opposition group in France composed primarily of Arabs.[137] However, because of strong objections by the Ottoman government and a lack of support from the French authorities, he did not succeed.[138] Later, Halil Halid and Fāris tried to revive the organization in London by publishing journals. Halil Halid published a periodical called *Hürriyet* in 1902 and sent copies to the palace in order to extort money from the Ottoman government.[139] Fāris gave money to Haydarpaşazâde Ârif, a Young Turk, requiring him to publish *Muhbir (Informer),* the same title as one of the periodicals of the Young Ottomans.[140] But these efforts bore no fruit. Further activities by Fāris should be examined in the context of the Arabist movement.

The organization that Fāris led under various names was entirely separate from the CUP. Although Fāris established sound relations with Ali Şefkatî,[141] who functioned as an intermediary between the Freemasons and the CUP, and although Şefkati's satirical journal quoted *Hürriyet* on a few occasions,[142] Ahmed Rıza and Murad Bey, the two leaders of the CUP, severely criticized Fāris and made an effort not to comment on Le Parti Constitutionnel en Turquie. Ahmed Rıza complained about Fāris's activities to Murad Bey and described Fāris as a selfish person who was working for himself.[143] Murad Bey depicted the publication of *Hürriyet* as an example of opportunism.[144] Before fleeing to Europe, he informed the Ottoman police about the distribution of Fāris's journal.[145] Later, in an editorial in *Meşveret*, Ahmed Rıza wrote that "the journal *Hürriyet* is not a Turkish newspaper and for that reason cannot represent Ottoman society."[146] He also refused to circulate copies of *Hürriyet* that had been sent to him for distribution to CUP members.[147] Only during the conflict between Ahmed Rıza and Murad Bey over the leadership of the CUP did the latter praise Fāris's journal and then only to win his support against the former's allies in the committee.[148] Fāris responded warmly.[149] Murad Bey's followers hated Fāris,[150] however, and their charge that Fāris's correspondents were Armenians[151] blocked Murad Bey's alliance with Fāris. The main reason for their antipathy seems to have been his separatist tendencies.[152] When, after his honeymoon with the Ottoman government, Fāris decided openly to rejoin the opposition and published an Arabic-Turkish journal called *Khilāfat-Hilâfet*,[153] CUP members openly inveighed against him, asserting that they had nothing to do with either this journal or its editor.[154]

The young nationalist members of the CUP considered Le Parti Constitutionnel Ottoman a separatist and old-fashioned palace coup organization. The other wing of the CUP, which had previously controlled the Istanbul center of the organization and had sought a similar coup d'état, considered it a rival in the competition for the loyalty of the same cliques. Although Fāris established ties with high-ranking bureaucrats, they had no intention of appointing him their spokesman. Since he did not receive enough support from either group, his efforts produced no results.

Le Comité Turco-Syrien and Its Relations with the CUP

A few months after its inception, the existence of the Comité Turco-Syrien was made public in an interview given by two Syrian intellectuals, who also mentioned their soon-to-be-circulated organ. In response to a question by a French journalist, the Syrians described their conciliatory role in the opposition movement as follows:

Notre parti, nous déclare le représentant du Comité Syrien, est médiateur entre celui des Arméniens, qui sont chrétiens et réclament leur autonomie, et celui des jeunes turcs qui sont musulmanes et désirent, comme nous, conserver l'intégrité de l'empire, mais en obtenant des réformes effectives et pour tous ses sujets.[155]

The Comité Turco-Syrien shaped its policy toward this end. Although inaccurately characterized in the western press as a Young Turk organization and even confused with the Young Turkey party (the CUP),[156] this Syrian organization, in contrast to the so-called party of Fāris, became intimately tied with the CUP and gradually dissolved into it.

The Syrian reform advocates began their activities in Europe simultaneously with the inception of the CUP, and some joined the efforts of Fāris, although the Arabist contingent of his venture was insignificant.

During the time that Fāris was active in London, a Lebanese intellectual named Habib Antony Salmoné often visited Syria, where he met with Syrian journalists.[157] He brought out a journal called *Ḍiyā' al-Khāfiqaīn (Eastern and Western Review)[158]* in 1892 which was bought for a handsome sum by the Ottoman embassy in London with intent to terminate its publication.[159] He also printed other works against the sultan's regime until 1897, emerging as a symbol of awakening Christian Arabs.[160] In that year he sought a promise of British help to counter an anticipated retaliation by the Ottoman government against his relatives in Beirut.[161] Following this appeal, he visited Paris to assist in joint CUP–Comité Turco-Syrien activities,[162] after which he suddenly withdrew from politics.

In 1893, Amīr Amīn Arslān, a member of a foremost Druze family in Lebanon, fled to Paris and, with the help of Syrians there, attempted to organize an opposition to the sultan's regime.[163] Although some members of his family had ties with the sultan's regime, many others assisted the opposition movement. One led the local opposition in Lebanon and was accused of being an accomplice in the assassination of a gendarmerie officer.[164] Another member, a diplomat at the Ottoman embassy in Brussels, was accused of disseminating seditious propaganda.[165]

In August 1894, Arslān spearheaded a group of Arab opponents by printing and circulating an Arabic daily called *Kashf al-Niqāb*.[166] The proclaimed aim of which was "to expose the oppressors who have betrayed the country and neglected the nation [*ummah*], and sold the fatherland for money."[167]

The first issues spoke rather prudently of the sultan and even praised him for devoting all his time to the country's affairs.[168] The journal was smuggled into the Ottoman Empire and circulated throughout Syrian communities in Europe and the United States, where, it was said, the Syrian community received it "like thirsty people being given water."[169]

A series of articles criticized the "tyrannical government"[170] and Khalīl Ghānim, who wrote for the journal, promoted the constitution for all Ottomans.[171] Although he claimed that "Turks exercise injustice, severity and harshness, whereas the Arabs sacrifice their blood in *Jihād*," Ghānim made it clear that "the injustice of the pashas is more beneficial for [the Arabs] than a takeover of [their] land by foreigners."[172] Thus the journal remained within the bounds of Ottomanism, although it revealed a disproportionate interest in events in Syria and Lebanon and made much of the Arab element in the Empire.

Arslān was pressured by the French because of the Ottoman government's unremitting complaints,[173] and when he found himself confronted by financial problems in July 1895, he ceased publishing.[174]

Khalīl Ghānim's activities against the sultan's regime had begun some years prior to his involvement in *Kashf al-Niqāb*. Using his prestige as a former Syrian deputy in the short-lived Ottoman parliament, he engaged in political activities as early as 1880. He wrote for the prestigious French organ *Le Journal des Débats* and published an Arabic journal called *al-Baṣīr*.[175] Prior to the publication of *Kashf al-Niqāb,* he founded another organ named *Hilâl-Le Croissant,*[176] published in both French and Turkish, advocating reforms, a constitutional regime, and Ottomanism.[177]

When financial problems thwarted him, he sold the journal to the Paris embassy after lengthy negotiations.[178]

Around this time, a Catholic priest from Lebanon named Alexis Kateb brought out another bilingual journal in Paris, called *al-Rajā'-L'Espérance.*[179] According the to Ottoman authorities, Kateb's primary objective was blackmail.[180] His publication was received with stormy protests by journals close to the CUP.[181] He later confessed that his ambition exceeded blackmail—he intended to serve French interests in the Middle East.[182] When his petitions captured the attention of the French[183] they began to support his publication; his goal was thus fulfilled.[184]

In early 1895, Salmoné, Arslān, Ghānim, and Kateb decided to organize a Syrian-Arab movement opposed to the sultan's regime. *Kashf al-Niqāb* informed its readership that a committee had been established in London, headed by a member of the former Ottoman parliament, undoubtedly Ghānim, and composed of Syrians and Europeans. The committee's aim was described as "general protest against the daily injustice in the Empire, and more particularly in Syria,"[185] and later the journal mentioned that a branch might be established in Paris.[186] To launch the Comité Turco-Syrien, Arslān delivered a series of lectures to appeal to French public opinion on subjects such as "Women in the East." Ironically, his assistant was an editor paid by the palace to write eulogies of the sultan.[187] Next, at Ghānim's instigation, an open letter was sent to the sultan inviting him to grant freedom of the press and thus to liberalize his regime. It was signed by Arslān, Ghānim, Fāris, and many editors of journals in Cairo and Alexandria.[188] Although the tone of the letter was respectful, the Ottoman authorities described it as a "seditious and malevolent publication" and authorized an investigation of its signatories and distributors in the Empire.[189] It is curious that the group's name, Comité Turco-Syrien, was omitted in these formative initiatives.

The first activity under this title was a memorandum presented to the six Great Powers.[190] Although the memorandum was undated, the earliest notice of it appeared in the European press on November 22, 1895; thus it must have been written a few days that prior to date.[191] The object of the memorandum was to draw the attention of European governments to the general problems of the Empire and to demonstrate that the Armenian problem was a very minor one. The Ottoman ambassador in Paris recommended the drafting of a letter by the grand vizier, presented as if all Syrians were behind it, in which assertions in the memorandum would be refuted, and dispatching it from Syria to all prominent news agencies.[192] On December 13, 1895, this new organization published a bilingual Parisian organ called *La Jeune Turquie-Turkiyyā al-fatāt*. Apparently the committee found it necessary to justify its publication in Arabic as well as French. They asserted that they had done so because "Arabic is the language of the Holy Quran."[193] This was undoubtedly done to shield them from a possible accusation of separatism. The journal noted that letters sent by Turks and Arabs would be published regardless of whether the content concurred with the views of the paper.[194] The journal was distributed free of charge, and payment was offered to those willing to submit articles for publication.[195]

The Ottoman authorities acted swiftly to halt its distribution in the empire, especially in the Arab provinces,[196] and declared that Fāris was behind the publication and that the British had abetted its circulation.[197] However, other sources did not support these assertions.

Letters addressed to the Syrians contained high praises, such as "The people of Syria are the most intelligent and knowledgeable among the [peoples] of the Ottoman Empire and have been the first to recognize the possibilities of modern times."[198] Also, a presentation in dialogue form depicted Arabs as the most unjustly administered group in the Empire, while the Turks were disparaged:

> We the Arabs comprise three quarters of the Ottoman subjects, but of the ninety thousand officials, eighty thousand are Turks and only ten thousand are Armenians, Greeks, etc., even though it is a well known fact that the Turks are less wise and poorer administrators than the others. So where is justice and where equality? . . . How easy it was for the Turks in their early conquests to give up their language for the beautiful Arabic language [in] religious and civil [matters], to embrace sublime Arabic poetry and elevated Arab science . . . and glorious history. Until then they [the Turks] had no complete language, no glorious poetry, no science, no tradition, and no epic tales other than war stories, which are like the stroke of a pen on the pages of history.[199]

Open letters to the Syrians paid special attention to Syria's problems, ignoring other regions of the Empire.[200]

In spite of these views, as expressed in the journal and by the society behind it, CUP leaders praised and endorsed both. Ahmed Rıza underscored the difference between *Turkiyyā al-fatāt* and other Arabic journals,[201] and Murad Bey hailed the efforts of Arslān and Ghānim.[202] Given the fact that the journal was more critical toward the Turks than other journals published by the Arabs, such as *Hürriyet*, and that there was not a single Muslim Syrian among the founders of the society—Arslān was a Druze and the other three were Christians[203]—it is difficult to make sense of the CUP's endorsements.

To discern the reasons behind them it is necessary to scrutinize the membership of the Comité Turco-Syrien. One wing of the organization, led by Salmoné and Kateb, pursued a hard-line policy on relations between the Turks and Arabs. Salmoné consistently asserted that the Turks had no right to produce caliphs, indirectly advocating an Arab caliphate.[204] He also presented the Comité as the central organization of the Young Turk movement.[205] In addition, along with several anonymous writers, he adopted a more pro-Christian flavor in articles analyzing the problems of the Ottoman Empire.[206] Ahmed Rıza criticized these claims through *Meşveret* and labeled them separatist.[207] The second wing, led by Ghānim and Arslān, adopted a policy more favorable to relations between the Turks and Arabs and more moderate toward the Arabs' role in the Empire. Arslān's perspective on the Armenian problem was consistent with the CUP's,[208] and although he expected France to play a more active role in the Middle East, he did not share Kateb's longing to see Syria and Lebanon become French protectorates.[209] Arslān remained within the spirit of the official ideology, Ottomanism, even when writing about his ethnic group,[210] and he frequently extolled Ahmed Rıza.[211]

As for Ghānim, a prominent writer for *Mechveret Supplément Français* as well, he adopted an emphatically Ottomanist line[212] and praised the Young Turks for their efforts.[213]

This second wing was doubtless more deeply involved in the policy-making of the Comité Turco-Syrien, for Ghānim was its president and Arslān its secretary. Its program, presented in detail in Salmoné's book, had neither separatist nor anti-Turkish tendencies,[214] and in the central organ any notion of European intervention in Ottoman politics was denounced in a manner consistent with Ahmed Rıza's ideas.[215] The journal further condemned European imperial politics,[216] undoubtedly with the opposition of Kateb and Salmoné.

An article by Ghānim in *Kashf al-Niqāb* on relations between Arabs and Turks was hailed by the CUP. Ghānim wrote:

> Yes, I do want to restore the constitution, for the life of the Ottoman nation depends upon it. To the same extent I also long for the success and progress of the Arab nation, but only under the banner of the *Amīr al-Mu'minīn*, who holds the bridle of the Ottoman sultanate, and this for two reasons:
>
> First, the Arabs will not be secure in their comfort and future if Istanbul is not in their [the Turks'] hands. . . .
>
> Second, the Arabs care for the Turks and do not hate them as do the Greeks, Armenians, and the Bulgarians.[217]

Such ideas, coupled with the fact that the CUP selected Syria as its main arena until the coup d'état attempt was foiled there in 1897, led to a merger of the Comité Turco-Syrien and the CUP.

In May 1896 the Ottoman ambassador in Paris bribed French officials to allow him to intercept Amīr Arslān's incoming and outgoing mail. The letters and a report by a political police officer named Ducas revealed that Arslān, representing the CUP, was attempting to mediate between the CUP and Armenian committees for common action.[218] Other Ottoman sources were apparently convinced that an alliance between the Young Turks and the Syrians existed at this time.[219]

Also in May 1896, when *La Jeune Turquie* disputed accusations against the Young Turks by the French ambassador Paul Cambon, it was clearly stated that the organization saw itself within the framework of the Young Turk movement, and this elicited the approbation of the CUP.[220] In December 1896, at a banquet given to celebrate the twentieth anniversary of the promulgation of the Ottoman Constitution, Amīn Arslān called the CUP "our party."[221] Salmoné, Ghānim, and Arslān signed a memorandum presented to the Great Powers on behalf of "Les Partis des Réformes Générales en Turquie"; this document also bears the CUP seal at the top.[222]

The name Comité Turco-Syrien was last used while it was defending Ahmed Rıza against Murad Bey during the August 1897 schism.[223] At that time Salmoné had already quit politics, and Kateb had decided to work for his true objective in the pay of the French. The Ottoman government's efforts to buy off Arslān had been fruitless.[224] He and Ghānim endorsed Ahmed Rıza and the CUP. Arslān's influence in the Young Turk movement after 1897 was marginal, while Ghānim emerged as a symbol of Ottomanist policy in the CUP until his death in 1903. His Ottomanist ideas, which were commended by all factions in the CUP,[225] heralded the dissolution of the Comité Turco-Syrien and its absorption into the CUP.

The Role of the Ulema and the Sufi Orders in the Opposition Movement—Their Relations with the CUP

An examination of the opposition to the absolutist regime in the Ottoman Empire prior to the advent of the Young Turks, such as the Young Ottoman movement and the proclamation of the first Ottoman Constitution in 1876, reveals that the ulema figured prominently in such ventures. Primarily because of their legitimizing power, the ulema were attractive to the opposition groups in the Empire. Relations between the opposition and the ulema displayed two salient characteristics. First, members of the new intelligentsia did not view the ulema as natural allies, because most regarded religion as an obstacle to social progress. Second, since the regime of Abdülhamid II legitimized itself through Islam, the opposition, in spite of its secular identity and for pragmatic reasons, sought religious dicta from the ulema in order to refute this claim. Thus there were awkward but significant relations between the Young Turks and elements of the ulema, who described themselves as "the guardians of the nation and its true trustees"[226] and claimed a "right to monitor the conduct of the sovereign"[227] on the basis of Islamic precepts.

Because the various opposition groups deferred to the authority of the ulema, the latter fell under the suspicion of the sultan. Nevertheless, many ulema served as his advisers,[228] thus eliciting the criticism of the opposition; this criticism was leveled at them in spite of the fact that many members of the ulema were exiled during the reign of Abdülhamid II.[229] For such reasons the ulema organized their own opposition groups even before the overt activities of the CUP had begun. Only later did they decide to join forces with the Young Turks and in particular with the CUP, with which their organization gradually merged. Before we consider their role in the movement, it should be noted that the ranks of the ulema were divided by complex internal factions. There existed not only conflicting political commitments among the representatives of orthodox Islam but also discordant political allegiances within the various Sufi orders. The sultan's policy of using these orders and folk-Islam groups to express his will in the periphery further complicated the situation.

The manner in which the CUP procured *fatwās* from the orthodox ulema will be discussed later. These *fatwās* were given to the CUP as part of a conspiracy to delegitimize the rule of Abdülhamid II among the Ottoman Muslims. The Young Turks also uncovered and published a collection of *fatwās* against absolutism issued many years previously.[230] Their intention was to undermine the legal basis of Abdülhamid II's rule among the Muslim populace. The sultan's supporters countered these arguments with religious literature that proclaimed the essential value of loyalty and obedience to a sovereign, supporting this with citations from Islamic texts.[231] For this reason, when the Young Turks invited the various social groups to unite under their banner, the ulema were the first to whom they turned. As early as 1894, Hüseyinzâde Ali and İshak Sükûti, who led the organizational branch of the first nucleus of the CUP, secured a promise of support from Ubeydullah Efendi, a prominent member of the ulema.[232] However, in spite of this promise and the improved relations between the ulema and the Young Turks, the ulema continued to organize independent activities until 1897 and only subsequently began to join the ranks of the Young Turk opposition.

According to an Ottoman document, some committees were formed in Antalya before the Young Turks started to publish *Meşveret* in Paris:

> It was reported from Antalya that due to the provocations and incitements of a number of agitators, some hodjas are daring to disobey the imperial government and are forming committees. God forbid that some sort of unseemliness might ensue; British [war]ships may come to this region.[233]

When we consider this report in light of the activities of Hoca Muhid-din Efendi, who became the leader of the Cemiyet-i İlmiye (later dissolved into the CUP), it becomes clear that Hoca Muhiddin and the ulema were working behind the scenes and were responsible for these movements. As he himself wrote,

> At that time [1893–1894], when this lover of freedom was among the civil servants in Antalya, he [and his friends] had distributed patriotic publications throughout the province. We even made Hafız Mehmed Bey the first chamberlain of Sultan Abdülaziz, and Brigadier General Hasan Pasha, the brother-in-law of Hüseyin Avni Pasha, members of this association.[234]

Following these activities, leaflets were widely distributed in Istanbul claiming that "Abdülhamid is a usurper of the caliphate" and "to call him caliph is tantamount to infidelity." *Mizan* described the leaflets as the work of other opposition groups, and nowhere was it hinted that the CUP might have had a hand in it.[235] The fliers were undoubtedly authored and circulated by the organization of the ulema, and although members of the ulema continued to write to *Mizan*[236] and to send their protests to both *Mizan*[237] and *Meşveret*,[238] they acted independently for a while.

As late as 1896, the *talebe-i ulûm* (students of Islamic learning) tried to organize an independent demonstration,[239] and in January 1897, when the British ambassador spoke to a prominent ulema member, the latter made it clear that although he "is not much in favour of the revival of Midhat Pasha's constitution," he "considers that the people are not yet fit for a parliament, but of course even that, with any abuses it might bring with it at the outset, would be better than the continuance of the present tyranny."[240] Yet another activity of the ulema was the publication of an open letter to Lord Salisbury by the so-called Vatanperverân-ı Islâmiye Cemiyeti (Patriotic Muslims' Association).[241] Members of this association sent the Turkish translation of this text to Fâris's journal,[242] since it was assumed that he was involved with them[243] and not with the official organs of the CUP. Nor did they wait for the publication of Hoca Muhiddin's journal. It therefore seems improbable that substantial ties existed between this religious group and either the CUP or Hoca Muhiddin. The group's last known activity was its distribution of a leaflet in Istanbul after the Greco-Turkish War of 1897. The Ottomans were obligated on religious grounds to rebel against the regime of Abdülhamid II:

> What happened to Egypt, which is the way to Mecca? Who possesses Tunis? Where did Bosnia and Herzegovina and Eastern Roumelia go? To whom was Crete given? O! The Arabs, Bosnians, Kurds, Circassians, Albanians, who constitute the military divisions at Yıldız! I am addressing you, I am inviting you to [perform your] duty. By protecting Sultan Abdülhamid, you are forsaking your religion, God forbid, you are going to give up your ghosts as unbelievers. Are you betraying your religion for the fifty piasters that you receive monthly

and the rice and *zerde* that you have occasionally? Will you not be ashamed when you have the audience of God and the Prophet in the future? Will not the believers who shed their blood for the establishment of Islam spit in your face because you protect Sultan Abdülhamid, who annihilates Islam, with your swords? In the next sermon [we shall] speak about the constitution, and declare and prove that the Prophet recommended the constitutional regime.[244]

In his memoirs, Hoca Muhiddin recounts his flight to Europe, how he joined the opposition there, and how he discussed his group's prospective role in the movement with the Young Turk leader Ahmed Rıza in a conference that lasted forty days. They decided that Hoca Muhiddin should publish a journal in Egypt that would be the organ of the ulema; its purpose would be to "incite the religious feelings of people."[245] The ulema provided their full support,[246] and the Young Turks acknowledged this development in one of their journals, calling Hoca Muhiddin's decision "an initiative of patriotic members of the ulema who have recognized that this is the time to discharge their responsibility to lead the faithful."[247] Hoca Muhiddin also promised the Young Turks that he would publish articles proving that a parliament is necessary according to Islam.

After this agreement, Hoca Muhiddin insisted on publishing his journal as an independent organ, in spite of several instances of connections between the ulema and the CUP: articles had been appearing in the CUP journals written by members of the ulema, one of whom introduced himself as "a member of the ulema who is proud of being a member of the CUP"[248]; police had caught the *talebe-i ulûm* with *Meşveret*[249]; a lecturer at a Muslim theological school was an active correspondent for the CUP[250]; and the Ottoman ulema were appealing for help to Murad Bey or the Egyptian ulema.[251]

Intending to demonstrate its independence as well as its close links to the CUP, the official organ of Hoca Muhiddin's organization published letters received from CUP members, because, as was said, "the policy of the CUP is in accordance with [their] policy."[252] The arrival in Egypt of Hoca Kadri, a member of the ulema with even more direct relations with the CUP,[253] had a profound impact on the absorption of the organized ulema into the CUP.[254] During this process, the central committee of the CUP was controlled by a more conservative group than before, and there were many disagreements between this group and the positivist leader Ahmed Rıza. Under these conditions the collaboration between the ulema and the CUP developed relatively easily, and Hoca Muhiddin turned over his journal to an editorial board, which published it as the organ of the CUP in Egypt.[255]

In the wake of these events, the Egyptian branch of the CUP, with its strong Islamic underpinnings and insistence that the ulema lead the revolutionary movement,[256] now became even more conservative. Although more secular members of the CUP who had fled the Empire also participated in this branch, the CUP continued to attack the Ottoman government from an Islamic perspective in its journals. At this time the CUP had nothing to do with the ulema; nevertheless, it published articles to silence criticisms made by ordinary people that CUP constituents adhered to positivist and materialistic philosophies. Between 1900 and 1903, the ulema supported the Young Turks who were publishing the central organ *Osmanlı*, and not Ahmed Rıza and his followers. Nevertheless, the Committee of Progress and Union, which dominated the movement after 1902, no longer regarded the ulema as a legitimizing power. Whereas before 1902 the ulema had been cultivated by the Young Turks, they were now ignored by them and were unable to play a significant role in the Young Turk revolution of 1908. Though the ulema supported the Young Turks by declaring themselves the most ruthlessly suppressed group under the regime of Abdülhamid II[257] and by announcing that their society was an association directly linked to the CUP,[258] they experienced a change of heart after observing the CUP's lack of interest in Islam and its positivist tendencies. They decided instead to undertake independent activities once again.[259]

Another noteworthy relationship that was at least as important was that between the CUP and various Sufi orders. As European scholars and officials pointed out, Sufi orders played prominent political roles in Muslim countries, particularly in Ottoman society.[260] In late Ottoman times, orders seeking to influence politics constantly vied with one another. Although it is difficult to pinpoint the influence of any given order, it can be said that the heterodox orders favored the Young Turks, whereas the more orthodox ones were inclined to support the sultan. An exception to this pattern is the case of two Naqshbandī sheikhs who joined the opposition while their order as a whole backed the sultan.[261] One of them, Erbilli Sheikh Mehmed Es'ad, was exiled to his native town by Abdülhamid II[262] and praised the Young Turk movement after the revolution.[263] The other, a Naqshbandī sheikh at Constantsa, Şevki Celâleddin, actually joined the Young Turks and was the only active Sufi member at the Congress of Ottoman Opposition in Paris in 1902.[264]

The Sufi orders who opposed the existing political regime in the Ottoman Empire now came to the aid of the CUP. The strongest of them, the Bektashi sect, had played a very important role in Ottoman politics and had been suppressed in 1826[265]; for a decade after, "even the name Bektashi could not be mentioned."[266]

Following the coronation of Sultan Abdülmecid, the Bektashi order made an attempt at revival. At the initiative of Halil Revnakî Baba Efendi, the *tekke* (dervish lodge) at Merdivenköyü was reinstated, followed by other *tekkes*.[267] In 1872 the Bektashis published Fadl-allah Hurufi's *'Işknâme*,[268] one volume of an esoteric six-volume reference set known as the *Cavidannâme*.[269] This publication provoked Hoca İshak Efendi to compose a book in which he accused the Bektashis of having infiltrated the Sa'dīyyah, Rifā'īyyah, Qādirīyyah, and Naqshbandīyyah orders; of continuing their former practices, and of putting out "anti-Islamic" propaganda.[270] When the Bektashis published a book refuting Hoca İshak

Efendi's claims,[271] "the absolutist regime of Abdülhamid II banned the distribution of this book."[272] Besides taking measures against Bektashi propaganda,[273] the government forbade publication and distribution of any Bektashi material.

Bektashis were kept under close surveillance between 1878 and 1908[274] for other reasons as well: Their role in the Albanian nationalist movement of 1878–1881[275] and their efforts to fashion an Albanian national identity.[276] After the suppression of the Prizren League, from the beginning of the Young Turk movement until the revolution of 1908, the Bektashis worked closely with the Young Turks[277]; in 1899 Ahmed Baba, an Albanian Bektashi in Egypt, published an opposition journal in both Turkish and Albanian.[278]

It was claimed that this close affiliation was due to the affinity between the heterodox tendencies of the Bektashis and the liberal ideas of the Young Turks, and that the Bektashis were affiliated with the Freemasons, who let the Young Turks use their lodges after 1906.[279] The visit paid by the revolutionary officers to the Bektashi *tekke* at Rumelihisarı after the revolution of 1908 is an instance of tribute paid by the officers.[280] When in 1909 Rıfkı Baba's *Bektaşi Sırrı* appeared, it was the first Bektashi publication since Abdülhamid II's accession to the throne[281]; likewise, the new regime closed newspapers publishing articles against the Bektashi order and punished their owners,[282] while new Bektashi *tekkes* in Istanbul, such as Takkeci Mahallesi Tekkesi at Topkapı, were given permission to open.[283] In Albania after the revolution, the Bektashis gave their full support to the CUP.[284]

The same relationship is also in evidence between the Melâmîs, who were also allegedly affiliated with the Freemasons,[285] and the Young Turks during their later activities in the Balkans. Colonel Sadık Bey (leader of the CUP branch in Monastir in 1908) later told Andrew Ryan (the former dragoman and intelligence officer of the British embassy in Istanbul) that a large number of officers in Macedonia were Melâmî devotees and figured prominently in the movement.[286] Another case was that of Bursalı Tahir, one of the founders of the Ottoman Freedom Society in Salonica in 1906 and a prominent devotee of this order.[287] These two cases illustrate that the CUP had significant relations with the Melâmî order, which had always been against the establishment—in contrast to Bektashis, who had remained within the system until 1826.

There was also an association between the CUP and the Mevlevîs. The membership in this order of the heir apparent Reşad Efendi was significant. The Mevlevî *tekke* at Galata acted as an intermediary between the Young Turks and the heir apparent during the attempted coup d'état of 1896.[288] The other Mevlevî *tekke* at Yenikapı, which was under close surveillance and frequently searched by police and intelligence agents,[289] distributed the CUP organs published in Paris, and Celâl Efendi, its sheikh, was invited to participate in the coup d'état. He and his fellow conspirators discussed technical details such as "how to transfer the heir apparent from Beşiktaş to Istanbul."[290] But the role this *tekke* played actually in the venture is unclear.

Another hint of the bond between the Young Turks and the Mevlevîs in the capital was the ongoing effort of Tahir Dede, a Mevlevî dervish, to take over publication of a journal called *Resimli Gazete*. This was a journal to which the Young Turks of the Royal Medical Academy had contributed[291] but which had been suspended[292] on the grounds of "the participation of immoral people in its publication."[293] Again, the Young Turks in Izmir, led by Refik Nevzad, held organizational meetings at the home of a Mevlevî sheikh also known as Reşad Efendi for the purpose of forming a branch in Izmir.[294] These Young Turks and the sheikh himself were arrested by the police and exiled.[295] At about the same time Mehmed Efendi, another Mevlevî sheikh, was banished to Angora by the government, along with his Young Turk compatriots.[296] Finally, the Çelebi (the religious authority of the Mevlevî dervishes) requested asylum from the British vice-consul in Konya, telling him that he feared for his life for political reasons and because of the sultan's enmity, which had been aroused during the Young Turk revolution.[297]

The Young Turks also capitalized on the palace's support of those orders which the sultan believed would help block western penetration into the Arab provinces. The western powers, for their part, feared and opposed the orders.[298] If the sultan endorsed orders such as the Tījānī-yyah[299] and Sanūsīyyah,[300] which dominated large parts of North Africa, the Young Turks would have no chance of gaining the allegiance of the regions before the revolution. But the sultan's plan for a pan-Islamic policy aided by the Rifāʿīyyah and Madanīyyah orders, by which he intended both to block penetration by western powers and to achieve unity among his Muslim subjects, stimulated intense rivalry between these two orders and that of the Qadirīyyah order, especially in Syria. Two sheikhs of the Rifāʿīyyah and Madanīyyah orders, Abū al-Hudā al-Ṣayyādī and Ẓāfir al-Madanī [Muḥammad ibn Muḥammad Ḥasan], became the sultan's advisers; in return for promoting the sultan's policy, their orders were granted various privileges.[301] Sheikh Ẓāfir al-Madanī became a strong player in Ottoman politics[302] and received the help of the sultan in establishing a number of *tekkes*[303] because of the scant membership of the Madanīyyah order[304]; however, Abū al-Hudā al-Ṣayyādī and the Rifāʿīs gained a more prominent status. Like Ẓāfir al-Madanī, Abū al-Hudā al-Ṣayyādī had come to Istanbul before Abdülhamid II's accession and had impressed him in several ways.[305] Abū al-Hudā al-Ṣayyādī had authored pamphlets enjoining the faithful to unite under the rule of the caliph[306] and had argued that the Rifāʿīyyah order was the most excellent of all the Islamic orders.[307] Many of his works were translated into Turkish by the palace, and the ministry of education obtained copies of his books for public libraries.[308] Since the Rifāʿīs had established numerous *tekkes* in Macedonia,[309] the sultan may have wanted to use them against the Bektashis, the dominant order in that part of European Turkey. But the sultan's real aim was to back Abū al-Hudā al-Ṣayyādī's ambition to establish the Rifāʿīyyah as the dominant order in the Arab provinces and thereby to expand his own hegemony.[310] According to a contemporary, the sultan and al-Ṣayyādī launched a plan to accomplish this:

> La première partie du plan, action en Mésopotamie, mobilisait les Rifāʿyin contre les Qâdiryîn restés jusque-là maîtres à Baghdad.
>   La campagne fut menée par Abou'l Houdâ par la publication de textes imprimés et l'érection ou transformation d'édifices religieux, les deux moyens de propagande en Islâm, l'apostolat populaire étant mal vu.[311]

In addition, thanks to the efforts of al-Ṣayyādī, the Ottoman press openly criticized ʿAbd al-Qādir al-Jīlānī, the founder of the Qādiri order, on the occasion of the publication of the Turkish edition of his famous work *al-Ghunyah li-ṭālibī ṭariqat al-ḥaqq*. Further attacks on Jīlānī were forbidden by imperial order.[312] These attempts, plus the rivalry between Rifāʿīs and Qādiris, cemented a noteworthy alliance between the Young Turks and the Qādiris of Syria, and in 1897 they jointly attempted an abortive coup d'état.[313] Qādiris were arrested afterward and exiled. Their goal had been to prevent the expansion of the Rifāʿīyyah order in that region. The Young Turks, exploiting the rivalry between Qādiris and Rifāʿīs, argued that Abū al-Hudā al-Ṣayyādī was trying to diminish the influence of the Qādiris.[314] (A more detailed examination of this attempted coup is given in the following chapter.) For their opposition to the Rifāʿīyyah order and Abū al-Hudā al-Ṣayyādī, the Young Turks also received the support of the modernist ulema[315] and the Salafis, who were also working for reform within Islam.[316]

Another striking example of order involvement was the role played by the Badawī sheikh Nailî Efendi, also a member of the CUP branch in Istanbul, during the coup attempt of 1896.[317] When his *tekke* was stormed by the police, the sheikh and some of his devotees were sent into exile.[318] He returned to the capital twelve years later, following the revolution of 1908, and was revered within the circle of the orders.[319] Upon his death in December of that year, the CUP gave him a prestigious funeral attended by all their leaders.[320]

The sheikhs of various orders were banished and exiled along with the Young Turks on charges of collusion. Significant among these were the Khalwatī[321] and Sünbülî sheikhs[322] and the son of an Uşşakî sheikh.[323]

Because I lack further information, I cannot give a clearer picture of relations between the CUP and various orders. Nevertheless, the available sources indicate an interesting and significant relationship. An undated CUP circular, written about 1896, orders the members to convene organizational meetings, to draft new members, and to carry out propaganda activities in the *tekkes*. From this we can infer at least something of the nature of these relations.[324]

Another relationship to be considered is that between the Young Turks and the Babîs and Bahaîs, who played an important role in the Persian revolutionary movement.[325] The Babîs had established ties with the Young Ottomans as early as the 1860s.[326] We also know that Jamāl al-Dīn al-Afghānī, whose role in the Babî movement is even now a subject of controversy,[327] used to invite Young Turks to conferences in his mansion in Istanbul and influenced them deeply.[328] The journal *Kanun-i Esasî*, first published by the ulema and later the official organ of the CUP in Cairo, described al-Afghānī as "an important pillar and the perfect spiritual teacher for the CUP." The journal noted further that he had written an essay in both Arabic and Persian about the regime and personal life of Abdülhamid II and had given it to a prominent member of the CUP.[329] CUP organs published articles extolling him as an advocate of Islamic reform.[330] Nevertheless, although the sultan and al-Afghānī initially seem to have had close and favorable relations, eventually the sultan and the Ottoman government became very suspicious of al-Afghānī's political activities.[331] They accused him of "being a leader of the Babî Society and an agitator and of having relations and secret correspondence with Freemasons, Armenian committees, and Young Turks."[332] After making these vague accusations, the Ottoman grand vizier alleged that al-Afghānī was the mentor of 'Abd Allāh al-Nadīm, an Egyptian nationalist banished to Tripoli of Barbary, and that he had secret correspondence with three other Young Turks, also in Tripoli of Barbary.[333]

Babî militants were known to have helped distribute the Young Turk journals. The founder of the CUP, İbrahim Temo, revealed in his memoirs that he had received the banned and smuggled newspapers *Hayâl* and *İstikbâl* through the Babîs.[334] Later on, Mīrzā Riḍā Kirmānī, from whom İbrahim Temo received these newspapers and whom Temo depicted as a Babî, assassinated Nāṣir al-Dīn Shah of Iran.[335]

Although a small opposition group, the Babîs had always been under surveillance by the regime of Abdülhamid II. Thus it is unlikely that they conducted activities that have been attributed to the Young Turks.[336] Nevertheless, they obviously did not hesitate to help the Young Turks and the CUP. In return, the CUP organs, although officially critical of the assassination of Nāṣir al-Dīn Shah,[337] also made this conspicuous comment: "The vengeance of the Babîs, who were oppressed forty-eight years ago, opened a door of rejuvenation and progress in Iran. We do hope that the sighs and wails of the victimized [members] of the CUP will not be in vain."[338] In a like manner, İbrahim Temo wrote a eulogy for Mīrzā Riḍa Kirmānī, entitled "May Abdülhamid's Turn Come Next," and distributed it through the CUP network.[339] Doctor Nâzım, another central committee member, likewise praised the assassin in a private letter.[340] Another Young Turk, one of the founders of Le Comité Turco-Syrien, interviewed a Babî leader.[341] Later, in 1922, Abdullah Cevdet, one of the founders of the CUP, demanded that the Ottoman state substitute Bahaism as the state religion,[342] which occasioned a great outcry.[343] It may also be noted that 'Abd al-Bahā', the leader of the Bahaî movement, was released from prison after the Young Turk revolution, and many sources have attempted to link his freedom to the revolution[344]; there is, however, no clear evidence crediting the Young Turks for this, and amnesties were commonplace at the

time. Nevertheless the Young Turks and CUP members had been inter-
ested in the Babî and Bahaî movements and ideologies,[345] for all that the
Babîs with their sparse membership were only a *quantité négligeable* in the
Ottoman Empire.

The Supporters of a Palace Coup d'État and Their Connections with the CUP

High-ranking Ottoman officials seeking to realize a palace coup made up
the fifth important group opposing the regime of Abdülhamid II. Their
significance cannot be gainsaid, even though they never created a formal
organization with a name and program.

According to an account by Ardern G. Hulme-Beaman, the Young
Turkey party was "recruited mostly from the Softas," or theological students and from the naval and military colleges, whilst it also embraces a
considerable number of the old aristocracy, such as it exists in Turkey."[346]
The involvement of people described as "aristocrats" in the opposition
movement goaded the sultan into suppressing the Young Turk movement
in 1895. The sultan had been unconcerned with student movements up
to that time, pardoning by imperial decree any students who took part. In
1895, however, he began to fear a coup d'état by high-ranking officials
reminiscent of that of 1876.

In spite of the growing representation of a new intelligentsia in the
opposition membership, the old-style palace coup factions remained viable
during the reign of Abdülhamid II as late as 1895 and conducted their
own independent opposition.

When a foreign observer wrote that "Ten miles beyond the walls of
Constantinople the ordinary Turk knows nothing about the Young Turkey
Party or the softas," he implied that the hotbed of the movement was at
that time the palace.[347] This observation helps us understand why a clandestine pamphlet criticizing contemporary conditions and calling for the
sultan's abdication and the restoration of a parliamentary regime "cause
un grand émoi dans les sphères officielles et surtout au palais du Sultan."[348]
It is true that rival factions among high-ranking bureaucrats and palace
officials flourished within the Yıldız Palace. Sir Henry Layard, British
ambassador to the Ottoman Empire, had informed Lord Salisbury about
the formation of a so-called Palace party as early as 1879.[349] Since the
beginning of Abdülhamid II's reign, rival factions had tried to merge with
the Palace party and to control that body.

An opponent of the regime of Abdülhamid II who published several
journals and books claimed the following:

Préoccupé exclusivement de la conservation de son pouvoir chancelant, il par-
aît qu'Abd-ul-Hamid aurait institué une société secrète, à l'instar de la franc-
maçonnerie. Cette nouvelle institution de Yildiz-Kiosk aurait un mot d'ordre
sacré, des signes distinctifs et des obligations spéciales pour les adeptes. Cette
société aurait notamment pour but suprême la fidélité au souverain et l'ab-

stention de toute affiliation des initiés dans d'autres associations qui pourraient viser un changement de dynastie ou des attentats subversifs contre l'hôte impérial actuel de Yildiz-Kiosk.[350]

He asserted that this society, called Lâ İlâhe İllallah (There is no god but God), had a code consisting of twenty-seven articles, the first being, "Les membres s'obligent à combattre solidairement, par tous les moyens en leur pouvoir, les associations de toute nature ayant pour objet de se réunir dans des lieux communs pour délibérer en secret."[351] The sultan was also accused of "[de] former une sorte de nouvelle franc-maçonnerie orientale."[352] It is obvious that the author exaggerated the event, but he correctly pointed out that the sultan felt personally threatened, even in the palace,[353] and was trying to take measures against opposition factions. Foreign observers had mentioned that palace officials were banished for being active members of the so-called Young Turkey party.[354]

The traditional factions, so typical in Ottoman palaces, were reactionary groups that favored either the deposed Sultan or the heir apparent. An English newspaper reported that the Young Turks too were divided in their loyalties, either to the deposed Sultan Murad V or to Reşad Efendi, the heir apparent. Accordingly, the group around Salīm Fāris was supporting the heir apparent, whereas the group publishing *Meşveret* was backing the movement to reenthrone the ex-sultan.[355] Articles published in *Hürriyet*[356] and the official organs of the CUP[357] support this assertion. Even though various Young Turks were endorsing both candidates, the factions did not dominate the intent of the opposition movement per se.

The second and most important group to be considered is that of the Sublime Porte bureaucrats. On the advice of Said Pasha, the sultan began to rule with the help of the special commissions established in the palace, thus transferring power away from the Sublime Porte.[358] By this maneuver, the group known as the Old Turkey party achieved control over the instruments of bureaucracy. The Young Turks took great exception to this.[359] Most of the bureaucrats, who belonged to the so-called Young Turkey party previously headed by Midhat Pasha,[360] also wanted power restored to the Sublime Porte and to return to the efficient methods that had been in place for almost forty years.[361] These bureaucrats were also cognizant of the fact that no palace coup could succeed without the cooperation of the generals. In fact, in 1895, high-ranking palace officials, generals, and bureaucrats had agreed to seek to bring about conditions similar to those obtaining in 1876. We have seen that Fāris had tried to become the spokesman of these high-ranking conspirators. Although they welcomed every kind of opposition movement and activity that they thought might foster a milieu conducive to their prospective coup, they had no intention of allowing Fāris to become their leader.

Foreign diplomatic reports described the revolutionary activities as movements receiving support from palace circles.[362] At the same time Max Müller, the third secretary of the British embassy in Istanbul, obtained a pamphlet from a Turkish friend who had received it through one of the chamberlains. Written against the regime of the sultan and widely distributed in the palace, its title was translated as "La Religion et le Gouvernement s'en vont; c'est au Peuple d'agir maintenant." The style bears no similarity to the early CUP pamphlets and appeals.[363] The pamphlet proclaims: "Nous sommes une Société qui a decidé de mourir et de devenir victorieuse pour assurer la liberté du Chériat." Although Müller commented that the pamphlet had been written by the *softas*,[364] it contains themes never used by the ulema in their political writings. Moreover, its style is similar to that of an interview given to a British journal by a high-ranking, most probably bureaucratic Young Turk.[365] Possibly this pamphlet was written by supporters of a palace coup who sought to create an atmosphere similar to that of 1876. From our point of view, at least as significant as the author and place of publication is the fact that this pamphlet was read in the palace.[366]

The number of high-ranking officials and officers alleged to be involved in the Young Turk movement was also increasing in 1895. British intelligence received reports through the Russian embassy describing the Muslim Revolutionary party as being supported by four colonels and two generals.[367]

At last the conspiracy had found its leader: Gazi Ahmed Muhtar Pasha, one of the two heroes of the Russo-Turkish War of 1877–1878.[368] Fearful of his prestige among the people, the sultan sent this pasha to Egypt as the Ottoman high commissioner. Gazi Ahmed Muhtar Pasha was considered to be the most prominent Ottoman statesman who had been involved in the opposition movement.[369] His son Mahmud Muhtar Pasha was likewise thought to be connected to the Young Turks.[370] The Young Turks repeatedly solicited the participation of the high commissioner in the opposition and even invited him to become their leader.[371] Further appeals to Gazi Ahmed Muhtar Pasha were made in the Cairo-based Young Turk journal *Sancak*, published by Ahmed Saib, his former aide-de-camp.[372] Later, however, the Young Turks began to complain about Pasha's "hypocrisy" and to claim that although he had allied himself with the Young Turks, he was also trying to maintain his connection with the sultan.[373] But even as late as 1906, opposition circles were anticipating his help and writing open letters to him requesting his participation.[374] Evidence that Şevki Bey, his son-in-law, negotiated with the Young Turks in 1899 regarding a proposed Young Turk congress[375] and that Gazi Ahmed Muhtar Pasha himself wrote and published reform proposals in the local Egyptian press in 1900 proves that he tried to maintain his ties with opposition forces.[376] But the CUP members could not comprehend that he had no desire to become the leader of their movement; rather, he aspired to lead a coup by the high-ranking bureaucracy. When these people failed in their attempted coup in 1895, he tried to make a display of his loyalty and obedience to the sultan, just as did most of the bureaucrats involved in the conspiracy. After the crisis faced by the CUP in 1897, he began to limit his contacts with them; when the CUP reorganized in 1906, it ceased to regard him as an important ally.

Incidentally, a secret letter among the papers of Sir (later Lord) Thomas Sanderson, who was the permanent undersecretary of the British Foreign Office and had paid special attention to the affairs of the Ottoman Empire, gives a clear understanding of the aims of the coup organizers and of the leading role of Gazi Ahmed Muhtar Pasha in the conspiracy:

> Lord Northbrook came to see me last night, having come red hot from Cromer. He repeated to me the conversation that has already been reported from Cairo betweem [sic] Moukhtar and, I think, Major [General] Wingate, as well as himself.
>
> Moukhtar left on his mind the impression that the conspiracy which was present to his thoughts might break out at any moment. That is also my impression, for I doubt if any Turkish general would speak so openly, unless events justifying his tone were close at hand. He only mentioned one particular which I do not think is in Cromer's report, which is that in the event of the deposition of the Sultan, it should be the care of the British ambassador that a minor should be chosen to succeed him, so that some form of constitutional system on the Midhat plan should at once be set on foot, which would acquire sufficient stability during the Sultan's minority to survive his majority.
>
> My point, however, in writing all this is that the crisis is urgent. A conspiracy might break out today, or to-morrow. It might also not break out for months. But Moukhtar's outspokenness makes me think it will be sooner rather than later.[377]

French diplomats had reached a similar conclusion about the intentions of the Ottoman high commissioner after an interview with him.[378]

A change in British policy toward Russia and the Ottoman Empire, beginning with Lord Rosebery's appointment as the British prime minister,[379] with his extreme pro-Armenian and anti-Turkish approach in policymaking,[380] bolstered high-ranking Ottoman officials' belief that foreign intervention led by Great Britain was inevitable. In Great Britain, the same public reaction as was observed in the Bulgarian crisis of 1876 occurred in response to the Armenian crisis of 1894.[381] Prominent British statesmen's criticism of the Ottoman government's policy[382] provoked Lord Rosebery to increase his commitment to dealing with the problem.[383]

Observing Lord Kimberley's strong reaction and his initiative to organize a joint diplomatic initiative with Russia and Austria-Hungary in December 1894,[384] as well as the diplomatic interventions that followed,[385] Ottoman statesmen led by Gazi Ahmed Muhtar Pasha decided to embark on their venture: they offered a constitutional coup project to the British government through Lord Cromer. The payoff to the British government would, they argued, be a solution to the Eastern Question. A reformist Ottoman statesman stated to a western observer:

> The Armenians have lived in our midst for centuries, and they have never, until recently, been massacred or especially oppressed. On the contrary, they were found holding honourable situations in all our Administrations, and they pros-

pered as our "*Sarrafs*". It would be the same again if the government of the country were, as in former times, at the Sublime Porte and not at Yildis [sic].[386]

For the British government, a coup seemed the easiest way to solve the problem. On the one hand they had secret negotiations with the Sublime Porte,[387] but on the other hand they wanted to maintain the alternative radical solution. Lord Rosebery, who "would probably have been hailed as the greatest foreign minister of the nineteenth century, the man who solved the Eastern Question,"[388] made anti-Turkish statements after he left office,[389] and Lord Kimberley, who was described as a British foreign secretary "with full sympathy for the sufferers [Armenians] but without the power, against the rest of Europe,"[390] later declared "that for the future the Liberal Party will wash its hands of the doctrine of the integrity of Turkey."[391] These comments indicate that British policymakers had every reason to support a constitutional coup d'état in Turkey and to oppose the regime of Abdülhamid II. Unfortunately there seem to be no further documents concerning the bargain between the British cabinet and the Ottoman statesmen headed by Gazi Ahmed Muhtar Pasha. None of the studies of Lord Rosebery provides any information about this attempt. Since Lord Northbrook had completed his service in Egypt in 1885, he might have been sent by his government exclusively to discuss the matter with Lord Cromer and Gazi Ahmed Muhtar Pasha. His biography gives no information about his activities in Egypt in 1895.[392] Especially noteworthy is the presence of Major General Wingate, head of the intelligence department of the Egyptian army, which suggests a conspiratorial involvement on the part of the British.[393] Although Lord Cromer described Gazi Ahmed Muhtar Pasha as "a distinguished soldier" and praised "his high personal character," he wrote nothing about this venture in his book on Egypt.[394] When we reflect upon the role Gazi Ahmed Muhtar Pasha played in controlling the Islamic press against the British,[395] the description and praise by Lord Cromer gain import.

The derailment of this attempt and the resignation of Lord Rosebery did not extinguish revolutionary aspirations among Ottoman statesmen. Amid the continuing Armenian crisis, the interventionist policy of Lord Salisbury, the new prime minister, came as no surprise to the sultan or to the Ottoman statesmen, who still remembered the role he played in the Istanbul Conference of 1876–1877. This active policy inspired these statesmen to organize new ventures.[396] Indeed, the British government prepared a detailed plan for a naval demonstration during the last days of Lord Rosebery's ministry,[397] and the French drew up similar plans later.[398] Graf Goluchowski, the foreign minister of Austria-Hungary, was promoting an initiative for intervention,[399] and even the German Kaiser pointed to the great likelihood of a "palace revolution" and encouraged Lord Salisbury to intervene directly in Ottoman politics.[400] When rumors of such an intervention spread, Ottoman statesmen were convinced that this time foreign intervention was inevitable. At the height of the crisis, Kâmil Pasha, the newly appointed grand vizier, who had consistently counseled the sultan to count heavily on the British and to a minor degree on the French,[401] himself took the initiative. On November 4, 1895, he submitted a memorandum to the sultan requesting a drastic overhaul of the administrative and bureaucratic systems. He presented these demands as the will of the two Great Powers:

> The policy, which has been adopted by the Sublime State for a while, caused discontent among the public. The dissatisfaction, which was hidden in the hearts of the people, has come to the surface now when [the Great] Powers have decided to protect the Armenians, and the outburst and the complaints of people have spread even to Europe, and in this matter both Muslims and Christians speak with one voice. Although some states that are trying to exploit the opportunity are happy with the situation, the other states for which the maintenance of His Majesty's dominions as they are today is in accordance with their interest, pay great attention to the developments and intend to try to effect a disappearance of the causes which may harm the balance of power through a revolution in the Sublime State. The French ambassador [Paul Cambon] with whom I met the other day gave serious warnings as I submitted to His Majesty and it was clear from the way that he expressed himself that the British ambassador is of the same opinion."[402]

According to Kâmil Pasha, the two Great Powers required a transfer of power from the palace back to the Sublime Porte, and hence the reestablishment of a responsible government similar to its counterparts in Europe.[403] This memorandum placed the sultan in a predicament. To gain time, he ordered the grand vizier to discuss the matter at a cabinet meeting two days later. During these two days he tried to gather information about whether these requirements were really the will of the two Great Powers or a maneuver by Kâmil Pasha.[404] Further, on November 5, Michael Herbert, the British chargé d'affaires, instructed Adam Block, first dragoman to the embassy, to call at the palace and warn the sultan through the first secretary that the situation was dangerous. Later that evening Herbert received a message from the sultan informing him that "the reforms will be published in to-morrow's newspapers, and will be followed by an *Iradé* stating that all possible measures will be taken to secure the prosperity and welfare of all classes."[405] The European press even claimed that a communication announcing the sultan's intention to reestablish the constitution had been sent to Turkish journals.[406] But when the sultan discerned that the requirements of Kâmil Pasha were not an expression of the will of the two Great Powers[407]—although Cambon truly favored the reestablishment of a responsible government in Istanbul[408] and had encouraged Kâmil Pasha in his efforts—this communication was withdrawn. In addition, when on November 7, Herbert sent Block to the palace to express his dismay at the sultan's empty promises, he received another message, telling him that Abdülhamid II "had intended to make the publication, but now hesitate[s] from fear that the result would be an increase of jealousy on the part of the Muslim subjects."[409] The next day Kâmil Pasha received an appointment as a provincial governor; it was *de facto* exile.

Meanwhile, British and French circles were describing the Young Turk party as an organization of high-ranking bureaucrats,[410] and even after the dismissal of Kâmil Pasha, those bureaucrats persisted in their quest for a foreign intervention led by the British. However, when the sultan succeeded in preventing foreign intervention, these people, who did not regard the student organizations as more than tools, followed two divergent paths. The majority came to the conclusion that there was no chance of dethroning the sultan by a coup d'état and began to exhibit effusive loyalty toward their ruler. A smaller group decided to develop stronger ties with the CUP, which had become the main organization of the Ottoman opposition both within the country and abroad. Actually, the CUP, with the help of the palace coup organizers, attempted a similar coup d'état in 1896; its failure was a terrible blow to the high-ranking bureaucrats.

However, the pro-British and proreform Ottoman statesmen took another initiative, this time at the height of the diplomatic crisis over Crete immediately preceding the Greco-Turkish War of 1897. İsmail Kemal, described as a statesman who "professes to be a partisan of England and is said to have defended our [British] interests at the Palace on many occasions,"[411] instigated a new action against the palace regime.

İsmail Kemal had tried to establish favorable ties with the British authorities as early as 1892, with the aim of obtaining their support for reform in the Ottoman administration. In an interview of 1892 with C. M. Hallward, the British consul in Beirut, he complained about the "universal centralization" of the Empire and told Hallward that he supported British policy toward Egypt.[412] After İsmail Kemal was appointed governor of Tripoli of Barbary, Sir Philip Currie, the British ambassador to the Ottoman Empire, commented that the "Sultan has come to this decision in view of the English proclivities of Ismail Kemal."[413] But due to strong opposition by the French to the appointment of a prominent pro-British governor to Tripoli of Barbary, the sultan could not send him there.[414]

During the Armenian crisis of 1895, İsmail Kemal played a significant role in the coup d'état attempt led by Kâmil Pasha. On September 28, 1895, a detailed memorandum concerning administrative reforms and a proposed protocol were submitted to Sir Philip Currie. Sir Philip described the author of these papers as "a mussulman gentleman who has been governor general of several provinces. He is one of the few Turks [Muslims] who ventures to advocate a change in the present system of government and who has persistently advised the sultan to follow the counsels of England."[415] In view of the similarities between these two texts and İsmail Kemal's ideas as presented in his memorandum of 1897 and in various interviews with the British authorities, it may be concluded that these proposals were also written by him. The protocol proposal expresses a point of view similar to İsmail Kemal Bey's famous memorandum of 1897 on the establishment of a representative body:

S.M.I. le Sultan sera muté à convoquer immédiatement un conseil extraordinaire composé de manière à constituer la représentation. . . . Ce Conseil Extraordinaire sera appelé à exprimer les vœux des populations relativement à l'organisation définitive du province et à la constitution fondamentale du pays. . . . Un Hatt Impérial conforme à l'entente constituera définitivement le droit public de l'empire placé désormais sous la garantie collective de toutes les puissances signataires.[416]

According to İsmail Kemal, "Sir Philip, in the name of his government, insisted that the Empire should return to the old form of Government from the Porte, with an independent ministry responsible for its acts."[417] At the peak of the crisis, İsmail Kemal was dispatched by the sultan to the British embassy. He described the ensuing events as follows:

Unfortunately, Sir Philip Currie was at the moment *en route* on his return from London, where he has been on leave. Sir [Mr.] Michael Herbert . . . was Chargé d'Affaires, but I did not know him personally. At midnight I went to the house of Adam Block, the First Dragoman, and together we went to the Embassy, where Sir Michael Herbert, roused from his bed, received us. We had a long conversation, which, unfortunately, bore no fruit. I tried my utmost to persuade the Chargé d'Affaires that it was a unique occasion to profit by the Sultan's disposal to grant what would never be obtained from him under other circumstances, which would assure real government to the country and establish order throughout. . . . But Sir Michael Herbert could not make up his mind to submit the matter immediately and confidentially to Lord Salisbury.

In face of this obstinacy, I then advised Sir Michael, no longer as the Sultan's messenger, but in my private capacity as a patriot, to allow the whole fleet, which was then at Lemnos, to enter Constantinople harbour to force on the Sultan the will of Great Britain whose only desire was salvation for the Empire and peace for her people. But after five hours of conversation I was compelled to return to the Palace and announce that my mission had failed.[418]

In 1897, after the Armenian crisis and when most of the reformist Ottoman statesmen had new cause for hope because of the imbroglio over Crete, İsmail Kemal sent a memorandum to the sultan asking him for administrative reforms. He wrote to

"beg to propose to Your Majesty that you should immediately convoke a constituent assembly of the representatives of the people of your capital and provinces. This assembly will submit to Your Majesty the changes they deem it essential to introduce into the Constitution. When these modifications have been adopted, the new charter can receive the approval of Your Majesty and be promulgated by a special *Hatt*.[419]

This memorandum was smuggled to the European press by İsmail Kemal and published by *Le Temps* on April 8, 1897.[420] The *Times* of the same day gave a long summary of it and attributed great importance to it.[421] Publication of the memorandum by the European press caused "une énorme sensation à Constantinople," and issues of *Le Temps* sold secretly for five francs (one *mecidiye*) per issue.[422] The central committee of the

CUP in Geneva immediately published a Turkish translation of the memorandum.[423] Contrary to what the European press claimed,[424] İsmail Kemal's aim was not to impress the sultan or to convince him of the necessity for a change in the administrative system but to raise this question in Europe at a critical time when the intervention of foreign powers into Ottoman politics was expected. Seven months before İsmail Kemal's initiative, the British conferred with the Russian sovereign over the future of the Ottoman Empire. The czar's refusal to authorize Russian participation in a European intervention[425] impelled the British to support reform from within, although British public opinion favored direct intervention.[426] İsmail Kemal received support for his proposals even from confidants of the sultan such as İzzet Bey.[427] However, the defeat of the Greeks in the Greco-Turkish War did not allow İsmail Kemal and his bureaucratic accomplices in the Sublime Porte to carry out their plan.

After his failure, İsmail Kemal applied to the British embassy for a document permitting him to take refuge on board a British warship in case his life was threatened; he received it on January 25, 1898.[428] He then began to wait for the outbreak of a new serious diplomatic crisis. Eight months later the admirals of the international force of the Great Powers in Crete decided to replace the Ottoman tax collectors with Cretan Christians beginning September 3, 1898, precipitating a Muslim insurrection and later the killing of British officers and privates.[429] İsmail Kemal now foresaw an opportunity to begin another venture in the hope that a British-led foreign intervention was in the offing. On the same day, he went to the British embassy in Istanbul and described his plans to the British chargé d'affaires, who then wrote to Sanderson:

> You know the name of Ismail Kemal Bey, a former Governor of Syria [sic], member of the council of state, and one of the few who have raised their voices openly against the present Yildiz system. He occasionally received advice and encouragement from Sir Philip Currie who believed in him, and he still comes from time to time to the Embassy.
>
> Yesterday he was in a state of unusual depression and called to tell me that he and his friends were in despair of bringing about an improvement by persuading the Sultan to reform, and that they were determined to form a party which should take the lead in demanding a constitutional reform and a return to the traditional friendship with England.
>
> He had already won over, he said, a number of influential people. At their head was Izzet Bey, the late trusted advisor of the Sultan. Izzet Bey, however, was to be kept dark for the present. He mentioned a number of others, well known at the Palace, but whose names would not convey anything in England. There were several of the ulema among them. One of their ideas was to maintain a newspaper, to be published of course abroad and surreptitiously introduced into Turkey. Reform all round, for Mussulmans and Christians alike, was the programme, and above all the restoration of some kind of responsible government at the Porte. Their plan had not been mentioned to any other Embassy, the new party, if it may be so called desiring to rely mainly upon the sympathy if not the material support of England.

The dissatisfaction of all right minded Turks with the Sultan's policy is undoubtedly assuming large proportions, but it is difficult to judge whether the plan sketched out to me in confidence by Ismail Kemal Bey is likely to be of any practical use.

The Sultan would certainly nip it in the bud if he heard of it, and its authors would disappear from the scene appealing helplessly to England to give help for them out of their difficulties.

Ismail Kemal Bey, however was very anxious that Lord Salisbury should know of his designs. I said I would write privately to the F[oreign] O[ffice], but that I could make no promises of support and must leave it to the new ambassador to judge how far the embassy could countenance the action proposed to be taken.[430]

To my knowledge no documents exist about Sir Thomas's answer and how much support was given to the proposed action. İsmail Kemal wrote in his memoirs that with the support of Sir Philip he had established a periodical at Plovdiv called *Mecra-yı Efkâr (The Course of Ideas)*.[431] The paper had been smuggled into the capital, and the public bought copies at double and triple the price. The sultan, furious at İsmail Kemal's action, asked him to stop publication, which he declined to do.[432] Abdülhamid II, probably afraid of British support given to İsmail Kemal, refrained from ordering his arrest. However, the lack of foreign intervention in Ottoman politics prevented İsmail Kemal from fulfilling his dreams and left him with only his journal as a forum for his ideas on reform. This problem—political tranquillity and the consequent absence of a diplomatic crisis until 1902—compelled many reformist Ottoman statesmen to abandon their antiregime activities after 1898.

The CUP remained the single organization with whom such statesmen could maintain contact.[433] The CUP organs claimed that their organization "was the object of great appreciation, not only by the entire population, but also by the Royal Palace," referring to their connections with the high-ranking officials who continued to conspire with them.[434] However, these relations were as far from yielding fruit as they had been in 1895 and 1896. The only positive outcome of this connection from the CUP point of view was money and information.[435]

We shall see how a number of prominent statesmen, including İsmail Kemal, took flight in the years 1899 and 1900. After 1898 the hope of support from the sultan's intimate circle was nothing but a utopian idea. Because the CUP reorganized its structure and propaganda style, there was no longer any value to associating with such groups from 1906 on.

Individual Initiatives and the CUP

As a famous Turkish poet mentioned in his memoirs,[436] most youths aspired to join the ranks of the Young Turk movement and to flee to Europe, and a considerable number of them fulfilled their dreams. Upon examining the lists of the fugitives one can easily conclude that few of them had any affiliation with the CUP or any other organization; indeed, they had little or no involvement with the opposition.[437] Thus, when these people returned to the Ottoman Empire after the reproclamation of the constitution in 1908, the CUP did not give them any credit. In response they decided to establish their own organization, which they called Feda-kârân-ı Millet Cemiyeti (the Society of People Loyal to the Nation). They tried to procure special rights from the government,[438] and because of this they should be regarded a distinct category.

One of the pioneers in this category was Hakkı Bey, who first published an opposition journal in Paris called *Teessüf (Sorrow)* and then edited another monthly in Geneva called *Gencine-i Hayâl (The Treasure of Imagination)*.[439] In these journals he expressed themes identical to those used by the Young Ottomans. I have not come across his name in any document between 1881 and 1898, which I take to mean that he was politically inactive. In 1898 he began to publish a new journal, called *Cür'et (Courage)*, which was printed in the CUP publishing house in Geneva. Clearly he had established good relations with the committee.[440] At the same time he prepared cartoons to be used as CUP propaganda.[441] In a private letter he criticized Ahmed Rıza and endorsed the CUP center in Folkestone against his followers within the movement and then described himself as an "old Young Turk."[442] He used the term "our Istanbul Branch" in his journal for the CUP branch in Istanbul.[443] Finally, Hakkı Bey was the first and probably best example among individuals who fled to Europe without any organizational affiliation and who then joined the Young Turk movement led by the CUP. This was also said in a roundabout way in *Osmanlı*.[444]

Another individual showing early initiative was Ibrāhīm al-Muwayliḥī, the former secretary to the ex-khedive Ismā'īl Pasha. After publishing pamphlets against the regime of Abdülhamid II in France and Belgium, he was prevented from engaging in further oppositional activities by the British authorities acting upon the request of the Ottoman government.[445] Later, in Egypt, he wrote articles against the regime of the sultan.[446] Afterward, he returned to Istanbul and accepted favors from the sultan.[447] Ismā'īl Pasha's other secretary, Wāṣif Bey, tried to carry out similar activities in Italy. However, after publishing a pamphlet entitled *Le Secret de Midhat Pasha* in Italy, his activities were stopped, again upon the request of the Ottoman Foreign Ministry.[448]

Also of interest is the increase in the number of opposition journals published in foreign countries by non-Turkish and non-Muslim individuals. Europeans assumed, incorrectly, that these publications were the Young Turks' papers. N. Nicolaïdès, the editor of the most prominent journal among these, *L'Orient*, and the real editor of the journal *Le Yıldız* (its editorship was publicly claimed by Demetrius Georgiadès), was editing both journals on behalf of Greek nationalists.[449] Nevertheless, since he had annoyed the sultan as a member of the "Young Turk opposition," and thanks to the consideration of the Europeans, he sat at the bargaining table with the palace and had no trouble becoming an ardent supporter of Abdülhamid II's regime once he was satisfied with the result of the negotiations.[450] A certain George Badis, who menaced the Ottoman government by threatening to publish a journal named *Genc Türkiye (The Young Turkey)*, also sat at the bargaining table and was similarly gratified.[451]

After 1890 the number of people fleeing from the Empire increased dramatically. They fall into two groups. The first group used bluff to blackmail the palace. It pretended to form serious opposition committees and to organize activities; later it agreed to "stop" this pseudoopposition in return for money or government posts.[452] Between 1893 and 1895, Athens served as a base for this pseudoopposition. Most of the fugitives there returned to the Ottoman Empire, where they received money and positions.[453] Bargains between such fugitives and the Ottoman embassies, consulates, and intelligence service officers continued until the Young Turk revolution.[454] But there were no ties between these people and the CUP.

The second group of fugitives escaped through its own initiative to Europe or to British-ruled Egypt. Hakkı Bey was an outstanding example of this group. Some of these fugitives returned to the Empire after negotiating with the palace, but obviously their aim was not so simple. Included in this group were Tevfik Nevzad, a famous journalist of Izmir, whose newspaper was shut down by the government for "propagating republicanism,"[455] and Emrullah Efendi, the director of education in Izmir. They fled together to Geneva and published a journal called *Hidmet (Service)*. [456] Their flight aroused the enthusiasm of the opposition within the country[457] and filled palace and government circles with dread. Following negotiations between the Swiss and Ottoman authorities, these two men were deported by the Swiss government.[458] The Ottoman government permitted them to return to Izmir, but they were to be kept under close scrutiny.[459] Nevertheless, Emrullah Efendi was tried by a local kangaroo court under the pretext that he had quarreled with the accountant of his office,[460] and Tevfik Nevzad, despite denials in his prison letters,[461] tried to organize the opposition in Izmir, including the son of the governor Kâmil Pasha, ex-grand vizier, and thus attracted the attention of foreign diplomats.[462] After a detailed investigation, and in spite of the protests of the French consul in Izmir,[463] the government exiled Tevfik Nevzad and his accomplices to Bitlis, a small town in eastern Anatolia.[464] This was one of the most important arrests made outside of Istanbul. Two clues reveal that Tevfik Nevzad had close ties with the CUP (although when he fled to Europe he had no apparent affiliation). One is the participation in the cell founded by Tevfik Nevzad of Abdülhalim Memduh, the Government dragoman of Izmir, and also of Tokadizâde Şekip, both of whom later joined the CUP[465]; the other is a private letter sent by Tevfik Nevzad to Ahmed Rıza through the former's brother.[466] Tevfik Nevzad was later imprisoned in Adana, where he died in 1906.[467]

Another person closely related to the CUP was Tarsusizâde Münif, a student at the Royal Administrative Academy. He fled to Athens and there published a journal called *Hakikat (Truth),*[468] which he continued to publish in Geneva after moving there a few months later.[469] Foreign investigators described the journal as the organ of an organization, but this was not the CUP.[470] Tarsusizâde Münif continued to publish his journal even after the publication of *Meşveret* and *Osmanlı,* and later he edited two other journals named *Yıldız (Star)* and *Osmanlı (2).*[471] He established close ties with the CUP but did not become a member.

Others too fled to Europe and tried to establish movements against the regime of Abdülhamid II before the publication of *Meşveret:* Ârif Bey, who wanted to publish a journal with Ali Şefkatî,[472] but returned to the country after negotiations,[473] and Ahmed Fevzi, who—with the help of some Armenians—published a journal in Athens called *Vatan (1) (Fatherland)* causing the palace great anxiety.[474] Ahmed Fevzi also tried to start a publication in London but failed.[475] Both men had only limited contact with the CUP.

We have examined the activities of the six opposition categories and their relations with the CUP. The first three—the Freemasons, Le Parti Constitutionnel en Turquie, and Le Comité Turco-Syrien—tried to form distinct, well-organized movements and sought to establish ties with the CUP. The fourth group consisted of members of the ulema acting independently for a while and then dissolving into the CUP. As mentioned, the ulema are a group characterized by complicated internal factions; clearly not all dissident ulema were collaborating with the CUP. This is also true for the Sufi orders. The fifth group comprised the palace coup organizers, who were very active, especially in 1895, when foreign intervention in Ottoman politics seemed likely. Later some of them established ties with the CUP. Finally, there are the individual initiatives. The importance of this last category is minimal in comparison with the others. The European press, however, tended to attribute even acts of individual criminality to the Young Turks, incorrectly categorizing them as "Young Turk activities."[476] Nonetheless, the CUP became the most important opposition organization.

4

The Rise of the CUP in Ottoman Politics: The Formative Years of the Committee

The Founding of the CUP and Its Early Activities

The first nucleus of the CUP can be traced to the Royal Medical Academy. In 1889 an active student movement began there and spread even to the Empire's high schools.[1] This political opposition movement had its inception at a medical school because of the impact of biological materialist ideology prevailing there, which evoked for the students a vision of an ideal society far removed from their experience.

In the mid-1880s, students at the Royal Medical Academy began to take an active interest in ways to organize an opposition to the regime of Abdülhamid II. Even prior to establishment of the CUP, the doings of antiestablishment students were discussed among other students of this school[2] and other royal colleges.[3] These discussions were formalized in 1888.[4] Leaders of the student movement—İbrahim Temo, Abdullah Çevdet, and Mehmed Reşid— distributed to the other students back issues of Ali Şefkatî's *İstikbâl* and newspapers published by the Persian opposition in Europe.[5] Later İbrahim Temo and İshak Sükûti held confabulations,[6] and eventually these two medical students invited two classmates, Abdullah Cevdet and Mehmed Reşid to join them in founding the nucleus for an opposition committee. With their concurrence, the CUP was formed on June 2, 1889.[7] The four founders titled their society İttihad-ı Osmanî Cemiyeti (Ottoman Union Society). A meeting known as *Hamamönü İctima'ı* (Meeting in Front of Bath) or *Hatab Kıraathanesi*

71

İctima'ı (Meeting at the Firewood Reading Room) followed, during which the founders expounded their ambitions to other close schoolmates and urged them to join their nucleus.[8] In the summer of 1889, after increasing their membership with other medical students, İbrahim Temo and Asaf Derviş led a boycott at the school, protesting the disorder in the laboratories and the quality of the food. The Ministry of Education ordered the expulsion of İbrahim Temo and other leaders, but a petition by Marko Pasha, the principal, and İbrahim Pasha, an Albanian professor, secured their pardon by imperial decree.[9]

Later, while members of the new society were disseminating antiestablishment propaganda among college students in Istanbul and in their hometowns, news of İbrahim Temo's activities reached the palace. He was arrested in Ohrid and brought to Yıldız Palace on July 17, 1890,[10] where he was interrogated by the intelligence and released.[11]

After acquiring a sizable membership consisting of students and several bureaucrats,[12] the founders convened a new meeting, known as *Onikiler İctima'ı* (Meeting of Twelve) or *Midhat Paşa Bağı İctima'ı* (Meeting in Midhat Pasha's Vineyard),[13] chaired by Ali Rüşdi, a bureaucrat at the Ministry of Justice. Participants decided to hold weekly seminars at various places to draft bylaws, collect dues, organize branches, and assign membership numbers.[14]

This meeting transformed the society from a student group lacking structure into a sophisticated organizational framework. İbrahim Temo received membership number 1/1 (first member of the first branch) and other numbers were likewise assigned.[15] Although it seems possible that the founders formed the society after the Carbonari organizational framework, as various sources have claimed,[16] we lack information verifying that the Young Turks were acquainted with the ideas of the Carbonari. In the case of the Young Ottomans such an interest and knowledge are evident.[17] Since Hüseyinzâde Ali required the founders to replicate the organizational framework of Russian Nihilists[18] and because İbrahim Temo expounded on the Greek secret society Filiki Eteria with the other founders during the early meetings,[19] it is clear that to the Young Turks the interesting aspect of revolutionary societies was not their political ideas but their organizational frameworks.

The society drew up a twenty-one-article regulation[20] and recruited students from the Royal School of Administration and the Royal War Academy. In the former school, and prior to the activities of the Ottoman Union Society, a student, later to play an important role in the movement, formed a society in 1889 after a trip to Geneva and Paris. He modeled this group on the student associations in these two cities,[21] but the police stormed an early meeting and found a translation from a book by Jean Jacques Rousseau on one of the students.[22] Seven students were arrested.[23] Ali Kemal, the leader of the group, wrote that they were arrested for their "liberal ideas."[24] The government decided to exile the students who had joined in the venture and to banish Ali Kemal to Aleppo.[25] Soon after,

Amīr Arslān set up meetings for the students of the Royal School of Administration.[26]

Meanwhile students at the Royal War Academy organized a nucleus led by Major Batumlu Mustafa, a staff officer.[27] Both student groups asked the Ottoman Union Society leaders to organize a joint meeting so they could be accommodated into the organization. In the beginning İbrahim Temo and his friends expressed reluctance to so reorganize, but when Amīr Arslān threatened to turn the branch at the Royal School of Administration into an independent organization and to retain its dues,[28] the founders acquiesced and set up a new meeting, leading eventually to a merger of the groups. The participants of the *Onikiler İctima'ı* except İbrahim Temo, who was sick,[29] and the representatives from the Royal School of Administration and War Academy were present. In this meeting, known as *Rumelihisarı* or *Boğaziçi İctima'ı* (Bosphorus Meeting), a larger organizational framework was a subject of discussion.[30] The founders gave a memorandum to those spearheading the movement at the Royal School of Administration, Ali Münif and Mehmed Rauf, authorizing them to draft bylaws, and after altering this text the new regulations of the society were prepared.[31]

Following these events the society dedicated its efforts toward expanding its sphere of influence and accumulating influential members. However, this new policy allowed the intelligence network at the palace to acquire more information about the society and its activities. Four Royal Medical Academy students submitted a spy report to the palace revealing that "all students of the Royal Medical Academy have ideas against the establishment. Those poisoning them are some ninth grade students. The school is full of banned publications and in the near future seditious activities will be undertaken."[32] In July 1894 the government decided to attach the Royal Medical Academy, which until then had been an independent school, to the Ministry of Military Schools. Saib Pasha, the principal, was transferred to another post and Zeki Pasha, minister of military schools and a close confidant of the sultan, was put in charge of military discipline. Ahmed Hilmi Pasha was appointed principal of the school but control was in the hands of Zeki Pasha. As soon as the school became attached to the ministry, Zeki Pasha began a major investigation. The military searched the closets of the students, uncovering banned newspapers. Zeki Pasha ordered a court-martial to be set up, which decided to expel nine leaders of the society from the school and to sentence them.[33] However, the palace—which still viewed the movement as a student activity—pardoned them.[34]

A month later a second spate of arrests occurred at the Royal Medical Academy and Law School.[35] The police uncovered a "seditious" organization, and some pupils fled to Europe while the arrests were under way.[36] In spite of the government's measures, the recruitment of influential figures gained momentum. İshak Sükûti obtained the support of important ulema such as Ubeydullah Efendi and Hoca Kadri[37]; the latter smuggled issues of *Le Temps* from Paris and translated them for *softas* to convert them to the goals of the movement.[38] İshak Sükûti also met with İsmail Kemal and Murad Bey and reported back to his friends that he had enrolled them in the society.[39] However, these people were expecting a palace coup d'état and so took little notice of student activities. Murad Bey especially dreamed of becoming an *éminence grise* of the sultan and of holding meetings with the followers of Salīm Fāris[40]; therefore he declined an invitation to become the leader but helped them edit their appeals.[41] Another bureaucrat who entered the coterie was former Minister of Education Münif Pasha, known for his liberal ideas.[42]

The ranks of society members fleeing to Europe or Egypt also swelled during this period. Ali Zühdi and Ahmed Verdanî, a medical student, stowed away for Europe.[43] The latter was sent to Cairo to contact opponents, and Doctor Nâzım was stowed away to Paris to establish relations with Ahmed Rıza, a notable opponent of Abdülhamid II's regime who had taken refuge in Paris since 1889.[44] A document among the papers of İbrahim Temo reveals that the society communicated with Ahmed Rıza during its inception.[45] However, since Ahmed Rıza applied to the Paris embassy for research grants,[46] he considered the efforts of the students insignificant. Later, especially following an exchange of letters on the regulations of the society,[47] he began to exhibit a more critical approach to the Ottoman administration. His publication in the French press[48] and his conferences about the "emancipation of Ottoman women"[49] caused trepidation in government circles. His memoranda on reforms, sent directly to the sultan, later won him popularity among opponents of the regime.[50] In 1894 he became the leader of an Ottoman colony in Paris, antagonistic to the regime of Abdülhamid II,[51] and after lengthy discussions with Doctor Nâzım, he donned the leadership of the organization in Europe.[52] As a devoted adherent to positivism, he asked the founders in Istanbul to rename the society Nizam ve Terakki, a translation of Auguste Comte's famous motto *Ordre et Progrès*. The founders insisted on the term *İttihad* (Union) and the title Osmanlı İttihad ve Terakki Cemiyeti (The Ottoman Committee of Union and Progress) was agreed upon.[53]

Following this agreement, the society's activities abroad blossomed, especially in Paris. The government increased the allowance of the French press in return for writing favorably about it.[54] Also, for the first time, a pamphlet published by CUP was brought out in Paris,[55] sending tremors through government circles.[56]

About this time intelligence uncovered the society's activities among cadets at the Royal War Academy. In May 1895 a member of the society who had graduated the previous year fled to Athens[57] and raised great concern.[58] Police found a picture of ex-Sultan Murad V in the academy library.[59] Initially forty students were sequestered in the academy's prison.[60] A thorough investigation followed, and ninety-one cadets were taken to the police ministry and placed under arrest.[61] The government attempted to suppress news of these events, but CUP members informed the *Daily News* correspondent,[62] and later the Italian press described the arrests.[63] In spite of the government's efforts, the CUP branch at this school distributed leaflets in October, openly using the watchwords "Your predecessors helped the people. Are you sleeping?"[64] Also, banned newspapers and secret correspondence were found on the naval officers who were imprisoned but released two months later[65] as well as on the students of the Naval Academy who were imprisoned.[66]

At the Royal School of Administration, notes penned by the students satirizing the government and the sultan were uncovered.[67] At this point the government began to view this kind of student activity seriously because of the great diplomatic crisis of 1895 regarding Armenian affairs. As stated in a British daily, "The action of the Young Turkey Party is causing far more uneasiness at the Yildiz Kiosk than ever did the presence of the British fleet at Lemnos."[68] The sultan feared that high-ranking bureaucrats might capitalize on student activities and employ them as their tool.

When W. G. Max Müller, the third clerk of the British embassy in Istanbul, who had contacts with the Ottoman opposition,[69] interviewed two central committee members of the CUP in Istanbul, they innocently revealed that unbeknownst to themselves they were working for the palace coup d'état project of the high-ranking bureaucrats:

> The immediate object of this Society is the dethronement of the Sultan and the proclamation of the Constitution. The dethronement of the Sultan . . . would not necessarily entail any bloodshed except perhaps the judicial execution of some of the miscreants who surround His Majesty. On an appointed day one regiment, whose officers had been won over to the cause, would march into the square in front of the Seraskeriat (War Office), seize the Minister for War, appoint in his stead a man of their choice (probably Fuad Pasha, the man we call *Deli* or mad Fuad), send a messenger to Yildiz to inform the Sultan of his deposition and telegraph the news to the various provinces.[70]

Müller remarked that "this seemed a singularly simple plan" and shared his concerns about "the fanatical population." However, his informants assured him that "as no fetva had ever been published dethroning Mourad, and Abdul Hamid had come to the throne only as Prince-Regent, he was therefore in the eyes of the strict Moslems only Sultan *de facto* but not *de jure*." They also told Müller that they were thinking of appointing Gazi Ahmed Muhtar Pasha as grand vizier and Fuad Pasha as minister of war.[71] Müller secured a copy of the regulations of the CUP,[72] which were later discussed in the European press[73] according to the information given by a committee member in Istanbul.[74]

The regulations, most probably drafted by Ahmed Rıza, clarify the organizational framework of the CUP as well as the political leanings of its leaders.[75] The first article explains the reason for the formation of such a committee:

The Ottoman Committee of Union and Progress, created by all Ottomans, is composed of men and women with the aim of warning our compatriots and reforming the administrative system of the existing Ottoman government, which violates individual rights, such as justice, equality, freedom, stops all Ottomans from progress, and precipitated the fall of the fatherland into the hands of foreign molestation and coercion.[76]

The society, which appointed new members cooptively[77] and required them to take an oath,[78] had a centralized organization. In spite of the members' right to make suggestions,[79] all decision making was the prerogative of the central committee. Seniority determined rank within this hierarchical society.[80]

By escalating the spread of its activities, the CUP endeavored to exploit the great diplomatic crisis of 1895. CUP branches were set up in Paris and Cairo, and Ahmed Rıza and İsmail İbrahim became their respective leaders.[81] Opposition journals published in installments the memoranda of Ahmed Rıza in Cairo,[82] and Ali Kemal, who had taken the first initiative to organize students at the Royal School of Administration, fled from Aleppo,[83] traveling to Paris and joining the opposition there.[84] In the capital, for the first time, the CUP prepared an appeal to play upon the Armenian demonstration at the Sublime Porte on September 30, 1895, and on October 5, 1895, distributed it throughout the city, especially in mosques.[85] The appeal had been written by İbrahim Temo, İshak Sükûti, and İsmail İbrahim. They lithographed over a thousand copies.[86] While protesting the Armenian venture, the CUP adjured all Muslims of the empire to take revolutionary action.[87] Although the government stepped up its measures, a new manifesto was written. This was a terser but more fiery appeal, according to İbrahim Temo, and was distributed primarily to the officers.[88]

Following on the heels of the second appeal, a third one, written by the CUP organization in the capital, focused on government corruption, and contrary to the first two, asked the Muslims and Christians to unite against the common enemy and accused the sultan of preferring foreign intervention to forming a consultative body of capable statesmen.[89] A fourth and similar manifesto was distributed in the capital on December 8.[90]

Another important development in the capital was the flight of Murad Bey. He had asked the sultan to abandon the conservative groups in the palace. According to Murad Bey, he exchanged ideas with the sultan for two hours following the presentation of his memorandum, and the sultan "charged [him] to submit a draft constitution—moderate but liberal."[91] Max Müller claimed that the sultan asked Murad Bey to prepare a reform memorandum but that the sultan's advisers, Abū al-Hudā al-Ṣayyādī and Ragıb Bey, prejudiced the sultan against Murad Bey, calling him a nihilist.[92] When he again presented himself at the palace, the sultan refused to receive him. In reality the sultan discounted Murad Bey's reform proposals and found them absurd.[93] Losing all prospect of becoming the sultan's adviser, Murad Bey fled to Europe.[94] Although he refused membership in the CUP, he was known as a liberal for a long time by the European public,[95] and he had discussed the future of the Empire with "five persons, the choice spirits of the Young Turkey Party, [who had] joined [him] on the Bosphorus" before he fled Europe. Formulas such as the assassination of the sultan and revolution were dismissed, and "the majority decided to try to convince Europe of the true remedies for the actual situation."[96]

The activities of the CUP and other opposition groups raised enormous popular expectations, not only in the capital but also in the provinces[97]; however, when the sultan triumphed over foreign intervention, a major campaign of investigations and arrests was launched. Thirty-four CUP leaders and many sympathizers were taken into custody.[98] Some European newspapers cited as many as 900.[99] After a new wave of arrests, Abdullah Cevdet, a founder, and Mustafa Efendi, a prominent author of the first CUP appeals, were exiled.[100] Doctor İsmail İbrahim, who later became director of the Egyptian branch, was also arrested and banished.[101] İbrahim Temo fled to Romania.[102] Of those who understood the CUP network, only İshak Sükûti remained in the capital. Soon he too was caught and exiled to Rhodes, and this caused the total collapse of the CUP in the capital.[103] Before his apprehension, İshak Sükûti transferred his position as coordinator in the capital to Doctor Mekkeli Sabri.[104] Under the circumstances, he decided to form a new central committee. But since Lieutenant Colonel Şefik Bey, the leader of the military wing of the CUP, had also been exiled in early 1896,[105] the new coordinator visited him in exile in Acre in order to acquire information about the military members of the organization.[106] Then a new coordinating committee was formed led by Hacı Ahmed Bey, a high-ranking bureaucrat at the War Office, joined by Doctor Mekkeli Sabri and Hüseyin Avni[107] a new executive committee was appointed, composed of Marshal Fuad Pasha, Marshal Kâzım Pasha (Military commander of Istanbul), Sheikh Abdülkadir, Sheikh Nailî, Hakkı Bey (a member of the Council of State), Necib Pasha (a former ambassador), and Es'ad Bey (a high-ranking bureaucrat at the Ministry of Public Works). In this manner the CUP in the capital was transformed from a student organization into a committee of high-ranking bureaucrats and ulema.[108] İbrahim Temo later confessed that he did not even know the new director of the Istanbul branch.[109] This caused problems in relations between the Istanbul organization and the Paris branch.

While these vital events were occurring in Istanbul, Ahmed Rıza took the initiative of organizing the Young Turk movement in Europe. A necessary step was the establishment of a central organ, for which he arranged a meeting with young Ottoman students who were taking refuge in Paris. Khalīl Ghānim and Amīr Arslān also attended the meeting. But they could not agree on a common program. However, Ahmed Rıza managed to collect Fr 500 from the students and so was able to start the journal.[110] He later wrote a manifesto and "addressed the civilized world" thus:

> We ask for reforms, not only for this or that province but for the Empire as a whole, not in favour of any one nationality, but in favour of all Ottomans, Jews, Christians, and Mahometans. We desire to advance in the path of civilization, but above all we do not wish to advance save by strengthening the Ottoman element, while respecting the general conditions of Ottoman life. We are eager to preserve the peculiar originality of our Eastern civilization, and therefore to borrow from the West only the general results of its scientific evolution, which are necessary to enlighten a people aiming at liberty.[111]

Also he and those in his coterie told European journalists that their simple aim was the reproclamation of the constitution and reconvention of the parliament, and so they underscored their nonrevolutionary commitment.[112] Their remarks accorded with information given to a journalist by the Istanbul center of the organization. They averred that they "must not be confounded with Midhat's Young Turkey Party. [They] are simply malcontents not theorists . . . and have no antipathy to Abdul Hamid except on the ground of his odious methods of misgovernment."[113]

Finally on December 1, 1895, Ahmed Rıza printed the first issue of the central organ of the CUP, and on December 7 its French supplement, each with a different preface. In the preface to the Turkish organ he denounced the situation that resulted from Muslims living under the French and British administration and Turks living under the Russian and Bulgarian rule, and he underscored the significance of the Turkish element of the Empire: "*Meşveret* is a Turkish newspaper. It will give the Turkish explanation, i.e., the truth, about everything."[114] In the much longer French preface, he delineated the positivist basis for the CUP.[115] He also penned a manifesto, in which he appealed for material contributions to the committee, and distributed it through the CUP network in Istanbul. He said that the CUP "has become a real political association with branches in every province."[116] In comparison with the earlier stages of the CUP, the first part of this claim was accurate, although the second part was somewhat exaggerated.

The CUP as a Political Organization, 1895–1897

The CUP Organization in Europe and in Egypt, 1895–1896

Although the Istanbul branch of the CUP was the executive committee for the entire organization according to its regulations, this duty was performed *de facto* by the Paris branch after the collapse of the Istanbul section.[117] Later this was recognized by all branches, and Ahmed Rıza temporarily became the *de jure* leader of the movement.[118] He firmly opposed any revolutionary change and advocated a more conservative policy for the CUP:

> Most of the letters that I have received from Istanbul and the provinces since *Meşveret* began publication speak with sighs and tears about the necessity for

a revolution. [They are saying that] "the CUP is unaware of its prime duty. It takes no action. It gives no punishment to the spies butchering members of the society with the axes of absolutism. What nation has reclaimed its liberty without using weapons? What nation could save its administration from the hands of absolutism? You ought to join the general public. Do not become annihilated while advocating silly ideas such as 'it is possible without bloodshed.'" Previously people attacked the palace without knowing what they were doing and why they were revolting and they shouted [we do not want this]. Today it is impossible to materialize a great revolution by these [kinds of] blind revolts. The nation ought to have a strong ideology and a great ideal. This ideology and ideal should direct the nation toward a national aim.[119]

Ahmed Rıza defined his policy as positivist in letters to the European press written on behalf of the CUP.[120] A second characteristic of his approach was a stiff opposition to foreign intervention:

The British Government has sent a formidable fleet before the Dardanelles. It is without a doubt that such a succession to the throne with the help of a foreign hand will cause some hazardous new privileges [to be given to the Europeans]. If the Ottomans were united on a single aim regardless to their religion and ethnicity there would be no need for interposition and intervention by the foreigners.[121]

This viewpoint was underscored by the followers of this group in interviews given to European newspapers.[122]

The formation of a new central committee in Istanbul— composed of high-ranking bureaucrats, military generals, and ulema—and their adoption of a palace coup d'état policy gradually led to a major altercation between them and Ahmed Rıza. The Istanbul branch backed some secondary opponents in Europe, such as Halil Ziya, recognized as the secretary general of the Brussels branch of the CUP by Istanbul, although unknown to members in Europe.[123] This person's appeal for a palace coup d'état echoed the sentiments in the Istanbul center.[124]

Under these circumstances Murad Bey fled to Europe. European diplomats assigned tremendous significance to his personality and ideas,[125] and although they described him as a "liberal,"[126] he also received credit from the ulema.[127] Besides, he had been a key player in palace coup d'état attempts and favored European intervention.[128]

Thus Murad Bey became a balancing power between the Istanbul center and Ahmed Rıza. Since he believed that the solution of the problem was foreign intervention that should be effected by the Great Powers, he undertook negotiations upon his arrival in Europe. He obtained the audience of Graf Goluchowski and explained his viewpoint. However, he found the Austria-Hungarian foreign minister ignorant about these matters and decided to go to Paris.[129] He gained popularity there and, during an interview with *Le Figaro*, advocated a responsible government in Istanbul and backed Said, Kâmil, and Gazi Ahmed Muhtar Pashas in the establishment of such a government.[130] The first chapter of his book, entitled *Le Palais de Yildiz et la Sublime Porte le Véritable mal d'Orient*, was published in both *Le Figaro* and the *Pall Mall Gazette*.[131] In it, he emphasized the importance of returning power to the Sublime Porte. However, Ahmed Rıza gave him a cold reception.[132] Ahmed Rıza also criticized Murad Bey's approach, which required a responsible government and foreign intervention instead of the immediate convening of the Ottoman parliament.[133] Murad Bey then met with the leaders of the Armenian revolutionary committees in London for the purpose of forming a united front. However, his efforts were fruitless.[134] He also met with Lord Salisbury but was disappointed by the British statesman's outlook on the Eastern Question.[135] Murad Bey also failed to make an impact on the pro-Armenian policy of Gladstone.[136] At the same time the palace decided to win over Murad Bey and to compel him return to Istanbul.[137] However, he refused these offers[138] and promised the Ottoman ambassador, Anthopulos Pasha, that he would pursue a course different from the other opposition newspapers and write nothing against the sultan.[139] Upon his return to Paris, the young members of the organization clamored for Murad Bey to lead the Paris branch of the CUP, replacing Ahmed Rıza.[140] But again he declined. He met with Ahmed Rıza and told him that he had chosen to publish his journal, *Mizan (Balance)*, in Egypt[141] and departed for Cairo on December 29, 1895.[142]

In the wake of these events, Ahmed Rıza maintained his leadership in Paris. The Ottoman administration, understanding his consequential role, attempted to persuade him to return to the Empire, but he refused.[143] Then the Ottoman government targeted fugitives[144] and students[145] who were rallying to the Young Turk cause in Paris. Students protested the government's interference[146] and the CUP declared that it would grant a limited number of stipends to those willing to be protected by the committee.[147] The French government decided to withhold the help requested by Ottoman administration.[148]

The CUP's action was made possible by the financial support of high-ranking officials.[149] In fact, the CUP bought a printing plant in June 1896 and began to publish its central organ not by lithography but by letterpress, and it opened a bank account.[150] New donations were announced in the central organ with the intent of provoking anxiety in government circles.[151]

Meanwhile, in contradiction to frequent complaints that the European press underreported the activities of the CUP,[152] the group and its positivist leader became major newsmakers due to the French government's measures against them under the pressure of the Ottoman administration.

On April 11, 1896, the Léon Bourgeois government decided to ban the circulation of the Turkish version of *Meşveret* and to extradite Ahmed Rıza.[153] Ahmed Rıza called upon editors of various Paris journals,[154] protesting a new procedure of sentencing CUP members in Ottoman courts and then requesting their extradition from foreign governments.[155] Since an Istanbul court had condemned him for life,[156] he defined the dilemma as a question of freedom, and this provoked outrage. French journalists, led by Paul Granier de Cassagnac of *L'Intransigeant* and Clemenceau of *Libre Parole*, denounced the French government's action.[157] The French government amended its decision and limited its response to merely banning circulation of the Turkish version of *Meşveret*.[158] Consequently, Ahmed Rıza went to Geneva, where the journal was published under the editorship of Albert Karlen, a radical Swiss journalist.[159] In this issue, Ahmed Rıza denounced the sultan's policy toward the CUP.[160]

Following this development, the European press paid closer attention to the Young Turks and, despite their conservatism, the Young Turks were given respect and support by radical and revolutionary political figures in Europe. Among these was Karl Blind, who had participated in revolutionary activities with Giuseppe Mazzini and Garibaldi.[161] He published a lengthy article based on information provided by the Young Turks and paid tribute to their movement.[162]

While these events were transpiring in Europe, Murad Bey journeyed to Cairo and took over the publication of *Mizan* as the director of the Egyptian branch. Murad Bey's arrival, in Cairo allowed the Islamic group in the Egyptian branch to conduct the movement there. Upon his arrival, he applied to Paris and required Ahmed Rıza to extend his own authority.[163] Then he published a detailed and lengthy new program entitled "The Line of Conduct for Our Party,"[164] different from the two programs published by the central organ and its French supplement. This program provoked extensive discussions among the Young Turks[165] and showed the independent action of Murad Bey, who believed it was his prerogative to publish a program. Although Murad Bey and Ahmed Rıza praised each other meticulously,[166] they were subtly carrying on an intense rivalry with one another.

Murad Bey was slipping into the role of manager of the entire organization, although he was only the director of the Egyptian branch. An official letter to Ahmed Zeki, a leader of the Young Turk movement in the Balkans, demonstrates this; advising the Balkan Young Turks on organizational procedure, he wrote as if he were coordinator of the CUP, proffering guidance from an Islamic viewpoint in complete contradiction to the Paris branch.[167] In a short period, *Mizan* overshadowed *Meşveret*. The interrogation documents demonstrate that both journals were distributed indiscriminately in the capital and provinces by the CUP network.[168] However, according to the Young Turk documents, more people were demanding Murad Bey's organ than any other opposition journal or pamphlet,[169] and those subscribing to all Young Turk publications found *Mizan* to have the most profound impact.[170] Documentation on intercepted Young Turk publications further indicates that Murad Bey's journal was the most frequently smuggled publication.[171] Later the publishers of the new central organ of the CUP proudly announced that their circulation had surpassed even that of *Mizan* in 1896–1897.[172]

Murad Bey, so as to gain full advantage from these developments, stepped up his efforts to don a leadership guise. He was still proposing a palace coup d'état led by high-ranking bureaucrats and issued an appeal to them.[173] He also dispatched copies of his journal to influential officials in the regions.[174]

Murad Bey also strove to maintain sound relations with the British, since he deemed their help essential in reforming administration in the Ottoman Empire. He received a promise from Lord Cromer that "he would be protected during his stay in Cairo against the encroachments." Murad Bey further claimed that he presented a letter by Lord Salisbury to introduce himself to Lord Cromer.[175] This appears different from the general protection given to the Ottoman opposition in Egypt because of their pro-British policies.[176] However, Lord Cromer had a low opinion of Murad Bey and wished to use him as a tool in his relations with the sultan and the khedive. He wrote that "Mourad is an impecunious scamp. Most of what he says about the Sultan is quite true; but this is beside the point. . . . I dare to say that he will do what I tell him."[177]

This attitude began to shift in a negative direction under pressure from the Ottoman government. The British carefully weighed Murad Bey's impact on relations between the two countries.[178] Then the sultan himself informed the British that Murad Bey's activities were damaging his prestige as the caliph of all Muslims.[179] The sultan then asked Anthopulos Pasha to tell the British that Murad Bey was an impediment to a rapprochement between the Ottoman and British governments.[180] But the British responded simply that they could not intervene in the domestic affairs of Egypt.[181] Meanwhile Ottoman diplomats and statesmen were reiterating their allegations against Murad Bey.[182] In March 1896 the sultan asked the British to dispose of Murad Bey and to resolve the Armenian affairs and the Egyptian problem.[183] In the meantime, the Ottoman high commissioner to Egypt made applications to the khedive,[184] and when the local police discovered that a young acquaintance of Murad Bey was hatching a plot against the Egyptian ruler,[185] he found himself surrounded. Murad Bey also realized that his influence on European public opinion might diminish unless he spent time in Europe. After being warned to soften the language he had been using against the sultan,[186] he made the incident an excuse to move to Europe. On July 16, 1896, he arrived once again in Paris.

Two weeks before Murad Bey boarded a ship bound for Europe, the opposition against Ahmed Rıza among the Paris branch culminated with a protest by young CUP members against the positivist leader, accusing him of "publishing *Meşveret* without *meşveret* [consultation]."[187] According to an opponent of Ahmed Rıza, author of an unsigned letter to İbrahim Temo, the main reason for the action against the positivist leader was his absolutist tendencies:

> The philosophers of mankind devised the method of *meşveret* [consulting] to inquire into the opinions of everyone in order to discover a way to transform the unrealistic theory of total equality into the practice of relative equality.

During our time it can be proven that there is no other way to ensure peace among people. We humbly joined this human crowd . . . and amicably request [Ahmed] Rıza Bey to depart in this spirit . . . We begged him and sacrificed our authority and human dignity in order to direct him onto the true path. These efforts bore no fruit; he continued his absolutism. While he was inveighing against Sultan Hamid to institute consultation, he became the most extreme despot. . . . We even served him as obedient servants but instead of regarding our modesty as an aspect of our patriotism he took it as evidence of his personal talent, which is meager, and began to act the bully as a turkey, which is the stupidest of all animals. When he so elevated himself, we bowed to the ground, and then he elevated the more.[188]

Most of his opponents claimed that there was no difference between the absolutism of the sultan and that of Ahmed Rıza,[189] and they looked forward to Murad Bey's return. Upon his arrival, Ahmed Rıza's opponents again implored him to replace the positivist leader. Murad Bey eventually consented, and the members planned an extraordinary meeting.

Events immediately prior to this meeting dramatically worsened Ahmed Rıza's position. He was constantly assailed by the newly organized Istanbul center for his staunch opposition to any revolutionary attempt and to foreign intervention. In order to relax the opposition against him, he met with Armenian revolutionary leaders in London and with British statesmen,[190] to no avail. Besides, the Armenian leaders would not recognize the CUP.[191] The only warm response came from the British positivists,[192] but this was valueless in easing the opposition against him. Following his failure to impress his opponents, who had been anticipating a more revolutionary platform, the Paris branch, on September 16, 1896, applied to the Istanbul center and other branches requesting their help in developing a more active approach and obtaining more funding under the guise of a "patriotism tax."[193] However, to Ahmed Rıza this final attempt seemed empty.

At this time the CUP rescued its prominent members from prison. Şefik Bey, who had led the military organization in Istanbul, was sprung from Acre prison,[194] and İshak Sükûti, Çürüksulu Ahmed, and Salih Cemal escaped, with the help of the CUP, from a Rhodes dungeon.[195] İshak Sükûti first went to Beirut and then sojourned in Paris[196]; Salih Cemal was assigned to reorganize the Egyptian branch.[197] These flights occasioned hilarity among members,[198] and İshak Sükûti's long-standing role as committee coordinator and founder—until his banishment—brought him the ultimate prestige in the European branch. Ahmed Rıza's letters inviting him to Paris for common efforts indicate this.[199] But for Ahmed Rıza there was disappointment because these prominent members lacked the respect for him that the Ottoman students in Paris had. This, combined with the opposition against him, made it clear that any decision at the extraordinary meeting was sure to be negative.

At this meeting, held around mid-November, a decision was made to form a Committee of Inspection and Execution for "administrating the full scope of the committee in accord with the regulations and under its own aegis."[200] This committee was to have a director, an assistant director, and three members. By a secret ballot, Murad Bey was elected director. He later wrote that he had voted for Ahmed Rıza, but all other votes balloted had named him.[201] Çürüksulu Ahmed became the assistant director, and Doctor Nâzım, Şerafeddin Mağmumî, and İshak Sükûti were nominated members.[202] Doctor Nâzım and İshak Sükûti were also appointed director of correspondence and cashier respectively.[203] Recognition of the Paris branch's director as the leader of the organization was denied, and this branch was demoted to a normal one.[204] Çürüksulu Ahmed replaced Ahmed Rıza. Ahmed Rıza, who entered the meeting as leader of the movement, departed as editor of *Mechveret Supplément Français* on the condition that each issue be subject to the review and control of a board.[205] The topic of the central organ generated lengthy arguments. First it was decided that *Meşveret* would be published under the editorship of Murad Bey. But contradictory claims surfaced regarding ownership of the journal. Ahmed Rıza denied the claim that it was owned by the CUP and protested that he was the owner.[206] Then it was determined that only *Mizan* would represent the CUP as its central organ and that Ali Kemal, Şerafeddin Mağmumî, Şefik, and Şerif Beys would be members of the editorial board.[207]

Ahmed Rıza accepted these alterations and wrote in his journal that this had happened because "there was no need for two journals in Turkish for one society,"[208] and he expressed similar views in his correspondence.[209] However, the restructuring proved vital for the CUP. Other opposition journals also repudiated allegations of a discord in the CUP,[210] but letters sent to Ahmed Rıza requiring him to adopt censorious language of the new central organ make clear that there was greater disharmony than ever.[211]

The first appeal published in the new central organ on behalf of the new Committee of Inspection and Execution, undoubtedly penned by Murad Bey, illustrates the shift in policy. It claimed that the immediate task of the CUP was to "salvage the state and the caliphate" and urged the high-ranking bureaucrats to join them in a coup d'état.[212]

The Istanbul Branch and the 1896 Coup d'État Attempt

As we have seen, a new central committee of high-ranking officials, officers, and ulema replaced the CUP center in the capital, which had been composed of college students and young medical doctors. In a short time this branch obtained support from many officers, and the War Office became a CUP center. Meanwhile, European public opinion launched another pro-Armenian campaign.[213] The bureaucratic members of the center assumed that even if foreign intervention did not materialize, their attempt to depose the sultan might be supported by Europe. They gave interviews to the representatives of the Great Powers advocating reforms and "a favourable change in the state of affairs."[214]

Under these conditions the center undertook an initiative for the venture. A secret correspondence with the heir apparent, relayed through the Mevlevî tekke at Galata, led to his agreement. Doctor Mekkeli Sabri has provided a detailed description of their plans:

> When the [new] central committee decided to dethrone Abdülhamid using troops under the command of Marshal Kâzım Pasha, it was considered the [action of] self-sacrificing volunteers. In the event Abdülhamid had ventured to resist and ordered the Arab and Albanian divisions at the Chamberlain's office to open fire on national troops, then those volunteers would have assassinated him. The central committee arrived at this decision unanimously. Also we had corresponded with the heir apparent, Reşad Efendi, and a room of *bi'at* at the War Office had even been arranged. Abdülhamid was going to be dethroned and the constitution was going to be reproclaimed.[215]

The Istanbul branch also communicated with its Paris counterpart and asked the latter's approval. However, Doctor Nâzım gave a dubious answer within the description of a dream. The former reapplied, and Ahmed Rıza told them through another Paris branch member that "even if this event brought no result, it might open a door to revolution."[216] Upon this second vague answer, the central committee in Istanbul decided to expel Ahmed Rıza from the CUP, but because their branch had been dispersed, they were impeded from taking the necessary steps.

The preparations gathered momentum after pressure from the military faction. Again Doctor Mekkeli Sabri gives valuable information:

> The War Office branch was pressuring us terribly saying, "Either carry out the coup d'état or withdraw." In our branch there were high-ranking officers such as Kâzım Pasha and Fuad Pasha. Minister of War, Ali Rıza Pasha, is awaiting like a double-edged sword for a coup d'état. Once he told his aide-de-camp, Şefik Bey: "If these men succeed, I will be on their side; however, if they fail, damn them! I will stomp all over them." In case this branch carries out the coup d'état before us and succeeds, the fatherland would be saved from Abdülhamid, but look who lies waiting to seize it.[217]

The Istanbul center organized a special unit of self-sacrificing volunteers, as it had been ordered to do in a circular distributed in mid-1896.[218] Sheikh Abdülkadir, who had received privileges from the palace, since the sultan feared his power among the ulema[219], led the establishment of this unit, and ulema gave a weighty endorsement to the venture.[220] Sir Philip Currie commented that he could not comprehend how fanatical and anti-European groups and westernized people who read publications such as *Meşveret* could work together.[221] His comment was well taken because there were no similarities between the group surrounding Ahmed Rıza and the leaders of the Istanbul center. Also, the latter, influenced by distinguished ulema, asked the committee not to enroll Christians in the organization,[222] in opposition to Ahmed Rıza's efforts to unite the opponents around the Ottoman Constitution of 1876.

In late 1896, conditions for a coup d'état had again ripened. Dissatisfaction among the War Academy cadets had reached a pinnacle,[223] and the number of exiles from all classes escalated.[224] On September 17, 1896, the *softas* undertook a demonstration against the sultan, but they were stopped by military and police.[225] Meanwhile, the Dashnaktsutiun Committee distributed leaflets exhorting Muslims to unite with them in their struggle against the establishment.[226]

Finally, the Istanbul center agreed to initiate the coup d'état. However, Nadir Bey, the secretary of the Istanbul center, revealed its plans to İsmail Pasha, a confidant of the sultan, who immediately informed the palace about this venture.[227] A mammoth campaign of arrests ensued. Sir Philip Currie informed the Foreign Office that 350 people were arrested, including Kâzım Pasha, the military commander of Istanbul; the police commissioner; Hüsni Bey, and Salih Pasha, the gendarmerie commander.[228] Later Sheikh Abdülkadir, Sheikh Nailî, Doctor Sabri, Hacı Ahmed, and various bureaucrats and officials were apprehended and exiled forthwith.[229] Sheikh Abdülkadir's family was deported to Medina, and the other participants were relegated to remote corners of the Empire under the strictest control.[230] The sultan feared a military effervescence and limited reciprocity against high-ranking officials, appointing them to faraway places.[231] Fuad Pasha was exempted from this because of his popularity in European public opinion, suffering only dismissal.[232]

Following this failure, the Istanbul branch of the CUP again collapsed, and college students formed a new central committee. However, this branch would never attain the power and importance it had in 1896. Also, the CUP would never again have as many high-ranking officials and officers.

The only action of the CUP center in Istanbul following these developments was to apply to the embassies of the Great Powers, demanding their help. However, they received no affirmative answer.[233] The Freemasons also maneuvered to take advantage of the developments by dispatching a letter of protest to Jean Jaurès and the French government under the title Comité Libéral Ottoman.[234] But these events could not belie the need for the activities of the CUP to be transplanted to Europe.

The CUP Organization in the Regions

An essential document on the CUP network reveals that the CUP formed branches in Beirut, Damascus, Crete, Lesbos, Rhodes, Salonica, Izmir, Trabzon, Tripoli, and Tripoli of Barbary, as well as a general branch to oversee the city branches in Syria.[235] Two other branches were in Cyprus and Bosnia. Nominally they were in Ottoman lands; however, since they were under British and Austro-Hungarian rule respectively (according to the Cyprus convention and the Berlin Congress), these two can be considered branches abroad. The same is true for the Bulgarian central branch and local branches linked to it. According to this document, 100 secret committee numbers were assigned to Beirut, Damascus, and Tripoli of Barbary, thirty to Rhodes, fifty to Izmir, 100 to Lesbos, forty to Salonica, and 100 to the Syrian central organization. One number was assigned to a leader in Cyprus, and the numbers assigned to Trabzon were described as "beginning with 6/941 and 6/942."[236] Branches established after this document was written and those mentioned in Ottoman official papers were Adana, Adrianople, Angora, Crete, Erzurum, Hama, Homs, Kastamonu, Mamuret el-Azîz, and Mersin. The numbers the CUP organs provided concerning the membership seem somewhat exaggerated,[237] yet the CUP network undoubtedly was significant.

The regulations accorded coordinating responsibilities to Istanbul, but with its collapse, most new branches were established by the Paris section. It is possible to divide these branches into two types.

The first type was formed with the effort not of the CUP but of members who were in exile in those cities. Later such organizations were uncovered in Angora,[238] Kastamonu,[239] and Mamuret el-Azîz.[240] However, general conditions in those towns precluded any significant Young Turk activities. Similar organizations formed by the exiles, however, gained prominence due to the presence of military divisions there and more suitable conditions. For example, the Erzurum branch, working under the orders of Murad Bey, tried to establish ties with local Armenian organizations.[241] However, the interception of a letter sent to this branch from the Syrian center of the CUP prompted an in-depth investigation.[242] When local police stormed the residence of the exiled officers, they uncovered instructions sent by Murad Bey. A certain Armenian, Setrak Pastırmacıyan, was arrested for his role in receiving money from Europe and distributing it to CUP members.[243] More arrests followed. CUP members told interrogators that many of the sultan's confidants—such as Ragıb, İzzet, Lütfi, and Said Beys—were backing their movement. Certainly Murad Bey had been claiming this and had endeavored to convince CUP members.[244] Meanwhile police intercepted a blank paper sent by the Paris branch of the Dashnaktsutiun Committee in Erzurum via Russia. When police submerged it in a chemical bath, they discovered a message saying that since Armenian organizations and the CUP had a common aim, they should unite, in spite of their differences, to dethrone the sultan and should require all members in the region to act accordingly.[245] The Ottoman administration had the branch dismantled, and in spite of the fact that the arrests and investigation caused anxiety in town and rumors were being spread concerning the CUP activities in Istanbul,[246] the branch collapsed and died.

A second type of branch was formed directly by CUP members under the instructions of the central committee, and these constituted a significant local network. One example was the central branch in Syria.

With regard to the other branches, the Rhodes branch, which had many CUP expatriates, became a center for the distribution of banned publications within the Empire. İshak Sükûti's banishment to Rhodes and subsequent work there strengthened its prominence.[247] Although the governor of the Province of Cezaîr-i Bahr-i Sefid underestimated the value of the branch in the movement,[248] it had strategic utility for distribution of CUP publications into western Anatolia. The government sent intelligence agents to the island, who scrutinized the activities of the exiles.[249] Following the flight of İshak Sükûti and other prominent members, the branch lost its importance and collapsed in the fall of 1897.

The Adrianople branch became closely allied with branches in Salonica and Monastir and also communicated with the Balkan organization established by İbrahim Temo. However, interception of CUP documents sent from Adrianople to Salonica prompted an extensive investigation.[250] Seventeen members, ten of whom were officers and one a prominent Albanian *âlim*, İbrahim Efendi, were arrested.[251] Since the branch was foremost in military recruitment, this caused great distress to CUP leaders.[252] Also, the number of contributions flowing from this branch indicates a large membership.[253] After the initial arrests, low-ranking officials, including Talât Bey (who later became grand vizier Talât Pasha), were caught bearing the coded instructions of the CUP.[254] Despite its valuable function in European Turkey, this branch was annihilated by the palace, and the CUP's efforts to revitalize the organization in Adrianople came to nought.[255]

Another branch in European Turkey that held strategic importance was in Salonica. In 1896 the CUP organs began to publish news about its activities. As Leskovikli Mehmed Rauf mentioned,[256] this publication was directed to the followers of Sabatay Sevi, who had converted to Islam in the seventeenth century and were known as "dönmeler" (converts). Doctor Nâzım, a native of Salonica, openly commended their efforts for the Young Turk movement in *Meşveret*.[257] These praises were echoed in members' letters sent from Salonica,[258] and in mid-1896 a branch was born there.[259] Major Ahmed, whose pen name was Tarık, was appointed director upon the demise of previous administration.[260] Leskovikli Mehmed Rauf and the journalist Kudret Bey were members of the executive committee.[261] The branch enrolled large numbers of officers and distributed CUP publications.[262] It also asked the Paris center to pursue a more active policy, and upon the center's refusal, commissioned a volunteer to Istanbul to assassinate the sultan. The attempt, however, failed.[263] Leskovikli Mehmed Rauf wrote that their efforts halted after the Greco-Turkish War of 1897.[264] The palace later gave him a new post,[265] so it is possible that the activities of this branch were not known by the palace in detail.

Due to the schism between the followers of Ahmed Rıza and Murad Bey, a second CUP branch in Salonica was formed. Neither the documents of this branch nor a member's memoirs mention any activities of the above-mentioned branch. This substantiates the accusation of Şerafeddin Mağmumî that Ahmed Rıza continued to correspond with some branches as if he were the leader of the movement.[266] The second branch was established on January 28, 1897; Ferdinand Efendi was appointed director, Fikretî Bey the cashier, and Archbolo Efendi and Enver Bey secretaries.[267] According to a second communiqué, sent from Salonica to the central committee, the *dönmeler* joined the branch *en masse,* but they refused to pay dues, on the grounds that they were sending Fr 100 weekly to the Paris center. Later this branch planned to assassinate palace spies and intelligence officers in Salonica, and the local Armenian committee drew up a pact with them. However, because the Armenian committee insisted on writing threatening letters to the wealthy people in order to extort money, the plans were never realized.[268]

During the diplomatic crisis of 1897 the branch decided to curtail its activities.[269] There are no further documents on the activities of this branch after the Greco-Turkish War; this may be symptomatic of its inactivity. In 1901 *Meşveret* accused the Ottoman government of dispatching special agents to Salonica to investigate the activities of the branch; thus it might have survived beyond 1897.[270] However, no significant activities occurred until the reorganization of the CUP in 1906.

A similar branch was formed in Crete and for a while operated under the title Girid İttihad-ı Osmaniyan Cemiyeti (Ottoman Union Society in Crete).[271] Ottoman documents on the discovery of some branch documents on the officers[272] and the distribution of illegal publications[273] prove that the branch was active until late 1897. Like other branches in the Empire, this branch went into decline after the Greco-Turkish War. The reorganization of the CUP in 1906 allowed it to become again one of the most active in the organization.

Establishment of the CUP Network in the Balkans, 1895–1896

A salient event in the history of the CUP was the establishment of its Balkan branches by İbrahim Temo. He had some ties with the Aromenis organization in Macedonia; thus when the Ottoman police pursued him, he fled to Romania and arrived there on November 1, 1895.[274] After spending some time in Bucharest, he went to Dobruja in 1896 and spearheaded the formation of a CUP branch there. He was joined by Kırımızâde Ali Rıza, a native of Dobruja and a navy lieutenant who had fled from Istanbul to his hometown[275]; Sheikh Şevki Celâleddin; Hüseyin Avni, a teacher; and Mahmud Çelebi, a native of Constantsa who had come back to Romania from Paris.[276] This organization flourished for a short time,[277] during which İbrahim Temo wrote a pamphlet entitled *Hareket (Action)* with the help of Ottoman officials working at the consulates, Şefik Bey, and Alfred Rüstem, both secretly promoting the Young Turk cause. *Hareket* was a critique of Abdülhamid II's regime, and it is possible to find a discussion about almost everything, from Pan-Islamism to the Albanian committees, from the Armenian Question to relations between the Ottoman Empire and Great Britain in this small essay. Despite its eclectic and unrefined character, it won enormous popularity. The Balkan organization distributed a vast quantity through its network,[278] Egyptian[279] and European branches required more and more copies of it,[280] and the branch in Tripoli of Barbary initiated a translation into Arabic.[281]

İbrahim Temo also founded the CUP branches in Bulgaria under the direction of a central Bulgarian branch in Ruse, which was formed prior to Murad Bey's flight to Europe.[282] Temo also formed small branches in Plovdiv, Slivno, Lom, Pazardzhik, Shumen, Tutrakan, Varna, Vidin, and Yambol.[283] All the branches acknowledged İbrahim Temo as their leader in the Balkans.[284]

Another key organizer of the Young Turks in Bulgaria, Mustafa Ragıb, formerly a student at the Royal Medical Academy, produced a play denouncing Abdülhamid II's regime to win over the Muslim population in Ruse[285]; he also carried out various propaganda campaigns in the region.[286] The Vidin branch distributed CUP publications in Bulgaria with the help of the local Armenians,[287] and a local leader and the director of the Shumen branch, Talât Bey, traveled all around Bulgaria and Adrianople to enroll subscribers in the central organs.[288] CUP pamphlets vilifying the sultan from a religious viewpoint, such as *Ulema-yı Din-i İslâma Da'vet-i Şer'iye (An Islamic Invitation to Ulema)*, were widely distributed, and Muameleci Emin Ağa, a member of the central branch in Ruse, gave oral readings to illiterate people.[289] Also the local members concocted anti-Ottoman government slander in various cities.[290]

To win over this powerful organization, Murad Bey established ties with it when he was the director of the Egyptian branch. Later he sent Doctor Ali Hikmet to Bulgaria to carry out his propaganda, but Ottoman officials in Ruse put him under close surveillance and intercepted his letters, so he had no opportunity to carry out the intensive propaganda he intended.[291]

A final attempt by the Balkan organization was to establish ties with the Bulgarian and Macedonian committees. Committee members extolled the Young Turk movement during their demonstrations,[292] and this sent tremors through Ottoman government circles.[293]

In order to curtail Young Turk propaganda in Bulgaria and influence the people in Macedonia and Adrianople, the Ottoman government ordered the close scrutiny of travelers arriving from Bulgaria[294] and banned most Turkish publications printed there. This created an impression among officials that all publications printed in Bulgaria were prohibited; however, the grand vizier disabused them of this, saying that only publications with "seditious" passages had been banned.[295]

The CUP under the Direction of Murad Bey

The European Organization

Murad Bey shared the opinion of many high-ranking Ottoman bureaucrats that the failure of the movement was due to the lack of foreign intervention. This was the motive behind his appeals to the Armenians,[296] his unrealized attempt while in London in 1896 to gain the audience of Lord Salisbury with a joint Muslim-Armenian delegation,[297] and his later efforts to win over Armenian revolutionary leaders such as Armen Garo.[298]

However, at this point Murad Bey confronted another dilemma. The flights of many officers and military medical doctors altered the composition of the CUP in Paris. As an opposition newspaper wrote, they were seeking a military revolution, and although Murad Bey decried Ahmed Rıza's inactivity, his only sincere objective was a palace coup d'état:

> With the flight of many prominent Ottoman officers to France, the above-mentioned party's board was transformed from a civil into a military one. Beyond any doubt the military cannot be regarded as pen and ink users. They relate better to sword and rifle. Our commanders both in the Ottoman dominions and in France began to view the deliverance of speeches and use of the pen as impractical vehicles to the attainment of their goals, and began seriously to consider among themselves that the time had come for action instead of chitchat. Although some pen users among themselves stuck to the belief that to consume ink with a swift pen would solve the problem more easily than using "powder and weapon," finally they retrenched from this idea and accepted the aims of their military comrades to take initiative for serious action.[299]

The "activists," as they were known, led by Tunalı Hilmi, formed a special branch named Osmanlı İhtilâl Fırkası (Ottoman Revolution[ary] party) and claimed that "eighty percent of all members favored action."[300] This was directed by a secret executive committee of three people with the single aim of "active actions."[301] Since Tunalı Hilmi remained a member of the CUP until 1899,[302] this special branch was formed within the CUP. They undertook their initiative while Ahmed Rıza was leading the Paris branch. He wrote:

> The separatist committee which was formed here ten months ago, named "Partisans of action" but a more accurate title would be "On the pretext of action," fragmented our committee and caused its demise. However, we kept the commotion to ourselves and revealed nothing to the outside world.[303]

Ahmed Rıza also denounced every anarchist and revolutionary movement on behalf of the CUP in *Mechveret Supplément Français.*[304] There is no doubt that this special branch had expressed the feelings of many young members who thought that "all around the world progress is a consequence of revolution, and bloodshed is the price of liberty. The law issued by nature is inexorable."[305] These members thought that Murad Bey's election as director would enable them to act openly. They announced the establishment of their branch on December 21, 1896,[306] inscribed a different set of regulations for their branch, carved a seal reading "Ottoman Revolution[ary] party—Justice or Death,"[307] and penned fiery appeals to incite the Muslim Ottoman population. They addressed the ulema and the military in a ponderously religious language, markedly different from CUP appeals in the central organs drafted under the direction of Ahmed Rıza:

O Military! Do you still unwaveringly defend an unbelieving sultan who denies God, despises our Prophet Muḥammad, a peace be upon him, sold our beloved fatherland to the Russians, neither performs the *namaz* nor fasts? Think the better on this. Pity your household and the elderly fathers and mothers in your home towns. If you do not want to see your children, whom you cannot bear to kiss, and our sacred religion being trodden upon by the enemy, aim your weapons at Abdülhamid. Help the people, led by the ulema, in their attacks on Yıldız and bemoan Abdülhamid. Because: This is what God decrees.

O Commanders! . . . Those who bear the title "soldier" must endeavor to die with honor, not with disgrace. Don't you possess this courage?[308]

This appeal was circulated in various provinces, such as Adana[309] and Trabzon,[310] as well as in the capital,[311] and was widely read among the Muslims,[312] while a shorter appeal was also extensively distributed.[313] The same kind of language was found in appeals circulated by the Istanbul center too, which demonstrates acceptance of the branch's new policy:

Thank Heaven, our cry has not been in vain. Now the time has come for the good news. We have all understood that the greatest enemy of the Islamic and Ottoman world is the great assassin Abd-ul-Hamid and his crew . . . brothers, most of the ulema of our faith and the chiefs of our army belong to our Society; they share our ideals and aspirations. . . . Oh brothers and Ottomans! The day of judgment is at hand. Know that to die is blessed martyrdom, to slay is heroism! We have obtained from the ulema a fetva authorizing the destruction of the traitors. The ulema of the four sects agree that the strife is lawful in order to free our faith and state and country. They have given us the permit of victory. The victory will be ours, for God is the helper of the oppressed.[314]

The branch began to publish a journal in Geneva named *Ezan*,[315] which claimed that "no transformation is possible without revolution."[316] It also tried to establish ties with the Macedonian committees and the Balkan organization of the CUP. It proposed a venture involving bombings of various places including the palace,[317] and many volunteers immediately applied.[318] However, this revolutionary branch failed to win over the Armenians for common action, and the executive committee for the CUP found these plans too venturesome and withheld its endorsement.[319] As early as January 1896, members of this "activist" group had been negotiating with European anarchists over plots to assassinate the sultan,[320] and they continued their efforts until June 1897, when Murad Bey sat at the bargaining table with the sultan's agents.[321] The *raison d'être* of this group was revolutionary activity. Its failure in the short run effected its dissolution.

Murad Bey resolved that an effective way of managing this extremist wing was to allow it to carry out its program independently. He foresaw that its actions could be useful in his coup d'état plans, and to this end he published letters sent to *Mizan* from the Empire even though they contradicted his own ideas.[322] He also published extreme revolutionary articles, which caused the French consul in Geneva to label his journal as a "plus violent et plus nettement révolutionnaire" organ.[323]

Along with the recent power seizure within the CUP by new and military elements, the percentage of military membership in CUP branches in the Empire rose dramatically during this period.[324] However, since most of them were low-ranking officers, their value for Murad Bey was limited and he regarded them only as pawns in his grand designs, in which all the actors were prominent statesmen and the Great Powers.[325] On the one hand he used themes that could impress those low-ranking officials,[326] while at the same time underwriting a reform from within. He promised prominent statesmen and popular war heroes seats in the future cabinets if they took action against the sultan.[327] He claimed that this would also appease the Great Powers. From one of them Murad Bey received a promise of a large sum for his designs through the Ottoman ambassador to Sweden, Şerif Bey.[328] Murad Bey wrote:

> To permit Muhtar, Şakir, Ziya and Fehmi Pashas and Hacı Âkif or İsmail Kemal Beys to form a cabinet and to approve their cabinet list and reform program without hesitation. . . .
> At once to write a note to the Great Powers that we have come to trust in their sincerity and from now on we are pleased to accept all measures recommended by them and reveal the above-mentioned development as an introduction to it.[329]

Murad Bey further proposed the formation of an *Assemblée Délibérante* to include participation by statesmen and representatives of non-Muslim religious groups (Armenian Gregorian, Armenian Catholic, Bulgarian Orthodox, and Jewish) instead of a parliament elected by universal suffrage.[330] This exemplifies his attempts to impress the high-ranking bureaucracy in his efforts for a palace coup d'état aided by the Great Powers. Writing in *Mizan*, he threatened that high-ranking officers who were preserving their posts instead of resisting the regime of Abdülhamid II would be dismissed and never allowed to serve again after the coup d'état, which he claimed was imminent.[331] Also, he demanded that every high official emulate those who donated to the CUP.[332] Murad Bey's approach was doubtless a contrast to the revolutionary ideas of the military and "activist" groups dominating the movement. However, his grandiloquent language gave the impression that he would win over high-ranking officials, while Ahmed Rıza's drastic pacifism impelled revolutionary members into Murad Bey's camp. Concomitantly, they independently carried out their more revolutionary program, which Murad Bey did not denounce, as Ahmed Rıza had done.

The Ottoman administration perceived Murad Bey's actions as utterly perilous and labored to placate him.[333] A delegation of three was dispatched, one of whom was his relative. After a long argument Murad Bey placed three adamant conditions upon his return to the Empire. A general amnesty, the privilege of forming a cabinet free from palace control for one of the well-known statesmen, and the replacement of censorship with independent courts.[334] Upon the failure of this mission, a new delegation was sent by the palace composed of liberal statesmen and journalists who had been prominent in the Young Ottoman movement, such as Yusuf Ziya Pasha and Ebüzziya Tevfik. However, Murad Bey insisted on his former conditions, and this mission failed too.[335] Apparently Murad Bey believed that the sultan could be pressured into accepting a reform program through these kinds of negotiations and did not decline to bargain with his representatives, as Ahmed Rıza had done.

This new CUP policy was endorsed, albeit halfheartedly, by members who wanted to prevent Ahmed Rıza from controlling the movement. However, the positivist leader and his followers initially adopted a wait-and-see policy[336] and later stalwartly opposed Murad Bey's program. On many occasions they rejected orders or instructions imposed by the Committee of Inspection and Execution, and in spite of warnings, they persistently pursued their program. Ahmed Rıza and his followers were vociferous in denouncing the prointerventionist policy of Murad Bey. Although *Mechveret Supplément Français* had published appeals to the Great Powers, contrary to what Ahmed Rıza's opponents later claimed,[337] these appeals presumed to define the policies of the CUP, depicting it as a nonrevolutionary society, in order to receive sympathy and moral support from European public opinion.[338] Themes expressed contradicted Murad Bey's policy of tackling reform in the Ottoman administration as a matter of European balance of power.[339]

The discord between the two groups came to a climax at a Young Turk banquet celebrating the twentieth anniversary of the Ottoman Constitution. First Ahmed Rıza refused to wear a fez but donned a European hat, thus drawing criticisms from his opponents.[340] After the banquet, Murad Bey condemned his rival's coverage of the event in his journal and presented his resignation to the CUP.[341] This was obviously a ploy, since the positivist leader published Murad Bey's speech verbatim in one and a half pages[342] after summarizing his own in three paragraphs.[343]

Following Murad Bey's resignation, which the Committee of Inspection and Execution rejected, a new attack was leveled against the positivist leader. According to Murad Bey, he was even subjected to face-to-face attacks.[344] Also, in order to undermine Ahmed Rıza and prevent him from acting as leader of the movement, it was declared in *Mizan* that the CUP would not welcome documents or letters sent to addresses other than the official letterhead.[345] Murad Bey and his friends were certainly aiming at Ahmed Rıza and the offices of *Mechveret Supplément Français* with this description of "other addresses." Yet another measure followed. In February 1897, Murad Bey and his followers transferred the printing plant of *Mizan* and the executive committee to Geneva.[346] They announced that the Committee of Inspection and Execution was moved in order to extinguish ties with the positivist leader and his followers.[347] Ahmed Rıza described this move in a note in his journal as a seasonal move—that Murad Bey and Çürüksulu Ahmed had gone to Geneva for the summer.[348]

Murad Bey offered the directorship of the Paris branch to Ahmed Rıza for a designated period under the supervision of the central committee.[349] Ahmed Rıza responded by deleting the famous motto of Auguste Comte, *Ordre et Progrès*, which had been the apothegm of his organ.[350] Other signs of rapprochement occurred. In late February, the two groups concurred on a note sent to the European press.[351] Later they cooperated in a campaign of sending notes to various addresses in the Empire.[352] However, Ahmed Rıza's publication of a new program retaining his antirevolutionary approach and laying out a positivist foundation for their program demonstrates his insincerity.[353] As an added measure against the positivist leader, Murad Bey and his friends decided to set forth a French supplement to *Mizan*.[354]

When the executive branch was transferred from Paris to Geneva along with its most active and prominent members—except the few supporters of Ahmed Rıza who remained behind—the former members who had previously gone to Geneva in protest against the positivist leader[355] now returned to the fold.[356] The branch established in Geneva remained ineffective until the transference of the Committee of Inspection and Execution occurred.[357]

Another important point was the augmentation of the power of İshak Sükûti. Founders and members of the first nucleus at the Royal Medical Academy little heeded the power struggle between Murad Bey and Ahmed Rıza, describing it as a "quarrel among the chicly dressed gentlemen over women."[358] A member who had joined the movement during its onset told İshak Sükûti that it was not the time "for scrutinizing the obduracy of [Ahmed] Rıza or the shortcomings of Murad Bey."[359] A founder advised Sükûti to manipulate both leaders toward the success of the movement without regard to the problems they were meanwhile creating.[360] İshak Sükûti's assignment as coordinator of the society and editor of the central organ testifies to his swift ascent.[361]

While these disputes between the Paris and Geneva groups were taking place, the crisis between the Ottoman Empire and Greece over Crete and the ensuing war caused great difficulties for the organization. The executive headquarters in Geneva expected the Ottoman government to pursue an inactive policy, as it had done during the diplomatic crisis over Eastern Rumelia in 1885; therefore it censured the Ottoman administration for losing Crete, at that time a battleground for Turkish and Greek nationalisms, to the Hellenes.[362] They even considered publishing a special journal to discuss the subject and blame the sultan.[363] Murad Bey and his friends, as well as many European statesmen and journalists, fully anticipated that this crisis would become an avenue to British intervention,[364] perhaps to organize a new conference around either this problem[365] or the entire Eastern Question.[366]

Neither expectation was fulfilled. First, the crisis produced a war between the Ottoman Empire and Greece, and it became meaningless to accuse the government of not pursuing an active policy. As a final effort, an appeal penned and distributed in Istanbul condemned Abdülhamid II of conducting the war from his palace and of restraining Ottoman troops from gaining victory over the Greeks,[367] but the Ottoman victory then rendered the accusations absurd. When it became obvious that Ottoman triumph was imminent, Murad Bey and his friends declared that they had arrived at "a decision to suspend all agitation until the war is ended and to abstain from any movement whatever that might trouble or embarrass the government."[368] Second, because of the crisis and the war, the Great Powers avoided intervening in Ottoman domestic politics.

Murad Bey and his associates were jubilant over the Ottoman success.[369] However, a long-awaited military victory and the palace's extraordinary use of it as propaganda[370] maneuvered them into an untenable position, enabling the palace to launch an offensive against its opponents and compel them to return to the bargaining table.

Another consequence of this war was a deterioration in relations between the Geneva center and the Paris branch. First, Murad Bey asked Ahmed Rıza to reprint in *Mechveret Supplément Français* a letter written by Ahmed Midhat at the behest of the sultan and published in a French daily protesting the biased policies adopted by the Great Powers.[371] The patriotic themes employed by Ahmed Midhat were acceptable to the Young Turks, but Murad Bey was confident that the positivist leader would not publish any article by Ahmed Midhat, who had been the sultan's spokesman against the Young Turks and had been denounced by Murad Bey himself and other Young Turks less than a year before.[372] Murad Bey seized this opportunity to accuse Ahmed Rıza of disobeying the instructions issued by the Committee of Inspection and Execution. Meanwhile a columnist of *Mechveret Supplément Français*, an Ottoman of Greek descent, published an article favoring the rebel Greeks in Crete.[373] The article carried a distinctly separatist language, so an Armenian journal published it verbatim.[374] The Geneva center published an official decision requiring Ahmed Rıza to declare that the publication of this article "had taken place due to an error in typesetting."[375] With this decision the discord between the two groups became pronounced,[376] and when Ahmed Rıza refused to publish any such note, this produced a sensation at the Geneva center, where the positivist leader was accused of representing a cosmopolitan group and of promoting a misunderstanding of the aims of the CUP. One of his ardent opponents wrote:

> Not one person of more than fifty members of the society in Paris and in other European cities is likeminded or sharing his ideas nor does anyone visit him nor have the members of the society within [the Empire] ever corresponded with him. Although these events are as clear as day, this expelled and repulsed individual's announced publication of his nonsense-paper, in which he was aided by a Syrian who has resided in Paris for eighteen years and lost his [Ottoman] citizenship [Khalīl Ghānim]; a Greek who is an enemy of our state and religion and uses the pseudonym Ümid [Aristidi]; an Armenian [Pierre

Anméghian]; and a Jew [Albert Fua]. To call this the organ of a society was vileness, cowardice.[377]

Ahmed Rıza's answer was that Murad Bey and his followers represented a conservative and Islamic viewpoint and thus deviated from his liberal policy of uniting various religious groups in the Empire.[378] Murad Bey and his friends disclaimed these allegations and published an open letter in refutation.[379]

Finally, at a meeting of the executive branch, a protocol was accepted requiring Ahmed Rıza to give assurance and to publish his journal under supervision of two other CUP members and, in the event of his refusal, expelling him from the organization.[380] But the crisis did not end. Murad Bey became irate and denounced these developments as reflecting the "pro-Greek attitude of Ahmed Rıza's co-religionists—the positivists,"[381] and then presented his resignation to the Committee of Inspection and Execution.[382]

The committee dismissed his resignation, but Murad Bey demanded it, saying that "he was offered representation by many high-ranking statesmen before he left Istanbul and he intended to make applications and publications on their behalf."[383] The committee decided to assign leadership to three members collectively, but Murad Bey was still considered the "honorary leader."[384] The CUP correspondence reveals that the three were Çürüksulu Ahmed, Şerafeddin Mağmumî, and Reşid Bey.[385]

Despite these announcements Murad Bey corresponded with many branches through Tunalı Hilmi, who had become his private secretary. The latter once wrote that Murad Bey "was still supervising committee affairs in his capacity as a member."[386] Most probably he would have returned to his post if agents of the sultan had not intervened and started bargaining in Contrexéville.

The organization in Europe did its best to convince the European public that no serious discord existed within the committee. Notes and letters were dispatched to European newspapers.[387] But these efforts made little impact except for causing anxiety among palace officials, who began to await the collapse of the CUP.[388]

Meanwhile a lawsuit filed against the positivist leader in Paris by the Ottoman government forced the central committee to relax its objections toward Ahmed Rıza.[389] As İshak Sükûti wrote to the original founder,[390] this prompted it to review its decision and make a new offer to Ahmed Rıza:

> All members of the [Committee of Inspection and Execution] are first and foremost afflicted and regretful because of the action taken for securing the orderliness demanded by the committee. If he abandons his meaningless insistence, Ahmed Rıza is a desirable person in our eyes in view of his service and his special merit. Therefore if he promises that he will offer up his selfish ideas to the system of consultation, which is the main pillar of our committee, he will be reinstated to his former post with pleasure and gratitude.[391]

The lawsuit was not the only reason for this retraction. Although expulsion of the positivist leader from the CUP brought immense relief to the Young Turks in Europe, it was received coldly in the branches.[392]

The Egyptian branch, which was having problems with the central committee, firmly opposed the decision of expulsion, contrary to the expectations of Murad Bey and his friends. They had anticipated the Egyptian branch, which was under the control of ulema, to support the measure accusing Ahmed Rıza of offending religious sensitivities.[393] However, this branch asked the central committee to apologize to the positivist leader.[394] The Barbary Coast branch contacted Ahmed Rıza directly, promising full support were he to reestablish *Meşveret*.[395] Although the original founder shared the ideas of the Young Turks in Geneva,[396] the Romania branch avoided any unequivocal decision. Abdullah Cevdet, another founder, required the Committee of Inspection and Execution to publish a new note as soon as possible, declaring that "the disagreement between Ahmed Rıza and [itself] had been resolved."[397] Another prominent member wrote:

> Undoubtedly Ahmed Rıza's expulsion had horrible consequences. . . . Perhaps [Ahmed] Rıza merited expulsion. However, it should not be made known to everyone. You did just the opposite. That article's unfair severity caused us to forget every fault of [Ahmed] Rıza. The reason shown for this was very simple: The previous blunders of *Meşveret* [*Mechveret Supplément Français*] were unnoticed. Very well, [this time] attention is drawn. Announce in *Mizan* that *Meşveret* [*Mechveret Supplément Français*] is not the official organ of the society—that's enough. But you did not act so. You expelled [Ahmed] Rıza from the society. When those ignorant of the truth of the matter compare his service in the formation of the society with *Mizan*, his side weighs heavier in the balance. The letters [we have] received from Salonica, Bulgaria, and Istanbul illustrate this. Even [the central branch in] Bulgaria had officially requested an explanation. The Cyprus [branch] strongly opposed the decision. Even here Doctor Mehdi, Suad Bey etc. are behaving incorrigibly.[398]

The central committee received neither encouragement nor support from any branch. According to an opposition journal, two independent organizations formed around Murad Bey and Ahmed Rıza in Geneva and Paris.[399] Nevertheless, the importance of the Paris branch was limited from an organizational viewpoint. The Ottoman embassy found five Young Turks in Paris actively communicating with other branches. One was Şerafeddin Mağmumî, an ardent supporter of Murad Bey, and another was Haşim Bey, a Young Turk bought off by the palace.[400] According to another investigation by the same embassy, the numbers of actual Young Turks, not mere sympathizers, were eight in Paris and fourteen in Geneva.[401] It is more accurate to say that there was no one in the group surrounding Ahmed Rıza other than columnists for the French supplement. As Şerafeddin Mağmumî wrote, "Thank God Ahmed Celâleddin Pasha [intelligence service chief] does not know the reality. Although [some people are] telling him, he mistrusts [what they say]. If it continues like this our publication will be read only by those living abroad—in other words, ourselves."[402]

Under these circumstances the sultan, who was trying to cash in on the victory over the Greeks, decided to launch a peace campaign requiring the Young Turks to terminate their publications. Ahmed Celâleddin Pasha was designated as the negotiator and sent to Europe on the pretext of a change of air.[403]

The desperate Young Turks in Geneva, aware of Ahmed Celâleddin Pasha's mission, were looking forward to his visit.[404] Murad Bey initially declined an invitation to sit at the bargaining table.[405] Undoubtedly this gesture was made to impress the hard-liners in the movement and demonstrates his intention of translating the negotiation into an institutional one between the government and the CUP. On July 5, 1897, the central committee assigned Fuadpaşazâde Hikmet to propose a counteroffer to Ahmed Celâleddin Pasha and that he be apprised of the CUP's readiness to sit at the bargaining table conditional to a declaration of general amnesty.[406] When this decision, along with a private note from Ahmed Celâleddin Pasha, was presented to Murad Bey by a committee member and the interpreter of the Pasha, he agreed to start the negotiations.[407]

In order to even negotiate with Ahmed Celâleddin Pasha, the CUP had to compromise and withdraw its condition of general amnesty. At that point the central committee elicited viewpoints from the branches. Although we do not have all the answers, we know that at least one of the more conservative branches—the branch in Romania—warned the society against the "tricks" of Ahmed Celâleddin Pasha.[408] Doctor Nâzım Bey, acting on behalf of the Paris enclave[409] and Mehmed Reşid, a founder, acting on behalf of the Istanbul branch,[410] presented additional critical opinions and required the central committee to rebuff offers by Ahmed Celâleddin Pasha unless the sultan himself provided a guarantee of reforms.

Since the sultan imposed the strictest measures in order to prevent the circulation of *Mizan* during the bargaining,[411] those who warned the central committee understood the sultan's plan better than did Murad Bey and the CUP leaders in Geneva.

During negotiations, Münir Bey, the Ottoman ambassador to France, whose foremost duty was to instigate appropriate measures against the Young Turks and other opponents of the sultan,[412] entered into negotiations with Murad Bey through an embassy officer.[413] During this bargaining, the CUP asked for Fr 600,000 and demanded the proclamation of a general amnesty in return for closing *Mizan*.[414]

Following this meeting, Murad Bey returned to Contrexéville and continued bargaining with Ahmed Celâleddin Pasha.[415] The CUP demanded that the palace purchase the printing plant and all non-circulated back issues of *Mizan* at an exorbitant price to cover refunds to subscribers and to provide a large sum to the organization for distribution to the surviving relatives of dead CUP members.[416] The situation was discussed at a central committee meeting, and despite Murad Bey's tendency to reach an agreement quickly, other members compelled him to demand more substantial guarantees from Ahmed Celâleddin Pasha. However, Murad Bey informed them of his decision to return to the Empire.[417] He also conferred with prominent European leaders such as Generals Ignatief and Türr and requested their support.[418] In a letter to a French daily, he wrote that "rien d'étonnant d'ailleurs que quelqu'un de nous ait cause avec les honorables généraux dont vouz parlez, hommes d'Etat ayant passé une partie de leur carrière en Orient."[419] The central committee had solicited views from branches through a posted circular, in which they were asked to send a telegram in case of approval reading "envoyez marchandise"; otherwise "envoyez pas merchandise."[420] Murad Bey and many members were preparing to return while the central committee was thinking of maintaining the publication. From this point on Murad Bey no longer held his dominance over the movement. On July 15, 1897, Çürüksulu Ahmed was assigned to discuss the matter with the branches and other prominent figures in the organization.[421] Murad Bey formally agreed to return on July 20, 1897.[422] Two days later, the Paris embassy announced that all fugitives would be pardoned upon return to the Empire.[423] Bargaining between the CUP and Ahmed Celâleddin Pasha proceeded. The committee decided to end publication but refused to discontinue correspondence with its branches, claiming that there was an "armistice" between the palace and the CUP and it would be expecting reforms and the proclamation of a general amnesty.[424] The branches reluctantly obeyed this decision.[425] Those who disobeyed were expelled from the CUP.[426] However, almost all the branches decried the agreement. The Egyptian branch wrote to the central committee that

> the efforts of two years have been lost in a strange bargain transacted in one month. . . . A bargain that could only have come about for three reasons: Either extreme simplemindedness or impotence or sluggishness and selfishness. . . . The business from every point of view was a criminal blunder. God will certainly hold you culpable in this matter.[427]

The Bulgaria branch sent a censorious letter to Murad Bey.[428] The Romania branch demanded that the central committee reach an accord over a number of issues—all unacceptable to Ahmed Celâleddin Pasha—and announced that it might take independent action.[429] Abdullah Cevdet, who had recently fled from Tripoli of Barbary, insulted Murad Bey at the train station in Paris.[430] The others expressed despair in letters mailed to the central committee or in private meetings held among themselves.[431] Ahmed Rıza's followers launched an attack on both Murad Bey and the accord. Open letters by Khalil Ghänim[432] and Albert Fua[433] to Murad Bey were printed in French dailies and in *Mechveret Supplément Français*, accusing Murad Bey of betraying the movement. Similar letters penned by less important members of the CUP in Europe[434] and Istanbul[435] were also prominently recorded in the French press.

Murad Bey's retort to each allegation was to say he made the decision because "salus imperii summa lex esto," typical of his bombastic language.[436] But beside his great designs and indomitable confidence, reality stood in stark contrast to his claims. When he called for calmness among CUP members and rode by train to Istanbul, the situation for the organization had become precarious. On the one side, members of the Geneva branch awaited their stipends so as to return to the Empire,[437] the official CUP newspapers terminated publication, a lawsuit was initiated against *Mechveret Supplément Français* by the Paris embassy on the sultan's behalf, and—according to the foreign embassies[438] and foreign press[439]—the Young Turk movement was finished. On the other side, reforms were promised by the sultan. The growing disparity was obvious.

The Egyptian Branch

Following Murad Bey's departure for Europe, the Egyptian branch briefly underwent a period of waffling. Murad Bey's directorship of the Egyptian branch had transformed it into a central decision-making division. With his departure, the section was once again degraded to a regular branch. However, for several reasons, this branch was essential to the organization, so it was again impelled to power within the movement. First, Egypt had enormous strategic importance, since it allowed publications banned in the Empire to be smuggled easily. Second, many groups and individuals working against the regime of Abdülhamid II were active under the protection of the khedive and the British. Beginning in 1894, the smuggling of banned publications reached an all-time high, and the sultan ordered the punishment of those who were simply reading or distributing them or helping the smugglers to the same degree as if they were members of secret organizations.[440] Requests and petitions to the British high commissioner and the khedive were simply rebuked on the grounds of "lack of a press law in Egypt."[441] Third, Egypt was crucial for the CUP's relations with the ulema. Finally, the Egyptian notables supported the Young Turks financially, especially in the beginning of the movement.

As we have seen, Murad Bey arrived at the branch with a letter of authorization from the Paris center and immediately became its director. Although he claimed that his official induction to the CUP occurred three months later,[442] he had already been signing official documents as director. This exasperated those members who considered themselves to be the founders of the CUP. They attempted to publish a second organ in Cairo; however, the Paris center denied their petition.[443] After this rejection, the group, led by Doctor İsmail İbrahim and the pharmacist Mustafa, preferred to stand aside because of Murad Bey's prestige among the public and his alleged overrated stature in the eyes of the British.

Following Murad Bey's egress, İsmail İbrahim again assumed directorship, and prominent opposition leaders began to flow into Egypt: Hoca Kadri, whose articles in *Mechveret Supplément Français* received high acclaim from the Young Turks; Salih Cemal, who had been sprung by the

CUP from a Rhodes dungeon; and Hoca Muhiddin, who once led the ulema in the formation of a society. Impelled by the participation of two prominent ulema leaders, in spite of the fact that they did not officially enroll in the society for the next couple of months, and of many al-Azhar students, a more religious and conservative element seized control over the branch. A new organization emerged as a result. Immediately prior to the collapse of the Istanbul branch, the Egyptian section secured the amendment of the ninth article of regulations, establishing the Paris and Egyptian branches as a single section under the title sixth branch of the CUP,[444] thus allowing the Egyptian branch to become the central branch in the fall of 1896. This annoyed Ahmed Rıza, who refused to recognize the Egyptian branch as a section sharing power with the Paris branch under his dominance. Nevertheless, the Egyptian branch exerted their rights.

In order to find a means for compromise, Ahmed Rıza sent İshak Sükûti to Cairo, and he brought the two groups to an agreement.[445] Thanks to the amendment, the branch now had the right to publish a journal without the permission of the Paris section. Hoca Muhiddin refused to join an official organ of the CUP, and according to his memoirs, Hoca Kadri supported him in this matter.[446] Under circumstances such as these, the branch asked them to publish their organ as an ulema journal and promised support. Thus *Kanun-i Esasî (Constitution)* was born. At that time the organization was altered by the formation of the Committee of Inspection and Execution. However, since the new journal was presented as "the journal of a society composed of ulema and *talebe-i ulûm*,"[447] still no official sanction by this new committee was necessary.

So, Hoca Muhiddin and his ulema cohorts gained control over the Young Turk movement in Egypt, and the CUP branch became a group under their control, although they insisted on maintaining the journal as an organ of their ulema society. This effected a profound change on this branch's policy. In an official report sent to Bulgaria, the aims of the society were presented as follows:

> First . . . to chasten and ameliorate those who endanger the perpetuity of the religion and nation for their abominable personal ideas. . . . Second: Following the blessed revolution . . . to diffuse Islam and to glorify the word of God [*kelimetullah*] by founding political schools for religion and to produce a moral "Islamic Union" by sending officials to Islamic countries.[448]

When the branch asked the ulema leaders to become official members of the CUP and to dissolve their organization into it, they agreed on the condition that the CUP stop enrolling Christians.[449] Also, a strong policy for union among Muslim elements in the Ottoman Empire and an Islamist policy were assumed by the branch, and the central committee was enjoined to do likewise:

> Greeks advance the interest of Greece and Bulgarians advance the interest of Bulgaria. The Armenians are pursuing the utopia of establishing Armenia and etc., etc. The sermons and the lessons expounded by the priests and teachers

of these nations in churches and schools and [even] the lullabies sung by the governesses to babies in cradles are all against Islam. It is these nations who tell Europe that the Muslims are savage and barbarous. . . . This is the perplexing dilemma of the Christian nations [of the Empire]! Then what is the meaning of salvation? Since the Ottoman State is an Islamic state, as recognized by the Great Powers, the directing power in reforming her present condition should belong to the Muslim element.[450]

The branch also reviled the pro-British policy of *Mizan* and denounced efforts spent to secure foreign intervention in Ottoman politics.[451]

With the adoption of this new course, this branch presented a third alternative policy for the CUP. The first was Ahmed Rıza's policy of uniting all Ottoman elements under a constitution and of building a new avenue for Ottomanization by secularizing the state, and the second one was Murad Bey's more conservative and pro-Great Powers' intervention policy.

This new program called for a reconciliation between Islam and modern constitutional theory[452] intended to bombard the regime of Abdülhamid II with his own artillery by using language almost verbatim to that used by the palace. For this reason the Ottoman high commissioner could make no sense of Hoca Muhiddin's aim when he requested a permit "for the publication of a journal on Islamic affairs,"[453] and only after upturning police records on Hoca Muhiddin's previous journal, *İstikamet (Integrity)*, was it discernible that he was an authentic candidate for publishing an opposition journal.[454] The palace banned this "extraordinarily seditious journal," which was aiming at its Achilles' heel by employing an Islamic jargon.[455]

Soon a disagreement arose between Hoca Muhiddin and other members of the branch because of his strong Islamist policy and his insistence on the maintenance of their ulema society. Members of the branch withheld official correspondence from him,[456] and he turned over the administration of the organ to a new committee, which agreed to transfer it to an official CUP organ, and departed from Egypt.[457] At that point everyone anticipated that Doctor İsmail İbrahim would reassume leadership, but he was attending the khedive's visit to Paris for the purpose of establishing sounder relations with him and acquiring monetary support for the movement. Meanwhile Murad Bey had an unpleasant confrontation with the khedive's officials over securing an audience with him, and a confidant of the khedive denounced Ahmed Rıza's positivist tendencies. İsmail İbrahim told the khedive that neither of them was a founder or a member of the first nucleus. However, he could not convince the sovereign of Egypt.[458] İsmail İbrahim despaired and resigned from the CUP. Later he was pardoned by the Ottoman administration and appointed as a medical doctor and returned to the Empire.[459]

As a result of this unexpected resignation, Hoca Kadri assumed leadership of the branch, which persistently advocated a strong Islamist policy. In an important document prepared about this time, the leading members of the branch were listed as follows: Hoca Kadri; Doctor Câzım; Doctor Bahaeddin; Doctor Ermenak; Salih Cemal; Safvet Efendi; Mehmed Efendi; Farac al-Şūdānī[460]; Ahmed Efendi, a student at al-Azhar; 'Abd Allāh Efendi, an *ālim* at al-Azhar; Doctor Ilyā, columnist of *al-Muqaṭṭam*; Ḥājī Mīrzā Efendi Işfahānī, the correspondent of the branch in Iran[461]; and Yusuf Efendi, a student at the Law School in Cairo.[462]

The branch continued to be a mouthpiece for the ulema during Murad Bey's directorship in Geneva. The most salient feature of its policy was strict opposition to any intervention by the Great Powers, which they thought would favor the Christians of the Empire at the expense of the Muslims.[463] Murad Bey never acknowledged the significance of this, which no doubt underlay the preference of the Egyptian branch for a positivist over Murad Bey's conservative ideas.

The Istanbul Center

The Istanbul center suffered tremendous oppression after its failed coup d'état attempt. Spy reports wildly exaggerated the center's power,[464] and as a result the palace did not hesitate to punish even peripheral sympathizers as well as every statesman who favored CUP activities.[465] The new center formed by medical doctors and college students successfully circulated new leaflets and, on February 16, 1897, presented a note to the embassies of the Great Powers.[466] Meetings were held in mosques to incite Muslims against the sultan.[467] The British ambassador underscored relations between the Young Turks and *softas* and dervishes[468] and expected a serious attempt by them.[469] Similarly, Affaires Étrangères received information from many dependable sources regarding a CUP plot, scheduled for February 15, 1897.[470]

However, in spite of claims by CUP members in Istanbul extolling the power of this new central committee,[471] the society became prominent only within the circle of college students. The strongest local section during this period was in the Royal Military Academy. Special divisions were named after the military leaders of the 1876 coup d'état, Hüseyin Avni Pasha and Süleyman Pasha, which plotted to assassinate Zeki Pasha, the minister of military schools.[472] They also corresponded with the director of the Paris branch, Çürüksulu Ahmed, their former instructor. Another CUP cell consisting of twenty students was formed in the College of Engineering.[473] The students of the Naval Academy were also actively distributing appeals.[474] These fervent students composed a new anthem for the committee[475] and distributed appeals prepared by the Geneva branch.[476] But it became impossible to enroll high-ranking officers in the Istanbul center, as previously.[477]

Mehmed Reşid confessed to another founder the impossibility of taking any significant action without a sound organizational network.[478] In a short time his fears were realized. First a spate of arrests in the Royal Military Academy followed the informing by a student who was an active member.[479] Another betrayal occurred at the Royal Medical Academy.[480]

Similar arrests were made among the ulema.[481]

The palace ordered the strictest measures against anyone who distributed or carried out "seditious publications."[482] The low-ranking officers were arrested and tried in a court-martial.[483] Since figures about these arrests are not given in official statistics, we are ignorant as to the numbers of Young Turks and ulema arrested.[484] A Belgian daily provides these figures: seven prominent sheikhs, 106 high-ranking ulema, 324 students, and 630 other members of secondary importance.[485]

A tremendous blow struck the Istanbul center one more time and demoralized the leaders of the movement. A founder wrote:

> Even at the Royal Medical Academy, where we have our strongest roots, a profound desperation and languor prevail. Look how many brothers have been arrested. They are subjected to torture and exile. On the other hand Thessaly, which was acquired, is about to return [to the Greeks]. When will the CUP manifest its existence if it doesn't reveal it now? Or is it merely a nonsensical commotion? To stay in Europe and lament is no longer fashionable. Complaints such as "where are the practical consequences of the threatening appeals and placards?" most of the time we were unable to post them, have increased. What response is going to be given to those [complaints]? Some are even requesting that those residing in Europe should come over and unite with those here and then to undertake a general rebellion. . . . At least a hundred persons would be needed in order to lay siege to the Sublime Porte during a cabinet meeting; however, they are nonexistent.[486]

Mehmed Reşid asked the European center to hire some "bloodthirsty anarchists," and send them to the Ottoman capital to assassinate the sultan.[487] Meetings held at Süleymaniye with the ulema were fruitless.[488] The arrests also broke the organizational chain. Mehmed Reşid, the last founder in the country and one who played an essential coordinating role[489] was also arrested and exiled.[490] Those who were suspected of sympathizing with the Young Turk movement were appointed to remote corners of the Empire.[491] Two classes of the Royal Military Academy were expelled, and students of royal colleges were forbidden to loiter in the capital.[492] When Murad Bey rode the train from Paris to Istanbul, the CUP organization in the capital was in total disarray.

The Provincial Organization of the CUP
and the 1897 Coup d'État Attempt in Syria

Although the Ottoman Foreign Ministry had complained about the increase in activities of the CUP in Europe during this period,[493] even greater expansion occurred in the provincial organization. In May 1897 the official organ published a note warning people in the provinces against giving donations to bearers of forged CUP notes.[494]

The CUP organization in the Balkans prior to the Young Turk revolution has long held the attention of researchers. Certainly it conditioned the most stunning occurrence in the history of movement. However, the greatest organization of the CUP took place in Syria between 1895 and

1897; a coup d'état attempt there was undertaken by an alliance of military officers, local governors, notables, and the Qādiriyyah order.

A tremendous advantage was provided to the CUP organization in Syria in the form of aid by the Comité Turco-Syrien, which later dissolved into the CUP. As early as 1895, Şerafeddin Mağmumî, who had been sent to the region as a medical doctor, formed branches in various towns.[495] In a letter, he provided information on advancement in the movement: "The letter that I received is from Hama. The seed we planted with [Doctor Besim] when I was there became a tree with seventy branches and sprouted a tendril in Homs. The letter tells me that their branch is attached to Damascus and receives journals from there."[496]

In early 1896 the official CUP organ published letters from the region relating how the society had become popular[497] and had been endorsed there.[498] Special traveling agents were sent to the region to infiltrate military divisions and disseminate propaganda among its officers.[499] The French consul in Damascus commented later that discord among high-ranking officers provoked some to conspire with the Young Turks against the palace regime.[500] Another stunning example was the frequency of letters sent from Syria[501] and the demand for a more active policy.[502] In 1896 the officer members of the CUP conducted overt local propaganda against the sultan.[503] *Mizan* and the other CUP publications were read out loud in coffeehouses and bars.[504] On one occasion a skirmish took place between CUP members and other people when a member cursed the sultan.[505] In early 1897 the Syrian central branch provided the central committee with the addresses of many recently enrolled members.[506] Prior to the mass arrests, the CUP managed to enroll 500 members from this region.[507] To expand its activities, the CUP translated its regulations into Arabic, and many copies were sent to the province.[508] Especially in Hama, under the leadership of Sheikh Yahya, the local governor, qadi, police director, director of the post office, and almost all military officers in the town became CUP members.[509] Many officials and officers and local ulema in various small towns enrolled likewise.[510]

The expansion of the CUP in the region endangered new governmental measures. In June 1896 the results of a government investigation of the military officers in the Fifth Ottoman Army were released.[511] In March 1897, Şem'azâde Ahmed Refik Pasha provided detailed and invaluable information on the involvement of military leaders in the CUP in Syria and Lebanon.[512] Soon after, Edhem Pasha, the commander-in-chief of the victorious Ottoman troops at Alasonya, supplied information about the CUP organization in Aleppo.[513]

In addition to a large military participation, the CUP secured the support of the Qādiriyyah order in the region. When the Sublime Porte asked the governor of Syria and the commander of the Fifth Army for information about a "seditious society which was according to rumors secretly formed," they responded that the only possibly dangerous clique was the one formed against the Rifā'iyyah order by the Qādiris and the famous

Kaylānī family. They further claimed that high-ranking officials in the region had endorsed their cause.[514] The British consul underscored the fact that the commander of the Fifth Army, Abdullah Pasha, was at the service of Abū al-Hudā al-Ṣayyādī.[515] Salafi leaders such as 'Abd al-Ḥamīd al-Zahrāwī also supported the Young Turk cause. Zahrāwī published a journal called *al-Munīr* (*al-Mushīr* in Ottoman documents) in Homs and backed the Young Turk movement, especially the CUP.[516] Saman Efendi, a member of ulema who later became leader of the CUP Barbary Coast branch, worked for the Young Turk organization in Syria and frequently corresponded with the central organs.[517] 'Abd al-Qādir Badrān, a prominent member of ulema and reformer, joined in the "seditious" activities.[518] When the government decided to replace the *mutassarıf* because of his alleged participation in opposition activities, the ulema spearheaded the drafting of a petition sent to the Sublime Porte.[519]

In addition to the military, salafis, ulema, and the Qādiriyyah order, members of two prominent families—al-'Azm and Kaylānī—supported the movement.[520] This was consistent with Murad Bey's appeal to local town notables.[521] Both families were very active in local politics, and members of the former were involved in antiestablishment activities.[522] Their doings as well as their relations with the Young Turks had been investigated many times.[523] Rafīq al-'Azm, a prominent member and an advocate of Arab autonomy, participated in Young Turk activities in that region in the early 1890s.[524] Later he emigrated to Egypt, continuing to work with the Young Turks.[525] Haqqī al-'Azm, another leading figure of the family, also participated in Young Turk activities in Egypt and published the proceedings of the first Ottoman parliament in a Young Turk press there.[526] Members of the Kaylānī family had introduced political petitions enumerating instances of alleged misconduct by local officials and officers.[527]

A final group apparently involved in CUP activities in Syria was composed of Egyptians engaged in opposition against the sultan.[528] Also, according to Ottoman authorities, the CUP organization in the region allegedly had established ties with the local Armenian revolutionary groups and the British.[529]

Before it could organize a coup d'état attempt, this widespread CUP organization was destroyed by the palace. The palace ordered Bedri Bey,[530] the *mutasarrıf* of Hama, who had asked to resign before the impending developments,[531] and Hasan Bey, governor of Syria,[532] to take necessary action against the "seditious" activities. Then the commander of Aleppo bought off an officer in the regional CUP administration who provided the names of prominent officers in the organization.[533] The next day the sultan ordered the formation of a court-martial and trials began for military officers who had taken part in the organization and also for "everyone" opposing the regime. He also instructed the acting commander of Aleppo not to stir up excitement in the region over the trial.[534] At the same time Cudizâde Sabit Hoca, a "self-sacrificing volunteer" of the CUP branch in Adana, was apprehended,[535] after which some military members were arrested during a thorough investigation ordered by the sultan.[536] An in-depth investigation was undertaken in Beirut, and the CUP branch, led by Es'ad Efendi, formerly a participant in the Ali Suavi incident of 1878, was arrested along with many members from Damascus working with this branch.[537] The Beirut post office's notebook in which the names of those receiving "seditious publications" had been listed was used for mass arrests.[538] In a short period, hundreds of CUP members were taken into custody, and many were exiled at once.[539] Following the trials, all military leaders, ulema, and officials who had taken part in the venture were either imprisoned or exiled to remote corners of the Empire.[540] Thus the greatest provincial organization of the CUP was undone by the palace.

The dismissal of such local officers as Tawfīq Kaylānī and Rashīd Kaylānī, the director of birth registrations,[541] and the founding of opposition nuclei[542] reveal the persistence of the movement in that region despite the Palace's efforts. The foreign press continued to publish news chronicling unrest within the military,[543] and in 1899 Freiherr von der Goltz underscored Young Turk sympathy among the officers in the Fifth Army.[544] In 1898 the central organ published a message from the Aleppo branch concerning their receipt of the journal.[545] Another Young Turk sought asylum at the French consulate in Damascus in late 1898 and created a diplomatic problem.[546] However, compared with the enormous CUP network of officials, military, ulema, notables, and Egyptians, this new organization was only a small branch.

Regarding the activities of contemporaneous regional organizations, the salient issue was the interception of CUP publications in various military divisions.[547] However, activities in other military divisions had not encroached upon the organization of the Fifth Army.

During the interrogations, CUP members in Syria confessed that the committee had established branches in Iraq.[548] A document reveals that Câzım Bey, the governor of Mosul, was a CUP member.[549]

In British-ruled Cyprus, the CUP gained momentum. Messages sent to Şevket Bey, which were published in the central organ, demonstrate a direct relationship between the European center and this branch.[550] The momentum can be attributed to Hoca Muhiddin's arrival on the island. After breaking off with the Egyptian branch, he journeyed to Cyprus dressed as a *hodja*, organized meetings with young students, penned CUP propaganda, and denounced the sultan's regime. The mufti of Cyprus, Ali Rıfkı, informed the Sublime Porte that Hoca Muhiddin had come to the island "with the encouragement of the British," and "held meetings with ten or twenty ignorant people." Ali Rıfkı held a meeting at Ayasofya Mosque in Nicosia and recommended that Muslims not listen to this "non-well-wisher of the state."[551] The opposition journals informed their readers that "Hoca Muhiddin had become the honorary leader of the branch."[552] He himself claimed to have organized a group of eighty people.[553] This group held demonstrations on the island, in which more than two hundred people allegedly participated, clashing with local British police.[554] Finally, this branch began to publish a local satirical opposition organ, *Kokonoz*,[555] which managed to attract more than a hundred subscribers[556] and ridiculed the mufti's campaign against them through a use of Islamic rhetoric.[557]

The Balkan Organization

The CUP organization in the Balkans endorsed the activist wing, which formed the Ottoman Revolutionary party. Tunalı Hilmi's fierce pamphlets were widely distributed and read in the region.[558] We have also seen that the organization in the Balkans took an active role in the activists' venture to assassinate the sultan.

Mustafa Ragıb, under the pseudonym İsmail Raci, and Tahsin Bey, a member of the Vidin branch, went to Medgidia and talked over the planned assassination with İbrahim Temo, the leader of the organization.[559] He commented on their discussion thus: "Turkish blood, which was drained, again became hot."[560] Later Mustafa Ragıb and Tahsin Bey went to Calais to obtain dynamite for the assassination attempt.[561] However, these efforts bore no fruit.

The local committee in Vidin appointed Mustafa Ragıb as a French-language instructor at a high school in spite of complaints by the Ottoman commissioner.[562] The Paris center sent instructions to the central branch in Ruse via traveling agents.[563] There craftsmen such as Emin, Mehmed Teftiş, and Yorgancı İbiş controlled the movement and focused on Turks' local problems in Bulgaria.[564] A petition was launched among the Turks against the Ottoman representative in Ruse.[565] A second one intended to prevent the Bulgarian government from dismissing Cevad Bey, a CUP member and an instructor at a high school in Shumen, because of pressure by the Ottoman government.[566]

The CUP organization in Bulgaria also participated in the opposition movement there. Ahmed Zeki joined demonstrations by Bulgarian opposition parties and delivered speeches on behalf of the local CUP organization.[567]

At the European center, both before and after Murad Bey's seizure of power,[568] efforts were made toward the advancement of CUP activities in the region, from which vast numbers of CUP publications were smuggled into the Empire.[569] İbrahim Temo sustained leadership of the movement in the region, and local conditions promoted an alliance of fugitives with educated elite among Turks in Bulgaria—most of whom were teachers and craftsmen. The new central organ's subscription list contains many names of educated elite, grocers, slipper makers, and quilt makers as well as the names of the coffeehouses in which CUP publications were read aloud to illiterate people.[570] This was the reason for the creation of a "local" CUP ideology and activity in Bulgaria. Due to the forming of this activity, although it diminished in strength, CUP activities in the region proceeded with vitality.

5

Petty Intrigue and Conspiracy: The CUP, 1898–1900

The Reorganization of 1898

The European Organization

Although the Young Turks viewed the Contrexéville agreement an "armistice" and a "change in opposition style,"[1] outside observers saw the movement as terminating except for the work of Ahmed Rıza and his comrades in Paris.[2] Salīm Fāris tried to exploit the situation and to dominate the movement by claiming that his "was the only opposition journal in Europe published in Turkish."[3] To destroy the Young Turk movement in England, the palace launched a campaign against the opposition groups in London,[4] resulting in negotiations that effected withdrawal of Salīm Fāris from the movement and the closure of *Hürriyet*.

Under these conditions Ahmed Rıza decided to revitalize the movement. His friends sent letters to French newspapers refuting claims reported in those dailies that Murad Bey and his associates were the legitimate representatives of the Young Turk movement.[5] Ahmed Rıza also published an open letter to French deputies and senators to promote the aims of the movement.[6] The stalwartness of his views earned him wide support among the Young Turks, even among members of Murad Bey's faction who had decided to return to the country.[7] Some members wrote that in their eyes "there is no difference whether one uses the years 108, 1312, or 1896. An atheist of conscience is preferable to a religious person without conscience [Murad Bey].''[8] Encouraged by these praises and endorsements, Doctor Nâzım informed İshak Sükûti that the positivist leader had decided to republish *Meşveret* and use the title *Organ de la Jeune Turquie.* According to him, the CUP center in Geneva had no right to complain about his use of this title—it referred to all members of the opposition.[9]

The sultan's initial target had been the CUP center in Geneva,[10] and Ahmed Rıza and his friends refused to meet with Ahmed Celâleddin Pasha. On July 7, 1897, at a secret meeting with Münir Bey at Pâtisserie Gagé, Ahmed Rıza rejected the ambassadors requirement saying that "il changerait le ton du journal [*Mechveret Supplément Français*] quand le Sultan changerait sa manière de gouverner."[11] The palace then tried to pacify the small group surrounding the positivist leader with a lawsuit filed during the crisis in the CUP.[12]

This trial, however, in addition to popularizing the Young Turk cause in Europe again propelled Ahmed Rıza to *de facto* leadership of the movement. Many French intellectuals, inspired by Clemenceau,[13] rushed to defend Ahmed Rıza and turned the court into an arena for polemical discussion.[14] At the end of the trial the court imposed a fine of Fr 16, and even this frivolous fine was rescinded.[15] Clearly this was a victory for the Young Turks, who listened with elation to the judge's recitation of the vilifying words they used to describe the sultan in the previous issues of *Mechveret Supplément Français.* At the end they shouted "Long live France! Long live the court! Long live the Young Turkey! Down with the Sultan!" and left the courtroom as champions and freedom fighters.[16]

While these events were transpiring, developments in Istanbul vindicated the words of Ahmed Rıza and his friends. Arrests continued in Istanbul during the negotiations between Ahmed Celâleddin Pasha and the CUP[17] and gained momentum after Murad Bey's arrival in Istanbul.[18] Murad Bey was coerced by the government into giving an interview to an important daily, denouncing Young Turk activities against the sultan[19]; after this interview, the sultan's favorite journalist attacked Murad Bey in *Malûmat,* the palace's mouthpiece.[20] Under the circumstances it became almost impossible to call the agreement of Contrexéville an armistice.

The palace also banished seventy-seven CUP members to Tripoli of Barbary and Fezzan; this was a terrible shock to relatives of prisoners who had been awaiting a general amnesty since Murad Bey's return.[21] Most of the exiles had been students at royal colleges,[22] and the ship *Şeref* set sail from Istanbul for Tripoli of Barbary on September 8, 1897. Although upon their arrival the exiles penned a petition requesting an imperial pardon, this went unheeded.[23] Thus the CUP's most important demand was rejected and no one could even mention the promised reforms. Murad Bey stubbornly dispatched peculiar memoranda to the sultan: "In order to take on the Young Turkey party as an opponent to your Imperial will, then recognize that it is time for you to become master of this party in order to imbue fresh life to your state."[24] For a while he dreamed of winning over the sultan,[25] but even though he obtained good positions and salary raises, he lived under virtual house arrest.[26] Profoundly disillusioned, he abandoned Young Turk activities.

At that point all eyes turned toward Ahmed Rıza. His best move would be to publish an organ in Turkish; however, the printing plant had been sold to Ahmed Celâleddin Pasha in accord with the Contrexéville agreement, despite Ahmed Rıza's protests.[27] Further, the Ottoman agents had bought the house that published *Meşveret* in Geneva.[28] These setbacks notwithstanding, Ahmed Rıza handwrote the journal and lithographed it. The new issue of *Meşveret* was published on September 23, 1897, with the subtitle *The Organ of the CUP*. The positivist leader started the new era of campaigns with this striking introduction:

> The [members of the] faction who found it unnecessary to publish two organs in Turkish and published *Mizan* in Geneva instead of *Meşveret*, were summoned by the glow of a promised reward offered by the head of intelligence service, Ahmed Celâleddin Pasha, and returned to Istanbul. I found it an extraordinary humiliation for my friends to meet a servant of Abdülhamid who is doubly culpable—first he is a spy, second the servant of a tyrannical sultan. However, some of them not only met with him but also accepted gifts. They withdrew from the field of *gaza* and combat. They sold the printing plant, which had been entrusted to them for safekeeping, and also the seal of the committee, and stopped the publication of *Mizan*. In the same way that the shameful acts of a handful of vile persons, who spied for the palace and became a tool for massacres would not blemish the honor of a great nation, just so the return of five, ten disabled persons who had mistakenly joined the Young Turks, would not undermine the power and the policy of the CUP.[29]

In reality Ahmed Rıza did not have the right to publish an organ on behalf of the CUP, because the central committee sent a circular halting all publications, but no copy had been sent to the positivist leader, because he had been expelled from the CUP. His friends continued to be CUP members, but they too lacked the right to publish an official organ. The assignment of Abdullah Cevdet, a recent refugee from Tripoli of Barbary,[30] as administrator of *Meşveret* demonstrates a *de facto* situation. Doctor Nâzım informed İshak Sükûti that they were refusing to recognize the monopoly of the Geneva center over the CUP.[31] Since the few remaining members in Geneva were no longer able to answer letters by sending their messages through a central organ, Ahmed Rıza became the central correspondence address for the Young Turks in the Empire.

Although members of the central committee and the Geneva branch led by Şerafeddin Mağmumî protested this, they could do nothing vis-à-vis a *fait accompli*.[32] Mağmumî retired from political activities and went to Egypt,[33] Şefik Bey was appointed to the Ottoman embassy in Bucharest,[34] and Ali Kemal to Brussels. İshak Sükûti moved to Egypt to reorganize the Egyptian branch, and the Committee of Inspection and Execution became a mere placard.

Ahmed Rıza's unimpeded rise in the movement alarmed the Ottoman administration. Although the sultan and his confidants considered this subject closed in view of the Contrexéville agreement, the positivist leader attempted to alter this picture. The Ottoman administration took stringent measures to prevent the circulation of *Meşveret* and tried to stop its publication.[35]

Because of the ban on the Turkish version of his journal, Ahmed Rıza could not publish his organ in France, so the next best place to publish seemed to be Geneva. Wishing to dissociate himself from the branch there, he announced that "he had no friends in Geneva"[36] and published his journal in Brussels under the pseudoeditorship of Georges Lorand,[37] a socialist Belgian deputy whom he had met through a positivist friend.[38] The Ottoman administration sprang to action.[39] After lengthy discussions,[40] the Belgian government told its Ottoman counterpart that it would be a near impossibility to close down the journal under prevailing laws; however, it might be possible to extradite Ahmed Rıza from Belgium on grounds of "anarchist activities."[41] In spite of the campaign by the Belgian press[42] and opposition deputies in the Belgian chambers,[43] Ahmed Rıza was extradited from Belgium on December 13, 1897.[44] The Ottoman ambassadors and consuls renewed their applications regarding Ahmed Rıza's activities wherever he went.[45] However, these developments helped Ahmed Rıza propagate the Young Turk cause and claim that the movement was not dead. German diplomats shared this view.[46] Moreover, his steadfastness, described by one of his opponents as "d'une énergie, d'une vivacité auxquelles les Turcs ne nous ont pas habitués," which was attributed to his European origin,[47] along with his harsh suppression by the Ottoman government, worked together to make him a charismatic personality.

Capitalizing on his repute, Ahmed Rıza attacked his opponents on two fronts. First, he used his frequent theme of "being bought off by the palace":

> The sultan does not take seriously those who request the reproclamation of the constitution, when he observes that he can silence those selfish profiteers who made publishing in Europe a capital of trade for themselves in exchange for an unimportant post, a small sum of money, or a concession. He throws a bone to them. The disgraceful act of those who grab this bone and lick it unfortunately demonstrates that Sultan Abdülhamid is correct.[48]

Second, the positivist leader altered his language, which the activists and members of various branches supporting activist ideology described as "cold-blooded"[49]: "I am confident that I am not mistaken, and I guess also that the sultan has not been deceived. He does everything deliberately and with full knowledge of consequences. To hell with him!"[50]

He also catered to the activists by assuring them that he accepted revolutionary activities under certain circumstances. He found religious grounds for such action and did not categorically decline to work with the activists:

> We quickly understood the real nature of those mock heroes, who lately separated from me in protest on the grounds that I oppose action and refused to publish articles inciting the people to bloodshed. They kept saying that noth-

ing can be achieved through publication. Nothing can be seen except publication all around!

In our society people are accustomed to expect everything from the government, an assembly or a committee. Great things were anticipated from the Ottoman Committee of Union and Progress. It was thought that the Mahdi would reappear, the Wall of Gog and Magog would be razed to the ground. . . . When nothing appeared to impress those fanticizers the guilty referred to the impotence and stubbornness of the leader of the Committee. It was said that the leader hinders action, revolution, and all kinds of success. I never repudiated the necessity for a legitimate revolution and its advantages. . . . If those who depicted me as an atheist were grieving about the religion they should have executed this religious decree. . . . I mentioned why I was against action. Nevertheless, I held back nobody's hand.[51]

Then Ahmed Rıza dispatched a message to the branches in the Empire and in the Balkans to the effect that he was ready to work with them. The image of "the leader whom the sultan could not buy off," also used after the reorganization of the CUP, continued to stir members in the Empire.[52]

Although some leaders, led by Abdullah Cevdet, required the appointment of Ahmed Rıza as director,[53] İshak Sükûti, who gained control over the official CUP center, was unwilling to hand over the CUP to Ahmed Rıza.

As early as August 17, 1897, the remaining members of the CUP center in Geneva—İshak Sükûti, Tunalı Hilmi, Nuri Ahmed, Çürüksulu Ahmed, Ali Kemal, and Midhat Bey—held their first meeting after the Contrexéville agreement and decided to reinstate their publication in early September.[54] However, members led by Ali Kemal asked the center to wait for the reforms promised by the sultan.[55] Ali Kemal maneuvered to organize a society called Teavün (Mutual Assistance) with the intention of transferring remaining members there and then selling this new society to the sultan.[56] He even published a pamphlet as the organ of this new society,[57] and several young CUP members joined him. But İbnürreşad Mahmud, who was appointed secretary, later confessed that "most of the people who attended the meetings could not fathom why they were there or what was the goal of the society."[58] The experienced CUP members, however, regarded this organization as "serving the interests of Ali Kemal" and paid no heed to it.[59]

In mid-October members who wanted a new organ began to pressure İshak Sükûti, presenting him with a deadline of November 15, 1897, unless the sultan granted a general amnesty.[60] İshak Sükûti decided to collect enough money to found a new central organ and publish it by letterpress. He traveled to Egypt and sat at the bargaining table with Ahmed Celâleddin Pasha in order to sell the printing plant and back issues of the journals and pamphlets of the Egyptian branch.[61] The khedive, who "is making great efforts to get on better terms with the sultan," also offered money to the Egyptian branch in exchange for back issues.[62] At the end of the bargaining, a protocol was signed by İshak Sükûti, Reşid, and the cashier of the Egyptian branch, Rauf Ahmed. The seal of the branch was presented to İzzet Bey, Ahmed Celâleddin Pasha's representative, and the CUP leaders promised "never to undertake any publication contrary to the will of the sultan" in exchange for £ 1000.[63] İshak Sükûti gave £ 260 of this sum to the Egyptian branch for the reorganization of that section and the publication of a new organ,[64] some money was spent sending members of the branch to Europe,[65] and the remaining funds were invested in bonds in an Egyptian bank for the future expenses of the central committee in Geneva.[66] In this manner financial problems were more or less solved.[67]

On December 1, 1897, during the bargaining between İshak Sükûti and the sultan's agents in Cairo, the Geneva center published the first issue of a new central organ, under İshak Sükûti's instructions, called *Osmanlı*. Thus a new chapter began in the history of the CUP.

The sultan ordered the Ottoman diplomats to launch an offensive diplomatic campaign asserting that the publication of *Osmanlı* violated the Contrexéville agreement.[68] The CUP refuted this claim in its organ,[69] before the Swiss administration,[70] in the European press,[71] and to the Great Powers by publishing an open letter in which it accused the sultan of luring the Young Turks with promises of reform that he never fulfilled.[72] In this way the Young Turks obtained the support of the European public.[73] The Geneva center dispatched various notes on their aims and activities[74]—as well as their journal and its French supplement—to prominent European dailies, statesmen, and intellectuals.[75]

A new center was born in Geneva. Members included Abdullah Cevdet, İshak Sükûti, Tunalı Hilmi, Nuri Ahmed, Reşid, Halil Muvaffak, Âkil Muhtar, and Refik Bey.[76] The publication of the new organ also recalled most branches to the Geneva fold.[77] Thus İshak Sükûti managed once again to transfer power from Paris to Geneva. As a countermeasure to prevent Ahmed Rıza from using his French supplement against the Geneva center, a French supplement to the official organ was established four days after the publication of *Osmanlı*. Under the circumstances, the Geneva branch offered Ahmed Rıza the status quo before his expulsion from the CUP. He accepted this offer and closed down *Meşveret*.[78] Thus, after seemingly endless battles and crises, the CUP organization in Europe returned to the status quo of late 1896. In order to clear their names and to withhold from Ahmed Rıza his most effective weapon, the new center condemned former CUP members who had accepted government positions[79]; in defending themselves, however, they played into the hands of the accusers, because this issue then came to be discussed at greater length.[80]

The new center penned a manifesto rebuking the sultan from a religious vantage point and expressing a startlingly activist position. They circulated this in the capital and provinces:

Muslims!
Abdülhamid is neither the sultan nor the caliph according to our religion. Those who doubt our words should look into the Holy Quran and sunnah.

Our committee revealed the orders of God and the Prophet to the government and the people by [publishing] sacred verses and ḥadīths. Abdülhamid turned away from them and proved that he is a tyrant and does not hesitate to disobey God. Therefore our people should have resorted to arms; sadly they have not done so and thus have proven that they were also unrighteous. . . . Last year our committee signed the treaty with Abdülhamid that gained renown as [Contrexéville Treaty]. We silenced ourselves as if we believed the reform promises of Abdülhamid. However, he seized the opportunity and attained an apogee in inflicting suffering, destruction on our country and abasement of the state and caliphate. Our committee declared war on Abdülhamid, who has not kept his word as is enjoined by the Holy Quran. At that point Trikkala was bestowed upon the Greek. . . .

Be reasonable, Muslims be reasonable! . . .

Abdülhamid is annihilating the religion and the state. Please rise and slash this fake caliph and his accomplices to pieces. Give up your lives and kill.[81]

Similar appeals decrying the withdrawal of the Ottoman troops from Trikkala and Crete were frequently circulated to outrage the Muslim population.[82]

It is easily gathered from the perusal of these appeals that the activist group, ignored by Ahmed Rıza and striving independently under Murad Bey, rose to dominance in the new center[83] and once again sought ways to reach an agreement with Armenian revolutionary committees for common action, in spite of profound differences between them, including their commitment to the use of an Islamic rhetoric.[84] On January 20, 1897, the Dashnaktsutiun had invited the Young Turks "to join the Armenians and by assassinating the sultan to overthrow the Hamidian tyranny." In 1898 *Droshak* repeated the summons for alliance with the Geneva center and received a favorable response.[85] In June an affirmative answer was given only in the French supplement,[86] since the people whom the CUP hoped to win over opposed any alliance between the CUP and the Armenian revolutionary committees. But even rumors of such an alliance provoked mistrust among CUP members in the Empire,[87] and negotiations with the Armenians proceeded in secret.

With regard to the internal organization, İshak Sükûti apprised branches of a new bylaw.[88] Also a circular was distributed:

From many sides there comes the question: To whom does the leadership here, directorship, editorship belong?

1. Whoever stays here stays on behalf of the committee.

2. A . . . [left blank in the original text] person is assigned as honorary director. The most important and hard-to-solve matters of the committee are to be overseen by this esteemed person.

The real directorship is assigned to a member of the Istanbul branch. But since he bears this title only before the executive committee there . . . the title of director has been abolished totally, and from now on correspondence will be held on behalf of the executive committees.

3. Yet since a complete fraternity prevails among members here, there is no need for the assignment of a director. . . .

4. There is no editor.[89]

A new code was assigned among the branches.[90] With these changes, the Geneva center spread its control over the internal organization. Each branch was given power over its domestic issues because correspondence from various branches had to be directed through Geneva. Another advantage of this new arrangement was the isolation of Ahmed Rıza and his friends in Paris, thus denying them access to important decision making in Geneva.

The Geneva center started to publish three additional journals. Key among them was an English supplement to *Osmanlı* that promoted British support for the constitutional movement[91] and denounced the sultan's anti-British policy.[92] The aim of this publication was to secure British support, wrote a CUP member in a private letter during the early preparations for the supplement[93]; this horrified the Ottoman administration.[94] The second journal, *Kürdistan*, was published by Abdurrahman Bedirhan[95] in Turkish and Kurdish under the guidance of the CUP[96] and printed articles by two founders, Abdullah Cevdet and İshak Sükûti; this also frightened Ottoman administrators.[97] The third periodical was a satirical journal called *Beberuhi* (named after the funny dwarf in the Turkish shadow-puppet show), also published under the direction of the CUP,[98] with the intent of disseminating propaganda in an easy-to-understand form to the Ottoman public.

These strong and swift initiatives led to counterattacks from the Ottoman government. Strict instructions were given to officials to halt the circulation of *Osmanlı* in the Empire.[99] The Ottoman government also paid off Armenian typesetters at the CUP printing plant. Several members learned typesetting and published the journals themselves.[100] Then a consulate was set up to scrutinize Young Turk activities in this city,[101] and special funds were allocated to hire secret agents for this new diplomatic body.[102] Later Necib Melhame, an Arab confidant of the sultan, was sent there to bribe leading Young Turks,[103] to no avail.[104] Finally Ottoman officials managed to install three agents: Jacob Hajan (Spanish), Arpiar Krikor (Ottoman Armenian), and Joseph Pergowski (Polish). When the CUP hired anarchists whom they planned to send to Istanbul, the agents leaked this valuable information to the Ottoman intelligence.[105]

Besides using provocative language, the new center took action. According to İshak Sükûti, this became the chief aim of the organization: "If it becomes necessary to terminate *Osmanlı* we will do so. We are applying all and any means to strike dread into Abdülhamid. Just yesterday we sent Fr 1000 someplace, these kinds of expenses will gradually increase. Simultaneously we have slashed the expenses of the journal. . . . If we can finish a job within the empire, then everyone will send us money."[106] Traveling agents were sent throughout the Empire to collect donations.[107] The financial records of the Geneva center demonstrate a gigantic increase in money sent to CUP agents in Istanbul and Bulgaria.[108] Under instructions from the Geneva center, the Istanbul branch held a meeting in March 1898 to discuss ways of assassinating the sultan.[109]

After preparations for a conspiracy, in late October 1898 the central organ published a menacing open letter to the sultan:

> Go mad! Become as rabid as a mad dog! Tremble, the tyrant, tremble! . . . Everybody trembles from fear because of the resolve of tenacious people! Those brothers who understand nothing from this—and so are unable to make sense of the fact that we printed this journal ahead of schedule and in only six pages—please wait patiently until the next issue.[110]

This threat probably accorded with a highly detailed plan drafted by military members in Geneva, in light of information given by a sultan's confidant acquainted with every specific regarding the Royal Palace at Yıldız.[111] The CUP also drew a detailed map for the proposed conspiracy,[112] and since this map is now in the Yıldız Palace Archives, we can guess what happened to the venturers. In fact, the central organ was silent and did not fulfill its promise in the next issue. The intelligence and police had already begun a spate of arrests among civilian members and several college students[113] and later among military members.[114]

Another development was the establishment of a branch in Berlin. İshak Sükûti encouraged Mustafa Ragıb, an Ottoman graduate student in chemistry, to prepare the ground for a new branch there.[115] Later İshak Sükûti secretly journeyed to Berlin to assist Mustafa Ragıb.[116] They decided to hold a meeting and conference in Bad Kissingen about the regime of Abdülhamid II in order to win over the Ottoman students studying in the German Empire. However, Tevfik Pasha, the Ottoman ambassador, obtained information about their scheme and applied to Auswärtiges Amt, requiring that the German Foreign Office bar these "revolutionaries" from propagandizing on German soil.[117] At this time Germans were attempting to win over the sultan for their *Drang nach Osten* policy with the visit of the kaiser and secured every measure against all proposed activities by the Young Turks,[118] consigning this attempt to failure. The branch later collected sizable donations from Ottoman students and helped the Geneva center.

These efforts strained relations between the center and Ahmed Rıza further. The isolation of the Paris group pleased many members and was described as the best way to avoid publicizing the domestic troubles of the CUP, as Murad Bey and his friends had done.[119] Ahmed Rıza vehemently protested and demanded that the Geneva center unite with his group in Paris to work toward a nonrevolutionary and nonactivist common agenda.[120] İshak Sükûti refused, and relations between the two groups deteriorated.[121] Although the Geneva center gave Ahmed Rıza's articles top billing in *Osmanlı*, the number of those articles gradually decreased. In April, *Osmanlı*, in response to inquiries from the Empire, published a note denying "rumors" of discord between them and Ahmed Rıza.[122] In July, Ottoman intelligence learned through spy reports that "there is no agreement between Ahmed Rıza and the leaders of the Geneva branch."[123] Their disagreement on "action" was so profound as to create a complete divergence: "For instance, both *Osmanlı* and *Mechveret* are the official journals of the CUP. Both are published by persons not only with diametrically opposed political tendencies but who are utterly opposed personally. Therefore you open *Osmanlı* and learn that something is white, then open *Mechveret* and read that the same is thing black."[124]

The Egyptian Branch

Less than five weeks after signing the protocol with palace agents and terminating its activities, the CUP branch in Cairo again published *Kanun-i Esasî*. In an open letter to the sultan, it claimed that "since the CUP was not established by an imperial decree, it is impossible to abolish it by an imperial decree." It further claimed that the sultan's agents had duped the old editorial board.[125] In accordance with the new CUP regulations, Salih Cemal was appointed director and was responsible only to the executive committee of that section.[126] With this maneuver, secular members of the branch seized power. The Ottoman government's requirement from the khedive to return Salih Cemal to the Empire because he was a draft dodger failed yet elevated his importance.[127]

Salih Cemal adopted a policy independent from the Geneva branch, and his efforts to influence the center there were fruitless. The Geneva center, in turn, prohibited the Cairo branch from calling their journal "the official organ of the CUP," but said they might publish it as a branch periodical—thus they denied any aid.[128] For his part, Salih Cemal accused the leaders of the Geneva branch of monopolizing the movement, of spending money that belonged to the CUP, and of not enabling the branches to participate in decision making—all under the guise of giving them more liberty.[129]

The Geneva center then resolved to send a leading member to Cairo as "Special Inspector for the CUP," and in response Salih Cemal threatened them by filing a lawsuit at the local court in order to gain legal possession of the printing plant.[130] These developments further paralyzed the branch,[131] which needed a loan of £ 40 per month for expenses and publication.[132] The Geneva center advised them to collect donations and not to rely on them.[133] While these events were transpiring, a Young Turk who had pursued an independent course while working closely with the CUP established a journal, also called *Osmanlı*, in Cairo. Despite its claim of being an independent organ,[134] it propagated the ideas of the CUP center in Geneva.

Under these circumstances the branch ceased publication in 1899.[135] At that time Hoca Kadri, pursuing an independent course, had already begun publishing a journal called *Havatır (Memoirs)* and employed a highly conservative and Pan-Islamic jargon,[136] sending tremors through government circles.[137] Another group that had splintered from the branch published *Nasihat (Advice)*, a more "activist" journal[138] printing instructive advice for both the sultan and the Young Turks.[139] However, *Havatır* represented only those ulema who had formerly worked for the branch, and *Nasihat* the initiative of a few persons led by Hayreddin Bey, a former sea captain.[140] Neither represented the CUP or its Cairo branch. At the end of these complex developments, Salih Cemal filed the lawsuit over ownership of the printing plant,[141] and the Egyptian branch continued in this appalling situation until July 1899.[142]

In Cyprus, also ruled by the British, a secular group within the movement led by Doctor Burhan Bahaeddin seized power over the branch. This section was corresponding with both the Geneva center and the Egyptian branch and circulated a plethora of CUP propaganda material, particularly a translation of Schiller's *Wilhelm Tell*.[143] However, the ulema dispatched to the island by the sultan launched an anti-CUP campaign among the Muslims.[144] They later accused the Young Turks of being "anarchists" and prevented CUP members from disseminating propaganda on the island.[145]

The Istanbul Center and the CUP Network within the Empire

Documents reveal that the Geneva center maintained direct contact with the Istanbul center.[146] Following mass arrests in April, October, and November, the Istanbul section fell to its lowest ebb in late 1898, by which time it had become powerless.

Those working in the CUP network in the provinces endeavored to expand in Syria and in nearby towns such as Mersin and Adana; however, they could not augment activities in Syria due to the tight security measures. Instead, therefore, CUP swelled its activities in Mersin and Adana. The Mersin branch was established prior to Murad Bey's return but could not expand until early 1898.[147] A document sent to the central committee reveals that the section maintained a large membership, and the circulation of the central organ was widespread.[148]

When the palace obtained information about CUP activities in the region, it again ordered thorough investigations,[149] and in both Mersin and Adana many military officials and Armenian members were uncovered and arrested.[150]

Afterward the Geneva center continued to send the central organ to Mersin and Adana[151]; however, the police captured a telegraph operator in Adana who distributed CUP publications in the region,[152] and a spate of new arrests of sympathizers ensued.[153] Since the central committee received large donations from Mersin even after these arrests,[154] it is possible that the branch prevailed despite the capture of many members.

Similar events transpired in Diyar-ıbekir, where in 1894 Abdullah Cevdet had formed the first CUP branch nucleus with some preparatory schoolteachers and officers who had helped him.[155] He disseminated propaganda extensively, and while he was thus employed a loyal officer attempted his assassination.[156] After his return, the branch found further expansion impossible and confined its activities to the distribution of banned publications.[157] In 1898 the branch found rejuvenation, especially with the participation of a former student of the Veterinary School in Istanbul.[158] Ziya Bey (Gökalp), the ideologue of the CUP after the revolution, entered the branch at its inauguration.[159] He later worked in the CUP organization in Istanbul.[160] Following his dismissal from the school, he returned to his hometown and joined CUP activities there. The branch and its activities were uncovered early in 1899 and members were tried; however, the local court released most prisoners.[161] At this time the palace called for a court-martial,[162] and most members were exiled. After this event a local governor, a lieutenant colonel, and an intellectual who was exiled to Diyar-ıbekir instituted a new branch, but this too was uncovered two years later, and CUP activities in the region ceased until 1905.[163]

A burgeoning branch during this period was Tripoli of Barbary. With the arrival of the ship *Şeref*, most of the members of the Istanbul center transferred there. Şevket Bey, the aide-de-camp of Commander Receb Pasha and distributor of documents and publications while in Baghdad,[164] assumed leadership when he received an appointment there along with his commander. Şevket Bey had corresponded with Murad Bey while in Baghdad and worked with him on a reform project before Murad Bey's flight.[165] However, the arrival of Mehmed Reşid, a founder, generated a new organization, whose *de facto* leader he became.[166]

Exiles and convicts in the town published two journals, one lithographed and the other handwritten, named *Hatıra (Recollection)* and *Merhale (Stage)*, respectively.[167] The CUP organs published in Geneva and Cairo, as well as instructions given by the Geneva center, freely reached the fortress where most CUP leaders were interned.[168] This was due to the help of Receb Pasha, an opponent of the sultan.[169] However, under strict instructions from the palace, Edhem Ruhi, who was in charge of correspondence with the Geneva center and the Cairo branch, was put in solitary confinement, causing an uprising in the prison.[170] The palace ordered the prison commander to place the leaders of the uprising in irons and to open fire on them if they resisted.[171]

Later many prisoners escaped with the help of officers who were also members of the CUP.[172] Governor Namık Bey wrote to the palace that the number of police officers was insufficient for controlling so many exiles and prisoners.[173] When flights reached a peak, the palace questioned the commander and the governor.[174] However, more than half of the prisoners and exiles succeeded in fleeing to Egypt or Europe. Although Tripoli of Barbary became a tremendous center for Young Turk activities during this period, these did not significantly contribute to the success of the CUP's grand designs.

In European Turkey the most important development was the establishment of a branch in Durazzo under Derviş Hima's direction and dominated by Albanians. Another branch was formed in Tirana by military officers.[175] In the beginning, the Durazzo group was small and merely provided small donations to the European center[176]; later it organized as a branch under the direction of the Geneva center.[177] We lack further information on the Tirana branch except that it distributed CUP publications in the vicinity of Tirana. The Geneva center also received encouraging letters from Albania in praise of efforts by the CUP in that region.[178]

Nuri Bey, a lawyer member of the CUP in Ioánnina, published a pamphlet entitled *Hukuk-i Milliye ve Şahsiye (National and Personal Rights);* however, he was caught by the police before he could distribute it.[179] Hasan Bey, the mayor of Yenişehir, and his comrade Major Süleyman were caught by the police while distributing a CUP pamphlet entitled *Yaşasın Hürriyet (Long Live Freedom).*[180] After their interrogations, other military members of the CUP were arrested and exiled.[181] Military members in Salonica and Monastir were arrested and discovered to have corresponded with the Geneva center, and Hâzım Bey, the local governor of Dedeağaç, was found to be acting under instructions from Ahmed Rıza.[182] The activities in the Asiatic provinces had not yet attained a level beyond the actions of small groups or individuals. Among those worth mentioning was one in which members of the Egyptian branch attempted to extort money from Âbidin Bey, governor of Cezaîr-i Bahr-i Sefîd Province,[183] and the distribution of the CUP propaganda material in towns such as Aydın,[184] Izmir,[185] and Beirut.[186]

The CUP organization in the Empire was turning into a network of exiles distributing propaganda conceived in the Geneva center. This network became useless in bringing down the regime and also a severe impediment to the CUP organization in Europe. Most military members were serving in exile, and it became nearly impossible to enroll high-ranking officials. The salient causes of this gloomy picture were the Ottoman victory over the Greeks in 1897 and the ongoing siege waged by the Ottoman intelligence against all CUP domestic branches. The Geneva center's weak ideological propaganda and adoption of an activist but very simplistic policy also account for the CUP's loss of former allies.

The Balkan Organization

The Balkan organization had evolved into a distinct local Young Turk movement and ideology prior to the Contrexéville agreement. The changes in the administration of the CUP in Europe had almost no impact on it.

İbrahim Temo, the *de facto* leader of the movement in the region, donned Romanian citizenship in April 1898 so as to remove the Ottoman government's pressure on the Romanian administration over his activities.[187] Later he toured the region, visiting local centers and spreading the movement.[188] He opened new local branches, the most noteworthy one being in Sofia.[189] He also attempted to publish a journal with the help of two Turkish notables in Dobruja, but Ottoman diplomats thwarted their enterprise.[190] Nevertheless he won over the ulema and schoolteachers in Romania who were Albanians and Turks, such as Derviş Hima, Ahmed Vehbi, and Ali Şâkir, and he propagated the local Young Turk ideology.[191]

Following these developments İbrahim Temo established a journal called *Sada-yı Millet (Voice of the Nation)* with the help of Vasile M. Kogăl-niceanu, deputy of Constantsa. Although in the introductory article İbrahim Temo espoused the local Young Turk ideology without referring to the CUP,[192] an article written by Kogălniceanu subtly revealed that the journal belonged to the CUP.[193] However, the palace obstructed its publication[194] and circulation within the Empire.[195]

The journal was acknowledged to be the official CUP organ in the Balkans by both the Geneva center and the Paris branch.[196] But the Romania branch corresponded only with the Geneva center.[197]

Under the constant pressure and demands of the Ottoman diplomats, the Romanian government decided to extradite Kadri and Kemal Beys, who were on the editorial board.[198] Despite protests from the Romanian press,[199] the editor was obliged to stop publication after the ninth issue. The Ottoman government also demanded the surrender of the editorial board to the Ottoman authorities, however, the Romanians refused.[200]

Then Necib Melhame, one of the sultan's confidants, was sent to either bribe İbrahim Temo or to coerce him into giving up his activities. İbrahim Temo challenged him to a duel, and Necib Melhame's ensuing flight dramatically elevated Temo's prestige among the Young Turks in the region.[201]

While CUP activities in Romania were causing alarm in Istanbul, weightier events evolved in Bulgaria. Ali Fehmi, a graduate of the Royal School of Administration, had established a journal in Plovdiv named *Muvazene (Equilibrium)*, which in a roundabout way revealed itself to have ties with the CUP[202]; this journal also carried messages sent to members of Geneva center.[203] A journal named *İttifak (Alliance)* disseminated similar propaganda in Sofia and defended the Young Turk cause. The Ottoman administration failed to buy out its printing houses.[204] Meanwhile the palace sent loyal ulema members to Bulgaria to sermonize against the CUP and the Young Turks.[205]

In 1896 a reading room containing CUP organs, named Millî Türk Kıraathanesi (Turkish National Reading Room) was established in Shumen,[206] and one named Şefkat (Compassion) was instituted in Vidin—both by Hasan Aziz, a local CUP member. Here CUP propaganda material was read to illiterate Muslims.[207] In Ruse and Sofia, cottages were converted into reading rooms[208]; *Osmanlı*, which had been sent to the region regularly,[209] was read to the illiterates, and many copies were sold to villagers.[210] In Ruse, the Macedonian committee, under the instruction of its leader Georgi Kaptchef, helped CUP members read articles from *Osmanlı*.[211]

Mustafa Ragıb, who became the CUP traveling agent in the Ruse, Vidin, and Medgidia triangle, also disseminated CUP propaganda. Every effort by the Ottoman government to deport him to the Empire or dismiss him from his post at a high school failed.[212]

Ahmed Zeki, another local leader of the Ruse center, joined meetings held by Macedonian committees in Sofia and expounded the Young Turk cause.[213] He later published a journal named *Balkan* in Ruse, which provided information about CUP activities in Europe without revealing his organic link with it.[214] The journal focused on local problems and promoted campaigns against the mufti of Ruse[215] and the local Ottoman representative.[216] Bulgarian authorities, provided by Ottoman representatives, issued him an "unofficial warning."[217] In June 1898, Muslims, provoked by the ulema sent by the Ottoman government, demonstrated against his journal and activities.[218] Meanwhile, Ottoman representatives in Bulgaria reiterated demands that he discontinue the journal.[219] Finally Ahmed Zeki yielded and on July 30 shut down his journal.[220]

The CUP branch in Varna circulated a petition among Muslims against the Ottoman representative there. Many Muslim tradesmen and craftsmen joined the campaign, to the dismay of the Ottoman government.[221]

In response to the encroachment of conservative Muslims on CUP members and their meetings, under instructions from Geneva the central CUP branch in Bulgaria held a meeting at the mosque in Ruse, with 2000 people in attendance. It erupted into a demonstration, with participants demanding the dismissal of the mufti.[222] Also in the central organ an Islamic tone began to ring out in writings relevant to Bulgaria, Bosnia-Herzegovina, and Cyprus: "Those who claimed that the publication of the CUP is against the Sharia are ignorant of Islam."[223] The adoption of this rhetoric was recommended by local CUP leaders such as Ali Fehmi and Yunus Bekir, who believed the use of a more religious style would appeal to local Muslims.[224] Letters sent by the ulema or conservatives, apologizing for the fact that "they had cursed the Young Turks and called them atheists previously," demonstrate that this propaganda was helping the CUP gain more support[225] and even encouraging some local ulema to take up the Young Turk cause.[226]

The final attempt of the CUP in the region was made by İbrahim Temo. He formed a Society for Muslim Education and collected donations from governors and high-ranking officials by telling them that "the society was under the protection of H.I.M. the Sultan." However, when the governors checked this with the palace, they were told that this was a "seditious organization" finagling money for its revolutionary ends, and thus its fund-raising scheme failed.[227]

The Activities of the Geneva Center in Late 1898 and Negotiations with the Palace

The expectations of the CUP leaders and members soared after the publication of the new central organ, but ten months later found them plunged into despair. Discord with the Paris branch reemerged, the Egyptian branch adopted an independent course, and a lawsuit was filed against an inspector sent by the Geneva center; mass arrests were made throughout the Empire. Conspiracy plans proved fruitless, and an enormous sum had been squandered on unrealistic schemes. The only positive point was the vitality of the Balkan organization; however, this affected affairs in the Empire only peripherally.

Therefore the Geneva center again began negotiating with the government and Necib Melhame met with Abdullah Cevdet to discuss a new truce.[228] CUP leaders in Geneva announced in their journal that they had negotiated with the agents of the sultan and complained that the palace used imprisoned members as a wild card.[229] Letters which had been sent by CUP prisoners begging the committee for help were used by the leaders of the Geneva center as a device for bargaining.[230] However, the welfare and release of prisoners were only of minor concern to the Geneva center, its main interest being its finances and new conspiracy plans.

Palace agents proposed that the three leaders of the Geneva center, Abdullah Cevdet, İshak Sükûti, and Tunalı Hilmi, cease contributing to the central organ and that other members be ordered to relax the inflammatory language used against the sultan in *Osmanlı*. They, in turn, asked for the release of all CUP members exiled in Tripoli of Barbary and Fezzan before the onset of negotiations; this requirement was made by the branch in Tripoli of Barbary.[231] The Ottoman government agreed to this, and an imperial decree was issued on July 5 stipulating that the exiles must swear, in the presence of a committee of mufti and high-ranking officers headed by the governor, "not to become involved in seditious activities"; in return, they would be released.[232] The palace considered the word *release* to mean "freely to go around within the borders of the town." Nevertheless, even this constituted a serious "détente."[233] The Geneva center perceived it as an authentic rapprochement.[234]

At the bargaining table, the CUP leaders asked for money in exchange for easing their language against the sultan. On August 20 the three leaders agreed not to write for the central organ and other newspapers in exchange for a lifetime payment of £t 12 per month, guaranteed by an imperial decree.[235] In spite of bureaucratic problems, which were overruled by the sultan,[236] they began to receive this sum in early September.[237] Although the government further required the eleven CUP leaders to take up posts at the Ottoman embassies, they refused,[238] because it would endanger their standing among other CUP members in the country, especially after the denouncement in the central organ of Murad Bey and those who had accepted posts at the Contrexéville agreement.

In spite of the agreement, the three leaders continued to write for the central organ and to coordinate activities for the center. Salaries paid to Tunalı Hilmi and İshak Sükûti were cut, yet Abdullah Cevdet continued to receive his for eight months because he sent his articles secretly from Paris.[239]

With things at such a pass, the Geneva center again sat at the bargaining table, this time in the presence of Münir Bey. On November 9, Abdullah Cevdet presented the central committee's conditions to the ambassador: A general amnesty for CUP members, their appointment to jobs outside the capital, and a payment of Fr 50,000 to each of the three leaders. In return they promised to forego all activities and to hand over all back issues of the central organ and other publications.[240] When Münir Bey rejected this scheme, a final meeting was arranged, and on November 16, İshak Sükûti presented a new plan. The only change was an agreement to ease the language against the sultan until the settlement of the matter.[241] Münir Bey, however, refused this blueprint too.

The 1898 negotiations were suspended on this date. The Geneva center gained a respite from financial pressures since the three leaders received £t 12 for three months and Abdullah Cevdet received it for five more months. However, rumors about these negotiations and blackmailing activities by some members for their personal account[242] disappointed members in the country. Even İbrahim Temo, the closest friend of the three leaders, advised them to exercise greater caution and not to allow Ahmed Rıza and other opponents of the Geneva center to use the theme of "bought-off individuals."[243]

Following the break in negotiations, a rapprochement between the Geneva center and Ahmed Rıza was made through a meeting of Albert Fua and Abdullah Cevdet, and because of their numerous disappointments, the Geneva center agreed once more in favor of coexistence.[244] Meanwhile, aware of the impossibility of continuing activities without receiving financial backing, they looked into new ways to force the palace to the bargaining table once again. An open letter to Ottoman cabinet members in a style similar to that of Murad Bey was typical,[245] and although this did not accord with the activist tendencies of the Geneva center, it was considered an ideal way of threatening the sultan with a palace coup d'état. Another attempt involved the publication and distribution of a series of documents concerning Midhat Pasha's death, a subject that the sultan did not even want discussed before the European public.[246]

The CUP and the Young Turks until the Flight of Damad Mahmud Pasha

The Geneva Center and the Paris Branch

The CUP center was begun in 1899, a critical year in its history, under conditions so unpleasant that, as a leader described the group, "It is not a committee but a scandalous [organization]."[247] The year opened with an alleged Young Turk plot against the sultan[248]; an allegation that the palace denied.[249] Although we lack information, these allegations prodded the sultan to hasten his new, this time diplomatic attack on the Young Turks.

Due to increasingly cordial relations between the Ottoman and German empires, the sultan requested the help of German diplomats and thus elevated the Young Turk movement from a mere domestic problem into a matter of European diplomacy. This shift might have created an extremely dangerous situation for the CUP, since it was unlikely that the new administration would obtain diplomatic support from any Great Power. Their requests of humanitarian intervention for the political prisoners were rebuffed by Great Britain.[250]

In March the Germans asked the Swiss authorities to apply methods used formerly against Italian anarchists to the Young Turks.[251] The Swiss authorities told them that due to the likelihood of a conspiracy against the sultan, they had tightened surveillance of all Young Turk activities.[252] Afterward the Swiss foreign minister announced that "the strictest measures will be taken against the Young Turks, and anyone who continues such activities may be extradited."[253] It seems that at that point the German diplomats expected a cessation of Young Turk activities.[254]

Then, upon the personal application of Staatssekretär von Bülow, based on information received from Istanbul, the Swiss government intensified its suppression.[255] The Swiss political police prepared a detailed investigation of the activities of the Young Turks and the Armenians.[256] Meanwhile, Münir Bey, under instructions from the palace, prepared French translations of various articles previously published in *Osmanlı* and *Beberuhi* and submitted them to the Swiss embassy in Paris.[257] Upon examining those translations, which made the attacks on the sultan seem more harsh because in most cases derogatory and threatening words had been quoted out of context, the Swiss Ministry of the Interior prepared a new investigation report which led to a stronger ruling against the activities of the Young Turks.[258] At the same time Münir Bey presented photos of documents submitted to him by Abdullah Cevdet, İshak Sükûti, and Mustafa Refik during the negotiations, and asked the Swiss authorities to extradite them for blackmail.[259]

The sultan personally requested the assistance of Constans, the French ambassador, concerning the circulation of *Osmanlı* through French post offices in the Ottoman Empire. In order to please him, the French post office returned copies of the central organ stamped "*Osmanlı*'s entrance to the country is forbidden."[260] This development paralyzed the circulation network in the Empire, and instructions in disguised sentences could not reach the members for whom they were written.

Another application was made to the French authorities to suppress the delivery of *Mechveret Supplément Français*.[261] However, they rejected the demand.[262]

Yet another application was presented to the French for the extradition of two Young Turks, Şükrü [Léon Gattegno] and Mazlum Hakkı, residing in Paris but having contacts with the Geneva center, on the grounds of blackmail.[263] They had published a journal called *Reşad* (the name of the Ottoman heir apparent), and an appeal promoting foreign intervention in favor of the heir apparent, which they sent to the ambassadors of the Great

Powers. However, they left France before French police could fully investigate their activities.[264]

To ease pressure on themselves, the CUP leaders decided to publish a book in German denouncing the regime of Abdülhamid II and thus to impress German speakers. A leader of the newly established Berlin branch was assigned this task and penned a pamphlet detailing the history of the liberal movement in the Ottoman Empire.[265] This was presented as the CUP's official viewpoint[266] and drew attention in diplomatic circles.[267]

Later Tunalı Hilmi was sent to European capitals to describe the policies of the organization.[268] He also claimed authority to represent the Egyptian ulema.[269]

To win over European public opinion, the Geneva center decided to take further steps in its rapprochement with Ahmed Rıza, whose relations with European intellectuals, particularly positivists, had gained currency under these circumstances. His leading articles, which were deemed "unfit for publication" a year before,[270] began to reappear in the central organ.[271] In return he visited the Geneva center and praised its efforts.[272]

During this second honeymoon period between Paris and Geneva sections, articles with contradictory themes were printed simultaneously in *Osmanlı*. On the one hand an extremely pacifistic and antirevolutionary view was expressed: "We had never tried violent means until now and we never will."[273] On the other hand the CUP traveling agents were sent from Geneva to other branches in the Empire and abroad to gather donations for "the preparation of a final attack on the present administration."[274]

Like the themes in the central organ, CUP policies took two divergent paths during this period. First were efforts to prevent the sultan from suppressing their movement with the help of the German diplomats. During the kaiser's visit to the Ottoman Empire, Ahmed Rıza started just such a campaign by sending him a letter.[275] The central organ participated in the campaign by publishing articles criticizing the *Drang nach Osten* policy of the German Empire.[276] However, these articles expressed a strong pro-British tendency—never acceptable to Ahmed Rıza.

Also, with Ahmed Rıza's initiative, the CUP decided to join in The Hague Peace Conference in 1899. Although uninvited, Ahmed Rıza organized a joint delegation and presented a memorandum to the representatives. He convinced Minas Tscheraz, a prominent figure in the Armenian movement, to join the delegation; however, Albanians to whom he had also applied spurned the offer.[277] Besides having authorization from all branches of the CUP, he allegedly received authority from the ulema of al-Azhar to represent them.[278] He journeyed to The Hague with Pierre Anméghian and met with Minas Tscheraz, whose activities were being scrutinized by Ottoman diplomats.[279]

The Ottoman administration, in order to block the *de facto* participation of the joint CUP-Armenian delegation, asked the assistance of the German diplomats[280] and sent the Ottoman diplomats and agents to The Hague to hinder Ahmed Rıza from attending meetings.[281]

Their presentation and their labeling of the sultan as an "assassin" (Gladstone's expression) drew the attention of the representatives[282] and annoyed the Ottoman administration.[283]

Ahmed Rıza's presentation of the goals of the CUP as being peaceful and legitimate[284] was highly publicized and praised by the press.[285]

By delivering their memorandum, although unofficial, since they were uninvited, for the first time the CUP addressed the representatives of the powers.[286] Also for the first time publicly the CUP and the Armenians took joint action.[287] This is why the sultan ordered the participation of Diran Kelekyan to the Ottoman delegation in The Hague.[288]

The Ottoman representatives' allegations of violent attacks on Ahmed Rıza were also used as propaganda material by the CUP to prove their own peacefulness.[289]

Ahmed Rıza and Tscheraz also organized meetings and talks against the regime of Abdülhamid II, during which the former depicted the CUP as a positivist organization.[290] Tscheraz's proposed speech against the sultan, under the auspices of Christelijke Vereeniging voor Jonge Mannen, was not banned, but he was prohibited from using any pictures.[291] Later he adopted a religious tone and focused on the "peril of Pan-Islamism," accusing the sultan of inciting the Muslims in Java against the Dutch.[292] The sultan protested against both the Young Turks and the accusations of Tscheraz,[293] and the Ottoman administration applied heavy pressure to its Dutch counterpart to extradite them. However, they left the country before any action could be taken against them.[294]

After his activities in the Netherlands, Ahmed Rıza went to Christiania (now Oslo) to join the Ninth International and Interparliamentary Peace Conference, having published the eighty-first issue of *Mechveret Supplément Français* in Copenhagen.[295] The Ottoman ambassador Şerif Bey protested the *de facto* participation by the Young Turks and applied to the Swedish authorities asking for their censure. They passed his letter on to the secretary of state for Norway.[296] During this diplomatic procedure, besides presenting the cause of the CUP to many intellectuals and statesmen,[297] Ahmed Rıza succeeded in delivering a speech similar to the one he had presented in The Hague depicting the CUP as a nonrevolutionary organization:

> Our Committee is trying to change the present administration and to rule our country through a Sublime Porte responsible to a house of representatives and a senate. In order to achieve this goal we do not possess cannons or rifles; now our power consists only of publications.[298]

Ahmed Rıza also attempted during this time to persuade prominent French deputies and statesmen to write for *Mechveret Supplément Français* so as to impress European public opinion during this period.[299]

Meanwhile, on the second path, the activists were engaged in several ventures. The palace was receiving news about "a violent action that was certainly planned by the conspiratorial committee of Young Turks."[300] In early April, Ottoman diplomats tried to produce information from an anarchist named Jan Jacobovich, who went by the pseudonym Kropotkin, regarding the plans of the anarchist societies against the rulers of European countries.[301] On April 13, 1899, the sultan's private secretary sent an urgent telegram to Anthopulos Pasha in London about a joint Young Turk–Armenian plot to assassinate the sultan.[302] The following events read like a detective novel. The next day an anarchist named Alexander Dembski appeared at the Ottoman embassy in London claiming to have been part of a conspiracy against the sultan. According to Dembski, the anarchist committee was planning to send a Spanish and an Italian anarchist to Istanbul by train to assassinate the sultan five days hence. He said he knew everything about the plot and could provide the names of the anarchists and of the people they would be contacting in the Ottoman capital. In return he asked for Fr 100,000 so he might depart and settle in a remote African town, because he would otherwise be murdered for betraying anarchist friends in Europe.[303] A sum of £ 400 was given as a down payment to Dembski.[304] Then he revealed the story:

> Le 12 Mars le groupe d'anarchistes militant[s] à Londres a reçu une invitation de Francfort sur Mein [Francfort sur le Main] d'un moncieur [monsieur], qui a signé d'invitation par no. 6 Francfurterhof, d'envoyer un émissaire pour causer une affaire sérieuse. Le compagnon Messislas Goldberg était envoyé par la partie à Francfort et a trouvé à l'hôtel un espagnol se nommant Pouello et disant qu'il est secrétaire articulaire de Don Carlos et proposant aux anarchistes de faire un attentat contre la Reine régente Christine en admettant que l'attentat doit avoir un caractère pur anarchiste. Il a proposé une somme de cent mille francs à la caisse des anarchistes. Le dit compagnon est revenu à Londres, et le 30 Mars au club Victor Emmanuel Old Compton Street, il y avait une réunion où il a déposé le résultat de son voyage. Par le discours du compagnon Kazarianz un professeur révoqué de Tiflis, à l'unanimité on a refusé la proposition de M.Puello. Dans la même réunion, le compagnon Nazarbeck a prononcé un brillant discours sur la sauvagerie inouie [inouïe] avec laquelle le Sultan traite la jeunesse libérale à Constantinople et sur la manière de la Police turque d'influencer la Police européenne pour qu'on sévisse les hommes échappés au carnage. On a cité avec effroi des exemples d'arrestations surtout à partir du temps du voyage de Gillaume II [Guillaume II] et à la fin il a donné lecture d'un discours du deputé Charles Lorand à la Chambre Belge à la suite d'incident Riza à Bruxelles. On a résolu d'envoyer l'émissaire compagnon Dembski à Paris pour qu'il se ... son relation avec les compagnons révolutionnair [révolutionnaires] de Paris et après avoir pris la date les compagnons suivants Vartanianz (une femme), Ciancabilla, Potel, Dembski et Nazar-Bek sont partis pour Paris et le 3 avril se sont réunis à la rue Nollet no. 10, dans l'appartement d'écrivain Pierre Quillard sans que celui-ci prît part à la conférence, avec les compagnons Parmeggiani et Geoffroy et ils ont résolu sur la proposition de Parmeggiani de supprimer l'assistance de Riza à la conférence pour qu'il par sa sentimentalité n'empêche pas la résolution éventuelle qu'on va prendre. Après avoir pris la connaissance de la [du] protocole de la conférence de Londres on a résolu de supprimer Abdul-Hamid. Pendant la discussion de la manière de l'exécution et de la difficulté de préparer et fabriquer les

bombes, le compagnon Ciancabilla s'élève et prononce le discours finissant par les mots: mon compatriote Luccheni a tué sans toute [doute?] votre conférence et si on me laisse faire je me charge sans aucun ballotage de la résolution de la Compagnie. Sa proposition fut acceptée. On a balloté et on lui a choisi comme aide sur la place le compagnon Portet. Après avoir donné connaissance de la réunion très grave sans indication du résultat on a touché de M.Pierre Quillard trois mille francs et quinze mille francs de le [du] groupe d'arméniens à Paris à titre de secours pour les arméniens. A la fin on a résolu de munir les compagnons choisis d'argent et d'effets et annonçant la résolution à Constantinople aux trois compagnons sûrs, on est reparti pour Londres. A Constantinople il y a Kérim, professeur des langues, Rue Yorgandjilar no. 38. On lui a envoyé des letters pour les 2 autres compagnons. Dans la Grande rue de Péra ou dans une rue intermédiaire demeure levantin Brokar qui tient une maison louche. Aussi il y a à Constantinople un bijoutier Juif se nommant Ravul Decloix mais son vrai nom est Bernard. Ces trois personnes ont reçu connaissance de la résolution. Par la voie des chemins de fer via ces jours-ci à Constantinople Ciancabilla, porteur d'un passeport Anglais no. 834, livré le 28 Novembre [18]98 sous le nom de Dr. Robert. C'est un petit brun bien fait, visage vérolé avec une fraise à la joue garçon, l'âge de 30 ans. Le second Portet, porteur d'un passeport belge, livré par la commune Ixelles no. 32, le 4 février [18]99 sous le nom Jules Martin, sculpteur, un homme de 40 à [ou] 45 ans, taille moyenne, rasé, brun clair, portant des lunettes et il a le tic. On trouvera chez ces deux personnes les révolvers à sept charges avec tambour automatique, branche en bois avec une marque un cheval ou relief avec inscription Piper, Liège. On trouvera des poignards sans manche à rivière et marque. M. X. Sollingen Les lettres qu'on trouvera dans leurs poches aussi les lettres qu'ils trouveront à la poste restante Péra se lisent par les moyens de la dernière édition (18.ème-1899) de Zola Paris. Les lettres portent des chiffres et on procède au déchiffrement de la manière suivante: on prend un groupe de chiffres et on ouvre la page du livre qui porte le même chiffre et là on prend le premier mot et ainsi de suite.

L'attendat se prépare pour le Baïram.[305]

This amazing story appears accurate. Dembski was an anarchist and had participated in the movement since his youth. He was wounded in a explosion while he was manufacturing bombs with three friends in March 1889[306] the other persons mentioned in his story are verifiable. Avetis Nazarbek, a founding leader of the *Hnchakian* organization in Geneva, had advocated anarcho-socialist methods for the Armenian movement.[307] The Ottoman administration scrutinized his activities and the persons he met.[308] Giuseppe Ciancabilla had participated in anarchist activities in Geneva and became a prominent anarchist in the late 1890s.[309] Luigi Luccheni had ties with the Young Turks while in Geneva, and a book concerning his activities, entitled *L'Affaire Luccheni,* was published by Yusuf Fehmi, a Young Turk.[310] Luigi Parmeggiani had been a member of the anarchist group in Paris called *Intransigenti* and was at that time residing in London.[311] Pierre Quillard was a socialist-anarchist and had written for *La Révolution* and *Les Temps Nouveaux* in defense of the Armenian cause[312]; later he became the chief columnist of *Pro Arménia.* Unfortunately we lack further information about succeeding events in this venture, yet it seems obvious that this was another failed conspiracy.

Later the activist faction discussed a new venture with the radical wing of the Albanian committees; however, they could not carry their plans into the field of action.[313]

After the activist faction's repeated failures, Ottoman diplomats fabricated a conspiracy in order to extradite CUP members from Switzerland. Doctor Edmond Lardy, an ardent supporter of CUP activities who had publicized the Young Turk cause in his articles in Swiss journals, was attacked in his consulting room by two persons named Fauriat and Booz. The former threatened the doctor requiring him to furnish information about activities of CUP members. However, Lardy drew his revolver, subdued the men, and called the police.[314] During his interrogation, Fauriat told police that Lardy had been accumulating dynamite for a proposed CUP plot against the sultan.[315] Following this assertion, Resul Bey, the Ottoman consul, in a letter to the Swiss press, wrote that they "did not need spies or provocateurs," but they had been informed by two French persons that Lardy and Nuri Ahmed, a prominent member of the Geneva center of the CUP, were plotting to assassinate the sultan.[316]

The Swiss police arrested the two leading lights in the venture, Fauriat, Booz, as well as their friend Claude Pascal, and Visco Babatashi, the secretary of the Albanian Committee in Brussels, who had been advocating the union of all Albanians for cultural autonomy and maintained close relations with İbrahim Temo.[317] He had come to Geneva four months prior to the event and begun to work for the Geneva center.[318] Later, police interrogated leaders of the Geneva branch asking them to provide information. Abdurrahman Bedirhan,[319] Âkil Muhtar,[320] Nazmi Salih,[321] and Nuri Ahmed[322] denied all the allegations. Since Lardy had told the police that Visco Babatashi was an agent of the sultan who had been installed in the CUP,[323] the political police interrogated Babatashi twice.[324] Two detailed reports were prepared by the Geneva and federal political police authorities; both documents reveal that CUP members made no serious attempt against the life of the sultan and that the Ottoman consul had fabricated the story.[325]

The event drew enormous attention in diplomatic circles[326] and enabled the Geneva center to improve its image in Swiss public opinion. The palace recalled Resul Bey, and letters calumniating the Young Turks were published in French in the local Ottoman press.[327]

Meanwhile, new negotiations had gotten under way between the Geneva center and the palace. The palace again targeted the center, which by then had fifty active members.[328] The leaders of the Geneva center were desperate and floundering, as Abdullah Cevdet wrote to another founder:

> We became really aged. For God's sake, we might be dying and nobody would give us a loaf of bread. Oh, the people say a lot when it comes to speech-making. I spent the entire winter in Geneva with a ten-piece undershirt. They

all knew that we had no money or income. Who sent us a hundred francs [?]. . . There is no need for further words. We would never resign from serving the people. But we have trodden upon our own interests long enough. Therefore the committee is being transformed into a soup kitchen for the poor.[329]

This time instead of assigning a high-ranking intelligence officer, the palace dispatched Doctor Bahaeddin, a former Young Turk, to Geneva.[330] He met with many Young Turks and asked their requirements for halting publications and activities.[331] Once again the condition was a general amnesty; however, the leaders were now ready to accept posts in embassies and consulates, which they had been categorically refusing to do a year before.[332] Cognizant of their desperation, this time the Ottoman government stated its primary condition as the return of the all CUP leaders to Istanbul, and so the first stage of negotiations ended in a stalemate.

Following this failure, the palace reassigned Ahmed Celâleddin Pasha as negotiator. Rumors about his new mission made the barely improved relations between the Geneva and Paris branches very tense.[333] Members of the Paris branch were worried about the consequences of any accord between the head of the Ottoman intelligence service and the Geneva center:

> Most probably you heard that Ahmed Celâleddin Pasha is in Paris and intends to go to Geneva. The uproar that Ahmed Rıza's The Hague [activities] caused is spreading throughout the world. No European now remains who has not heard the title of our committee and no daily remains which has not issued publication concerning the affairs of our committee. In short, so great was this uproar for the committee that we should not count on a new one happening. Now after this uproar if they would hold negotiations with Celâl[eddin] Pasha and stop the journal, the disgrace besmirching the committee would destroy all the efforts spent until now.[334]

Ahmed Rıza sent a message to İshak Sükûti, through Doctor Nâzım, reminding them that his primary condition for a rapprochement was that neither would negotiate with the sultan's agents.[335] Under such heavy pressure, İshak Sükûti declined to meet with the head of the intelligence service,[336] who initially expected that he and other leaders would apply to him. Then Ahmed Celâleddin Pasha sent intermediaries to the CUP leaders.[337] He thought that most leaders would return to Istanbul.[338] However, Abdullah Cevdet, who had negotiated with him, refused such a settlement and threatened to move CUP headquarters to London.[339] Then the head of the intelligence service worked out a temporary settlement.[340] A telegram reveals that an agreement was concluded in mid-August, but the conditions were vague.[341] The CUP leaders in Geneva were to be given monthly stipends on the condition that they write nothing against the sultan. Small amounts of money were distributed to the lesser members of the Geneva branch.[342] Although this gave the Geneva center breathing time, stipends were cut twenty days later, since Ottoman agents uncovered their ongoing activities.[343]

The leaders of the Geneva center then found themselves in a predicament. On the one hand it had become impossible for them "to carry out
[their] opposition activities without financing by Abdülhamid."[344] On the
other hand the Paris branch was pressuring them heavily not to accept any
agreement with the sultan's agents, and the palace was asking them officially to accept posts which, if they took them, could not be hidden from
the Paris branch or other members in the country, although they might
disclose receipts of money after secret negotiations. Also the leaders of the
Geneva center were aware of a special investigation of their activities by
Swiss political police which resulted seven months later in a stern warning
to limit their activities.[345] The typesetter for the central organ faced extradition from Switzerland because he had participated in an incident in Bulgaria the year before.[346]

The Paris branch once again pressured the leader of the Geneva center
not to reach an agreement with the palace:

> In the course of the conversation we had begun to discuss your appointment
> to some posts. [Ahmed Rıza] said, "I would never have believed that Sükûti
> would leave the committee." . . . Why are you wearing that beard, a symbol
> of masculinity? Do you not feel yourself as forceful as Ahmed Rıza's description
> in a letter that he wrote to his mother: "I will never compromise my principles
> in the slightest degree even if they would furiously burn you and my entire
> family up in front of my eyes."[347]

However, the conditions mentioned above compelled the leaders of
the Geneva center to accept the sultan's terms. On September 26, 1899,
an imperial decree announced the appointment of the center's two leaders
to positions at Ottoman embassies in Europe.[348] İshak Sükûti and Abdullah Cevdet became medical doctors at the Ottoman embassies in Rome
and Vienna; soon after, Tunalı Hilmi was appointed clerk to the Ottoman
embassy in Madrid.[349] A new and "direct imperial decree" followed, com-
manding the Ottoman Foreign Ministry to finish the bureaucratic for-
malities quickly.[350] But the leaders did not go to the capitals to which they
had been appointed and tried to finagle money from various Ottoman
diplomatic representatives, including the ones who had appointed them.[351]
Even as late as December 1899, none of them had begun his new occupation. This was part of a plan they had, to collect enough money to
continue their publication for a considerable period.[352]

In order to gain time and to accumulate more money, a new plan was
launched. Abdullah Cevdet and Mustafa Rahmi announced the formation
of a society called Reşadiye Committee. A regulation on the organizational
framework of the committee was published in Geneva[353] and was made
available in various languages, including English, threatening the palace
with a claim of British support.[354] The so-called founders immediately
assumed center stage.[355] The Swiss political police began an investigation
of the committee[356] and the Ottoman consul applied to the Swiss authorities to instate measures against the organization.[357] However, the Swiss

political police easily uncovered the simple truth—that "this committee had been formed so as to influence Ahmed Celâleddin Pasha and to gain importance in his eyes."[358] Abdullah Cevdet confessed this during his interrogation on October 17, 1899.[359] After the failure of this project, no alternative remained but to take up new occupations. The leaders succeeded in extorting more money from Ahmed Celâleddin Pasha and turned it over to the organization.[360] Later final negotiations between the Ottoman government and the leaders took place in Berlin in February 1900, and after receiving yet more money, they promised to go to the towns to which they had been appointed.[361]

The most difficult time for the leaders started afterward. Although they had not, as Murad Bey had done, gone to Istanbul and endured humiliation by the domestic press, many unimportant Young Turks had returned to the Empire.[362] At that point the leaders related to members in the other branches that none of those who returned had held a significant position in the organization. However, now they were at gunpoint, and it was impossible to conceal this in the way they kept other bargains with palace agents secret. Rumors in Young Turk circles about the blackmailing activities of unimportant CUP members during the same period worsened the image of the Geneva center in the eyes of the participants in the Empire.[363]

From the leaders' viewpoint it had been the committee's policy.[364] Each CUP member had to give two-thirds of his salary and stipend to the organization in order to keep his membership current, according to a decision taken by the central committee in early 1898.[365] Some prominent leaders, including İbrahim Temo, had advised the Geneva center's leaders to accept positions for at least one year in order to accumulate enough money for a long-term publication.[366] However, it was too difficult to explain this arrangement to most of the members in the Empire, who deemed it a betrayal similar to that of Murad Bey.

Hoping to mollify these members,[367] the leaders published a special article in *Osmanli Supplément Français* claiming that they had accepted these posts only so as to impel the Ottoman government to release CUP members imprisoned in Tripoli of Barbary; a list of the prisoners' names accompanied the article.[368] It is true that imperial decrees concerning their release were enacted only after this settlement[369]; nevertheless, this did not justify the action of the conductors in the eyes of most members, who sent letters addressing these leaders as "vile persons."[370] Leading members confessed this made the work of the Geneva section very difficult.[371]

During the negotiation period, Tunalı Hilmi took another important initiative for a general congress for Ottoman opposition. In his capacity as inspector in Cairo, he conducted secret negotiations with Muḥammad 'Alī Ḥalīm Pasha, and they decided to reorganize the CUP, with financial backing from the latter. On August 15, 1899, Tunalı Hilmi presented this offer to Ahmed Rıza and the Paris branch.[372] Muḥammad 'Alī Ḥalīm Pasha wanted Ahmed Rıza to come to Cairo and discuss the matter directly with him.[373] Numerous branches, led by Tripoli of Barbary, urged Ahmed Rıza to accept the offer.[374] He detested the activist faction,[375] which undoubtedly contributed to his negative response. However, as his confidant Doctor Nâzım stated, the real reason was his mistrust of the non-Turkish elements of the Empire:

> As regards the matter of a proposed congress in Brindisi: When someone says "congress" the thing that comes to mind is a society composed of the gathering together of many people working toward a common goal. How many people can be found to attend a congress which would convene on behalf of our committee? What sort of advantages can be derived from a congress for our fatherland [consisting of] some people who might accept the invitation in good faith and join and *four-and-a-half* Arabs, Armenians, Greeks, and Albanians?[376]

In spite of this refusal, Tunalı Hilmi kept up his efforts. He had already sent an invitation to many CUP leaders, prominent opponents of the regime, and high-ranking Ottoman officials. He required the prospective participants to prepare their memoranda beforehand and issued a deadline of October 5, 1899, informing them that the three-day congress would convene on October 20, 1899.[377]

A new circular was published secretly in Istanbul by Ebüzziya Tevfik[378] and was distributed within the Empire and abroad. The Geneva and Egyptian branches prepared memoranda for the convention.[379] News alleging British support for the congress was published in European dailies.[380]

When the Ottoman government applied to its Italian counterpart[381] and posited similar demands to the Italian ambassador in Istanbul,[382] the Italian government forbade the convention, and the coordinators decided to move the meeting to Corfu.[383] However, the Ottoman government blocked their gathering there through diplomatic maneuvers.[384]

Muḥammad 'Alī Ḥalīm Pasha's contacts with the CUP leaders about a congress continued until mid-1900.[385] Toward the end of 1899, the situation altered profoundly, and Tunalı Hilmi's appointment to the Madrid embassy prevented him from carrying out this mission.

By late December the CUP and the Young Turk movement had been all but annihilated by the sultan, and most members probably thought that only a miracle could revitalize the movement. Nevertheless, this miracle occurred. The sultan's brother-in-law and his two sons fled, and their participation in the movement saved it from demise.

The Egyptian Branch

By the end of 1898 the Egyptian branch had nearly terminated its activities, and the dispute between the branch director, unrecognized by the Geneva center, and the members loyal to it had been transferred to a local court.

Following the lawsuit, which lasted more than a year, judgment was given in favor of Salih Cemal and Hoca Kadri, his partner, but all the documents of the branch remained sealed by local authorities because the court did not decide to which side to award their possession.[386] In January 1899 the Geneva center opted to commission Abdullah Cevdet with extraordinary authority and dispatch him to Cairo in order to reorganize the branch. However, the vital importance of the salary paid to him prevented the central committee from realizing this idea.[387] Tunalı Hilmi, was sent instead as the special inspector for the CUP. He was allowed two weeks to reorganize the branch. However, Salih Cemal's resistance to his authority[388] and the continuing lawsuit eventuated a longer stay.[389] Hoca Kadri, the former branch leader, at that point supported Salih Cemal and also protested against the idea of an inspector sent to Cairo.[390]

On July 7, Tunalı Hilmi organized a new and extraordinary executive committee consisting of nine members and "a virtuous and prominent person residing in Egypt" who was appointed as the "honorary director."[391] Although the name of this person was not revealed in documents, in light of Tunalı Hilmi's other activities in Egypt and this description, it must have been Muḥammad 'Alī Ḥalīm Pasha.[392] Tarsusîzâde Münif was assigned as the temporary director.[393]

On August 31, the committee decided to publish a new branch organ called *Hak (Justice)*.[394] The Geneva center required them to publish it as the official organ of the branch only, independent of the central committee in Geneva,[395] and they even announced this.[396] The introductory article carried an Islamic tone and an activist tendency, undoubtedly due to Tunalı Hilmi.[397]

In late September the extraordinary executive committee was replaced by a regular one founded in accordance with CUP regulations.[398]

Salih Cemal and Hoca Kadri, spearheading a faction of the old branch, started a campaign against this committee, declaring all their decisions void.[399] They protested the events and especially the role of Tunalı Hilmi, accusing him of being the sultan's agent. The new center reacted by publishing an appeal praising Tunalı Hilmi's work in the movement and decrying measures against him by the sultan and the intelligence service.[400]

With the flight of Hüseyin Tosun,[401] Ali Fahri, Bahriyeli Fahri, Haydar, Edhem Ruhi, Nazmi, Bahriyeli Rıza, Kadribeyzâde Fâzıl, and Mehmed Emin from Tripoli of Barbary[402] and their participation in the branch, the section came to be dominated by military officers.

The financial crisis continued to be the branch's greatest problem. A fund- raising campaign was instituted,[403] and the Tripoli of Barbary branch began to remit monthly payments to Cairo.[404] These funds, however, were inadequate for the journal, which became a problem after two months:

> You wrote that the enemy is great. It is great and not merely one. You should see how we here are besieged by immigrants cursing with a swift pen. There is no need to tell you that Hoca Kadri is heading them. We now have this much. If we close down the publishing house, things would be dynamically

worsened. The existence of *Hak* is imperilled; if it disappears he will yell osten-
tatiously to the entire Ottoman world about our lack of firmness and our zeal
for returning to Istanbul—the very themes that he already uses against us.

We need £ 2 per month [to publish] *Hak*. If it would be met by someone,
I would wish for nothing more in the world. My friend, do you understand
how much the publication by the Egyptian branch adds to our moral strength
within the Empire? Believe me, if *Hak* ceases [its publication] the despair and
hopelessness that you are witnessing will be increased five [or] ten fold. I swear
to God I am ready to give my life if only *Hak* will continue to be published.[405]

As stated in the introductory article, *Hak* revealed two tendencies: (1)
an Islamic perspective as required by the Geneva center,[406] although the
new members of the section were against this style of propaganda, and (2)
a demand for a strong activist policy.[407]

The most dramatic change in Egypt during this period was the great
criticism leveled against the branch. Arab and Circassian nationalists, most
dailies in Cairo (such as *al-Muqaṭṭam* and *al-Mirṣād*), and ulema led by
Hoca Kadri, the former leader of the branch, jointly opposed the CUP.[408]

The Egyptian branch was also subjected to pressure from the palace,
which was trying to cut off financial support that the khedive secretly provided. On March 28, 1899, the sultan sent a message to the British ambassador informing him that "there were in Egypt certain ill-advised and fool-
ish persons who called themselves Young Turks, but who were merely
animated by a wish to extort money." He further claimed that he "could
prove to [the British ambassador] that they were supported and instigated
by the Khedive." Sir Nicholas R. O'Conor advised the Foreign Office to
send "a civil answer to His Majesty saying that . . . Her Majesty's Government cannot interfere with the liberty of the press." The significant aspect
of the sultan's message was, as Sir Nicholas pointed out, "his direct appeal
to Her Majesty's Government and the studied way in which he ignores
the Khedive's authority."[409] The khedive told Cromer that "he had never
in any way supported or subventioned either 'Young Turks' or their newspapers."[410] Cromer recommended to the Foreign Office that they turn the
issue into a bargain by asking whether "the sultan will give instructions to
Moukhtar Pasha to abstain from encouraging the Anglophobe press."[411]
The sultan expressed his satisfaction to the British ambassador, and following this initiative a rapprochement took place between the sultan and
the khedive concerning the Young Turks.[412] Although the former could
not prevent the CUP branch from publishing their newspapers, the latter
succeeded in removing one financial source.

The CUP Organization within the Empire

During the first half of this period there was complete inactivity at the
CUP section in the capital. Later, appeals with a strong nationalist tone
calumniating the sultan for his policy over Crete and Macedonia were

pinned up and distributed by the members there and in some provincial towns.[413]

In the second half of this period pro-British CUP members organized more serious activities. British victory over the Boers in Transvaal provided an opportunity for a small demonstration. Most pro-British CUP members wrote articles for a literary journal called *Servet-i Fünûn (Wealth of Sciences)* favoring Great Britain and claiming the superiority of the British social structure.[414] In November 1899, at the instigation of Hüseyin Siyret, a leading author of the journal and a CUP member, and İsmail Kemal, an appeal praising the British was written.[415] İsmail Kemal requested of Sir Nicholas that he receive a delegation with the prepared appeal. At first the ambassador did not want to receive the delegation, since he understood that it was a "Young Turk" one. Upon the insistence of various well-known people, İsmail Kemal being the foremost one, the appeal praising the British was presented to Sir Nicholas.[416] It was signed by twenty-nine persons including İsmail Kemal, several naval officers, ulema from Baghdad and Mosul, bureaucrats, and authors of *Servet-i Fünûn*; a total of 150 people carried out a silent demonstration.[417] Many leading CUP members in Europe praised the ideas expressed in the text.[418]

The palace depicted the demonstration as a great venture by the Young Turks. The British ambassador, anxious about the consequences, reported the event to Ahmed Tevfik Pasha, the Ottoman foreign minister, and the latter expressed his regrets regarding the development.[419] Also, the palace directly instructed Anthopulos Pasha to discuss the matter with the Foreign Office.[420] Four days later, new instructions delivered to him at the behest of the sultan underscored the "anarchist" tendencies of the participants and protested agaist the British ambassador's objection to their arrests.[421] The British, however, did not give a clear answer to Anthopulos Pasha and thus expressed their obdurate objection to the demonstrators' arrest.[422]

Rumors about the Muslim population's endorsement of the appeal struck dread in the palace and government circles.[423] İzzet and Ragıb Beys, the sultan's confidants, informed Marschall von Bieberstein that the sovereign's abiding fear was of an "overt political demonstration," perhaps the first in many years, and its organizers' ties with Great Britain.[424] Baron Calice described the demonstration as Anglophile, supported by some high-ranking bureaucrats and ulema, and as setting the stage for a grander design.[425] The Paris ambassador of the German Empire also noted the increase in pro-British sentiments in Istanbul among high-ranking bureaucrats.[426] The sultan did not dare punish İsmail Kemal, the architect of the demonstration; however, the two other heroes of the event, Hüseyin Siyret[427] and İsmail Safa,[428] were exiled, and later the other participants were also banished.

A short time before the pro-British demonstration, a less important event occurred. Ali Haydar Midhat, the son of Midhat Pasha and a champion of pro-British policy, fled to Europe,[429] and this was also depicted as an initiative by the pro-British group within the Young Turk movement.[430] The palace asked him to return and offered money and other privileges, but he turned them down.[431]

In late 1899 a correspondence between Kemaleddin Efendi, a brother of the sultan, and the CUP was discovered.[432] Many CUP members, ulema, and high-ranking bureaucrats known as the opponents of the palace regime were arrested. The total number of those arrested was estimated in various sources to be around sixty.[433] Among them were Sahib Molla, a well-known dervish[434]; Said Bey, a member of the State Council; Ziya Molla, a member of the State Council, and his two brothers[435]; and Ferdi Bey, another member of the State Council.[436]

Except for the initiatives of the pro-British faction, the CUP could not undertake anything of real importance. An attempt to distribute new appeals in the capital was abortive because they were intercepted at the house of a college student.[437] The only achievement was the distribution of the central organ and of the official journal of the Egyptian branch, which was deliberately using Islamic jargon, throughout the provinces.[438]

The Balkan Organization, New Branches in North Africa and Central Asia, and the CUP in Cyprus

During this period, the Geneva branch intended to transform the Balkan organization from a network focusing extensively on the internal problems of that region to one carrying out propaganda activities similar to those of the central committee. Halil Muvaffak, one of the leading members in Geneva, had been sent to Bucharest for this purpose and met with Şefik Bey, a former CUP member who had left the movement after the Contrexéville agreement, and the two traveled all around the Balkans and met with the leaders of the local branches.[439] However, the Ottoman diplomats forced them to leave the region by applying diplomatic pressure on the Balkan governments.[440]

In Bulgaria in June, a skirmish broke out between conservatives loyal to the sultan and Young Turks at a café because the latter wanted to hang a picture of Ali Suavi, a Young Ottoman. The Young Turks begged for the help and protection of the Bulgarian Macedonian committee.[441] Soon after, Ahmed Zeki, leader of the Bulgarian central branch in Ruse, founded a new journal called *Islah (Reformation)*. He again used restrained wording in implying he was tied with the CUP.[442] However, this did not prevent the Ottoman government from asking the Bulgarian authorities to stop the journal.[443] Ahmed Zeki once again decided to stop the publication and to move to Geneva and participate in the activities of the center there.[444]

Those who had fled to various towns in Greece, primarily to the Piraeus and Athens, formed a CUP branch for Greece, and military members published a journal called *Seyf-i Hakikat (The Sword of Truth)* and communicated with the Geneva center.[445] With the arrival of more refugees, this branch expanded; yet despite the annoyance of the Ottoman government, it carried out no significant activities except the smuggling of CUP publications from Greece into the Empire.[446]

Despite diminishing CUP activities in the Balkans, the organization managed to form new branches in North Africa and Central Asia.

A new and larger Barbary Coast branch was formed, which included Algeria, Tunisia, and Morocco. The Geneva center warned the indigenous Muslims against people claiming CUP membership and collecting donations.[447] A CUP member given a position in the Marrakesh government's army[448] organized extensive propaganda in the region.[449] The central organ and its French supplement disseminated active CUP propaganda among the Muslim population[450] using an Islamic rhetoric in order to obtain more donations,[451] and articles against the sultan were published in the local press with the help of the Young Turks.[452] These activities continued into 1900.[453]

In Central Asia a CUP branch was formed in Bukhara in late 1898.[454] A certain Şakir Muhammedof journeyed from Orenburg to Siberia and visited many towns and villages inhabited by Turkic people, collecting donations from many Muslims before returning to Habarovsk, his hometown.[455] Later, through him as mediator, another Central Asian Turkic person asked the CUP to provide donation tickets so he might collect money.[456] Şakir Muhammedof also dispatched regular news from Central Asia and the Far East to *Osmanlı*.[457] In Turkestan a certain Hâris Feyzullah collected donations and supplied information on the Central Asian affairs to the central committee.[458] He also sent large sums of money to the Geneva center.[459] Similarly a certain Mehmed Fatih Kerimof had collected large donations from the Tatars in Crimea.[460]

The Cyprus branch founded a newspaper called *Feryad (Cry)* and printed in installments pamphlets previously advertised by the central committee.[461] The upsurge in CUP's activities and the mufti's constant claims of their "seditious" activities caused British officials there to consult on their prospective attitude toward Young Turks and their insistence on establishing journals denouncing the regime of the sultan.[462] The Colonial Office applied to the Foreign Office, and Lord Salisbury proposed that they "refuse certain applications for permission to publish newspapers in the Island, and to intimate to the publisher of a newspaper already in existence that unless he discontinues his attacks upon the Sultan he will be prosecuted."[463] The Colonial Office softened this attitude slightly: "Instead of threatening prosecution, it would be more advisable to notify the publisher that, unless he ceases to give offence, his paper will be suspended."[464] This new policy led to a decrease in CUP activities in Cyprus.

6

The CUP in the Hands of the High-Ranking Conspirators

The Flight of Damad Mahmud Pasha and Its Consequences

Contrary to the Ottoman government's expectations, *Osmanlı* remained in publication after an agreement with the leaders of the Geneva branch and the palace,[1] and the leaders continued to author unsigned articles for it.[2] After the leaders' acceptance of posts at various Ottoman embassies, in order to provide moral support to members in the Empire, the Geneva center adopted a strongly activist rhetoric.[3] It also published a German supplement to *Osmanlı* in order to relax diplomatic pressure on the CUP. This was İshak Sükûti's idea.[4] The articles about Germany were so laudatory[5] that Ahmed Tevfik Pasha, the Ottoman ambassador in Berlin, endeavored to exploit the event to advance relations with Germany.[6] But this new publication provoked vehement opposition among pro-British members.[7] The leaders then decided to use it as a blackmailing tool.[8] After printing the second issue, all back issues were sold to Ottoman agents in a bargain initiated by Abdullah Cevdet.[9] However, neither the strong rhetoric nor the German supplement went far in restoring hope to supporters, and some important members were even inclined to believe that the movement had ended.[10]

At that point, Ahmed Rıza once again took the initiative and applied to the French Ministry of the Interior for the publication of *Meşveret*.[11] Affaires Étrangères consulted on the matter with Constans, the ambassador in Istanbul, and Ahmed Rıza was again left unanswered.[12]

The flight of Damad Mahmud Pasha, the sultan's brother-in-law, and

Sabahaddin and Lûtfullah Beys, his two sons, on December 14, 1899, to Europe altered the picture drastically.[13] They made immediate headlines in the European press,[14] with Pasha claiming that his liberal ideas had impelled him to flee.[15] German diplomats watched the event closely, as they considered it a new venture by the pro-British group.[16]

Germans were well aware that Damad Mahmud Pasha's flight was a result of his failure to obtain a concession on behalf of a British company.[17] His well-known British sympathies accorded with his economic interests, and everybody in Istanbul thought that the flight was a final initiative by the pro-British Ottoman statesmen.[18] Soon after his flight, Damad Mahmud Pasha sent a note to the British through an intermediary requesting their backing of the opposition movement he was preparing; in return, he offered his support in their economic interests:

> Je me permets à cette occasion de vous exposer certaines idées qui me viennent et qui peuvent également vous intéresser. Il me semble très à propos dans la situation où je suis de me vouer entièrement à la propagande de la politique anglaise en Orient d'en faire ressortir les côtés avantageux et les utilités immédiates au point de vue du salut de l'Empire Turc, d'attirer la sympathie du Sultan sur la nation britannique et de l'amener à préférér dans les concessions à accorder le capital anglais au français, à l'allemand et à je ne sais quel autre; ce qui pourrait assurer nos intérets respectifs. Mais ce résultat ne peut être réalisé que par un long séjour en Europe et surtout en Angleterre.
>
> . . . Je viens donc vous proposer pour me faciliter d'organiser cette compagne à l'intérêt du gouvernement Britannique, campagne dans laquelle la pleine victoire sera la prédominance absolue des droits commerciaux et industriels anglais sur ceux des autres nationalités en Turquie de me faire prêter ce qui veut dire de vouloir bien conclure un emprunt de 12 000 livres Sterling à mon propre nom.[19]

The German press's concern with Damad Mahmud Pasha's flight was understandable in light of this information.[20] The sultan, in order to prevent him from revitalizing the Young Turk movement and translating it into a movement of the pro-British wing of the Ottoman bureaucracy, instructed Ottoman diplomats to scrutinize the affairs of his brother-in-law.[21] Later the palace tempted Damad Mahmud Pasha for return with an offer of £t 50,000 and shares in the concession that he had been trying to acquire for a British company.[22] Later in England, Anthopulos Pasha made him a new offer,[23] and finally Turhan Pasha added another inducement in order to persuade him to return.[24]

As pointed up in a French intelligence report, the main reason for the unease at the Yıldız Palace was that

> En attendant il y a parmi les jeunes turcs à Constantinople une activité significative. La police a beau en arrêter un assez grand nombre, les softas deviennent de·plus en plus remuants et se croient assez forts pour présenter une pétition au Sultan en faveur des réformes. Leur chef est un Mollah (prêtre) du nom d'Abdullah et il sont bien déterminés à donner à leur mouvement un caractère religieux. Ils s'adressent à Abdul-Hamid plus comme Calife que comme Sul-

tan. Ce nouveau développement de la cause de la Jeune Turquie impressione beaucoup les musulmans.[25]

The flight of Pasha raised Young Turks' expectations. Messages analyzing the flight and its value to the movement urged the CUP center to do everything possible to prevent Damad Mahmud Pasha's return.[26] Many other fierce letters were published in *Osmanlı*.[27] Some opposition newspapers called on Damad Mahmud Pasha to unite all the opponents of the regime, which Ahmed Rıza and other leaders had failed to do.[28] Others beseeched him to breathe new life into the movement.[29] Later many opponents confessed that the deciding event which impelled them to join the Young Turk movement was Damad Mahmud Pasha's flight.[30]

Since Damad Mahmud Pasha did not have a carefully outlined agenda, he was unable to determine his next action. Ottoman diplomats were under the impression that he planned to publish a new opposition journal in Turkish, Arabic, and Persian.[31] Instead, he sent a letter to *Mechveret Supplément Français* and invited Ahmed Rıza and his group to common action, thereby establishing his first overt tie with the CUP.[32] This sent tremors through government circles, as Damad Mahmud Pasha's flight gave birth to its frightening consequence for the Ottoman government.[33]

Damad Mahmud Pasha decided to take a second step, which would be more terrifying to the sultan. His sons went to London to procure British support. Anthopulos Pasha was issued a directive requiring him to demand the British to withhold any endorsement of the fugitive and his sons.[34] But on December 20, the Foreign Office had already been informed by Sir Nicholas that "apart from his position as the brother-in-law of the Sultan he [Damad Mahmud Pasha] is not a man of any weight of influence although he was Minister of Justice [sic!] some twenty years ago."[35] Damad Mahmud Pasha's sons were given a cold reception in Britain. Sabahaddin and Lûtfullah Beys attempted to contact Lord Salisbury in order to meet with him, and when their letter was presented to him with a note by a secretary at the Foreign Office, reading, "they were anxious to see your Lordship and they are 'faisaient la politique Anglaise,' " the British prime minister responded "They should be introduced by their ambassador who certainly would not do such a thing. Regret absence."[36] Four days later, they tried again with a new letter in which they wrote:

> Toutefois une raison plus forte encore nous permettait d'espérer une réponse favorable de votre part Monsieur le Ministre, c'est, et certainement vous ne l'ignorez pas, la préférence très marquée avec laquelle notre cher père S. A. Damad Mahmoud Pasha, a tojours soutenu comme Ministre et comme homme privé la politique anglaise en Turquie. . . . Anglais et Turcs peuvent attendre d'une entente cordiale et il y avait peut être quelque courage à soutenir à haute voix cette thèse . . . notre père et nous n'avons pas voulu tenir compte de cet état d'esprit, nous avions compris paraît-il mieux que tout autre nôtre rôle de patriotes ottomans et nous avons continuellement défendu nos principes anglophiles. . . . Les peuples d'Occident et l'Angleterre particulièrement auront fait justice eux-mêmes.[37]

But again they received an icy reception.

This time the sultan launched a diplomatic counterattack on the three imperial fugitives. He requested the direct help of the kaiser[38] and secured the aid of German diplomats.[39] Later he bargained with the French, offering them unrestricted circulation of French journals that had been banned by the Ottoman government.[40] Following this, British and French post offices were required to prevent Damad Mahmud Pasha from sending letters to his family and friends through the director of l'Agence Nationale.[41] However, the two powers rejected this.

In response Damad Mahmud Pasha sent a second letter to Ahmed Rıza's organ and while discussing his great designs for solving the Empire's problems, he implied that he would not return and had decided to participate in the opposition movement.[42] At that point the sultan offered him all the shares in the concession through Bernard Maimon, an intermediary for British economic interests in the Ottoman Empire.[43] But Damad Mahmud Pasha rejected this impressive new offer too.[44]

Damad Mahmud Pasha and the Geneva Center

Up to this point the Geneva center, struggling with its own collapse, had witnessed these developments from the sidelines while warding off a new diplomatic campaign by Karatodori Pasha, the Ottoman ambassador in Brussels, who was supported by German diplomats.[45] However, after Damad Mahmud Pasha's inviting signals, they contacted him and his sons. In February 1900 Damad Mahmud Pasha agreed to write for *Osmanlı*, and this reestablished it as an important organ in the eyes of both the members in the country[46] and the foreign diplomats.[47] Damad Mahmud Pasha journeyed to Geneva in late March,[48] where Sabahaddin Bey declared that "there are people with courage, but it is not possible to form a serious party for action unless they gather under the leadership of a single person."[49] This was also a response to articles published in the European press about the economic reasons of their flight.[50]

The coverage by the Swiss press, which included discussions about Damad Mahmud Pasha's leadership in the Young Turk movement, provoked the anxiety in the Ottoman government.[51] The information proved true, and a new center was formed in Geneva under the leadership of Damad Mahmud Pasha. It consisted of his sons; Hüseyin Siyret, one of the expatriated heroes of the pro-British demonstration[52], Muhammad 'Alī Halīm Pasha, who tried to organize a congress for Ottoman opposition; and Ali Haydar Midhat.[53]

Damad Mahmud Pasha was considered the conductor for this body, but the former leaders of the Geneva center objected to the idea of leaving the CUP and the movement to the fugitive brother-in-law.[54] In their eyes Damad Mahmud Pasha was an important source of funds and prestige.[55] The original founder had a very low opinion of him. He wrote: "Mahmud Pasha's plan is not to unite with us and do something. He will knock on all doors in order to reach a personal goal, and finally will return to his prison in the form of a palace without serving our aim even as much as Murad Bey, or he will squander the treasury of the nation at the luxurious hotels of Europe."[56]

Under the circumstances, İshak Sükûti decided to appoint Edhem Ruhi, who had recently fled from Tripoli of Barbary,[57] a man who was liked by everyone because of his industriousness,[58] as the new director of the central committee in Geneva, and Nuri Ahmed as the editor of *Osmanlı*. Edhem Ruhi's appointment was comparable to the assignment of Alfred Rosenberg to the leadership of the Nazi party. Edhem Ruhi's simple ideas represented those of the average Young Turk,[59] but he could not pose a threat to the leadership of İshak Sükûti and was ready to abdicate to the real leader when asked. In this way the real control remained in the hands of İshak Sükûti. He also instructed his remaining friends in Geneva to maintain contacts with Damad Mahmud Pasha and secure his financial support.

During his stay in Geneva Damad Mahmud Pasha met with Nuri Ahmed and told him that he wanted to publish *Osmanlı* with the help of friends, yet he asked Nuri Ahmed to continue his work as the editor, which he accepted.[60]

An example of the coexistence of two distinct committees was the separate denunciation of Karatodori Pasha by the leaders of both groups. Damad Mahmud Pasha sent a letter to the Swiss press on behalf of Ottoman liberals in Geneva concerning the event,[61] and later Nuri Ahmed dispatched a second one on behalf of the CUP center in Geneva.[62]

On April 1, 1900, *Osmanlı* announced that it would publish the literary works of Damad Mahmud Pasha.[63] This project, however, went far beyond the publication of literary works—*Osmanlı* came under the control of the fugitive brother-in-law, his sons, and friends.[64] Diplomats asserted that the journal had been bought by Damad Mahmud Pasha,[65] and some members of the CUP in the Empire believed that he had become the editor of the journal.[66] The remaining members of the old committee in Geneva became a group of protégés under the dominance of Damad Mahmud Pasha's circle. They had the seal of the CUP and legal possession of the central organ, but the financial power of the other group made it dominant.

The most important change in *Osmanlı* was a new series of more decidedly pro-British articles, which were also more critical of Germany.[67]

The Rise of the Pro-British Group under Damad Mahmud Pasha and the CUP Center in England

In mid-1900, the Young Turk movement—except for the Paris branch under the control of Ahmed Rıza—had become a crusade led by the pro-British group. The Ottoman government began to arrest those who had taken part in the pro-British demonstration, along with well-known pro-

British bureaucrats.[68] Following these arrests, İsmail Kemal was appointed governor of Tripoli. This was the most that the sultan could do against the leader of the pro-British group, who was under the protection of the British embassy. In 1895 the sultan had tried to send him to Tripoli; however, the objections of the French, who did not want an Anglophile governor next to Tunis, made the appointment impossible.[69]

İsmail Kemal applied to the British, telling them that his life was in danger. The British ambassador requested the opinion of the Foreign Office on this critical matter.[70] With the intervention of Sir Nicholas, the matter seemed resolved. On April 25, the ambassador wrote to the Foreign Office that İsmail Kemal would go to Tripoli.[71] However, the next day İsmail Kemal took refuge on the *stationnaire* (i.e., ship docked at Istanbul harbor) of the British embassy.[72] The sultan told Adam Block through a place officer that

> "If Ismail [Kemal] desired to leave the country he was free to do so . . . if that was his object he could have gone like anyone else by train or by steamer or by caïque or by horse; there was never any necessity for concealment. . . . He could walk down the quay 'swinging his arms' in all liberty and do just as he pleased. If he liked to remain he could do so, if he preferred to go to Tripoli the post was still open to him; if he did not want it he need not to take it.[73]

İsmail Kemal, however, asked for more British protection and expressed his desire to leave the Empire in letters he wrote on board *HMS Salamander*.[74] The British ambassador remained unconvinced by İsmail Kemal's report of a threat against his life, and informed the sultan about the developments.[75] On May 1, İsmail Kemal was transferred to an Egyptian ship without intervention by Ottoman authorities and left the Empire.[76]

This flight was another great venture of the pro-British statesmen, who were trying to dominate the movement. For the first time British support had been clearly witnessed and was underscored in independent dispatches sent by Damad Mahmud Pasha and the CUP central committee in Geneva to Sir Nicholas.[77] German diplomatic reports focused on the significance of this overt endorsement and the fact that İsmail Kemal had once worked under Midhat Pasha.[78] The information from Sir Thomas exposing his pro-British sentiments substantiated this approach.[79] In the eyes of many diplomats, the Young Turk movement under the control of Damad Mahmud Pasha was the struggle of the pro-British group of bureaucrats led by İsmail Kemal and their alleged ally Gazi Ahmed Muhtar Pasha, a most prestigious military figure.[80] İsmail Kemal's domination over the Albanian movement darkened this gloomy picture for the sultan. However, the British received information that İsmail Kemal's flight had nothing to do with the effervescence in Albania.[81]

Both the dominance by the pro-British faction and the practical problems in Geneva, the foremost of which was the sultan's purchase of the publishing house printing *Osmanlı*,[82] prompted the decision of the central committee and Damad Mahmud Pasha's group to transfer the CUP head-quarters to England, thereby announcing that an ideological change had occurred which embodied a pro-British stance.[83]

The *Osmanlı*'s sixty-second issue was published in London, and the two groups continued to work together in England. However, as the activities of the pro-British group gained momentum, the title of the CUP was almost forgotten.

With the participation of İsmail Kemal, extolled in the British press[84] and praised by British diplomats in Istanbul,[85] the pro-British group launched a diplomatic campaign against the regime of Abdülhamid II.

The first act was an open letter by Sabahaddin and Lûtfullah Beys, written while the headquarters were still in Geneva. After criticizing the internal and financial policies of the sultan, it focused on the importance of good relations with Britain, although it omitted the name of the country:

> Au lieu de suivre un système politique honorable et solide qui soit de nature à attirer le respect et la confiance des Puissances avec lesquelles nous sommes en rapport, vous avez travaillé à établir une politique à votre détestable usage personnel; aux actions des gouvernements européens vous avez opposé ruses médiocres, qui avec le respect dû au Souverain, ont fait perdre le respect dû au pays et ont discrédité l'honneur national de la Turquie. Vouz avez détourné l'amitié d'une grande puissance alliée naturelle de la Turquie, qui n'avait pas manqué de nous soutenir en chaque occasion jusqu'au jour de votre avènement.[86]

A copy of this was sent to Sir Nicholas to elicit his support.[87] Following this, Damad Mahmud Pasha and his sons again requested Lord Salisbury's audience through J. Charlier. The former's secretary appended a note of refusal on the ground that "[Damad Mahmud Pasha] is a political exile."[88] Ten days later Damad Mahmud Pasha himself penned a letter to Lord Salisbury saying "sur l'instance de l'ambassadeur d'un despote, ignorant, incapable de souveraineté et de Khalifat, d'une ennemi implacable des Anglais, vous avez répondu par un refus à une lettre de recommandation que j'avais présentée avec la prière d'être admis dans une interview avec Votre Excellence." He commented further: "je ne juge pas non plus digne du caractère éminemment civilisateur et humain du gouvernement anglais."[89] Once again he was rejected. Later he published a note protesting against a decision concerning the rights of fugitives and inquired of the Great Powers, "eux aussi, avaient démontré à Abdul Hamid l'urgence de l'application des réformes dans son pays; ils avaient même envoyé leur flotte jusqu'à Béchiké pour le menacer."[90] Neither this prointerventionist policy nor the direct application of the fugitive brother-in-law and his sons to the queen, complaining because their correspondence with Seniha Sultan, the wife of Damad Mahmud Pasha, was being intercepted by the sultan, gave them an avenue by which to secure British support.[91] The sultan expressed satisfaction to the British that a cold reception had been given to Damad Mahmud Pasha.[92] Abdülhamid II also tried to impress and appease the British after the flight of İsmail Kemal by exhibiting friendly feelings toward England, such as an unusual observation of the queen's birthday.[93]

Similar rejection was given to other prominent members of this group who tried to secure British assistance. Ali Haydar Midhat's letters to Lord Salisbury[94] and to Sir Nicholas[95] evoked neither a positive response nor a meeting with high-ranking British statesmen. When he sent an old letter from his late father, Ahmed Midhat Pasha, and asked a former secretary to Lord Salisbury to submit it to him, Lord Salisbury refused the letter.[96]

Even İsmail Kemal, who had been described by the palace as "the tool of conspiracy of the British"[97] and was highly esteemed by British diplomats in Istanbul, could do little to advance the situation. The sultan had been shaken by stories fabricated by the Young Turks concerning İsmail Kemal's accusations of the Ottoman government during an audience with the queen.[98] However, Anthopulos Pasha denied them.[99] Besides, İsmail Kemal's later application for British citizenship or "British protection" was rejected.[100] His extreme pro-British opinions, expressed in British journals[101] and published as pamphlets,[102] were insufficient in securing direct British support between 1900 and 1901.

Osmanlı also expressed an extravagantly pro-British and anti-German position in England,[103] which was noted in the foreign press.[104] Members of the group surrounding Damad Mahmud Pasha published similar articles in popular journals[105]; however, even this made no serious impact on the British.

Following the failure to secure British support, through pro-British publications and personal contacts, Damad Mahmud Pasha and his friends decided to gain recognition by pursuing two policies.

The initial step undertaken, over the objections of İshak Sükûti, was the adoption of a pronounced Islamic rhetoric in *Osmanlı*[106] in order to gain the support of the ulema. Excellent examples of this new style were drafted by Damad Mahmud Pasha himself.[107] The journal began to be distributed to the pilgrims in Hedjaz,[108] and a new Young Turk faction began to assemble in the capital under the leadership of Abdullah Efendi, a member of ulema.[109] Also *talebe-i ulûm* began once again to lead the opposition movements in Istanbul,[110] and pamphlets with the seal "Union of Muslims" were distributed throughout the capital.[111]

The second strategy was an appeal to the Armenians for common action. Since Damad Mahmud Pasha knew that British intervention hinged upon the participation of the Christian groups in the Empire, he cultivated relations with the Armenian leaders as soon as he reached Europe.[112] Later Armenian journals offered "moral support" to the new group dominating the Young Turk movement.[113] Meanwhile, the Dashnaktsutiun branch in Boston initiated an alliance between the CUP and their organization.[114] At the same time a certain Martos Ferciyan provided the central committee with an article he had written containing the same offer.[115] Although, in September 1900, the palace received news of a rapprochement between Young Turks and Armenian revolutionaries,[116] Armenian spies for the Ottoman government in London denied this claim.[117] Finally, in the fall of 1900 Damad Mahmud Pasha published an open letter to the Armenians inviting them to common action.[118] A favorable answer published in *Droshak* read "Dashnaktsutiun would not accept the re-establishment of the Constitution of Midhat as a solution of the Turkish problem, but look to a democratic federative policy as the way out." It further stated that Dashnaktsutiun "would fortify the Young Turks if first it received a guarantee that the situation of the peoples would be bettered."[119] In this way Damad Mahmud Pasha achieved an understanding with the Armenians, which no other Young Turk leader had ever done. An additional attempt was made to secure the support of an Armenian society called Murad Committee in Manchester, which was, strangely enough, publishing *fatwās*.[120] However, since the leaders of the organization were more interested in blackmailing the palace than in forming an alliance with the Young Turks, they declined the offer and were later bought off by the palace.[121]

Almost simultaneous with this success, Damad Mahmud Pasha petitioned the khedive for permission to continue his efforts in Cairo.[122] The khedive guaranteed his protection and financial support,[123] and with the intention of carrying out activities in a British-ruled and predominantly Muslim country, Damad Mahmud Pasha went to Egypt.

Despite the Young Turks' great expectations,[124] the sultan's persistent efforts rendered it impossible for Damad Mahmud Pasha to complete any activity there. While he was on his way to Egypt, the sultan had asked the khedive to warn him in advance if Damad Mahmud Pasha's landing at an Egyptian fort would be denied.[125] The cabinet advised the khedive that "it would be impossible to prevent Mahmoud Pasha from landing in Egypt or to send him to Constantinople without a previous sentence having been passed to that effect in the Egyptian courts."[126] The British ambassador Rodd requested authorization from the Foreign Office "to convey to [Damad Mahmud Pasha], if necessary, a message to the effect that it is undesirable that he should remain in Egypt, and that he would do well to return as quickly as possible to Europe."[127] Two days later the sultan sent a new message to the khedive revealing that "the British government had given no encouragement to Mahmoud when in London" and he "must either return to Europe or be sent back to Constantinople. . . . Egypt must never be considered as a place of refuge for disloyal subjects of the Ottoman Empire."[128] Under such circumstances Damad Mahmud Pasha told the British ambassador that he desired to return to Istanbul with his two sons and his retinue, "on the condition that he is fully pardoned and allowed to remain in possession of his property," and he inquired "whether the British Ambassador could be allowed to approach His Imperial Majesty on the subject."[129] Lord Salisbury, however, found it undesirable for the British to act as intermediaries.[130]

Under the sultan's persistent personal demands,[131] Lord Cromer "prohibited the Egyptian press from opening their columns to this [all kind of calumnies and falsehoods against the sultan] under the threat of suspension."[132]

Damad Mahmud Pasha became a prisoner in Egypt instead of a conductor of activities against the sultan.[133] In April 1901, after lengthy negotiations, the khedive persuaded Damad Mahmud Pasha to return to the Empire.[134] His sons requested the protection of Lord Cromer, who told them that "as they are both of age, they are free to go wherever they please and that no force should be used whilst they remained in Egypt."[135] Later his sons persuaded Damad Mahmud Pasha to reconsider, and they returned to Paris.[136] However, the cutting off of the khedive's stipend[137] and his declining prestige due to negotiations with the palace, transformed Damad Mahmud Pasha into a burden on the Young Turk movement. A Young Turk leader wrote, "there is no hope for him, but I do not abandon hope for his sons."[138]

Witnessing the decline of Damad Mahmud Pasha's prestige, İshak Sükûti wanted, even as early as August 1900, to make İsmail Kemal the leader of the CUP. İshak Sükûti described İsmail Kemal in a letter as "a person who is extraordinarily efficient in business and a serious statesman."[139] Although İsmail Kemal had visited the committee while in England,[140] he expended his best efforts on the Albanian instead of the Young Turk movement.[141] His flight had raised expectations among the Albanian nationalists.[142] He met with Faïk Bey Konitza and Albanian leaders for a common program; however, soon after he began to pursue his own agenda. He went to Egypt and attracted the interest of both Albanians and Young Turks and was warned by the Ottoman high commissioner to shun involvement in the Albanian separatist movement.[143] He had established ties with the Albanian separatist committee in Rome[144] and discussed the future of Albania with Greek statesmen,[145] even delivering speeches for "the independence of European Turkey."[146] The palace reciprocated to the Muslim Albanian leaders, who penned an open letter condemning his activities.[147] Later he was sentenced to death in absentia by an Ottoman court and his property was confiscated.[148]

Ali Haydar Midhat, the other leader of the pro-British group, had worked with the central committee in England during the period. Although the official editor described his articles as "utterly absurd,"[149] they were published because he had made regular donations to the central committee.[150]

The CUP pursued two often divergent agendas during this period. The first was activities outlined by the leaders of the pro-British group of statesmen, especially Damad Mahmud Pasha and İsmail Kemal. The second was a series of designs formulated by the remaining members of the old committee.

Activities under the instructions of the pro-British statesmen were designed to impress the Great Powers, especially Great Britain, and to solicit their intervention in Ottoman domestic policies; efforts were also made to inflame Muslim sentiment against the sultan and thereby to create a crisis that would be an occasion for foreign intervention.

Toward the first goal, the CUP published a note of protest on the twenty-fifth anniversary of Abdülhamid II's accession to the throne: "This blood-thirsty tyrant's countless victims caused the whole civilized world to weep. But unfortunately the Great Powers did nothing but give him some friendly advice. . . . The civilized governments bear an enormous responsibility because of the tolerance they have shown for the crimes of the Red Sultan."[151]

The two sons of Damad Mahmud Pasha sent similar appeals directly to European statesmen, calumniating the regime of Abdülhamid II and asking for foreign intervention:

> Si le Sultan Abdul Hamid a suscité l'indignation la plus légitime par les grands massacres d'Ottomans-Arméniens en 1895–1896, il ne mérite pas moins la réprobation universelle pour ces disparitions et ces meurtres de[s] sujets (chrétiens ou musulmans), qui, sur diverses parties de l'empire, ont lieu presque quotidiennement, sans que tant de souffrances, de ruines, de larmes et de deuils aient seulement un écho d'indignation d'humanité, près de toutes les âmes honnêtes de l'Europe, à qui, sans doute, ces horreurs ne restent pas cachées. . . .
>
> Ce dernier incident si regrettable cet oubli, ce mépris d'une parole donnée par le Sultan Abdulhamid II au représentant d'une grande puissance comme la France, peut faire comprendre au monde comment notre peuple, si patient, si 'loyaliste,' si respectueux de la Dynastie régnante, a pu être amené, peu à peu, à désirer avec nous, un régime plus humain, plus honnête et plus digne, à le vouloir, à l'éxiger d'une manière de plus pressante et impérieuse.[152]

The most significant attempt, however, was made at the behest of Damad Mahmud Pasha: The acquisition of a *fatwā* given by Sheikh Muḥammad b. Yūsuf al-Marrākushī, who was also known as Badr al-Dīn al-Ḥasanī,[153] declaring that Abdülhamid II was unfit for the caliphate.[154] This was a final attempt in this arena, after many articles had appeared to the same end in the central organ.[155]

Copies of the *fatwā* were sent to the British queen and the British ambassador in Istanbul with an explanatory note from the CUP.[156] British statesmen paid little attention to the *fatwā*, contrary to the expectations of the pro-British group.[157] The central committee also succeeded in delivering sermons in the name of the heir apparent as the caliph and the new sultan—only outside the country. Thousands of copies of the *fatwā* were smuggled into the Empire by the CUP branch in Athens under the eye of its director, Yaşar Bey.[158] An Arabic version was sent to the Arab provinces.[159] In Greece and other neighboring countries, this event caused tremendous excitement and was viewed as the start of a revolution.[160] It also stimulated discussions among the Young Turks in Europe and in the Empire. A CUP member in Crete wrote to Ahmed Rıza that "if we had not trusted the journal *Osmanlı*, we would have assumed that a foreign hand had intervened. As it is known, the British were consulting on this matter with the Sharif [of Mecca] for a long time."[161] Contrary to these discussions and the impact abroad, the *fatwā* produced no significant consequence except the arrest of CUP members in the Empire.[162]

A month later a new *fatwā* was allegedly secured from the ulema of al-Azhar. The CUP claimed that it was acquired against the sultan. The *fatwā* was a response to a question about

> what should the Muslims do if the commander of the faithful Zayd will not abandon his absolutist style of administration, even after being warned by his subjects and, if on the contrary, he violated the peace and security of all the subjects by amassing a power for the aggrandizement of his administration. What then ought to be done against the *āmīr* Zayd and his accomplices by the subjects?

The response was that "the subjects had to arm and assassinate the tyrannical [administrative] body according to a *ḥadīth*."[163]

A second undertaking under the instructions of Damad Mahmud Pasha and İsmail Kemal involved revolutionary activities in Albania. As early as May 1900 the *Drita* organization, working for Albanian autonomy, applied to Damad Mahmud Pasha to secure his help for common action.[164] Around the same time local Albanians established a CUP branch in Scutari.[165]

In the summer of 1901, with the initiatives of İsmail Kemal, a joint Albanian-CUP movement started up in southern Albania.[166] The two CUP members, while continuing to serve on the Albanian committee in Corfu, moved to Dulcigno in Montenegro and founded a center for propaganda and revolutionary activities.[167] Later Damad Mahmud Pasha participated in the activities. His conduct, as well as frequent passages by Albanians who voyaged across the narrow strait between Albania and Corfu, heightened the sense of dread within the Ottoman government.[168] Rumors of a joint Albanian-Greek-CUP activity spread.[169] Most striking is the support of Damad Mahmud Pasha and his comrades to the Albanian Revolutionary Committee, which "had lately come to terms with the Epirote Revolutionary Society." A British diplomat underscored this event by writing that "these two bodies, if not actually fused into one, are now working together with the object of putting an end to Turkish rule in Albania."[170]

These activities created tension between the Ottoman and Greek governments,[171] and the Ottoman side, as a diplomatic device, withheld its signature from the treaty of commerce which had been drawn up.[172] Although the Greeks did not comply with the Ottoman demand to extradite Damad Mahmud Pasha on grounds that he was carrying out "anarchist activities,"[173] they asked him to leave the country of his own will and with a payment of Fr 5000.[174]

A final point regarding activities of the pro-British group using the title CUP was that they attracted some high-ranking bureaucrats who developed an interest in the CUP: Ali Nuri (Gustaf Noring) who published a satirical journal in which he praised Damad Mahmud Pasha,[175] Alfred Rüstem, another diplomat, who was so aptly described by a French diplomat who said "jusqu'il en soit la cause qu'il a embrassée n'a rien à gagner à être défendre par un tel avocat,"[176] and İzzet Pasha, the Ottoman ambassador in Madrid.[177] However, their activities had no significance other than becoming an irritation to the sultan.

With regard to the activities of the CUP itself, in September 1900 its headquarters were transferred from London to Folkestone, which conserved funds for other expenses.[178] Members tried to solve the financial problems of the center by obtaining regular donations from Muḥammad 'Alī Ḥalīm Pasha and Muḥammad Ibrāhīm Bey of Egypt.[179] These donations, however, did not cover all their expenses. Damad Mahmud Pasha could not fulfill his promise of donating £t 25 of his £t 800 stipend paid to him by the khedive.[180] The financial records of the CUP, held by Halil Muvaffak, state that Damad Mahmud Pasha donated only £ 20 out of £ 158.10, the entire income of the CUP for four months.[181] Further, the Ottoman government's termination of payoffs to CUP members appointed to posts in Europe, based on the claim that they helped the Young Turk cause, worsened the situation.[182]

In order to solve the financial problems, the central committee, under the instructions of İshak Sükûti, struck a bargain with Memduh Pasha, the Ottoman minister of the interior, and extorted a small sum from him, which later funded CUP propaganda.[183] At the same time, unsold issues of the translation of Vittorio Alfieri's work *Della Tirannide* under the title *İstibdad* were sold to the Ottoman government.[184] The Ottoman ambassador in Paris obtained information about a new scheme for extorting money by threatening the government with the publication of a new journal.[185] After its failure, the central committee decided to publish a satirical journal for blackmailing purposes.[186] The journal, named *Dolab (Merry-Go-Round)*, received attention, and many people subscribed to it.[187] However, since the real purpose of its publication was to extort money for the committee, Abdullah Cevdet and Edhem Ruhi negotiated with Ottoman agents and diplomats and in due course sold it to the government.[188] Although it was announced that the journal was not an official organ,[189] this development greatly diminished the prestige of the central committee in the eyes of the members.[190]

With money thus derived, the CUP prepared two leaflets. One was a short appeal to the Ottoman people claiming that "the struggle for salvation [was] ahead" and "everyone should be ready to carry out his duty."[191] This was nothing more than moral support to members in the country using the CUP name, which had not be seen for a while.

The second appeal was sent to CUP members at the Royal Medical Academy, and was distributed only among college students.[192]

As regards the CUP branches, the situation was not heartwarming. The Paris branch had become an independent body. After the move of the headquarters to London, those who remained in Geneva established activist organizations, and only the Berlin branch sent donations collected from Ottoman students.[193]

Another problem of the central committee was the poor quality of articles in the central organ. All but those penned by Damad Mahmud Pasha and Sabahaddin Bey were written by young CUP members.[194] It would be hard to say that these articles expressed a comprehensive viewpoint; most of them did little more than condemn the regime of Abdülhamid II. Under the direction of Damad Mahmud Pasha, some fabricated stories based loosely on articles previously published in the Turkic journals in Russia, such as *Tercüman (Interpreter)*, appeared in *Osmanlı*. Typically the CUP author would falsely claim that a certain sheikh had sent an important letter to the committee, telling the details in a scribbled story.[195]

A final ordeal facing the CUP leaders during their stay in England was pressure by the Ottoman ambassador on the Foreign Office to procure the publications of the organization. Legal advisers to the Ottoman embassy employed a famous detective bureau, Fullex, which supplied them with daily reports of the activities of Damad Mahmud Pasha, his sons, and other CUP members.[196] These legal advisers urged the Ottoman ambassador to investigate both *Osmanlı* and *Dolab*, hoping to uncover a basis for blackmail, since neither periodical had been registered. The Foreign Office discussed the matter with the Home Office.[197] In December 1900 Anthopulos Pasha cited his accusation, at which point the British police visited the printing plant and the CUP headquarters and warned the editor of the central organ, who promised to obey the law in future issues.[198] However, Anthopulos Pasha claimed new irregularities, and Ottoman authorities sought the help of the British chargé d'affaires in Istanbul.[199]

After securing only a warning from the British authorities, Anthopulos Pasha reapplied to the Foreign Office regarding a telegram of condolence and its response. The CUP had sent its condolences to Edward VII after the death of Queen Victoria and published the response, signed "Edward."[200]

The Ottoman ambassador stated that the telegram was forged, since the king was not supposed to write back to the CUP.[201] The Home Office determined that the telegram was genuine, and although not endorsed by the king, it had in fact been signed by a secretary named Edward.[202] The Ottoman ambassador also complained that CUP organs were sent regularly to the British Museum.[203] Although it was the British authorities' policy to support the Ottoman ambassador, they confessed to him that "without evidence of criminal acts or intentions on their part it will be impossible to interfere with their liberty of action or appeal to the public press."[204]

The official activities of the CUP during this period were less significant than those under the orders of Damad Mahmud Pasha, İsmail Kemal, and their friends.

The Paris Branch of the CUP

After the flight of Damad Mahmud Pasha, everyone paid close attention to his doings and those of his friends. Although he often wrote to Ahmed Rıza requesting common action, Damad Mahmud Pasha's objective—changing the regime with the assistance of the Great Powers—was unacceptable to the positivist leader,[205] whose sharp criticisms of the old center in Geneva for their goal of foreign intervention were a veiled calumniation of Damad Mahmud Pasha's ideas.[206]

Although Ahmed Rıza's publications were limited to *Mechveret Supplément Français*, his strong anti-interventionist policy and his steadfast refusal to so much as speak with the sultan's agents fueled his dramatic rise in the movement. His comrade, Doctor Nâzım, made this apt comparison between the Geneva and Paris centers:

> Look, my dear Sükûti, let's make a comparison between the conditions under which you and [Ahmed] Rıza were operating two years ago and your present situations. Financial strength was on your side—a large sum of around eighteen or twenty thousand [French] francs, a nice printing plant. [Ahmed] Rıza had not even eighteen centimes. As to courage (morale): [Ahmed] Rıza was known as an atheist within the country, and abroad as a person who thinks only of his self-interest, an obstacle to the union, and a despot. As opposed to this, the Turkish publication that could secure correspondence with the members within the fatherland and the seal [of the CUP] were in your hands. In addition to this, as opposed to the two friends of [Ahmed] Rıza, most of the people with ability of working for the committee were your friends.
>
> Present situation: As regards financial strength: You are unable to sleep because of the need to secure [money], in order to revive the committee for a couple of more months. [Ahmed] Rıza is receiving more than enough money in a month to cover expenses to publish for one year. As regards morale, my respect for you prevents me from delving into the details of this matter.[207]

In fact, Ahmed Rıza drew financial support from Ottoman statesmen such as Şerif Bey, who was secretly supporting Young Turk activities.[208] His greatest problem, however, was his lack of an organ in Turkish, but this was solved in an unexpected way.

Ahmed Saib, one of the aides-de-camp of Gazi Ahmed Muhtar Pasha, decided to join the opposition and published a journal called *Sancak (Standard)*.[209] He criticized the blackmailing activities of the CUP center in Geneva and declared his journal independent from CUP organs.[210]

In mid-1900 Ahmed Saib and Ahmed Rıza agreed to act together.[211] The first evidence of their association was the publication of a sequence of open letters by Ahmed Rıza to the sultan,[212] followed by articles in *Sancak* strongly denouncing the CUP center:

> The Ottoman Committee of Union and Progress was founded upon the aspiration of serving the fatherland and operated for some time in loyal dedication

to this sacred cause, but has lately been usurped and overrun by evil people who have their own interests at heart. The committee has become prey to the conspiratorial aims of those scoundrels.[213]

The journal and the positivist leader criticized the CUP center and declared that the only real Young Turk group was theirs.[214] *Sancak* wrote:

> Today genuine liberals [Young Turks] are rare. . . . However all of them are fellows who have sacrificed their lives and happiness to the profession of liberalism. None of them behaves as a liberal one day and then converts to a praying subject [of the sultan] with a proper salary on another.[215]

This unlooked-for assault distressed CUP members, who concluded that Ahmed Rıza was pulling the strings from behind the scene.[216] They requested that Ahmed Saib deny the accusations.[217] Upon his refusal, the central organ brought out a statement to the effect that only the CUP represented the Young Turk movement and that *Osmanlı* was its only official organ.[218] Later a pamphlet was published accusing Ahmed Saib of developing a separatist activity within the movement and of appointing Ali Kemal, who blackmailed the palace in 1897, as the Paris correspondent for his journal.[219]

In response, in November 1900, *Sancak* began to use the title *Journal Promoting Young Turk Ideas*,[220] and its editor enjoined Ahmed Rıza to form a new organization to replace the CUP:

> One of the most important matters is the issue of the committee. . . . This is a matter of life and death. I do not know your thoughts on this subject, but I have solved the problem for myself. . . . I do not recognize the Committee of Union and Progress. The only thing that I acknowledge is the courage and grace you have shown during the times of interregnum. If you accept, I will regard you as a leader. I am ready to obey [your orders] to the degree a trained soldier obeys [the commands of] his officer. . . .
>
> So what needs to be done?
>
> What is to be done is obvious to me. A party [committee] should be formed. To begin with a center should be established. . . . This center can be formed nowhere but around yourself. . . .
>
> Now let's speak about the obstacles standing before the founding of such a committee! . . . I hope you don't construe the company and *Osmanlı* to be the party of the Committee [of Union and Progress]. Because in the present state of affairs these two are dead. Their vivification is impossible. In reference to the other aspect, please at least form the fictitious committee which you mentioned in your last letter. I am sure that in a short period of time an authentic organization will be born out of that committee.[221]

Ahmed Saib and Ahmed Rıza also distributed similar propaganda among Ottoman opposition circles, accusing the CUP center of blackmail.[222] They later invited some CUP members to join in the creation of a new committee, declaring that "its leaders would be Ahmed Rıza and Ahmed Saib."[223] Ahmed Rıza also obtained financial support from the khedive for the new committee's publication expenses.[224] However, most of those whose participation was essential declined the invitation.[225]

Ideologically, the most important aspect of this initiative was an anti-interventionist policy. Both Ahmed Rıza and Ahmed Saib denounced İsmail Kemal's requests for foreign intervention.[226] They viewed him as being subservient to the interests of imperialistic western powers.[227]

The Young Turks dwelling in Paris while supporting the CUP center in Geneva and then in England could not organize significant activities. Their appeals sparked a diplomatic crisis between France and the Ottoman Empire and could not be sent to the Empire because the French police intercepted them.[228] They formed a society called Tahsil Cemiyeti (Society for Education), which fronted as a cultural organization while secretly being an active political committee.[229] They contacted İshak Sükûti and provided him with details about their doings[230]; however, they were unable to effect significant activities.

The "Activists" in Geneva

During this period the activists, functioning as a faction within the CUP, assumed a more independent course and established numerous committees in Geneva, although most of them maintained membership in the CUP. Tunalı Hilmi, their long-time leader, described the conditions under which the activists, along with many other groups, found themselves compelled to remain within the fold of CUP although they found the CUP policies insupportable. Upon the weakening of the CUP center, they gained the authority to form their own organizations and to defend their own program:

> In every society political parties and opposition groups are assembled and created by people following divergent ideals and programs. Therefore each member has a center, formed according to his own idea and program. If he likes it and thinks that it merits participation, he makes it his center. . . .
> Although there are various groups among the Young Ottomans [Turks], such as revolutionary, peaceful, for the constitution, against the constitution, thus far only this particular committee [CUP] existed and every liberal [Young Turk] found an advantage in participating.[231]

Immediately prior to Damad Mahmud Pasha's flight, the activist faction of the CUP decided to form an executive committee for planning action, but with his unwillingness to take part, their decision was postponed.[232] However, when Damad Mahmud Pasha looked down on activists and refused to meet their representatives,[233] they were propelled to independent action. In response, the CUP center sent a letter to the Swiss president accusing those activists who had remained in Geneva of being agents of the Ottoman government.[234] In addition, Dr. Edmond Lardy, defender of the Young Turk cause before Swiss public opinion, began to favor Damad Mahmud Pasha and his followers over the activists.[235]

The notable Young Turks in Geneva named in a secret memorandum were Selâhaddin Bey, Naim Gergor, Babanzâde Hikmet Süleyman, Kadri Hikmet, İhsan Namık, Ali Fahri, and Âkil Muhtar.[236] We should include Burhan Bahaeddin, whose role was acknowledged in another letter,[237] and the Young Turks Âsaf Nazmi, Kemal, Şefik, Ahmed Muhtar, Hamid Hüsni, and Doctor Câzım. An Austrian report claimed that about twenty Young Turks and forty Armenians were behaving "incorrigibly" in Geneva.[238]

Besides Naim Gergor, who had links with Arab groups,[239] all others had taken part in CUP activities. Gergor appeared in Geneva with his pamphlet propagating activist views in mid-1900,[240] but we lack information about any previous participation in the movement.

The first activist journal published in this period was *İnkılâb (Revolution)*.[241] Its editor, a young activist named Ahmed Muhtar, called for "vengeance through a revolution" but made minor impact and the journal could sustain only a brief existence.[242] In mid-1900 Kemal Bey, another young activist, announced the establishment of İstikbal-i Vatan ve Millet Cemiyet-i Osmaniyesi (the Ottoman Committee for the Future of the Fatherland and Nation), which published *Vatan (Fatherland)* as its organ. Following this Şefik Bey, another activist, assumed the publication of an organ named *İstikbâl (Future)*[243]; however, neither these journals nor the committees held much attraction for the activists.

In August the more prominent activist leaders decided to organize a branch called Osmanlı İttihad ve İcraat Şubesi (Ottoman Union and Action Branch).[244] Points of interest are these: They were careful to call themselves a branch, never a committee, and they selected a name similar to that of the CUP. In September they published the journal *Darbe (Coup d'état)* as the organ of this branch and propagated an activist program:

> Intellectual slavery and moral decrepitude can be viewed as the temporary illnesses of a nation which can be healed. Although these illnesses can spread because of their contagiousness, their cure lies in the destruction of the dangerous rabble. However, the only way for their extradition and suppression is "action by the people," and this depends upon the awakening of the potential for the "desire for freedom" and the "love of vengeance" within a nation.[245]

While these events were occurring, Tunalı Hilmi, the ideologue of the activist movement, asked Ali Fahri, who played important roles in the CUP's Egyptian branch, to travel to Geneva and organize the activists there into a new committee. Ali Fahri journeyed to Geneva and after lengthy discussions İntikamcı Yeni Osmanlılar Cemiyeti (the Committee of Avenging Young Ottomans) was formed.[246] This new organization published *İntikam* (Vengeance)[247] as well as a satirical journal called *Tokmak (Mallet)*.[248]

Both *İntikam* and *Tokmak* are filled with activist and "anarchist" articles. Here are samples:

> We have drunk blood from dawn to dusk
> Twenty-five years have passed
> We want vengeance, vengeance!
> The entire world has seen nothing like this!
> The dogs will wrench his carcass![249]

> The shamelessness and effrontery of the Yıldız puppet have become unbearable. Advice, reprimand, and even sometimes cudgeling made no impression. So we considered at length and decided: Either this head moderates his stubbornness or we shall break it into pieces. We decided to [mallet] it.[250]

This new committee, which claimed to be an umbrella organization for the activists, tried to win over some members of the CUP by saying "they are for the creation of a union, however they also foster rebellion."[251] They obtained support from a small anarchist group in Istanbul that called itself Türabis.[252] The branch in Romania eventually endorsed this new committee.[253] Later the former sent the printing plant, which had published *Sada-yı Millet* in 1898, to this new organization, which had until then lithographed its central organ.[254]

With regard to the propaganda of this new committee, the activists were reassured that the best way to incite people was to implement a religious jargon,[255] a policy that was the main pillar of activist propaganda; it can be seen in their outstanding appeal distributed in the Ottoman capital in 1901[256]:

> Oh Muslim [*Muvahhid*]!
>
> Your religion and faith make every hidden thing clear to you. . . .
> Oh Muslim, stand up and come forth to save your religion and faith which are being held in the hands of the oppressors.
> Oh Muslim, save yourself!
> Oh Muslim, save your nation, they are destroying it!
> Over these despicable events, standing as a last straw, there stands a commander, a cruel commander, a bloodthirsty, crowned devil.
> Your religion and faith are in his hands.
> As if your religion and faith—there is no power or strength but in God— were taken from your sacred heart and thrown into the muck in the heart of that devil.
> Save, Muslim, save!
> Cut through to this filthy heart and salvage your religion, faith, state, country!
> God helps a person who helps Him.
> Oh Muslim: To help God means to obey Him. Obey Him!
> We hear this continually.
> We are hand in hand. Please hear this and give your hand to us!
> Oh brother! We suffer casualties of property, lives, military, country, and

nation. It is the duty of all to save those survivors and to undertake revenge
for those we have lost.
    Oh Muslim! The place of vengeance is the filthy heart of Abdülhamid.
                                    The Committee of Avenging Young Ottomans[257]

In addition to this theme, which the activist faction played upon since
its formation, The Committee of Avenging Ottomans adopted two new
and significant themes: A call for "personal anarchist activities"[258] and an
appeal to the provinces requiring them to rebel against "the gendarmerie
sergeant who snatches away [their] ox, the tax collector who steals [their]
provisions, the local governor."[259]
    Although most activists joined this new committee, problems began
to arise. A group led by Babanzâde Hikmet Süleyman splintered from the
main body and established its own committee, İstirdat Cemiyeti (Restitution Committee), publishing an organ called *İstirdat (Restitution)*.[260]
They claimed to have formed a branch in the Empire[261] and distributed
appeals in the mosques of Istanbul.[262]
    In the summer of 1901, Tunalı Hilmi wanted to reorganize and reu-
nite the activists. A meeting was held at Hôtel Métropole in Geneva, and
Tunalı Hilmi tried to coerce the activists into forming a new umbrella
organization called Bîtaraf Yeni Osmanlılar (Neutral Young Ottomans).[263]
When this failed, he cut all ties with the activists.[264]
    The CUP viewed all these activities as treacherous. In letters
exchanged among members, these organizations were described as "fictitious committees"[265] and their members as "God damn liberals."[266]
However, some activists who had remained close to the CUP center and
maintained their membership joined İshak Sükûti in the blackmail of
Münir Bey, the Ottoman ambassador;[267] however, this plan failed and the
Committee of Avenging Young Ottomans sold *Tokmak* to Haydar Bey,
the Ottoman consul in Geneva, for Fr 3000 and spent this money for
future activities.[268]
    Activists extolled Ahmed Rıza and the group surrounding him in their
journals while criticizing the CUP center.[269] We shall see how these two
groups united during the Congress of Ottoman Opposition in 1902.
    Münir Bey, meanwhile, dispatched several petitions to the Swiss
authorities. He compiled translations of articles published in the various
activist journals in a file which contained threats and derogatory phrases
against the sultan and the Ottoman government.[270] These journals were
replete with such themes and statements, and this made Münir Bey's
endeavors much easier than his previous attempts. Also, the activists' anarchist themes worked in his favor, since after 1900 the Swiss police became
concerned with the activities of foreign anarchists in general.[271] Münir Bey
began his solicitations in April 1900 while the CUP center was still in
Geneva,[272] but at first they produced unsatisfactory results. Initially, as we
have seen, a strong warning was issued to CUP leaders on May 18, and
the Swiss authorities deemed this sufficient. Next a controversy among

Ottoman diplomats enabled the Young Turks in Geneva to win over Swiss public opinion.

Baron Richtofen, the Ottoman consul general who was accused of spying and bribing Swiss police in order to gain information about the Young Turks and who was ridiculed by the press,[273] had a disagreement with the Ottoman government and barred Haydar Bey, the new Ottoman consul, who had been sent to Geneva to replace him, from entering the consulate.[274] This event was described as a power struggle among Karatodori Pasha, Münir Bey, and other low-ranking Ottoman diplomats concerned with acquiring more awards and financial prizes from the sultan because of their efforts against the Young Turks and Damad Mahmud Pasha in particular.[275] The Swiss press used material supplied to them by the Young Turks in satirizing this event[276] and accused their own government of collaborating with agents of the sultan.[277] This provided a breathing space to the activists while their enemies were being heavily criticized.

In the following year Münir Bey again filed petitions, one on May 4 and another on May 8 in a letter to the Swiss president.[278] He issued additional claims on June 21 and July 1.[279] Now circumstances were altered dramatically from what they had been a year earlier. German diplomats applied intense pressure on the Swiss authorities.[280] Again the Swiss police launched a detailed surveillance of the Young Turks remaining in Geneva,[281] leading to an interrogation of every activist leader.[282] The umbrella organization of the activists sought support in Swiss public opinion,[283] and although the Swiss press was helpful,[284] it had no effect on Swiss authorities. A new warning was issued to the activist leaders,[285] and the Swiss decided to extradite Ali Fahri, the editor of *İntikam*,[286] giving the activists and Ali Fahri an opportunity to elucidate their cause in the Swiss press through interviews and articles. However, the Young Turks failed to rescind the decision.[287]

Prior to the Congress of Ottoman Opposition, the activists suffered from great financial pressure and factiousness within their sparse ranks and so were compelled to ally themselves with a major faction.

The Young Turks in Egypt

In 1899 the CUP branch in Egypt became burdensome to the central committee when prominent members filed lawsuits against one another. They had not received financial support from the center for 2½ years and spent most of their time working out outlandish projects to extort money from the palace.[288] After their failure, Bahriyeli Rıza, who became the leader, sat at the bargaining table with Ottoman officials and intelligence agents for the sale of *Hak*. However, this gave an opportunity to his opponents, who were backed by Salih Cemal, the former director of the branch. They explained the events as follows:

> Six members of the CUP were sitting in the café next to the Crédit Lyonnais Bank in Cairo at five p.m. on Wednesday, July 9th of the European calendar,

and wanted to understand why the journal *Hak* was not being published. They wondered because a rumor was spreading those days about the sale of the journal to Yıldız and this rumor was on everyone's lips. At that time Bahriyeli Rıza, who was one of them, suddenly said in an unbelievably arrogant and domineering manner: "Yes, we are not publishing it for the present because we are bargaining with the government with the intention of selling the journal. If we fail in this then we shall publish it again."

This bold action and insolent expression of Rıza Efendi and his supposition that he was the committee perhaps with the addition of some of his accomplices, offended the members of the committee. It was decided hereafter to remove [Rıza Efendi and his accomplices] from the committee and to establish and publish the journal *Hakk-ı Sarih [Genuine Justice]* as the official organ of the committee.

Hakk-ı Sarih does not and cannot have any sort of relationship with "Sold *Hak*."[289]

With this new development both sides of the lawsuit renewed their campaign against each other in June 1900. Edhem Ruhi informed İshak Sükûti that Salih Cemal was organizing this movement behind the scenes against the CUP center.[290] The CUP center instructed the Egyptian branch to declare that "there is no official organ of the CUP other than *Osmanlı,* and *Hak* is the organ of the CUP branch in Egypt, and the publishers of *Hakk-ı Sarih* were malicious."[291] The branch published a denial and declared that those who published *Hakk-ı Sarih* had no association with the CUP.[292]

Conversely the other group published an appeal in Arabic entitled *Bāyān,* accusing Tunalı Hilmi, who had been sent as an inspector to Egypt, and the CUP center of blackmail.[293] The branch immediately denied these accusations.[294] All these events, however, lessened the prestige of the CUP and the Young Turks in Egypt, which was already very low.

At this point twelve members of the branch were bought off by the khedive and sent to Istanbul, leaving only three prominent Young Turks in the Cairo branch, namely Bahriyeli Rıza, Ali Fahri, and Ziya Efendi.[295] Tunalı Hilmi made several visits to Cairo to refuel the aspirations for a general congress of Ottoman opposition; however, his official position at the Ottoman embassy in Madrid and the collapse of the CUP branch in Egypt hindered him from fulfilling his goal.[296] His dispatching of Ali Fahri to Geneva to organize the activists left Bahriyeli Rıza alone, a man on bad terms with every remaining Young Turk in Cairo, who could do nothing else except publish the journal.[297]

However, Damad Mahmud Pasha's and later İsmail Kemal's visits raised Bahriyeli Rıza's expectations and drew the attention of foreign diplomats.[298] Activities to organize an opposition front in Egypt headed by former prominent statesmen such as Damad Mahmud, Bedirhanpaşazâde Osman, Said Halim Pashas, and İsmail Kemal[299] led Bahriyeli Rıza to think that the time had arrived for new action.

With İsmail Kemal's initiative and the khedive's help,[300] Bahriyeli Rıza formed a new committee named Şafak Osmanlı İttihad Cemiyeti (Dawn of Ottoman Union Committee); its membership included unimportant refugees, Hüseyin, Bedirhanzâde Mahmud, and Hilmi Beys.[301] This new society maintained that "the CUP had completed its natural life span and had failed because it lacked a strong program," and this necessitated the formation of their own committee.[302]

The new society published an open letter to the sultan[303] and applied to the Great Powers, delineating their great designs for the Ottoman Empire[304]; later they invited the Armenians to common action.[305] However, contrary to their claims,[306] this committee, as eccentric as their emblem—a camel carrying a crescent flag and a fountain pen—could accomplish nothing and collapsed after former high-ranking Ottoman statesmen left Egypt.

The group publishing *Hakk-ı Sarih* tried to establish ties with the group surrounding Ahmed Rıza and published articles praising the positivist leader.[307] They received favorable answers from Ahmed Saib,[308] who was working as the representative of Ahmed Rıza in Cairo, and these two groups built an alliance in Egypt to counter the CUP center in England. However, the khedive's refusal to support Salih Cemal and his associates prevented them from continuing their publication, and soon *Hakk-ı Sarih* left circulation.[309]

Thus the CUP lost its Cairo branch, and its activities were limited by the assignment of Celâleddin Ârif to Cairo to meet with the khedive on behalf of the CUP.[310] The khedive, however, gave no credit to the CUP.

In order to prevent these minor ventures in Egypt, the sultan applied to the Germans to use their diplomatic influence on the khedive to curtail Young Turk activities.[311] The khedive, who used the Young Turks as a card in his game with the sultan, took steps against them in spite of Lord Cromer's discouragement.[312] A group of Young Turks were invited to the khedival palace and deported to the Ottoman Empire by boat at the behest of the Egyptian ruler.[313] Later, Egyptian authorities issued a warning to the printing houses publishing Young Turk material. Finally Léon Fehmi, triple agent working for the khedive, the sultan, and the Young Turks— and, more important, on his own account—was invited to the khedival palace and placed under *de facto* arrest. Five days later, with the intervention of the British, he was released and extradited to appease Abdülhamid II.[314]

The CUP Center in Istanbul and Activities in the Empire

During this period, because of unfavorable conditions, a new, semiautonomous CUP center was established in the capital. This center's most outstanding activity was a plan approved on December 6, 1901, to assassinate the sultan. However, since one of the members was spying for the palace and furnishing documents to the sultan,[315] the plan was leaked to the sovereign and the Istanbul center once again collapsed.[316]

Later two members of the former Istanbul center, Silistireli Hacı İbrahim Paşazâde Hamdi (whose code name was Ağabey, Big brother) and İbrahim Bey (whose code name was Çoban, Shepherd) formed a new center; however, they were unable to accomplish anything of significance before 1906.[317]

Another activity in the capital was the establishment of a branch of the Dawn of Ottoman Union Committee. Some low-ranking officers and officials took part in the venture and distributed an appeal of the organization in mosques[318]; however, all of them were later arrested and exiled.[319]

The Young Turks in the other parts of the Empire had a tranquil period. The most important event was the refuge given at the Russian consulate in Beirut to two Young Turks who had been low-ranking officials. Although initially given asylum, they were later sent to Istanbul by the Russians.[320]

A final development worthy of note was the springing from the Rhodes dungeon of Lieutenant Colonel İsmail Hakkı,[321] a military member of the CUP who had been supplying information to the organization from the War Office prior to his arrest.[322]

The Balkan Organization

The Balkan organization also had a tranquil period. Discussions among members in Europe created no schisms there and it remained loyal to the center. This was due to İbrahim Temo's firm control over the movement in the Balkans, where he acted as an independent leader.[323] In Romania, İbrahim Temo and his friends sent many copies of the CUP central organ and publications to Istanbul via Constantsa[324] and propagandized in Dobruja.[325] As early as May 1900, the Ottoman government began to pressure its Romanian counterpart to bar the Young Turks from engaging in activities and smuggling CUP material into Ottoman ports. Later the Romanian police stormed İbrahim Temo's house and interrogated his father regarding Young Turk activities.[326]

In Bulgaria the central branch remained loyal to the center, supporting Damad Mahmud Pasha[327] and maintaining the distribution of the central organ in the region.[328] The central committee dispatched Celâleddin Ârif and later Silistireli Hamdi, a former staff officer, to the region.[329] The latter especially was assigned to create propaganda countering the claims made in the journal *Sancak*, which was being sent to the region by Ahmed Rıza.[330] Silistireli Hamdi labored toward this end until he joined the activists, leaving Bulgaria for Geneva. The Ottoman government also made repeated applications to its Bulgarian counterpart and eventually succeeded in closing down the publishing house where *Muvazene* was printed.[331]

These developments forced İbrahim Temo and the CUP leaders in the Balkans to set up a fictitious society named Terakki-i Maarif-i İslâmiye (Progress of Islamic Education); they continued their propaganda activities under this front organization[332] and transferred the smuggling operation of CUP publications to Greece. Meanwhile, the CUP branch in Greece had also attempted to contact the Armenian organizations and had drawn up plans for a terrorist action.[333] The Ottoman government sent special intelligence agents to Athens to investigate the activities of this branch.[334]

The CUP and the Ottoman Opposition prior to the 1902 Congress

When news agencies informed their subscribers of the demand by the "Young Turk Committee in Istanbul from Damad Mahmud Pasha to take the initiative for convening a general congress that would include all dissatisfied Young Turks, Armenians, and Macedonians," the CUP and the Young Turk movement were in a disarray.[335] The sons of Damad Mahmud Pasha had already appealed to the opponents of the regime of Abdülhamid II for such a convention through Young Turk journals.[336]

The CUP center welcomed the development.[337] It was aware of its impotence and aspired to become the new center of the activities following the convention, as the seal of the CUP was in its hands.

Ahmed Rıza and his followers adopted a disinterested approach. They were about to cut all ties with the other groups. Such a congress would be a platform for them from which they could express their ideas.

The activists hailed the decision.[338] This had been their objective all along,[339] while their intolerable situation had compelled them to ally themselves with a strong faction in the movement.

Little can be said about the Young Turks in Egypt, where the movement was in even greater disarray. The best remark was made by İsmail Hakkı, who had been sent to Cairo to reorganize the movement: "These people [Young Turks in Egypt] are a group of paupers."[340]

Former statesmen such as İsmail Kemal and Damad Mahmud Pasha were taking the initiative to secure the Great Powers' intervention in Ottoman politics.

Neither the Young Turks in the Empire nor those working in the CUP network in the Balkans understood the schisms among the elite of the movement. They fully anticipated the convention to unite all opponents of the regime.

For Armenian, Albanian, and other organizations seeking separatism or autonomy, the convention would be an ideal opportunity to make their voices heard by the European public.[341]

All these groups, although pursuing dissimilar goals, expected an outcome that would facilitate the advancement of their own policies as well as the formation of a common front for dethroning the sultan. However, the convention had an unexpected outcome—a split in the Young Turk movement. This gave birth to a reorganization of many groups with widely divergent agendas into two new organizations.

7

Organizational Transformation of the CUP, 1889–1902

The weft of the fabric of the Young Turk movement was its distinct ideology. During the CUP's formative phase, this positivist, social Darwinist, and biological materialist dogma was conspicuous. Later, as various groups gathered beneath the CUP banner, the motivating ideology had to be submerged, and evidence for it was barely visible, as if veiled by a mist. Today only a careful reader able to ferret meaning from between the lines will discern that this philosophy continued to lead during the later phase of the CUP.

Intellectual members came to the CUP already knowledgeable about its ideological basis. An entire generation having become imbued with western ideas while attending college in the Ottoman Empire had embraced this philosophy, so fundamental to the original Young Turks.[1] It is misleading, therefore, to study the "lists of detrimental individuals" prepared by Ottoman ambassadors. Because evidence of support for the Young Turks cannot be found in the highly censored Ottoman press, one might easily conclude that every intellectual was an admirer of the sultan—there are so many praises of the sovereign. For instance, a person who praised the sultan lavishly in a domestic journal[2] expressed his enmity only after he fled to Egypt and became a participant in the Young Turk movement.[3] The widespread flights of officials, even from the chamberlain's office, which was labeled "ungratefulness" by the sultan,[4] demonstrate this.

Another consequence of the unification of various social and political elements under the CUP banner was that it became possible to speak about more than one CUP with a single agenda. For instance, while the CUP center proudly announced that its members were "aghas, beys, pashas, aides-de-camp of the sultan, officers of the chamberlain's office,"[5] the CUP Balkan network declared a war against "the impudent individuals veiled as notables who have become a dreadful calamity to our people . . . Inhuman aghas, unscrupulous beys, fake pashas [and] wicked müftis."[6] In Bulgaria, where the Ottoman government had almost no impact on politics, the CUP network was maintained by an alliance of local intellectuals—most of whom were high school teachers—and craftsmen such as İbiş Bey, a quilt maker; Mehmed Bey, a slipper maker; and Emin Bey, a realtor. The CUP organization in Syria, by contrast, was formed as an alliance among the military, intellectuals, and prominent families such as al-'Azms and Kaylānīs. Another contrast is that between a joint Muslim-Armenian CUP executive committee in Mersin and one of the most important branches in the movement in Cairo continually asking the central committee to bar Christian membership. In spite of the strong religious concerns of the ulema members of the CUP, the Salonica branch worked under the auspices of the *dönmeler*.

It was very difficult to find anything in common among these various groups, pursuing divergent goals, other than the wish to dethrone Abdül-hamid II. In an oppressive political system whose aim was to penetrate every aspect of political and social life, all opponents of the regime felt compelled to unite under a common banner. This can be observed in later opposition movements in Ottoman-Turkish history, such as the unification of opponents of the CUP including the ulema and secular ethnic nationalists in Hürriyet ve İtilâf Fırkası (Liberal Entente) in 1911 and the opponents of the new republican regime in Serbest Cumhuriyet Fırkası (Liberal Republican party) in 1930. The CUP became the voice of opposition everywhere, speaking for dissidents of many persuasions. For instance, in the Balkans and especially in Bulgaria, it became an organization of craftsmen whose markets were taken over by Christian tradesmen importing similar goods from Europe and selling them more cheaply, whereas Turkish notables and big landowners there favored the sultan.[7] The CUP also echoed the Turkish nationalist opposition to the Bulgarian government. In Syria, members of the Kaylānī family who were not "adept at adjusting themselves to political change"[8] backed the CUP. Also, some Sufi orders who were discriminated against by the sultan and his confidants in favor of other rival orders became ardent supporters of the Young Turks. Some orders, independent of their heterodoxy or orthodoxy, joined the ranks of the CUP without regard to their differences and in response to the rise of their rivals.

As to the support given by various ethnic groups, we observe an interesting fact. None of the founders of the CUP was of Turkish origin, and they represented the important Muslim groups in which a strong sense of nationalism was yet to develop—Albanians, Kurds, and Circassians. These ethnic groups also relied on Ottoman protection against Christian groups promoted by the Great Powers' diplomacy—Greeks, Serbs, and Armenians. The participation in the CUP of Turks in large numbers and a sizable constituency of pro-Ottoman Arabs established the committee as a defender of the Muslims of the Empire. The CUP organizations further allied themselves with pro-Ottoman non-Muslim groups who were pitted against more powerful Christian groups of the Empire, backed by the Great Powers. An outstanding example was İbrahim Temo's flight, made possible with the help of prominent Albanians and Apostol Margarit,[9] who had been one of the leaders of the Aromenis movement in Macedonia against the Greeks.[10] İbrahim Temo received help from not only Albanians, Tatars, and Turks living in the region but also Kutzo-Vlaks, who were extolled by the CUP for their struggle against the Greeks and Bulgarians.[11] Vasile M. Kogălniceau, who helped İbrahim Temo to publish his organ, was also trying to win over Turks and Tatars of Dobruja against the Bulgarians.[12]

This is the reason an amnesty for Bulgarians was denounced in the journal of the Romania branch while the CUP center was in favor of it.[13] Muslim Bosnians also endorsed the CUP, and their *kıraathanes* subscribed to the official organs,[14] most probably to read and translate them to the illiterates as in Bulgaria.

Long controlled by non-Turkish but Muslim intellectuals, the CUP strove to unify Muslims in the Empire. The best article written to this end was penned by İshak Sükûti, who asked the Albanians and Kurds to unite with the Turkish element of the Empire against the "menace" of the Armenians and the Balkan Christians.[15] Many similar warnings were issued to the Muslim Albanians and Kurds of the Empire during the period.[16] Even the Arab and Albanian revolts initially were praised in the official organ.[17] Many CUP leaders had dual allegiances to the Ottoman state and to their ethnic group. İshak Sükûti and Abdullah Cevdet also wrote for Abdurrahman Bedirhan's *Kürdistan*,[18] which sometimes featured an ethnic viewpoint.[19] İbrahim Temo was also working for Albanian committees by preparing their appeals for autonomy[20] and donating money to them.[21] Since he used the phrase "I hate Turks" in a private letter, it is likely that he viewed himself primarily as an Albanian.[22] His journal made use of laudatory phrases about Albanians, such as "the noble Albanian nation"[23] and "brave Albanians."[24] Nevertheless, the CUP was simultaneously expressing delight over İbrahim Temo's prestige among the Albanian committees[25] while vehemently denying that it was "a Turkish committee"[26] and accusing the sultan of provoking the separatist movements among Ottoman elements.[27]

The failure of its leaders' initiative to obtain positive answers from the non-Turkish Muslim groups[28] and the participation of many Turks in the movement allowed another group that considered itself as Turkish to gain control of the movement. This group, similar to those intellectuals who used the same themes in the domestic Ottoman press,[29] although with more careful language, began to emphasize a single "dominant element of the empire."[30] Later they wrote that while the people of the Empire were composed of different nationalities, it was natural that the Turkish element, being the most numerous, would dominate and rule.[31] Also, by using popular race theories still inherent in CUP ideology, distinctions between Turks and Arabs began to emerge,[32] and Turks were lauded:

> What remains are the Turks, who are also underdressed, underfed and are suffering. This nation, which is obedient, patient, easygoing, and mild mannered, is branded by some as leprous and lazy. As one of our great men has remarked, the Turks are in fact like a bullet in a gun. They have a difficult time getting out, but once they are out, they will go as far as they can.[33]

Later Tunalı Hilmi's writings, in which Turkishness was regarded synonymously with Ottomanism, echoed the rise of this sentiment in the CUP.[34] Examples are from private letters: "It wounds the feelings of Nuri Ahmed to work under an Armenian typesetter,"[35] and "To publish Abdurrahman Bedirhan's *Kürdistan* is a nuisance."[36] Members of this group vehemently denounced[37] İsmail Kemal's journal and Albanian nationalist themes expressed there,[38] in spite of the guarantee announced in *Osmanlı* that it would never promote Albanian nationalism.[39] Similar condemnations were made[40] of a journal established by Mehmed Emin which propagated the ideas of a Cemiyet-i İttihadiye-i Çerâkese (Committee for Circassian Union).[41] Also *Sūriya al-fatāt*'s policies[42] and a claim by *al-Muqaṭṭam* that "it was the Arab Empire who conquered North Africa while the Sublime Porte lost it to the western imperialist powers" were denounced by members of this group,[43] and it was required of them "to find the true path."[44] The most striking fact was that these remonstrations were leveled against groups that the Ottoman government was targeting.[45]

Until the 1902 congress, two groups could be recognized within the CUP network—an Ottomanist group composed of non-Turkish but overwhelmingly Muslim members and a group whose members were Turks and who viewed the world with tinted Turkish glasses. But from the onset of the movement to late 1901, the second group had grown, often at the expense of the first.

Factiousness within the CUP was caused by three factions that began to emerge at the onset of the movement. One was led by Ahmed Rıza and defended a constitution and a parliament for all Ottomans as a means of solving the problems of the Ottoman Empire, meanwhile rejecting any foreign intervention in Ottoman politics.[46]

The second group promoted a different agenda by recommending an advisory council to the sultan, not a parliament. Most members of this faction had been high-ranking statesmen. Murad Bey led the group between 1895 and 1897, until his dramatic return; after two years in which this group was ineffective, Damad Mahmud Pasha and İsmail Kemal assumed leadership, and once again theirs became the dominant faction in the committee. Their program was simple and based entirely on securing the Great Powers' intervention. Most of the time they looked to Great

Britain for such intervention, never realizing that British public opinion on the Eastern Question had reversed. An examination of Gladstone's, Rosebery's, and even Salisbury's opinions on the Eastern Question reveals that to expect such an intervention was entirely unrealistic. Whether Tory or Liberal, the British public's shift from a pro-Turkish viewpoint to an anti-Turkish one made it impossible for British statesmen to intervene in Ottoman politics in the way that Murad Bey and İsmail Kemal expected them to do. It should be also remembered that even Disraeli had been unable to intervene in Ottoman politics during the Eastern crisis of 1876–1877. In the beginning, Murad Bey naïvely believed that Great Britain and other Great Powers could intervene in Ottoman politics without favoring a non-Muslim group in the Empire. Later, Murad Bey tried to obtain support from Armenians to elicit such an intervention. Although this policy was maintained as a pillar in this group's agenda, Damad Mahmud Pasha and İsmail Kemal failed because there was little they could offer the Armenians without offending the Turkish nationalist group that was emerging in the movement and other conservatives who opposed such an alliance.[47]

A third faction consisted of young college students who formed the nucleus in the Royal Medical Academy. It is hard to say that they had a clear political agenda, and their most important tenet was that the committee should remain a progressive organization under their control. However, in spite of İshak Sükûti's control over the movement, due to his outstanding organizational capacity, it was impossible for them to maintain their hegemony with their "scientific" ideology in a political organization of complicated alliances.

Later two other factions emerged. One was the activists who had been sparked by the anarchist movement in Europe, and despite the central committee's ongoing criticisms of anarchism as an ideology,[48] the activist wing freely exhibited its interest in anarchism.[49] As early as 1899 one of the founders had begun to write articles for Jean Grave's *Les Temps Nouveaux*.[50] However, from his writing one cannot tell the degree to which he understood anarchist ideology.[51] Eventually many Young Turks were influenced by Grave's ideas.[52] It is quite understandable that Grave's solidarist theories impressed the Young Turks.[53] However, when the activists began to form their own committees, they laid aside anarchist ideas and began to promulgate an absurd activist agenda, in which only the shedding of blood was promoted.

The second faction was the Balkan network, which became an independent organization under the leadership of İbrahim Temo, represented the Turkish nationalist ideology and pursued a course of solidarity among Muslim elements in the Balkans and European Turkey. Clearly the most comprehensive and consistent agenda in the movement was theirs, along with that of the group surrounding Ahmed Rıza.

Thus before 1902 the CUP became an organization of loosely affiliated groups and factions. Some members even formed other committees, as in the case of activists, while maintaining CUP membership. Therefore participants in the Young Turk movement took up the initiative of forming a more effective organizational body. The congress of 1902 marks the end of the CUP organization that had existed since 1889, and although this label was used by other organizations afterward, the construction and ideological framework of their enterprises were fundamentally different from those of the CUP during this period.

8

The First Congress of
Ottoman Opposition in
Paris
and Its Consequences

One of the most momentous events in the life of the Young Turk movement was undoubtedly the First Congress of Ottoman Opposition, held in Paris in 1902.[1] This meeting yielded two significant results. First, various member groups that had banded together under the framework of the CUP split apart. Second, several Turkish nationalist organizations and the group surrounding the positivist leader Ahmed Rıza merged in opposition to a policy adopted by the majority of the congress. This meeting is thus pivotal in the history of the CUP.

Final Activities before the Congress

In late 1901, Sabahaddin and Lûtfullah Beys reprinted their appeal for a general congress of Ottoman opposition, previously published only in journals; this time they put it out in both Turkish and French and distributed it among the opponents of the regime of Abdülhamid II; they also began to work on the election of representatives.[2] Before examining this process and its relevance, let us consider the activities of the various groups within the movement just prior to the convention.

The Young Turk organization in Egypt had nearly collapsed, and the one in the Balkans was faltering. The others however, were still engaging in political activities.

The group surrounding Damad Mahmud Pasha stepped up its activities in Albania aided by İsmail Kemal, who had become an influential member. According to Italian diplomats, the group was also involved in a conspiracy (allegedly supported by the British and led by İsmail Kemal and Gazi Ahmed Muhtar Pasha) to promote Reşad Efendi, the heir apparent.[3] A similar venture was launched to establish a Young Turk committee in Nish. Controlled by local Albanians, it disseminated propaganda in support of the heir apparent.[4] This attracted the attention of German diplomats[5] but yielded no results.

The remaining members of the old committee—assigned too much importance by the Ottoman government[6] and kept under close scrutiny—continued to rail against each other. Nuri Ahmed, resentful of Edhem Ruhi's indirect control of the official organ *Osmanlı*, transferred all CUP assets to his own name.[7] He vigorously denied this but was never believed,[8] and a furious controversy broke out among the members.[9] This group, in response to an appeal of their few supporters in the Empire, prepared a "Manifesto for Ramadan"[10]—a calumniation of the sultan on religious grounds,[11] which was distributed in both the capital and the provinces. Finally the members planned to assassinate the sultan: They considered sending an anarchist to Istanbul[12] or acquiring a boat and arming it with two cannons in order to bombard the Hamidiye Mosque during a Friday prayer or to open fire on Dolmabahçe Palace.[13] The attempts ended in failure, as had previous similar ventures.[14]

The few active Young Turks within the Empire established a new society called Cemiyet-i Hayriye-i İslâmiye (Islamic Benevolence Society) and published a pamphlet entitled *Yıldırım (Lightning)*. Police and intelligence service agents discovered them soon enough,[15] and Edhem Bey, their leader, fled to Greece and continued his activities there.[16]

Tunalı Hilmi, the former leader of the activist organizations, who had been inactive since 1900, proposed an initiative. While maintaining his post at the Ottoman embassy in Madrid, he voyaged to Athens under the pseudonym Behlûl and established contacts with anarchists there.[17] His efforts produced no significant results, and as soon as the Ottoman government got wind of what he was doing, he was ousted from his post and an Istanbul court sentenced him to death in absentia.[18] As a Young Turk who had been advocating a general congress since 1899, Tunalı Hilmi this time proposed an alternative convention to the one planned by the sons of Damad Mahmud Pasha. In his published eleventh sermon he challenged Sabahaddin, Lûtfullah Beys and İsmail Kemal's plan and began to himself promote a congress that would be a "Chamber of all Ottomans," in which all ethnic groups in the Empire would participate.[19] He denied allegations that he was "in competition with the sons of Damad Mahmud Pasha in the field of organizing a separate congress," but it was obvious that he was challenging their efforts.[20] By characterizing "his aim as being not only to organize a congress at any cost but to create a specific and sound policy and to lay a firm foundation for it to rest upon," he was criticizing his rivals' proposal of having been too hastily put together.[21] He tried on the one hand to influence the activists by lauding revolutionary methods[22] and on the other hand to win over radical members of the movement by advocating the declaration of the caliphate of the heir apparent.[23] He also decried the willingness of Sabahaddin Bey and the ex-statesmen to change the regime with the help of the Great Powers; he extolled the masses, presumed by his rivals to be incapable of revolting against the sultan.[24] Finally, by insisting that "the language of communication at the congress be Turkish, which is the Ottoman language," he took a stand against nationalist groups in the movement.[25] Despite these efforts, however, his deteriorating position within the Young Turk movement gainsaid any serious consideration of his proposal by the factions he was courting.

The Young Turks' efforts to organize a general congress created near panic within government circles in Istanbul. Ottoman intelligence learned that the Young Turk, Armenian, and even the Macedonian organizations would join forces and organize a joint committee after the meeting.[26] After Sabahaddin and Lûtfullah Beys' summons for a congress, the government imposed tighter measures on Young Turks within the Empire and increased the number of communiqués questioning foreign cabinets about Young Turk activities. In addition, it established collaborative efforts with the Swiss police[27] and initiated new and expanded measures to sever communication networks linking the Young Turks abroad with their sympathizers in the Empire.[28] It combed the civil officialdom, kept suspects under close surveillance,[29] and launched a major investigation to suppress circulation of "seditious publications," which were rumored to be distributed through tobacco shops.[30]

Then, Ottoman intelligence was informed of a plot involving three prominent Young Turks—Damad Mahmud Pasha, Hoca Kadri, and Siyret Bey[31]— to assassinate the sultan by dynamite.[32] On the basis of a detailed investigation by Ottoman intelligence as well as information supplied by the khedive of Egypt,[33] the Ottoman Foreign Ministry initiated efforts to extradite these Young Turks and their comrades from countries where they were living and engaging in "seditious" activities. Biographical information about the leaders was given to the German Foreign Ministry, whose assistance in the matter had been requested[34]; the British Foreign Office was warned not to allow Damad Mahmud Pasha to enter Britain[35] and was provided with detailed information about the assassination plot.[36]

Subsequently, Damad Mahmud Pasha left Corfu for Brindisi, with Ottoman diplomats and intelligence agents on his tail.[37] The Ottoman ambassador to Rome applied to the Italian Foreign Ministry for Damad Mahmud Pasha's extradition and secured a promise from the Italian foreign minister that he would be kept under close surveillance.[38] The Ottoman Foreign Ministry similarly applied to every country where Damad Mahmud Pasha might sojourn.[39] Unable to effect further political assignations, Damad Mahmud Pasha found himself under the watchful eye of the Italian police and barred from entering any other country. While these diplomatic efforts were under way, the Ottoman press publicized the decision to arrest the three leaders.[40] An Istanbul court sentenced them to death in absentia during the time the Congress of Ottoman Opposition was sitting in Paris.[41]

The Ottoman government, hoping to frustrate the opposition while it was organizing a convention, perceived the value of extraditing Damad Mahmud Pasha's sons and İsmail Kemal from France,[42] and to this end it negotiated with the French government.[43] In addition, an Istanbul newspaper was ordered to publish an article calling for the extradition of these Young Turks—a singular instance of an Ottoman daily commenting on the Young Turks, albeit without mentioning names: "Since the strong measures taken by these governments, able to identify the hypocritical feelings of these malicious individuals, are also good for their own interests, the new police measures which we heard have been implemented are recommended strongly and are a source of happiness."[44]

While the Ottoman government was waging its campaign to "prevent the rabble [Young Turks] in France from carrying out their seditious and malignant acts,"[45] the Young Turks launched a counteroffensive. First, they described to French journalists the pressure exerted on the Greek government to harass Damad Mahmud Pasha while he resided in Greece, and the latter published articles sharply critical of the Ottoman government.[46] Then the Young Turks repeated one of their classic accusations,[47] that by maligning the Young Turks the Ottoman ambassador to Paris was promoting his personal financial interests.[48] In addition, *Osmanlı*[49] and other opposition journals[50] denounced the measures against Damad Mahmud Pasha, Hoca Kadri, and Siyret Bey, calling them a perversion of justice.

Sabahaddin, Lûtfullah Beys, and İsmail Kemal had completed their preparations, and the chosen representatives were arriving in Paris. The invitations announced that the first session of the congress would be held on January 15, 1902. However, the "hesitation of the Armenian representatives" occasioned a delay.[51]

Ottoman intelligence received information about the departures for Paris of representatives from the Armenian and Macedonian committees and of Ali Fehmi, the editor of the journal *Muvazene*.[52] The event most alarming to the Ottoman government—the participation of representatives of the Macedonian committees—never occurred. Upon learning that the congress would be held on January 17 or 20, and that thirty revolutionary Turks and Armenians would participate, the Ottoman embassy petitioned the director of the Paris police,[53] claiming that some of the delegates had come to present conspiratorial plans against the life of the sultan: Three Young Turks—Damad Mahmud Pasha, Hoca Kadri, and Siyret Bey—who stood accused of anarchist activities and were being tried in Istanbul in absentia, and Armenian anarchists who had participated in takeover of the Ottoman Bank in Istanbul. French political police began monitoring the residence of Sabahaddin and Lûtfullah Beys; they were interested in every detail, down to the time the lights were turned off and the comings and goings of visitors at any hour.[54]

Münir Bey applied to Delcassé, informing him that the real aim of Damad Mahmud Pasha's two sons was to overthrow the legitimate Ottoman government in conjunction with adventurers and "maître chanteurs" summoned from Britain, Switzerland, and Romania. He asked why the French government had not extradited the Young Turks as the Swiss government had done, and why the French government did not stop those engaged in criminal schemes against the Ottoman State at the time when it was trying to establish good relations with France.[55] When on the following day Nabi Bey, a councillor at the Ottoman embassy, repeated this demand to the Affaires Étrangères,[56] the French minister demanded that these charges be investigated.[57] He then contacted the French diplomatic agent in Cairo, requesting all available information about the activities of Damad Mahmud Pasha and his sons while in Egypt.[58] He asked the French ambassador in Rome to describe steps taken against Damad Mahmud Pasha in Italy,[59] and of his counterpart in Bern about measures taken against Young Turks in Switzerland. The responses from the first two sources arrived late and in any event yielded no new information. But the French ambassador to Bern sent a lengthy dispatch in which he underlined the Swiss government's 1900 warning to the Young Turks and described how Brenner, head of the justice and police departments of the Swiss Federal Government, had provided him with information. Brenner identified the names Abdurrahman Bedirhan and Nuri Ahmed from a list, labeling them "maître chanteurs" who tried to extort money from the sultan by threatening him. Brenner added that he shared Münir Bey's judgment about most Young Turks residing in Switzerland. The French ambassador was also shown Nuri Ahmed's letter in which he had accused the activists in Switzerland of blackmail.[60]

In light of this evidence, Préfet de Police Louis Lépine summoned the two sons of Damad Mahmud Pasha to his office and informed them that the French authorities had decided to ban the convention.[61] Sabahaddin Bey objected to Lépine's characterization of certain participants and enjoined him not to bar a congress in France, which the prince portrayed in glowing terms as a land of justice and freedom.[62] Lépine reiterated that the French authorities would not permit the meeting. Sabahaddin Bey called upon various newspapers, explaining to their editors that the Young Turks' program was in full accordance with the reforms demanded by Delcassé in the French parliament, and he challenged Lépine's designation of the convention as "the congress of conspirators."[63] He concluded by stating that the convention might take place in London. *Osmanlı* printed accusations that the French government was prisoner to the desires of the sultan and repeated Sabahaddin Bey's assertion that a convention in London was possible.[64]

At this point the Young Turk leaders had given up all hope of holding the congress in Paris.[65] Reşid Sadi, who continued to support the Young Turk movement even after his appointment to a new post at the Ottoman embassy in London, contacted Ahmed Rıza requiring him to urge the princes to give interviews to British journalists before going to Britain, cautioning them to say that "they were neither anarchists nor socialists nor liberals and that their sole aim was to demand the restoration of the Ottoman Constitution."[66] Anthopulos Pasha, the Ottoman ambassador, alarmed by information about the Young Turks' plans, presented a recent communiqué sent by Tevfik Pasha, the Ottoman foreign minister, to the British Foreign Office, describing "conspiratorial" designs by Damad Mahmud Pasha, Hoca Kadri, and Siyret Bey.[67] Two days later he officially applied to Lord Lansdowne to deny permission for assembly.[68]

It looked as though the Ottoman government would be able to prevent the congress as it had done in 1899, when the Young Turks had tried to organize a meeting in Brindisi; but the Young Turks now took action to reverse the French decision.

They drew the attention of the French public to the situation, presenting the problem as one of freedom. Tensions between the French and Ottoman governments[69] and the mounting protest in France against the regime of Abdülhamid II, because of the latest Armenian crisis, worked in their favor.

A debate arose over an interpellation given by Marcel Sembat on November 15, 1901,[70] concerning France's relations with the Ottoman Empire. Sembat told French deputies that an agent had been caught engaging in espionage for the sultan. He maintained that Abdülhamid II had formed a secret police organization with the sanction of the French government to track down Young Turks and Armenians. Sembat found the idea of foreign police spying in France intolerable.[71] Soon after this debate, he described to the minister of the interior in parliament how the detention and expulsion of Ottoman agents, who had been apprehended while pursuing liberal students in Paris, had yielded full information about activities of those agents. The minister responded that several Ottoman subjects involved in seditious activities had been expelled some time before but that there had been no recurrence of the problem. Dissatisfied with this answer, Sembat again went to the podium and asserted that those who were expelled had been involved not in sedition but in espionage.[72]

During the final preparations for the Congress of Ottoman Opposition, Denys Cochin, a proponent in the French parliament of the Armenian cause since 1897,[73] together with Gustave Rounet, another radical deputy, and others, proposed a motion to issue a resolution favoring the Armenians and censuring the Ottoman government. After fierce discussions in which the Ottoman government was condemned, the proposal was carried with 280 voting in favor and 235 against.[74]

Sabahaddin Bey then reiterated an old, oft-repeated complaint of the Young Turks, hoping to gain the support of the radical segment of French public opinion[75]: A long-standing collaboration existed between the sultan and the French police against the Young Turks. He also claimed to have been followed by an Ottoman agent for some time and to have reported the incident to the police.[76] The French Foreign Ministry, eager to curtail discussion of this issue, obtained information from the police[77] that those who were monitoring Sabahaddin Bey's activities were not Ottoman agents but their own officers.[78] They added that the sultan's agents had been inactive in Paris for some time.[79] Meanwhile, Sabahaddin Bey with his brother Lûtfullah Bey drafted a letter in which they expounded their reasons for convening a congress in Paris.[80] The letter, which they sent to Delcassé, included the veiled threat that they would create a scandal by going public over the police incident. Meanwhile, the police department revised the report on the activities of Damad Mahmud Pasha and his sons; now none of their activities was described as illegal or extreme.[81] Thus the organizers of the congress were transformed from "conspirators" into "victims."

Besides these developments, "the applications and interventions of some foreign friends" persuaded the French government to reverse its decision.[82] The names of these "foreign friends" were not mentioned in any source relating to the congress. Some newspapers drew attention to the role played by several French deputies and prominent statesmen.[83] They may have included Joseph Denais, the secretary general of the French journalists' union and an admirer of Sabahaddin Bey,[84] Clemenceau,[85] and Rhône deputy Francis de Pressensé, an ardent supporter of the Armenian cause. Another source claimed that 'by getting the support of some members of the French cabinet, the approval of the Minister of the Interior was obtained.'"[86]

Although these explanations carry some weight, they do not elucidate how and why this development occurred. A telegram by the French Foreign Ministry sent to Istanbul during the congress expressed the Ottoman government's satisfaction with the original decision.[87] A British daily claimed that this decision had originated with Delcassé but that Prime Minister René Waldeck-Rousseau reversed it.[88] German diplomats commenting on the issue shared this view,[89] which gains import in light of the fact that Delcassé was a remarkably independent cabinet minister and often made decisions contrary to the policies of Waldeck-Rousseau.[90] While the congress was being organized, Delcassé was preoccupied with the Bagdadbahn project. He still hoped that the French capital would play a role[91] and avoided anything that would jeopardize this opportunity, including a congress of the Ottoman opposition. It is also plausible that Waldeck-Rousseau, who was being bombarded with criticism by his political opponents over several issues (among which the Dreyfus affair was prominent), chose to sidestep this new controversy in order to avoid fanning the flames of this opposition during the election campaign of May 1902.[92]

Another person who played a salient role in the matter was Louis Lépine. His part in satisfying Münir Bey was underscored in a British daily,[93] although Lépine wrote nothing about these events in his memoirs.[94] Some of his contemporaries denounced him, condemning his approach to the political opposition and left-wing organizations and alleging that he wielded nearly unlimited power in internal affairs.[95] Left-wing

journals leveled similar criticisms against him for his role in the French
government's decision against the Young Turks.

Further condemnations erupted when the sultan decorated high-ranking police officials in Paris only a few months after the congress.[96] Nonetheless, although it was obvious that Lépine was not fond of the Young
Turks, the decision against them seems far beyond the scope of his authority, and speculation about his influence should be viewed with skepticism.
In fact, the organ of the Dashnaktsutiun Committee claimed that it was
not Lépine but the government that had granted the permit to the con-
gressional organizers—on the conditions that the sessions be held at a
private house and not in a public place, that they remain closed to the
public, and that all official proceedings of the congress be presented to the
French Ministry of the Interior before publication.[97]

Even to convene their congress seemed a great feat for the Young
Turks, considering the obstacles they had faced. The Ottoman government even tried to suppress the news that the Congress of Ottoman Opposition had met.[98]

The two important elements of the meeting are the appointment procedure of representatives and the lobbying activities of the two factions,
which followed divergent paths after the congress. To understand the consequences of the convention, let us consider these aspects.

The Organization of the Congress

The two sons of Damad Mahmud Pasha, who convoked the Congress of
Ottoman Opposition, also controlled its organization. They conferred
only with İsmail Kemal, and Lûtfullah Bey traveled to Brussels to consult
with him.[99] İsmail Kemal agreed to participate in the convention only
under specific conditions. He required "that all the ethnic elements in
Turkey should be represented, so that the desiderata of all the people in
the Empire might be formulated, the Powers signatory of the Treaties of
Paris and Berlin should know that in the eyes of the Ottoman people they
had pledged their honour concerning the adoption of reforms for the good
of the Empire." He claimed that "if the aid of Europe were invoked the
congress might be of some value, but if it stopped at the mere expression
of opinions and nothing more was done [he] could not see any use in it."
The sons of Damad Mahmud Pasha accepted his conditions.[100]

Thus the coordinating committee was formed. Its members, Sabahaddin, Lûtfullah Beys, and İsmail Kemal, held a banquet, attended by the
close friends of Sabahaddin and Lûtfullah Beys, in which they chose the
delegates—"prominent opposition figures."[101] Afterward they sent letters
of invitation to the prospective delegates, most of which were drafted by
Sabahaddin and Lûtfullah Beys; the format of the congress was meant to
galvanize a new committee whose influence would spread throughout the
Ottoman Empire and its autonomous provinces. The letters delineated a
blueprint for an updated Constitution of 1876, which was strongly cen-

sured by Ahmed Rıza and his disciples.[102] İsmail Kemal also wrote letters to prominent Young Turks with whom he had personal relations.[103]

The salient point in this process is that all the invitees had been chosen by the coordinating committee. Although the committee met with Ahmed Rıza, who had led the Young Turk movement nominally or actually for years, they did not invite him to all of their planning sessions.[104] At the conclusion of the preparations, Ahmed Rıza sent a note to the coordinating committee advising them not to send personal invitations from one person only. He warned that those not attending would be within their rights to ignore decisions taken by a convention so invited. He demanded that all participants be Ottoman citizens and know Turkish and that the Ottoman Constitution of 1876 form the basis for discussions.[105] The coordinating committee ignored his requirements. Since the delegates were designated and invited by a committee of three, the constructs of "majority" and "minority" were controversial.

The list of representatives reveals that the primary criterion for inclusion was editorship or authorship of articles in Young Turk journals. However, this criterion was not applied across-the-board, and editors living in France or in central Europe had the advantage of proximity. One such person was Doctor Lütfi, who earlier had tried to establish a multilanguage journal called *İttihad-ı İslâm (Pan-Islam),*[106] probably with the aim of extracting money from the palace. When it failed,[107] he assumed the editorship of *Moniteur Ottoman,* a negligible bilingual periodical. He sought help with his journal from Sabahaddin and Lûtfullah Beys[108] and extolled the efforts of İsmail Kemal.[109] Ahmed Saib, editor of *Sancak,* which became the Young Turks' most important journal in Egypt, was also invited but hindered by distance from attending. Never even invited was Tunalı Hilmi,[110] a long-time advocate of a general congress of the Ottoman opposition and editor of *Ezan,* which he could publish only irregularly; between 1896 and 1899 he had been a prominent writer for various Young Turk journals.

A second criterion was membership in a distinct professional group in the Empire, such as the military. But again questions arose over the view that İsmail Hakkı—who had been sprung from prison by the group surrounding Damad Mahmud Pasha[111] and then had joined their group—was the most eligible person to represent Ottoman officials. Other members of the military at the convention, such as Silistreli Mustafa Hamdi and Ali Fahri, were also on the editorial boards of Young Turk journals and had been active in the movement. It can be concluded that invitations to the congress were sent only to the leaders of activist organizations, to those in the group surrounding Ahmed Rıza, and to those individuals whom it was impossible to omit because of their prominence in the movement.

When the coordinators became aware that the remaining members of the old organization that still controlled *Osmanlı* were planning to act as a group independently of Sabahaddin and Lûtfullah Beys,[112] they decreased the number of delegates invited from this group. Another reason for this was that the coordinating committee feared their animosity toward the Armenian committees, especially toward the Dashnaktsutiun,[113] whose participation, the coordinators believed, would bring the backing of the Great Powers.[114]

None of the three living founders of the first nucleus of the CUP attended the meeting. İshak Sükûti and Abdullah Cevdet had official posts at the Ottoman embassies in Rome and Vienna, and İbrahim Temo was not a member of the delegation sent from the Balkans. Edhem Ruhi, the official chairman of the CUP, who had had a disagreement with Sabahaddin Bey,[115] did not attend either.

As regards representation of every ethnic element in the Empire—İsmail Kemal's primary requisite for the convention—it cannot be said that meaningful participation was achieved. The most meaningful compliance was achieved by the Armenian committees. Indeed, for a while friends of Damad Mahmud Pasha were advocating a rapprochement between the Young Turks and the Armenians. The organizers invited all three major Armenian committees—the Dashnaktsutiun, Verakazmial (Reformed) Hnchakian, and Hnchakian committees. The first two responded favorably, but the third did not bother to answer.[116] The first two held a special meeting and discussed taking a united stance at the convention. Later they met with the princes and with İsmail Kemal separately, requiring acceptance of their terms as a condition for their participation: Recognition of the sixty-first article of the Berlin Congress of 1878 and the Great Powers' memorandum of May 11, 1895.[117] Although *Droshak* gave no information about the organizers' response and Young Turk sources wrote nothing about these negotiations, it is likely that the results were positive, because the two Armenian committees sent a joint delegation to the convention.

In addition to this institutional representation, two prominent Armenians had been personally invited to the convention: Minas Tscheraz, the editor of *Armenia*, who had represented the Ottoman opposition with Ahmed Rıza at The Hague Peace Conference, and Garabet Basmacıyan.[118]

Albanians had a large representation at the convention. İsmail Kemal represented the pro-Greek Albanians, and Derviş Hima, who had been denounced by the nationalist wing of the Young Turks[119] for his role in promoting the adoption of the Latin script for Albanian,[120] represented the pro-Italian Albanians. To represent Albanian nationalist organizations in Serbia and Romania, Yaşar Erebera, who worked with Hima both at the central committee of the Albanian Muslim organization in Serbia[121] and in the Albanian nationalist movement in Bucharest,[122] was sent to the convention.[123] Hoca Kadri, mistakenly referred to as an Albanian representative,[124] had been invited for his editorship of several Young Turk journals and as a prominent writer for *Mechveret Supplément Français*. Besides this, he described himself as a Herzegovinian and not an Albanian,[125] as did the Ottoman press.[126] Also, contrary to the claim some Albanian researchers made,[127] Albanians at the congress did not adhere to a common line by supporting Sabahaddin Bey's idea of "decentralization."

The Greeks at the convention were Konstantinos Sathas, Vasileos Musurus Ghikis, Georges Fardis, and Anastase Adossidis. Ghikis, the son-in-law of Musurus Pasha, former Ottoman ambassador to London, had once been a member of the State Council and had fled to Europe on the heels of Damad Mahmud Pasha and his sons,[128] He maintained sound relations with them and with İsmail Kemal.[129] More recently he had secretly applied to the British embassy in Istanbul to obtain a passport; he was another example of the pro-British Ottoman statesman.[130] As for the other Greek participants, their eligibility to represent Ottoman Greeks comes to mind. A reasoned answer to this question is provided by a Greek scholar:

> We do not know anything else but their names. Did they represent any orga-
> nization, or were they only influential Greek personalities? Even more, one
> may ask whether they were Ottoman Greeks. The case of Sathas and Adossidis,
> whose names appeared in the resolution of the Congress suggest[s] that they
> were not afraid of Abd-ul Hamid's revenge. We may conclude, therefore, that
> their links with Ottoman Turkey were rather weak.[131]

Besides failing to represent the Greek element of the Empire, these delegates had no ties to the Greek committees of Macedonia, and their role in the Young Turk movement was nonexistent. Adossidis later published a journal called *L'Hellénisme* and defended the Greek nationalist cause. Ghikis played a minor role in the coup d'état attempt of the Osmanlı Hürriyetperverân Cemiyeti following the congress. Sathas was a prominent scholar known for his essays on Byzantine history. But it is hard to understand why he was invited to the convention, given his lack of awareness of Ottoman politics. Fardis was the editor of the journal *Archives Diplomatiques* in Paris at the time of the congress, and he was studying constitutional theories, on which he later became an expert.[132] One might suppose that he was invited because of his knowledge in this field.[133] But neither Sathas nor Fardis participated in any Young Turk activities after the congress.

For the other ethnic groups there was no meaningful ethnic representation. The emphasis on broad representation as underlined in the official text of the resolutions published after the congress[134] and considered highly significant by the European press[135] was a mere fabrication intended to impress the Great Powers.

It was claimed, for instance, that the Jews had taken part in the convention. However, the only Jew at the assembly, Albert Fua, had been invited because of his long-time involvement in the movement and in deference to his distinguished contributions to *Mechveret Supplément Français*. Besides, the name of his ethnic-religious community was never referred to at the meeting. The same can be said of Khalīl Ghānim, who claimed to represent the Arabs in the convention. But the degree to which

Ghānim, a Catholic Arab, could represent the Arab element of the Empire is highly questionable. Also, even if one does accept him as an ethnic representative, there is still the impossible task of explaining the poor representation of the Arabs, in contrast to the overrepresentation of the Armenians and Albanians, whose populations in the Ottoman Empire were relatively small. In fact, Ghānim had been invited to the congress because he was a major writer for *Mechveret Supplément Français*. Recent claims about the representation of the Circassians[136] and the Kurds[137] with the participation of Hüseyin Tosun, Kemal Bey, and Abdurrahman Bedirhan, Baban-zâde Hikmet Süleyman, respectively, do not reflect the actual situation. These men were invited for their roles in the movement quite apart from their ethnic origins.

Finally, as was underlined in an Armenian journal[138] that led the Armeno-Macedonian Conference and in an Austrian daily,[139] the Slav and Walachian elements of the Empire were not represented. Following Sisyan Efendi's speech in which he "expressed regrets at seeing no delegate from the Macedonian committee,"[140] the Armenians demanded that the organizers invite them. The organizers issued an invitation through *Droshak* to the "Ottoman Bulgarians living in Europe" but received no response. The Armenian delegates took umbrage at the short notice of this invitation and asked the organizers to mention this circumstance in the proceedings, which they refused to do.[141]

For all these reasons the composition of the representatives, despite the organizers' claims,[142] was arbitrarily created by the three organizers, and besides the Armenians, Greeks, and to some extent Albanians, there was no ethnic representation. Undoubtedly other participants had ethnic identities along with their Ottoman identity, but their participation was not based on ethnic considerations.

As regards organizations, the coordinating committee refused such representation for any but the Armenian and Albanian groups. Participation so derived would undoubtedly have served the interests of the many activist groups in Geneva and the CUP, which was still controlled by the remaining members of the old organization. To prevent this, the organizers asserted that the congress would be organized by the Serbest Osmanlılar Fırkası (the Party of the Ottoman Liberals)—a title never before used by any opposition group, including all opponents of the regime then present in the Ottoman Empire.[143] They also decided not to use the title CUP, both during the preparations and at the meeting. An underlined statement in each invitation affirmed that a new committee would be formed after the congress. Thus a new schism arose; the organizers, their friends, the Greek and Armenian delegations, and the Albanian participants were in one camp, and the alliance of activists and the group surrounding Ahmed Rıza were in the other.

At the first sign of lobbying activity prior to the congress, almost every participant visited the sons of Damad Mahmud Pasha. Most of these were social visits, however, at which organizational matters were not discussed.[144] In contrast, police reports reveal that the princes were holding almost constant audience at their residence—with İsmail Hakkı, Ali Haydar Midhat, and Hüseyin Tosun.[145] Ali Fehmi, a self-described "impartial" delegate, wrote that he had observed large-scale lobbying activity in Paris.[146] However, according to police reports, he was holding the same kind of meetings at the apartment he had rented with Hoca Kadri and Celâl Bey; usually these meetings continued late into the night.[147] Other meetings were held at Ahmed Rıza's apartment with the aim of shaping a common policy.[148] One may therefore conclude that the issues discussed and voted on at the congress were familiar to the delegates and that they had a fairly clear idea of the activities and policies of the other groups.

According to the organ of the activists, their efforts and those of Ahmed Rıza's followers, were thwarted by the inexperience of the young princes, the opposition of the Armenian committees, and the "machinations" of İsmail Kemal.[149]

A conclave consisting of Hoca Kadri, Sheikh Şevki Celâleddin, Khalīl Ghānim, Ahmed Rıza, Ali Fahri, Mahir Said, Babanzâde Hikmet, Celâleddin Rıza, Hüseyin Tosun, Zeki, Yaşar Sadık Erebera, Derviş Hima, Ali Fehmi, Silistireli Mustafa Hamdi, and Nâzım Bey convened at the offices of *Mechveret* and drafted a four-article program,[150] essentially a summary of general principles:

> 1. The existence and enthronement of the Ottoman Royal House and the obligation of obedience and loyalty to this dynasty of illustrious name within the orders legitimately vested.
> 2. The exalting of the religion of Islam along with civilization and the protection of other religions.
> 3. The granting to Muslim and non-Muslim Ottoman subjects an equal share in the material and moral benefits by trying to unite them politically.
> 4. The acceptance of the Constitution that had been proclaimed in the year 1293 [1876] as grounds for unity and a guiding principle in the administration of domestic and foreign policies.[151]

The primary intention of the last article was to prevent any change in the constitution of 1876. The leaders of this effort next sought the approbation of the leaders of the other group, and the two factions convened at Khalīl Ghānim's apartment on January 31, 1902. After lengthy negotiations, they agreed on a more detailed text. This document was signed by Ahmed Rıza, Ali Haydar Midhat, Khalīl Ghānim, Hüseyin Tosun, Hüseyin Siyret, İsmail Hakkı, İsmail Kemal, Musurus Ghikis, and Sabahaddin Bey.

A compromise was also drawn up, as part of the second article of the program, by Ahmed Rıza and his followers on behalf of non-Muslim groups. As part of the same article, however, they prevented their opponents from acting on their intention to change the constitution by a resolution of the congress. The two sides also compromised on the fourth article. Ahmed Rıza and his followers amended the text to include the resolutions of the Berlin Congress; they also upset the Armenians, who were seeking special reforms for the six provinces in eastern Anatolia, by saying "à toutes les provinces de l'Empire":

> 1. Nous repoussons toute solidarité entre le peuple ottoman [in the printed text:les peuples ottomans] et le régime d'oppression, sous lequel nous vivons depuis 25 ans, cette unique source des méfaits qui se commettent dans l'Empire et qui soulèvent l'indignation de l'humanité tout entière;
> 2. Nous entendons établir entre les différents peuples et races de l'Empire une entente qui assurera à tous, sans distinction, la pleine jouissance de leurs droits reconnus par les Hatts impériaux et consacrés par les traités internationaux, leur procurera les moyens de satisfaire d'une manière complète leur légitime aspiration, de prendre part à l'administration municipale et provinciale [in the printed text: l'administration locale], les mettra sur un pied d'égalité au point de vue des droits comme des charges incombant à tous les citoyens, leur inspirera le sentiment de fidélité et de loyalisme envers le trône et la dynastie d'Osman, qui seule peut maintenir leur union;
> 3. Nous nous appliquerons en toute circonstance à faire converger les vœux de tous les peuples ottomans et les efforts de tous les patriotes vers ce triple but: a) maintien de l'intégrité et de l'indissolubilité de l'Empire ottoman; b) rétablissement de l'ordre et de la paix à l'intérieur, condition essentielle du progrès; c) respect des lois fondamentales de l'Empire, notamment de la Constitution promulguée en 1876, qui en est incontestablement la partie la plus importante et qui offre la garantie la plus sûre et la plus précieuse des réformes générales, des droits et des libertés politiques des peuples ottomans contre l'arbitraire;
> 4. Nous proclamons notre ferme résolution de respecter les traités internationaux et particulièrement le traité de Berlin, dont les dispositions, en ce qui concerne l'ordre intérieur de la Turquie, devront être étendues à toutes les provinces de l'Empire.[152]

A letter drafted by Ahmed Rıza provides the details of the negotiations:

> I categorically reject the intervention of foreigners in the domestic affairs of [our] fatherland under whatever name or title. This article concerning foreign intervention was included in the first draft prepared by İsmail Kemal and Musurus Beys and approved last night. Later, due to the objections of the princes and of Hoca Kadri it was removed. Only the fourth article has remained. I had objected to the fourth article, saying that the constitution recognizes international treaties and that this was enough. In response they said that our Armenian citizens would not participate unless this article, especially the [resolutions of] the Berlin Congress, were mentioned [in the text]. Since their participation was requested by everyone, I had to accept this article.[153]

Once an agreement was reached; the text was printed and distributed to the delegates.[154] In spite of his complaints about the negotiations, Ahmed Rıza and his followers continued to hold sway at the meeting. Undoubtedly the arrival in Paris of the activists Babanzâde Hikmet Süleyman, Mahir Said, and Hamid Hüsni, who supported Ahmed Rıza, was an important factor in his ascendancy to a position of leadership not only over his own followers but also over a nationalist-activist alliance.[155] As we have seen, the text that had been prepared at the offices of *Mechveret* was signed by all activists. Naturally these developments were a profound disappointment for İsmail Kemal; the group opposing his ideas had exhibited drive and organizational strength beyond anyone's expectations. The final text was a far cry from the themes he had proposed before the congress,[156] which prompted European diplomats to anticipate a plea from the congress for the Great Powers' intervention.[157] Aided by Armenian, Greek, and some Albanian delegates, he drafted a supplemental statement, which so altered the original intent of the text that Sabahaddin Bey agreed to endorse it.

As the activists described it, this maneuver brought all their and Ahmed Rıza's efforts to nought:

> Everyone had arrived and the all arrangements were completed for the Congress, when His Excellency İsmail Kemal's participation in the Congress on a specific condition, contrary to resolutions drawn up during the first stage [of the preparations for the Congress], revealed that the general union which was yearned for by all of us was impossible. Most particularly, due to a supplement containing an invitation to foreign powers to intervene, the nobility and dignity of patriotism came to be viewed with contempt. Through this development, all hopes for the congress were dashed.[158]

However, the nationalist-activist alliance had no intention of yielding to İsmail Kemal. Thus, when letters by İsmail Kemal were published in the European press just prior to the convention favoring European intervention in Ottoman domestic affairs[159] (they were republished in Armenian journals),[160] those who had opposed him during the congress reiterated their adamant stand against his position. A prime example of this antagonism is a letter drafted by Ahmed Ferid:

> To İsmail Kemal Bey,
> His Benevolently Disposed Excellency,
>   To occupy the post of the grand-vizierate under the protection of foreign authorities who are our great enemies is not an honor but a disgrace. I read the letter which you sent to [*Le*] *Matin* on behalf of all easterners and every Ottoman regardless of their ethnicity and religion. I want to learn upon what [authority] you have been authorized the expression of your ideas and your promise of support given on behalf of the entire populace. For instance, I am an Ottoman too but in no way do I share Your Excellency's ideas. I assume that there are probably others sharing my ideas among the Ottomans. Or maybe Ottomanism extends only to the Albanian committee, and I am unaware of this fact. I find it unnecessary to prove the baseness and senselessness of the praise which you made in order to impress them [the Great Powers] in your above-mentioned letter. The history of Poland, the affairs of Crimea lie before us. . . . We want to undertake our own reform without the intervention by the deceitful and usurping hand of Europe.[161]

İsmail Kemal's ideas were depicted as collaborationist and pandering to the imperialist designs of the Great Powers. The condemnation of European imperial ambitions was fast becoming a cornerstone in burgeoning nationalism; predictably, the two factions were unable to find any ground for compromise.

As the opening of the congress approached, each camp strove to assemble a list of resolutions that accorded with its own political ideology. Ahmed Rıza's indefatigable efforts yielded a text—albeit a short-lived one—omitting any reference to foreign intervention in domestic affairs. Even though his opponents overrode his wishes, the effort can be counted a success when seen in light of the process for delegate selection. An eleventh-hour maneuver by İsmail Kemal transformed this picture. As was abundantly clear even before the convention, the members of this meeting were unable to create a united opposition front.

The First Congress of Ottoman Opposition

The first session of the congress was held on February 4, 1902, at 8 p.m., at the house of Germain Antoin Lefèvre-Pontalis, a member of the Institut de France, in compliance with the conditions set by the French government—that the Ottoman opposition hold its congress at a private residence and that it remain closed to the public. Forty-seven delegates attended.[162]

Lûtfullah Bey gave the first speech in French and thanked Lefèvre-Pontalis for "his humanitarian treatment of the Ottoman liberals."[163] Lefèvre-Pontalis gave an extemporaneous response and was loudly applauded.[164]

A decision was then made about the official language at the congress: Speeches were to be delivered in either French or Turkish.[165] The Armenians objected, insisting on French as the only official language, but after a short discussion they acceded to the general wish for two languages.[166] Nevertheless, most members of the majority group chose to speak French, something castigated by *Kürdistan*.[167]

After the language issue had been settled, Sabahaddin Bey delivered the opening address. According to him, an ongoing war was being waged between liberty and absolutism, and every problem facing the Ottoman state had its origin in the administrative system. Sabahaddin Bey also declared that "the Turks who constitute the greater majority ask nothing for themselves alone and have no desire to interfere in the ethnic characteristics of other groups living in the Empire." He closed with a warning that "the perception that Europe has acquired about our country is derogatory."[168] Hüseyin Siyret took the stand next, hailing the efforts of Sabahaddin and Lûtfullah Beys and thanking them on behalf of the delegates.[169] So far, except for the brief discussion between the Armenians and other delegates about the official language, both sides had avoided any name-calling. The official organ of the activists described the discourses made up to this point as "fiery speeches."[170]

Following this exciting introduction, Sabahaddin Bey proposed that the congress appoint a number of officers to the convention. İsmail Kemal moved that the chairmanship be offered to Sabahaddin Bey, who accepted. Konstantinos Sathas and Sisyan Efendi were made vice-chairmen, an acknowledgment of the preferential treatment accorded to the Armenians and Greeks.[171] Ali Fahri and, after Albert Fua had refused the position, Anastase Adossidis were nominated to be the recording secretaries.[172] By these assignments the pro-interventionist group led by İsmail Kemal demonstrated that the convention was under its control; except for Ali Fahri, all the appointees were its members. Although İsmail Kemal personally made no bid for power at that time, Ahmed Rıza later claimed that a schism occurred then as the second faction mobilized around İsmail Kemal.[173]

After the appointment of officeholders, Sabahaddin Bey again addressed the delegates. He read out the program which he said "had been prepared by some prominent personalities,"[174] and added İsmail Kemal's supplement:

Conclusion:

Tels étant les principes sur lesquels l'entente est établie, nous constituons un Comité permanent qui s'efforcera de faire prévaloir ces principes et se livrera aux démarches nécessaires, auprès des puissances signataires du traité de Paris de l'année 1856 et du traité de Berlin de l'année 1878, afin d'obtenir leur concours moral et une action bienveillante de leur part, ayant pour objet la mise à exécution des engagements internationaux stipulant l'ordre intérieur en Turquie, ainsi que de tous les actes internationaux découlant des susdits traités et leur adaptation à tous les vilayets de l'Empire, de la manière la plus profitable à chacun d'eux.[175]

This French supplement was lithographed and distributed to the delegates in Turkish,[176] but it had an explosive impact on the convention.[177] According to the activists, the prointervention group forbade its rivals to criticize the supplement, and they further claimed that "the right of free criticism, which customarily reigns at congresses, had been suppressed by a majority ignorant of it."[178] The majority agreed to discuss the program and the supplement and, fearing their opponents' withdrawal, denied İsmail Kemal's demand that it be approved immediately. At this point the Armenians wanted to read an appeal, but when their request was denied, they walked out.[179] By the end of the first session, it had become clear that the convention would soon deteriorate into a feud between the two camps.

The second session, held at the princes' residence, was undoubtedly the most animated of all. Those rejecting the supplement launched an offensive with a speech delivered by Albert Fua in French. Fua focused on the dangers of foreign intervention in Ottoman domestic affairs and called attention to some of the vague wording of the supplement.[180] By making Fua, a non-Muslim and a non-Turk, their first speaker, the anti-interventionist group intended to demonstrate that their opposition was not rooted in a nationalist ideology. Following this speech Ahmed Rıza took the stand next and condemned the idea of foreign intervention:

> I categorically refuse intervention by the foreigners, under any title whatever, in the domestic affairs of our fatherland. Because:
>
> 1. Every nation is free to conduct its domestic affairs in conformance to its own will. This right is recognized all around the world and by all nations. Even the Serbians and the Bulgarians are rejecting foreign intervention.
>
> 2. The foreign interventions which have taken place until now never respected our national interests. In each case such interventions were made in order to separate an element from us or to acquire new privileges for profiteers and missionaries, and they have invariably inflicted harm on us. The right of intervention which Europe employed against us is nothing less than the application of the principle of *al-ḥukmu lī man ghalaba* to us, in a disgraceful manner.
>
> 3. Each time foreign powers have intervened in our domestic affairs they have been contemplating their own interests. Their brutal atrocities in China and Africa and especially their protection of Abdülhamid's regime are evidence for our claim.
>
> 4. Besides their own deplorable faults, the Great Powers of Europe are under the malicious influence of Russia concerning Eastern affairs. Even those desirous of our reform would fear giving offense to Russians and be constrained in executing the reforms to accord with Russian interests. Therefore, to invite the intervention of Europe which is under the Russian influence means to invite Russian intervention.
>
> 5. To demand European intervention means to present a mandate to Europe [and] to confess our inability and impotence. Can't we see the fact that even the smallest permit given to the Europeans in a spirit of hospitality is interpreted by them as treaties or capitulations and it is impossible to recall a privilege once it has been granted?
>
> 6. We are asking for European intervention, however Europe will never help us [in doing so] unless she finds a material interest. Thus I ask, are the rights and privileges we are going to relinquish equal to the interest we are going to gain [?] It is obvious that we are going to lose. If one says that Europe is intervening [in our domestic affairs] regardless of our will [we respond to this by saying]: It is beyond our power to hinder Europe. However, to not summon her intervention is within our power. Patriotism and national dignity charge us to act in this way.[181]

Hoca Kadri, Khalīl Ghānim, Ahmed Ferid, Doctor Nâzım, and Mustafa Hamdi made similar declarations.[182] Ahmed Ferid's speech was inaudible over the commotion by members of the majority.[183] Another scathing denunciation was presented by Abdurrahman Bedirhan.[184] Hours of discussion were spent on minutiae.[185] The debates became so ferocious that the recording secretary, who was taking minutes of the proceedings in French, resigned three times and Sabahaddin Bey resigned once, but their resignations were not accepted.[186]

According to the majority, the minority made the following statements:

> [Our] Constitution is the guarantor of the prosperity and security of the various Ottoman nations. We do not need the supportive actions of the Great Powers and the assistance which has been demanded will be impossible [to obtain]. Even if given as imagined, it would be contrary to our interests. This kind of assistance would injure our national dignity. We should work for ourselves. We have to trust and rely on our own strength.[187]

Also according to the majority, members of this faction responded to these comments in the following manner:

> The Constitution is our utmost desire. The European intervention will be realized eventually. [This is] because some elements in the Ottoman nation so persistently demand the execution of [the terms of] the international treaties, while displaying the oppression that has been inflicted on them before the tender and merciful ear of Europe.
>
> We will demand assistance from Europe [the Great Powers] in concert with all Ottoman nations. In doing so we hope to transform the intervention from one hostile to us into one favoring us. The interventions previously made in favor of Serbia, Montenegro, Bulgaria, Eastern Rumelia, and Crete will tomorrow be implemented in the middle of Anatolia, at the gates of our capital.[188]

When members of the minority inquired "whether by saying 'European intervention' they meant a military one,"[189] Sabahaddin Bey once again rose to the podium. After emphasizing the foreign interventions that some ethnic groups of the Empire had provoked, he claimed that the moment had arrived for demanding such intervention on behalf of all "Ottoman nations." He said that he respected the sincerity of those who perceived foreign intervention to be irreconcilable with national dignity but averred that such an intervention was nevertheless necessary:

> In order to make our voice heard, we must demonstrate that we hear the voice of Europe. Therefore, I propose that, as our nationalist duty, we apply for the benevolent mediation of the Great Powers, with a serious delegation of members from all Ottoman elements, inviting them to execute the terms of the treaties, and to bring force to bear against the present absolutist regime that rules against the general will in our fatherland. . . . As regards your question whether the intervention that we are demanding would be a military one, our response is to consider the testimony of history. How many times have [the Great Powers] intervened in our domestic affairs, how many times even have parts of our country been taken away? Why do we not want to transform these interventions, which most of the time took place without even a military action, into one favoring our own interests?[190]

The striking point here is that whereas Sabahaddin Bey described foreign intervention in Ottoman domestic affairs as "benevolent mediation" or "equitable action" and Sisyan Efendi presented it as the *sine qua non* of any alliance between the Young Turks and the Armenians,[191] opponents such as Ahmed Ferid characterized it as a "deceitful and usurping hand." The disagreement was not over details, as the central organ claimed, but over substance. Thus all efforts to harmonize the discord were fruitless. Abdurrahman Bedirhan and Silistireli Mustafa Hamdi asked that the term *action bienveillante* be replaced with the phrase *concours moral.*[192] Another document reveals that the term *benevolent conduct* was proffered by the opponents.[193] Ahmed Rıza's notes, penned during the congress, reveal his predilection for a more neutral phrase: "to require the moral aid of the Great Powers."[194] İsmail Hakkı tells us that the term *action bienveillante* was invented by Khalīl Ghānim, but that Ahmed Rıza firmly opposed it.[195] According to Fua the majority acquiesced to the incorporation of both terms in order to satisfy the minority group.[196] Soon afterward the majority revealed a letter from Ahmed Midhat Pasha to Lord Derby written at the peak of the crisis of 1876–1877; it was the property of his son Ali Haydar Midhat, also a delegate at the congress.[197] In order to lay to rest any doubts about the letter's authorship, it was presented for examination by all delegates.[198] In the letter Ahmed Midhat Pasha proposed the *concours moral* of Great Britain, using the phrase *action morale* and hoping to enlist British support.[199] However, the minority group brought forward a motion censuring the term *action=harekât*, with the claim that "the people would strongly oppose a foreign intervention."[200]

Another important aspect of the congress was the vote for the program and supplement. Various sources provide differing and fragmented pieces of information. Ali Fehmi wrote that "the four-article program and its supplement were endorsed by a majority of the vote." He claimed that "articles of the program were accepted unanimously but, as for myself, I abstained."[201] *Droshak* wrote that the Armenians did not participate in the vote.[202] However, *Kürdistan* claimed that "the Armenian delegates abstained in the first sitting but voted for foreign intervention [in the following session] with the majority."[203] İsmail Hakkı wrote that Khalīl Ghānim was sick at the time, and sent his vote in an envelope.[204] We might conclude that the program and supplement were voted on separately and that the former was accepted by forty-two votes against one abstaining vote by Ali Fehmi (assuming we can trust his account of his own behavior). The supplement was accepted by a majority, but I found no clear record of this in any source. The activists claimed that votes were cast for both texts without lengthy discussion.[205] In spite of the coordinating committee's efforts to create a strong majority in the convention by blocking participation of many of their opponents, an overwhelming consensus did not emerge during the congress. Since no verifiable results of the voting have been found in any source,[206] the only way to determine who voted against the supplement is to examine the organs of the various groups that covered the meeting.

A document among the papers of Bahaeddin Şakir provides information: those who addressed the convention against the supplement or were depicted as opponents of the minority group by various journals were Abdülhalim Memduh, Abdurrahman Bedirhan, Ahmed Ferid, Ahmed Rıza, Ali Fahri, Ali Fehmi,[207] Albert Fua, Khalīl Ghānim, Hamid Hüsni,

Babanzâde Hikmet Süleyman, Hoca Kadri, Mahir Said, Mustafa Hamdi, Doctor Nâzım, Nuri Ahmed, and Yusuf Akçura.[208] The document contains a list of nineteen delegates, all belonging to the majority group, with the number twenty-five in parentheses.[209] Since it is still unclear how some delegates voted, we may conclude that the majority consisted of twenty-five delegates opposing the eighteen representatives of the minority; two delegates are unknown to us. The minimum number for the minority is sixteen.

At the end of the second session Sabahaddin Bey announced that he and his brother had put up Fr 25,000 toward the new society that was to be established after the convention. The munificence of this sum captured the attention of foreign diplomats observing the convention[210] and was applauded by all delegates.[211]

During the third session, which took place the following day at the princes' residence, the minority attempted to reopen the discussion about foreign intervention. The majority, however, disallowed this, noting "the impossibility of the alteration or modification of a decision once made."[212] Then the Armenian delegation, which opposed the "réformes générales" described in the third article of the program,[213] presented its declaration:

> 1. Que les Comités arméniens sont prêts à collaborer avec les libéraux ottomans à toute action commune ayant pour but de transformer le régime actuel;
>
> 2. Qu'en dehors de l'action commune, les Comités arméniens continueront leur action particulière, étant bien entendu que cette action est dirigée contre le régime actuel et non contre l'unité et l'existence organique de la Turquie;
>
> 3. Que leur action particulière n'a, d'ailleurs, d'autre but que d'obtenir l'exécution immédiate de l'article 61 du traité de Berlin, du mémorandum du 11 Mai 1895 et de son annexe, ainsi que les réformes mentionnées dans les mémoires remis par voie diplomatique au gouvernement français au nom des Comités arméniens.[214]

This text reveals how antithetical the vantage point of the members of the Armenian committees[215] was to the rest of the movement and how they had divorced themselves from the notion of "libéraux Ottomans" by emphasizing their willingness to work with them. Sabahaddin Bey declared that the Armenians' response had been accepted by the majority:

> Les représentants des peuples de l'Empire Ottoman, qui ont pris part au Congrès ouvert le 4 Février 1802 [sic] à Paris, après avoir pris connaissance des déclarations ci-dessus, protestant contre le régime actuel de la Turquie:
>
> S'engagent à travailler en commun en vue:
>
> 1. De transformer le présent régime de gouvernement en un régime de liberté et de justice tel que l'assurerait le rétablissement de la Constitution;
>
> 2. De rappeler aux Puissances Européennes qu'il est de leur devoir et de l'intérêt général de l'humanité de faire exécuter les clauses des traités et actes internationaux intervenus entre elles et la Sublime Porte, de manière à en faire profiter toutes parties de l'Empire Ottoman.[216]

With this declaration, the majority used elastic language to accept the execution of reforms for six provinces as decreed by article sixty-one of the Berlin Congress, but it also tried to satisfy the minority by asking that these reforms apply to the entire Empire. This was a compromise intended to prevent the Armenians from walking out. *Osmanlı* wrote that "the majority and the Armenians had reached a perfect accord at this point."[217] Nevertheless, the minority first claimed that "the memorandum of May 11, 1895, was annulled"[218] and later "employed an allusive and caustic language for Armenians,"[219] saying "the Armenians had been subjected to wrath and oppression by the present administration. But are the Turks who compose the dominant element less oppressed or more equitably treated than the Armenians?" With this statement members of the minority proclaimed the dominance of the Turkish element.[220] At that point Ahmed Rıza returned to the podium and fulminated against the declaration:

> Here you are dismissing the program of the Armenians. On the other hand they are rejecting ours. While Armenians cannot reach any accord over principles with a group that accepts many aspects of their program, it is certainly unlikely that they would reach an agreement on a program aiming at foreign intervention. How is it possible for any real agreement to be accorded by two committees that reject each other's program? According to their own words the Armenians want to reach an agreement with us in order to overthrow the present regime. This type of agreement can be reached between sovereign states or in the most extreme case between the Ottomans and the Bulgarians. But I cannot imagine it between the citizens of the same state who are living in different areas of the Empire.[221]

After his speech, the third session was adjourned. Although the delegates convened the next evening, the Armenian representatives begged a day of grace, to await instructions from their headquarters on whether to accept the declaration. The fourth session was postponed until the next day.[222]

At this session, held in the evening of February 8, 1902, the members of the minority once again brought up the subject of foreign intervention, but as before the "majority" silenced them by repeating that once a decision was made it could not be changed. Here Sabahaddin Bey rose to speak. When he said "the Constitution will be a substantial source for delineating the limits of [their] sacred duty,"[223] Sisyan Efendi interrupted him, exclaiming that they "did not consider the Constitution as the single tool for their national liberation."[224] Other Armenian delegates further averred that they "would never wish to see the six provinces of Anatolia subjected to the Ottoman Constitution."[225] The tension rose in the atmosphere. İsmail Kemal stood up and made a shocking indictment against the Armenians. He said:

> I refute these comments on behalf of the majority. We are searching for suitable grounds for reforms that can benefit all parties and might be proper for you, and we do acknowledge that you are justified in your cause.

But if you wish the creation of an [organic] law exclusively unto your-
selves, I say, no! No! Always no will be your answer, and we will oppose you
on every occasion from this point onward. As long as you remain an element
of the Ottoman state there will be a constitution for you, just as for us.

I defend your cause, not in an effort to appease you. I am defending it
on behalf of the interest of my state and government. I will defend it even if
you do not want me to do so. I recognize you not as an independent element
but as Ottomans. You have rights as Ottomans. [However,] you do not have
the right to bargain with us and make offers as if you were [representatives of
a] state. The [authority] who granted the constitution was not Europe but
our state. You should also bear in mind that we are not only Turks here.
Greeks, Albanians, Arabs, and others are present.[226]

After this speech the Armenian delegates walked out one by one.[227]
By saying, "if you will unite, then we shall come over and discuss with
you," they left the door open.[228] Sabahaddin Bey endeavored to prevent
a dissolution of the congress by arguing that the Armenians' action "would
not damage the union."[229] But because he understood the value of Armenian backing for obtaining support from the Great Powers, he and his
friends negotiated a new resolution for Armenians. Thus they gave a favorable response to the Armenians and so kept the door open between themselves and the Armenians:

> 1. L'accomplissement des vœux légitimes des Arméniens relativement à
> l'organisation de l'administration locale des provinces qu'ils habitent et de
> toutes les autres provinces;
> 2. L'établissement d'un gouvernement central s'appuyant sur les idées
> libérales et qui serait la meilleure garantie du maintien des droits nationaux,
> comme du fonctionnement régulier des administrations provinciales et dont
> les Arméniens bénéficieraient au même titre et dans la même mesure que tous
> les peuples de l'Empire.[230]

Ahmed Rıza challenged even this compromise by charging that "the
Armenians are offering their right hand to the revolutionary Bulgaro-Mac-
edonian Committee [IMRO] and their left hand to the Young Turks, who
are promoting the reproclamation of the Ottoman Constitution." He further denied any possibility of true accord with the Armenians.[231] Following
this speech, and in response to the Armenians' action, a rapprochement
was attempted between majority and minority groups. According to the
activists, both sides considered forming a new and joint organization.[232]
But according to the majority, due to "the stubbornness of the minority,"[233] and according to their opponents, due to "the inflexibility of the
majority on the subject of intervention,"[234] this rapprochement failed.
İsmail Kemal gave a two-hour speech during which he sought some
grounds for a compromise, but his efforts were in vain.[235]

The next day the delegates convened for the final session. There was
a secret ballot to elect members of the central committee of the new organization; one delegate unable to join the voting sent his decision in a
letter.[236] The new central committee was set up under the honorary lead-

ership of Damad Mahmud Pasha, with Sabahaddin Bey, İsmail Kemal, Ali Haydar Midhat, İsmail Hakkı, Hüseyin Siyret; Musurus Ghikis; and Georges Fardis.[237]

Before the close of the convention, the minority read their appeal, announcing that they had found the principles of the majority a threat to the national interest; they stated their intention to found an independent program of action:

Our Dear Compatriots,

While participating in the Congress, we have been hoping to close our convention with a unanimous accord. To use the power derived from our unity was our utmost aim. Our final offer proves how steadfastly we favored unity. Our offer was this: "The congress will inform the Great Powers by an appeal that we will concentrate our work toward progress and general reforms by reproclaiming the constitution in our fatherland and we hope for the favorable inclination and the benevolence of European powers." But unfortunately, our goal has been thwarted. The majority of the congress preferred to enlist the assistance of the foreigners, or according to their own words, to invite them to fulfill their duties as stated in treaties, acknowledging their right to intervene in our domestic affairs and to pursue their rights by such action. It was decided that the most consequential among the duties enumerated by the new permanent committee, in short, the essence of the regulation that was designed and accepted, was to demand foreign intervention.

We assume that at the present stage of civilization, national interest remains the primary determining factor for the actions of governments. We are not confident that the interests of the powers will always concur with our own in the field of reforms. We agree that foreign intervention is hazardous to our interests, to the maintenance of our independence, and to our territorial integrity. The majority should also concede that they could not produce a single example of beneficial foreign intervention during peace-time. Second, we failed to comprehend how European intervention will be secured in light of our national interests. We are unable to imagine how an Ottoman association, to be founded in Paris, would formulate the policies of the Great Powers toward the Eastern Question.

We are not against Europe as we are unjustly accused. On the contrary, to imitate their progress throughout our country is our prime and sacred aim. We want to enlighten our people by their education and to equip our government with their constitution[alism]. We desire to follow the policies of the developed nations in all public works. Thus, what causes the disagreement between us is not that [we are against Europe]—it is the pro or con stand toward foreign intervention. We find the consummate patriotism in categorically refusing [foreign] intervention and hope that our patriotism will be pursuant to our national interests and commended by Europe.

Thus we proclaim that we must work independently and wish with our hearts that the future committee to be founded by the majority will bring forth good works for our fatherland.[238]

The split at the end of the convention forced the majority, which was allied with various groups seeking divergent goals, to sit once more at the bargaining table with the Armenians. The subject of their meeting is unknown. The discord and the Armenians' threats to organize a common front with the Macedonian committees left even foreign observers baffled as to how the two sides reached an agreement.[239] Further, the Armenians had pointed out that it was useless for them to participate in a new organization since they already had functioning committees.[240] On February 14, after a consensus was reached between the Armenians and the majority, the former sent a letter to Sabahaddin Bey indicating that they had relaxed their policy toward a joint action. The letter stated that they "were ready to participate in all efforts to overthrow the present regime" and that "they did not oppose the establishment of a constitutional central administration that would execute" special reforms for the six provinces.[241] Although they took the additional step of using the term *constitutional central administration,* they insisted on special reforms. The majority, under the direction of Sabahaddin and İsmail Kemal Beys, halfheartedly accepted this modest compromise. They decided to appoint an Armenian representative in the central committee, replacing Siyret Bey. They offered the seat to Kılıçyan Efendi, who had not participated in the convention; when he refused, they authorized the Armenian committees to choose their own representative.[242]

This was a victory for the Armenians, since most parts of their program had now been endorsed by the majority.[243] The minority, however, vehemently opposed this new development.[244]

With the last bridge between the majority and the minority destroyed, the Young Turk movement, which until then had maintained a united front despite difficulties, was split.

Consequences of the Congress

In spite of the fears of the Ottoman government, the congress emerged divided into a majority and a minority faction. But one should be cautious about these terms. First, the majority did not represent a truly dominant position. The minority and its supporters consisted of a group that existed since the adoption of the title CUP and had long held sway over the movement[245]; all the societies had been founded by the activists, the most important among which were İntikamcı Yeni Osmanlılar and İstirdat committees; and the active element of the Young Turk establishment in the Balkans. Those groups were publishing six journals, namely, *İntikam, İstirdat, Kürdistan, Mechveret Supplément Français, Muvazene,* and *Sancak,* or seven if one includes *Meşveret,* which Ahmed Rıza had hoped to republish.[246] By contrast the majority had not even one journal representing the movement. The editor of *Osmanlı,* controlled by the remaining members of the old organization, had voted with the minority at the convention. Therefore, the only course available to the majority was to take over the central organ. Again, the minority dominated the Young Turk network in Paris, Geneva, Egypt, and Bulgaria while the majority's only relationships were with high-ranking bureaucrats in Istanbul.

When Ahmed Rıza demanded that the president of the convention identify the participants in the meeting and tell why they had been invited, the majority's "commotion" silenced the positivist leader. According to the journal reporting this event, "the identities of those [who did this] were uncertain; nor were they in the register of Ottoman patriots."[247] Besides, it was problematic for the majority to obtain the support of such elements as the Armenians, Albanians, and Greeks. The Armenian committees' official support was meager and a disappointment to Sabahaddin Bey and İsmail Kemal. Though the Armenians calumniated Ahmed Rıza and his followers for their anti-interventionist stance, predicting that "they are going to annihilate the Christian nations of the empire upon the death of Sultan Abdülhamid II, and the Constitution is a mask that they use,"[248] they withheld a full endorsement of the majority wing of the Young Turks, and some Armenian journals openly criticized Damad Mahmud Pasha.[249] As for the Greek delegates, it was unclear which group they were representing. The only significant support came from some Albanian organizations, but their support was of slight value in attracting the Great Powers, since the endorsement was by Muslim Albanians. Under these circumstances the European press continually emphasized the fact that Damad Mahmud Pasha and his followers were trying to impose changes in favor of the Christian elements in order to receive the backing of the Great Powers.[250]

The majority was a coalition of various groups seeking divergent goals. In this majority, composed of Turks, Greeks, Albanians, and Armenians, the last three identified themselves with their ethnic group. Even the Armenians expressed a reluctance to don the Ottoman mantle. By contrast the minority had not a single Christian member, and the only person claiming an ethnic identity above his Ottoman one was Abdurrahman Bedirhan, a Kurd. Those aware of his published appeals to the Kurds asking them to treat Armenians well[251] and who had learned that he was demanding the support of the British diplomats for his publication and activities,[252] assumed that he intended to act with the majority. Probably the pro-Armenian attitude of the majority impelled him to join the minority.

Another obstacle for the majority was the endorsement of an inactive program. Their only aim was to secure the intervention of the Great Powers in Ottoman domestic politics. Ali Haydar Midhat, a member of the new central committee, wrote that the reason for this was that "the people bemoan the oppression by the sultan and are powerless to make their voice audible to the civilized world; therefore it was necessary to become their interlocutor."[253] But to effect such an intervention for the entire Empire, which had gone unrealized even during the dire events of 1895, was an arduous task. Securing it even for one region depended on the level of influence of the Christians living in that area.

The majority had no alternative but to establish relationships with separatist groups and with those who viewed western intervention not as an act of imperialism but as the benevolent and humanitarian assistance of the Great Powers. However, neither group exerted sufficient influence to lead the majority to overthrow the regime. Thus whereas Damad Mahmud Pasha and his friends formed ties with the Egyptian ulema and issued joint publications,[254] anti-British Egyptian nationalists such as Muṣṭafā Kāmil Bey, leader of the Nationalist party, accused those Young Turks who voted for foreign intervention in the congress of being agents of foreign powers.[255] A less radical Arab journal shared this point of view.[256] On the other hand periodicals, published later by the minority, supported the Egyptian nationalists' cause.[257] Although European admirers of Sabahaddin Bey ascertained that his efforts would yield positive results for "European Peace" and "World Civilization,"[258] their praise was not useful in overthrowing the sultan's regime.

For all these reasons the majority would face more difficulties than the minority. As one journal put it "the group called minority is indeed the majority."[259]

An important consequence of the convention was that it was a stimulus for the union of two groups, the activists and the group surrounding Ahmed Rıza, for despite their differences, both opposed foreign intervention. This unification, however, may have materialized later without the catalyst of the convention.

When the European press applauded the victory of Damad Mahmud Pasha and his sons, heralding them as the "individuals of the day,"[260] the losers of the Congress undertook an initiative to build a stronger organizational network for controlling the movement.

A final result of the congress was that, until August 15, 1903, no group was in a position to carry the title of the CUP. Only then did the remaining members of the old organization who retook the official organ *Osmanlı* assume that title.[261] However, this title remained alive and well in the alliance established between the activists and the followers of Ahmed Rıza.

9

The Political Ideas of the Young Turks

Islam as a Tool of Modernization

Foreign scholars commenting on the Young Turks' writings, even after
the revolution of 1908, had difficulty deciphering the heavy Islamic rhetoric and references used.[1] Even the titles of Young Turk organs—*Ezan,
Hak, İctihad, Meşveret*—had been selected for their appeal to a Muslim
readership. In the CUP anthem, the sultan was accused of being "an atheist,"[2] and in an early propaganda pamphlet, the CUP leaders described an
imaginary trial—not in a modern court, which they professed to admire,
but on Judgment Day when the Prophet, famous caliphs, Ottoman sultans,
and statesmen tried Abdülhamid II and sentenced him to death according
to Islamic law.[3]

Whereas in their open writings the CUP leaders extolled and pro-
moted Islam,[4] their private letters reveal the disregard in which they held
Islam, especially in its institutionalized form. Here is a letter from Ahmed
Rıza to his sister:

> Though many famous scholars emerged among the Arabs in the fields of
> geometry, algebra, astronomy, geography, and medical sciences during the
> times of Prophet Muhammad and of his successors, a thousand years later the
> *ummah* of Muhammad have descended so low as to request a shopping tally
> of three and a half gurush from the clerk of grocer Georgos. This is due to the
> fact that the Prophet's words have been so misconstrued by our God damn
> ignorant imams and softas as to claim that when the Prophet used the term

science he referred only to readings from the Quran. . . . It is for such reasons that nobody read the works of the Western scholars. . . . These cowardly scoundrels effected the annihilation and wretchedness of a great *ummah*! . . . Today the Muslims have declined to the level of Jews. If you ask my own opinion: From the viewpoints of education and knowledge they are certainly at a level lower than the Jews. The *ummah* is dissolved, weakened, and from this point it will never recover and regain vitality. The believers in the heaven which has houris, cold sherbets, and rivers are decreasing. Were I a woman, I would embrace atheism and never become a Muslim. Imagine a religion that imposes laws always beneficial to men but hazardous to women such as permitting my husband to have three additional wives and as many concubines as he wishes, houris awaiting him in heaven, while I cover my head and face as a miller's horse. Beside these I would not be allowed to divorce a husband who prevented me from having any kind of fun, but would be required to submit to his beatings. Keep this religion far away from me.

How strange that this should be a sort of mental illness for me—whenever the discussion turns to religion I lose control of myself. . . . My dear Fahire the times will change. However, we were either born too early or in an unlucky country.[5]

Abdullah Cevdet was disgruntled when the central committee required him to add footnotes to his translation of Alfieri's *Della Tirannide*, which denied any Islamic basis to absolutist regimes. Yet in doing so he seemed to defend Islam so ably[6] that later scholars assumed his own real views had been reflected,[7] when in fact he had found those passages in Alfieri's work to be entirely cogent.[8]

The reasoning behind this double standard toward Islam was twofold. First, the Young Turks as modernists thought that the only way of infusing modernization and westernization into their Empire was to present them to Muslim masses as Islamic concepts. For instance, parliament was often alluded to as the final stage of the Islamic concept of *mushāwara*,[9] and to send girls to school was presented as observing a *ḥadīth* of the Prophet.[10] From this viewpoint Islam was nothing other than a device.

Second, the Young Turks perceived their society as being an *ummah* of Muslims and so they sincerely undertook to develop the means of converting the "psychology of Muslims." In their application of Gustave Le Bon's theories they assumed just such a reference, and Abdullah Cevdet referred to it as "Muslim spirit." Islam was the tool for molding this Muslim soul. A popular saying among the Young Turks was: "Science is the religion of the elite, whereas religion is the science of the masses."[11] Again, Abdullah Cevdet wrote:

Nous avons constaté par nos longues expériences: l'esprit musulman fermera toute ouverture à la clarté si elle vient immédiatement du monde chrétien. Il nous faut donc à nous qui assumons le soin de transfuser un sang nouveau dans les veines musulmanes, de chercher et trouver tous les principes progressistes dans l'institution de l'Islam même, et l'islamisme en déborde. Telle est la raison qui nous amène souvent à parler des musulmanes et de l'islamisme.[12]

For this reason Abdullah Cevdet asked the following questions while omitting those about ways of saving the Ottoman empire: "What are the reasons and conditions for the decline of the Islamic World? And what is the most effective measure to save the Islamic World from total extinction and to pour a fresh vitality on the Muslims?"[13] İsmail Kemal claimed that "brilliant and clever Muslims should enlighten the masses . . . and such a service to Muslims can be rendered only by Muslims."[14] Ahmed Rıza raised a similar point when he criticized missionary activities in the Ottoman Empire, asserting the impossibility of converting a Muslim to Christianity.[15] He thought that the way to convert Muslims was to transform them into positivists. He wrote: "Un lien scientifique, une morale universelle, dégagée de toute conception théologique, me semble le seul remède capable de réaliser l'harmonie et la bonne entente internationales,"[16] and therefore "il y a promesse de mariage entre la civilisation musulmane et la civilisation *scientifique*."[17] Young Turks concurred with this idea; however, they also admitted that this should be a gradual conversion, and that their initial goal was to infuse a new *Weltanschauung* into the Muslim spirit. A Young Turk wrote of the impossibility of promoting positivism in the Empire in spite of its fundamental humanism because of fanaticism among the masses. However, since their immediate objective was to make a revolution, eradicating fanaticism could gradually be effected later.[18] "An enlightened Muslim elite," as the Young Turks envisioned it, would accomplish this mission,[19] which when completed would enable anyone to cast Islam aside. Ahmed Rıza dreamed of an Ottoman flag modeled on the flag of Brazil and of substituting positivism for Islam. Abdullah Cevdet later asked the Muslims to convert to Bahaism, which he regarded as an intermediary step between Islam and materialism,[20] and Young Turks' efforts to create a very liberal and progressive Islam reflected a core endeavor.[21] The Young Turks approached an extreme when they manipulated Islamic values in an attempt to convince their readership that Islam was a kind of materialism. They drew parallels between Islamic thinkers of earlier times and modern materialists. For instance they claimed that the philosophical definition of al-Jurjānī contained the very substance of the sayings of Jacoby: "Les hommes descendent des animaux et son destinés à devenir des Dieux[22];" Abū al-'Alā' al-Ma'arrī was presented as someone who wrote books "on the laws of evolution, which today are called Darwinism."[23] "Striking" similarities were seen between the ideas of Ibn al-'Arabī and Bacon,[24] and finally specific writings by Massillon were presented as if taken directly from *ḥadīths*.[25] A scholar of Islam might find wide disparities between this "Islam" and the religion of Islam. However, this was far more than a device for countering accusations of atheism, which many participants of the movement believed it to be,[26] rather it was the creation of a brand new ideology presented as Islam.

Striking similarities can be found between some texts written by the Young Turks and those written by the Salafis and the followers of 'Abduh and al-Afghānī. Especially interesting is the idea of relying on the original sources of Islam. The Young Turks, however, did not attempt to reconcile Islam with modern sciences and ideas, and they developed a positivist-materialist ideology by deliberately misinterpreting Islamic sources. Theirs was an original contribution to Ottoman political thought, and it distinguishes them from members of other liberal movements among Muslims who were also trying to use Islam as a device for modernization by claiming the Islamic roots of modern European laws.[27] For this reason the Young Turks gave a delayed answer to the question raised years ago by the ulema against the leader of the Young Ottoman movement. When he claimed that religion and faith were secondary determinants of a society and that their primary importance was to the individual,[28] the ulema had simply asked: "so what are the important determinants [of the society] if not religion [Islam]?"[29] He and the other members of the movement were unable to respond to the ulema. Later the Young Turks answered, saying to their adherents that it is "science" and to the masses "Islam, but not the one that you know—the real Islam."[30]

The Young Turks and Positivism

Auguste Comte himself had high regard for the Turks and the Ottoman ruling elite as opposed to the other nations of the Middle East.[31] In 1853 he even solicited the help of Reşid Pasha to promote positivism in the Orient.[32] Later, positivists trying to establish ties with Midhat Pasha received a warm response from him.[33] However, these attempts led to no substantial results for the positivists.

Nevertheless, positivism emerged as the underpinning of Young Turk thought. Ahmed Rıza, who led the movement intermittently from 1895 to 1908, became a student of Pierre Laffitte and later a leader in the international positivist movement.[34] Numerous Young Turks admitted that their knowledge was founded on positivism.[35] For their part positivists supported the Young Turks during their opposition in exile[36] and after the Revolution of 1908, which they regarded as a triumph of positivism.[37]

Direct references to positivism are scant in Young Turk journals. Once Ahmed Rıza wrote that space limitations prevented him from commenting on positivism in his journal.[38] but the real reason was a precaution against alienating the religious allies of the Young Turks.

There are many reasons behind the popularity of positivism among the Young Turks. The most important is that positivism, which claimed to be a new religion, was an ideology for which the Young Turks, who were trying to replace religion with science, were ripe. Besides, as Ahmed Rıza demonstrated, it was easy to claim common elements between Islam and positivism on the subjects of property, family, and government.[39]

The Young Turks considered their ideal society an *ummah*, and positivism's refutation of the individual as the simplest unit of society and the importance that it attributed to the division of labor were corroborated by Islam. Ahmed Rıza wrote: "The Government of Islam is a collective authority in which every free citizen . . . is bound by a common destiny, and shares in its responsibilities."[40]

Until now researchers have emphasized the significance of the term *progress* in the title of the main Young Turk organization. Actually, it is more important to examine the reason why the term *union* replaced *order* in the famous apothegm of Comte. Unity among the Ottomans was always agreed upon and was promoted as the primary aim of the CUP.[41] Its leaders assumed that in a society of united people there would be duties and responsibilities for each member. Murad Bey wrote that "duties are sacred. The heavy duties are undertaken by important people and lighter ones by lesser people."[42] Ahmed Rıza asserted that the shining difference between a civilized society and a gang of savages in a jungle is that "the sultans, princes, women, religious and military leaders—in short, important, unimportant—are equally charged with a duty to society."[43] He published a series of pamphlets on the "duties and responsibilities" of members of various social groups and intended to write more such pamphlets about sultans, princes, women, ulema, military, non-Muslim subjects, civil officials, authors, the elite and the masses.[44] By the time of the Young Turk revolution, in addition to an essay about sultans and princes, he had authored two more pamphlets—one on the military and the other on women.[45]

Abdullah Cevdet and İshak Sükûti took another initiative before fleeing to Europe. At a private elementary school, which they had established in Mamuret el-Azîz, they attempted to instill a collective sense of responsibility by punishing every student in class whenever someone failed an exam.[46] The Young Turks' approach was similar to the thesis of Mexican positivists, led by Miguel S. Macedo, on relations between "superiors and inferiors."[47] Like the Young Turks, this wing of the Mexican positivists—so-called Científicos—tried to establish a society grounded on the laws of science. The idea of union among members of a society each of whom had duties and responsibilities, also has roots in traditional Ottoman thought.[48] Ahmed Rıza and his friends were able to draw on the established goal of a strong government for maintaining "order" and regulating every aspect of private life in such a society. This was undoubtedly the lesson that they learned from their teacher Pierre Laffitte,[49] which accorded well with traditional Ottoman thought. Therefore they preferred the name "Committee of Union and Progress" and not to reconcile positivism with liberal ideas by adopting names like "Liberty and Progress" by Victorino Lastarria or "Love, Order, and Progress for Liberty" by Gabino Barreda.[50]

A second advantage of basing the Young Turk ideology on positivism was that they could embrace it as "scientific." Recall that when Young Turks became the adherents of positivism, positivistic organicism was the prevailing ideology in Europe and that the separation between organicism and positivism was manifested long after the Young Turk Revolution. It was also fashionable in the 1890s to undertake a positivistic course using as banners Le Bon's, Moleschott's, Vogt's, Büchner's, and Haechel's theories. This was expressed in the Latin American positivist movement[51] and was also true for the positivists in Italy.[52] Like the Young Turks, many "freethinkers" of Europe found it natural and interesting to convert from "unbelief" to "Comte's religion."[53]

A third reason for adopting positivism was that its adherents were critical of contemporary European values and imperial politics, and they drastically departed from general European public opinion on the Eastern Question.[54] The nationalist faction of the CUP and Ahmed Rıza based their anti-imperialistic jargon on this non-Eurocentric positivist rhetoric. He thought that "le positivisme seul est capable de sauver, aux yeux des peuple orientaux, le prestige de la civilisation occidentale et l'honneur de la grande Révolution française."[55] He created an antithesis to the approach of western scholars and diplomats on the Eastern Question through an application of positivist ideas to the issues.[56] Later Ahmed Rıza authored an outstanding work refuting European imperial politics based on his positivist ideas,[57] which was reprinted by the Tunisians without a new preface, even as late as 1979, in an attempt to benefit from it.[58] Besides the anti-imperialist rhetoric, Ahmed Rıza employed positivism to legitimize his Turkish nationalist ideas. He carried out a dispute on the Macedonian Question with a French positivist and expressed the official Turkish perspective on the matter.[59] In that sense Ahmed Rıza and his friends' efforts were similar to Charles Maurras's synthesis of positivism and French nationalism.

The Young Turks and Elitism

Although the Young Turk movement has been defined as a political opposition activity, little in the writings of CUP members was political, and the leaders rarely commented on their political tendencies. Once Murad Bey, to refute accusations of anarchism, wrote that the Young Turks "can be considered conservatives."[60] On another occasion he claimed that "the CUP was similar to the conservative parties in Europe."[61]

Despite their many complaints about absolutism, the Young Turks rarely discussed the types of regimes they admired. Sabahaddin Bey characterized the entire body of Young Turk publications as "the wail of a bitten man."[62] The only exceptions are Tunalı Hilmi's three works in which he drew a detailed state model based on the principle of the people's sovereignty and their socialization as Ottomans through the use of a Turkish symbology[63]; there were also scattered references to the theory of social contract with quotes from Rousseau and Locke.[64] The official CUP organs paid no attention to such issues; however, and they never became significant elements in Young Turk thought.

Also, CUP leaders never provided a clear definition of absolutism, against which they railed and plotted; they usually referred to absolutism simply as an impediment to progress and neglected to examine it in any political context. Although the most serious effort to define absolutism

was the translation of *Della Tirannide*, the Young Turks were more interested in Alfieri's anticlericalism and his accusation that tyrants become
enemies of science in order to keep their subjects ignorant.[65] Besides these,
the accomplished assassination of the tyrant in Alfieri's poem *L'Etruria
vendicata* certainly impressed the activist faction of the Young Turks.

A single persistent strain running throughout Young Turk publications was their elitist perception of the masses as despicable. Even in their
earliest writings, published during expatriation, the Young Turks drew
upon Le Bon's theories when proposing solutions to various dilemmas
facing Ottoman society. From Ahmed Rıza[66] to Hoca Muhiddin,[67] and
from the nationalist faction of the Young Turks[68] to the official organs of
the CUP,[69] Le Bon's ideas were regularly cited. Even *Osmanlı* once
claimed that the shortcomings of the movement were "due to an ignorance of *psychologie [des foules]* and the inability of members to define their
own enemies accordingly."[70] Le Bon was considered the greatest living
sociologist.[71] His book *Les lois psychologiques de l'évolution des peuples* was
translated by Abdullah Cevdet in 1907.[72] Le Bon's simple language and
plausible generalizations, in addition to the perceived scientific nature of
his work, satisfied the Young Turks.[73] The Young Turks never mentioned
Tarde and Durkheim, whose seminal theories were popularized by Le Bon.

Le Bon's antipathy toward revolutions, especially the French Revolution, became intrinsic to the Young Turk *Weltanschauung*, which viewed
"the people" as a "foule." Early criticisms decried the people, whom they
blamed for "not appreciating the efforts of these distinguished individuals
[the Young Turks]."[74] In their private papers "people" were labeled
"senseless."[75] The inability of a crowd to reach correct decisions was contrasted with the value of superior individuals,[76] culminating in a condemnation of the people. Eventually people were judged guilty: "To whom
does the guilt belong? To the people! Because every nation is worthy of
the government that administrates it."[77]

Young Turks' adherence to Le Bon's theories also posed problems.
First, their espoused aim was to reopen the Ottoman parliament. Second,
a strong faction in the movement was praising revolutions, and from the
onset of the movement the French Revolution was given exemplary status.[78] The first dilemma was relatively easy to solve. They asserted that if
a parliament could be a "national assembly to which people sent the most
intelligent individuals," it might be valuable.[79] Therefore, the task to
which the Young Turks dedicated themselves was the creation of an elite.[80]
This elite could guide the masses by imposing their ideas on them through
constant repetition.[81] The problem before them was described as the creation of the elite, because the masses, if guided wrongly, could bring
unwished-for results.[82] The Young Turks underscored the importance of
an "intellectual elite" by implementing various *ḥadīths* and succeeded in
creating a "scientific," elitist theory, which they then stitched into an
Islamic jacket. The best explanation of their accomplishment based on Le
Bon's theories was later summarized in *Şûra-yı Ümmet*:

In one of his works the French philosopher Gustave Le Bon likens nations to a pyramid. The base of that pyramid was made of masses called *peuple*, and the top was composed of the class of intelligentsia. . . . Therefore, it is necessary to search for the reasons for changes in the conditions of the nations not among the masses that composed a great majority, but in the psychology of their intelligentsia. . . . Since in chemistry two elements need a connection such as that provided by thermal or electrical energy, in order to blend, the people need such a guiding channel so as to be able to be constructively influenced by the events. . . . In France, people are indebted to Clemenceau, Rochefort, Jaurès, Drumont, Anatole France, who control public opinion. . . . The people of Istanbul endures its most sacred rights being trodden upon, and the shame that derives from this belongs not to the masses but to the intelligentsia of the Muslim society.[83]

This undoubtedly describes the emergence of the Republican Public party's populist platform "for the people" but never "by the people," as expressed in the mid-1920s and 1930s.

The problem of how to change the regime without a revolution was deemed paramount. Until 1902 the only solution the Young Turks envisioned was to educate the masses about their goal of replacing the regime of Abdülhamid II with a dictatorship of intellectuals. Many Young Turks worked in education, despite their varied backgrounds. Ahmed Rıza preferred to be the director of education of Bursa after receiving a degree in agricultural engineering from Grignon University.[84] Murad Bey taught political history at the Royal School of Administration even though he was only an amateur historian and had held positions in the public debt administration. Abdullah Cevdet and İshak Sükûti established a private elementary school and tested original methods in education. Furthermore Abdullah Cevdet penned an interesting pamphlet on education, which he presented as a *mémoire* at the International Congress of Social Education in Paris.[85] Mehmed Reşid prompted the CUP exiles in Tripoli to open a library in which lectures were given to the local inhabitants on basic subjects.[86] İbrahim Temo spearheaded the establishment of a cultural society to educate Muslims in the Balkans.[87] Also, CUP journals proposed to members in small towns that they embark upon educational projects, as if these organs represented a society for education[88]; the importance of education was frequently underscored.[89] Another reason they emphasized education was their belief that "through education [the application of scientific method to the solution of social problems and secularly grounded principles of social morality] could be fixed in a race and transmitted thereafter by heredity."[90] The Young Turks took this idea from a treatise by Jean-Marie Guyau entitled *Education et hérédité: Étude sociologique.*[91] In this way it became possible to merge Le Bon's theories with those of Guyau and to find a "scientific rationale" for promoting education.

This attitude left the CUP with no revolutionary praxis except that of the activists. Therefore, the convergence of Ahmed Rıza's followers with the activists held great significance. The emerging new group hesitated to adopt a revolutionary course, however, until 1906, when Bahaeddin Şakir perceived this flaw in the CUP, and under his direction the society was transformed into a nationalist-revolutionary organization in which tasks like the education of the masses were entirely absent.

Materialism, Race, and Nationalism

We have observed that from its inception the Young Turk movement lacked allegiance to any political doctrine and despised "pure politics." Politics played a minuscule role in the Young Turks' grandiose agenda, while "science," a term Young Turks usually employed when referring to "materialism," informed their particular definition of life. According to the founders, "life, resulting from chemical and physical events, is qualified by becoming a living organism and of reproducing."[92] Interestingly, this description does not distinguish between biological and social entities. As Ahmed Rıza expressed it, "society is a complex organism dependent solely upon natural laws. This body is subject to cyclic illnesses." According to him, social problems could be healed through an application of scientific methodology.[93] One of his opponents described his extradition from the CUP in 1897 as the "amputation of a gangrenous organ from the body of the CUP."[94]

The most arresting feature is the extremely bioorganistic slant of the Young Turks' version of materialism, certainly influenced by René Worms's works.[95] When later Abdullah Cevdet translated an essay by Jacques Novicow, another foremost name in the field of bioorganistic theory, entitled *La guerre et ses prétendus bienfaits*, he commented that Novicow's treatise *La critique du Darwinisme Social* was the more scholarly and enlightening work.[96] However, no comment by any Young Turk about a solidarist ideology from a bioorganistic viewpoint has yet been unearthed. Most probably, just as they lost interest in Narodnik ideas, their immersion in and allegiance to Le Bon's theories impeded their thorough examination of solidarism. However, using bioorganistic theories, the Young Turks propounded a full array of elitist claims and endeavored to build a revolutionary praxis:

> A society is like a human body, because each is composed of varied and numer-
> ous living cells. Just as an individual requires therapy to recover from an illness,
> so a society needs to take cures for its special illnesses—the doctors are dubbed
> lawmakers, administrators, and politicians. If a society is without such doctors,
> or if in spite of their presence an oppressive group dares to violate the balance
> of order and aided by luck attains strong power . . . the remedy to save a nation
> from so dangerous an illness, which would surely reap grave effects, is the
> rebellion of the violated people against their oppressors. Rebellion is the only
> way in which a weak and sick nation may heal itself.[97]

They also maintained that the reason the people were obedient to Abdülhamid II's regime—a phenomenon they deemed irrational—was that the sultan attempted to alleviate the physical discomfort of his subjects. They claimed that this provided them with the obligation to augment the general poverty, thus allowing the people to have a sensory experience of the oppression they endured.[98]

In this treatise one recognizes the belief that society is governed by an organic balance controlled by a natural flow. It is possible—but only if aided by luck—for oppressors to reverse the flow, although this would be an irrational and unnatural development, and under such circumstances the enlightened elite would be obliged to resist the oppressors. This was an interesting theory, although, contrary to the belief of the Young Turks, not a revolutionary one. Had they created a solidarist theory dependent on bioorganicism, as Léon Bourgeois had, this would have furnished them with a political device to attract people. Since they declined to do so, their ideas on bioorganicism were not useful to them in their political struggle.

Another salient aspect of the Young Turk *Weltanschauung* was its comments on race. The Young Turks were adherents of popular biological materialist theories of the mid-nineteenth century, which were especially concerned with race. Le Bon's war against democracy was an attempt to protect the superior race—white, European—from the danger of mob rule.[99] Letourneau, who deeply influenced the Young Turks, examined the evolution of various subjects within different races.[100] Also, Edmond Demolins's book *A quoi tient la supériorité des Anglo-Saxons?*, because of its title, drew the interest of the Young Turks,[101] even though its examination of superiority was not drawn from a biological perspective; later Sabahaddin Bey became a disciple of Demolins.

Besides these influences, the two Young Turks—Abdullah Cevdet and Sabahaddin Bey—who credited thinkers who had influenced them, gave the same name: Ernst Haeckel.[102] The Young Turks were impressed not only by his and his monist followers' bioorganistic ideas but even more so by his theories proposing to liberate the Germans from western civilization through a new educational curriculum and "to teach Germans that the universalist assumptions of western culture had been founded upon religious and metaphysical illusions."[103] Haeckel also detailed the importance of the inequality of men and opposed socialist movements from the same vantage point as Le Bon.[104] Therefore, Haeckel's ideas, resumed in a superior race (German), could provide a solid basis for the Young Turks.

However, despite their adherence to Le Bon's, Letourneau's, and Haeckel's theories, the Young Turks refrained from formulating a nationalist theory involving race during the formative years of their movement. Although in their scientific writings they frequently discussed the importance of race, they proposed no theory evaluating "the Turkish race." There is little doubt that this was because, in the Darwinist racial hierarchy, Turks were always assigned to the lowest ranks. Darwin himself had a low opinion of "the Turkish race."[105] This, coupled with the participation of many non-Turk members in the nascent movement, prevented the Young Turks from focusing on the race issue.

However, a strong focus on race did emerge immediately after Japan's first victories over Russia in 1904. Yusuf Akçura pointed out that one of the choices before the Ottoman Empire was to pursue a course of Turkish nationalism based on race,[106] and the organ published by the nationalist faction required Ottomans to follow the advice given to the Japanese by Herbert Spencer: To eschew marriage with Europeans in order to preserve racial purity.[107] When Abdullah Cevdet met Gustave Le Bon in 1905, he questioned him about where the European thinkers had erred when they placed the Japanese at the bottom of the racial schema.[108] The Japanese victory had cast serious doubt on the way the races had been hierarchically categorized.

The Young Turks embraced the race theories except for the placement of Turkish and Asian peoples in the lowest rungs. With Japanese successes, they achieved a new freedom to use race theories, because now they could rearrange the hierarchical assignments:

> Some Europeans and some Ottomans, who imitate whatever they see without understanding, regard us as a race in the lower part of the racial hierarchy. Let's say it in plain Turkish: They view Turks as second-class human beings. Japanese people, being from the stock of the yellow race, are obliterating this slander against nature with the progress in their country, and with their cannons and rifles in Manchuria.[109]

During the period of 1889 to 1902, however, the Great Powers' economic penetration and political intervention in the Empire were catalytic forces that propelled the Young Turks' development of nationalism and were among the most frequently used themes in their publications.[110] But an even more compelling force behind this development was the organizational structure of the CUP. Since CUP branches within the Empire were short-lived because of the spy network, more regular branches were established in the Balkan countries, which had recently gained independence or autonomy from the Ottoman Empire. These branches had the further advantage of regularly corresponding with the CUP center in Europe, and besides the branches, many people living in the Balkans, Cyprus, Crete, the Caucasus, and Central Asia sent letters to the CUP center.[111] The people in those lands identified themselves with an ethnic identity of Turkishness or Turkicness rather than with an extraethnic identity of Ottomanness. The disproportionate number of nationalist applications sent to the CUP center made a profound impact on the CUP administration. It is not coincidental that Yusuf Akçura, who for the first time focused on "a Turkish nationalism based on race," was a Tatar, and although he emigrated to the Empire when young, his initial socialization took place in Russia. Another, less important factor in Young Turks' shift to nationalism was that most Young Turks lived in Paris and witnessed an invigoration of French nationalism after the French defeat in 1871. They also witnessed the emergence of L'Action Française and soaring nationalist sentiment. It should also be remembered that Yusuf Akçura was a student of Albert Sorel and Emile Boutmy at l'École Libre des Sciences Politiques.

However, those at the CUP center could not comprehend the fact that Islam played a protonationalist role in lands such as the Balkans and Russia. Articles in Balkan Turkish journals claimed that Islam and nationalism had merged into a single construct,[112] and even lauding the Turks[113] did not convince the CUP center of this phenomenon. The organizations formed against Armenian committees[114] and Greek organizations[115] were anticipating stronger nationalistic propaganda from the CUP center. However, since CUP leaders were unable to recognize the protonationalist role of Islam, they continued to cloak their programs in a strongly religious rhetoric, which was unpalatable and never believed in. A shift to nationalism was gradually accomplished between 1902 and 1906, and in 1906 CUP propaganda realized a nationalist focus.

An examination of the Young Turk *Weltanschauung*—although expressed not in political ideas but rather in great sociological theories that had political ramifications—provides a picture diametrically opposite to the declared aims of the CUP, namely the reopening of the parliament and reproclamation of the constitution.[116] However, these were only devices to obscure their true agenda: A strong government, the dominant role played by an intellectual elite, anti-imperialism, a society in which Islam would play no governing role, and a Turkish nationalism that would bloom later. The last item on the agenda was controversial, since some CUP members were not Turkish. While Turkish members gravitated toward Turkish nationalism, which became the guiding ideology of the CUP, especially after 1906, the non-Turkish members leaned toward their own respective nationalist movements. İbrahim Temo and İsmail Kemal later participated in the Albanian nationalist movement, and Abdullah Cevdet became a leader in the Kurdish one.

The true agenda of the Young Turks was equally inviting to the military, who generally had a less serious interest in philosophy than did intellectuals. Many officers were influenced by their instructor Colmar von der Goltz's book *Das Volk in Waffen*, which was translated and recommended to all Royal Military Academy cadets by the War Office.[117] The book promoted a strong government and asked the military to play a more significant role in reshaping society. The only theories known to the military were those of Le Bon, but this should not surprise us, since his theories had made a similar impact on the French military.[118] It appears contradictory that Enver Bey, who had taken his division into the mountains in June 1908 to force the sultan to reproclaim the constitution and reopen the parliament, wrote four years later:

Alors il faut écraser toutes les têtes moyennes (mittelmassig) qui désirent partager le pouvoir, comme un français [Le Bon] disait très justement: Avant la république il y avait en France un seul despote, et maintenant il y en a des centaines parce que tous les députés veulent faire sentir leur pouvoir.[119]

Therefore, the military was prepared to embrace the Young Turk *Weltanschauung* upon accepting Turkish nationalism, ready to promote a strong government and a superior ruling elite. The CUP's shift to nationalism and securement of the military's endorsement was realized in 1906, and the military's new role was ably described by Ahmed Rıza.[120] The injection of a strong nationalism into the Young Turk *Weltanschauung* also gave this military-intellectual alliance a revolutionary praxis that it had lacked for nearly two decades. However, we can say that except for the injection of nationalism, all aspects of this *Weltanschauung* were shaped between 1889 and 1902.

10

Conclusion

Until 1902, the CUP was an umbrella organization composed of loosely affiliated factions. The term *faction* is insufficient to describe the component groups of the CUP, because they functioned almost as independent groups and some eventually adopted independent courses, even severing ties with the center. This was far beyond the simple factioning typically observed in political parties, such as that within the Russian Social Democratic Labor party. One can find remarkably little in common among the factions composing the CUP other than the Young Turk *Weltanschauung* and the wish to dethrone Abdülhamid II. With the exception of members who were ulema and who joined the CUP when the founders were trying to expand, all members embraced the common *Weltanschauung*, regardless of their various political activities.

Many important figures in the CUP later undertook diverse political roles. Two of the founders—İbrahim Temo and Abdullah Cevdet— became fierce opponents of the CUP after 1908 and together inaugurated the Ottoman Democratic party. Mehmed Reşid remained loyal to the CUP and served as governor after the revolution. As to the most notable Young Turk figures, Sabahaddin Bey led an opposition against the CUP and thus became a symbolic figure, and Hoca Kadri and Hoca Muhiddin launched an ulema opposition against the CUP.

The balance among the factions fluctuated between 1889 and 1902. Conservative units retained the upper hand until 1902, when a more radical faction, the activist-nationalist, gained control of the movement by allying themselves with the followers of Ahmed Rıza. Conservatives

213

formed their own independent organization in 1906, allowing this alliance to use the title "Committee of Progress and Union" and thereby to inherit the previous movement.

Except for small donations and the support given by the khedive of Egypt—this fluctuated depending on his relations with the sultan—it is ironic that the Young Turk movement was subsidized by the palace, with money extorted by the sale of journals and by the blackmail with which some members obtained state positions.[1]

The inaccurate use of the term *Young Turks* over the past nine decades has confused the topic considerably and many activities carried out by various organizations or groups were falsely attributed to the Young Turk organizations, especially to the CUP. When the CUP emerged as the fore-most opposition organization, many other dissidents of the regime of Abdülhamid II joined it. By 1897, with the exception of the nationalist-separatist organizations of the various ethnic groups of the Empire, the CUP had succeeded in gathering almost all the opponents of the regime under its roof.

Around the time Damad Mahmud Pasha and prominent Ottoman statesmen fled the Ottoman Empire, the Young Turk movement became an affair of European diplomacy. The sultan accepted the support of German diplomats in combating the movement. One faction in the movement continually awaited British help to dethrone the sultan and form a pro-British government. The available British documents reveal that British statesmen were interested in the intrigues of the Ottoman statesmen in office, such as Kâmil Pasha, Gazi Ahmed Muhtar Pasha, and İsmail Kemal, and backed them in their ventures. However, they did not similarly endorse the CUP or former statesmen who fled to Europe or Egypt and joined the movement there. This was the general policy of the British, and it was consistent until 1908, except for the support given by British statesmen to a Young Turk coup d'état venture planned in 1902–1903, which was never executed.

Although the European public and many scholars commonly labeled the Young Turks "liberals" and "constitutionalists," these traits were never aspects of the Young Turk *Weltanschauung*. A detailed analysis of their ideas reveals that the Young Turks did not adopt liberal ideas, and under the influence of the theories of Gustave Le Bon, who became their idol, they devalued parliaments as hazardous bodies. Although a rhetoric promoting constitutionalism was implemented by the Young Turks, this scheme was merely a device to stave off any intervention by the Great Powers in the domestic politics of the Empire. It was for the Young Turks a guiding purpose to develop an intellectual elite to govern the Empire—they never envisioned participation of the masses in policy-making or administration.

Another guiding principle for the Young Turks was the transformation of their society into one in which religion played no consequential role. In this materialistic structure, science was to replace religion. However, the Young Turks soon recognized the difficulty of spreading this idea and began to work at developing claims that Islam itself was materialism. As compared with later intellectual activities by Muslim intellectuals, such as the attempt to reconcile Islam and socialism, this was an extremely difficult task, because its aim was to reconcile a religion and an antireligious thought. Although some former members of the CUP continued to make efforts in this field after the revolution of 1908, they were severely denounced by the ulema, who accused them of "trying to change Islam into another form and create a new religion while calling it Islam."[2]

Positivism, with its claim of being a religion of science, deeply impressed the Young Turks, who believed it could be more easily reconciled with Islam than could popular materialist theories.[3] Positivism also provided an anti-imperialist agenda for the Young Turks and an avenue for conforming their society to modern culture without acquiring a taint of Christianity; the strongly Christian bias toward the Eastern Question and the Young Turks[4] drove the Young Turks to search for intermediary ideologies by which they could enter the stream of western culture. Positivism also served as a base for the desired strong government. The Young Turks favoring a strong government—which also contradicts what is commonly believed today—simply stitched their ideas in this field into a "scientific" jacket with the help of positivism. To the Young Turks, all political ideas necessarily needed "scientific" bases. For instance, while Gneist's ideas on *Der Rechtsstaat* might have provided legal bases for strong government, the Young Turks had no interest in legal theories as a basis for government—in their eyes everything stemmed from natural laws, not man-made precepts.

A further note on the Young Turks' desire for a strong government is that the nature of the Young Turk body distinguished it from other European intellectual movements. During the late Ottoman Empire, all the intellectuals were state officials. This was true for both the Young Ottomans and the Young Turks. All Young Turks earned money as state officials, and when some members of the CUP reached an agreement with the palace, they showed no hesitation in accepting state positions. Their participation in the government apparently had led them to value the state. This, on the one hand, may help to explain why the Young Turks created a thesis of strong government out of positivism (as we have seen, it was possible for South American positivists to found a more liberal ideology). On the other hand the Young Turks were reluctant to approach theories against the state, such as Marxism or anarchism.

As regards nationalism, the CUP underwent a gradual transformation. With many Muslim but non-Turkish members participating at the outset, the CUP embraced the official state ideology—Ottomanism. During this period Young Turk publications focused on patriotism and skirted any mention of nationalism. Typical of this policy is the CUP's translation of Schiller's *Wilhelm Tell*.[5] However, Ottoman patriotism jarred many non-Turkish Ottoman intellectuals because of its exclusive use of Turkish symbols. For instance, İsmail Kemal claimed that the reform program and Ottomanization efforts during the Tanzimat period "almost seem to have been the beginning of the political programme of the Young Turks."[6] In Tunalı Hilmi's detailed plans for socializing Ottomans, the symbols used were all Turkish; therefore Yusuf Akçura later called these writings the earliest fruits of Turkish nationalism.[7] In modern times this can be compared with the employment of Javanese symbols in inventing a pan-Indonesian symbology, which annoyed the non-Javanese.[8]

Turkish nationalists gradually gained the upper hand in the CUP, and following the Congress of 1902, a stronger focus on nationalism developed. It was no coincidence that at this very time Ahmed Rıza chose to replace the term *Ottoman* with *Turk*.[9] However, it was not until 1904 that nationalism came to be based on a "scientific" theory, and following the Japanese victory over Russia, the Young Turks began to base their nationalism on the "scientific" race theories of Europe.

A thorough examination of the *Weltanschauung* of the Young Turks between 1889 and 1902 leaves no doubt that, except for the shift in focus on nationalism, the official ideology of the early modern Turkish state was shaped during this period. The Young Turks who lived long enough to witness the coming into being of the Turkish republic saw many of their dreams fulfilled—it was a regime based on a popular materialist-positivist ideology and nationalism. The new regime worked to be included in western culture while exerting an anti-imperialist rhetoric and convened a parliament composed not of elected politicians but of virtually selected intellectuals working on behalf of the people without cooperating in any capacity with the "ignorant" masses. The impact of the Young Turks on shaping the official ideology of early modern Turkey went far beyond the political changes they effected.

Abbreviations

A & P	Accounts and Papers (State Papers)
AE	Affaires Étrangères
AQSh	Arkivi Qendror Shtetëror—Tirana
BBA	Başbakanlık Arşivi—Istanbul
BEO	Bâb-ı Âli Evrak Odası
CAB	Cabinet Papers
CTF	Cerrahpaşa Tıp Fakültesi
CUP	Ottoman Committee of Union and Progress
CP	Correspondance Politique
EI	Encyclopaedia of Islam
F.O.	Foreign Office
HHStA	Haus-, Hof-u. Staatsarchiv—Vienna
H.O.	Home Office
IJMES	International Journal of Middle East Studies
İ.M.K.İ	İbnülemin Mahmud Kemal İnal
IUL	Istanbul University Library
MES	Middle Eastern Studies
NLS	National Library of Scotland
NS	Nouvelle Série

PA	Politisches Archiv
PAAA	Politisches Archiv des Auswärtigen Amtes der Bundesrepublik Deutschland—Bonn
PRO	Public Record Office—London
SL	Süleymaniye Library
T	Turquie
TPL	Topkapı Palace Library
VGG (2)	Vilâyetler Gelen Giden (2)
YEE	Yıldız Esas Evrakı
YMGM	Yıldız Mütenevvî (Günlük) Marûzat
YP	Yıldız Perâkende
YSHM	Yıldız Sadaret Hususî Marûzat
YSRM	Yıldız Sadaret Resmî Marûzat

Notes

Chapter 1

1. The roles that former CUP members played in early Turkish political life are well examined in Erik J. Zürcher, *The Unionist Factor: The Rôle of the Committee of Union and Progress in the Turkish Nationalist Movement (1905–1926)* (Leiden, 1984).

2. See my "Jön Türklerin Yabancı Dilde Çıkardıkları Dergilerde İşledikleri Temalar," in *Türkiye'de Yabancı Dilde Basın* (Istanbul, 1986), 93–109.

3. See *Tanzimat I* (Istanbul, 1940).

4. Yusuf Hikmet Bayur, *Türk İnkılâbı Tarihi* 2/4 (Ankara, 1952), 1–397.

5. Ahmed Bedevî Kuran, *İnkılâp Tarihimiz ve Jön Türkler* (Istanbul, 1945), *İnkılâp Tarihimiz ve İttihad ve Terakki* (Istanbul, 1948), *Osmanlı İmparatorluğunda İnkılâp Hareketleri ve Millî Mücadele* (Istanbul, 1956) [Second and enlarged edition, Istanbul, 1959], *Harbiye Mektebinde Hürriyet Mücadelesi* (Istanbul, [1960?]).

6. Tarık Zafer Tunaya, "Türkiye'nin Gelişme Seyri İçinde İkinci Jön Türk Hareketinin Fikrî Esasları," *Tahir Taner'e Armağan* (Istanbul, 1956), 167–88.

7. Şerif Mardin, *Jön Türklerin Siyasi Fikirleri* (Istanbul, 1983). The first edition was published in 1964.

8. Ernest Edmondson Ramsaur, Jr., *The Young Turks: Prelude to the Revolution of 1908* (Princeton, 1957).

9. Iu. A. Petrosian, *Mladoturetskoe dvizhenie (vtoraia polovina XIX-nachalo XX v)* (Moscow, 1971), 137–316.

10. Donald Quataert, "The 1908 Young Turk Revolution: Old and New Approaches," *MESA Bulletin* (1979), 22–29, and "The Economic Climate of the

'Young Turk Revolution' in 1908," *Journal of Modern History* 51, no. 3 (September 1979), 1147–61.

Chapter 2

1. Dukakin-zadeh Basri Bey, *Le monde Oriental et l'avenir de la paix* (Paris, 1920), 3–10.

2. Paul Fesch, *Les Jeunes Turcs* (Paris, 1909), 15 ff.

3. *Avrupa'dan Düvel-i Muazzamadan Addolunan Fransa ve Rusya ve İngiltere ve Avusturya ve Prusya Devletlerinin ve Sair Zayıf ve Sagir Düvelin Ahvâl ve Keyfiyet-i Mülkiyeleri* TPL MS R.1615, 2. This translated pamphlet is a further example of efforts by Ottoman statesmen to collect data about Europe and Europeans. For another sound example see *İcmâl-i Ahvâl-i Avrupa* TPL MS R.1648.

4. See İbrahim Müteferrika, *Usûl ül-Hikem fî Nizâm ül-Âlem* IUL, Turkish Manuscripts, no. 6694, 19–20; *Tarih-i Cevdet* 6 (Istanbul, 1309 [1891–92]), 4.

5. An early text praising the radical methods of transformation in Russia was the account of his ambassadorship by Rasih Mustafa Pasha, who was sent to Russia after the Iaşi Treaty of 1792. See *Sefaretnâme-i Rasih Efendi* IUL, Turkish Manuscripts no. 3887, 7. The establishment of embassies in Europe revealed that a change of mind had occurred along with and an acquiescence to the principle of "acting according with European custom." See Faik Reşit Unat, *Osmanlı Sefirleri ve Sefaretnâmeleri* (Ankara, 1968), 168.

6. Mehmed Emin Behic, *Sevanih el-Levâyih* TPL, H.370, 65; also see *Lâyiha-i Tatarcıkzâde Abdullah Molla Efendi* (1228 [1813]), IUL, Turkish Manuscripts, no. 6930, 202.

7. For examples see *Taife-i Nasaranın Sefer ve Harb ü Darb ve Hıfz-ı Memlekete Müteallik Bâzı Tedbirleridir ki Tercüme Olunub İşbu Safahata Şebt Olundu* IUL, Turkish Manuscripts, no. 3984, passim, and *Tahrir-i Asker Maddesine Dair Lâyihadır* SL, Hüsrev Paşa Manuscripts, no. 807-10, 29-32.

8. See *Devlet-i Aliyye'nin Ahvâl-i Hâzırasına Dair Risâledir* SL, Hüsrev Paşa Manuscripts, no. 851, 2.

9. *İngiltere Seyahatnâmesi* IUL, Turkish Manuscripts, no. 5083, 5. Also see *Mühendishâne-i Sultanî'nin Te'sisi ve Küşadını Âmir Sultan Selim Han-ı Sâlis Fermanı* (Istanbul, 1328 [1910]), 1.

10. Topkapı Sarayı Müzesi Arşivi, E. 1518/1. This document bears no date; however, its content gives the impression that it was an early-nineteenth-century text. For the appointment of ulema to teach Islamic learning to the Ottoman students in Paris, see BBA-İrade-Dahiliye, 6 C 1273/no. 24340.

11. For the distress of Ottoman statesmen because of the French Revolution, see "Muvazene-i Politikaya Dair Reis'ül-küttab Âtıf Efendi'nin Lâyihası," in *Tarih-i Cevdet* 6, 394–401; for measures taken to prevent the spread of revolutionary ideas following the 1848 revolutions in Europe, see Topkapı Sarayı Müzesi Arşivi, E. 9321/32-25708, 1265 [1849], and BBA-Bâb-ı Âsâfi; Mesâil-i Mühimme-129/VIII Avrupa İhtilâlinden Dolayı Memâlik-i Şâhânede Bâzı Tedâbîr İcrasına Dair.

12. The following example is typical of reactions by persons confronted with social and political structures fundamentally different from their own: "At European banquets many women are present, sitting at the table while the men sit behind them, watching like hungry animals as the women eat. If the women pity them, they give them something to eat, if not, the men go hungry." *Sefaretnâme-i Vahid Efendi* [1806], IUL, İ.M.K.İ Manuscripts, no. 3040/1, 7–8.

13. See *Ebubekir Râtib Efendi'nin Seyahatnâmesidir* IUL, Turkish Manuscripts, no. 6096, 14.

14. *Avrupa Medeniyeti ve Ûmranı Hakkında Risâle*, IUL, Turkish Manuscripts, no. 6623, 3–4, 6.

15. See Enver Ziya Karal, "Nizam-ı Cedide Dair Lâyihalar," *Tarih Vesikaları* 1, no. 6 (1942), 425.

16. See *İcmâl ül-Sefain fî Tüccar ül-Âlem* SL, Es'ad Efendi, no. 2062/2, 46, *İcmâl-i Ahvâl-i Avrupa* SL, Es'ad Efendi, no. 2062/1, 29.

17. *Devlet-i Aliyye'nin Ahvâl-i Politikasına Dair Bâzı Malûmat* TPL, Y.242, 1. Although this is a translated work, these comments, contrary to custom, remained uncensored.

18. Kadri, "Avrupa Kıt'asının Mevki'-i Coğrafisi ve Ahvâl-i Tarihiyesine Dair Bâzı Malûmat-ı Mücmeledir," *Mecmua-yı Fünûn* 1, no. 3 (August-September 1862), 111.

19. *Bir Osmanlı Zabiti ile Bir Ecnebî Zabitin Mükâlemesi* IUL, Turkish Manuscripts, no. 6623, 23–24, and *Sual-i Osmanî ve Cevab-ı Nasranî* TPL, H.1634, 2.

20. "The Ottomans should increase their knowledge by reading works written in European languages." Hamdi, *Beyân-ı Fâide-i Cedide: Bera-yı Hall-i Muahedât-ı Adide-i [Adediye-i?] Âliye Tercümesi* (1266 [1849]), Atatürk Library, Muallim Cevdet Manuscripts, no. K. 51, 1. For a similar explanation, see Hüseyin Rıfkı-Mühendis Salim, *Usûl-i Hendese* Atatürk Library, Muallim Cevdet Manuscripts, no. K.118, 2–3.

21. See *İngiltere Memleketiyle Londra Şehrinin Bâzu Usûl ve Nizamâtını Bildiren Seyahatnâme* [1833?] IUL, Turkish Manuscripts, no. 5085, 27–28. For similar information about industry and technology in Great Britain, see 16–18. Also see *Journal du voyage de Mahmoud Raif Efendi en Angleterre écrit par lûy même* (1793), TPL, III.Ahmet 3707, 63.

22. *İngiltere Memleketiyle*, 62–63.

23. *Zaman-ı Kadîmde Umûr-i Âlemin Nizam Üzerine Olub Şimdi İhtilâl Üzerine Olduğunun Hikmet ve Sebeblerini Beyân Zımnında Risâledir* (1191 [1777]) IUL, Turkish Manuscripts, no. 6939, 4–15.

24. See Sarı Abdullah, *Tedbir en-Neş'eteyn ve Islâh en-Nüshateyn* TPL, E.H.1359.

25. Sarı Abdullah, *Telhis en-Nesayih* TPL, R.358, especially 2 ff.

26. For an example written during the westernization movement, see *Nizam-ı Devlete Dair Risâle* IUL, Turkish Manuscripts, no. 2905.

27. For an example, see *Tedâbir-i Umûr-i Saltanata Dair Bir Lâyiha*, IUL, Turkish Manuscripts, no. 6925, 2–4.

28. E. J. W. Gibb, *A History of Ottoman Poetry* 5 (London, 1907), 7, 19–20.

29. See Enver Ziya Karal, *Halet Efendi'nin Paris Büyük Elçiliği 1802–1806* (Istanbul, 1940), 31–40; Elhac Mustafa Efendi, *Nemçe Sefaretnâmesi* Fatih Millet Library, Trh. MS, no. 844, 29–30, *1205 Senesinde Sefaretle Prusya'ya Gönderilen Ahmed Azmi Efendi'nin Sefaretnâmesidir* İ.M.K.İ Manuscripts, IUL, no. 2491, 23–24.

30. Bernard Lewis, *The Emergence of Modern Turkey* (London, 1965), 69.

31. *Avrupa'ya Dair Tarihce: Tarih-i Es'ad Efendi* SL, Es'ad Efendi, no. 2063, 53–54.

32. *Avrupa'nın Ahvâline Dair Risâle: Âsâr-ı Rıfat Paşa* (Istanbul, 1275

[1858–59]), 10–11; Mustafa Sami, *Avrupa Risâlesi* (Istanbul, 1256 [1840–41], 26, 30–31, 35.

33. Mehmed Şevki, "Avrupa Devletlerinin Ahvâl-i Hâzırası," *Mecmua-yı Fünûn* 3, no. 25–36 (1281 [1864–65]), 186.

34. Münif, "Mukayese-i İlm ve Cehl," *Mecmua-yı Fünûn* 1, no. 1 (June-July 1862), 29–30.

35. Münif, "Mukaddeme-i İlm-i Jeoloji," *Mecmua-yı Fünûn* 1, no. 2 (July-August 1862), 65. Many popular journals opened their pages to the teaching of geology; see Ahmed Reşad, "Tarih-i Tabiî," *Âsâr-ı Perâkende*, no. 2 (March 2, 1873), 40–46.

36. *Zeyl-i Risâle-i Ahlâk-Âsâr-ı Rıfat Paşa* (Istanbul, 1275 [1858–59]), 11.

37. Münif, "Darülfünûn Dersleri," *Mecmua-yı Fünûn* 1, no. 8 (January-February 1863), 332.

38. For an example, see *Risâle fî Fazilet ül-İlm ve'l Ulema* Istanbul Devlet Library, MS no. 7891/2, 24–31.

39. Sadık Rıfat Paşa, *Zeyl-i Risâle-i Ahlâk*, 21–22.

40. Şerif Mardin, "Tanzimat Fermanının Manâsı," *Forum* 8, no. 90, (December 15, 1957), 13.

41. Azîz, "İntihar," *Mecmua-yı Fünûn* 4, no. 34 (May-June 1866), 218–28.

42. See Mehmed Emin, *İlm-i Hıfz-ı Sıhhat* (Istanbul, 1289 [1872]), 15.

43. See M. Nadir, "İtikadât-ı Bâtıladan," *Mir'at-ı Âlem* 1, no. 15 (1882), 236 ff.; Münif, "Mukayese-i İlm ve Cehl," *Mecmua-yı Fünûn*, 53.

44. See Kadri, "Hikmet-i Tabiîyeden Alâim-i Semaviyeye Dair Bir Hoca ile Şakird Beyninde Muhaveredir," *Mecmua-yı Fünûn* 1, no. 1, 39.

45. Edhem, "İlm-i Kimya," *Mecmua-yı Fünûn* 1, no. 7 (December 1862–January 1863), 289 ff.

46. Ahmed Cevad, *Kimyanın Sanayi'e Tatbikini Havî Mebâhis-i Müfîde* (Istanbul, 1295 [1878]), 2; Ahmed Hilmi, "Acaibât-ı Kimyeviye," *Vekayi'-i Tıbbiye*, no. 52 [March 27, 1882], 202.

47. [Şemseddin Sami] "Semerât-ı İlm," *Hafta*, no. 19 [December 27, 1881], 291–92.

48. See Hikmet, *Terakkiyat-ı Cedide-i Bahriye* IUL, Turkish Manuscripts, no. 4177.

49. For examples see *Risâle der Beyân-ı Lüzûm-i Temeddün ve İctima'-yı Beni Âdem* SL, Halet Efendi Manuscripts, no. 765/13, especially 1–3, and *Risâle der Beyân-ı Temeddün ve İmaret* TPL, R. 2044.

50. "Terakki ve Maarif," *Hafta*, no. 1 [August 19, 1881], 2.

51. David Apter, *The Politics of Modernization* (Chicago, 1965), 83–87.

52. Hermann [Arminius] Vámbéry, *Der Islam im Neunzehnten Jahrhundert* (Leipzig, 1875), 101, A[bdolonyme] [Jean Henri] Ubicini, *La Turquie actuelle* (Paris, 1855), 360–61, John Welsh, "Last Days of the Ottoman Empire," *The Fortnightly Review* 46, no. 274 (October 1889), 543.

53. "Tarih-i Hükema-yı Yunan," *Mecmua-yı Fünûn* 4, no. 34 (May-June 1866), 255 ff.

54. Hüseyin Avni, "Spinoza-Hayat ve Mesleği," *Güneş* 1, no. 5 (1301 [1883]), 231; no. 8 [1883], 384; and no. 9 [1883], 432.

55. *Spinoza Mektebine Reddiye* TPL, H.372.

56. See "Lisanların Ensâb ve Taksimatı," *Hafta*, no. 1, 11.

57. See "Dünya'da İnsanın Zuhuru," *Dağarcık*, no. 4 (1288 [1871]), 109–117.

58. Bernard Lewis, "The Impact of the French Revolution on Turkey," *Journal of World History*, no. 1 (January 1953), 109.

59. "Medeniyet," *Hafta*, no. 11 [October 28, 1881], 164–65.

60. "Voltaire ile Rousseau," *Hafta*, no. 18 [December 5, 1881], 273–74.

61. Mehmed Emin Fehmi, *İlm-i Hıfz-ı Sıhhat*, 16–17.

62. See "[Müşteri Listesi]," *Mecmua-yı Fünûn* 1, no. 4 (August-September 1862), 167–68.

63. See Ali Muzaffer, "Fünûn," *Hazine-i Fünûn*, no. 3 [July 27, 1893], 23–24. Also see idem, "Fennin Lüzûm-i Tahsili," *Hazine-i Fünûn*, no. 6 [August 17, 1893], 42–43.

64. See Necib, *Malûmat-ı Muhtasara* (Istanbul, 1287 [1870–71]), 37–38, İbrahim Edhem Giridî, *Makalât-ı Hakîmiye* (Istanbul, 1304 [1886–87]), 4.

65. Şerif Mardin, "Super Westernization in Urban Life in the Ottoman Empire in the Last Quarter of the Nineteenth Century," in *Turkey: Geographic and Social Perspectives*, ed. Peter Benedict et al. (Leiden, 1974), 403–42.

66. For an example see [Emin], *Kethüdazâde Efendi'nin Tercüme-i Hali ve Zeyl-i Âcizidir: Menâkıb-ı Kethüdazâde Elhac Mehmed Ârif Efendi Hazretleri* (Istanbul, 1305 [1887–88]), 241–42.

67. See İsmail Ferid, *İbtâl-i Mezheb-i Maddiyûn* (Izmir, 1312 [1894]), passim. For a similar comparison between Büchner's work and Islam see "Tercih-i Bend," *Mırsad*, no. 6 [April 30, 1891], 43n.

68. E. I. Jacob Rosenthal, *Islam in the Modern National State* (Cambridge, 1965), 28–29.

69. Şerif Mardin, *Din ve İdeoloji* (Istanbul, 1983), 98.

70. For an excellent analysis of his political ideas, see Şerif Mardin, *The Genesis of the Young Ottoman Thought* (Princeton, 1962), 254, 260 ff.

71. *Ziya Paşa'nın Rüyanâmesi* IUL, İ.M.K.İ Manuscripts, no. 2461, 1–2.

72. [Namık Kemal], "Bizde Adam Yetişmiyor," *Hürriyet (1)*, no. 25, December 17, 1868, 1–2. Accordingly the CUP organ chose the following title for an article about the arrest of CUP members in Izmir. "Zekâ Bu Ahdde Müstelzim-i Ceza Oluyor [Intelligence is requiring punishment in these times]," *Osmanlı*, no. 44, September 15, 1899, 7.

73. "Türkistan'ın Esbâb-ı Tedennisi," *Hürriyet (1)*, no. 5, July 27, 1868, [1].

74. Nuri, "Bâtıl Zehâb," *İbret*, no. 10 [June 26, 1872], 1; see also [Namık] Kemal, "İzah-ı Merâm," *İbret*, no. 10, 2, idem, "Mukabele," *İbret*, no. 12 [June 29, 1872], 1–2, idem, "Maarif," *İbret*, no. 16, [July 4, 1872], 1.

75. Reşad, "Frenklerde Bir Telâş," *İbret*, no. 13 [July 1, 1872], 1.

76. See Celâl Nuri, "Şime-i Husumet," *İctihad*, no. 88 [January 22, 1914], 1949–51. For an analysis of this movement, see my *Bir Siyasal Düşünür Olarak Doktor Abdullah Cevdet ve Dönemi* (Istanbul, 1981), 357–65.

77. "Atufetlû Kemal Bey Hazretlerinin Bir Mektublarından Alınub Makabli Derc Edilen Fıkranın Ma'badıdır," *Gayret (1)*, no. 33 [October 1, 1884], 1.

78. For an analysis of his political ideas see Mardin, *The Genesis*, 385 ff.

79. Hayreddin Paşa, *Mukaddime-i Akvem ül-Mesâlik fî Ma'rifet-i Ahvâl ül-Memâlik Tercümesi*, trans. Abdurrahman Efendi (Istanbul, 1296 [1878–79]), 4. He wrote that "if Voltaire had not been disrespectful to religion he would have doubled his reputation and everybody would have benefited from his works." (104).

80. [Şemseddin Sami], "Medeniyet-i Cedidenin Ümem-i İslâmiyeye Nakli,"

Güneş 1, no. 4 (1301 [1883–84]), 179–84. For the similar ideas expressed by the same author see "Tarih," *Güneş* 1, no. 4, 171–75. He was praised by the Young Turks; see Abdullah Djevdet, "Ch[emseddin] Samy Bey," *İctihad* 2, no. 2 (January 1905), 10–12, and "Şemseddin Sami Merhum," *Osmanlı*, no. 141, November 15, 1904, 1–2.

81. "Felsefe," *Hafta*, no. 9 [October 14, 1881], 142.

82. Yenişehirlizâde Halid Eyüb, *İslâm ve Fünûn* (Istanbul, 1315 [1897]), 3–7.

83. "Bâzı Zevat Tarafından Cemiyete Verilen Hedaya," *Mecmua-yı Fünûn* 2, no. 22 (March-April 1864), 432–35.

84. Ahmed Midhat, *Beşir Fuad* (Istanbul, 1304 [1886–87], 13, and [idem], *Müntehabât-ı Ahmed Midhat* 3 (Istanbul, 1307 [1889–90], 14–15.

85. Ahmed Midhat, *Schopenhauer'in Hikmet-i Cedidesi* (Istanbul, 1304 [1886–87]), passim.

86. John W. Draper, *Niza-i İlm ü Din*, trans. Ahmed Midhat (Istanbul, 1313 [1895]).

87. Adıvar draws our attention to the preface of Ahmed Midhat; see Abdulhak Adnan-Adıvar, "Interaction of Islamic and Western Thought in Turkey," in T. Cuyler Young, ed., *Near Eastern Culture and Society* (Princeton, 1951), 124. It was also claimed that Draper's conciliatory attitude toward Islam increased the popularity of his book in the Ottoman Empire; see Cyrus Hamlin, *Among the Turks* (New York, 1878), 347. A similar comment was made at the Ottoman parliament during the discussion on the budget of the Ministry of Education in 1917. See *Meclis-i Meb'usan Zabıt Ceridesi* 3/8 (1333/1917), 50/3, 771.

88. See Donald Flemming, *John William Draper and the Religion of Science* (Philadelphia, 1950), 134–35, Tomás Cámara, *Contestacion à la Historia del Conflicto entre la Religion y la Cienca de Juan Guillermo Draper* (Valladolid, 1883), and "Draper's Religion and Science," *The Presbyterian Quarterly and Princeton Review* 4, no. 1 (January 1875), 158–65. For a criticism by a Tatar see Abdullah Bubi, *Terakki-i Fünûn ve Maarif Dinsizliği Mucib mi?* (Kazan, 1902), 3 ff.

89. Ahmed Midhat, *Beşir Fuad* (Istanbul, 1304 [1886–87]), 15, 28.

90. See M. Orhan Okay, *Beşir Fuad: İlk Türk Pozitivist ve Natüralisti* (Istanbul, 1969), 93.

91. For the acceptance of his ideas by the Young Turks, see Berna Kazak, "Ömrüm: Ali Kemal'in Hatıratı," senior thesis, IUL, no. 7528 (1954), 75–76.

92. Ahmed Midhat, *Avrupa Âdâb-ı Muaşereti Yahud Alafranga* (Istanbul, 1312 [1894–95]), passim.

93. An excellent example was a cartoon in a satirical journal. The conversation occurring between a traditional and a modern lady was as follows:

"—Woman, what kind of dress is this? Aren't you ashamed?
—You are the one who should be ashamed of her dress in this century of progress."

See *Hayâl (1)*, no. 157 [June 17, 1874], [4].

94. Enver Ziya Karal, *Selim III'ün Hatt-ı Hümayûnları: Nizam-ı Cedit 1789–1807* (Ankara, 1946), 43.

95. *Tarihî Notlar* TPL, Y.Y.89, 21 ff; Ziyaeddin Fahri Fındıkoğlu, "Tanzimatta İçtimaî Hayat," *Tanzimat*, 627; Éd[ouard] Engelhardt, *La Turquie et le Tanzimat ou Histoire des réformes dans l'Empire ottoman depuis 1826 jusqu'à nos jours* 1 (Paris, 1882), 79–87.

96. See Jocelyn to Derby, Constantinople, February 9, 1877/no. 115, PRO/F.O. 424/49, Stanton to Derby, Munich, February 9, 1877/no. 9, PRO/ F.O. 424/49. Also see "Varaka," *Vakit (1)*, September 25, 1876.

97. Un ami de la Turquie [Albert Fua], "Pourquoi les Turcs ne bougent pas," *Mechveret Supplément Français*, no. 21, October 15, 1896, 1.

98. "Jön Türk ve Ermeni," *Hak*, no. 31, November 30, 1900, 1.

99. See BBA-BEO/Mahremâne Müsvedât, no. 129 [July 8, 1901]. Also see Münir Bey to Müfid Bey, July 11, 1901/no. 37, and Müfid Bey to Münir Bey, July 17, 1901/no. 30, Archives of the Turkish Embassy in Paris, D. 244.

100. Süleyman Nazif, *Yıkılan Müessese* (Istanbul, 1927), 6.

101. See Celâl Bayar, *Ben de Yazdım* 1 (Istanbul, 1965), 179–80. For the smuggling of the pamphlets of Ahmed Rıza, see Hasan Bey to the Chamberlain's office, Bursa [February 25, 1896]/no. 28, *Boğaz Vekâleti, İnebolu, Çölemerik Kangırı, Kal'e-i Sultaniye, Bursa, Cisr-i Mustafa Paşa, Sapanca, Sarışaban, Pazarköy ile Muhaberata Mahsus Defter*, BBA-YEE, 36/2470-22/147/XVI.

102. Yusuf Kemal Tengirşek, *Vatan Hizmetinde* (Istanbul, 1967), 28–34.

103. See BBA-YMGM, 21 M 1305/no. 158.

104. "Ta'ziye," *Osmanlı*, no. 100, January 15, 1902, 8.

105. This couplet became an apothegm used by the journal *Kanun-i Esasî*, the organ of the Egyptian branch of the CUP. The initial article of the CUP central organ *Osmanlı* also ended with this couplet. See "İfade-i Mahsusa," *Osmanlı*, no. 1, December 1, 1897, 1. For similar aphorisms in the Young Turk journals, see "İdare-i Hâzıra Semereleri," *Mizan*, no. 176, May 14, 1896, 2491; "Kahire," *Osmanlı*, no. 112, September 15, 1902, 5; Edhem Ruhi, "Ümid-i İnkılâb," *Osmanlı*, no. 142, December 8, 1904, 1.

106. "Vak'a-i Sultan Azîz," *Sancak*, no. 10, December 20, 1900, 7; "Cümle-i Siyasiye," *Mizan*, no. 163, February 13, 1896, 2386–87.

107. "Lâyiha," *Osmanlı*, no. 108, July 15, 1902, 2.

108. Fuad, "Les discours de M. Gladstone et de Lord Rosebery," *Mechveret Supplément Français*, no. 21, October 15, 1896, 3.

109. Ahmed Riza, "Une explication," *Mechveret Supplément Français*, no. 10, May 1, 1896, 1; "La visite de S.A. la Princesse Nazli au Comité," *Mechveret Supplément Français*, no. 20, October 1, 1896, 1; and "Mustafa Fâzıl Paşa," *Osmanlı*, no. 119, March 15, 1903, 7.

110. Besides drawing from the works of the Young Ottomans for their publication (see BBA-YEE, 15/74/74-10/74/15), the Young Turk journals reprinted articles that had appeared in Young Ottoman journals. See Ziya Paşa, "Ikhtilâfu Ummatin Rahmatun," *Osmanlı*, no. 44, September 15, 1897, 1.

111. Le Comité, "Lettre adressée à MM. les députes Français," *Mechveret Supplément Français*, no. 22, November 1, 1896, 1.

112. Abdullah Cevdet, "Şime-i Muhabbet," *İctihad*, no. 89 [January 29, 1914], 1984.

113. M[ehmed] Sabahaddin, "Gençlerimize Mektublar: İntibah-ı Fikrîmiz," *Terakki*, no. [1], [April, 1906], 1.

114. "Anadolu Mektubları: 3," *Osmanlı*, no. 114, October 15, 1902, 4.

115. See Şerafeddin Mağmumî, *Seyahat Hatıraları: Brüksel ve Londra'da* (Cairo, 1908); idem, *Paris'den Yazdıklarım* (Cairo, 1911), idem, *Seyahat Hatıraları: Fransa ve İsviçre'de* (Cairo, 1914); and Ali Kemal, *Paris Musahabeleri* 1 (Istanbul, 1329 [1912]), 2 (Istanbul, 1331 [1914]).

116. For examples employed by urban planners and municipality officials, see

BBA-BEO/Şehremaneti Giden, 689-27/7, 137 [May 20, 1895]/46881, and 265 [August 26, 1895]/50518.

117. Ahmed Saib, *Rehnüma-yı İnkılâb* (Cairo, 1318 [1900]), 37.

118. Ahmed Salâhi, *Osmanlı ve Avrupa Politikası ve Abdülhamid-i Sânî'nin Siyaseti* IUL, Turkish Manuscripts, no. 9521, 4.

119. For an example, see "Adam Olalım," *Osmanlı*, no. 102, February 15, 1902, 5.

120. Abdullah Cevdet, *Hadd-ı Te'dib: Ahmed Rıza Bey'e Açık Mektub* (Istanbul, 1912), 65–66.

121. Abdullah Cevdet's, *Fizyolociya-yı Tefekkür: Mehazımın Esası C[K]raft und Stoff Ünvânlı Kitabın Tefekkür Bahsidir* (Istanbul, 1308 [1890]) was the translation of a chapter of Ludwig Büchner's, *Kraft und Stoff: Empirisch-naturphilosophische Studien* (Frankfurt am Main, 1858). Later he summarized Büchner's *Natur und Geist: Gespräche zweier Freunde über den Materialismus und über die realphilosophischen Fragen der Gegenwart* (Frankfurt am Main, 1857), in a pamphlet entitled *Goril* (Ma'muret-el-Azîz, 1311 [1893]). The chapter translated from Büchner's *Kraft und Stoff* received praise from Ottoman intellectuals. See Ş[ükrü] Kâmil, "Fizyolociya-i Tefekkür: Mütalâa ve Tefekkür Hakkında Nesâyih-i Sıhhiye," *Maarif*, nos. 41–42 [April 28, 1892], 234–37. Translation of the entire text was made in 1911 by Baha Tevfik and Ahmed Nebil in two volumes: *Madde ve Kuvvet* (Istanbul, 1911).

122. A[bdullah] Cevdet, "Herkes İçün Kimya," *Musavver Cihan*, no. 4 [September 23, 1891], 30 ff.

123. For interesting examples, see "Ziya ve Hayat," *Musavver Cihan*, no. 18 [December 30, 1891], 140, "Uyku," *Maarif*, no. 7 [October 8, 1891], 107–108, "Seyr-fi'l-menâm," *Maarif*, no. 8 [October 15, 1891], 123–24; "Hıfz-ı Sıhhat ve Fizyolociya-i Dimağ Yahud Fenn-i Terbiye-i Etfale Mukaddeme," *Musavver Cihan*, no. 32 [April 13, 1892], 250, "Başın Büyüklüğü," *Maarif*, no. 47 [June 2, 1892], 323–25, "Vezn-i Dimağ," *Maarif*, no. 49 [June 16, 1892], 358.

124. İ[brahim] Edhem [Temo], "Tagaddi ve Devam-ı Hayat," *Musavver Cihan*, no. 31 [April 6, 1892], 244n.

125. Şerafeddin Mağmumî, "Kalb ve Dimağ," *Maarif*, no. 32 [March 23, 1891], 83. For a discussion that this article occasioned see Ş[ükrü] Kâmil, "Kalb mi, Dimağ mı?" *Maarif*, no. 116 [October 12, 1893], 180–82.

126. Tevfik Nevzad's undated [1906?] letter to his daughter, Benâl. Private Papers of Tevfik Nevzad.

127. Şerafeddin Mağmumî, *Başlangıç* (Istanbul 1307 [1889–90]), 22–23.

128. Abdullah Cevdet, "Teselsül-ü Saltanat Mes'elesi," *İctihad*, no. 6 (May 1905), 86–87. All the claims made here were based on Théodule Ribot's book *Hérédité: Étude psychologique* (Paris, 1882).

129. For examples, see "İlm-i Kitabetin Mekâtib-i Askeriyece Lüzûmuna Dair Bir Genc ve Zeki Zabitin Mütalâasıdır," *Resimli Gazete*, no. 2 [April 2, 1891], 17–18; Genc Zabit, "Fenn-i Kitabetin Lüzûmuna Dair Olan Makaleye Zamime," *Resimli Gazete*, no. 6 [May 10, 1891], 78–79.

130. Ömer Subhi bin Edhem, *Yunanistan-ı Kadim Mader-i Medeniyet Midir?* IUL, Turkish Manuscripts, no. 3225, 12. For a similar criticism of sociology and psychology see Rıza Tevfik, "İbn-i Haldun'dan," *Maarif*, no. 188 [July 4, 1895], 275.

131. For the best example see his poem in *Ma'sumiyet* (Istanbul, 1311 [1893]), 18–19.

132. Rıza Nur, *Tıbbiye Hayatından* (Istanbul, 1327 [1909]), 7.

133. This information appears in a letter from Doctor Mekkeli Sabri to Edouard Herriot on November 18, 1912, published in [Feridun] Kan Demir, *Jön Türklerin Zindan Hatıraları 1848–1903: Bir Devrin Siyasî ve Fikrî Tarihi* (Istanbul, 1932), 106.

134. See "Les manifestations," *Le Moniteur Oriental*, July 27, 1908. Another placard prepared by the students for a ceremony at the academy read: "La science fait le salut des peuples." See "Les manifestations," *Le Moniteur Oriental*, August 6, 1908.

135. See Niyazi Berkes, *The Development of Secularism in Turkey* (Montreal, 1964), 116–18.

136. İbrahim Temo, "Darwin'in Ellinci Ölüm Yıldönümü," *İçtihat*, no. 347, June 15, 1932, 5736.

137. "Dr. İbrahim Themo Bey'in Mektubu," *Yolların Sesi*, no. 6, February 28, 1933, 131. A good example of how the study of natural sciences influenced the students is a letter written home by a freshman. See *Dersaadet'de Mekteb-i Tıbbiye-i Şâhâne Talebesinden Bir Zât Tarafından Diyar-ıbekir'de Akrabasından Bir Zâta Yazub Gönderdiği Mektubdur ki Aynen Bu Mahalle Derc ve Tahrir Olundu* (1305 [1890]), Princeton University Islamic MS (S. 3), no. 276-II, 1–4.

138. İbrahim Temo to Karl Süssheim, Medgidia, August 9, 1933, Nachlaβ Süssheim, Staatsbibliothek Preussischer Kulturbesitz: Orientabteilung.

139. İbrahim Temo to Karl Süssheim, Medgidia, July 22, [1]933, Nachlaβ Süssheim. This was Félix Isnard's (Temo erroneously refers to the author as Félix Bernard) *Spiritualisme et matérialisme* (Paris, 1879). This popular pamphlet explained the value of the supplantation of religion by experimental science. See especially 154 ff.

140. See Rıfat Osman, *Hayat ve Hatıratım* 1, Cerrahpaşa Medical School Manuscripts no. 213/69, 48 ff.

141. See Abdullah Cevdet, *Ma'sumiyet*, and idem, *Türbe-i Ma'sumiyet* (Istanbul, 1308 [1890–91], idem, *Hiç* (Istanbul, 1307 [1889–90]). For the eulogy see idem, *Ramazan Bağçesi* (Istanbul, 1308 [1890–91]), 2–6.

142. For the ideas and political career of Raspail see Dora B. Weiner, *Raspail: Scientist and Reformer* (New York, 1968), passim.

143. For Şakir Pasha's life, ideas, and his transmission of Bernard's ideas to Ottoman intellectuals, see Z. Fahri Fındıkoğlu, *Claude Bernard ve Şakir Paşa* (Istanbul, 1963), 36–51.

144. The first edition of the first volume of Şakir Pasha's work was published in 1892. A second and enlarged edition was published in 1901. The second volume was published in 1904. The third and fourth volumes appeared in 1906 and 1909, respectively.

145. Claude Bernard, *Introduction à l'étude de la médecine expérimentale* (Paris, 1865), 75.

146. P. Q. Hirst, *Durkheim, Bernard, and Epistemology* (London, 1975), 26–28; Reino Virtanen, *Claude Bernard and His Place in the History of Ideas* (Lincoln, 1960), 56–59.

147. Claude Bernard, *Introduction*, 159; idem, *Principes de médecine expérimentale* (Paris, 1947), 142–43. Also see Otakar Poupa, "Le problème de l'évolution chez Claude Bernard," *Philosophie et méthodologie scientifiques de Claude Bernard* (Paris, 1967), 109–116; Joseph Schiller, *Claude Bernard et les problèmes scientifiques de son temps* (Paris, 1967), 139 ff.

148. Dieter Wittich, *Vogt, Moleschott, Büchner: Schriften zum kleinbürgerlichen Materialusmus in Deutschland* (Berlin, 1971), vi and lxxi.

149. See Ludwig Büchner, *Herr Lasalle und die Arbeiter, Bericht und Vortrag über das Lasalleische Arbeiterprogram* (Frankfurt am Main, n.d.), passim; idem, *Darwinusmus und Sozialismus oder der Kampf ums Dasein und die moderne Gesellschaft* (Leipzig, 1910), passim.

150. See Ludwig Büchner, *Der Mensch und seine Stellung in Natur und Gesellschaft in Vergangenheit, Gegenwart und Zukunft oder: Woher kommen wir? Wer sind wir? Wohin gehen wir?* (Leipzig, 1889), 192–95.

151. Carl Vogt, *Untersuchungen über Thierstaaten* (Frankfurt am Main, 1851). For his criticism of Marx and Engels, see 212–13.

152. For an analysis of these elements in Büchner's work see Friedrich Albert Lange, *Geschichte des Materialusmus und Kritik seiner Bedeutung in der Gegenwart* 2 (Leipzig, 1898), 89 ff. However, in spite of these characteristics of Büchner's work, it was praised by Darwin, Haeckel, and Bölsche. See Dieter Wittich, *Vogt, Moleschott, Büchner*, v and lxxi.

153. For Büchner's usage of Darwinism see *Die Darwinische Theorie von der Entstehung und Umwandlung der Lebe-Welt* (Leipzig, 1876).

154. Besides *Kraft und Stoff,* Büchner underscored this idea in other popular pamphlets. See *Der Gottes-Begriff und dessen Bedeutung in der Gegenwart* (Leipzig, 1874), *Über religiöse und wissenschaftliche Weltanschauung* (Leipzig, 1887), and *Gott und die Wissenschaft* (Leipzig, 1897). However, the Young Turks' work demonstrates that they were influenced only by one chapter in Büchner's main work entitled, "Die Gottes-Idee," and they were unaware of the above-mentioned popular pamphlets.

155. Abdülhak Adnan Adıvar, *Tarih Boyunca İlim ve Din* 1 (Istanbul, 1944), iv.

156. Boşnak, "Bosna-Hersek'den," *Rumeli*, no. 8 [January 26, 1906], 3–4.

157. "Rumeli," *Rumeli*, no. 8, 4.

158. Münir Bey to the Chamberlain's office, April 22, [18]96/no. 38, *Paris [Sefaretiyle Muhabere Defteri]*, BBA-YEE, 36/2468/141/XII.

159. Âsım Bey to the Paris embassy, July 10, 1903/no. 165, Private Papers of Salih Münir Pasha.

160. Âkil Muhtar to İshak Sükûti, October 21, [18]98, AQSh, 19/106-1//471/378.

161. For an example see Mağmumî, *Başlangıç*, 14–15.

162. "İstanbul'da Akademi Te'sisine Dair Ahmed Rıza'nın Arizası (August 6, 105 [1893])," BBA-YEE, 14/1234/126/9.

163. "Esbâb-ı Teşekkül," *Hak*, no. 32, December 15, 1900, 1.

164. M[ehmed] Sabahaddin, "Genclerimize Mektub: Rus İhtilâlinin Ma'nâ-yı İctimaîsi," *Terakki*, [no. 1], 7–8.

165. See L. Pierce Williams, "Science, Education, and the French Revolution," *Isis* 44/4, no. 138 (December 1953), 311–30; C. Coulston Gillispie, "Science in the French Revolution," *Behavioral Science* 4, no. 1 (1959), 67–73.

166. "Hakîm, Edîb Ali Bey Hüseyinzâde," *İctihad* 2, no. 4 (April 1907), 294-96.

167. See Franco Venturi, *Roots of Revolution* (London, 1964), 285, 288. For the popularity of Büchner, Vogt, and Moleschott among the Russian intellectuals, also see Fyodor Dostoyevsky, *The Possessed* (New York, 1963), 353. In this novel the protagonist disposed of icons in his room, replacing them with three lecterns

on which he displayed the works of Büchner, Vogt, and Moleschott, and to which he lit votive candles.

168. O[tto] Hachtmann, "Türkische übersetzungen aus europäischen Literatur," *Die Welt des Islams* 6 (1918), 8.

169. *Dürûs-i Hayat-ı Beşeriye* (Istanbul, 1319 [1901]), 360.

170. Gustave Le Bon, *La civilisation des Arabes* (Paris, 1884).

171. See Kandıralı Nusret Hilmi, "İslâmiyetin Hâl-i Hazırı," *Maarif*, no. 117 [October 19, 1893], 199. Also at the sultan's behest, the first chapters of this book were translated into Turkish. This manuscript translation is in IUL Turkish Manuscripts, no. 9928. Le Bon's favorable view of Arab civilization was cited by Aḥmad Ṭabbārah at the Arab congress of 1913 in Paris. See *al-Mü'tamar al-'arabī al-awwal* (Cairo, 1913), 85.

172. His highly acclaimed work is *Recherches anatomiques et mathématiques sur les variations de volume du crâne et sur les rélations avec intelligence* in 8 vols. (Paris, 1879). Also see "Recherches expérimentales sur les variations de volume du crâne et les applications de la méthode graphique à la solution de divers problèmes anthropologiques," *Comptes rendus de l'Académie des Sciences* 87 (1879), 79 "Gustave Le Bon adresse les résultats fournis par la mesure des capacités de crânes conservés au Muséum d'Histoire naturelle," *Comptes rendus de l'Académie des Sciences* 89 (1879), 870. It is interesting to note that Vogt wrote about the "unscientific" character of phrenology, and Büchner, although placing a higher value on it, held a similar viewpoint. See Lange, *Geschichte des Materialismus* 2, 339.

173. Abdullah Cevdet, *Fizyolociya-yı Hıfz-ı Sıhhat-i Dimağ*, 29 ff.

174. Ibid., 41.

175. Ibid., 22–23. See also idem, *Dimağ*, 17–18.

176. Abdullah Cevdet, *Fizyolociya ve Hıfz-ı Sıhhat-i Dimağ*, 19.

177. Two books by Abdullah Cevdet, *Dimağ* and *Fizyolociya ve Hıfz-ı Sıhhat-i Dimağ*, were influenced by Letourneau's theories on biology. See *La biologie* (Paris, 1876). For his explanation based on race, also see *La sociologie d'après l'etnographie* (Paris, 1880), 3 ff.

178. An interesting definition of "loyalty" (*sadakat*) was proposed by a former statesman, Grand Vizier Mahmud Nedim Pasha as follows: "Loyalty is honesty in words and deeds, [it is] material and moral safekeeping. The following concepts are all derived from loyalty: Blessedness, compassion, probity, and patriotism. Possessors of these qualities are called loyal and those who prefer their opposites are liars and traitors. Happiness and peace in the affairs of state originate from loyalty" (*Sadr-ızâm Mahmud Nedim Paşa'nın Âyine-i Devlete Dair Kitabı* Fatih Millet Library, MS Trh. 1022, 7.)

179. BBA-YEE, 31/1221-IV/104/88. The memorandum bears the date [January 31, 1903].

180. BBA-YEE, 31/1221-IV/104/88. The memorandum bears the date [December 2, 1907].

181. Tahsin Paşa, *Abdülhamit Yıldız Hatıraları* (Istanbul, 1931), 6.

182. This short list drawn from over five hundred examples provides us with details:

1. The petition by Marshal Zeki Pasha, the Grand Master of Artillery, for a building site of 160.000 square meters as an imperial gift. BBA-YP, 11 Ca 1326/no. 465.

2. The petition by Said Pasha, The Minister for Foreign Affairs for a *yalı*

(a mansion on the shore of the Bosphorus) as an imperial gift. BBA-YP, 5 Ra 1303/no. 152 and his petition for some money as an imperial gift. BBA-YP, 4 Za 1303/no. 995.

3. The petition by the imperial aide-de-camp Derviş Pasha for some money as an imperial gift. BBA-YP, 16 L 1311/no. 1244.

4. The petition by the Minister of Commerce and Public Works Mahmud Celâleddin Pasha for a house as an imperial gift. BBA-YP, 13 R 1314/no.no. 6320.

5. The petition by the Chamberlain Kâmil Bey for a house as an imperial gift. BBA-YP, 10 N 1314/no. 894.

6. The petition by Hayreddin Paşazâde for the house left by Jamāl al-Dīn al-Afghānī as an imperial gift. BBA-YP, 17 L 1314/no. 1056.

7. The petition by Enver Bey, the local governor of Beyoğlu for the same house. BBA-YP, 8 Z 1314/no. 1339.

8. The petition by General Ali Rıza Pasha for the same house. BBA-YP, 30 Ca 1315/no. 591.

9. The petition by Marshal Ârif Pasha for a mansion at Nişantaşı as an imperial gift. BBA-YP, 1 R 1320/no. 436.

10. The petition by Marshal Abdullah Pasha for a *yalı*, which he currently rented, as an imperial gift. BBA-YP, 17 B 1325/no. 1536.

11. The petition by the imperial aide-de-camp Ruşen Pasha for the grant of privilege for running the port of Beirut. BBA-YP, 6 B 1304/no. 549-2 and 10 B 1304/no. 549-1.

12. The petition by Münir Pasha for grant of a contract to drain a swamp in Drama. BBA-YP, 27 S 1395/no. 686.

13. The petition by Ziya Pasha, the Minister of Land Registry, for a grant of privilege for the coal mines in Amasya and Bartın. BBA-YP, 1 N 1306/no. 22

14. The petition by Memduh Pasha, the Minister of the Interior for a grant of privilege for certain copper mines. BBA-YP, 23 Z 1317/no. 2183.

15. His petition for a grant of privilege for a tobacco monopoly. BBA-YP, 19 C 1320/no. 1521-1.

16. The petition by Marshal Zeki Pasha for a grant of privilege for the electricity of Istanbul. BBA-YP, 6 N 1324/no. 774.

183. For an example, see Mehmed Galib, lieutenant governor of Kastamonu, to the sultan, dated [March 5, 1901], in *Tahrirat Mecmuası* IUL, İ.M.K.İ Manuscripts, no. 2522, 5.

184. Ö[mer] N[aci], "Jurnaller," *Tanin*, December 10, 1909.

185. BBA-YMGM, 12 Ra 1311/no. 631-2308.

186. See Ibrahim Hakki, "Is Turkey Progressing?" *The Imperial and Asiatic Review* (April, 1892), 268–69.

187. *Sultan Abdülhamid'in Kime Hitaben Yazıldığı Anlaşılamayan Tezkere-i Serzeniş-âmizi* IUL, İ.M.K.İ Manuscripts, no. 3310, 217. The note was written to Münif Pasha, the minister of education.

188. See "Havâdis," *Mizan*, no. 174, April 30, 1896, 4280; Tevfik Sağlam, *Nasıl Okudum?* (Istanbul, 1981), 43–44.

189. Şerafedin Mağmumî, "İfadem," *Kamus-i Tıbbî* (Cairo, 1910), iv; Tunalı Hilmi, "Anarşizm Nedir mi Dediniz?" *Mizan*, no. 172, April 16, 1896, 4260.

190. Hüseyin Enver Sarp, "Türk Ocağı Nasıl Kurulmuştu?" *Türk Yurdu*, no. 242 (March 1955), 666.

191. "İstanbul'dan," *Osmanlı*, no. 44, September 15, 1899, 2.

192. H[abib] Antony Salmoné, *The Fall and Resurrection of Turkey* (London, 1896), 252–54. For similar requests by the Young Turk journals see "Bir Memurun Hasbihali," *Şûra-yı Ümmet*, no. 32, July 11, 1903, 2, and "Sultan Abdülhamid ile Memurin-i Devlet," *Hürriyet*, no. 19, July 17, 1895, 1.

193. "Şam'dan," *Osmanlı*, no. 75, January 1, 1901, 6–7.

194. See "Muarızîne Cevab," *Osmanlı*, no. 68, September 15, 1900, 1.

195. "Amerika Terakkiyatına Bir Nazar," *Osmanlı*, no. 110, August 15, 1902, 3.

196. "Japonya'da İttihad Cemiyeti," *Osmanlı*, no. 17, August 1, 1898, 8.

197. See "Hakkaniyet Badi-i Selâmetdir," *Bedreka-i Selâmet*, no. 17 [July 29, 1897], 1, and "Nankörlük," *Zaman* (Nicosia), no. 138, February 12, 1895, 1.

198. The hatred of lower-ranking officials and military officials was observed by foreign diplomats. See Romels to Goluchowski, Salonica, October 18, 1898/ no. 50, HHStA, PA XXXVIII 406 Konsulat Saloniki, 1898, and Currie to Salisbury, Constantinople, August 26, 1897/no. 512-572, PRO/F.O. 78/4806.

199. BBA-YEE, 31/111-26/111/86.

200. BBA-YMGM, 22 Ca 1314/no. 3885 and 6 Za 1317/no. 8195.

201. See BBA-YMGM, 27 C 1313/no. 4448, 4 N 1317/no. 1255-6043, and 26 S 131/no. 61-1460.

202. "İstibdad," *Tercüman-ı Hakikat*, July 3, 1878.

203. "Hürriyet-i Kanuniye," *Tercüman-ı Hakikat*, July 4, 1878.

204. See Ferid Pasha's memorandum dated [March 10, 1906], BBA-YEE, 5/ 1699/83/2.

205. [Sidney] Whitman, "Abdul Hamid an Autocrat not a Despot," *New York Herald* (Paris), August 17, 1896. Since Whitman became closely acquainted with Ahmed Midhat, and they exchanged ideas on philosophical and political matters, it seems plausible that Whitman's claims reflect Ahmed Midhat's views. The sultan asked Whitman to resign from the *Herald* and work for him, but he refused. See Sidney Whitman, *Turkish Memoirs* (London, 1914), 25–28, 216–24, 34.

206. Un Jeune Turc [Murad Bey?], "Young Turkey's Views," *New York Herald* (Paris), August 29, 1896.

207. Ahmed Midhat, "Ahmed Midhat's Letter: Reply of a Distinguished Mussulman Author to 'A Jeune Turque,'" *New York Herald* (Paris), September 4, 1896.

208. Fuat et Réchid, "Reply to Ahmed Midhat," *New York Herald* (Paris), September 9, 1896. For further criticism by the Young Turks and the CUP see Mehmed Murad, *Müdafaa Niyetine Bir Tecavüz! : (Kırkanbar'a Cevab)* (Paris, 1134 [1314-1896]), and Comité Ottoman d'Union et Progrès, *Affaires d'Orient: Réponse au ' New York Herald ' et à Mahmoud Nedim Bey ambassadeur de Turquie à Vienne* (Paris, 1896).

209. See "Tasfiye-i Rüteb-i Askeriye Kanunu," *Düstûr* (2d ser), 1 (Istanbul, 1329 [1911]), 421–23.

210. Raymond Aron, *Essai sur les libertés* (Paris, 1965), 70.

211. *Ziya Paşa'nın Rüyanâmesi*, 2.

212. Said Halim Paşa, *Buhranlarımız: Meşrutiyet* (Istanbul, 1329 [1915]), 3–4.

213. See [Âli Pasha], *Réponse à son altesse Moustafa Fazil Pacha au sujet de sa lettre au Sultan* (Paris, 1867), 24.

214. This was also underscored in the first Ottoman pamphlet on "constitutional government." See Tarık Zafer Tunaya, "Osmanlı Anayasacılık Hareketi ve 'Hükümet-i Meşruta'," *Boğaziçi Üniversitesi Dergisi(Beşeri Bilimler)* 6 (1978), 236.

215. Elliot to Derby, Constantinople, December 19, 1876 (telegraphic), PRO/F.O. 424/46.

216. Salisbury to Derby, Pera, January 1, 1877/no. 78 (confidential), PRO/F.O. 424/37.

217. Derby to Salisbury and Elliot, January 10, 1877/no. 18, PRO/F.O. 424/37.

218. *Bazı Hususî İradeleri Havî Defter*, BBA-YEE, 24/11/162/VII.

219. Ahmed Midhat, "Parlâmentolar," *Tercüman-ı Hakikat*, May 1, 1896. Identical language was employed by pro-palace journals published abroad. See Tchyplak-Moustafa, "La Jeune Turquie," *L'Orient* 8, no. 19, May 23, 1896, 6–7, and no. 21, June 6, 1896, 8. About a rare occasion on which the sultan himself commented on parliamentary regimes, Sir Nicholas R. O'Conor recorded the following: "The Sultan then went on to speak of parliamentary systems praising the British Constitution and saying that if he could have a parliament upon which he could rely as the King of England can rely upon the British Parliament, he too, would travel about Europe and be very glad to be relieved of the heavy burden of the cares of state, but *Allah* forfend his having a Parliament like the French Chamber of Deputies." See O'Conor to Lansdowne, Constantinople, May 6, 1905/no. 309 (confidential), PRO/F.O. 78/5394.

220. "Encümen-i Mahsus-u Vükelâ Kararı, [December 17, 1895]/no. 1563," BBA-Tezâkir-i Samiye Dosyaları, 1536/1563 and BBA-YSRM, 1 B 1313/no. 1563, BBA-İrade-Dahiliye, Receb 1313/no. 63-1409.

221. [Faïk Bey Konitza], "Les Jeunes-Turcs et leur panacée," *Albania*, vol. F, no. 10, October 15, 1901, 165. Almost identical accusations were made by Armenians against Ahmed Rıza. See Dikran Elmassian, "Une entente entre les Ottomans est-elle possible? Une conversation avec M. Ahmed Riza," *Le Courrier Européen*, no. 37, July 21, 1905, 42–43.

222. See Sigm[und] Freud, *Massenpsychologie und Ich-Analyse* (Vienna, 1921), 5–24.

223. Gustave Le Bon, *Psychologie des foules* (Paris, 1895), 181.

224. Şevket Süreyya Aydemir, *Suyu Arayan Adam* (Istanbul, 1979), 277.

225. Mehmed Murad, *Mücahede-i Milliye: Gurbet ve Avdet Devirleri* (Istanbul, 1324 [1908]), 153, 180.

Chapter 3

1. Portions of this section have been published as an article. See my "Notes on the Young Turks and the Freemasons," *MES* 25, no. 2 (April 1989), 186–97. The articles are Elie Kedourie, "Young Turks, Freemasons and Jews," *MES* 7, no. 1 (1971), 89–104; Paul Dumont, "La Turquie dans les archives du Grand Orient de France: Les loges maçonniques d'obédience Française à Istanbul du milieu du XIXe siècle à la veille de la Première Guerre Mondiale," in *Colloques internationaux du CNRS*, no. 601, *Économie et sociétés dans l'Empire Ottoman*, 171–202; idem, "La Franc-Maçonnerie d'obédience Française à Salonique au début du XXe siècle," *Turcica* 16 (1984), 65–94. The book is by Ramsaur, *The Young Turks*, 103–109.

Kedourie's article focuses on relations between Freemasonry and the CUP after the 1908 revolution. Dumont's second article discusses the activities of the Grand Orient de France in the Ottoman Empire. Two other recent books dealing with the Freemasons and the Young Turks are journalistic and popular histories; not scholarly works: Orhan Koloğlu, *Abdülhamit ve Masonlar 1905'e Kadar* (Istanbul, 1991); and idem, *İttihatçılar ve Masonlar* (Istanbul, 1991).

2. *Mahmud Şevket Paşa Su-ikasdi İddianâmesi*, [1913]. Manuscript copy of the court proceedings, private collection, 30. Similar claims were also made in the European press. See "Hostility to the Jewish Freemasonry," *Morning Post*, October 7, 1911; and "Salonica Committees Arms Jewish Freemasonry and Turcification," *Morning Post*, October 11, 1911. For the criticisms of ulema see "Fran Masonlar," *Beyan'ül-hak*, no. 19 [January 6, 1909], 435–36, and no. 21 [February 22, 1909], 484–86. The religious groups holding a more strongly fundamentalist stand, such as İttihad-ı Muhammedî Fırkası (The Union of Mohemmadans party), criticized Freemasons and their relations with the CUP even more severely in their organs. See Vahdetî, "İstanbul'da Farmason Locası," *Volkan*, no. 36, February 5, 1909, 2–3, Vahdetî, "İttihad," *Volkan*, no. 54, February 23, 1909, 1, "Volkan," *Volkan*, no. 55, March 19, 1909, 2. Şerif Pasha, who led the Ottoman ex-patriots in Paris, accused the CUP leaders of being Freemasons and Zionists. See Şerif Paşa, *Millet-i Osmaniye Bir Hitabe* (Paris, 1914), 15. For a similar condemnation of Freemasons, which appeared in the journal published by Şerif Pasha in Paris; see "Le Comité et la Franc-Maçonnerie," *Mècheroutiette*, no. 48 (September 1913), 56–57.

3. Ebüzziya, "Farmasonluk," *Mecmua-yı Ebüzziya*, no. 100 [June 12, 1911], 681–82. See also Tarık Zafer Tunaya, *Türkiye'de Siyasal Partiler 1*, *İkinci Meşrutiyet Dönemi: 1908–1918* (Istanbul, 1984), 381–82.

4. Μαρίνος Πολλάτος, *Διακόσια χρόνια 'Ελληνικού Τεκτονισμού (1740–1940)* (Athens, 1952), 51–52.

5. Στέρφανος 'Ι. Μακρυμιχαήλος, "Ψήγματα ἀπό τήν Δρᾶσιν τοῦ 'Ελληνικοῦ 'Ελευθεροτεκτονισμοῦ ἐν Τουρκία κατά τόν 19ον Αιώνα," *Τεκτονικό Δελτίο* 1 (1954), 602–603. Thus Malcom Khan, who figured significantly in activities generated by Masonic lodges in the Orient and endorsed the Young Turk movement in the late 1890s, claimed that the Young Turk movement emerged during the 1870s. See Prince Malcom Khan, "L'Orient," *La Revue de Paris* 1, no. 4, (February 1, 1897), 539. For Young Turks' praise of his article, See Ahmed Riza, "Variétés," *Mechveret Supplément Français*, no. 35, May 15, 1897, 6–7. Armenians, however, were annoyed by Malcom Khan's endorsement of the Young Turks. See D. S. Kirakosian, *Mladoturki: Pered sudom istorii* (Erevan, 1986), 84.

6. Πολλάτος, *Διακόσια Χρόνια*, 52–53.

7. 'Α. Χ. Χαμαδόπουλος, *Ή Νεωτέρα Φιλική Έταιρεία: 'Αγνωσται Σελίδες τῆς 'Εθνικῆς μας 'Ιστορίας* (Athens, 1946), 12.

8. For an excellent summary of his efforts, see Constantin Svolopulos, "L'initiation de Mourad V à la Franc-Maçonnerie par Cl[éanthi] Scalieri: Aux origines du mouvement libéral en Turquie," *Balkan Studies* 21 (1980), 441–56. The author is the grandson of Cléanthi Scalieri.

9. See the Private Papers of Cléanthi Scalieri, private collection. The details are contained in Scalieri's letter dated June 17, 1876, which begins, "Mon cher ami." For the role of the ulema and the softas in the revolt, see a letter addressed to Scalieri by Louis [Aimable] from Paris, dated May 29, 1876. I am indebted to

Professor C. Svolopulos for allowing me to examine Cléanthi Scalieri's private papers.

10. The deposition of Sultan Murad V on the grounds of "mental instability" caused great controversy. The Freemasons claimed that the ex-sultan's "illness" had been temporary and that he had recovered. They demanded that he be reenthroned. See Kont E. de Kératry, *Mourad V, Prince, Sultan, Prisonnier d'état* (Paris, 1878). Counterarguments were put forward by Dr. L. Capoleone in his book *Une réponse à M. de Kératry à propos de son ouvrage intitulé Mourad V, Prince-Sultan-Prisonnier d'état* (Istanbul, 1878). For a more scientific and neutral study on the subject, see Schlager, "Die psychiatrische Begutachtung des Sultans Murad V und dessen Thronensetzung," *Zeitschrift für Psychiatrie* 34 (1878), 1–48.

11. For details of the committee's futile efforts, see İsmail Hakkı Uzunçarşılı, "V. Murad'ı Tekrar Padişah Yapmak İsteyen K. Skaliyeri-Aziz Bey Komitesi," *Belleten* 8, no. 30 (1944), 260–78.

12. [Cléanthi Scalieri], Ὁ Σουλτάνος Χαμίτ καί τά Ὄργανα αὐτοῦ ἐν Ἀθήναις (Athens, 1882), 4.

13. Ibid., 5–7. According to the Ottoman press, Es'ad had previously participated in the "seditious" and "separatist" activities in Syria. The press also implied that he had received support from former grand vizier Ahmed Midhat Pasha. See "Atina'da Bir Türk Gazetesi," *Tercüman-ı Hakikat*, December 17, 1880. Ahmed Midhat Pasha himself denied this claim, however. See "Midhat Paşa," *Muhibban*, no. 12 [September 5, 1909], 102.

14. Cléanthi Scalieri, *Appel à la Justice Internationale des Grandes Puissances par rapport au procès de Constantinople par suite de la mort du Sultan Aziz, adressé par Cléanthi Scalieri au nom du Sultan Mourad accusé de Midhat Pacha et des autres condamnés* (Athens, 1881), passim.

15. Cléanthi Scalieri to Goschen, British high commissioner, June 1880, and another letter dated June 18, 1880. PRO/F.O. 195/1332.

16. This organization published the speeches and confidential correspondence of numerous European statesmen concerning Russia's influence in the East. [Georges Giacometti], *Les responsabilités* (Istanbul, 1877). A Turkish edition exists; see *Mes'uliyet* (Istanbul, 1294 [1877]). This book was also translated into English. See *Russia's Work in Turkey: A Revelation* (London, 1877).

17. For the palace's investigation of the Freemasons and their activities and the measures taken against them, see BBA-YMGM, 1 S 1308/no. 551. This document deals with the Freemasons in Syria. Also see BBA-YP, 5 Ra 1308/ no. 1476-1032, and BBA-YMGM, 1 S 1308/no. 1476–551.

18. This comment was used to describe the activities of the Freemasons' lodge in Beirut. See BBA-YMGM, 23 Ca 1310/no. 400-2470. For the government reaction to the Masonic activities in favor of former Sultan Murad V, see BBA-YP, Z 1310/no. 1695. For the pressure applied on the Freemasons, see BBA-YP, 9 S 1307/no. 930-3. For measures against the Freemasons in Beirut, see Mehmed Kâmil to the governor of Beirut, March 19, 1895/no. 2, *Beyrut Vilayetiyle Muhaberata Mahsus Defter*, BBA-YEE, 36/2470/6/147/XVI.

19. On the renewed activities of the Freemasons in the Beyoğlu section of Istanbul, see the comments of First Chamberlain Mehmed Süreyya in a letter dated October 31, 1894. The letter is reproduced photographically in Kan Demir, *Zindan Hatıraları*, 96.

20. Πολλάτος, *Διακόσια Χρόνια*, 129–31, and Paul de Régla [Paul André

Desjardin], *La Turquie officielle: Constantinople, son gouvernement, ses habitants, son présent et son avenir* (Paris, 1891), 406 ff.

21. "From an Armenian Correspondent," *Daily News*, September 11, 1890.

22. Said Pasha to Rüstem Pasha, September 16, 1890/no. 98271-126, BBA-HNA/ End:S-III, D.7, K.105.

23. For the British report on the activities and establishment of the newspaper, see PRO/F.O. 78/4463, report no. 180, dated September 26, 1892.

24. For samples of the intelligence work spawned by this journal, and information on Marengo, see BBA-YSHM, 5 Ca 1309, 23 Ca 1309, 27 C 1309, 8 Z 1309, 5 S 1310/no. 1638, 8 S 1310/no. 1652, 16 Ca 1311/ no. 1739, 17 Ca 1311/no. 1750, 24 Ca 1311/no. 1862, 2 C 1311/no. 1977, 3 C 1311/no. 1990, 8 C 1311/no. 2957, 7 M 1313/no. 63; BBA-YP, 29 B 1309/no. 981, 8 S 1311/ no. 1691; BBA-BEO/Zabtiye Giden, 663-21/13, 55–102 [May 8, 1892], and 176-3653 [August 13, 1892]; BBA-YMGM, 11 R 1310/no. 359–2981.

25. Justin Marengo, "Une expulsion Turque en France," *La Turquie Libre*, no. 3, January 27, 1892, 2.

26. "Sur les bords du Bosphore," *La Turquie Libre*, no. 4, February 5, 1892, 5.

27. For samples of these declarations, see Le Comité Libéral Ottoman, "Traduit du Turque," *La Turqie Libre*, no. 9, July 20, 1892, 1; and "L'Approche d'une solution," *La Turquie Libre*, no. 13, August 17, 1892, 1.

28. See "La dynastie Ottomane," *La Turquie Libre*, no. 2, January 1, 1892, 8 "Les Osmanlis et Abd-ul-Hamid II," *La Turquie Libre*, no. 5, February 17, 1892, 2; and no. 6, March 18, 1892, 1. For the conspiracy revolving around Murad V, see "Arrestations à Constantinople," *La Turquie Libre*, no. 4, February 5, 1892, 8.

29. "Mourad V et la Franc-Maçonnerie," *La Turquie Libre*, no. 15, October 13, 1892, 6–7. For more information about this conference, see Paul de Régla [Paul André Desjardin], *Au pays de l'espionnage: Les Sultans Mourad V et Abd-ul-Hamid II* (Paris, [1902]), 219 ff.

30. *The Armenians and the Turks under Abdul Hamid* (Printed by the Ottoman Committee of "Young Turkey" at Constantinople, [1893]). There is also a Turkish version in manuscript form, translated by an official at the Sublime Porte for official use. See *Sultan Abdülhamid Hazretlerinin Ahd-i Hümayûnlarında Ermenilerle Türkler*, BBA-YSHM, 20 R 1311/ no. 283-31.

31. Draft of the note sent from the Sublime Porte to the under-secretary of the Ottoman Foreign Ministry [August 16, 1893]. BBA-HNA-End: MT, K.729.

32. Said Pasha to Rüstem Pasha, August 27, 1893/no. 5797-4155, BBA-HNA-End: S.III, K.281, D.7; the draft of the undated note sent from the Ottoman Foreign Ministry to the Sublime Porte BBA-HNA-End: MT, K.728; and Lambemment to the Ottoman ambassador, Brussels, September 14, 1893 (confidentielle), BBA-HNA-End: S.III K.289, D.12/1, E.5400-241.

33. *La Turquie sous Abd-ul-Hamid* (Imprimerie du Comité de la Jeune Turquie à Constantinople, [1893]).

34. See, for example, the reaction in Rome: Consul in Livorno to Mahmud Nedim, November 28, 1893/no. 332–38. Archives of the Turkish Embassy in Rome, Box 52 (1).

35. "La Turquie et Abdul Hamid," *L'Italie*, November 28, 1893.

36. N. Nicolaïdès, "La Turquie sous Abd-ul-Hamid," *L'Orient* 6, no. 1, January 1, 1894, 6–7.

37. See [Desjardin], *Au pays de l'espionnage*, 269 n.1.

38. *The Armenians and the Turks*, 3 ff., and *La Turquie sous Abd-ul-Hamid*, especially 13–15.

39. The fact that this was the first book is attested to on the back cover of *La Turquie sous Abd-ul-Hamid*. Two more books were announced to be forthcoming: *Comment on ruine un empire* and *De la presse Anglaise et Française le Sultan Abd-ul-Hamid*.

40. See "A Turkish Manifesto," *Times*, November 26, 1895. For a discussion of Le Comité, see "Les affaires de Turquie," *Le Temps*, November 19, 1895.

41. Currie to Salisbury, November 27, 1895/ no. 891, PRO/F.O. 78/ 4623. The text of the manifesto is included in the report. According to the manifesto, Le Comité was founded in 1875. In a petition sent to Edward VII, Le Comité identified itself as "Les membres Franc-Maçons du Comité Libéral Ottoman de Constantinople." See Lansdowne to O'Conor, May 8, 1901/no. 107 (confidential), PRO/F.O. 78/5119.

42. BBA-YP, Za 1314/no. 1239, and *Le Temps*, May 25, 1900.

43. One such manifesto is enclosed with a letter from O'Conor to Salisbury, July 4, 1900, PRO/F.O. 78/5060. For another manifesto written on December 22, 1900, and sent to the British embassy in Istanbul, see PRO/F.O. 195/2108. For the reaction of the Young Turks to these manifestos and other activities of this organization, see "L'Intervention des étrangers," *Mechveret Supplément Français*, no. 107, December 1, 1900, 1, and Ahmed Riza, "Respectons la constitution," *Mechveret Supplément Français*, no. 101, July 15, 1900, 1.

44. On Şefkati's activities, see Kemal Salih Sel, "Masonluk Âleminin Meşhur Meçhulleri," *Mimar Sinan*, no. 18 (1975), 34–44.

45. For palace information on the publication of *İstikbâl* in Naples, see BBA-YSHM, 16 S 1297/no. 76.

46. For the implementation of both these strategies, see BBA-YSHM, 4 L 1297/no. 825 and 16 S 1297/no. 76.

47. For his activities in Geneva, see BBA-YSHM, 24 Za 1297, 8 Za 1297, 12 R 1306, 14 Ra 1306. For his activities in Paris, see BBA-İrade-Dahiliye, 26 Ca 1301/no. 72-383.

48. For the subsidies paid by the former khedive, see BBA-YSHM, 8 B 1298, 9 S 1298, 18 S 1301. These stipends were cut off when relations between the sultan and the former khedive improved. See BBA-YP, 18 Ca 1306/no. 818 and 12 L 1308/no. 2425.

49. For his activities in London, see Allen [the spy of the Ottoman embassy in London] to Morel Efendi, June 15, 1895/no. 73, July 9, 1895/no. 32, October 10, 1895/no. 214, and Rüstem Pasha to Turhan Pasha, September 5, 1895/no. 764-20128, Archives of the Turkish Embassy in London, Box 303(3); the notes of the Ottoman embassy in London dated October 5 and 10, 1895, Private Papers of Sir Philip Currie (Constantinople-Reports), PRO/F.O. 800/114; BBA-BEO/ Hariciye Âmed, 155-5/11, 2851 [September 8, 1895], 3340 [September 10, 1895], 3605 [November 2, 1895], BBA-BEO/Hariciye Reft, 185-5/39, 1049 [September 9, 1895]/ 50895.

50. [Ali Şefkatî], "Mukaddeme," *İstikbâl*, no. 27, June 21, 1895, [1]. Şefkati's paper was smuggled into the empire. See the note of the Ottoman government dated July 4, [18]95/no. 55, *Turkey: Stoppage of Newspapers by British Post Offices in Turkey*, PRO/F.O. 78/5259.

51. For information on this meeting, see Rüstem Pasha to Turhan Pasha,

June 19, 1895/no. 541-19824. Archives of the Turkish Embassy in London, Box 303 (3).

52. BBA-YSHM, 17 Ra 1315/ no. 372.

53. Ramsaur, *The Young Turks*, 15; Peter Bartl, *Die albanischen Muslime zur Zeit der nationalen Unabhängigkeitsbewegung (1878–1912)* (Wiesbaden, 1968), 153; Hasan Kaleshi, "Dr. Ibrahim Temo—der Gründer des Jungtürkischen Komitees Einheit und Fortschritt: Ein Beitrag zur Erhellung der Rolle der Albaner in der Jungtürkischen Bewegung," *Sudost-Forschungen* 35 (1976), 117. Temo does not say anything to corroborate this either. See his letter in Cerrahpaşa Tıp Fakültesi Tıp Tarihi ve Deontoloji Arşivi, I-1935, and the draft of his letter to Karl Süssheim in AQSh, 19/31//108-110

54. See Ahmed Rıza's letter to the Masonic lodge in Paris, dated November 17, 103 [1892]. Ahmed Rıza used the positivist calendar in his correspondence. Private Papers of Ahmed Rıza (1).

55. Le Comité sent a note of protest to the British ambassador in Istanbul on December 22, 1900, calumniating the regime of Abdülhamid II. See PRO/F.O. 195/2108.

56. For the appeal of the Freemasons to the king, see BBA-YEE, 17/952/63/22, "Turkish Masons to the King," *Daily Mail*, April 9, 1901, "Turkish Freemasons Send an Appeal on Behalf of ex-Sultan Murad to King Edward VII," *New York Times*, April 9, 1901.

57. "Protestation de la Ligue des Droits de l'Homme," *Mechveret Supplément Français*, no. 114, May 1, 1901, 2–3.

58. AE-NS-T, 3 (1899-1901), 270–71.

59. [Desjardin], *Au pays de l'espionnage*, 277–78.

60. Anthopulos Pasha to Tahsin Bey, April 26, 1901 (confidential), Archives of the Turkish Embassy in London, Box 383 (6).

61. Lansdowne to Currie, May 8, 1901/no. 107, PRO/F.O. 78/5119, and Anthopulos Pasha to Tahsin Bey, May 9, 1901, Archives of the Turkish Embassy in London, Box 362(10).

62. See AE-NS-T, 2 (1898), 52–53, and "Sultan Murad-ı Hâmis Hakkında Düvel-i Muazzama Hükümdârânına Cemiyetimiz Tarafından Gönderilen Mektubun Suret-i Mütercemesidir," *Osmanlı*, no. 12, May 15, 1898, 1.

63. See Necmeddin Ârif to İshak Sükûtî, February 19, 1901, AQSh, 19/106-5//296/1644, and İshak Sükûti to Doctor Nâzım, February 24, 1901, Private Papers of Bahaeddin Şakir.

64. "Paris'de Osmanlı Hürriyetperverân Kongresi," *Osmanlı*, no. 104, April 16, 1902, 1.

65. Ibid.

66. Report of the Superintendent of the Paris Police, M. Leproust, dated May 7, 1902, Archives de la Préfecture de Police de Paris (Sabaheddin et Loutfullah)/no. B. A(1653)-171154.

67. See the minutes of the September 12, 1908, meeting of this lodge, Ἡσίοδος, no. 49: Πεντηκονταετηρίς (Athens, 1958), 1.

68. O. Pontet, "La Franc-Maçonnerie et la question d'Orient," *L'Acacia*, no. 3 (February 1903), 203–207.

69. In 1894 the Armenian committees had asked to make common cause with the Greek Freemasons, but their suggestion was turned down. (See *Cevad Paşa Merhumun Zaman-ı Sadaretinde Takdim Olunan Tezâkir-i Hususiyenin Suretlerini Havî Defter* [September 4, 1894], BBA-YEE 36/419/146/XV.) Then

in 1903 they applied to the Grand Orient of France. See M. Hiram, "La Franc-Maçonnerie et la question d'Orient," *L'Acacia*, no. 4 (March 1903), 325–27.

70. [Ahmed Rıza], "Franmasonlar," *Şûra-yı Ümmet*, no. 27, April 29, 1903, 3.

71. "Une intervention Maçonnique," *Mechveret Supplément Français*, no. 139, April 1, 1903, 3.

72. "Freemasonry in Egypt," *Crescent*, 17, no. 454 (September 1901), 203.

73. For the reports to the sultan on Egyptian Freemasonry, see BBA-YP, 3 B 1306/no. 925-1, 1 Za 1318/ no. 1549, and report of Gazi Ahmed Muhtar Pasha, 220 (Dossier 120)-557/4 S 1315, BBA-BEO/Mısır Hülâsa Defteri (26)-1040-86/12.

74. Πολλάτος, *Διακόσια Χρόνια*, 138.

75. Major General Şakir to Âsım Bey (confidential), [1905]/no. 79, *Umum Kayda Mahsus Defterdir*, no. 4, BBA-YEE, 36/139-74/139/XIX. For the comment appearing in the newspaper on the Young Turks, see "Καί οἱ Νεότουρκοι Ζητοῦν Σύνταγμα," *Σκρίπ*, October 28, 1905.

76. He gave a talk at a Young Turk conference held at a Dutch Freemason organization in 1899. See *Conférence du Parti de la Jeune-Turquie* (one page handbill signed by Ahmed Riza on behalf of "Le Comité Central de la Jeune Turquie"). The handbill is in Algemeen Rijksarchief: Tweede Afdeling: Kabinet en Protocol (1871–1940): 60 (141). Also see Ahmed Riza, "La Jeune Turquie à La Haye," *Mechveret Supplément Français*, no. 79, July 1, 1899, 2. Later an important Young Turk, Reşid Bey, met him to discuss the possible use of the letters of Murad V for propaganda purposes. Young Scalieri had an important collection of these letters. See undated letter from Reşid Bey to İshak Sükûti, AQSh, 19/106-1//834/1853. After the revolution he published a book about decentralization and endorsed Sabahaddin Bey's ideas. See Georges Cléanthe Scalieri, *La régeneration constitutionelle: La décentralisation et la réforme administrative* (Istanbul, 1911), especially 1–7, and 102 ff.

77. Πολλάτος, *Διακόσια Χρόνια,*, 131–32.

78. BBA-YP, 17 Z 1322/no. 2655-645/2858.

79. Report from the inspectorship of Rumelia, dated [November 19, 1907], and the memorandum of the governor of Salonica dated [November 18, 1907]. BBA-YEE, 30/1190/51/78.

80. For details, see T. Nadir [Haydar Rıfat], *Beyn-el-Milel İhtilâl Fırkaları* ([Istanbul], 1326 [1908]), 6; Ebüzziya, "İtalyan Franmason Locaları ve Siyonizm," *Mecmua-yı Ebüzziya*, no. 131 (1912), 131; "Farmasonluk Hakkında Tetimme-i İzahat," *Mecmua-yı Ebüzziya*, no. 102 (1911), 742–43 "Le Grand Orient Ottoman," *Mècheroutiette*, no. 49 (December 1913), 39–40.

81. See Eduardo Frosini, *Massoneria Italiana e Tradizione Iniziatica* (n.p., 1911), 158.

82. *Dictionnaire de la Franc-Maçonnerie*, s.v. "Turquie" (Paris, 1987), 1203.

83. Jean Rodes, "L'Origine et les causes du mouvement constitutionnel: Conversation avec Refik Bey et le major Niyazi," *Le Temps*, August 20, 1908.

84. O. Pontet, "La Franc-Maçonnerie de Turquie," *L'Acacia*, nos. 68–69 (September 1908), 135–38; and N. Nicolaïdès, *L'Empire Ottoman: Une année de constitution* (Brussels, 1909), 143 ff.

85. D. Margaritti, "Du rôle de la Franc-Maçonnerie dans la révolution de Turquie," *L'Acacia*, no. 71 (November 1908), 321–22.

86. For the support of the Greek Great Orient leader A. Alexandropulos, see "La Franc-Maçonnerie et S.M.I. le Sultan," *Le Moniteur Ottoman*, August 11, 1908. The lodges Lobor et Lux in Salonica and Socrates in Alexandria sent telegrams at the time of the reopening of the Ottoman parliament. See *Takvim-i Vekayi'*, December 23, 1908, 7. In return, Doctor Nâzım praised the Freemasons, particularly the Grand Orient, during his speech delivered at the Grand Orient de France on October 7, 1908. See Paul Dumont, "Une délégation Jeune-Turquie à Paris," *Balkan Studies* 28 (1987), 321–24.

87. Marling to Grey, Constantinople, December 27, 1909/no. 992 (confidential), PRO/F.O. 424/222.

88. For the endeavors of Greek intellectuals, see A. J. Panayotopulos, "The 'Great Idea' and the Vision of Eastern Federation: A Propos of the Views of I. Dragoumis and A. Souliotis-Nicolaïdis," *Balkan Studies* 21 (1980), 331–65.

89. For example, see Mevlan Zadé Rifaat Bey, *L'Empere* [sic] *Ottoman et les Sionistes, les Juifs qui ont ruiné la Turquie* (Constantsa, 1923), 5–11, Friedrich Wichtl, *Weltfreimaurerei Weltrevolution Weltrepublik: Eine Untersuchung über Ursprung, Verlauf und Fortsetzung des Weltkrieges* (Munich, 1936), 150–52, and Khayrī Ridā, *Shadharah 'an tārīkh al-Māsūnīyah mundhu aqdam 'uṣurihā ilā hādhā al-yawm* (Damascus, 1928), 29.

90. For his publication in Istanbul see Muḥammad al-Hādī Matwī, *Aḥmad Fāris al-Shidyāq 1801–1887: Ḥayatuhu wa āthāruhu wa āra'uhu fī al-nahdah al-'Arabiyah al-ḥadīthah* (Beirut, 1989), 149–71, Atilâ Çetin, "El-Cevaib Gazetesi ve Yayını," *İÜEF Tarih Dergisi*, 34 (1984), 475–85. For his pro-British and anti-French policy see Layard to Derby, Therapia, June 9, 1877/no. 588 (confidential), PRO/F.O. 424/55, Gabriel Charmes, *La Tunisie et la Tripolitaine* (Paris, 1884), 378–79.

91. *The Decline of British Prestige in the East* (London, 1887). The book had been praised by the European politicians and denounced by the pro-Ottoman journals. See G. D['orcet], "Projets d'allience Turco-Russe," *L'Orient* 1, no. 4, November 4, 1889, 102.

92. BBA-YSRM, 1 B 1311/no. 2356, 13 B 1311/no. 2485, 23 B 1311/no. 2589.

93. BBA-YSHM, 9 S 1309, 22 S 1309, 21 Ra 1309/no. 1760, BBA-YP, 4 Ra 1308/no. 767.

94. Rüstem Pasha to Süreyya Pasha, February 10, 1890, BBA-YEE, 18/75-4/75-4/51; Cooke (one of the British spies of the Ottoman embassy in London) to Morel Bey, February 27, 1890, and a coded note dated January 22, 1890, Archives of the Turkish Embassy in London, Box 259 (2).

95. Rüstem Pasha to Süreyya Pasha, February 27, 1890, BBA-YEE, 18/75-4/75-4/51.

96. Es'ad Pasha to Rüstem Pasha, Paris, February 14, 1890/no. 13676, and Rüstem Pasha to Es'ad Pasha, London, February 17, 1890, Archives of the Turkish Embassy in London Box 259 (2).

97. BBA-YSHM, 4 Z 1307, 5 M 1308, 11 M 1308, 25 M 1308.

98. "The Sultan and the New English Ministry," *Morning Advertiser*, August 20, 1892. For other claims relating to activities of constitutional groups among the Muslims, see Ali-Ahmed, "Lettres de Turquie," *Le Yildiz*, no. 7,

December 10, 1892, 4, and "The Discontent in Turkey," *Daily News,* June 16, 1892.

99. "Turquie," *Le Temps,* June 1, 1892.

100. For the establishment of the journal and its publication, see Rüstem Pasha to Süreyya Pasha, March 3, 1894 and March 30, 1894, Türk İnkılâp Tarihi Enstitüsü Arşivi 1c./nos. 340 and 344, Rüstem Pasha to Said Pasha, December 17, 1894/no. 620-19026, Archives of the Turkish Embassy in London Box 295 (2). It was even claimed that the journal had been published in the Ottoman Empire with Fāris's money. See BBA-YMGM, 29 S 1311/no. 4320, and BBA-YSHM, 5 S 1311/no. 3119.

101. Civanpîr [Salīm Fāris], "Gazetemizin Esbâb-ı Te'sisi," *Hürriyet,* no. 1 [February 1, 1894], 1.

102. "Dersaadet Havâdisi," *Hürriyet,* no. 8 [March 22, 1895], 1. Also see "Abdülhamid'in Hal'i Hakkında Rivâyât-i Muhtelife," *Hürriyet,* no. 17, July 3, 1895, 1–2.

103. See "Fransa Matbuatının Suriye'deki Efkârı," *Hürriyet,* no. 1, 6, "Gavâil-i Mündefi'a ve Gavâil-i Gayr-i Mündefi'a," *Hürriyet,* no. 2 [February 16, 1894], 1–2.

104. "Hürriyet'in Hurûfâtı," *Hürriyet,* no. 1, 9.

105. Halil Halid to Ahmed Rıza, London, September 9, 1895, Private Papers of Ahmed Rıza (1).

106. Halil Halid, *The Diary of a Turk* (London, 1903), 186–99.

107. Mehmed Murad, *Mücahede-i Milliye,* 30–31.

108. BBA-YSHM, 17 S 1312/ no. 3163.

109. BBA-YSHM, 21 S 1312/ no. 3219, 26 S 1312/ no. 3318, 6 N 1312/ no. 3449, 15 M 1312/ no. 115.

110. BBA-Mahremâne Müsvedât, 4 Ş 1312/no. 14.

111. BBA-BEO/Telgrafve Posta Nezareti Giden, 585-17/10, 1/43882, and 208 [January 15, 1895]/54657; BBA-BEO/Dahiliye Giden, 94-3/43, 2966 [January 3, 1895]/54657; BBA-BEO/Zabtiye Giden, 662-21/13, 1 [March 14, 1895]/48883; BBA-BEO/Hariciye Âmed, 156-5/11, 3643 [November 5, 1895]; BBA-İrade-Hususî, Cemaziy'ülevvel 1313/no. 37-779.

112. BBA-BEO/Hariciye Reft, 155-3/11, 1871 [February 24, 1894]/ 43323. The British authorities were discontented with Fāris's publication. See Kimberley to Rüstem Pasha, March 28, 1894, Archives of the Turkish Embassy in London, Box 295 (2); Arminius Vambéry to the Foreign Office, June 4, 1894, Vambéry Papers, PRO/F.O. 800/33. The British tried to take some measures under constant pressure from the Ottoman government. See General Post Office to Currie, June 14, 1895/no. 466. PRO/F.O. 78/5259. The sultan thanked the British authorities when they took initial measures. See Said Pasha to Rüstem Pasha, May 22, 1894/no. 174. PRO/F.O. 78/4744.

113. BBA-YMGM, 16 L 1311/no. 809-8464; Sanderson to Anthopulos Pasha, March 28, 1895, PRO/F.O. 78/4744, and an undated note from Morel Bey to Worland (director of the publishing house), Archives of the Turkish Embassy in London, Box 295 (2).

114. "Statement against the Sultan and Turkish Government in the Turkish Paper Hurriyet, Printed in England L.O.O 967 as to Prosecution of Printers," PRO/H.O. Registered Papers, 45:9741-A. 55743. The embassy also tried to hire the famous lawyer George Lewis as defense for the suit. See Anthopulos Pasha to

Tahsin Bey, February 26, 1895. Archives of the Turkish Embassy in London, Box 319 (2).

115. BBA-BEO/Dahiliye Giden, 95-3/44, 578 [May 5, 1896]/58054; BBA-BEO/Hariciye Reft, 183-5/39, 312 [May 5, 1896]/58054; "Nouvelles de l'étranger, "*Le Temps*, May 10, 1896.

116. See coded telegram dated December 12, 1894/no. 240a–244, Archives of the Turkish Embassy in London, Box 295 (2). Even regional British press had expressed sympathy with the journal. See "Hurriyet," *Eastern Daily Press* (Norwich), March 2, 1894.

117. "The 'Hurriyet' in London," *Armenia*, no. 73, November 1, 1894, 3.

118. BBA-BEO/Hariciye Âmed, 155-3/11, 837 [May 9, 1895], 864 [May 11, 1895], 909 [May 13, 1895], 1053 [May 23, 1895], 1134 [May 30, 1895], 1215 [June 8, 1895]; BBA-BEO/Hususî İrade-i Seniye, 377-8/100, 1265/1184; "Dersaadet Muhabirimizden Mevrud Mektubun Tercümesidir," *Hürriyet*, no. 4 [March 21, 1894], 4.

119. Tahsin Bey's telegram, dated September 20, 1895. Archives of the Turkish Embassy in London, Box 303 (1).

120. Comité du Parti Constitutionnel Ottoman à Constantinople, *Lettres ouvertes: A la Majesté Impériale le Sultan Abd-ul-Hamid: Première lettre* (Paris, 1895). Archives of the Turkish Embassy in Paris, D. 176; BBA-YP, 28 B 1312/no. 866-2.

121. See "Telgrafnâmeler," *Hürriyet*, no. 39, October 16, 1895, 3, "Türkiya'da Osmanlı Hürriyetperverân Fırkası," *Hürriyet*, no. 59, October 1, 1896, 2, "Islahât-ı Osmaniye Fırkasının Beyannâmesi," *Hürriyet*, no. 64, December 15, 1896, 3.

122. [April 19, 1895]/no. 4090, *Cevad Paşa Merhumun Zaman-ı Sadaretinde Takdim Olunan Tezâkir-i Hususiyenin Suretlerini Hâvî Defter*, BBA-YEE, 36/419/146/XV; Şakir Bey to the Chamberlain's office, Athens, May 27, [18]95/ nos. 22–23, *Atina Sefaret-i Seniyesiyle Muhaberat Kaydına Mahsus [Defter]*, BBA-YEE, 36/2470-4/147/XVI.

123. BBA-BEO/Hariciye Âmed, 155-3/11, 831 [May 8, 1895], 948 [May 15, 1311], 989 [May 19, 1895].

124. "The Author of the Stamboul Placards," *Pall Mall Gazette*, October 11, 1895, "The Armenian Question," *Times*, October 11, 1895.

125. Diran Kélékian, "La Turquie et son souverain," *The Nineteenth Century* 40, no. 237 (November 1896), 696.

126. "La Situation en Turquie," *Le Temps*, October 20, 1895, "Uneasiness at Yildiz Kiosk," *Pall Mall Gazette*, November 5, 1895.

127. BBA-BEO/Zabtiye Giden, 662-21/13, 432 [December 8, 1895]/ 53427.

128. BBA-BEO/Adliye Giden, 23-1/23, 805 [December 15, 1895]/53617.

129. BBA-BEO/Hariciye Âmed, 155-5/11, 3360 [October 13, 1895]; "The Armenian Crisis," *Standard*, October 24, 1895.

130. "Avukat Acem İzzet Bey," *Osmanlı*, no. 44, September 15, 1899, 3. İzzet Bey died in prison. It was claimed that he was killed by the agents of the sultan. See Henry Thompson, "His Majesty Jekyll-and-Hyde," *World's Work* 7 (November 1903), 4091–92.

131. "Âlem-i Hakikatden Bir Sada," *Hürriyet*, no. 62, November, 15, 1896, 2.

132. For the negotiations, see Anthopulos Pasha to Tahsin Bey, October 17, 1896; Tevfik Pasha to Anthopulos Pasha, June 9, 1896/no. 170-19062; Anthopulos Pasha to İzzet Bey, January 16, 1896/no. 21, February 9, 1896/no. 28, Archives of the Turkish Embassy in London, Box 319 (2); BBA-BEO/Hariciye Reft, 184-5/40, 958 [September 16, 1897]/75540.

133. Anthopulos Pasha to Tahsin Bey, July 17, 1897, and Tahsin Bey to Tevfik Pasha, June 27, 1897/no. 15, Archives of the Turkish Embassy in London, Box 332 (4).

134. Anthopulos Pasha to Mahmud Celâleddin Pasha, December 2, 1897/ no. 23140, Archives of the Turkish Embassy in London, Box 332 (3).

135. BBA-Divan-ı Hümayûn: Muhtelif ve Mütenevvî Defterler: Muharrerât-ı Umumiye, 84, 17 C 1315/no. 135, BBA-YMGM, 2 B 1315/no. 1918, protocol dated [November 18, 1897], Archives of the Turkish Embassy in London, Box 332 (3).

136. To Goluchowski, Büyükdere, October 7, 1897/no. 42, HHStA, PA XII 168, Türkei Berichte 1897 (VI-XII)/679 3182.

137. Affaires Étrangères to Barthou, January 7, 1898, AE-NS-T, 2 (1898), 9.

138. Barthou to Affaires Étrangères, February 8, 1898. Ibid., 44.

139. Rauf Bey to Anthopulos Pasha, July 3, [1901], Archives of the Turkish Embassy in London, Box 362 (10).

140. Haydarpaşazâde Ârif to Anthopulos Pasha, March 10, 1902, enclosed with the letter from Anthopulos Pasha to Tahsin Bey, June 24, 1902. Ibid., Box 347 (2).

141. BBA-YSHM, 22 S 1313/no. 457.

142. See. "İstitrad," *Hayâl (2)*, no. 6, September 15, [18]95, [4].

143. Mehmed Murad, *Mücahede-i Milliye*, 166, and Ahmed Rıza to Doctor Nâzım, undated [July 1897] letter, Private Papers of Bahaeddin Şâkir.

144. Mehmed Murad, *Mücahede-i Milliye*, 28–29.

145. "İstibdat devrinde, hürriyetperverlerin takibine ait bir vesika," *Resimli Tarih Mecmuası*, no. 2/74 (February 1956), 88–89.

146. Ahmed Rıza, "Osmanlı İttihad ve Terakki Cemiyeti ve Avrupa Matbuatı," *Meşveret*, no. 20, October 8, 1896, 2.

147. Ahmed Bedevî Kuran, *Osmanlı İmparatorluğunda İnkılâp Hareketleri ve Millî Mücadele*, 220, Mehmed Murad, *Mücahede-i Milliye*, 183–86.

148. "Havâdis," *Mizan*, no. 183, July 1, 1896, 2522.

149. "Hürriyet, Mizan, Meşveret," *Hürriyet*, no. 55, August 1, 1896, 3.

150. For an example, see Şerafeddin Mağmumî to İshak Sükûti, Paris, July 10, 1897, AQSh, 19/106-7//292/1950.

151. A letter, signed "Bende" and dated [December 9, 1896], AQSh, 19/135//157 626. Also see Arsen Efendi to Ragıb Bey, Varna, June 22, 1896, AQSh, 19/135//29/189.

152. See "İstanbul'dan Aynen Mektub," *Osmanlı*, no. 56, March 15, 1900, 7.

153. For Fâris's role in this publication, see the telegram sent from the Ottoman embassy in London to the Chamberlain's office, October, 12, 1904, Archives of the Turkish Embassy in London, Box 404 (1); Cavit Orhan Tütengil, *'Yeni Osmanlılar' dan Bu Yana İngiltere'de Türk Gazeteciliği 1867–1967* (Istanbul, 1969), 84.

154. See an unsigned, undated letter sent from a CUP member in Istanbul

to the central committee in Geneva, AQSh, 19/61//17/280. Also see Necmeddin Ârif to İshak Sükûtî, March 10, 1900, AQSh, 19/106-5//270/1711, "Osmanlı," *Osmanlı*, no. 55, March 1, 1900, 8.

155. "Interview de l'émir Arslan-Syriens, Arméniens et Jeunes Turcs," *L'Intransigeant*, November 29, 1895.

156. "The Situation in Constantinople," *Times*, December 16, 1895, "Young Turkey Party's Plans," *New York Times*, May 3, 1896, and, "The Turks Criticized the Sultan," *New York Times*, June 27, 1896.

157. H[abib] Antony Salmoné, "The Press in Turkey," *The Nineteenth Century* 36, no. 213 (November 1894), 720–21.

158. Chamberlain's office to the London embassy [December 26, 1891]/no. 3106, BBA-YEE, 18/75-4/75-4/51; BBA-YP, 22 Ş 1309/no. 1197-2, 14 L 1309/no. 1952, 12 Z 1309/no. 1580. Salmoné to Rüstem Pasha, May 3, 1892, Archives of the Turkish Embassy in London, Box 277 (8).

159. For a criticism of the sultan's policies by the journal see "al-Sulṭan 'Abd al-Ḥamīd al-Thānī wa wilāyāt al-Balqān," *Ḍiyā' al-Khāfiqain*, no. 5 (July 1892), 57ff.

160. See "The Turkish Press," *New York Times*, December 23, 1894.

161. His note dated January 15, 1897, PRO/F.O. 78/4840.

162. French intelligence note dated [London], January 19, 1897, AE-NS-T, 1 (1897), 7.

163. Es'ad Bey to the Chamberlain's office, October 30, 1893; Chamberlain's office to Es'ad Bey, November 26, 1893; Ziya Bey to the Chamberlain's office, November 27, 1894, and January 2, 1894, *Paris ve Viyana Sefaret-i Seniyeleri İle Muhaberata Mahsus Defter*, BBA-YEE, 36/2585/148/XVI.

164. BBA-İrade-Hususî, Cemaziy'ülâhir 1312/no. 49-1310.

165. BBA-YSHM, 18 S 1318/no. 250.

166. For its publication see Ziya Pasha to the Foreign ministry, August 11, 1894/ no. 194-9859, and August 14, 1894/no. 160-10950. Dışişleri Bakanlığı Hazine-i Evrak Arşivi, İdarî. D. 198.

167. "Kashf al-Niqāb," *Kashf al-Niqāb*, no. 1, August 9, 1894, [1].

168. "Sulṭan al-Ghāzī 'Abd al-Ḥamīd Khān," *Kashf al-Niqāb*, no. 1, [2].

169. "Murāsalāt al-wilāyāt al-muttaḥida," *Kashf al-Niqāb*, no. 19, January 17, 1895 [3].

170. See "al-ḥukūma al-istibdādiyya lī-faylasūf al-sharq," *Kashf al-Niqāb*, no. 9, October 4, 1894 [1] ff.

171. See Khalīl Ghānim, "al-qānūn al-āsāsī," *Kashf al-Niqāb*, no. 18, January 10, 1895, [1–2]; no. 27, March 21, 1895, [1–2], and "al-risāla al-thālitha," *Kashf al-Niqāb*, no. 32, May 2, 1895, [1–2].

172. Khalīl Ghānim, "al-qānūn al-āsāsī," *Kashf al-Niqāb*, no. 18, [1–2].

173. Arslān's note to the British authorities dated January 19, 1895/no. 491, PRO/F.O. 78/4646.

174. Türk İnkılâb Tarihi Enstitüsü Arşivi, 82/18112.

175. See Salmoné, *The Fall and Resurrection*, 250, and *Procès contre le Mechveret et la Jeune Turquie* (Paris, 1897), 60. In the beginning Ghānim received support from the Ottoman embassy in Paris to defend the Ottoman cause in French press. See BBA-YSHM, 5 L 1309/no. 6092.

176. For its publication see Foreign ministry to Es'ad Pasha [November 6, 1893]/no. 193, Archives of the Turkish Embassy in Paris, D. 176.

177. "Hatt-ı Hareketimiz," *Hilâl*, [December 1893], [2].

178. For the Ottoman authorities' measures against this journal and the ensuing negotiations see BBA-İrade-Hususî, Cemaziy'ülâhir 1311/ no. 4-864, Rebiy'ülâhir 1311/no.98-1105; BBA-YP, 5 L 1311/no. 1313; BBA-YSHM, 3 Ca 1311/no. 1536, 7 N 1311/no. 3143, 16 L 1311/no. 3606, 3 Za 1311/no. 3890, 25 Ca 1311/no. 1879; Foreign Ministry to Es'ad Pasha, April 24, 1894, Archives of the Turkish Embassy in Paris, D. 176; BBA-BEO/Hariciye Reft, 183-5/39, 1175 [October 23, 1893]/37536.

179. The French authorities claimed that Kateb was a defrocked priest. See "Note concernant M. A[lexis] K[ateb]," July 30, 1899, AE-NS-T, 3 (1899–1901), 140–41. However, since he later published articles in Arab journals under his ecumenical title, this claim seems erroneous. See "Nāwfiṭūs Muṭrān Ṣaydanāyā," *al-Mashriq* 3, no. 23, December 1, 1900, 1068–72. Arslān on the other hand recommended to his readership that they purchase Kateb's organ. See "jārīdat al-Rajā'," *Kashf al-Niqāb*, no. 29, April 4, 1895, [3].

180. Nabi Bey's letter to the Affaires Étrangères, March 17, 1899, AE-NS-T, 3 (1899–1901), 25.

181. "[El-Recâ' Gazetesi]," *Hayâl(2)*, no. 6, [3–4].

182. Alexis Kateb to the French premier, Paris, January 10, 1899, and to [Delcassé], January 22, 1899, AE-NS-T, 3 (1899–1901), 7–8. He even denied his participation in the establishment of the Comité Turco-Syrien. See "La Jeune Turquie et le Père Kateb," *L'Orient* 8, no. 3, January 18, 1896, 4.

183. Alexis Kateb to the Minister of commerce, Paris, May 30 and 31, 1899, to Delcassé, May 31, 1899, AE-NS-T, 3 (1899–1901), 124–25, 127–28.

184. See Deschanel to Delcassé, Paris, June 6, 1899 and "Note pour la Direction Politique, June 24, 1899," AE-NS-T, 3 (1899–1901), 133–36. His ideas were clearly presented in his pamphlet entitled *Œuvre patriotique de propagation de la foi Chrétienne et de pénétration Française en Syrie et dans tout l'Orient* (Paris, [1899]).

185. "Jam'iyya jadīda fī Lūndra," *Kashf al-Niqāb*, no. 21, January 31, 1895, [1]. The assertion that Europeans had joined the society is contradicted by a later announcement made by the organization. See "Nos derniers explications," *La Jeune Turquie*, no. 4, January 24, 1896, [2]: "Le Comité Turco-Syrien ne compte aucun membre étranger."

186. "al-jam'iyya al-sūriyya fī Lūndra," *Kashf al-Niqāb*, no. 25, March 7, 1895, [4].

187. He was James Sanū'a. He presented himself as Sheikh Abū Naẓẓārah and, at the sultan's behest, he praised Abdülhamid II and decried the British policy toward the Middle East. See Abou Nadarra, "A S.M.I le Sultan Ghazy Abd-ul-Hamid Khan," *Le Journal d'Abou Naddara*, no. 6, June 25, 1897, 26; "We Prefer Death to Fighting for Tyrants," *L'Attawadod d'Abou Naddara*, no. 1, March 1901, 10. Both the conference and Arslān's relations with Sanū'a provoked the enmity of the Ottoman authorities. See Ziya Pasha to Said Pasha, April 14, 1895/ no. 158-8797, Archives of the Turkish Embassy in Paris, D. 176 and BBA-YSHM, 16 Za 1312/no. 4320. For the conference see "Khiṭāb mudīr al-jarīda 'an al-mar'a fī al-sharq wa iktirāḥ," *Kashf al-Niqāb*, no. 29, [1–2].

188. *Memorandum présenté par la presse Ottoman libre à sa Majeste Impériale le Sultan Abdul-Hamid II*. A copy of it is in the Archives of the Turkish Embassy in Paris, D. 176.

189. See BBA-BEO/Hariciye Reft, 183-5/39, 813 [July 28, 1895])/49511,

1143 [September 25, 1895]/51393, 1192 [October 14, 1895]/51886; BBA-BEO/Hariciye Âmed, 155-3/11, 3202 [October 7, 1895].

190. For the text see "Le Comité Turco-Syrien aux Puissances," *Le Jour*, November 26, 1895, "Mémorandum aux six Grandes Puissances par le Comité Turco-Syrien des Réformes," *La Jeune Turquie*, no. 1, December 13, 1895, [1].

191. See "The Eastern Question," *Times*, November 22, 1895.

192. Ziya Pasha to the grand vizier [November 27, 1895], BBA-HNA-End: MT K.794.

193. See "Turkiyyā al-fatāt," *Turkiyyā al-fatāt*, no. 1, December 13, 1895, [1].

194. "I'lān," *Turkiyyā al-fatāt*, no. 6, February 21, 1896, [1].

195. See Amīn Arslān's letter dated March 20, 1896, *Turkiyyā al-fatāt*, no. 8, March 20, 1896, [1]; "Ilā qurrā'inā al-kirām," *Turkiyyā al-fatāt*, no. 1, [1]. Beginning with its seventh issue a subscription fee was required.

196. Coded telegram from Ziya Pasha to Tevfik Pasha, December 18, 1895, Archives of the Turkish Embassy in Paris, D. 176; BBA-İrade-Hususî, Receb 1313/ no. 69; BBA-BEO/Dahiliye Giden, 94-3/43, 2662 [December 18, 1895], BBA-BEO/Zabtiye Giden, 662-21/13 123 [December 18, 1895]/53773; BBA-BEO/Hariciye Reft, 183-5/39, 1496 [December 19, 1895]/53790. For the distribution of the journal in Egypt, see BBA-BEO/Mısır Hidiviyet-i Celilesinin Tezâkir Defteri (62)- 1036-68/8, 4459-173 [December 31, 1895], and BBA-BEO/Mısır Hülâsa Defteri (26)-640-68/12, 4459 [December 31, 1895].

197. BBA-BEO/Hariciye Âmed, 155-5/11, 4459 [December 30, 1895]. Fāris hailed *Kashf al-Niqāb* in his organ, however, he did not mentioned his relations with Arslān or other members of the society. See "Paris'de Bir Arabî Gazete," *Hürriyet*, no. 8 [March 22, 1895], 8.

198. "Ilā ikhwāninā al-sūrīyyin," *Turkiyyā al-fatāt*, no. 2, 27 December 1895, [1].

199. "Mawḍū' ta'ammul ilā ikhwāninā al-sūrīyyin," *Turkiyyā al-fatāt*, no. 3, January 10, 1896, [1].

200. "Ilā ikhwāninā al-sūrīyyin," *Turkiyyā al-fatāt*, no. 5, February 7, 1896, [1]; and no. 12, May 19, 1896, [1].

201. "Evrak ve Havâdis," *İlâve-i Meşveret*, no. 7, March 1, 108 [1896], 3.

202. "Teşekkür ve Memnuniyet," *Mizan*, no. 167, March 12, 1896, 2324.

203. This was at the heart of the criticism leveled by the pro-palace journals. See "Le Comité Syrien des Réformes," *L'Orient* 7, no. 38, December 28, 1895, 6, and "Le dédain de la Jeune Turquie des quatre Syriens," *L'Orient* 8, no. 1, January 4, 1896, 6.

204. See H[abib] Antony Salmoné "Is the Sultan of Turkey the True Khaliph of Islâm [?]" *The Nineteenth Century* 38, no. 227 (January 1896), 177.

205. Ibid., 176.

206. See "The Real Rulers of Turkey," *The Nineteenth Century* 37, no. 219 (May 1895), 721 ff.; Muslim 'uthmānī, "Ilā ikhwāninā al-Sūrīyyin," *Turkiyyā al-fatāt*, no. 6, February 21, 1896, [1].

207. [Ahmed Rıza], "Hilâfet ve Saltanat," *Meşveret*, no. 6, April 1, 1896, 3–4; "Une réplique," *La Jeune Turquie*, no. 9, April 3, 1896, [2].

208. See Emin Arslan "Les Arméniens à Constantinople," *La Revue Blanche* 11 (1896/2), 282–83; his undated letter to the European editors in *La Jeune Turquie*, no. 7, March 6, 1896, [1]. For similar ideas expressed by anonymous

writers, see "al-Arman wa al-Sūriyyūn," *Turkiyyā al-fatāt*, no. 4, January 21, 1896, [2]. This was the reason behind the hesitation of the Armenians to sign an appeal prepared by Arslān previously. See "Vox Clamentis in Deserto," *Armenia*, no. 83, September 1, 1895, 2–3. However, they spoke amicably about the publication of *Kashf al-Niqāb*. See "Miscellaneous News," *Armenia*, no. 88, February 1, 1896, 4.

209. Emin Arslan, "Les affaires d'Orient," *La Revue Blanche* 11 (1896/2), 240.

210. Emin Arslan, "Le troubles de Syrie," *La Revue Blanche* 11 (1896/2), 83–84.

211. See Amin Arslan, "Un coup d'épée dans l'eau," *La Jeune Turquie*, no. 10, April 17, 1896, [1].

212. Halil Ganem, "Lettre du Président de notre Comité," *La Jeune Turquie*, no. 3, January 1896, [2].

213. H[alil] G[anem], "Le Journal des Débats et la Turquie," *La Jeune Turquie*, no. 2, December 27, 1895, [1].

214. Salmoné, *The Fall and Resurrection*, 87 ff.

215. "Le controle Européen en Turquie," *La Jeune Turquie*, no. 2, [1–2].

216. "L'Europe et la politique coloniale," *La Jeune Turquie*, no. 12, May 19, 1896 [2].

217. Khalīl Ghānim, "al-qānūn al-āsāsī," *Kashf al-Niqāb*, no. 18, January 10, 1895, [1–2].

218. Münir Bey to Tevfik Pasha, Paris, May 23, 1896 (personelle et confidentielle), and the annexes, BBA-HNA-End: S.III, K.291, D.16/A.

219. BBA-BEO/Hariciye Âmed, 156-5/12, 1143 [June 2, 1896].

220. See "A nos lecteurs," *La Jeune Turquie*, no. 4, January 24, 1896, [1], "La Jeune Turquie," *L'Orient* 8, no. 8, February 1896, 4, and "Monsieur Cambon," *Mizan*, no. 178, May 28, 1896, 2509–10.

221. "Banquet de la Jeune Turquie," *Mechveret Supplément Français*, no. 26, January 1, 1897, 7.

222. The note dated January 27, 1897, PRO/F.O. 78/4840, and AE-NS-T, 1 (1897), 7–8.

223. "Comité Turco-Syrien des Réformes," *Mechveret Supplément Français*, no. 40, August 1, 1897, 5–6.

224. BBA-İrade-Hususî, Şa'ban 1314/no. 53-636, BBA-BEO/Hariciye Reft, 184-5/40, 1155 [October 14, 1896]/63857, 1621 [December 28, 1896]/67608, and 6 [March 14, 1897]/68825.

225. See "Halil Ganem," *Şûra-yı Ümmet*, no. 34, August 9, 1903, 1–2; and "Te'essüf ve Ta'ziye," *Osmanlı*, no. 121, September 1, 1903, 1.

226. Şeyh Ali Efendizâde Hoca Muhiddin, "Maksad-Meslek," *Kanun-i Esasî*, no. 1, December 21, 1896, 3.

227. Şeyh Alizâde Fatih Mezunlarından Hoca Muhiddin, "28 Cemaziy'ülâhir Sene 1314 tarihinde Zât-ı Şâhâneye Takdim Kılınan Ariza Suretidir," *Kanun-i Esasî*, no. 1, 3, and [Ka]d[r]i Nâsıh, "al-'ulamā warathatu al-anbiyā'," *Kanun-i Esasî*, no. 17, April 19, 1897, 3–5.

228. Salmoné, *The Fall and Resurrection*, 71 ff.

229. The ulema complained about this fact in their appeal, which they addressed to the soldiers during the counter revolution in 1909. See "Asker Evlâdlarımıza Hitabımız," *Beyan'ül-hak*, no. 29 [April 19, 1909], 670.

230. [Abdullah Cevdet-Hoca Şakir], *Ulema-yı İslâm Enarallahu Berahinehum Taraflarından Verilen Feteva-yı Şerife* (Geneva, 1314 [1896]), passim.

231. Nazif Sürûrî, *Hilâfet-i Muazzama-i İslâmiye* (Istanbul, 1315 [1897]), 6–23, Zeki, *Âlem-i İslâmiyet ve Şark ve Garb* (Istanbul, 1316 [1898]), 111–13, 'Abd al-Jamîl, *al-Zafar al-Ḥamīdiyya fī ithbāt al-Khalīfa* (1315 [1897]), Marmara University İlâhiyat Fakültesi Library MS no. 30, 2, 4–6, 19–21, Yūsuf b. Ismāʿīl al-Nabhānī, *al-Aḥādīth al-Arbaʿīn fī wujūb ṭāʿat āmīr al-muʾminīn* (Beirut, 1312 [1894]), passim.

232. Hüseyin Zâde Ali, "İttihat ve Terakki Cemiyeti Nasıl Kuruldu [?]" *Tan*, March 4 and 5, 1938. See also [Rıfat], *Beyn-el-milel İhtilâl Fırkaları*, 70–71.

233. BBA-İrade-Hususî, Şevval 1312/no. 38–73.

234. Hoca Muhiddin, *Hürriyet Mücahedeleri Yahud Firak ve Menfa Hatıraları* (Istanbul, 1326 [1908]), 2.

235. "İhtar," *Mizan*, no. 173, May 7, 1896, 2488.

236. For an example, see Eddaî Talib-i Selâmet Bir Mü'min, "Mekke-i Mükerreme," *Mizan*, no. 170, April 2, 1896, 2446.

237. Medrese-nişînlerden Fakir Bir Sohta, "Bu Ne Hilâfetdir Yârâb [?]" *Mizan*, no. 172, April 16, 1896, 2463.

238. Tarik-i İlmiyeden Hayreddin, "Hakk-ı Saltanat," *Meşveret*, no. 23, November 23, 1896, 1–2, and "Eâzım-ı Ulemadan Bir Zatın Mizan Kardeşimize Gönderdiği Mufassal Mektubu Fevkâlâde Ehemmiyetli Olduğundan Bâzı Parçaları Bervech-i Âti Dercedildi," *İlâve-i Meşveret*, no. 8, March 15, 108 [1896], 1.

239. BBA-BEO/Hariciye Âmed, 156-5/12, 3176 [October 27, 1896].

240. Currie to Salisbury, Therapia, August 26, 1897/no. 517–572, and enclosed memorandum. The interview was held on January 19, 1897. PRO/F.O. 78/4806. Similar ideas were subsequently introduced to the British authorities by high-ranking ulema. A remarkable example is Najm al-Dīn Efendi's, qadi of Baghdad, secret memorandum to the British consul, stating "the future of Islam is in security under British rule." See his memorandum enclosed with the letter from Ramsay to O'Conor, Baghdad, July 23, 1906/no. 642–62 (strictly confidential), PRO/F.O. 371/154, file 29027.

241. See Le Comité Musulman de Constantinople, *A sa Seigneurie le Marquis de Salisbury Premier Ministre et Ministre des Affaires Étrangères de sa très gracieuse Majesté la reine Victoria: Lettre ouverte* [Paris, 1896].

242. "Vatanperverân-ı İslâmiye Cemiyeti ve Lord Salisbury: Açık Mektub," *Hürriyet*, no. 56, August 15, 1896, 1–3. The original French text was summarized in an Armenian journal, "Le Sultan jugé par les Turcs," *L'Arménie*, no. 95, September 1, 1896, 3–4. This open letter caused anxiety among the government circles, see "Lord Salisbury'e Mektub-i Alenî," *Hürriyet*, no. 57, September 1, 1896, 2. Another appeal of protest by another ulema organization was sent to the same journal a month before. "Ulema ve Meşâyih-i İslâmiyenin İhtarâtı," *Hürriyet*, no. 78, July 15, 1897, 2.

243. Karl Blind, "Young Turkey," *Fortnightly Review* 60 (December 1896), 836.

244. Vatanperverân Cemiyetine Mensub Müderrisinden, *Birinci Va'az* (Istanbul, [1897]), a one-page handbill.

245. Muhiddin, *Hürriyet Mücahedeleri*, 3.

246. "İstanbul'dan," *Kanun-i Esasî*, no. 4, January 11, 1897, 7.

247. "Tebşir," *Hakikat*, no. 8, January 15, 1897, 3.

248. Müntesibîn-i İlmiyeden Biri, "Efradından Bulunmağla Müftehir Olduğum (Osmanlı İttihad ve Terakki Cemiyeti'nin) Mısır Şu'besi Tarafından Neş-

rolunan (Ulema-yı İslâma Da'vet-i Şer'iye) Nâm Risâle-i Mergubeye Zeyl İttihaz Edilmek Üzere Meşveret Gazetesi'ne," *Meşveret*, no. 21, 23 October 1896, 4.

249. Türk İnkılâp Tarihi Enstitüsü Arşivi, 82/18423.

250. Acting governor of Edirne to the Chamberlain's office [28 January 1897], *Edirne Vilâyetiyle Muhaberat Kaydına Mahsustur*, BBA-YEE, 36/139-32-IV/139/XVIII.

251. "Mekâtib," *Mizan*, no. 171, 9 April 1896, 2454. The relationship that the Young Turks tried to establish aroused dread at the palace. See Şerif Pasha, the Ottoman ambassador to Sweden, to the Chamberlain's office, June 17, [18]99/ no. 139. *Tahran, Petersburg, Stockholm Sefaret-i Seniyeleriyle Muhaberata Mahsus Defterdir*, BBA-YEE, 36/139-44/139/XVIII.

252. "İttihad ve Terakki Cemiyeti'nin Mesleği Cemiyetimizin Mesleğine Tevafuk Edegeldiğinden Efradından 'F.Ş.' İmzasıyla Aldığımız Varakayı Aynen Dercediyoruz," *Kanun-i Esasî*, no. 1, January 21, 1896, 5–6.

253. For his participation in the Young Turk movement and his short biography, see PAAA, 733/3, Die Jungtürken, 198 (Bd.1-2), A. 334, 7.1.1902, and the spy report entitled "Jön Türklerin Meşruhatlı Esamisi Olub fî. 10 Ramazan 317 Tarihli Tezkere-i Âcizâneme Melfufdur." Abbas II Papers, Durham University, F. 26/281. Later on he cut all ties between himself and the CUP and upbraided the Young Turks, accusing them of being Freemasons, Turkish nationalists, and atheists. See Mehmed Kadri Nâsıh, *Sarâyih*, (Paris, [1910?]), 38–39, 209–14.

254. Muhiddin, *Hürriyet Mücahedeleri*, 3.

255. Ibid., 5.

256. See Füzelâ-yı Müderrisinden Bir Zât, *Ulema-yı Din-i İslâma Da'vet-i Şer'iye* ([Cairo], 1314 [1896]), especially, 12–16, *İmamet ve Hilâfet Risâlesi (Cairo, 1312 [1896])*, 3–5, 43, [İbrahim Temo], *Hareket* (Istanbul [Bucharest], 1312 [1896]), 69–71, and Tunalı Hilmi, *İkinci Hutbe: al-'ulamā warathatu al-anbiyā'* ([Geneva], 1314 [1896]), 8 ff.

257. Mustafa Sabri, "{Beyan'ül-hak}'ın Mesleği," *Beyan'ül-hak*, no. 1 [November 5, 1908], 2–3; Fatih Dersiâmlarından Hafiz Mehmed, "Makale-i Mahsusa," *Beyan'ül-hak*, no. 3 [October 18, 1908], 11–13; Ali Nazmi, "Makale-i Mahsusa," *Beyan'ül-hak*, no. 17 [December 25, 1908], 380. Banishment of many members of the ulema on the grounds that they were "taking part in the activities which are not in accordance with the sultan's imperial will" supports these claims. For an interesting example see BBA-Tezâkir-i Samiye Dosyaları, 400, no. 1451 [December 9, 1895].

258. "Cemiyetimiz," *Beyan'ül-hak*, no. 1, 11.

259. "[İhtar]," *Beyan'ül-hak*, no. 14 [January 4, 1909], 298.

260. Octave Depont-Xavier Coppolani, *Les confréries religieuses Musulmanes* (Algiers, 1897), 257–77; Ernest Meyer, "Les associations Musulmanes," *Annales de l'École Libre des Sciences Politiques*, 1 (1886), 294–98, d'Estournelles de Constant, "Les sociétés secrètes chez les Arabes et la conquête de l'Afrique du Nord," *Revue des deux Mondes* 74 (1886), 100 ff.

261. One of the prominent sheikhs of the Naqshbandīyyah order, Gümüşhanevî Ahmed Ziyaeddin, who had been invited to the palace during the reign of Sultan Abdülâziz, and had received even more respect from Abdülhamid II, who requested his opinion on various matters. See [Mustafa Fevzi bin Numan], *Hediyet ül-Halidîn fî Menâkıb-ı Kutb ül-Ârifîn Mevlâna Ahmed Ziyaeddin bin Mustafa el-Gümüşhanevî Kuddise Sırrahu* (Istanbul, 1313 [1895]), 51.

262. For his relations with the sultan, see Hamid Algar, "Political Aspects of Naqshbandī History," *Naqshbandis: Cheminements et situation actuelle d'un ordr-*

mystique Musulman ed. Marc Gaborieau, Alexandre Popovic, and Thierry Zarcone (Istanbul, 1990), 141. For his banishment see "Tasavvuf," *Tasavvuf,* no. 4 [April 13, 1911], 4–5.

263. Mehmed Es'ad, "Makale-i Mahsusa," *Beyan'ül-hak,* no. 17 [December 25, 1908], 371–73.

264. For his relations with the Young Turks, see Müstecib Ülküsal, *Dobruca ve Türkler* (Ankara, 1966), 143. General information about him is given in Alexandre Popovic, *L'Islam Balkanique: Les Musulmans du sud-est Européen dans la période post-Ottomane* (Berlin, 1986), 236, and idem, "Les ordres mystiques musulmanes du Sud-Est européen dans la période post-ottomane," *Les Ordres mystiques dans l'Islam: Cheminements et situation actuelle* ed. A.Popovic and G.Veinstein, (Paris, 1985), 96 n.141.

265. For their punishment see Es'ad, *Üss-i Zafer* (Istanbul, 1241 [1826]), 199–207.

266. A[hmed] Rıfkı, *Bektaşi Sırrı* 1 (Istanbul, 1325 [1909]), 147.

267. Ibid., 148.

268. This work was translated into Turkish in 1429 by Tirevî 'Abdülmecid İbn-i Ferişteh İzzeddin (see TPL, H.263). (For more information about Tirevî and his writings, see Abdülbaki Gölpınarlı, "Hurufilik ve Mîr-i 'Alem Celâl Bik'in Bir Mektubu," *Türkiyat Mecmuası* 14 (1965), 94), and had become the most widely read volume of *Cavidannâme* among the Bektashis. (See *İzah ül-esrar,* IUL, Turkish Manuscripts, no. 4382, 42). It was published by lithograph in 1288 [1872]. (*'İşknâme* [Istanbul, 1872].)

269. The *Cavidannâme* was translated into Turkish in 1648 by Dervish Murtaza under the title *Dürr-i Yetim.* But this manuscript could not be printed after the advent of printing because the presses were state controlled. See Abdülbaki Gölpınarlı, "Bektaşilik-Hurûfilik ve Fadl-Allah'ın öldürülmesine düşürülen üç tarih," *Şarkiyat Mecmuası* 5 (1964), 15.

270. İshak Efendi, *Kaşif ül-Esrar ve Dafi ül-Eşrar* ([Istanbul], 1291 [1874]).

271. Esseyid Ahmed Rıf'at, *Mir'at ül-Makasid fi Def' ül-Mefâsid* (Istanbul, 1293 [1878]).

272. Rıfkı, *Bektaşi Sırrı* 1, 113.

273. BBA-YSHM, 28 N 1321/no. 3098-1.

274. Despite false rumors of his membership in the Bektashi order (see Odysseus [Charles Norton Edgecumbe], *Turkey in Europe* (London, 1900), 196), Abdülhamid II was deeply fearful of the seditious activities of the Bektashis, and they were kept under continuous scrutiny.

275. F[rederick] W[illiam] Hasluck, "Geographical Distribution of the Bektashi," *The Annual of the British School at Athens,* no. 21 (1914–1916), 116.

276. See Naïm Bey Frasheri, "Le 'Livre des Bektashis' de Naïm Bey Frasheri," *Revue du Monde Musulman* 49 (1922), 119, Norbert Jokl, "Die Bektashis von Naim Be Frashëri," *Balkan-Archiv* 2 (1926), 231–32. Max Choublier, "Les Bektachis et la Roumélie," *Revue des Études Islamiques* (1927– Cahier III), 443, Gabriel Louis-Jaray, *Au Jeune Royaume d'Albanie: Ce qu'il a été = Ce qu'il est* (Paris, 1914), 100. For the participation of some prominent Bektashi babas such as Baba Zeynel and Baba Hacı in the national activities see Ippen to Goluchowski, Scutari, January 31, 1901/no. 1, HHStA, PA XIV 7 Albanien.

277. Ernest Ramsaur, "The Bektashi Dervishes and the Young Turks," *The Moslem World* 32, no. 1 (January 1942), 7–14. Contemporary Turkish authors have described the Young Turk and the Kemalist movements as Freemason-Bek-

tashi conspiracies. See Klaus Kreiser, "Notes sur le présent et le passé des ordres mystiques en Turquie," in *Les ordres mystiques dans l'Islam*, 52, 60.

278. "Havâdis," *Albania*, vol. D, no. 10, October 30, 1899, 16.

279. W. S. Monroe, *Turkey and the Turks: An Account of the Lands, the Peoples and the Institutions of the Ottoman Empire* (London, 1908), 281, and Richard Davey, *The Sultan and His Subjects*, vol. 1 (London, 1897), 97: " They are [the Bektashis] even said to be affiliated to some of the French masonic lodges. One thing is certain; the order now consists almost exclusively of gentlemen of education, belonging to the Liberal, or Young Turkey party." The alleged relations between the Bektashis and the freemasons had been discussed by many accounters. See John P. Brown, *The Dervishes or Oriental Spiritualism* (London, 1868), 59–60. Edmund Naumann, *Vom Goldnen Horn zu den Quellen des Euphrat* (Munich, 1893), 195. Georg Jacob, *Beiträge zur Kenntnis des Derwisch Ordens der Bektaschis* (*Türkische Bibliothek*, B.9) (Berlin, 1909), 36–37. Even the Freemasons hinted at a kinship between them and the Bektashis. See "Turkey," *A Library of Freemasonry* 4, ed. Robert Freke Gould (Philadelphia, 1906), 126. The Bektashis regarded Freemasons as a secret society similar to their own and made the following comment: "Freemasonry is a derogatory phrase used among lower classes of our society when referring to those who appeared to be lax in their religious observations. However, Freemasonry is nothing other than a sect of fraternity and mutual assistance which binds its members." Rıfkı, *Bektaşi Sırrı* 1, 1n.

280. "Rumelihisarında Mahmud Baba Dergâhında: Nafi Baba ile Mukaddes Ordumuzun Gayur Zabitleri," *Muhibban*, no. 12, 97. For Nafi Baba's speech in which he criticized the old regime and praised the army, see Tarik-i Rıfaiyeden Osman Fevzi, "Aynen: Suret-i Nutk," *Muhibban*, no. 8 [April 28, 1910], 71. For some information about Nafi Baba see Georg Jacob, "Die Bektaschijje in ihrem Verhältnis zu verwandten Erscheinungen," *Abhandlungen der Philosophisch-Philologischen Klasse der Königlich Bayerischen Akademie der Wissenschaften*, 24 (III. Abteilung 1907–09), 29.

281. John Kingsley Birge, *The Bektashi Order of Dervishes* (London, 1937), 81.

282. "Yüzbaşı Şükrü Efendi'ye," *Muhibban*, no. 3 [March 16, 1911], 128.

283. R. Tschudi, "Bericht über die in der Umgebung von Konstantinopel vorhandenen Bektaschi-Klöster," *Abhandlungen der Philosophisch-Philologischen Klasse der Königlich Bayerischen Akademie der Wissenschaften* 24 (III.Abteilung, 1907–09), 52. Also the ancient rights of Cemaleddin Efendi (Çelebi), who was the true descendant of Hacı Bektaş and the *de jure* supreme head of the order were restored after the Young Turk revolution. See Hasluck, "Geographical Distribution," *The Annual of the British School at Athens*, 87–88. For the controversy and a discussion of the lineage, see Çelebi Cemaleddin Efendi, *Bektaşi Sırrı Nâm Risâleye Müdafaa* (Istanbul, 1328 [1910]), passim, and A[hmed] Rıfkı, *Bektaşi Sırrı'nın Müdafaasına Mukabele* (Istanbul, 1327 [1911]), 84–146.

284. Margaret Hasluck, "The Nonconformist Moslems of Albania," *Contemporary Review* 127 (1925), 601.

285. Brown, *The Dervishes*, 176–77, Lucy M. J. Garnett, *Mysticism and Magic in Turkey* (London, 1912), 132–33.

286. Ryan Papers, Miscellaneous (1908–1914), PRO/F.O. 800/240. İshak Sükûti had an interest in the philosophy of this order. See Doctor Nâzım to İshak Sükûti, December 12, 1901, AQSh, 19/106-5//767/1406.

287. Bursalı Mehmed Tahir, *Osmanlı Müellifleri 1299–1915*, ed. A. Fikri Yavuz and İsmail Özen, (Istanbul, n.d.), 66–67. For his participation in the order, see Abdülbaki [Gölpınarlı], *Melâmilik ve Melâmiler* (Istanbul, 1931), 328–29.

288. Kuran, *İnkılâp Tarihimiz ve İttihad ve Terakki*, 65.

289. Mehmed Ziya, *Yenikapu Mevlevihânesi* (Istanbul, 1329 [1911]), 220–27. Even the regular observances at the tekke were frequently forbidden by police.

290. Ibid., 229–31.

291. For an example see A[bdullah] Cevdet, "Harput'da Buzluk Yahud Bir Tabiî Buz Fabrikası," *Resimli Gazete*, no. 30 [October 15, 1891], 328–29.

292. For the government's decision of suspension, see *Mabeyn, Devâir ve Vilâyetlerle Bâzı Zevâta Yazılan Tezkere ve Muharrerat Müsveddelerini Havî Dosya Defteri*, BBA-YEE, 36/398/146/XIV, no. 268 [October 26, 1899], Memorandum to the Ministry of the Interior.

293. Ibid., no. 5271 [September 27, 1901], Memorandum to the under-secretary of the Ministry of the Interior. For the suspicions of the palace about Tahir Dede and the journal, see no. 5272 [September 27, 1901], and no. 5278 [September 28, 1901]. Memoranda to the Ministry of the Interior.

294. Glanstätten to Goluchowski, Smyrna, September 12, 1899/no. 98, HHStA, PA XXXVIII 313, Konsulate Smyrna 1899; and Samson to O'Conor, Smyrna, September 6, 1899/no. 55, enclosed with the letter from O'Conor to Salisbury, Constantinople, September [11], 1899/no. 426, PRO/F.O. 78/4995.

295. "Havâdis," *Osmanlı*, no. 45, October 15, 1899, 7.

296. Shipley to O'Conor, Angora, September 19, 1899/no. 30 (confidential), enclosed with the letter from O'Conor to Salisbury, September 28, 1899/no. 462 (confidential). PRO/F.O. 78/4995.

297. Doughty-Wylie to the British embassy in Istanbul, Konya, July 12, 1908/no. 82, PRO/F.O. 195/2280.

298. For instance Jules Cambon; gouverneur général de l'Algérie, commissaire du Gouvernement; claimed that: "En effet, messieurs, il faut considérer que jusqu'à présent nous n'avons peut être pas assez tenu compte des choses de l'esprit en ce qui concerne les indigènes. Ce que je vous disais du développement des zaouïas, du développement du fanatisme, de l'ignorance et des passions religieuses dans la masse des indigènes." *Journal Officiel*, June 19, 1894, *Sénat: Session ordinaire de 1894 (49e séance)*, 544. Combes, the *rapporteur* made similar comments see *Journal Officiel*, June 16, 1894, *Sénat: Session ordinaire de 1894 (48e séance)*, 532. For the fear of the orders on the part of the French, see Louis Rinn, *Marabouts et Khouan: Étude sur l'Islam en Algerie* (Algiers, 1884), 101–102; Napoléon Ney, *Un danger europeen: Les sociétés secrètes Musulmanes* (Paris, 1890), passim; Depont-Coppolani, *Les confréries religieuses Musulmanes*, xiii–xiv; L'Abbé Rouquette, *Les sociétés secrètes chez les Musulmans* (Paris, 1899), 26–27.

299. For the sultan's endorsement of Tijānīs, see Jamil M. Abun-Nasr, *The Tidjaniyya: A Sufi Order in the Modern World* (Oxford, 1965), 159, 161. A prominent member of this order Muḥammad b. Mukhtār, "while in Istanbul is said to have initiated Sultan 'Abdul-Hamid [II] into the Tidjaniyya." Ibid., 161.

300. It was even claimed that in the beginning "Abdülhamid II had endorsed a Shādhilīyyah order [the Madanīs] against the Sanūsīs, but later he regarded this to have been a great mistake." See Şehbenderzâde Filibeli Ahmed Hilmi, *Sünûsiler ve On Üçüncü Asrın En Büyük Mütefekkir-i İlmiyesi Seyyid Muhammed el-Sünûsi-Abdülhamid ve Seyyid Muhammed el-Mehdî ve Asr-ı Hamidî'de Âlem-i İslâm ve Sünûsiler* (Istanbul, 1325 [1909]), 70. Later Abdülhamid II recognized their

authority for the purpose of using them against western penetration (Italian in particular) of Tripoli and Cyrenaika. During the Ottoman-Italian War of 1911–12, the Young Turks led by Enver Bey received the full support of Sanūsīs in the struggle against the Italians. See Enver Bey's letters to a German woman with whom he frequently corresponded. Dated January 31, 1912, end of May [May 29, 1912], June 28, 1912, July 9, 1912, Ernst Jäckh Papers, Yale University Sterling Memorial Library, MS no.466; Enrico Insabato, *L'Islam et la politique des Alliés* (Paris, 1920), 104.

301. For their impact on Abdülhamid II, see Velī al-Dīn Yegen, *al-Maʿlūm wa al-majhūl* (Cairo, 1909), 98 ff.

302. Ẓāfir al-Madanī played an important role in the appointment of Tunuslu Hayreddin Pasha as grand vizier. See "Hayreddin Paşa," *Tercüman-ı Hakikat*, December 14, 1878; "New Turkish Ministry," *Times*, December 5, 1878, İbnül-emin Mahmud Kemal İnal, *Osmanlı Devrinde Son Sadrıazamlar* 6 (Istanbul, 1965), 897–901, G.S.Van Krieken, *Khayr al-Din et la Tunisie* (Leiden, 1976), 277. Ẓāfir al-Madanī wrote two important books supporting the idealized goal of pan-Islamism with Abdülhamid II as the caliph. See Ẓāfir al-Madanī Muḥammad ibn Muḥammad Ḥasan, *al-Nūr al-ṣāṭiʿ wa-al-burhān al qāṭiʿ* ([Istanbul, 1301 [1883–84]]), and *al-Anwār al-qudsīyah fī tanzīh ṭuruq al-qawm al-ʿalīyah [al-mushtami] ʿalā al-awrād wa-al azāb al-Shadhilīyah* (Istanbul, 1304 [1886]). Although the second book and its Turkish version (*El-envâr-ül kudsiye fī tenzih-it turuk-il-kavm-il aliyye* (Istanbul, 1302 [1882]) bore his name, the manuscript version presented to the sultan carried the name of his brother Sheikh Ḥamza. IUL, Turkish Manuscripts, no. 4648. He also openly praised the sultan in these two books, see 60–61 and 302–303 respectively. For his political influence, see A. Le Chatelier, *Les confréries Musulmanes du Hedjaz* (Paris, 1887), 112–16. Surprisingly, Sheikh Ẓāfir al-Madanī's brother Sheikh Ḥamza and his son Ḥamīd, who was a lieutenant, helped the Young Turks distribute their leaflets in 1895. This information appeared in two letters written by İbrahim Temo in Medgidia, which he had sent to Karl Süssheim, dated December 25, 1933, and October 9, 1935. Nachlaß Süssheim.

303. J. Spencer Trimingham, *The Sufi Orders in Islam* (Oxford, 1971), 126.

304. For a brief history of the order, see al-Madanī, *El-envâr-ül kudsiye* IUL, 200 ff.

305. B. Abu-Manneh, "Sultan Abdulhamid and Sheikh Abulhuda al-Sayyadi," *MES* 15, no. 2 (May 1979), 134–40; Frederick Jones Bliss, *The Religions of Modern Syria and Palestine* (Edinburgh, 1912), 242; Keçecizâde İzzet Fuad Paşa, "Abdülhamid'i Parmağı Üzerinde Oynatan (Ebulhüda) Kimdir?," *Büyük Gazete* 2, no. 60, December 15, 1927, 4–5; and "(Ebulhüda) Kimdir?," *Büyük Gazete* 2, no. 61, December 22, 1927, 4–5. Contrary to all these claims, Abū al-Hudā al-Ṣayyādī was shown great respect while staying in the provinces and before becoming an adviser to Abdülhamid II. The official letters signed by Es'ad Pasha, İzzet Bey, and Ahmed Midhat Pasha, dated [July 25, 1872], [November 25, 1876], and [December 6, 1876], respectively were given to a journalist by Abū al-Hudā al-Ṣayyādī. See "Ebulhüda Efendi," *Serbesti*, February 6, 1909.

306. The most important pamphlet written by him in this field was *Daï'r Reşad li sebil ül-ittihad ve inkıyad* trans. Halebli Kadri Efendizâde Abdülkadir (Istanbul, n.d. [1882?]). He praises the Ottoman caliphate and Abdülhamid II (13), and exhorts the faithful to obey the ruler on the basis of proofs drawn from Islamic texts (14 ff.) The explanations made by Butrus Abu-Manneh based on the claim that this book was never translated into Turkish are erroneous. See "Abdul-

hamid II and Abulhuda al-Sayyadi," *MES*, 143 and 152 n.128. For Abū al-Hudā al-Ṣayyādī's praise to Abdülhamid II, see also *Āyāt al-ʿirfān fī mawlid sayyid walad ʿAdnān* (Istanbul, 1302 [1884]), cover page; and O'Conor to Salisbury, Constantinople, February 14, 1900/no. 50 (secret), PRO/F.O. 407/190. His disciples, too, preached obedience to the sultan. See David Dean Commins, *Islamic Reform: Politics and Social Change in Late Ottoman Syria* (Oxford, 1990), 105.

307. *Hidāyat al-sāʾī bi-sulūk tarīqat al-ghawth al-Rifāʿī* ([Istanbul, 1872–3]), *al-Qawāʾid al marʿiyah fī uṣūl al-ṭarīqah al-Rifāʿiyyah* (n.p., n.d.); *al-ʿInāyah al-rabbāniyah fī mulakhkhaṣ al-ṭarīqah al-Rifāʿiyyah* (Istanbul, 1301 [1893]).

308. "Maarif Nezaret-i Celilesinden Tastîr Buyurulan Ruhsatnâmenin Suretidir," in Abū al-Hudā al-Ṣayyādī, *Ḍawʾ al-Shams fī qawlihi Buniya al-Islām ʿalā khams* 1 [Istanbul, 1300/1882–83], 8.

309. D. Gadzhanov, "Mohamedani Pravoslavni i Mohamedani Sektanti v Makedoniya," *Makedonski Pregled* 1, no. 4 (1925), 61 ff.

310. Some Istanbul Rifāʿīs, who did not think highly of Abū al-Hudā al-Ṣayyādī, endorsed the Young Turks. For an example, see "Muallim Sadık Paşa," *Muhibban*, no. 2 [October 28, 1909], 9–12.

311. L. Massignon, "La dernière querelle entre Rifāʿyin et Qâdiryîn," *Revue du Monde Musulman* 6, no. 11 (November 1908), 457. Similar claims were made by Ahmed Hilmi. See *Sünûsiler*, 69–70.

312. BBA-YP, 11 S 1304/no. 81658.

313. BBA-BEO/VGG(2), Suriye Giden, 352, 7 [April 8, 1897]/69883.

314. "Havâdis," *Mizan*, no. 173, April 23, 1896, 2472. Contrary to this information given by the Young Turks, European sources gathered information from the Qādiris before the 1908 revolution and revealed no data about the rivalry. See, for instance, Max von Freiherrn von Oppenheim, *Vom Mittelmeer zum Persischen Golf: Durch den Hauran, die syrische Wüste und Mesopotamien* 1 (Berlin, 1899), 74–75. (Massignon's above-mentioned article is the first European work on the rivalry between the two sects. See Martin Hartmann, *Der Islamische Orient: Berichte und Forschungen* 3, *Unpolitische Briefe aus der Türkei* [Leipzig, 1910], 194/n.16.) However, Frederick William Hasluck was told by one of the former British consuls at Mosul that "the Young Turks at the beginning of their régime made an attempt to destroy the tomb of Ahmed Rifai." F[rederick] W[illiam] Hasluck, *Christianity and Islam under the Sultans* 2 (Oxford, 1929), 620.

315. Jamāl al-Dīn al-Afghānī, whose relations with the Young Turks will be discussed later, had several controversial discussions with Ẓāfir al-Madanī and Abū al-Hudā al-Ṣayyādī. (See [Mîrzâ Aqa Khan], "Le livre In Cha Allah! Réfuté par Séyyèd Borhan ed-Din Balkhi," *Revue du Monde Musulman* 21 (1912), 239–62, Edward G. Browne, *Materials for the Study of the Bàbì Religion* (Cambridge, 1918), 224–25) Foreign observers claimed that these two sheikhs were intriguing against al-Afghānī. (See Bernhard Stern, *Der Sultan und seine Politik: Erinnerungen und Beobachtungen eines Journalisten* (Leipzig, [1906]), 30 ff, and "Šeik Dzemaluddin Afgani," *Ogledalo*, no. 2, June 7, 1907, 2 ff.) al-Afghānī's fellow Muḥammad ʿAbduh also criticized the intrigues of Abū al-Hudā al-Ṣayyādī (See Wilfrid Scawen Blunt, *My Diaries: Being a Personal Narrative of Events 1888–1914* 1 [New York, 1922], 285) and the Young Turks had interviews with ʿAbduh.(See Ibid., 225, Abdullah Cevdet, "Şâhzâde Şeyh-ül Reis Hazretleriyle Mülâkat," *İctihad*, no. 126 [January 27, 1914], 447.) ʿAbduh was praised by the Young Turks after his death in 1905.(See [Abdullah Djevdet], "Des morts qui ne meurent pas: Cheikh Mohamed Abdou," *Idjtihad*, no. 9, (October 1905), 135, Abdullah Cevdet, "Şeyh Muhammed Abduh," *İctihad* 2, no. 11 (April 1906), 164–65, and "Teessüf-i

Azîm," *Şûra-yı Ümmet*, no. 80, August 16, 1905, 4. These praises gain import in the light of 'Abduh's anti-Turkish feelings. See Wilfrid Scawen Blunt, *The Secret History of the British Occupation of Egypt* (New York, 1922), 191. Also the idea of "Arab Caliphate" presented by Blunt was 'Abduh's. See Wilfrid Scawen Blunt, *The Future of Islam* (London, 1882), vii–x, 89. For this idea, see also Gabriel Charmes, *L'Avenir de la Turquie: Le Panislamisme* (Paris, 1883), 182–87.) The only exception to the position taken by the Islamic reformers for Abū al-Hudā al-Şayyādī, was an article published in the journal of 'Abduh's disciple Muḥammad Rashīd Riḍā. In this article, Abū al-Hudā al-Şayyādī was presented as an authority on religious affairs. See "al-Ḥikmah al-sharʿiyyah fī muḥākamat al-qādiriyyah wa al-rifāʿiyyah," *al-Manār* 1 (1897), 598. Yet the same journal later inaccurately described his loss of prestige (See "Suqūṭ al-Shaykh Abī al-Hudā Afandī," *al-Manār* 4, no. 15, October 14, 1901, 592), and published a letter criticizing him, while informing the reader that the criticism was too mild. See "Maktūb min baʿḍi bulaghāʾ miṣr lī-samāḥati Abī al-Hudā Afandī al-shahīr," *al-Manār* 3, no. 20, November 4, 1900, 471–73.

316. For the relations between the Salafis and the Young Turks, see Commins, *Islamic Reform*, 92–95.

317. See Albert Fua, "Ahmed Riza Bey," *Mècheroutiette*, no. 40, (March 1913), 28–29.

318. "İstanbul'da Tevkif ve Teb'id," *Hürriyet*, no. 64, December 15, 1896, 4; "Minister-System of Espionage," *Daily Mail*, December 19, 1896. Badawīs had their *tekkes* mostly in Mecca, Medina, and Jeddah and were not very strong in Istanbul in the late nineteenth century. They had only eight small *tekkes* in the Ottoman capital, and Sheikh Nailî was the sheikh of the *tekke* at Koca Mustafa Paşa. See Depont-Coppolani, *Les confréries religieuses Musulmanes*, 335–36.

319. See Mustafa Kara, *Din, Hayat, Sanat Açısından Tekkeler ve Zaviyeler* (Istanbul, 1980), 283; and Klaus Kreiser, "Derwischscheiche als Publizisten: Ein Blick in die religiöse Presse zwischen 1908 und 1925," *Zeitschrift der Deutschen Morgenländischen Gesellschaft, Supplement* 6 (1983), 213–14.

320. See "Teessüf-i Azîm," *Şûra-yı Ümmet*, no. 71, December 15, 1908, 5, and "Şeyh Nailî Merhumun Cenaze Alayı," *Şûra-yı Ümmet*, no. 72, December 16, 1908, 4.

321. Edhem Ruhi, "Yine Bir Levha-i Dil-sûz," *Rumeli*, no. 14 [March 26, 1906], 3. Edhem Ruhi wrote this article on the occasion of the death of Khalwatī Sheikh Necmeddin, with whom he had been exiled.

322. The name of this sheikh was not given by the Young Turk organs, but it was noted that he had been exiled first to Bursa and then to Fezzan with his brother. See "Havâdis," *Osmanlı*, no. 68, September 15, 1900, 8.

323. This was Hüsameddin Bey, who died in 1901 in exile. See "Şühedâ-yı Hürriyet," *Osmanlı*, no. 83, May 1, 1901, 4.

324. AQSh, 19/60//445-30-1. Another document reveals that naval officers convened at various *tekkes* and "their real aim is not religious practice but to create gathering centers at those *tekkes*." Deniz Müzesi Arşivi-Şûra-yı Bahrî, 610-26-A, 29, July 29, 1902, and Deniz Müzesi Arşivi- Umumî Evrak, 125/1, 37, June 30, 1902.

325. For their role, see "Les Béhais et le mouvement actuel en Perse," *Revue du Monde Musulman* 1, no. 2 (December 1906), 198–206; and Arminius Vambéry, *Western Culture in Eastern Lands* (London, 1906), 334–37.

326. Juan R. I. Cole, "Iranian Millenarianism and Democratic Thought in the 19th Century," *IJMES* 24 (1992), 11.

327. Although the Ottoman authorities accused al-Afghānī of being a member and mentor of Babîs, Browne wrote that al-Afghānī "had no great opinion of Bábîs." See Edward G[ranville] Browne, *The Persian Revolution of 1905–1909* (Cambridge, 1910), 45.

328. T[ürk] Y[urdu], "Şeyh Cemaleddin Efganî," *Türk Yurdu* 4, no. 8 [June 25, 1914], 2263–67, and *Ethem Ruhi Balkan Hatıraları-Canlı Tarihler* 6 (Istanbul, 1947), 11. al-Afghānī also influenced "un groupe des Jeunes Persans" in Istanbul. See X [Taghizade, S. H], "Le Panislamisme et le Panturquisme," *Revue du Monde Musulman* 22 (1913), 185.

329. "Havâdis," *Kanun-i Esasî*, no. 15, April 5, 1897, 4.

330. Halil Ganem, "Djémal Eddin," *Mechveret Supplément Français*, no. 31, March 15, 1897, 5, and "Şeyh Cemaleddin Efganî," *Kanun-i Esasî*, no. 14, March 29, 1897, 4–5.

331. For his activities in Istanbul, see BBA-YEE, 18/553-586/93/36. Even the books mentioning his ideas and political activities were banned after his death. See BBA-BEO/ Hidiviyet-i Celile-i Mısriyenin Tahrirat Defteri, 1031-68/4, no. 291, and BBA-İrade-Hususî, Rebiy'ülâhir 1315/no. 101–444.

332. The note of the grand vizier Halil Rıfat Pasha dated [May 4, 1896], BBA-YEE, 31/1709-3/110/87. For al-Afghānī's relations with the Freemasons see A. Albert Kudsi-zadeh, "Afghani and Freemasonry in Egypt," *Journal of the American Oriental Society* 92, no. 1 (January-March 1972), 25–35.

333. Ibid., Although 'Abd Allah al-Nadīm was an Egyptian nationalist (see Muḥammad al-Makhzūmī, *Khātirāt Jamāl al-Dīn al-Afghānī* [Beirut, 1931], 129 ff; Nikkie R. Keddie, *Sayyid Jamāl ad-Dīn al-Afghānī: A Political Biography* [Los Angeles, 1972], 379), he was described as a Young Turk in this letter.

334. İbrahim Temo, *İttihad ve Terakki Cemiyetinin Teşekkülü ve Hidemati Vataniye ve İnkılâbı Milliye Dair Hatıratım* (Medgidia, 1939), 66–67. Although the Ottoman authorities had repeatedly complained about the role played by the servants in the Persian embassy in Istanbul, they never gave any information indicating the religious sects and orders to which these servants belonged. See BBA-BEO/VGG(2), Devâir-Mühimme, no. 4 (Hariciye), no. 5398 [March 23, 1894], Devâir: 16/8728. For a document about the Babî's involvement in the Young Turk publication, see Şem'azâde Ahmed Refik Pasha to the Chamberlain's office, no. 1153 [January 12, 1899], *Memurin-i Müteferrikaya Mahsus Kayd Defteridir*, BBA-YEE, 36/139-84/139/XX.

335. Temo, *İttihad ve Terakki*, 67. In his testimony Mīrzā Riḍā Kirmānī said that he was politically active in Istanbul and that some of his friends had been arrested by the Ottoman police. But he mentioned nothing about the distribution of the banned journals. See 'Alī Khān Ẓahīr al-dawla, *Tārīkh-i bī-Durugh* (Tehran, n.d.), 67–68. Mīrzā Riḍa Kirmānī's affiliation to the Babîs is a highly controversial issue. Although all official Ottoman and Young Turk sources depicted him as a Babî; authoritative Persian sources such as Yaḥya Dawlatābādī, *Hayāt-i Yaḥyā* 1, 4th ed. (Tehran 1342 [1983]), 126, claimed that "in this period, whenever there are political problems and an oppositionary undertaking from the nation to divert attention, the statesmen clothe the affair with the garb of immorality and display it as Babî [heresy]. [They do this] to conceal the advent of anti-government feelings on the part of the nation. At that time, resorting to the same politics they arrested a few well known individuals from the Babî sect and diverted public opinion from the Babîs' arrest. At the same time, they arrested a group from the assembly of the enlightened among which were, Hajj Sayāh-i Maḥallātī, Mīrzā 'Abd Allah Ṭabīb-i Khurāsānī, Mīrzā Riḍā-i Pīlihvar-i Kirmānī, etc." Grand Vizier Halil Rıfat Pasha

accused al-Afghānī of the assassination, see his note mentioned above. For the sensitivity of the Ottoman government to the possible role of al-Afghānī in the assassination see Tahsin Bey to Ahmed Bey, the Ottoman military attaché in Tehran, May 8, [18]96/no. 3; and Ahmed Bey to the Chamberlain's office, May 9, [18]96/no. 4, *Tahran Ateşemiliteri ile Muhaberat Kaydına Mahsus Defter*, BBA-YEE, 36/139-44/139/XVIII and BBA-YP, 18 Za 1313/no.1338, 24 Za 1313/no. 1348, 23 Z 1313/no.1490, 3 M 1314/no. 64. Some Persian sources in contrast accused Abdülhamid II and al-Afghānī of planning the assassination of Naṣīr-al-Dīn Shah. See Ismāʿīl Rāʾīn, *Faramūshkhānah va Frāmāsunrī dar Īrān*1, (Tehran, 1357 [1979]), 310–13; and Mahdī-Qulī Hidāyat, *Khāṭirāt va khaṭarāt*, 3d ed., (Tehran, 1361[1982]), 79. However, more reliable sources refuse this involvement. See Dawlatābādī, *Hayāt-i Yaḥyā* 1, 167, Keddie, *Sayyid Jamāl ad-Dīn al-Afghānī*, 404-16.

336. Even as late as 1908 the Babî groups throughout the Ottoman Empire were under close scrutiny by police. BBA-BEO/Dahiliye Giden, 107-3/56, 863 [June 18, 1908], and BBA-İrade-Hususî, Cemaziy'ülevvel 1326/no. 65–472.

337. "Ölmüşe Rahmet, Bakîlere Selâmet," *Mizan*, no. 175, May 7, 1896, 2484.

338. Ahmed Rıza, "İcmâl-i Ahvâl," *Meşveret*, no. 11, May 23, 108 [1896], 2.

339. AQSh, 19/60//814/8. Temo wrote a minute on the eulogy as follows: "This is the manifesto which was printed by lithograph in Bucharest and sent to Istanbul through foreign post offices."

340. Doctor Nâzım to İshak Sükûti, undated, AQSh, 19/106-5//916/1390. Doctor Nâzım also required İshak Sükûti to provide him with the couplet that Mīrzā Riḍā Kirmānī read during his execution. This couplet was published in Mahdī Bāmdād, *Sharḥ-i ḥāl-i rijāl-i Īrān dar qarn-i 12 va 13 va 14 hijrī* 3 (Tehran, 1347 [1968]), 17.

341. Emin Arslan, " Une visite au chef du Babisme," *Revue Bleue* 6, no. 10, September 5, 1896, 314–16.

342. Abdullah Cevdet, "Mezheb-i Bahaullah-Din-i Ümem," *İctihad*, no. 144, March 1, 1922, 3015–16.

343. Mustafa Sabri, "Abdullah Cevdet Bey Efendi'ye," *Peyâm-ı Sabah*, March 7, 1922, March 18, 1922; Ahmed Şîrânî, "Mebâhis-i Diniye," *Tevhid-i Efkâr*, June 19, 1922.

344. H. M. Balyuzi, *'Abdu'l-Bahà: The Centre of the Covenant of Bahà'u'llah* (London, 1971), 123, J[ohn] E[benezer] Esslemont, *Bahā' Allah wa al-ʿaṣr al-jadīd* [Cairo, 1928?], 65, "Morte del capo dei Baha'i," *Oriente Moderno* 1, no. 8, January 15, 1922, 511.

345. İshak Sükûti, had a deep interest in the Bahaî philosophy and studied its works. See Mehmed Ziyaeddin to İshak Sükûti, London, May 24, [18]98, AQSh, 19/106-4//520/1173.

346. Ardern G. Hulme-Beaman, *Twenty Years in the Near East* (London, 1898), 301. Vambéry made the following comment about the sultan: "The Sultan's fear of Young Turks was exaggerated, for in Turkey revolutions are not instigated by the masses, but by the upper classes." Arminius Vambéry, *The Story of my Struggles: The Memoirs of Arminius Vambéry* 2 (New York, 1904), 389.

347. James W. Gambier, "England and the European Concert," *Fortnightly Review* 62, no. 367 (July 1897), 65.

348. "Turquie," *Le Temps*, August 22, 1888. The pamphlet that was named

"Un Songe" could be Namık Kemal's "Rüya." This work was handcopied and widely read by medical students. For such a copy see Princeton University, Islamic MS (S. 3) no. 276-I. The work was republished by the Young Turks in 1907. See Namık Kemal, *Rüya ve Magosa Mektubu* (Cairo, 1907).

349. Layard to Salisbury, November 5, 1879 (private), Add. MS 39132, British Library. For the Young Turks' criticism of this development, see Ahmed Saib, *Abdülhamid'in Evâil-i Saltanatı* (Cairo, 1326 [1908]), 137.

350. Demetrius Georgiadès, *La Turquie actuelle: Les peuples affranchis du joug Ottoman et les intérêts Français en Orient* (Paris, 1892), 105. Cf. "Projet de réforme religieuse: Attribué A.S.M.I le Sultan," *La Turquie Contemporaine*, no. 4, May 21, 1891, 5–6. The claims made by Georgiadès were used by many authors even after the Young Turk revolution. For an example, see Vico Mantegazza, "Un Régime che Scampare," *Il Secolo XX* 7, no. 9 (September 1908), 50–51.

351. Georgiadès, *La Turquie actuelle*, 109.

352. "Dernière heure," *La Turquie Contemporaine*, no. 3, May 11, 1891, 7.

353. A foreign journalist reported that " the Sultan found on his table a letter in which he was threatened with death if he did not abdicate immediately, or if he did not make up his mind to grant reforms for the whole Empire in six days at the outside." See "A Threatening Letter to the Sultan," *Pall Mall Gazette*, November 22, 1895.

354. G[eorgina] Max Müller, "Letters on Turkey," *Longman's Magazine* 28, no. 164 (June 1896), 142.

355. "Ex-Sultan Murad V," *Daily Mail*, December 17, 1896.

356. For an example, see "Şehzâde Reşad Hazretleri," *Hürriyet*, no. 56, August 16, 1896, 3.

357. "Sultan Murad Mazlum," *Osmanlı*, no. 43, April 15, 1899, 1–3; and Abdullah Djevdet, "Le Sultan Murad V," *Mechveret Supplément Français*, no. 79, July 1, 1899, 5–6.

358. For an analysis of this development, see Carter V. Findley, *Bureaucratic Reform in the Ottoman Empire: The Sublime Porte 1789–1922* (Princeton, 1980), 227–39.

359. See "Sadr-ıâzam Said Paşa," *Osmanlı*, no. 99, January 1, 1902, 1–2; "Makale-i Mahsusa," *Şûra-yı Ümmet*, no. 31, June 27, 1903, 3, "Meslek-i Tahrib," *Sancak*, no. 7, December 30, 1899, 2.

360. "Report of Proceedings of the Grand Council on January 18, 1877," enclosed with the letter from Salisbury to Derby, Pera, January 20, 1877/no. 140, PRO/F.O. 424/37.

361. Mesafer-Bey, "L'Administration Ottomane," *La Revue de l'Islam* 2 (1897), 14.

362. Cambon to Hanotaux, October 31, 1895/no. 191 (confidentiel), AE-CP-T, 524 (October 1895), [234–39].

363. "Revolutionary Pamphlet entitled, 'La religion et le gouvernement s'en vont; c'est au peuple d'agir maintenant.'" enclosed with Müller's memorandum dated November 29, 1895. Both documents were enclosed with the letter from Currie to Salisbury, Constantinople, November 29, 1895/no. 881. PRO/F.O. 78/4623.

364. Müller's memorandum dated November 29, 1895. Ibid.

365. "Young Turkey: An Interview with a Young Turk," *Pall Mall Gazette*, July 2, 1895. For the anxiety among the Ottoman diplomats as a result of this

interview, see BBA-BEO/Hariciye Âmed, 155-5/11, 1690 [July 5, 1895], and 2635 [August 25, 1895].

366. Incidentally an English daily that had been employed by the Ottoman palace dwelt upon this very point see "The Turks and Their Troubles," *Morning Advertiser*, November 7, 1895.

367. Decipher from Herbert, Pera, November 10, [1895] /no. 650, PRO/ F.O. 78/4629.

368. For his biography, see Rifat Uçarol, *Gazi Ahmet Muhtar Paşa 1839– 1919: Askeri ve Siyasi Hayatı* (Istanbul, 1989).

369. Cambon to Berthelot, Pera, February 18, 1896/no. 38, AE-CP-T, 526 (January-February 1896), [292–94].

370. "An Important Arrest," *Pall Mall Gazette*, February 13, 1896; Clive Bigham, *With the Turkish Army in Thessaly* (London, 1897), 64–65.

371. Ali Fahri, *Kandil ve Muhtar Pasha* 2d ed. (Cairo, 1324 [1908]), 6–7, 13–14.

372. See "Gazi [Ahmed] Muhtar Paşa," *Sancak*, no. 22, April 28, 1900, 1.

373. Necmeddin Ârif to İshak Sükûti, [Cairo], April 18, 1901, AQSh, 19/ 106-5//244/1719.

374. Bir Osmanlı, *Mısır Fevkâlâde Komiseri Devletlû Gazi Ahmed Muhtar Paşa Hazretleri'ne* (Istanbul, 1322 [1906]), BBA-YEE, 30/1468/51/78.

375. Halil Muvaffak to İshak Sükûti, undated [1899?], AQSh, 19/106-3// 44/875.

376. For his reform proposal for the Ottoman Empire, see "Işlāh al-salṭana al-'uthmāniyya mashrū' dawlatlū Mukhtār Pāshā al-ghāzī," *al-Muqaṭṭam*, May 30, 1900. Western diplomats considered the proposal an important text and an indication of the high commissioner's relations with the opposition forces in the Ottoman Empire. See Cogordan to Delcassé, Cairo, June 6, 1900/no. 120, AE-NS-T, 3 (1899–1901), 98–100.

377. Rosebery to Sanderson, The Durdans, April 16, 1895, PRO/F.O. 800/ 1, Lord Sanderson's Private Papers. Another copy of this letter is at Rosebery Papers, MS. 10070, 62–63. NLS.

378. "Rapport en Caire du 30 Février [1896]: Vues de Muhtar Pasha sur la situation de l'Empire Ottoman," (très confidentiel), AE-CP-T, 526 (January-February 1896), [264–65].

379. Lillian M[argery] Penson, "The New Course in British Foreign Policy," *Transactions of the Royal Historical Society*, 25 (1943), 131–32, C[edric] J[ames] Lowe, *The Reluctant Imperialists: British Foreign Policy 1878–1902* 1 (London, 1967), 187–95.

380. Detailed analysis of his policy towards the crisis is given in Helmut Reifeld, *Zwischen Empire und Parlament: Zur Gedankenbildung und Politik Lord Roseberys (1880–1905)* (Göttingen, 1987), 136–42. Rosebery was strongly pro-Armenian but his approach can be considered an expansion of the type of policy followed by Gladstone. See A. Andréadès, "Lord Rosebery," *La Revue de France* 9 (4) (August 1929), 639.

381. Kenneth Bourne, *The Foreign Policy of Victorian England 1830–1902* (Oxford, 1970), 155.

382. A most severe criticism was leveled by Gladstone. See "Armenian Question," *Times*, December 31, 1894. For underlining made by Lord Rosebery on a copy of this article, see Rosebery Papers, MS.10242, 117. NLS. For George Douglas Campbell's criticism, see *George Douglas Eight Duke of Argyll (1823–1900):*

Autobiography and Memoirs, ed. Dawager Duchess of Argyll, 2 (London, 1906), 469–80, and Duke of Argyll [George Douglas Campbell], *Our Responsibilities for Turkey: Facts and Memories of Forty Years* (London, 1896), passim. To "satisfy public opinion" was a primary objective of Lords Rosebery and Kimberley. See Rosebery to Kimberley, May 1, 1895, Kimberley Papers, MS.10243, 226. NLS.

383. See *The Destruction of Lord Rosebery: From the Diary of Sir Edward Hamilton, 1894–1895,* ed. David Brooks (London, 1986), 195, 199; The Marquess of [Robert Offley Ashburton] Crewe [Milton], *Lord Rosebery* (London, 1931), 423–25, Robert Rhodes James, *Rosebery: A Biography of Archibald Philip, Fifth Earl of Rosebery* (London, 1963), 377.

384. Before organizing this joint diplomatic action, on November 24, 1894, Kimberley decided to send Colonel Chermside to Istanbul in order to prepare a detailed naval demonstration plan, claiming that they "should have a right to do this under Article LVI [sic] of the Treaty of Berlin which pledges the Porte to protect the Armenians against Circassians and Kurds." Kimberley to Currie, November 24, 1894/no. 99a; PRO/CAB. 37/37 (1894)/no. 41 (confidential). For Kimberley's preoccupied state of mind, see Kimberley to Rosebery, November 30, 1894, Rosebery Papers, MS.10042, 99–102, NLS.

385. At the outset of the crisis and in spite of his pro-Armenian approach, Lord Rosebery was reluctant to take the initiative because he feared Russia's involvement in the crisis and he refused Gladstone's encouragement by saying: "I do not see why we should bear the whole burden of this astute if pious race." But later British public opinion forced him to do so. See Gordon Martel, *Imperial Diplomacy: Rosebery and the Failure of Foreign Policy* (London, 1986), 142–45.

386. R. Hamilton Lang, "The Present Government in Turkey: Its Crimes and Remedy," *Blackwood's Edinburgh Magazine* 162, no. 991 (July 1897), 224; and An Eastern Resident, "Sultan Abd-ul-Hamid," *Contemporary Review* 67 (January 1895), 53.

387. Lord Kimberley's answer to Lord Connemara's question on March 30, 1895, at the House of Lords, *Hansard's Parliamentary Debates,* 34 (1895), col. 609. For further information see Kimberley to Rosebery, May 29, [18]95, Rosebery Papers, MS.10070, 130–31, MS.10042 ff.198–99. NLS, and Rosebery to Kimberley, May 21, 1895, MS.10243, Kimberley Papers, 234–35. NLS.

388. Lowe, *The Reluctant Imperialists,* 195. See also "Turkey and the Near East," *The Progressive Review* 1, no. 1 (October 1896), 31.

389. See *The Foreign Policy of Lord Rosebery* (London, 1901), 79–84, "Armenia," *The Liberal Magazine* 3 (1896), 540–41.

390. Thomas F. G. Coates, *Lord Rosebery: His Life and Speeches* 2 (London, 1900), 750. Lord Kimberley was also a member of the Anglo-Armenian Committee. See R. des Coursons, *La rébellion Arménienne: Son origine-son but* (Paris, 1895), 41.

391. Diplomaticus, "The Sultan and the Concert," *Fortnightly Review* 62, no. 368 (August 1, 1897), 318.

392. Bernard Mallet, *Thomas George, Earl of Northbrook G.C.S.I: A Memoir* (London, 1908).

393. Some information about him and his activities is given in Sir Francis Grenfell, "Introduction," F[rancis] R. Wingate, *Mahdiism and the Egyptian Sudan* (London, 1891), iii–iv.

394. Cromer, *Modern Egypt* 2 (London, 1908), 374, 380. Despite his son's criticism, Gazi Ahmed Muhtar Pasha was known to be a strongly pro-British Otto-

man statesman. Mahmoud Moukhtar Pacha, *Événements d'Orient* (Paris, 1908), 205–206.

395. K. Vollers, "Lord Cromer und sein Egypten," *Historische Zeitschrift* 102, no. 3 (1909), 63–64.

396. The best printed diplomatic sources about the diplomatic crisis of 1895–1896 are *A & P*, 109 *Turkey* 1 (1895), *A & P* 110 (1896), *Turkey* 5 (1896), *Die Große Politik der Europäischen Kabinette 1871–1914*, 10: *Das türkische Problem 1895* (Berlin, 1923), *Documents Diplomatiques: Affaires Arméniens: Projets de réformes dans l'Empire Ottoman 1893–1897* (Paris, 1897). An outstanding analysis based on published documents is given in Hugo Preller, *Salisbury und die türkische Frage im Jahre 1895: Eine Einzeluntersuchung zur Geschichte der deutsch-englischen Beziehungen der Vorkriegszeit* (Stuttgart, 1930), 35 ff. For another conventional analysis see Harold Temperley and Lilian M. Penson, *Foundations of British Foreign Policy: From Pitt (1792) to Salisbury (1902)* (Cambridge, 1938), 494–95. More revisionist and detailed analyses of Salisbury's policy are given in W[illiam] N[orton] Medlicott, "Historical Revisions: Lord Salisbury and Turkey," *History* 12 (October 1927), 244–47; Keith Wilson, "Drawing the Line at Constantinople: Salisbury's Statements of *Primat der Innenpolitik*," *British Foreign Secretaries and Foreign Policy: From Crimean War to First World War*, ed. Keith M. Wilson, (London, 1987), 198–213, and idem, *Empire and Continent: Studies in British Foreign Policy from the 1880s to the First World War* (London, 1987), 6–22.

397. Colonel Herbert Chermside's memorandum entitled "Observations to Naval Demonstration against Turkey and Possible Subsequent Action," enclosed with the letter from Currie to Kimberley, Pera, June 6, 1895/no. 368 (secret), PRO/F.O. 78/4613.

398. Cambon to Hanotaux, Therapia, October 10, 1895/no. 178, AE-CP-T 524 (October 1895), [114–18].

399. See Peter Martin, *Die Neuorientierung der österreichisch-ungarischen Außenpolitik 1895–1897 :Eine Beitrag zur europäischen Bündnispolitik im ausgehenden 19. Jahrhundert* (Göttingen, 1972), 80 ff.

400. Colonel L. V. Swaire, British Military attaché in Berlin, had the audience of the kaiser in August 1895, and the kaiser made the following remarks to Swaire: "We do not know what Lord Salisbury's policy is likely to be; but I am quite certain of one thing, and that is, if he does not intend gradually to withdraw from the inheritance of his predecessors in office, which would leave the condition of Turkey and its Pashas worse than it was before, that nothing will result until a British man-of-war appears in the Golden Horn with an ultimatum. Remember that you are dealing with Eastern people. They understand nothing but force." Colonel L. V. Swaire's memorandum, written in Berlin dated August 30, 1895. Enclosed with the letter from Mallet to Salisbury, Berlin August 30, 1895/no. 194 (secret). PRO/CAB. 37/40 (1895)/no. 44. Unaware of the kaiser's enmity, the sultan presumed that it had been the kaiser who protected him from dethronement through a European intervention. The kaiser indignantly added his own exclamation mark on the document expressing the sultan's gratitude. See von Saurma to von Hohenlohe, Therapia, October 23, 1895/no. 156, *Die Große Politik* 10 *Das türkische Problem*, 79–80. Likewise, in 1896, the kaiser put a minute reading "Der Sultan muß abgesetz werden!" on a telegram. See Marschall von Bieberstein to Kaiser Wilhelm II, Berlin, August 28, 1896 (entzifferung), *Die Große Politik* 12/1 *Alte und neue Balkanhändel* (Berlin, 1923), 20.

401. [Mehmed Kâmil Paşa], *Hatırât-ı Sadr-ı Esbak Kâmil Paşa* (Istanbul, 1329 [1911]), 108–109.

402. Ibid., 190, BBA-YEE, 34/1996/159/94.

403. Ibid.

404. İnal, *Son Sadrıazamlar* 9 (Istanbul, 1965), 1372.

405. Herbert to Salisbury, Constantinople, November 5, 1895 (Telegraphic), *A & P* 95 (1896), 106.

406. "The Situation in Turkey," *Times*, November 8, 1895, and Karl Blind, "The Crisis in the East," *North American Review* 162, no. 470 (January 1896), 85.

407. *Hatırat*, 196; and İnal, *Son Sadrıazamlar* 9, 1370, 10 (Istanbul, 1965), 1468–69. Also the claimed support of the British ambassador for Cambon's asserted encouragement does not seem probable in light of the curiosity of the British diplomats about "the maneuvers of Cambon." See Harold Nicolson, *Sir Arthur Nicolson, Bart. First Lord Carnock: A Study in the Old Diplomacy* (London, 1930), 89–90.

408. Cambon gives information about his opinion in two documents and also in a personal letter to his mother. Cambon to Hanotaux, Therapia, October 16, 1895/no. 182, *Documents Diplomatiques Français (1871–1914)*, 1 Série (1871–1900), 12 (Paris, 1951), 244–46. Hanotaux's minute to this document is as follows: "Cette lettre est extrêmement importante. Il y aurait lieu de demander M.Cambon ce qu'il entrevoit comme issue en cas de complication intérieure et de disparition du Sultan." Ibid., 246 n. In an earlier correspondence he focused on the same issue. See Cambon to Hanotaux, Pera, June 12, 1895, *Documents Diplomatiques: Affaires Arméniennes, Projets de réformes dans l'Empire Ottoman* (Paris, 1897), 77. In a letter dated February 15, 1895 which he had sent to his mother Paul Cambon also made a remarkable comment. See Paul Cambon, *Correspondance 1870–1924*, ed. Henri Cambon (Paris, 1940), 385–86. Although they give valuable information about Paul Cambon's diplomatic activities in Istanbul, his two biographers do not supply any information about his role in the government crisis of November 1895. See Un Diplomate, *Paul Cambon ambassadeur de France (1843–1924)* (Paris, 1937), 123–167 and Keith Eubank, *Paul Cambon Master Diplomatist* (Oklahoma City, 1960), 46–60.

409. Herbert to Salisbury, Constantinople, November 8, 1895, *A & P* 95 (1896), 107–108.

410. See "Confusion de pouvoirs en Turquie," *La Paix*, December 2, 1895.

411. Currie to Kimberley, Constantinople, April 22, 1895/no. 253 (confidential), PRO/F.O. 78/4611.

412. Draft written by C. M. Hallward, Beirut, August 1, 1892/no. 40 (very confidential). PRO/F.O. 226/214 (Beirut 1892).

413. Currie to Salisbury, Therapia, July 16, 1895/no. 471, PRO/F.O. 78/4614.

414. BBA-YSHM, 8 M 1313/no. 71.

415. Currie to Salisbury, Therapia, September 28, 1895/no. 632 (confidential), PRO/F.O. 78/4618.

416. "Mémoire," enclosed with the letter from Currie to Salisbury, Therapia, September 28, 1895/no. 632 (confidential), PRO/F.O. 78/4618.

417. [İsmail Kemal], *The Memoirs of Ismail Kemal Bey*, ed. Somerville Story (London, 1920), 265. Sir Philip Currie's comment on this issue was as follows: "I

hear from many quarters that the feeling against the irresponsible rule of the Palace is gaining strength among all classes of the population and that any action which England might take for placing some restraint upon it would be hailed with enthusiasm. The Turks complain that our efforts have hitherto been directed solely to the amelioration of the Christians, and they declare that if we were to demand a general reform of the administration we should meet with their hearty support." Currie to Salisbury, Therapia, September 28, 1895/no. 632 (confidential), PRO/ F.O. 78/4618.

418. *The Memoirs of Ismail Kemal Bey*, 267–68.

419. Ibid., 397.

420. "Les Cahiers de la Turquie: Rapport adressé à S.M.I. le sultan par Ismaïl Kemal bey, ancien gouverneur général de Tripoli, daté du 12/24 Février 1312/ 1897," *Le Temps*, April 8, 1897. The original text is in BBA-YEE, 14/88-42/88/ 13.

421. "Turkey," *Times*, April 8, 1897: "It is a document which very justly compares with the famous report of Necker in 1782."

422. "Turquie," *Le Temps*, April 21, 1897.

423. *Trablusgarb Vali-i Esbakı İsmail Kemal Bey Tarafından Atabe-i Ülyâ-yı Padişâhî'ye Takdim Olunan Lâyiha Suretidir* (Geneva, 1314 [1897]). There is also a version translated into Arabic by Syrians residing in New York. See "Lā'iḥa Ismā'īl Kamāl Bey," *al-Ayyām*, no. 29, January 20, 1898, 4–5, and no. 30, January 27, 1898, 4–5.

424. "Turkey," *Times*, April 15, 1897: "Ismail Kemal's letter to the Sultan delights and emboldens the Mahomedan malcontents, but scarcely impresses his Majesty, who is hardened against expostulation. Kemal fails to realize that the Sultan deliberately prefers the Hamidian system with its unworthy instruments, to statesmanlike Government conducted by men of character." This view presented in another article written after İsmail Kemal's death. See Beta, "A Great Albanian," *The Near East* 19, no. 506 (January 20, 1921), 85.

425. This matter was discussed between a British statesman and the Czar on September 27 and 29, 1896. See PRO/CAB. 37/42-(1896), no. 35 (very secret).

426. For instance see H[arry] C[raufuird] Thomson, *The Outgoing Turk* (London, 1897), 256–57. This idea was shared by some British diplomats. See [Adam Block?], "Private Memorandum by a member of Her Majesty's Embassy at Constantinople Respecting Turkish Administration," PRO/CAB. 37/43 (1896), no. 59 (confidential), 3: "I believe that the only way of effectively improving any branch of Turkish Administration is to put it somehow or other under European control."

427. Adam Block's confidential memorandum dated April 27, 1897. Enclosed with the letter from Currie to Salisbury, Constantinople, April 29, 1897/ no. 297 (confidential), PRO/F.O. 78/4801.

428. This document had been signed by İsmail Kemal and Adam Block, and dated January 25, 1898. A copy of it was enclosed with Adam Block's memorandum dated May 1, 1900. This memorandum was further enclosed with the letter from O'Conor to Salisbury, Constantinople, May 2, 1900/no. 161. PRO/F.O. 78/5058.

429. See *A & P* 110 (1899), *Turkey* 7 (1897), 1–7, 17–19, *Documents Diplomatiques: Affaires d'Orient: Autonomie Crétoise* (Paris, 1898), 137–41, Henri Lombard, *L'Occupation internationale en* **Crète** *de 1900 à 1906* (Paris, 1908), 83– 85. The assassination of the British officers and privates was described in a letter,

by grand vizier Damad Ferid Pasha to Şeyhülislâm Dürrizâde Abdullah Efendi, as having caused the loss of Crete by the Ottomans. Basing his remarks on this past example the grand vizier gave a plea to the Şeyhülislâm to prevent attacks by the nationalists against the allied troops. See "Sadr-ıâzam ve Hariciye Nâzırı Fehametlû, Devletlû Damad Ferid Paşa Hazretleri Tarafından Kaymakam-ı Sadaret ve Şeyhül-islâm Dürrizâde Abdullah Efendi Hazretlerine, an Versailles, July 3, [1]920," Bibliothèque Nationale (Paris), Supplément turc 1445, 42 (53).

430. To Sanderson, September 4, [18]98 (private and confidential), PRO/F.O. 195/2008.

431. *The Memoirs of Ismail Kemal Bey*, 277.

432. Ibid., 277–78.

433. To Goluchowski, Constantinople, December 7, 1899/no. 56, HHStA, PA, XII, 172 Türkei Berichte, 1899, VIII–XII.

434. "Osmanlı İttihad ve Terakki Cemiyeti," *Osmanlı*, no. 16, June 15, 1898, 3.

435. For the money donated to CUP by anonymous high-ranking officials, see "Erbab-ı Hamiyet Listesi," *Mizan*, no. 171, April 9, 1896, 2454.

436. Yahya Kemal, *Çocukluğum, Gençliğim, Siyasî ve Edebî Hâtıralarım* (Istanbul, 1973), 74–75. The author himself fled to Europe in order to become a Young Turk.

437. BBA-YSHM, 11 M 1324/no. 85.

438. A.V., *İhtilâl Fırkalarının Teşebbüs-i İhaneti Yahud Fedâkârân-ı Millet Cemiyeti* ([Istanbul], 1328 [1910]), 3–7.

439. See [Hakkı], "İ'tizâr," *Gencine-i Hayâl*, no. 3 [July 1881], [1–2]. For the efforts of the Ottoman authorities to stop his publication see BBA-YSHM, 10 R 1297/no. 156, and 19 R 1297/no. 170.

440. See [Hakkı], "Mütâliin-i Kirâma," *Cür'et*, no. 4, November 25, 1898, 1.

441. Hakkı Bey to İshak Sükûti, [Paris], February 15, 1898, AQSh, 19/106-3//732/9776.

442. Hakkı Bey to İshak Sükûti, Paris, November 27, 1901, AQSh, 19/106-3//732/9776. He used similar language in a letter to the central organ of the Geneva branch. See "Cür'et Gazetesi Sahib-i Hamiyetperveri Hakkı Beyefendi Hazretleri Tarafından Mektub," *Osmanlı*, no. 54, February 15, 1900, 4.

443. "Dersaadet Şu'bemiz Âzâ-yı Mütehayyizân ve Hamiyetperverânından Bir Zât-ı Âlicenâhın Mektubuna Taraf-ı Âcizîden Cevab," *Cür'et*, no. 7, February 28, 1899, 1–2.

444. "Teessür-i Azîm," *Osmanlı*, no. 127, December 1, 1903, 2.

445. PRO/H.O. Registered Papers: 45. 9650-A-38025 b.

446. Ibrāhīm al-Muwaylihī, *Mā hunālika min asrār balāt al-Sulṭan ʿAbd al-Ḥamīd* (Cairo, 1985), 84 ff.

447. Blunt, *My Diaries*, 98–99.

448. For his activities in Naples, see Ottoman consulate in Naples to Mahmud Nedim, October 5, 1894/no. 18-2107, and October 9, 1894/no. 19-2108. Archives of the Turkish Embassy in Rome, Box 52 (1).

449. N. Nicolaïdès' letter to Gennadios, Greek ambassador to Great Britain, dated August 14, 1889. Enclosed with is a copy of the journal *L'Orient* at Gennadion Library (Athens) (call. no. P 86 S).

450. For his publication and the negotiations, see BBA-YSHM, 20 S 1310/no. 263, 30 S 1310/no. 356, 24 Ra 1310/no. 558, 5 R 1310/ no. 687, 15 R

1310/no. 757, and BBA-YMGM, 3 L 1310/no. 504-7163. After his satisfaction, he organized meetings in Paris to celebrate the anniversaries of Abdülhamid II's day of accession to the throne. See "Dahiliye," *Sabah,* September 6, 1895.

451. BBA-İrade-Dahiliye, 26 Rebiy'ülevvel 1308/no. 93885.

452. For an example, see BBA-BEO/Zaptiye Giden, 662-21/13, 87 [June 22, 1892]/ 9738 (mühimme).

453. A good example was the case of Lieutenant Mahmud. See *Cevad Paşa Merhumun Zaman-ı Sadaretinde Takdim Olunan Tezâkir-i Hususiyenin Suretlerini Havî Defter,* BBA-YEE, 36/419/146/XV, 4606 [May 19, 1895].

454. For the proposed measures of the Ottoman government against the fugitives and their political and blackmailing activities, see BBA-YSHM, 13 Za 1316/no. 1708 and BBA-YP, 12 Za 1318/no. 1537.

455. BBA-YSHM, 21 S 1311/no. 2958.

456. Said Pasha to Mahmud Nedim, 7/7925, March 1, 1894/no. 7-7925; Mahmud Nedim to Said Pasha, April 14, 1894/no. 90-19567, Archives of the Turkish Embassy in Rome, Box 50 (2); and the note dated April 19, 1894 in Private Papers of Sir Philip Currie, PRO/F.O. 800/114.

457. Muhiddin, *Hürriyet Mücahedeleri,* 2.

458. BBA-YSHM, 21 B 1311/no. 2560, 29 S 1311/no. 3062, 30 S 1311/no. 3068, 12 L 1311/no. 3563, 20 L 1311/no. 3674, 19 Za 1311/no. 4094, BBA-BEO/Hariciye Reft, 183-5/39, 136 [April 19, 1894]/28988.

459. BBA-BEO/Hariciye Reft, 183-5/39, 141 [April 15, 1894] /29119, and BBA-YSHM, 5 L 1311/no. 3454, 30 S 1311/no. 3417, BBA-YMGM, 11 L 1311/no. 805-8294.

460. Sublime Porte to the Police ministry [July 26, 1894], BBA-Ayniyat Defterleri, no. 1689 (Zabtiye).

461. Undated letter from Tevfik Nevzad to his brother Refik Nevzad. Private Papers of Tevfik Nevzad.

462. Glanstätten to Goluchowski, Smyrna, September 1, 1899/no. 95, HHStA, PA XXXVIII 313, Konsulate Smyrna (1899).

463. Kâmil Pasha to the Chamberlain's office [September 8, 1899]/no. 2, *Aydın Vilâyet-i Celilesiyle Muhaberata Mahsus Defterdir,* BBA-YEE, 36/2470-15/147/XVI.

464. According to Hamson, the British consul, these dissidents were denounced by a certain Mustafa, who accused them of corresponding with the Paris branch of the CUP. Hamson to O'Conor, Smyrna, September 6, 1899/no. 55, enclosed with the letter from O'Conor to Salisbury, Constantinople, September [11], 1899/no. 426, PRO/F.O. 78/4995.

465. See Hüseyin Avni [Ozan], *Tokadîzade Şekip Hayatı, Felsefesi, Eserleri* (Izmir, 1938), 8, and İbnül Emin Mahmud Kemal İnal, *Son Asır Türk Şairleri* 2 (Istanbul, 1930–1942), 1782–85.

466. Tevfik Nevzad to Refik Nevzad [November 23, 1895], Private Papers of Tevfik Nevzad.

467. Although most of his accomplices were later released he was first sent into exile and then imprisoned. See Divisional General Şakir to the Chamberlain's office, Izmir [March 23, 1900]/no. 19, *1316 Senesi Müteferrika Kayd Defteridir,* BBA-YEE, 36/139-77/139-XIX. For this part of his life and political activities, see Ziya Somar, *Bir Adamın ve Bir Şehrin Tarihi: Tevfik Nevzad: İzmir'in İlk Fikir-Hürriyet Kurbanı* (Izmir, 1948), 63 ff.

468. BBA-İrade-Hususî, Rebiy'ülâhir 1314/no. 77-339, BBA-BEO/Hari-

ciye Reft, 183-5/39, 1110 [October 5, 1896]/63535, BBA-YMGM, 2 Ca 1314/ no. 2008.

469. Archives d'Etat-Genève-Chancellerie, B. 7 (October 27, 1896), 147.

470. French Ministry of the Interior to Delcassé, May 13, 1898, AE-NS-T, 2 (1898), 80–81.

471. For the publication of these two journals, see BBA-BEO/Dahiliye Giden, 96-3/45, 3717 [February 15, 1897] /80947, and BBA-BEO/Hariciye Reft, 184-5/40, 1410 [November 7, 1897]/78681, and 1705 [March 7, 1897]/ 80947. For his political activities during this period, see Fındıkoğlu Z. Fahri, *XIX. Asırda Türkiye Dışında Türk Gazeteciliği ve Tarsûsîzâde Münif Bey* (Istanbul, 1962), 12–32.

472. The investigation report of Allen, agent of the Ottoman embassy in London, enclosed with the letter from Rüstem Pasha to Said Pasha, May 30, 1895/ no. 434-196961, Archives of the Turkish Embassy in London, Box 303 (3).

473. BBA-İrade-Hususî, Safer 1313/ no. 341.

474. BBA-BEO/Telgraf ve Posta Nezareti Giden, 585-17/10, 16 [April 8, 1895]/4985, BBA-BEO/Dahiliye Giden, 94-3/43, 99 [March 29, 1895])/4922, BBA-YSHM, 5 L 1312/ no. 3763, 8 L 1312/ no. 3823, 20 Za 1312/ no. 4242, 3 Z 1312/ no.4746, 8 Z 1312/ no. 4842, 11 Z 1312/ no. 4875, 23 Z 1312/ no. 5027, BBA-YMGM, 2 Ca 1314/ no. 2008. This journal published articles favoring ex-Sultan Murad V. See "Sultan Murad Mes'elesi," *Vatan (1)*, no. 2 (April 1895), 3–4.

475. Rüstem Pasha to Turhan Pasha, May 25, [18]95/no. 425-19684, and June 19, 1895/no. 539-19822; and Said Pasha to Rüstem Pasha, May 29, 1895/ no. 192-12761, Archives of the Turkish Embassy in London, Box 303 (3).

476. For an example, see "Un Complotto contro il Sultano," *Il Corriere della Sera*, October 7, 1894. This "plot" had nothing to do with the Young Turk movement. See Said Pasha to Tevfik Pasha, October 11, 1894/no. 44-10949, Archives of the Turkish Embassy in Rome, Box 71 (3). For another example, see Mahmud Nedim to Said Pasha, June 27, 1893, Ibid., Box 50 (1).

Chapter 4

1. For instance, see *Bazı Hususî İradeleri Havî Defter*, BBA-YEE, 24/11/ 162/VII, no. 13 [July 28, 1900].

2. Doctor Mekkeli Sabri to Abdullah Cevdet, Le Mans, June 27, 1931, 3. Private Papers of Abdullah Cevdet.

3. Leskovikli Mehmed Rauf, *İttihad ve Terakki Cemiyeti Ne İdi?* (Istanbul, 1327 [1909]), 12–13.

4. Cevrî [Mehmed Reşid], *İnkılâb Niçün ve Nasıl Oldu?* (Cairo, 1909), 26.

5. İbrahim Temo to Karl Süssheim, Medgidia, August 9, 1933, Nachlaß Süssheim.

6. Saî [Şerafeddin Mağmumî], "Tohum ve Semereleri," *Meşveret*, no. 6, February 15, 108 [1896], 3.

7. This date was provided by İbrahim Temo. See the draft of a letter from Temo to Karl Süssheim, AQSh, 19/31//108/110. However, Sükûtî wrote in the draft of a letter, which he sent to Minister of the Interior Memduh Pasha, that the society had been founded in 1890. See AQSh, 19/104//214/1. The third founder, Mehmed Reşid, approved the date of June 2, 1889, in his pamphlet, which he penned after the Young Turk revolution. See [Mehmed Reşid], *İnkılâb*, 26.

8. İbrahim Temo to Karl Süssheim, Medgidia, August 9, 1933, Nachlaβ Süssheim; K[arl] Süssheim, "'Abd Allāh Djewdet," *EI-Supplement* (1938), 56. In three other letters İbrahim Temo wrote that a series of meetings were held at the place called *Hamamönü* or *Hatab Kıraathanesi*. See his letters to Karl Süssheim, Medgidia, September 2, [1]933, December 25, [1]933, and September 14, [1]935, Nachlaβ Süssheim. These meetings had acquired this name because the students were convened on the firewood in front of the bath of the Royal Medical Academy.

9. İbrahim Temo to Karl Süssheim, Medgidia, August 9, 1933, and December 25, [1]933, Nachlaβ Süssheim.

10. İbrahim Temo to Karl Süssheim, Medgidia, September 14, [1]933, Nachlaβ Süssheim.

11. İbrahim Temo's short autobiography entitled "Muhtasaran Tarihçe-i Hayatım," enclosed with his letter to Karl Süssheim, Medgidia, June 25, [1]933, Nachlaβ Süssheim.

12. İbrahim Temo's letter to Süheyl Ünver, "Doktor İbrahim Temo," CTF-Tıp Tarihi ve Deontoloji Enstitüsü Arşivi, I-1935, 4.

13. The participants were: İbrahim Temo, Abdullah Cevdet, İshak Sükûti, Mehmed Reşid, Ali Şefik, Ali Rüşdi, Âsaf Derviş, Besim Mehmed, Giridî Muharrem, Hikmet Emin, Hüseyinzâde Ali, and Şerafeddin Mağmumî. These names were drawn from the following sources: İbrahim Temo's letter draft, AQSh, 19/31// 108/110; his letter to Süssheim, Medgidia, August 9, [1]933, Nachlaβ Süssheim; Temo, *İttihad ve Terakki*, 20–21; and Rıza Tahsin, *Mir'at-ı Mekteb-i Tıbbiye* 1 (Istanbul, 1328 [1910]), 127.

14. [Mehmed Reşid], *İnkılâb*, 27–28.

15. AQSh, 19/31//108/110.

16. See A[hmed] R[efik], *Abdülhamid-i Sânî ve Devr-i Saltanatı: Hayat-ı Hususiye ve Siyasiyesi* 3 (Istanbul, 1327 [1909]), 1068–69, Ramsaur, *The Young Turks*, 15–16.

17. The Young Ottomans too imitated the organizational framework of the *Carbonari*. See Ebüzziya, "Yeni Osmanlılar," *Yeni Tasvir-i Efkâr*, June 20, 1909. They also had an interest in Silvio Pellici's ideas. See Mardin, *The Genesis*, 21–22, and Roderic Davison, *Reform in the Ottoman Empire* (Princeton, 1963), 193.

18. "Hüseyin Zade Ali, "İttihad ve Terakki Cemiyeti Nasıl Kuruldu[?]" *Tan*, March 4, 1938.

19. İbrahim Temo to Karl Süssheim, Medgidia, August 9, [1]933, Nachlaβ Süssheim, and to Süheyl Ünver, CTF-Tıp Tarihi ve Deontoloji Enstitüsü Arşivi, I-1935, 3. İbrahim Temo erroneously referred the society as Etniki Heteria.

20. Although two important figures in the movement referred to this regulation we have gleaned no mention of this first internal regulation. See AQSh, 19/ 31//179/180, and Doctor Mekkeli Sabri's letter to Abdullah Cevdet, Le Mans, June 27, 1931, 6 and 13. Private Papers of Abdullah Cevdet.

21. Berna Kazak, "Ömrüm: Ali Kemal'in Hayatı", 107-109, *Canlı Tarihler: Ahmet Reşit Rey (H.Nâzım)-Gördüklerim-Yaptıklarım (1890–1922)* (Istanbul, 1945), 42–44.

22. Berna Kazak, "Ömrüm", 111–12.

23. BBA-BEO/Hariciye Reft, 183-5/39, 1066-1294 [July 8, 1895]/ 47157.

24. His letter to the grand vizier dated [June 22, 1895], and the grand

vizier's note dated [July 14, 1889], BBA-BEO/Hariciye Reft, 183-5/39, 1066, 1294, 1732 [July 8, 1895])/47147 and 48854.

25. BBA-BEO/Hariciye Reft, 185-5/39, 1119 [August 22, 1895])/51318 and müsvedât: 37158.

26. Mehmed Rauf, *İttihad ve Terakki Cemiyeti*, 14.

27. Ibid., 21.

28. Ibid., 22–23.

29. İbrahim Temo to Karl Süssheim, Medgidia, August 9, 1933, Nachlaß Süssheim.

30. AQSh, 19/31//108/110.

31. Mehmed Rauf, *İttihad ve Terakki Cemiyeti*, 25.

32. Rıza Tahsin, *Mir'at-ı Mekteb-i Tıbbiye*, 128. Later it was claimed that thirty-two students out of 340 had become members of the organization at that point. See Ekrem Şadi Kavur, "Tıbbiyeli ve Genç Türklerin İstibdada Karşı Hürriyet Mücadelesi," *Dirim* 50 (8), August 1975, 378.

33. They were: Abdullah Cevdet, Ahmed Bahtiyar, Mehmed Reşid, Tekirdağlı Mehmed, Mihail Oseb, Naki Celâleddin, Rıza Servet, Şefik Ali, and Şerafeddin Mağmumî. [Mehmed Reşid], *İnkılâb*, 29. Rıza Tahsin gave the name Muammer Şevket instead of Tekirdağlı Mehmed. See *Mir'at-ı Mekteb-i Tıbbiye*, 128.

34. İbrahim Temo claimed that his persuasion of the members of the court-martial resulted in the issuance of the imperial decree. (See his letter to Süheyl Ünver, CTF-Tıp Tarihi ve Deontoloji Arşivi, I-1935, 4). However, another founder's explanation of the palace's action seems more accurate. See [Mehmed Reşid], *İnkılâb*, 30.

35. For information about these arrests see *L'Italie*, September 16, 1894, and *Moniteur de Rome*, September 17 and 18, 1894.

36. BBA-BEO/Zabtiye Giden, 662-21/13, 113(327/247)/35774, and *Cevad Paşa Merhumun Zaman-ı Sadaretinde Takdim Olunan Tezâkir-i Hususiyenin Suretlerini Havî Defter*, BBA-YEE, 36/419/146/XV.

37. Mehmed Rauf, *İttihad ve Terakki Cemiyeti*, 17.

38. The spy report of Adjutant Major İhsan Bey, dated [October 24, 1895] is in Asaf Tugay, *İbret: Abdülhamid'e Verilen Jurnaller ve Jurnalciler* 1 (Istanbul, 1961), 83.

39. Mehmed Rauf, *İttihad ve Terakki Cemiyeti*, 17.

40. For his meetings with Acem İzzet and other followers of Fāris see Alvarez to Currie, Bengazy, November 23, 1895. Enclosed with the letter from Currie to the Foreign Office, Constantinople, January, 28, 1896/no. 71. PRO/F.O. 78/4701. This information was given to the British Consul by Major General Dağıstanlı Hasan Bey.

41. Mehmed Murad, *Mücahede-i Milliye*, 25–28.

42. Mehmed Rauf, *İttihad ve Terakki Cemiyeti*, 18.

43. Rıza Tevfik, *Mir'at-ı Mekteb-i Tıbbiye*, 129. Ali Zühdi later coordinated CUP activities and died in 1897. See Bir Kürd [Abdullah Cevdet], "Ali Zühdi Bey'in Vefatı," *Kanun-i Esasî*, no. 23, June 28, 1897, 7.

44. Z. D. Imhoff, "Die Entstehung und der Zweck des Comités für Einheit and Fortschritt" *Die Welt des Islams* 1 (1913), H.3–4, 172.

45. AQSh, 19/31//179/180.

46. See Chamberlain's office to Paris embassy, June 19, 1889, Paris embassy to the Chamberlain's office, July 8, 1889, and the memorandum of the Ministry

of Imperial Treasury, [January 5, 1890]. Archives of the Turkish Embassy in Paris, D. 176.

47. AQSh, 19/31//179/180.

48. See BBA-YSHM, 13 L 1309/no. 3938, and Paris embassy to the Chamberlain's office, June, 24 1892. Archives of the Turkish Embassy in Paris, D. 176.

49. BBA-YSHM, 8 Za 1309/no. 3938.

50. Ahmed Rıza, *Vatanın Haline ve Maarif-i Umumiyenin Islahına Dair Abdülhamid Han-ı Sânî Hazretlerine Takdim Kılınan Altı Lâyihadan Birinci Lâyiha* (London, 1312 [1894]), and *Vatanın Haline ve Maarif-i Umumiyenin Islahına Dair Sultan Abdülhamid Han-ı Sânî Hazretlerine Takdim Kılınan Lâyihalar Hakkında Sadaret'e Gönderilen Mektub* (Geneva, 1313 [1895]).

51. Archives de la Préfecture de Police de Paris (La Colonie Ottomane de Paris), B. A (1653)- 1097003.

52. [Mehmed Reşid], *İnkılâb*, 30.

53. "İlk Meclis-i Mebusan Reisi Ahmed Rıza Bey'in Hatıraları (1)," *Cumhuriyet*, January 26, 1950.

54. "Tezkere-i Marûza Sureti [June 25, 1895]," BBA-Ayniyat Defterleri, no. 1637/14.

55. *Vatan Tehlikede!* [Paris, 1895].

56. BBA-BEO/Şehremaneti Giden, 689-27/7, 1176 [November 30, 1895])/8428 (mühimme), and BBA-BEO/Dahiliye Giden, 94-3/43, 2490 [November 30, 1895])/8428 (mühimme).

57. BBA-BEO/Hariciye Âmed, 155-3/11, 937 [May 15, 1895]), and 960 [May 16, 1895])/46700.

58. For the government's efforts to return him, see ibid., no. 1046 [May 23, 1895].

59. Divisional General Ali Rıza Pasha's note [January 21, 1896], *Tahrirat Mecmuası*, İ. M. K.İ Manuscripts, IUL, no. 2522.

60. Kâzım Karabekir, *İttihad ve Terakki Cemiyeti, 1896–1909* (Istanbul, 1982), 97.

61. BBA-BEO/Mahremâne Müsvedât, [July 15, 1895]/no. 38.

62. BBA-BEO/Hariciye Âmed, 155-5/11, 1573 [June 28, 1895], 1619 [June 14,1895], 1664 [July 3, 1895], 1673 [July 4, 1895], 1717 [July 7, 1895], 1726 [July 8, 1895], 1750 [July 9, 1895], 1934 [July 16, 1895], 1951 and 1975 [July 27, 1895], 2116 [July 18, 1895], 2132 [July 20, 1895], 2708 [August 31, 1895], Turhan Pasha to Mahmud Nedim Bey, July 1, 1895/no. 51, Archives of the Turkish Embassy in Rome, Box. 51 (1), BBA-BEO/Hariciye Reft, 183-5/39, 619 [June 30, 1895])/48518.

63. See "Una Smentita," *Opinione*, July 5, 1895, "Una Conspirazione alla scuola militare," *Il Corriere di Napoli*, June 26, 1895, "Une Conspiration," *L'Italie*, June 27, 1895.

64. "Agitation Spreading," *Daily Chronicle*, October 24, 1895, "The Young Turk Movement," *Pall Mall Gazette*, October 24, 1895, and "Turkish Students Held," *New York Times*, October 21, 1895.

65. The draft of a memorandum sent to the Chamberlain's office from the Ministry of Navy dated [October 29, 1895], Deniz Müzesi Arşivi—Mektubî Bölümü, I, 863/52, 161.

66. Ministry of Navy to the Chamberlain's office [September 16, 1895], Deniz Müzesi Arşivi--Mektubî Bölümü, I, 1036/48, 36.

67. BBA-BEO/VGG(2)- 1296: Jurnal; no. 3: Mühimme [April 23, 1895].

68. "Uneasiness at Yildiz Kiosk," *Pall Mall Gazette*, November 5, 1895.

69. Currie to Salisbury, Constantinople, November 27, 1895/no. 870 (confidential), *PRO/F.O.* 78/4623. Interestingly enough Müller's mother wrote about the Young Turks in 1893–1894, even before the Young Turks had begun any overt activities. See Mrs [Georgina] Max Müller, *Letters from Constantinople* (London, 1897), 194–95.

70. "Memorandum by Mr. Max Müller." Enclosed with the letter from Currie to Salisbury, Constantinople, November 27, 1895/no. 870 (confidential), PRO/F.O. 78/4623.

71. Ibid.

72. "Regulations of the Turkish Society of Union and Progress," enclosed with W. G. Max Müller's memorandum dated November 26, 1895, PRO/F.O. 78/4623. Müller's memorandum was discussed in the British Cabinet and was sent to the queen. Under-secretary Sir Thomas Sanderson thanked Max Müller for information concerning the Young Turks. See draft of the letter from Sanderson to Currie, December 14, 1895/no. 402, PRO/F.O. 78/4606.

73. BBA-BEO/Hariciye Âmed, 155-5/11, 4100 [December 4, 1895].

74. BBA-BEO/VGG(2)-1296: Jurnal; no. 3: Mühimme, 4100 [December 7, 1895], and BBA-BEO/VGG(2)-1345: Devâir Mühimme (Zabtiye), [December 7, 1895]/no. 4.

75. *Osmanlı İttihad ve Terakki Cemiyeti Nizamnâmesi* (n.p., n.d.).

76. Ibid., 1.

77. Ibid., 2. (Article 8.)

78. Ibid., 7. (Article 27.)

79. Ibid., 7. (Article 29.)

80. Ibid., 3. (Article 10.)

81. Mehmed Murad, *Mücahede-i Milliye*, 154.

82. Ahmed Rıza, "Vatanın Haline ve Maarif-i Umumiyenin Islahına Dair Sultan Abdülhamid Han-ı Sânî Hazretlerine Takdim Kılınan Altı Lâyihadan Birinci Lâyiha," *Basiret'üs-Şark*, no. 7, October 24, 1895, 3 ff. This newspaper was banned by the Ottoman Government. See BBA-BEO/Mısır Komiserliği Âmed: Mısır Komiseri Muhtar Paşa Hazretlerinden Gelen Tahrirat Defteridir, 746-36/4, 729/760 [September 6, 1895], and 743/764 [September 14, 1895].

83. BBA-BEO/Zabtiye Giden, 662-21/13, 314 [September 25 1895]/51374, BBA-BEO/Hariciye Reft, 183-5/39, 112 [October 24, 1895]/52185, BBA-BEO/VGG(2): Haleb Giden, 297; 102 [September 22, 1895]/51302 and BBA-Tezâkir-i Samiye Dosyaları, 398; 804 (September 26, 1895).

84. Ziya Pasha to Said Pasha, October 20, 1895/no. 9306, Archives of the Turkish Embassy in Paris, D. 195.

85. Cambon to Hanatoux, October 6, 1895/no. 139 (telegram), and Therapia, September 16, 1895/no. 182, AE-CP-T, 524 (October 1895), [71], [136–37].

86. Detailed information is provided by İbrahim Temo in his letter to Karl Süssheim, Medgidia, October 9, 1935, about the preparation and distribution of this appeal. Nachlaβ Süssheim.

87. A text is given in Temo, *İttihad ve Terakki*, 48–49. This text was written according to İbrahim Temo's recollections.

88. İbrahim Temo to Karl Süssheim, Medgidia, October 9, 1935, Nachlaβ Süssheim.

89. AQSh, 19/60//820/10-11. A copy of it is in BBA-YP, 19 C 1313/

no. 766. It was translated into English by the British embassy and sent to the Foreign Office. This text was enclosed with the letter from Currie to Salisbury, Constantinople, November 11, 1895. PRO/F.O. 424/184. The translation of this manifesto was also published in a British daily. See "A Secret Manifesto," *Pall Mall Gazette*, November 27, 1895.

90. "The Sultan Yields," *Times*, December 11, 1895.

91. Murad Bey, "The Yildiz and the Porte: The Real Evil of the East," *Pall Mall Gazette*, December 23, 1895.

92. Müller's memorandum dated November 26, 1895, PRO/F.O. 78/4623.

93. *Hatırât-ı Sultan Abdülhamid Han-ı Sânî*, ed. Vedad Urfî (Istanbul, 1340 [1922]), 11, 42. Murad Bey's ideas were also ridiculed by the sultan's confidant. See N. Nicolaïdès, "Le grrrrand réformateur Mourad-Bey," *L'Orient* 7, no. 38, December 28, 1895, 5.

94. See Mehmed Murad, *Mücahede-i Milliye*, 69 ff., and Birol Emil, *Mizancı Murad Bey: Hayatı ve Eserleri* (Istanbul, 1979), 115–20.

95. Murad Bey's proposals for solving the early Armenian problems (see [Murad], "Cümle-i Siyasiye," *Mizan*, no. 153, August 7, 1890, 1–2) attracted the attention of the foreign press. See "Lettres de Turquie," *Le Temps*, August 19, 1890.

96. Murad Bey, "The Yildiz and the Porte," *Pall Mall Gazette*, December 23, 1895.

97. Blakeney to Blunt, Prevesa, November 7, 1895 (confidential), and Blunt to Currie, Salonica, November 28, 1895 (confidential), PRO/F.O. 421/152.

98. BBA-BEO/Zabtiye Giden, 662-21/13, 475, 31/ 53871, and BBA-BEO/Harbiye Giden, 250-6/64, 1579/55364.

99. "La Situazione a Constantinopoli," *Il Secolo*, December 8, 1895.

100. BBA-İrade-Dahiliye, Receb 1313/no. 63/1409, BBA-YSRM, 2 B 1313/no. 1563, BBA-Tezâkir-i Samiye Dosyaları (Mazbata), 1536/1563 [December 17/18, 1895], BBA-YP, C 1317/no. 955-2(4702).

101. BBA-İrade-Dahiliye, Şa'ban 1313/no. 15-1705.

102. BBA-YP, C 1317/no. 955-II (4702).

103. [Rıza Nur], "San Remo'da İshak Sükûti," *Şehbâl*, no. 14, [October 28, 1909], 270.

104. Some information regarding his role in the organization of the CUP was given in Kadri Raşid, "Doktor Sabri," *Yeni Gazete*, September 4, 1908.

105. "Chéfik-Bey," *Tribune de Genève*, June 19, 1897, and "Turkey," *Times*, February 27, 1896.

106. Doctor Mekkeli Sabri to Abdullah Cevdet, Le Mans, June 27, 1931, 8. Private Papers of Abdullah Cevdet.

107. Ibid., 8, "1312'de Nümune-i Terakki Mektebinde Toplananlar Kimlerdi, Ne Yapacaklardı [?]" *Vakit*, May 19, 1930.

108. Ahmed Bedevî Kuran, *İnkılâp Tarihimiz ve İttihad ve Terakki*, 65.

109. İbrahim Temo to Karl Süssheim, Medgidia, August 9, 1933, Nachlaβ Süssheim. Similarly a member of the Istanbul branch later wrote that CUP activities had been started with their initiative in 1896. See [İhsan Şerif], "10000 Talebenin Hocası 44 Senelik Muallimlik Hayatını Anlatıyor," *Vakit*, May 7, 1930.

110. This information was found in a note sent from the Paris embassy to the Ottoman Foreign Ministry, November 10, 1895/no. 459. BBA-HNA-End: TS, K.101, E.298. Ahmed Rıza later wrote that he established the journal with Fr 100

collected from the Young Turks in Paris. Ahmed Rıza, "L'Inaction des Jeunes Turcs," *La Revue Occidentale* 27, no. 1 (January 1903), 91.

111. "The Situation in Turkey," *Times*, November 6, 1895.

112. Henri Bryois, "La Jeune Turquie," *L'Evénement*, November 6, 1895.

113. "Constantinople," *Times*, November 18, 1895; "Occasional Notes," *Pall Mall Gazette*, November 18, 1895; and "Les affaires de Turquie," *Le Temps*, November 19, 1895.

114. Ahmed Rıza, "Mukaddeme," *Meşveret*, no. 1, December 1, 107 [1895], 1.

115. "Notre programme," *Mechveret Supplément Français*, no. 1, December 7, 1901, 1.

116. *Muazzez Vatandaşlar*. A one-page handbill signed by Ahmed Rıza and Doctor Nâzım. Private Papers of Ahmed Rıza (2).

117. Ibid.

118. "İlân-ı Resmî," *Mizan*, no. 1, January 14, 1896, 2.

119. Ahmed Rıza, "İhtilâl," *Meşveret*, no. 29, January 14, 1898, 2; also see Ahmed Rıza, "İcmâl-i Ahvâl," *Meşveret*, no. 6, February 15, 108 [1896], 1.

120. "La Jeune Turquie," *La Paix*, November 9, 1895.

121. Ahmed Rıza, "İcmâl-i Ahvâl," *Meşveret*, no. 18, September 8, 108 [1896], 2.

122. "Young Turkey II: The Present Aims by a Member of the Young Turkish Party," *Pall Mall Gazette*, February 24, 1896: "Again as the avowed object of the Young Turks is to dispense with European control, we must suppose more magnanimity on the part of the Powers than they have exhibited of late before we can imagine them taking the initiative in the restoration of the Turkish Parliament. Therefore, it would seem that any movement must be started by the Turks themselves."

123. Halil Halid to Tunalı Hilmi, Wooking, July 5, 1896 in Kuran, *Osmanlı İmparatorluğunda İnkılâp Hareketleri*, 220.

124. For the echoes of this appeal in the movement and the European press, see "Bir Acayib Beyannâme," *Hürriyet*, no. 49, 2, and "Turkish Reform League," *Times*, April 13, 1896. The entire text of this strange appeal recommending the dethronement of Abdülhamid II and his banishment to Madeira Island under Portuguese protection was publish in *Svoboda* (Sofia) on June 19, 1896. A French and a Turkish translation of this Bulgarian text are given in BBA-BEO/Mümtaze: Bulgaristan Tasnifi Evrakı I, A MTZ (04), 34/96, 1314. 1. 29.

125. Von Saurma to Schillingsfürst, Therapia, August 8, 1897/A. 9800-no. 214, Geheimes Staatsarchiv-Berlin, III. HA, Nr. 1104, Bl. 2617–2619.

126. Cambon to Berthelot, Pera, December 26, 1895/no. 219, AE-CP-T, 525 (November-December 1895), [353–54]. The same viewpoint was expressed by western press. See "Mourad Bey's Condemnation," *New York Times*, March 11, 1896.

127. See Gulam Muhammed Ali, "Ey Din Karındaşı," *Mizan*, no. 177, May 21, 1896, 3001, and "Ser-efrâz-ı Ulema-yı Mütehakkikinden Bir Zât-ı Âli'nin İmzasıyla Dersaadet'den Alınmışdır Ma'el-Teşekkür Tezyîn-i Sehaif Eyliyoruz," *Mizan*, no. 165, February 27, 1896, 2406–407.

128. Mehmed Murad, *Yıldız Saray-ı Hümayûnu ve Bâb-ıâli Yahud Şarkın Derd-i Aslîsi* ([Cairo], 1313 [1896]), 94.

129. Mehmed Murad, *Mücahede-i Milliye*, 82–83.

130. Maurice Leudet, "Conversation avec Mourad Bey," *Le Figaro*, December 8, 1895.

131. *Le Figaro*, December 3, 1895, and *Pall Mall Gazette*, December 23, 1895. His views impressed European public opinion. See "Une brochure de S. Ex. Mourad Bey," *Le Figaro*, December 10, 1895, "The Voice of Turkey," *Pall Mall Gazette*, December 23, 1895.

132. Mehmed Murad, *Mücahede-i Milliye*, 88.

133. Ahmed Rıza, "[Murad Bey'in Risâlesi]," *Meşveret*, no. 3, April 1, 108 [1896], 2.

134. Mehmed Murad, *Mücahede-i Milliye*, 104–105.

135. Mehmed Murad, *Tatlı Emeller, Acı Hakikatler Yahud Batn-ı Müstakbele Âdâb-ı Siyasiye Talimi* (Istanbul, 1330 [1912]), 4–5.

136. "Once More," *Pall Mall Gazette*, December 28, 1895.

137. Ahmed İzzet Bey to the Ottoman embassy in London [January 4, 1896], Archives of Turkish Embassy in London, Box 339 (8).

138. See BBA-YSHM, 1 B 1313/ no. 1552, BBA-YP, 13 C 1313/ no. 796.

139. "Lettre à S.Ex[cellence] Izzet Bey Conseiller d'Etat résident à Yildiz concernant Mourad Bey le 14/26 Décembre 1895," Archives of the Turkish Embassy in London, Box 303 (3).

140. Halûk Y. Şehsuvaroğlu, "Mizancı Murad Bey'in Memlekete Dönüşü," *Akşam*, December 2, 1951.

141. Mehmed Murad, *Mücahede-i Milliye*, 106.

142. Anthopulos Pasha to Tahsin Bey, January 26, 1896, Archives of the Turkish Embassy in London, Box 303 (3).

143. "Lettre à S. Ex[cellence] Izzet Bey, Conseiller d'Etat concernant Ahmed Riza Bey," Archives of the Turkish Embassy in London, Box 303 (3).

144. BBA-İrade-Hariciye, Şa'ban 1313/no. 5-1643, Fuad, "Une question au gouvernement Ottoman," *Mechveret Supplément Français*, no. 4, February 1, 1896, 1–2.

145. Cambon to Berthelot, Péra, February 5, 1896/no. 24, AE-CP-T: 526 (January-February 1896), [204–207], BBA-İrade-Hususî, Zilkade 1313/no. 38-1266, and 44-1273; Currie to Salisbury, Constantinople, April 23, 1896, *PRO/ F.O.* 78/4706, Fuad, "Le Rappel des étudiants Ottomans," *Mechveret Supplément Français*, no. 15, June 15, 1896, 2.

146. BBA-İrade-Hususî, Şevval 1313/no. 55-1206.

147. "İlân," *Meşveret*, no. 5, February 1, 108 [1896], 4.

148. La Rédaction, "Remerciements," *Mechveret Supplément Français*, no. 5, February 15, 1896, 1.

149. Ahmed Rıza's letter dated London, July 17, 108 [1896], Private Papers of Bahaeddin Şakir.

150. Hey'et-i Tahririye, "Tebşir ve Teşekkür," *Meşveret*, no. 12, June 8, 108 [1896], 1.

151. Nâzım, "[İâne]," *Meşveret*, no. 21, October 23, 1896, 8.

152. Ahmed Rıza, "Osmanlı İttihad ve Terakki Cemiyeti ve Avrupa Matbuatı," *Meşveret*, no. 20, October 8, 1896, 2.

153. "Envoyer au Cabinet de M.Hanotaux," AE-NS-T, 2 (1898), 11, *Journal Officiel* 28, no. 100, April 12, 1896, 2072.

154. "Ahmet Rıza Bey'in Hatıraları (2)," *Cumhuriyet*, January 27, 1950.

155. For the details of this policy see the undated memorandum of [İbrahim] Hakkı Bey, law counselor of the Sublime Porte, BBA-YEE, 14/1291/126/10.

156. For the verdict, see Archives of the Turkish Embassy in Paris, D. 237, and BBA-YEE, 14/1291/126/10.

157. The articles written by the French journalists were republished in the special issue of the French supplement of the central organ. See *Mechveret Supplément Français*, no. 9, April 18, 1896, 1–12.

158. Obviously this was a minor effort, considering the expectations and anxiety of the Ottoman government concerning the journal and its editor. See BBA-YSMGM, 7 S 1314/no. 224-1422, BBA-YSHM, 16 S 1313/no. 384.

159. "Jung-türken in der Schweiz (Zeitung Mechveret)," May 19, 1896/von Genf (11.5.96), and May 21, 1896/von Genf (20.5.96), Bundesarchiv-Bern, E. 21/14'248.

160. See "Muvaffakiyet-i Cihanbânî," *Meşveret*, no. 10, May 1, 1896, 1–2, and "Tebşir," *Meşveret*, no. 10, 2.

161. See Giuseppe Mazzini's letter to Karl Blind dated August 1, 1870, published in "La Prusse fomentant des insurrections," *L'Agence Libre*, no. 2482, November 15, 1888. For more information about his activities see Archives de la Préfecture de Police de Paris (Karl Blind), B. A (963)- 58423235-RD.

162. Karl Blind, "The Young Turkey," *The Fortnightly Review* 60, 830–43. This article was republished in *Living Age* 13, no. 2471, January 16, 1897, 163–73, and summarized in the French supplement of the central organ. See "La Jeune Turquie," *Mechveret Supplément Français*, no. 25, December 1, 1896, 5–6.

163. Halûk Y. Şehsuvaroğlu, "Jön Türklerin Mısır Faaliyetleri," *Akşam*, November 21, 1951.

164. "Fırkamızın Hatt-ı Hareketi," *Mizan*, no. 159, February 1896, 2359–60.

165. "Hürriyet, Mizan, Meşveret," *Hürriyet*, no. 55, August 1, 1896, 2.

166. See Mehmed Murad, "Aziz Rıza Bey," *Meşveret*, no. 3, January 1, 108 [1896], 1–2. Murad, "Aziz Kardeşim Rıza," *Meşveret*, no. 18, September 8, 108 [1896], 2, "Murad Bey," *İlâve-i Meşveret*, no. 6, February 15, 108 [1896], 3. "Havâdis-i Siyasiye," *İlâve-i Meşveret*, no. 7, March 1, 108 [1896], 4, "Condamnation de Mourad Bey," *Mechveret Supplément Français*, no. 5, February 5, 1896, 1–2.

167. See *Mizan*, no. 43 [September 10, 1908], 187.

168. See the interrogation report of Mehmed Rıf'at bin Ârif, a student at the Royal Medical Academy. AQSh, 19/106-5//593/1143.

169. A letter signed "A naval officer, graduated from the naval academy this year" and sent to Şerafeddin Mağmumî and Doctor Nâzım, AQSh, 19/135//16/222.

170. Abdullah Cevdet to İshak Sükûti, Tripoli of Barbary, April 29, 1896, AQSh, 19/106//153/440.

171. See BBA-BEO/ Telgraf ve Posta Nezareti Giden, 585-17/10, 2 [March 19, 1896] 56443, Âbidin Bey, governor of Cezaîr-i Bahr-i Sefid Province to the Chamberlain's office, Rhodes [March 14, 1896]/no. 18, BBA-BEO/VGG(2)-Anadolu [Telgrafi Defteri]: 903, and the grand vizier to Gazi Ahmed Muhtar Pasha, BBA-BEO/Mısır Hidiviyet-i Celilesinin Muharrerat Defteri (71)-1032-68/4, S.13/E.5/ [March 25, 1896], BBA-İrade-Hususî, Şa'ban 1313/no. 87-1079, BBA-BEO/Hariciye Reft, 185-5/39, 1774 [February 13, 1896], BBA-BEO/Zaptiye Giden, 662-21/13, 519 [February 13, 1896]/55773.

172. "Osmanlı'nın Beşinci Sene-i İntişârı," *Osmanlı*, no. 97, December 1, 1901, 2.

173. Âbidin Bey, governor of Cezaîr-i Bahr-i Sefid Province, to the Chamberlain's office [May 13, 1896]/no. 13, *Cezaîr-i Bahr-i Sefid ile Muhaberat Kaydına Mahsusdur*, 1310/1311, BBA-YEE, 36/139-46/139/XVIII.

174. Avnülrefik Bey to the Chamberlain's office, Mecca [March 31, 1896]/ no. 23, *Haleb ve Adana Kumandan Vekâletine Mahsus [Defter]*, BBA-YEE, 36/ 2470-18/147/XVI.

175. This information is in Gazi Ahmed Muhtar Pasha's memorandum dated [January 30, 1896], which was enclosed with BBA-İrade-Dahiliye, Şa'ban 1313/ no. 29-1951.

176. See Earl of Cromer, *Abbas II* (London, 1915), 76.

177. Cromer to Salisbury, Private, Cairo, June 30, 1896/no. 260, Cromer Papers, Letters to Secretaries of State, PRO/F.O. 633/IV.

178. Decipher from Sir Philip Currie, Pera, January 17, 1896, PRO/F.O. 78/4723.

179. Decipher from Sir Philip Currie, Pera, February 10, 1896/no. 52, PRO/ F.O. 78/4723.

180. Tahsin Bey to Anthopulos Pasha, Yıldız, February 23, [18]96, Archives of the Turkish Embassy in London, Box 319 (2).

181. Anthopulos Pasha to Tahsin Bey, London, February 27, 1896, Archives of the Turkish Embassy in London, Box 319 (2).

182. See "Les Affaires de Turquie," *Les Temps*, January 29, February 3, and 20, 1896.

183. Currie to Salisbury, Pera, March 10, 1896/no. 94 (confidential), PRO/ F.O. 78/4723. A French daily claimed that the new crisis over Egypt was created by the sultan in order to force the British to extradite Murad Bey. See "La question d'Egypte," *L'Eclair*, February 29, 1896.

184. BBA-İrade-Dahiliye, Şa'ban 1313/no. 29-1951, and BBA-YEE, 15/74- 31/74/15.

185. Fevziye Abdullah, "Mizancı Mehmed Murad Bey," *Edebiyat Fakültesi Tarih Dergisi* 1, no. 1 (1950), 81–82.

186. "Karilerimize," *Mizan*, no. 184, June 8, 1896, 2553.

187. This action was led by Cemil, Refik, Hasan, Halil, Doctor Ahmed, and Georgos Efendi. See Fuad Şükrü to İbrahim Temo [Paris], June 26, 1896, AQSh, 19/135//136/1081.

188. An undated and unsigned letter to İbrahim Temo, AQSh, 19/135// 13/270.

189. See Şerafeddin Mağmumî's letter dated October 16, 1896 in Kuran, *İnkılâp Tarihimiz ve İttihad ve Terakki*, 92.

190. "Daily Chronicle Office," *Daily Chronicle*, July 22, 1896.

191. The following conversation transpired between Murad Bey and Ahmed Rıza after the latter's return to Paris:

> You spoke to the fellows. What have you decided?
> Nothing. They are incorrigible.
> What are they saying?
> Nothing. They do not recognize us.
> Whom did you see?
> All of them.
> Are they unanimous?
> Yes.

See Mehmed Murad, *Mücahade-i Milliye*, 166.

192. Ahmed Rıza to Doctor Nâzım, London, July 15, 108 [1896], Private Papers of Bahaeddin Şâkir.

193. The letter sent to the Istanbul center is in AQSh, 19/59//47/3. There are also two other letters sent to the Syria and Salonica branches. See, respectively, AQSh, 19/59//273/38, and 19/59//174/1.

194. BBA-YP, 2 Ş 1314/no. 830; "Meşveret," *Meşveret*, no. 18, September 8, 108 [1896], 4.

195. For their flight, see Âbidin Bey to the Chamberlain's office [November 3, 1896]/no. 556, [November 4, 1896]/nos. 557, [November 5, 1896]/nos. 559 and 560, [November 8, 1896]/no. 564, and [November 9, 1896]/no. 567, BBA-BEO-VGG(2)/ Anadolu Telgrafi Defteri: 903. For information supplied later see Âbidin Bey to the Chamberlain's office [March 18, 1899]/no. 90. *Cezair-i Bahr-i Sefid ile Muhaberat Kaydına Mahsusdur*, BBA-YEE, 36/139-46/139/ XVIII. For Çürüksulu's flight, participation in the movement, and his short biography see July 4, 1897/von Genf, June 3, 1897/no. 300. Bundesarchiv Bern, E. 21/14'248. For Salih Cemal's participation in the movement and his biography see the spy report entitled "Jön Türklerin Meşruhatlı Esamisi," Abbas II Papers, Durham University, F. 26/280-1.

196. K.A. to İshak Sükûti, Tripoli of Barbary [January 22, 1897], AQSh, 19/106-6//632/1793-1.

197. "Müesser Bir Ziya'," *Anadolu*, no. 1, April 24, 1902, 4.

198. See Müştak Vasfi to İshak Sükûti, Rhodes, October 8, [18]99, AQSh, 19/106-4//124/1235, "Tebşir," *Meşveret*, no. 22, November 8, 1896, 1, and "Prisonniers Turcs Délivres," *Mechveret Supplément Français*, no. 23, November 15, 1896, 4–5.

199. In two letters, dated October 4, 108 [1896], and November 20, 108 [1896], Ahmed Rıza underscored Sükûti's importance for the movement. See, respectively, AQSh, 19/127//809/3, and AQSh, 19/127//28/3.

200. "İlân-ı Resmî," *Mizan*, no. 1, 2.

201. Mehmed Murad, *Mücahede-i Milliye*, 192–93.

202. İsmail Edhem to İshak Sükûti, December 1, 1896, AQSh, 19/106-3/ /637/1111.

203. "Tebligat," *Mizan*, no. 1, 1–2.

204. "İlân-ı Resmî," *Mizan*, no. 1, 2.

205. Mehmed Murad, *Mücahede-i Milliye*, 193.

206. Ibid., 195–96.

207. Ibid., 193.

208. Ahmed Rıza, "İhtar," *Meşveret*, no. 23, November 23, 1896, 1.

209. Ahmed Rıza's letter dated November 17, 108 [1896], AQSh, 19/127/ /304/2.

210. See "Tebşir ve Tebrik," *Kanun-i Esasî*, no. 2, December 28, 1896, 6, "Meşveret ve Mizan," *Hürriyet*, no. 64, December 15, 1896, 3. Another opposition journal expressed its pleasure with the decision given for *Mizan*'s publication. See "Mizan-Teşekkür," *Hakikat*, no. 7, December 1, 1896, 3.

211. An unsigned letter to Ahmed Rıza from London, dated December 21, [18]96, Private Papers of Ahmed Rıza (1).

212. Hey'et-i Teftiş ve İcra, "Beyannâme," *Mizan*, no. 1, 2–3.

213. For examples see "Jolie civilisation," *La Justice*, January 22, 1896, "Turks Awaiting Reforms," *Daily Telegraph*, October 22, 1896.

214. Currie to Salisbury, Pera, April 14, 1896/no. 284 (secret), PRO/F.O. 78/4705. See also Chermside to Currie, Constantinople, March 30, 1896 (strictly confidential), *Conf.* 6853.

215. Doctor Mekkeli Sabri to Abdullah Cevdet, Le Mans, June 27, 1931, 5, Private Papers of Abdullah Cevdet.

216. See Kan Demir, *Zindan Hatıraları*, 153.

217. Doctor Mekkeli Sabri to Abdullah Cevdet, Le Mans, June 27, 1931, 7–8. Private Papers of Abdullah Cevdet.

218. AQSh, 19/60//445/30.

219. See BBA-Tezâkir-i Samiye Dosyaları, 400 [November 30, 1895]/no. 1360.

220. See "Şeyh Nailî Efendi," *Nevsâl-i Osmanî*, 1325 [1909], 184.

221. Currie to Salisbury, Constantinople, December 9, 1896/no. 1030 (secret), PRO/F.O. 78/4720.

222. AQSh, 19/60//445/30.

223. "Havâdis-i Askeriye," *Hürriyet*, no. 60, October 15, 1896, 3.

224. "İstanbul Havâdisi: Tevkif ve Nefy," *İlâve-i Meşveret*, no. 6, February 15, 108 [1896], 3, and "Memâlik-i Osmaniye'de Nefy ve Teb'id," *Hürriyet*, no. 58, September 15, 1896, 3.

225. "Dersaadet'de Hükümferma-yı Dehşet," *Hürriyet*, no. 59, October 1, 1896, 4.

226. A copy of this appeal was sent to the Paris branch from Geneva by a Young Turk who used the pen name Osmanoğlu. The letter with which the appeal was enclosed was dated September 4, 1896. Private Papers of Bahaeddin Şakir.

227. It is not entirely clear whether Nadir Bey deliberately revealed their plans to İsmail Pasha or whether the latter gathered information from the former. However, the accusations made in the central organ afterward imply that the first alternative was more likely. See "Casus-i Bînamus Nadir," *Mizan*, no. 28, July 19, 1897, 4, and "Tabaka-i Bâlâ Muhabirimizden," *Mizan*, no. 17, April 26, 1897, 4. See also "Jawāsīs al-Asitāna," *al-Ayyām*, no. 29, 1. A British document proves that the sultan was aware of the venture before Nadir Bey's informing. Currie cabled to Salisbury on September 22, 1896 (no. 406, secret): "An attempt by the Young Turkish Party to depose the Sultan is said to be imminent. I hear on reliable authority that large quantities of ammunition have been sent to the Palace where the battery guns have been prepared for action. But if an attempt is made it is not likely to take the form of an open attack on the Palace." PRO/F.O. 78/4724.

228. Currie to Salisbury, December 9, 1896/no.1030, PRO/F.O. 78/4720.

229. The list of the exiled individuals is in BBA-Mahremâne Müsvedât [December 6, 1896]/no. 84. More names are given in five other documents about banishments. See BBA-BEO/Dahiliye Giden, 95-3/44, 21 [January 10, 1897]/ 67265, 37/66891, and 71916, 49/71916, and 72480. More information about the venture and the names of the secondary people are given in the following articles: "İstanbul Muhabir-i Mahsusumuzun Mektubu," *Hürriyet*, no. 65, January 1, 1897, 3, "Nefy-Tagrib," *Kanun-i Esasî*, no. 2, December 2, 1896, 8, "İstanbul'dan Gelen Bir Mektubdan," *Kanun-i Esasî*, no. 3, January 4, 1897, 7, "Yine Müceddidin Fırkası," *Hürriyet*, no. 64, December 15, 1896, 1, "Hâlâ Bilâ Muhakeme Habs ü Nefy," *Hürriyet*, no. 65, 2.

230. The sultan gave special and strict instructions. See BBA-Mahremâne Müsvedât [December 3, 1897]/ no. 68, and [December 6, 1897]/nos. 80 and 81.

231. See "Merkez Kumandanı," *Kanun-i Esasî*, no. 1, December 21, 1896, 7, and "Garibe-i Siyasiye," ibid.

232. For measures taken against him, see BBA-YP, 1314/no. 798, Cambon to Hanotaux, Pera, January 14, 1897/no. 7, and January 26, 1897/no. 19, AE-NS-T, 1 (1897), 4–7. His dismissal caused protests in the European press. See Joseph Denais, "Les victimes du Sultan: La démission de Fuad Pasha," *La Nouvelle Revue* 106 (May 1, 1897), 71–72.

233. Currie to Salisbury, December 9, 1896/no. 1030, PRO/F.O. 78/4720.

234. "Mussulman Appeal to France," *Daily Graphic*, December 16, 1896, "Beyannâme," *Kanun-i Esasî*, no. 3, 8.

235. AQSh, 19/57//33/209.

236. Ibid.

237. It was claimed that "the number of those who were registered in the CUP has reached 18,000." See Hey'et-i Teftiş ve İcra, "Beyannâme," *Mizan*, no. 1, December 14, 1896, 2. The other official organ asserted that "130,000 individuals had been sent into exile because of their membership in the CUP." See "Dar-ül-harb," *Meşveret*, no. 22, November 8, 1896, 5.

238. For the first activities see Memduh Bey to the Chamberlain's office [February 21, 1896], *Ankara Vilâyetiyle Muhaberat Kaydına Mahsusdur*, BBA-YEE, 36/139-15/139/XVIII. Later more CUP members were exiled. (See Shipley to O'Conor, Angora, September 19, 1899/no. 30 (confidential), enclosed with the letter from O'Conor to Salisbury, Therapia, September 28, 1899/no. 462 (confidential), PRO.F.O. 78/4995.) This caused new activities in the town. See Governor Tevfik Bey to Âsım Bey at the Chamberlain's office [October 23, 1900], *Ankara [Vilâyetiyle Muhaberata Mahsus Defter]*, BBA-YEE, 36/1470-3/147/36.

239. Governor Enis Bey to Kâmil Bey [July 4, 1898]/no. 3, Kâmil Bey to Enis Bey [April 18, 1895]/no. 25, and September 3, 1899/no. 40, *Kastamonu [Vilâyetiyle Muhaberata Mahsus Defter]*, BBA-YEE, 36/2470-42/147/XVI.

240. Âsım Bey to the governor [July 21, 1901]/no. 14, and [March 21, 1904]/no. 26, *Mamuret el-Azîz Vilâyetiyle Muhaberata Mahsus Defter*, BBA-YEE, 36/2470-40/147/XVI.

241. Governor Rauf Bey to the Chamberlain's office, [February 9, 1897]/no. 26, *Erzurum Vilâyetiyle Muhabereye Mahsus Defterdir*, BBA-YEE, 36/2470-3/147/36.

242. Governor Rauf Bey to the Chamberlain's office [February 14, 1897]/no. 67, ibid.

243. The Russian consulate intervened in favor of Pastırmacıyan and inquired about his release to the local administration. See Mehmed Kâmil to the governor [March 10, 1897]/no. 72, and Governor Rauf Bey to the Chamberlain's office [March 30, 1897]/no. 74, ibid.

244. Governor Rauf Bey to the Chamberlain's office, February 19, 1897/no. 68, ibid.

245. Rauf Bey to the Chamberlain's office [April 1, 1897]/no. 76, ibid.

246. Graves to Currie, Erzurum, February 5, 1897/no. 4, enclosed with a letter from Currie to Salisbury, Constantinople, February 16, 1897/no. 107, PRO/F.O. 78/4798.

247. Yunus Nadi, "İshak Sükûti Bey," *Yeni Tasvir-i Efkâr,* October 5, 1909.

248. Âbidin Bey to the Chamberlain's office, July 5, 1897/no. 250-1951, BBA-BEO/VGG(2):Anadolu [Telgrafi Defteri]:903 / Rodos:4 (18).

249. BBA-İrade-Dahiliye, Safer 1314/no. 11-493, and BBA-BEO/Dahiliye Giden, 95-3/44, 1527 [August 3, 1896]/61493.

250. Kerim Bey in Monastir to the Chamberlain's office [January 27, 1896], *Manastır Valisi Abdülkerim Paşa Kullarına İhsan Buyurulan Şifre Miftahı [ve Şifre Halliyesini Havî Defter]*, BBA-YEE, 36/2470-8/147.XVI.

251. "Edirne'den Mektub," *İlâve-i Mesveret*, no. 9, April 1, 108 [1896], 4. For more information see "Edirne'den," *Mizan*, no. 2, December 2, 1896, 4–5, and "Havâdis-i Siyasiye," *Meşveret*, no. 8, March 15, 108 [1896], 4.

252. Abdullah Cevdet to İshak Sükûti, Tripoli of Barbary, April 29, 1896, AQSh, 19/106//153/440, and Abdullah Cevdet to Ahmed Rıza, May 30, 1896, Private Papers of Ahmed Rıza (1).

253. A donation, receipt no. 1444, AQSh, 19/62//113/1.

254. Information about Talât Bey's role in the early activities of the CUP is in "Lebensgeschichte Talaat Bey," 3–6, Ernst Jäckh Papers, Yale University, MS 466, Box 2, Folder 44. For more information see *Ebubekir Hâzim Tepeyran Hatıraları, Canlı Tarihler* 1 (Istanbul, 1944), 144–45.

255. Amedî [İshak Sükûti] to İbrahim Temo, Geneva, May 23, [18]97, AQSh, 19/106//23/1.

256. Mehmed Rauf, *İttihad ve Terakki Cemiyeti*, 79–82.

257. Nâzım, "Vilâyetlerimiz," *Meşveret*, no. 5, February 1, 108 [1896], 3. Their role in Young Turk activities was also underscored by the French consul. See his dispatch to Hanotaux, Salonica, February 12, 1897/no. 6, AE-NS-T, 1 (1897), 19.

258. Hak-Gû, "Selânik'den Mektub," *Meşveret*, no. 15, July 23, 108 [1896], 4. Martin Hartmann asserted the continuation of relations between the CUP and the *dönmeler* following the Young Turk revolution. *Unpolitische Briefe aus der Türkei*, 7–8.

259. Mehmed Rauf, *İttihad ve Terakki Cemiyeti*, 85.

260. Tarık, "Selânik'den," *Meşveret*, no. 17, August 23, 108 [1896], 4.

261. Mehmed Rauf, *İttihad ve Terakki Cemiyeti*, 85. Mehmed Rauf Bey was a prominent Albanian and described as one of the leaders of the Albanians in Salonica by Austrians. See Kral to Goluchowski, Monastir, December 10, 1900/no. 73 (geheim), Beilage F, HHStA, PA XIV/7 Albanien. His Albanian origin was also underscored by İbrahim Temo. See İbrahim Temo to Karl Süssheim, Medgidia, December 25, 1933. Nachlaß Süssheim.

262. Mehmed Rauf, *İttihad ve Terakki Cemiyeti*, 85–86, 94.

263. Ibid., 95–99.

264. Ibid., 96.

265. BBA-İrade-Dahiliye, Şa'ban 1317/no. 18-1769.

266. Şerafeddin Mağmumî, *Hakikat-i Hal* (Paris, 1315 [1897]), 26.

267. A document signed by Ferdinand and Archbolo Efendis and Fikretî and Enver Beys dated [January 28, 1897], AQSh, 19/59//235/53. Fikretî Bey previously sent donations to the Paris center. See "İlân," *Meşveret*, no. 23, November 22, 1896, 8.

268. The Salonica branch to the Paris branch, undated [March-April 1897?], AQSh, 19/59//32/484.

269. Ibid.

270. "Selânik'den İkinci Mektub," *Osmanlı*, no. 86, June 15, 1901, 5–6.

271. Zeynel Âbidin to the offices of Mizan, Canea [July 29, 1897], AQSh, 19/92//643/1.

272. The documents were uncovered at Doctor Major Mustafa's residence. See Commander of Crete to the Chamberlain's office [September 9, 1897], *Girid*

Fırka-i Hümayûn Kumandanlığıyla Muhaberat Kaydına Mahsus Defterdir, BBA-YEE, 36/139-45/139/XVIII.

273. Chamberlain's office to the Acting-governor's office [July 13, 1897]/ no. 28, and İsmail Bey to the Chamberlain's office [July 14, 1897]/no. 29, *Hudud-u Yunaniye Kumandanı Neş'et Paşa İle [Muhaberat] Kayd Defteridir*, BBA-YEE, 36/2470-9/147/XVI.

274. "Muhtasaran Tarihçe-i Hayatım," enclosed with İbrahim Temo's letter to Karl Süssheim, Medgidia, June 25, 1933, Nachlaβ Süssheim; Temo, *İttihad ve Terakki*, 58–60.

275. Some biographical information about Kırımîzâde Ali Rıza was given in İbrahim Temo's letter to Karl Süssheim, Medgidia, December 25, [1]933, Nachlaβ Süssheim.

276. Ülküsal, *Dobruca ve Türkler*, 149.

277. For a documented account of their activities, see Tahsin Cemil, "Asociatia din Romania a Junilor Turci," *Anuarul Institutului de Istorie şi Arheologie 'A. D.Xenopol'* 7 (1970), 180–88.

278. Talât Bey to Ahmed Zeki, Ruse, April 27, [18]96, and May 16, 1896, AQSh, 19/135//11/478, and 19/31//13/197.

279. Murad Bey required İbrahim Temo to send thirty copies of the pamphlet for distribution in Egypt. See the former to the latter, Cairo, May 4, 1896, AQSh, 19/135//195/423.

280. See Fuad Şükrü to İbrahim Temo, April 29, [18]96, AQSh, 19/135//352/73-3.

281. Abdullah Cevdet to Ahmed Rıza, Tripoli of Barbary, May 30, 1896. Private Papers of Ahmed Rıza (1).

282. The central branch in Bulgaria to Murad Bey [August 1897?], AQSh, 19/59//56/33.

283. "Muhtasaran Tarihçe-i Hayatım," enclosed with İbrahim Temo's letter to Karl Süssheim, Medgidia, June 25, 1933, Nachlaβ Süssheim, and Temo, *İttihad ve Terakki*, 59–60.

284. İbrahim Temo to İshak Sükûti, October 16, [18]98, AQSh, 19/106-3//270/1066.

285. BBA-BEO/Hariciye Âmed, 156-5/12, 109 [March 23, 1896]/ (Mümtaze: 1842), BBA-BEO/Zabtiye Giden, 662-21/13, 13 (Mümtaze [March 31, 1896]), 18 (Mümtaze [April 9, 1896]).

286. BBA-BEO/Hariciye Âmed, 156-5/12, 5527 [February 27, 1896]/ (Mümtaze: 99), 341/142 [April 5, 1896]/(Mümtaze: 18).

287. BBA-BEO/Hariciye Âmed, 156-5/12, 3406 [October 15, 1896].

288. BBA-BEO/Hariciye Âmed, 156-5/12, 3301 [November 7, 1896], and 3406 [November 15, 1896].

289. BBA-BEO/Hariciye Âmed, 156-5/12, 1503 [June 30, 1896], 1790 [July 19, 1896], BBA-BEO/Hariciye Reft, 183-5/39, 615 [July 2, 1896).

290. BBA-BEO/Bulgaristan Masasının Tezkere Kayd Defteri (73), 959-60/ 23, 4472/1051 [January 31, 1897].

291. BBA-BEO/Mümtaze: Bulgaristan Tasnifi Evrakı I, A MTZ (04), 36/ 39, 1314. 3. 18 and 37/11, 1314. 4. 13, BBA-BEO/Hariciye Âmed, 156-5/12, 2211 [August 24, 1896].

292. Doctor Ali Hikmet to Ahmed Zeki, [Ruse], June 1, 1896, AQSh, 19/ 135//13/464.

293. BBA-BEO/Hariciye Âmed, 157-5/13, 4490 [February 4, 1897].

294. BBA-BEO/Bulgaristan Masasının Tezkere Kayd Defteri (73)-959-60/ 23, 503/1007 [January 7, 1897].

295. BBA-BEO/Hariciye Âmed, 157-5/13, 4490 [February 4, 1897].

296. "Ermeni Vatandaşlarımıza Bir Da'vet," *Mizan*, no. 162, December 6, 1896, 2384: "O our Armenian Compatriots! O the committees of nation within [the fatherland] and abroad! We are addressing this invitation to you on behalf of the Ottoman Committee of Union Progress. Let's devote our efforts to the future by forgetting the past. Let's unite to rescue the fatherland from the calamity to which she is being subjected."

297. Tahsin Bey to Anthopulos Pasha, July 11, 1896/no. 23, Archives of the Turkish Embassy in London, Box 319 (2).

298. The report of the Commissaire Spécial in Annemasse to the Directeur de la Sûreté Générale, June 8, 1897/no. 709, AE-NS-T, 1 (1897), 116.

299. "Fransa'da Müceddidin-i Osmaniyenin Hakikat-i Hâli," *Hürriyet*, no. 67, February 1, 1897, 1.

300. *Tebliğnâme-i Hususî*, one-page appeal. AQSh, 19/60//645/15-2.

301. AQSh, 19/60//16/1.

302. Tunalı Hilmi, *Murad* (Geneva, 1317 [1899]), 277.

303. Ahmed Rıza to the director of the Romania branch, June 22, 109 [1897], AQSh, 19/59//35/30.

304. Le Comité, "Déclaration," *Mechveret Supplément Français*, no. 19, September 15, 1896, 1.

305. Süleyman Nazif to İshak Sükûti [January 4, 1897], AQSh, 19/106-5/ /137/1430.

306. Kuran, *İnkılâp Tarihimiz ve İttihad ve Terakki*, 98–99.

307. Tunalı Hilmi to İshak Sükûti, undated, AQSh, 19/106-1//635/571.

308. AQSh, 19/59//35/1.

309. Governor Hilmi Bey to the Chamberlain's office [June 5, 1897], *Gümülcine Mutasarrıfiyla, Adana, Diyar-ıbekir Vilâyetleri Muhaberat Kaydına Mahsus Defterdir*, BBA-YEE, 36/139-54/139/XVIII.

310. BBA-YSHM, 14 N 1314/no. 2226.

311. BBA-YEE, 15/74-25/74/15.

312. Currie to Salisbury, Pera, February 6, 1897, PRO/F.O. 78/4798, and BBA-YP, 4 M 1315/no. 59.

313. AQSh, 19/60//350/73.

314. "Manifesto of the Ottoman Society of Union and Progress," enclosed with a letter from Currie to Salisbury, Constantinople, March 4, 1897/no. 163, PRO/F.O. 424/191.

315. See Archives d'Etat Genève-Chancellerie, B. 8, 84.

316. [Tunalı Hilmi], "Bir Hutbe," *Ezan*, no. 1, February 2, 1897, 1.

317. BBA-YSHM, 12 L 1314/no. 2599.

318. Hacı Âdil's undated letter [1897], AQSh, 19/135//195/941.

319. Çürüksulu Ahmed to İshak Sükûti, undated [1897], AQSh, 19/106// 1228/1.

320. Reşid Bey to İshak Sükûti, January 4, [18]96, AQSh, 19/106-6//631/ 1819.

321. The Istanbul branch to İshak Sükûti, July 20, 1897, AQSh, 19/106-7/ /298/2039.

322. A. Y., "Şam'dan," *Mizan*, no. 172, April 16, 1896, 2462.

323. His dispatch to Hanotaux, Geneva, March 31, 1897, AE-NS-T, 1 (1897), 30. He later made a comparison between *Mechveret Supplément Français* and *Mizan* and described the former an "organ modéré" while characterizing the latter "représentant l'élément violent et révolutionnaire". See his dispatch to Hanotaux, Geneva, July, 2, 1897, AE-NS-T, 1 (1897), 177.

324. "Une conversation édifiante-Les déclarations de Chéfik Bey," *Mechveret Supplément Français*, no. 22, November 1, 1896, 7, "Askerî Muhabirimiz Harbî'den," *Mizan*,no. 8, February 22, 1897, 4, "Evrak ve Mekâtib," *Mizan*, no. 166, March 5, 1896, 2415.

325. Mehmed Murad, *Mücahede-i Milliye*, 154–55.

326. The most important publication during this period was an appeal to the naval officers and sailors written by a member. See [Süleyman Nazif], *Bahriyelilere Mektub* [Paris, 1896?]. For another striking article, see "Mehmed Namık Kemal," *Mizan*, no. 17, April 26, 1897, 1–3. Murad Bey also printed maps showing the territorial losses of the Ottoman Empire under Abdülhamid II to incite these officers. See "Avrupa-yı Osmanî," *Mizan İlâvesi*, no. 1, 1314 [1897], and "Asya ve Afrika-yı Osmanî," *Mizan İlâvesi*, no. 2, 1314 [1897].

327. See "Mühim Havâdis," *Mizan*, no. 12, 4; "Ey Zivin Kahramanı Gazi Ahmed Muhtar Paşa Hazretleri! Plevne Kahramanı Gazi Osman Paşa Hazretleri! Elena Kahramanı Fuad Paşa Hazretleri!" *Kanun-i Esasî İlâvesi*, February 18, 1897, [1]; and "Bir Muamma," *Kanun-i Esasî*, no. 7, February 1, 1897, 2.

328. Şerif Paşa, *İttihad ve Terakki'nin Sahtekârlıklarına, Denaetlerine Bülend Bir Sada-yı Lâ'netimiz* (Paris, [1911]), 30. Şerif Pasha wrote that a donation of £t 300 per month was promised by one of the Great Powers. However after Murad Bey's return to the Empire, that Power reneged on it. Murad Bey's pro-British declarations encourage us to believe that this great power was Great Britain. However, some information obtained by the French furnishes hints about a possible German assistance. On June 16, 1897, the French intelligence sources presented information to Affaires Étrangères that a letter and a check of DM 200 were given to Çürüksulu Ahmed by Freiherr von der Goltz. Çürüksulu Ahmed wrote a letter in response praising the efforts of the German military mission in the Ottoman Empire. This information, further underscored by the French Consul in Geneva, distressed to Affaires Étrangères. The latter obtained through a professor named Mouille, a copy of Çürüksulu Ahmed's response, dated June 19, 1897, which strongly denounced Abdülhamid II's treatment of young Ottoman officers. The French consul was also given a copy of the dedication which was written on the first page of Murad Bey's pamphlet and had already been sent to the kaiser. See intelligence note entitled "Parti jeune turc" and dated Geneva, June 16, 1897; Petlet to Hanotaux, Geneva, June 16, 1897; Affaires Étrangères to Petlet, June 30, 1897/no. 3 (très confidentiel); Petlet to Hanotaux, Geneva, July 2, 1897; Le Commissaire spécial to Directeur de la Sûreté Générale, Annemasse, July 3, 1897, AE-NS-T, 1 (1897), 110, 111–113, 126, 135–138, 171–172. Another event which seemed to support a possibility of German assistance was Şerif Bey (Pasha)'s close relations with the Germans. He had a long conversation with the kaiser while he was visiting Stockholm and after the Young Turk revolution Şerif Pasha took the initiative for a German-Young Turk rapprochement by introducing Ahmed Rıza to the German ambassador in Paris and advising the positivist leader to present a letter to the kaiser to this end. See von Lancken to von Bülow, August 15, 1908/no. 8, and August 18, 1908/no. 64. Nachlaß Fürsten von Bülow NL. 182, Bundesarchiv-

Koblenz. It is however difficult to be absolutely clear as to which Great Power had promised support to the Young Turk movement.

329. "Yangın Var! Cankurtaran Yok Mu?" *Mizan*, no. 12, March 22, 1897, 2.

330. Mourad, *Le palais de Yildiz et la Sublime Porte le véritable mal d'Orient* (Paris, 1895), 43 ff. He underscored the same themes in the central organ. See "Yangın Var!" *Mizan*, no. 17, 2.

331. "İhtar-ı Mahsus," *Mizan*, no. 12, March 22, 1897, 4.

332. "Şükran," *Mizan*, no. 11, March 15, 1897, 1.

333. The salient reason for this was the wide circulation of *Mizan* among high-ranking officials. For instance when the palace inquired of the governor of Salonica whether his son was reading the central organ of the CUP, he affirmed that this journal was widely distributed but swore that his son was loyal. (See Mehmed Kâmil to Rıza Bey [June 23, 1897]/no. 76, and Rıza Bey to the Chamberlain's office [June 24, 1897]/no. 77, *Musul, Van, Kastamonu, Selânik Vilâyetlerine [Mahsus Muhabere Defteri]*, BBA-YEE, 36/2470-16//147/XVI.) The chief judge of the court of appeals in the same city also confirmed the wide circulation but denied the allegations that he was reading the journal. (See Mehmed Kâmil to Reşad Bey [June 13, 1897]/no. 167; Reşad Bey to the Chamberlain's office [June 15, 1897]/no. 168, and [June 25, 1897]/no. 180, *Memurin-i Müteferrikaya Mahsus Kayd Defteridir*, BBA-YEE, 36/139-84/139/XX. For the measures aimed at stopping circulation of the journal see BBA-BEO/ Hariciye Reft, 184-5/40, 1466 [January 23, 1897]/66315, and BBA-BEO/Dahiliye Giden, 96-3/45, 1278 [June 18, 1897]/73451.) The impact of *Mizan* on people from various classes was underscored by the French ambassador too. See Cambon to Hanotaux, (Télégramme), Pera, April 16, 1897/no. 196 (confidentiel), AE-NS-T, 1 (1897), 31.

334. "Yüz ve Astar," *Mizan*, no. 4, January 11, 1897, 2.

335. "Hey'et-i Fevkâlâde," *Mizan*, no. 8, February 22, 1897, 3, "Yeni Bir Hey'et-i Murahhasa," *Hürriyet*, no. 69, March 1, 1897, 3, "Une mission extraordinaire," *Mechveret Supplément Français*, no. 29, February 15, 1897, 6. For Ebüzziya Tevfik's invitation asking the Young Turks to reach an agreement with the palace, see his letter to Şefik Bey, Paris, February 16, [18]97, AQSh, 19/135// 217/192.

336. Ahmed Rıza to the Romania branch, June 22, 109 [1897], AQSh, 19/ 159//35/30-16.

337. See Albert Fua, "Ahmed Riza Bey," *Mècheroutiette* (March 1913), 34 ff.; Paul Fesch, *Constantinople aux derniers jours d'Abdul-Hamid* (Paris, [1907]), 374–76.

338. See Le Comité, "Appel aux Cabinets Européens," *Mechveret Supplément Français*, no. 20, October 1, 1896, 1, and "Lettre adressée à MM. les députes Français," *Mechveret Supplément Français*, no. 22, November 1, 1896, 1.

339. Frederic Greenwood, "The Anglo-Russian Partnership," *Pall Mall Gazette*, December 18, 1896.

340. Mağmumî, *Hakikat-ı Hal*, 29.

341. Mehmed Murad, *Mücahede-i Milliye*, 203–204.

342. "Banquet de la Jeune Turquie: Discours de Mourad Bey," *Mechveret Supplément Français*, no. 26, 4–5.

343. "Discours de M.Ahmed Riza," *Mechveret Supplément Français*, no. 26, 4.

344. Mehmed Murad, *Mücahede-i Milliye*, 206–208, 211. This claim contradicts language used in letters sent to Ahmed Rıza by some prominent members of the CUP. See İshak Sükûti's letter dated February 25, [18]97/108. Private Papers of Ahmed Rıza (1).

345. "İhtar," *Mizan*, no. 14, April 5, 1897, 1.

346. "İ'tizar," *Mizan*, no. 6, January 25, 1897, 1; Archives d'Etat-Genève—Chancellerie, B.7, 146, "Mechveret Jung-türken Zeitung in der Schweiz," February 27, 1897/von Genf 25.2. 1897/no. 82, March 6, 1897/von Genf 4.3.1897/no. 90, March 16, 1897/von Genf 19.3.1897, Bundesarchiv-Bern, E. 21/14'248; "Le commissaire spécial l'Annemasse au Ministre de l'Intérieur: Publication turques," AE-NS-T, 1 (1897), 28.

347. "İhtar-ı Mahsus," *Mizan*, no. 19, May 1, 1897, 1.

348. "Avis," *Mechveret Supplément Français*, no. 35, May 15, 1897, 8.

349. Mehmed Murad, *Mücahede-i Milliye*, 211–12.

350. A[hmed] R[ıza], "Avis," *Mechveret Supplément Français*, no. 33, April 15, 1897, 1. The use of this motto was severely criticized by the opponents of Ahmed Rıza. See Mehmed Murad, *Mücahede-i Milliye*, 140–41, and Mağmumî, *Hakikat-i Hal*, 15.

351. "Note de la Jeune Turquie," AQSh, 19/58//669/21, and *Mechveret Supplément Français*, no. 30, March 1, 1897, 1.

352. Nuri Ahmed to İshak Sükûti, Geneva, February 9, 1897, AQSh, 19/135//175/188.

353. "Programme de la Jeune Turquie," *Mechveret Supplément Français*, no. 29, February 15, 1897, 1.

354. Doctor Nâzım to İshak Sükûti, undated [1897], AQSh, 19/106-5//759/1373. However, new developments prevented them from actualizing their decision.

355. Doctor Nâzım to Seraceddin Bey, June 8, 1896, AQSh, 19/129//47/238.

356. According to an investigation by Swiss authorities, the most active members of the CUP in Geneva were Çürüksulu Ahmed, Ahmed Hüsni, Ahmed Nuri, Ahmed Şerafeddin, Halil Muvaffak, Hasan Ârif, İshak Sükûti, Mehmed Şefik, and Zeki Bey. See "Mechveret: Jung-türken Zeitung in der Schweiz," Bundesarchiv-Bern, E. 21/14'248, and Dr. M. Kebedegg's letter dated April 13, 1897, Bundesarchiv-Bern, E. 21/14'251.

357. Mehmed Murad, *Mücahede-i Milliye*, 212.

358. İsmail Edhem to İshak Sükûti, January 24, 1897, AQSh, 19/106-3//811/1112.

359. Reşid Bey to İshak Sükûti, Cairo, April 18, 1897, AQSh, 19/106-6//262/1821.

360. L. Lâli [Mehmed Reşid] to İshak Sükûti [June 2, 1897], AQSh, 19/106-4//263/1134.

361. Fuad Bey to İshak Sükûti, June 13, 1897, AQSh, 19/106//150/1.

362. "Ey Vatandaşlar," *Mizan İlâvesi* [no. 3], February 16, 1897, Hacı Ali Bey's undated letter, AQSh, 19/135//105/941.

363. Ali Zühdi's letter dated March 6, 1897, AQSh, 19/135//31/254.

364. Vindex, "A Plot against British Interests in the Levant," *The Forthnightly Review* 61, no. 361 (June 1, 1897), 813–24.

365. Henry Norman, "The Globe and the Island," *The Cosmopolis* 6, no. 17 (May 1897), 394–406.

366. Ferdinanto Nunziante, "La questione d'Oriente e l'Arbitrato Internazionale," *La Rassegna Nazionale* 95 (May 1, 1897), 153–162, Francis de Pressenssé, "The Powers and the East in the Light of the War," *The Nineteenth Century* 41, no. 363 (May 1897), 686.

367. AQSh, 19/60//821/12. For a similar appeal issued by the CUP see "Geçmiş Zaman," *Muhibban*, no. 2 [October 28, 1909], 13–14.

368. "The Tide of the War," *Pall Mall Gazette*, April 24, 1897.

369. Kâmil Bey to İshak Sükûti, AQSh, 19/106-6//92/1778. For the similar attitude of the other opposition groups, see "[Teşekkür]," *Hürriyet*, no. 80, August 15, 1897, 1.

370. Two examples of these propaganda books are Müstecâbizâde İsmet, *Muvaffakiyet-i Osmaniye Yahud Yâdigâr-ı Zafer* (Istanbul, 1315 [1897]), and Vecihi ve Rüfekâsı, *Musavver Tarih-i Harb* (Istanbul, 1315 [1897]).

371. Ahmed Midhat's letter dated May 5, 1897 in *Le Journal des Débats*, May 10, 1897.

372. Mehmed Murad, *Müdafaa Niyetine;* Comité Ottoman d'Union and Progrès, *Affaires d'Orient;* "Kırkanbar'a Bir İhtar-ı Hâlis," *Mizan*, no. 18, May 3, 1897, 1–2; "Yine Kırkanbar," *Mizan*, no. 11, March 15, 1897, 2; "Ahmed Midhat Mel'unu," *Kanun-i Esasî*, no. 12, March 14, 1897, 8.

373. G. Umid [Aristidi], "Illusions et réalités," *Mechveret Supplément Français*, no. 35, May 15, 1897, 1. This author wrote similar articles prior to this one. See "Au feu!" *Mechveret Supplément Français*, no. 29, February 15, 1897, 1–2, and "Affaires d'Orient," *Mechveret Supplément Français*, no. 31, March 15, 1897, 1.

374. [Aristidi], "Illusions et réalités," *L'Arménie*, no. 104, June 1, 1897, 3–4.

375. "İlân-ı Mahsus," *Mizan*, no. 21, May 24, 1897, 2.

376. When, prior to this development, members in the Empire asked Murad Bey whether there was discord between the two groups (see "Tabaka-i Bâlâ Muhabirimizden," *Mizan*, no. 6, January 25, 1897, 3), Murad Bey categorically denied it. See Murad, "İzah-ı Hakikat," *Mizan*, no. 10, March 8, 1897, 1.

377. Mağmumî, *Hakikat-i Hal*, 31.

378. "Dans le monde de l'Islam: Recrudescence de fanatisme," *La Patrie*, July 4, 1897.

379. "İhtar-ı Hâlis," *Mizan*, no. 27, July 5, 1897, 2–3.

380. "Mazbata," *Mizan*, no. 22, May 31, 1897, 2.

381. Mehmed Murad, *Mücahede-i Milliye*, 214. Murad Bey's allegation was inaccurate in light of comments made by the positivists in their journals. See Editor [Edward Spencer Beesly], "The Turco-Greek War," *The Positivist Review* 5, no. 59 (June 1, 1897), 117–20.

382. "Aynen," *Mizan*, no. 22, 2.

383. "İlân-ı Mahsus," *Mizan*, no. 22, 2–3.

384. Ibid.

385. See AQSh, 19/59//102/16.

386. Tunalı Hilmi to the Romania branch, June 24, 1897, AQSh, 19/59//188/6.

387. Un membre du Comité des Jeunes-Turcs, "Jeunes Turcs," *Tribune de Genève*, June 14, 1897.

388. Mehmed Kâmil to the Paris embassy, June 29, [18]97/no. 74, *Paris*

Sefaret-i Seniyesiyle Muhaberata Mahsus Defterdir, BBA-YEE, 36/2468-2/141/XII.

389. "Au sujet du journal turc le 'Mechveret' (Paris, June 19, 1897)," and "Note pour le Ministre (Paris, June, 19, 1897)," AE-NS-T, 1 (1897), 107, 108–109.

390. İshak Sükûti to İbrahim Temo, Geneva, May 23, [18]97, AQSh, 19/106//601/1.

391. "İzah-ı Hakikat," *Mizan*, no. 25, June 21, 1897, 3.

392. Süleyman Nazif to İshak Sükûti, Paris, June 1897, AQSh, 19/106-5//280/1434.

393. Rıfat Bey to İshak Sükûti, undated letter [June 1897], AQSh, 19/106//72/736.

394. The decision was signed by Hoca Kadri, Midhat Bey, and Salih Cemal, AQSh, 19-106-4//309/1170.

395. Saman Bey's letter to Ahmed Rıza on behalf of the Barbary Coast branch and members from other close branches, June 26, 1897, Private Papers of Ahmed Rıza (1).

396. İbrahim Temo's undated letter, AQSh, 19/135//134/270.

397. He expressed his feelings in his two letters to İshak Sükûti, Tripoli of Barbary, June 3, 1897, and June 10, 1897, AQSh, 19/106//160/310, and 19/106//158/1.

398. Rauf Ahmed to İshak Sükûti, Cairo, July 12, 1897, AQSh, 19/106-6//300/1878. Identical feelings were expressed in another letter sent from the same city. See Cafer Bey to İshak Sükûti, undated [July 1897], AQSh, 19/106-7//298/2039.

399. "Müceddidin-i Osmaniyenin İnşikakı," *Hürriyet*, no. 77, July 1, 1897, 3.

400. Paris embassy to the Chamberlain's office, July 2, [18]97/no. 77, and July 4, 1897/no. 79, July 11, 1897/no. 82, *Paris Sefaretiyle Muhaberata Mahsus Defterdir*, BBA-YEE, 36/1468-2/141/XII

401. Lists entitled "Paris'de Bulunan Teb'a-i Şâhânenin Esamisini Mübeyyin Defterdir," and "Cenevre'de Bulunan Teb'a-i Şâhânenin Esamisini Mübeyyin Defterdir," Archives of the Turkish Embassy in Paris, D. 220.

402. Şerafeddin Mağmumî to İshak Sükûti, Paris, July 10, [18]97, AQSh, 19/106-7//292/1950. Also Murad Bey made the following comment in his memoirs: "I was desperate because of the situation. To quit publication honorably was so much the better and this might have made an impact [on my decision]." Mehmed Murad, *Mücahede-i Milliye*, 241.

403. The CUP center in Geneva to the Romania branch, undated, AQSh, 19/58//655/7, and Petlet to Hanotaux, Geneva, June 8, 1897, AE-NS-T, 1 (1897), 101.

404. Undated letter from Salih Cemal to İshak Sükûti, AQSh, 19/106-7//833/1972, and Şefik Bey to İshak Sükûti, Paris, September 25, [18]97, AQSh, 19/106-7//121/2024.

405. Mehmed Murad, *Mücahede-i Milliye*, 341–42.

406. Ibid., 248–49.

407. Ibid., 250.

408. Undated memorandum of the Romania branch, AQSh, 19/31//181/504.

409. Doctor Nâzım to İshak Sükûti, undated [July 1897], AQSh, 19/135//152/50.

410. Lâli [Mehmed Reşid] to İshak Sükûti [July 19, 1897], AQSh, 19/106-4//298/1132.

411. BBA-İrade-Hususî, Muharrem 1315/no. 29-312, and Safer 1315/no. 4-91.

412. İzzet Bey's coded telegram draft, BBA-YEE, 11/1194/120/5.

413. Mehmed Murad, *Mücahede-i Milliye*, 266–70.

414. Ibid., 268.

415. Detailed information about the bargains was given in two letters written by Şerafeddin Mağmumî to İshak Sükûti, dated July 20, 1897, and August 20, 1897, AQSh, 19/106-7//307/2023-2, and 19/106-4//577/1116.

416. Şerafeddin Mağmumî to İshak Sükûti, Contrexéville, July 30, 1897, AQSh, 19/106-4//298/1132.

417. The central committee to the Romania branch, AQSh, 19/58//655/7.

418. See Florian to Marcel, Contrexéville, July 27, 1897 (confidentiel); Florian to Hanatoux, Contrexéville, July 27, 1897 (très confidentiel), Florian to Hanotaux, Contrexéville, July 29, 1897 (très confidentiel), AE-NS-T, 1 (1897), 197–98, 199–201, 206–207, and "On nous écrit de Contrexéville," *Le Temps*, July 28, 1897.

419. His letter to the editor of *Le Temps* from Contrexéville, July 28, 1897. *Le Temps*, July 30, 1897.

420. The central committee to the Romania branch, AQSh, 19/58//655/7.

421. The decision of the central committee dated July 15, 1897, AQSh, 19/59//102/16.

422. Mehmed Murad, *Mücahede-i Milliye*, 282–83.

423. See Türk İnkılâp Tarihi Enstitüsü Arşivi, 82/19875.

424. Şerafeddin Mağmumî to İshak Sükûti, July 30, 1897, AQSh, 19/106-7//295/2004.

425. Rauf Ahmed to İshak Sükûti, Cairo, July 23, 1897, AQSh, 19/106-3//296/1881.

426. Mağmumî, *Hakikat-i Hal*, 34.

427. The Egyptian branch to Çürüksulu Ahmed, July 23, [18]97, AQSh, 19/58//8/1.

428. AQSh, 19/59//56/33.

429. The CUP branch in Romania to the central committee, AQSh, 19/31//181/504.

430. See Abdullah Cevdet, *Hadd-ı Te'dib: Ahmed Rıza Bey'e Açık Mektub* (Istanbul, 1912), 37.

431. Süleyman Nazif to İshak Sükûti, July 4, 1897, July 17, and August 4, 1897, AQSh, 19/106-5//59/1549, 19/106-5//293/1441, and 19/106-5//216/1449; Mithat Şükrü Bleda, *İmparatorluğun Çöküşü* (İstanbul, 1979), 18–19.

432. "La Jeune Turquie et le Sultan: Lettre de M. Halil Ganem," *L'Eclair*, August 9, 1897. He repeated his accusations later. See Halil Ganem, "Sây ü Amelimiz," *Meşveret*, no. 30, May 6, 1898, 1.

433. Un ami de la Turquie [Albert Fua], "Lettre ouverte à Mourad Bey," *Mechveret Supplément Français*, no. 40, August 1, 1897, 6. This letter was republished in *L'Eclair*, August 9, 1897.

434. "Un nouvelle protestation," *L'Eclair*, July 31, 1897.

435. "Les Jeunes Turcs et le Sultan," *La Justice*, August 14, 1897.

436. "Réponse de Mourad Bey," *L'Eclair*, August 9, 1897.

437. BBA-BEO/Hariciye Reft, 184-5/40, 1628 [January 22, 1898]/80352, and BBA-İrade-Hususî, Şa'ban 1315/no. 79-898.

438. To Goluchowski, Büyükdere, October 7, 1897/no. 42, HHStA, PA XII, Türkei Berichte, 1897 (VI-VII)/6793182.

439. "The Young Turkey Party," *Times*, August 12 and 14, 1897, "Murad Bey Returns," *New York Times*, August 18, 1897, "Orient-Chronik," *Monatschrift der Christliche Orient* 3, no. 10 (October 1897), 479–80.

440. BBA-BEO/Dahiliye Giden, 93-3/42 [September 4, 1894]/ (mümtaze).

441. BBA-BEO/Mısır Hidiviyet-i Celilesinin Muharrerat Defteri (71), 1032-68/4, E.821. S.119 [September 5, 1894].

442. Mehmed Murad, *Mücahede-i Milliye*, 150–51.

443. Ibid., 130–31.

444. The Egyptian branch to the central CUP branch in Bulgaria, August 4, 1897/no. 112, AQSh, 19/158//10/112.

445. Abdullah Cevdet to İshak Sükûti, January 17, 1897, AQSh, 19/106// 194/1.

446. Muhiddin, *Hürriyet Mücahedeleri*, 3.

447. "İlân," *Mizan*, no. 4, January 11, 1897, 2.

448. AQSh, 19/158//10/112.

449. Undated memorandum, AQSh, 19/60//233/15.

450. AQSh, 19/60//233/15.

451. Two broken-off pages of a memorandum penned by the Egyptian branch. AQSh, 19/60//238/621.

452. Arminius Vambéry, *La Turquie d'aujordhui et d'avant quatre ans* (Paris, 1898), 57–58.

453. BBA-BEO/Mısır Komiserliği Âmed: Mısır Komiseri Muhtar Paşa Hazretlerinden Gelen Tahrirat Defteridir, 764-36/4, 728/822 [December 3, 1896].

454. BBA-BEO/Hariciye Âmed, 157-5/13, 227 [March 31, 1898], and BBA-BEO/Hariciye Reft, 184-5/40, 128 [April 10, 1898].

455. See BBA-İrade-Hususî, Ramazan 1315/no. 16-1925, BBA-BEO/Tel-graf ve Posta Nezareti Giden, 585-17/10, 168 [January 17, 1898]/80888, BBA-BEO/Dahiliye Giden, 96-3/45 [February 12, 1898]/80888, BBA-BEO/Mısır Hidiviyet-i Celilesinin Muharrerat Defteri (71)-1032-68/4, S.154, E.102 [December 30, 1897].

456. Muhiddin, *Hürriyet Mücahedeleri*, 3–6.

457. Muhiddin, "İhtar," *Kanun-i Esasî*, no. 5, January 17, 1897, 4.

458. İsmail İbrahim to İbrahim Temo, Cairo, January 27, 1897, in Temo, *İttihad ve Terakki*, 96–100.

459. BBA-BEO/Dahiliye Giden, 97-3/46, 3425 [January 1, 1899].

460. He also took part in Egyptian domestic politics. For his letter to the sultan criticizing his policies, see "Abdülhamid'e Açık Ariza," *Yakın Tarihimiz* 4, no. 49, January 31, 1963, 292.

461. For his short biography, see Mahdī Bāmdād, *Sharḥ-i ḥāl-i rijāl-i Īrān dar qarn-i 12 va 13 va 14 hijrī* 4, 189–90.

462. AQSh, 19/58//1/2.

463. Ninth and tenth broken-off pages of a letter sent from Salih Cemal to İshak Süküti, AQSh, 19/106-7//929/1979.

464. BBA-YSHM, 25 B 1314/no. 1775.

465. BBA-BEO/ Hariciye Âmed, 157-5/13, 4145 [January 11, 1897]. An official organ claimed that more than five thousand *talebe-i ulûm* were sent into exile. See "Havâdis," *Kanun-i Esasî*, no. 5, January 17, 1897, 4.

466. "Havâdis," *Kanun-i Esasî*, no. 10, February 22, 1897, 7.

467. "17 Şubat İstanbul: Aynen," *Kanun-i Esasî*, no. 10, 7.

468. Currie to Salisbury, Pera, February 3, 1897/no. 74 (confidential). PRO/F.O. 78/4797.

469. Currie to Salisbury, Pera, February 18, 1897/no. 115, PRO/F.O. 78/4798.

470. See Télégramme, Tripoli [of Barbary], February 10, 1897/no. 4 (confidentiel), Cambon to Hanotaux, Pera, February 11, 1897/no. 31, Lacau to Hanotaux (Communiqué à l'Ambassade), Tripoli of Barbary, February 11, 1897/no. 13 (confidentiel), AE-NS-T, 1 (1897), 9, 10–13, 14–18.

471. "İdare-i Merkeziye'den Mevrud Bir Mektub'dan," *Mizan*, no. 6, January 25, 1897, 4.

472. G. Rizas, *Abdul Hamid: Sa vie politique et intime* (Istanbul, 1909), 442–43.

473. İshak Süküti to Doctor Nâzım, June 11, 1896, Private Papers of Bahaeddin Şâkir.

474. Grand Vizier's office to the Naval Academy [March 17, 1897], Deniz Müzesi Arşivi—Mektubî Bölümü, I, 1059/5-162.

475. There was a song composed for the CUP circa 1895. It was given in [İbrahim Temo], *Hareket*, [93]. The new and official anthem was given in Bahaeddin Sâî, *Güldeste-i Hatırât-ı Ahrar ve Eslâf-Refuge [Réfugié] Turc à Paris* Istanbul Hakkı Tarık Us Library, MS. D.38/I, 47-48. Members began singing this anthem in mid-1897. See Zahid, "İstanbul'dan," *Kanun-i Esasî*, no. 19, May 3, 1897, 6–7, Ali Fahri, *Emel Yolunda* (Istanbul, 1328 [1910]), 47–48.

476. Constantinos Dimitri to İshak Süküti, May 22, [18]97, AQSh, 19/106-4//1148/271.

477. "İstanbul'dan," *Kanun-i Esasî*, no. 6, January 25, 1896, 3–4.

478. L. Lâli [Mehmed Reşid] to İshak Süküti [July, 19 1897], AQSh, 19/106-4//198/1132.

479. Kuran, *İnkılâp Tarihimiz ve Jön Türkler*, 36.

480. Reşid, *Taşkışla Divan-ı Harbi Mukarreratına Dair Hakayık-ı Mühimme* (Istanbul, 1324 [1908]), 4–9.

481. For more information on the arrests, see Ali Fahri, *Emel Yolunda*, 5 ff.

482. See the "Warning to the Students," written by the director of the Royal School of Administration, dated [December 15, 1896], AQSh, 19/135//221/26, the note sent by the grand vizier's office to the Naval Academy [July 4, 1897], Deniz Müzesi Arşivi—Mektubî Bölümü, I, 1059/46-38.

483. See Currie to Salisbury, Therapia, August 26, 1897/no. 517-172 (confidential), PRO/F.O. 78/4806, and "Turkey," *Times*, August 5, 1897.

484. There is a socioeconomic survey prepared for the sultan by the Statistical Bureau of Ministry of Commerce and Public Works, entitled *Devlet-i Aliyye-i Osmaniye'nin Bin Üçyüz Onüç Senesine Mahsus İstatistik-i Umumisidir* IUL, Turkish Manuscripts, no. 9184/6. In pp. 65–66 of this manuscript a statistic was pro-

vided that read: "Those who endanger the internal security of the State." However, the numbers were very low (1 in Istanbul and its vicinity, 20 in Trabzon, 24 in Diyar-ıbekir, and 32 in Syria), and these do not include persons working in the Young Turk movement.

485. "Une nouvelle cour martiale en Turquie," *L'Indépendance Belge*, August 14, 1897.

486. L. Lâli to İshak Sükûti [July 5, 1897], AQSh, 19/135//262/703.

487. Çerkes Lâmi [Mehmed Reşid] to İshak Sükûti, undated, AQSh, 19/106-4//256/1141.

488. AQSh, 19/135//262/703.

489. AQSh, 19/106-4//256/1141.

490. Ali Fahri, *Emel Yolunda*, 64.

491. Most of them were under British protection. See Adam Block's memorandum dated July 7, 1897, enclosed with the letter from Currie to Salisbury, Therapia, July 9, 1897/no. 463, PRO/F.O. 78/4804.

492. The circular by the Ministry of education dated [November 11, 1897]/no. 4, *İstanbul Valiliğine Gelen Tahrirat-ı Umumiye Suretleri* IUL, Turkish Manuscripts, no. 9886, 38.

493. BBA-YSMGM, 15 Ra 1314/no. 2222.

494. "İlân-ı Resmî," *Mizan*, no. 18, May 3, 1897, 1.

495. Şerafeddin Mağmumî, *Seyahat Hatırâları: Anadolu ve Suriye'de* (Cairo, 1909), 300. The fact that the branches had been founded by him was stated in a confession by members of the CUP while being interrogated in Aleppo. See BBA-BEO/Harbiye Gelen, 221-6/29, 1 [March 14, 1902]/135853.

496. Şerafeddin Mağmumî to İshak Sükûti, July 10, [18]97, AQSh, 19/106-7//292/1950.

497. M.A., "Suriye'den Mektub," *İlâve-i Meşveret*, no. 9, April 1, 108 [1896], 3.

498. M.A., "Suriye'den Mektub," *İlâve-i Meşveret*, no. 5, February 1, 108 [1896], 3.

499. M.A., "Suriye'den Mektub," *Meşveret*, no. 22, November 8, 1896, 6.

500. To Hanotaux, Damascus, December 18, 1897/no. 29, AE-Politique Intérieure (Syrie-Liban)-Dossier Général, 2 (July-December 1897): 105, [116–17].

501. See "Suriye'den Mektub," *Meşveret*, no. 2, December 15, 107 [1895], 4, "Şam'dan Mektub," *İlâve-i Meşveret*, no. 11, May 13, 108 [1896], 3, "Suriye'den Mektub," *Meşveret*, no. 15, July 23, 108 [1896], 3–5, "Suriye'den Mektub," *Meşveret*, no. 17, August 23, 108 [1896], 3.

502. A.Y., "Şam'dan," *Mizan*, no. 172, April 16, 1896, 2462.

503. Commins, *Islamic Reform*, 94.

504. The Chamberlain's office to the commander of Aleppo and Adana [July 27, 1897]/no. 25, *Haleb ve Adana Kumandan Vekâletine Mahsus [Defter]*, BBA-YEE, 36/2170-18/147/XVI.

505. Ali Muhsin to the Chamberlain's office [July 27, 1897]/no. 26, ibid.

506. Nuri Ahmed's letter dated February 9, 1897, AQSh, 19/135//175/188.

507. The confession of Captain Galib during his interrogation. See Ali Muhsin to the Chamberlain's office [August 8, 1897]/no. 30, *Haleb ve Adana Kumandan Vekâletine Mahsus [Defter]*, BBA-YEE, 36/2170-18/147/XVI.

508. See Rauf Ahmed to İshak Sükûti, Cairo, May 28, [18]97, AQSh, 19/ 106-6//275/1875. For the text see *Osmanlı İttihad ve Terakki Cemiyeti Nizamnâmesi-Nizâm jam'iyyat al-ittihâd wa al-taraqqi al-'uthmāniyya* (n.p., n.d.).

509. Ali Muhsin to the Chamberlain's office [August 8, 1897]/no. 30, *Haleb ve Adana Kumandan Vekâletine Mahsus [Defter]*, BBA-YEE, 36/2170-18/147/ XVI.

510. BBA-BEO/Dahiliye Giden, 101-3/50, 50 [March 18, 1902]/135853; Ali Muhsin to the Chamberlain's office [April 10, 1899]/no. 31, *Haleb ve Adana Fevkâlâde Kumandanlığı Vekâletine Mahsus [İkinci] Defterdir, BBA-YEE, 36/ 39/139/XVIII.

511. "Cevab," *Mizan*, no. 179, June 4, 1896, 2520.

512. Şem'azâde Ahmed Refik Pasha to the Chamberlain's office [March 29, 1897]/no. 27, *Memurin-i Müteferrikaya Mahsus Kayd Defteridir*, BBA-YEE, 36/ 139-84/139/XX.

513. Edhem Pasha to the Chamberlain's office, June 27, 1313/no. 86, *Alasonya Ordu-yu Hümayun Umum Kumandanlığı ile Muhabere Defteridir*, BBA-YEE, 36/139-40/139/XVIII.

514. The Sublime Porte required information by a letter dated [April 8, 1897]/no. 257. The commander of the Fifth Army, Marshal Abdullah Pasha, responded the next day by sending a coded telegram. Both documents are in BBA-BEO/VGG(2): Suriye Giden: 352, 7 [April 8, 1897])/69883. The governor sent an identical telegram. See BBA-BEO/VGG(2): Arabistan Telgrafi: 956 [April 10, 1897]/no. 31.

515. Richards to Currie, Damascus, July 23, 1897/no. 38 (confidential), enclosed with the letter from Currie to Salisbury, Therapia, August 2, 1897, PRO/ F.O. 78/4805.

516. "al-Sayyid 'Abd al-Ḥamīd al-Zahrāwī," *al-Manār* 19, no. 3 (August 29, 1916), 169. For more information about al-Zahrāwī's ideas and political activities see Commins, *Islamic Reform*, 55–59, A. A. Duri, *The Historical Formation of the Arab Nation* (London, 1987), 194–98, Elie Kedourie, *Arabic Political Memoirs and Other Studies* (London, 1974), 126–29.

517. Saman, "Suriye'den Mektub," *İlâve-i Meşveret*, no. 9, April 1, 108 [1896], 1, idem, "Suriye Mektubu," *Meşveret*, no. 10, April 15, 108 [1896], 3–4, idem," Suriye'den Mektub 2," *İlâve-i Meşveret*, no. 10, 1.

518. Telegram sent by the governor of Syria, Hasan Bey, to the Chamberlain's office [July 12, 1897]/no. 105 (Suriye: 8158), BBA-BEO-VGG(2), Arabistan Telgrafi: 956. For more information about Badrān's work and activities see Commins, *Islamic Reform*, 47.

519. Telegram to the Sublime Porte [April 10, 1897]/no. 484-11860. This petition was signed by nine prominent ulema and thirty-five prominent merchants. BBA-BEO/VGG(2): Suriye Giden: 352, 7 [April 8, 1897]/69883.

520. For the political role these two prominent families played, see Linda Schatkowski Schilcher, *Families in Politics: Damascene Factions and Estates of the 18th and 19th Centuries* (Stuttgart, 1985), 136–44, 194–96.

521. "Açık Muhabere: Kastamonu'da (Lâ..) Bey'e," *Mizan*, no. 24, June 14, 1897, 4.

522. For the flight of a member of this family who was sentenced to death, see BBA-BEO/Hariciye Âmed, 155-3/11, 1275 [June 12, 1895]. 'Alī Bey, another member of this family, later led the establishment of an opposition society in Egypt called *Shams al-Islām*. See Reşid Bey, governor of Beirut, to the Cham-

berlain's office [September 17, 1899]/no. 216, *Beyrut Vilâyetiyle Muhaberata Mahsus Defter*, BBA-YEE, 36/2470-6/147/XVI.

523. See the telegram sent by the local governor of Hamidiye on the activities of 'Abd al-Qādir al-'Aẓm, who was accused of being a Young Turk. Hama [October 8, 1896]/no. 711, BBA-BEO/VGG(2): Arabistan Müteferrikası: 211. For other investigations see BBA-BEO/VGG(2): Suriye Gelen:345, 95 (telegram- [October 24, 1897])/77018, 96 and 100 [February 19, 1898]/ 81066, 73423, 5029 [December 4, 1897]/78528, and 76789.

524. See Commins, *Islamic Reform*, 93.

525. See his letter to Avram Galante, Cairo, July 27, 1908, Archives Galante, RP 112, Dossier 21, Central Archives of the Jewish People.

526. See Azimzâde Hakkı, *Türkiya'da Meclis-i Meb'usan* (Cairo, 1906).

527. See the petition by Muḥammad Rashīd Kaylānī signed by 120 persons and sent to the Sublime Porte protesting against a gendarmerie captain. Hama [March 20, 1897]/no. 11. BBA-BEO/Arabistan Müteferrikası: 211.

528. To Hanotaux, Beirut, September 28, 1897/no. 57 and no. 59, AE-T-Politique Intérieure (Syrie-Liban)- Dossier Général 2 (July-December 1897): 105, [125 and 131]; Richards to Currie, Damascus, July 23, 1897/no. 38 (confidential), enclosed with the letter from Currie to Salisbury, Therapia, August 2, 1897/no. 518, PRO/F.O. 78/4805. For the efforts of Ottoman intelligence to uncover the groups instructed by their centers in Egypt see coded telegram [September 14, 1897]/no. 47, BBA-BEO/VGG(2): Suriye-Giden: 352. For Yaḥyā Ṣa'id, who went to Egypt from Homs several times and printed antiestablishment publications, see coded telegram to the Commander of the Fifth Army [January 1, 1898]/no. 53, BBA-BEO/VGG (2): Arabistan Vilâyâtı Giden: 235.

529. See respectively Mehmed Kâmil to the Commander of Aleppo [July 27, 1897]/no. 25, and [August 23, 1897]/no. 36, *Haleb ve Adana Kumandanlığı Vekâletine Mahsus [Defter]*, BBA-YEE, 36/2470-18/147/XVI.

530. Telegram sent to Bedri Bey from the Sublime Porte, [May 6, 1897]/ no. 15, BBA-BEO/VGG(2): Arabistan Vilâyâtı Giden:235.

531. Telegram sent to the Sublime Porte from Bedri Bey [November 24, 1897]/no. 972 (Hama), BBA-BEO/VGG(2): Arabistan Müteferrikası: 211.

532. Currie to Salisbury, Therapia, August 26, 1897/no. 517-572 (confidential), PRO/F.O. 78/4806.

533. Ali Muhsin to the Chamberlain's office [June 2, 1897]/no. 22, *Haleb ve Adana Kumandan Vekâletine Mahsus [Defter]*, BBA-YEE, 36/2170-18/147/XVI.

534. Mehmed Kâmil to the acting commander of Aleppo [June 3, 1897]/ no. 23, ibid. For more information see the dispatch sent from Aleppo to Hanotaux, August 11, 1897/no. 22, AE-NS-T, 1 (1897), 219–20.

535. Chamberlain's office to the governor of Adana [June 10, 1897]/no. 20, *Gümülcine Mutasarrıfıyla, Adana, Diyar-ıbekir Vilâyetleri Muhaberat Kaydına Mahsus Defterdir*, BBA-YEE, 36/139-54/139/XXVI.

536. See Chamberlain's office to the governor of Adana, Hasan Hilmi Bey [September 20, 1897]/no. 25, and from the latter to the former [September 21, 1897]/no. 26, ibid.

537. The governor of Beirut, Nâzım Bey to the Chamberlain's office [July 6, 1897]/no. 50, *Beyrut Vilâyetiyle Muhaberata Mahsus Defter*, BBA-YEE, 36/2470-6/147/XVI; Chamberlain's office to the governor of Syria [July 7, 1897]/no. 48, *Suriye Vilâyeti ve Beşinci Ordu Kumandanlığıyla Muhaberata Mahsus Defterdir*,

BBA-YEE, 36/2470-14/147/XVI; Şem'azâde Refik Pasha to the Chamberlain's office [July 21, 1897]/no. 200, *Memurin-i Müteferrikaya Mahsus Kayd Defteridir*, BBA-YEE, 36/139-84/139/XX; to Hanotaux, Damascus, July 23, 1897/no. 14 and July 28, 1897/no. 15, AE-NS-T, 1 (1897), 193–94; 203–5.

538. The governor of Beirut, Nâzım Bey to the Chamberlain's office [July 13, 1897]/no. 51, *Beyrut Vilâyetiyle Muhaberata Mahsus Defter*, BBA-YEE, 36/2470-6/147/XVI.

539. Chamberlain's office to Şem'azâde Ahmed Refik Pasha [August 24, 1897]/no. 202, *Memurin-i Müteferrikaya Mahsus Kayd Defteridir*, BBA-YEE, 36/139-84/139/XVI; Lacau to Hanotaux, Tripoli of Barbary, September 3, 1897/no. 48, AE-NS-T, 1 (1897), 222–23.

540. A list of exiles and imprisoned leaders of the venture is provided in BBA-BEO/Harbiye Gelen, 221-6/29, 1 [March 15, 1902]/135853. For further information and additional names of the less important persons who took part in the attempt see BBA-YSMGM, 4 Z 1316/no. 1055-9180, 14 Z 1315/no. 7670, 18 Za 1319/no. 85-8786; BBA-BEO/Harbiye Giden, 259-6/67, 213 [April 16, 1902]/137166, 296 [May 1, 1902]/137834, 142317, and 162579; BBA-YP, 5 L 1316/no. 1023-8093.

541. Telegrams numbered 58, 65 (1315 [1899])/ 117521 and 118661, BBA-BEO/VGG(2): Suriye Gelen: 345.

542. For such a nucleus established by an exile in Hama, Avnullah Bey, see the governor of Aleppo to the Sublime Porte, 10 [May 9, 1898], Arabistan Müteferrikası:184/85325, BBA-BEO/VGG(2): Haleb Giden: 297.

543. See "Konstantinopel," *Pester Lloyd*, December 16, 1897.

544. Freiherr von der Goltz's memorandum dated Berlin, August 14, 1899, A. 9137, and Marschall von Bieberstein to Schillingsfürst, Pera, December 22, 1899/no. 253, A. 14945, PAAA, 645/2, Türkische Militärs, 159/3, (Bd.2-3).

545. "Haleb'den," *Osmanlı*, no. 4, December 15, 1898, 6.

546. Constans to Delcassé, Pera, November 17, 1898/no. 240, AE-NS-T, 2 (1898), 97–101.

547. For the interception of these publications in the residence of a major in the Third Army, see the commander of the Third Army, Kâzım Bey to the Chamberlain's office [January 22, 1896]/no. 13, *Üçüncü Ordu-yu Hümayun ve Kosova ve Selânik Umum Kumandanlığıyla Muhaberat Kaydına Mahsusdur*, BBA-YEE, 36/2470-7/147/XVI. During the arrests in Syria various divisions were asked to supply information about discipline in their units and the "circulation of seditious publications." See Vehbi Pasha to the Chamberlain's office [August 8, 1897]/no. 69, *Memurin-i Askeriyeye Mahsus Üçüncü Muhabere Defteridir*, BBA-YEE, 36/2470-5/147/XVI.

548. Mehmed Kâmil to the governor of Syria [July 7, 1897]/no. 48, *Suriye Vilâyeti ve Beşinci Ordu Kumandanlığıyla Muhaberata Mahsus Defterdir*, BBA-YEE, 36/2470-14/147/XVI.

549. Necmeddin Ârif to İshak Sükûti, March 17, [18]99, AQSh, 19/106-5//169/1691.

550. "Kıbrıs'da Şevket Bey'e," *Mizan*, no. 23, June 7, 1897, 3.

551. See Mufti's letter to the grand vizier [August 6, 1897], BBA-BEO/Mümtaze Kalemi: Kıbrıs, 2/45 (1315. 3. 29). For more information see BBA-BEO/Zabtiye Giden, 663-21/14, 876 [August 29, 1897])/Mümtaze:475/183. His story about his arrival in Cyprus is given in Muhiddin, *Hürriyet Mücahedeleri*, 5–6.

552. "Kıbrıs'da Vatanperver Osmanlılar," *Hürriyet*, no. 79, August 1, 1897, 3.

553. Muhiddin, *Hürriyet Mücahedeleri*, 4.

554. "Kıbrıs Müceddidlerinin Muvaffakiyetleri," *Hürriyet*, no. 82, September 15, 1897, 4. Also clashes occurred when conservative Muslims protested the demonstrations. See Muhiddin, *Hürriyet Mücahedeleri*, 4.

555. BBA-BEO/Telgraf ve Posta Nezareti Giden, 585-17/6, 72 [August 11, 1897]/mümtaze:417, BBA-İrade-Hususî, Rebiy'ülevvel 1315/no. 116–228.

556. "İhtar," *Kokonoz*, no. 5 [January 3, 1897], 1.

557. "Kokonoz'un Ciddî Birkaç Sözü," *Kokonoz*, no. 7 [March 3, 1897], 1–2.

558. BBA-BEO/Hariciye Âmed, 157-5/13, 1805 [July 28, 1897]/ Ruscuk: 2, 142 [July 31, 1897]/ Mümtaze:19, BBA-BEO/Zaptiye Giden, 663-21/14, 49 [April 19, 1897]/70217. For the distribution of appeals published by "activists," see "Vatan Havâdisi," *Hakikat*, no. 10, February 15, 1897, 4.

559. For their relations with İbrahim Temo see BBA-BEO/Bulgaristan Hülâsası, (41)-941-60/5, 91/270 [June 4, 1897], 3687/1484 and 175/500 [August 4, 1897], A MTZ HR (04). (1315.15.21), (1315.3.7). BBA-BEO/Hariciye Reft, 184-5/40, 740 [August 5, 1897] and 1318 [October 18, 1897]; BBA-BEO/Hariciye Âmed, 157-5/13, 1671 [October 14, 1897], BBA-BEO/Bulgaristan Masasının Tezkere Kayd Defteri (73), 959-60/23. To the Ottoman Foreign Ministry [August 5, 1897]/no. 175-500, and [October 16, 1897])/no. 305-844.

560. İbrahim Temo to Ahmed Zeki [November 5, 1897], AQSh, 19/31// 16/17.

561. BBA-BEO/Bulgaristan Masasının Tezkere Kayd Defteri, (73), 959-60/23, to the Ministries of police and navy [July 1, 1897]/no. 1184–368.

562. BBA-BEO/Bulgaristan Hülâsası (41), 941-60/5, no. 368/1484 (1313 [1897]).

563. BBA-BEO/Hariciye Âmed, 157-5/13, 3017 [November 14, 1897]/ Mümtaze:780; BBA-BEO/Hariciye Reft, 184-5/40, 1173 [October 23 1897]/ Mümtaze:780.

564. For an investigation of their activities see BBA-BEO/Bulgaristan Komiserliği Gelen, 672-24/1, 72 [May 9, 1897], BBA-BEO/Bulgaristan Masasının Tezkere Kayd Defteri (73), 459-60/23, to the Police Ministry, 1747/469 [August 8, 1897], BBA-BEO/Bulgaristan Hülâsası (41), 941-60/5, 803/140 [April 25, 1897], 907/190 [May 8, 1897].

565. BBA-BEO/Bulgaristan Masasının Tezkere Kayd Defteri (73), 959-60/23, 72/225 [May 22, 1897], to the Ottoman Foreign Ministry. BBA-BEO/Bulgaristan Muharrerat Defteri (90), 965-20/69, 140/803 [April 25, 1897].

566. BBA-BEO/Bulgaristan Masasının Tezkere Kayd Defteri (73), 959- 60/23, 566/1103 [February 22, 1897], 7/118 [April 22, 1898], 100/294 [June 14, 1897]. All three dispatches were sent to the Ministry of education.

567. BBA-BEO/Bulgaristan Hülâsası (41), 941-60/5, 3159/898 [December 2, 1897].

568. Ahmed Rıza to Doctor Nâzım, London, July 24, 108 [1896], Private Papers of Ahmed Rıza (1).

569. To Mustafa Bey, undated [December 1896], AQSh, 19/135//148/ 491-487.

570. Bundesarchiv-Bern, E. 21/14'248.

Chapter 5

1. Mağmumî, *Hakikat-i Hal*, 34—35. This was also underscored in the CUP communiqué sent to the press. See "Le compromis des Jeunes-Turcs," *Journal de Genève*, September 17, 1897.

2. Currie to Salisbury, Therapia, August 26, 1897/no. 517–572 (confidential), PRO/F.O. 78/4806, and 429/192.

3. "Avrupa'da Türkçe Matbuat," *Hürriyet*, no. 82, September 15, 1897, 1.

4. "Ahmed Celâleddin Paşa ve Kâmil Bey," *Hürriyet*, no. 81, August 15, 1897, 2.

5. See chapter 4 for letters written by Halil Ganem and Albert Fua. For the French press' viewpoint regarding Murad Bey and his friends' representation of the movement, see "Les Jeunes-Turcs: La décision du Parti sur les propositions du Sultan," *L'Eclair*, August 7, 1897.

6. A copy is in the Private Papers of Ahmed Rıza (2).

7. Süleyman Nazif to Ahmed Rıza, Paris, August 13, 1897, Private Papers of Ahmed Rıza (1).

8. To Doctor Nâzım, signed "your brother", and dated [June 28, 1897], Private Papers of Bahaeddin Şâkir.

9. Doctor Nâzım to İshak Sükûti, undated [1897], AQSh, 19/106-5// 121/1416.

10. Ali Vehbi Bey, *Pensées et souvenirs de l'ex Sultan Abdul-Hamid* (Paris, 1910), 28–29.

11. Political Police note, Paris, July 19, 1897, AE-NS-T, 1 (1897), 186.

12. Münir Bey reiterated his claims against Ahmed Rıza and his journal before Hanotaux on August 7, 1897, See AE-NS-T, 1 (1897), 214–16.

13. *Procès contre le Mechveret et la Jeune Turquie*, 24–29. Ahmed Rıza's good relations with Clemenceau and the latter's support of the movement continued afterward. As a matter of fact Ahmed Rıza's petition for republishing *Meşveret* was submitted to the French Ministry of the Interior with a note by Clemenceau to the Minister. See AE-NS-T, 3 (1899-1901), 165. However his relations with the Young Turks went unmentioned in the life story of Clemenceau written by his private secretary. See Jean Martet, *Le silence de M. Clemenceau* (Paris, 1929).

14. *Procès*, 6 ff. For more information concerning the trial see "Notre procès," *Mechveret Supplément Francais*, no. 44, August 15, 1897, 5; Bir Kürd [Abdullah Cevdet], "Meşveret Aleyhine Edilen İkame-i Da'va," *Meşveret*, no. 24, September 23, 1897, 1–2.

15. *Procès*, 92. This fine was found "absurd" by foreign observers. See William Miller, *Travels and Politics in the Near East* (London, 1898), 488.

16. *Procès*, 91-92; Un ami de la Turquie [Albert Fua], "Vive la France!" *Mechveret Supplément Français*, no. 44, 5.

17. "İstanbul'da Devam-ı Ahz ü Girift," *Hürriyet*, no. 81, 2; "İstanbul Muhbir-i Mahsusumuzun Mektubu," *Hürriyet*, no. 82, 3.

18. Cihadî, the military representative of the CUP in Istanbul, to İshak Sükûti and Tunalı Hilmi, August 19, [18]97, AQSh, 19/106-7//314/2072.

19. "Murad Beyle Mülâkat," *İkdam*, August 20, 1897. Translated into French and published in the organ of Ahmed Rıza, "Une interview de Mourad Bey," *Mechveret Supplément Français*, no. 42, September 1, 1897, 6–7. Also pub-

lished in *Le Soleil*, September 2, 1897, and *L'Orient* 9, no. 34, August 24, 1897, 7.

20. Mehmed Tahir, "Mazi ile Hâl," *Malûmat*, no. 81, August 22, 1897, 1–2.

21. Ali Fahri, *Emel Yolunda*, 31.

22. A list is given in three sources: A petition secretly sent to the French consul (enclosed with the dispatch from Lacau to Hanatoux, Tripoli of Barbary, September 24, 1897/no. 55), AE-NS-T, 1 (1897), 231–35; Ali Fahri, *Emel Yolunda*, 58–65, and *Şeref Vapuruyla Trablusgarb'a Nefyedilen Mağdurînin Millet Meclisine İstida'larıdır* [Istanbul, 1908?], passim.

23. The petition was dated September 15, 1897, and enclosed with the dispatch from Colonel Mustafa Bey to the Chamberlain's office [September 17, 1897], *Memurin-i Müteferrikaya Mahsus Kayd Defteridir*, BBA-YEE, 36/139-84/139/XX.

24. "Murad Bey Tarafından Yevm-i Cülûs'da Takdim Olunan Ariza-i Tebrikiye," [1898], BBA-YEE, 15/74-76/74/15.

25. Maurice Leudet, "Mourad Bey," *Le Figaro*, October 17, 1897.

26. For his appointments and salary increases, see BBA-İrade-Dahiliye, Safer 1317/no. 21-151, and Cemaziy'ülâhir 1318/no. 32-1054. Since his brother-in-law was prevented from an appointment in the military (see İsmail Bey at Golos to the Chamberlain's office [March 24, 1898], *Memurin-i Askeriyeye Mahsus Beşinci Defterdir*, BBA-YEE, 36/139-36/139/XVIII), it was impossible for him to carry out any activity. However, the stories circulated by his opponents concerning his arrest were fabricated. See "Dahile Girenlere Bir İbret," *Osmanlı*, no. 35, May 1, 1899, 2.

27. Doctor Nâzım to İshak Sükûti, undated, AQSh, 19/106-5//706/1401.

28. "Avis," *Mechveret Supplément Français*, no. 42, September 1, 1897, 1.

29. Ahmed Rıza, "İfade-i Mahsusa," *Meşveret*, no. 24, September 23, 1897, 1.

30. For his flight see BBA-YP, 5 Ca 1315/no. 586-3074, "Die Schicksale eines Übersetzer," *Pester Lloyd*, February 23, 1899.

31. Doctor Nâzım to İshak Sükûti, July 30, 1897, AQSh, 19/106-5//257/1426.

32. Şerafeddin Mağmumî to İshak Sükûti, 25 [September? 1897], AQSh, 19/106-7//831/2021.

33. "Doktor Şerafeddin Mağmumî," CTF-Tıp Tarihi ve Deontoloji Enstitüsü Arşivi, 3.

34. BBA-BEO/Hariciye Âmed, 157-5/13, 2367 [September 18, 1897]-Bucharest: 191), BBA-YSHM, 21 R 1315/no. 575.

35. See BBA-İrade-Hususî, Cemaziy'ülevvel 1315/no. 10-164, BBA-BEO/Hariciye Reft, 184-5/40, 1040 [September 30, 1897]/76104, BBA-BEO/Posta ve Telgraf Nezareti Giden, 585-17/20, 108 [September 30, 1897].

36. Ahmed Rıza, "[İhtar]," *Meşveret*, no. 25, November 9, 1897, 4.

37. BBA-YMGM, 17 B 1315/no. 2129, and 20 B 1315/no. 5038; Münir Bey to the Chamberlain's office [December 1, 1897]/no. 137, *Paris Sefaretiyle Muhabereye Mahsus Defter*, BBA-YEE, 36/2468/141/XII.

38. "İlk Meclisi Mebusan Reisi Ahmed Rıza Beyin Hatıraları(2)," *Cumhuriyet*, January 27, 1950.

39. Tevfik Bey's undated note to the sultan, BBA-YEE, 15/74-19-ç/74/15; to Hanotaux, Brussels, October 27, 1897/no. 85, AE-NS-T, 1 (1897), 274–75.

40. See BBA-BEO/Hususî İrade-i Seniye, 378-8/100, 100-675 (8169)/78201. Unfortunately it is impossible to obtain more information about the bargain between the two governments. There is a file on Ahmed Rıza in Archives Générales du Royaume Belgique, L'Administration Publique- Police des Étrangers-Dossiers Individuels: 619796. However, the documents in this file have been transferred to the cabinet of a ministry. I could not find them in the files of foreign, interior, and justice ministries.

41. BBA-YSHM, 1 Ca 1315/no. 1124.

42. See "Le Mechveret: La publication de l'édition turque à Bruxelles," *La Réforme*, December 12, 1897, "Belçika Basını," *Meşveret*, no. 28, December 24, 1897, 2.

43. BBA-YMGM, 21 C 1315/no. 1753-625, 27 B 1315/no. 5077-654; A[hmed] R[iza]," Le Mechveret Turc à la chambre Belge," *Mechveret Supplément Français*, no. 48, November 1, 1897, 3–7. Later an interpellation was given by George Lorand on Ahmed Rıza's extradition. See "Belgique," *Le Temps*, February 11, 1898.

44. BBA-BEO/Hariciye Âmed, 157-5/13, 3401 [December 21, 1897], BBA-YP, 1 B 1315/no. 857, "Un défi policier," *Mechveret Supplément Français*, no. 50, January 1, 1897, 6–7.

45. See BBA-YSHM, 1 Ca 1315/no. 640, 8 C 1315/no. 736, 13 Ş 1315/no. 1124.

46. To Schillingsfürst, Brussels, February 10, 1898/no. 16, A. 1814, PAAA, 732/3, Die Jungtürken, 198 (Bd.1-2).

47. Fesch, *Constantinople*, 337.

48. Ahmed Rıza, "Ben mi Aldanıyorum Padişah mı Aldanıyor[?]" *Meşveret*, no. 25, November 9, 1897, 1.

49. Rauf Ahmed to İshak Sükûti, March 17, [18]97, AQSh, 19/106-6//275/1873.

50. Ahmed Rıza, "Ben mi Aldanıyorum."

51. Ahmed Rıza, "İhtilâl," *Meşveret*, no. 29, January 14, 1898, 2–3.

52. See Doctors Nâzım and Bahaeddin Şakir to the director of the CUP branch in Kızanlık, Paris, June 2, 1906: "The reason for the dissolution of the old committee was not Ahmed Rıza but the covetousness and vice of Murad Bey, Sükûti, and Abdullah Cevdet. When Sultan Hamid bought those converts off with a salary of Fr 1500, he sent ambassadors to Ahmed Rıza promising him an ambassadorship." *İttihad ve Terakki Cemiyeti Merkezi'nin 1906–1907 Senelerinin Muhaberat Kopyası*, Atatürk Library, Belediye Manuscripts, no. O. 30, 49.

53. Süleyman Nazif to İshak Sükûti, Istanbul [October 29, 1897], AQSh, 19/106-5//208/1445.

54. The proceedings of this meeting are in, *Şûra-yı Ümmet-Ali Kemal Da'vası* (Istanbul, 1325 [1909]), 96–99.

55. Ali Kemal to Murad Bey, November 21, 1897, in Birol Emil, *Jön Türklere Dair Vesikalar I-Edebiyatçı Jön Türklerin Mektubları* (Istanbul, 1982), 38–39.

56. See BBA-YEE, 15/74-32-b/74/15, BBA-İrade-Hususî, Cemaziy'ülevvel 1315/no. 64-52, and Ali Kemal's letter to Ebüzziya Tevfik Bey, Paris, September 26, 1897, in "Genç Türklerin ve Millî Mücadelenin Aleyhdarı Ali Kemal'in Mektubları," *Resimli Tarih Mecmuası*, no. 3/75 (March 1956), 156–58.

57. BBA-BEO/Posta ve Telgraf Nezareti Gelen, 579-17/4, 69 [August 21, 1897].

58. "Paris Hatırâlarından-Ali Kemal Bey," *Serbestî*, December 17, 1908.

59. "Ali Kemal Bey," *Şûra-yı Ümmet*, no. 67, December 11, 1908. For more information concerning Ali Kemal's activities and his opponents' criticism, see Ali Fahri, *Açık Mektub: Ali Pinhan Bey'e* (Cairo, 1322 [1904]), 8-10, and "İttihat ve Terakki!" *Milliyet*, April 11 and 12, 1934.

60. Abdullah Cevdet to İshak Sükûti, Geneva, October 17, 1897, and Paris, October 27, 1897, AQSh, 19/106//157/211, and 19/106//155/1.

61. Detailed information about these negotiations is in a letter from Salih Cemal to İshak Sükûti, November 3, 1897, AQSh, 19/106-7//47/1963.

62. Cromer to Salisbury, Cairo, December 11, 1897/no. 290 (private), Cromer Papers, Letters to the Secretaries of State, PRO/F.O. 633/IV.

63. The protocol is dated December 2, 1897, BBA-YEE, 15/74-31-e/74/15.

64. AQSh, 19/102//156/2.

65. AQSh, 19/106-7//155/1991.

66. AQSh, 19/106-6//201/1939, and 19/102//83/1.

67. Besides the money obtained from the sale of the periodicals, pamphlets, and the seal of the Egyptian branch, the central committee was also given money by Ahmed Celâleddin Pasha. No source provides clear information about this money. Münir Pasha informed the palace that "the Young Turks succeeded in accumulating Fr 40,000, adding money from the salaries given to them, to the sum given by Ahmed Celâleddin Pasha." Münir Pasha to the Chamberlain's office, December 7, [18]97, *Paris Sefaret-i Seniyesiyle Muhaberata Mahsus Defterdir*, BBA-YEE, 36/2468/141/XII-2. Many CUP members received these salaries and gave two-thirds of the money to the organization. A list of those who received salaries is in Türk İnkılâp Tarihi Enstitüsü Arşivi, 82/18343. Another source wrote that £t 8000 was given by Ahmed Celâleddin Pasha to induce Murad Bey to return. See Edmond Fazy, *Les Turcs d'aujordhui ou le grand Karagheuz* (Paris, 1898), 270.

68. Mehmed Kâmil to the Paris embassy, August 29, 1898/no. 37, *Paris [ve Viyana Sefaret-i Seniyeleriyle Muhaberata Mahsus Defter]*, BBA-YEE, 36/2468/141/XII.

69. "İfade-i Mahsusa," *Osmanlı*, no. 1, December 1, 1897, 1, and "Teessüf mü Edelim İftihar mı?" *Osmanlı*, no. 24, November 15, 1898, 1.

70. January 8, 1898/von Genf, January 6, 1898/no. 12 and January 19, 1898/von Genf, January 17, 1898/no. 29, Bundesarchiv-Bern, E. 21/14'248.

71. AQSh, 19/61//10/1. Also see "Les réformateurs de la Turquie," *Le Temps*, January 5, 1898.

72. See "Lettre adressée à LL. EE. ministres et ambassadeurs des Grandes Puissances," *Osmanli Supplément Français*, no. 3, February 5, 1898, 1. Open letter was also sent to the ambassadors of Great Powers see AQSh, 19/60//22/66, AE-NS-T, 2 (1898), 13, PRO/F.O. 78/4943, Bundesarchiv-Bern, E. 21/14'248. Also the third issue of the French supplement was sent to the British ambassador in Istanbul. See PRO/F.O. 78/4912.

73. The most important articles in this vein were: [Edmond Lardy], "Un agent Turc à Genève," *Journal de Genève*, March 20, 1898, and Comtesse Colonna's article "La Jeune Turquie," published in two periodicals, *L'Union Républicaine du Havre*, April 11, 1898, and *Dimanches Littéraires*, April 23, 1898.

74. AQSh, 19/106//128/265.

75. "Liste d'adresses de l'Osmanli et du Mechveret, 11.8.[18]99," Bundes-archiv-Bern, E. 21/14'248.

76. Abdullah Cevdet, *Hadd-ı Te'dib*, 53; December 21, 1897/ von Genf, December 20, 1897/no. 863, Bundesarchiv-Bern, E. 21/14'248.

77. See "İstanbul'dan," *Osmanlı*, no. 2, December 15, 1897, 6, "Üsküb'den," *Osmanlı*, no. 3, January 1, 1898, 6.

78. Ahmed Rıza, "İhtar," *Meşveret*, no. 30, May 6, 1898, 1. He also praised the publication of the new central organ. See "Osmanlı ve Kanun-i Esasî Gazete-leri," *Meşveret*, no. 29, January 14, 1898. 3.

79. "Darbe-i Hak," *Osmanlı*, no. 17, August 1, 1898, 8.

80. Ali Kemal, *(Cenevre)'de Neşredilmekde Bulunan Osmanlı Gazetesinin (17) Numerolu ve (1) Ağustos 1898 Tarihli Nüshasında (Darbe-i Hak) Unvânı ile Neşredilmiş Bir Fıkra-i Müfteriyâneye Cevabdır* (Paris, [1898]).

81. AQSh, 19/60//25/1. A copy of it is in Bundesarchiv-Bern, E. 21/14'249. Bd.4.

82. Calice to Zwiedinek, Pera, November 21, 1898/no. 196-9792 (tele-gram), HHStA, PA XII 170 Türkei Berichte 1898 (X-XII), and "Affaires de Crète," *Le Temps*, November 14, 1898.

83. However, an extreme activist group also advocating foreign intervention splintered from the CUP, formed a society named Comité d'action Ottoman under the leadership of Bahri Bey, and presented a memorandum to the Great Powers. See their appeal entitled "Aux généreuses puissances protectrices de l'humanité," in AE-NS-T, 2 (1898), 46–47. It was claimed that the Armenians and the Greeks took part in the ventures of this committee. See Mehmed Kâmil to Münir Bey [March 31, 1898]/no. 162 and Münir Bey to the Chamberlain's office, April 1, [18]98/no. 163, *Paris Sefaret-i Seniyesiyle Muhaberata Mahsus Defterdir*, BBA-YEE, 36/2468/141/XII.

84. Marschall von Bieberstein to Schillingsfürst, Pera, April, 20, 1898/no. 265, A. 4822 and Berlin, April 29, 1898/no. 3704, zu.A. 4822, PAAA, 732/3, Die Jungtürken, 198 (Bd.1-2).

85. This information is in J. Michael Hagopian, "Hyphenated Nationalism: The Spirit of the Revolutionary Movement in Asia Minor and the Caucasus, 1896–1910," Ph.D. diss., Harvard University (1942), 207–209.

86. "Rapprochement des Comités," *Osmanlı Supplément Français*, no. 7, June 15, 1898, 4.

87. K.A. to İshak Sükûti, Tripoli of Barbary [September 6, 1898], AQSh, 19/106-6//276/1781. Rumors also spread throughout the provinces concerning an alliance between Young Turks and the Armenian committees. See lieutenant governor of Aydın to the Chamberlain's office [August 3, 1898]/no. 761, *Memurin-i Müteferrikaya Mahsus Kayd Defteridir*, BBA-YEE, 39/139-84/139/XX.

88. BBA-İrade-Hususî, Zilhicce 1315/no.91-1355, BBA-BEO/Hariciye Reft, 184-5/40, 315 [May 22, 1898]/84253, and BBA-BEO/Dahiliye Giden, 97-3/46 [May 22, 1898]/84253.

89. AQSh, 19/60//675/5.

90. AQSh, 19/57//143/1.

91. "Our Aim," *English Supplement to the Osmanli*, no. 1, July 15, 1898, 5–9.

92. "England and Turkey," ibid., 10–17.

93. Reşid Bey to İshak Sükûti, February 21, 1898, AQSh, 19/106-6//590/1826.

94. BBA-BEO/Hariciye Reft, 185-5/41, 767 [August 15, 1898]/88199.

95. For his participation in the Young Turk movement, see Abdurrahman, "Sultan Abdülhamid Han-ı Sânî Hazretlerine Arzuhalimdir," *Kürdistan*, no. 7 [October 19, 1898], 1.

96. "Kürdistan Gazetesi," *Osmanlı*, no. 35, May 1, 1899, 4, and "İlân," *Osmanlı*, no. 65, August 1, 1900, 8.

97. BBA-İrade-Hususî, Rebiy'ülâhir 1318/no. 48-280; Münir Bey to the Chamberlain's office, February 21, [18]99/no. 101, *Paris [ve Viyana Sefaret-i Seniyeleriyle Muhaberata Mahsus Defter]*, BBA-YEE, 36/2468/141/XII-1.

98. "Teşekkür," *Beberuhi*, no. 2, March 1, 1898, 1. For its publication and circulation within the empire see Archives d'Etat-Genève-Chancellerie, B. 8, 18; Headquarters of Geneva Political Police to Federal Attorney General, May 18, 1898/P.P.200, Bundesarchiv-Bern, E. 21/14'248, Bundesarchiv-Bern, E. 21/14'249. Bd.2 (Beilage:4); BBA-BEO/Dahiliye Giden, 96-3/45, 3357 [February 7, 1898])/80803.

99. To the Ottoman Foreign Ministry [January 12, 1899], and from Tevfik Pasha to Âtıf Bey, March 13, 1899/no. 48; and from the latter to the former, March 16, 1899, Dışişleri Bakanlığı Hazine-i Evrak Arşivi, Siyasî D. 178; BBA-YP, 11 S 1315/no. 267.

100. AQSh, 19/60//675/5.

101. BBA-BEO/VGG(2), Devâir Mühimme: 1347, (6)-Hariciye [December 1, 1896]/no. 3892-11661; memorandum dated August 13, 1898 "Création d'une consulat Ottoman à Genève," AE-NS-T, 2 (1898), 88 ff. The story of the establishment of an Ottoman consulate in Geneva was well summarized in a German newspaper later. See "Das türkische Generalkonsulat in Genf," *Frankfurter Zeitung*, December 28, 1900. Also a Swiss daily gave similar information. See "Lettre de Turquie," *La Gazette de Lausanne*, December 1, 1900. The Young Turks and their Swiss sympathizers denounced this development. See "A propos de l'installation du consulat Turc à Genève," *Osmanli Supplément Français*, no. 5, April 5, 1898, 2–4, D.E., "L'Activité consulaire!!" *Osmanli Supplément Français*, no. 7, June 15, 1898, 2–3, and "Le commissaire spécial de surveillance administrative au Ministre de l'Intérieur, Annemasse, August 10, 1898," AE-NS-T, 2 (1898), 89.

102. BBA-İrade-Hususî, Zilkade 1315/no. 18-1140.

103. AE-NS-T, 2 (1898), 89. Prior to this mission he had been sent before the Armenian committees and some prominent Young Turks. See Currie to Salisbury, Constantinople, July 9, 1897/no. 464, PRO/F.O. 78/4804.

104. His activities as the chargé d'affaires of the Paris embassy created a diplomatic problem between the French and Ottoman governments. See BBA-YSHM, 7 S 1315/no. 161, 24 S 1315/no. 250, 29 S 1315/no.282, 29 S 1315/no. 286, 8 Ra 1315/no. 341, 18 C 1315/no. 839.

105. AE-NS-T, 2 (1898), 91–93.

106. İshak Sükûti to Doctor Nâzım, February 21, 1898, Private Papers of Bahaeddin Şakir.

107. "Beyân-ı Hâl ve İlân," *Osmanlı*, no. 4, January 15, 1898, 1.

108. Fr 20,000 was sent to the agents in "Istanbul, Bulgaria, and other places." AQSh, 19/102//348/22.

109. "İstanbul'da Hürriyetperverân-ı Osmaniyenin İctima'-yı Hafîsi ve Ermeniler," *Sada-yı Millet*, no. 4, March 27, 1898, 2.

110. "Açık Muhabere," *Osmanlı*, no. 23, October 28, 1898, 1.

111. *Saraya Karşı İcra Edilecek Harekât-ı Taarruziyeyi Müberhen Ta'limat*, Bundesarchiv-Bern, E. 21/14'248.

112. BBA-YEE, 19/328 (mükerrer)/130/57.

113. Currie to Salisbury, Constantinople, April 3, 1898/no. 207, PRO/F.O. 78/4914.

114. Romels to Goluchowski, Salonica, October 19, 1898/no. 50, HHStA, PA, XXXVIII 406 Konsulat Saloniki 1898.

115. Mustafa Ragıb to İshak Sükûti, Berlin, March 15, [18]98, AQSh, 19/106-4//566/1284.

116. Mustafa Ragıb's undated [1903?] draft, AQSh, 19/103//657/688.

117. The copy of Tevfik Pasha's letter to von Bülow, Berlin, June 23, 1898, Bayerisches Hauptstaatsarchiv, Bayerische Gesandtschaft in Berlin, no. 1174 (Politische Versammlungen 1876–1914).

118. See the note sent from Königliches Bayerisches Staatsministerium to Königliche Gesandschaft in Berlin, Munich, August 27, 1898/no. 481, ibid., and their notes dated September 5, 1898, A. 10295, enclosures dated October 13, 1898, A. 11769, and zu.A. 11769, PAAA, 732/2, Die Jungtürken, 198 (Bd.1-2).

119. Ferah Şadi to İshak Sükûti, May 6, [18]98, AQSh, 19/106-2//298/330.

120. See Âkil Muhtar to İshak Sükûti, Paris, April 1, [18]98, AQSh, 19/106-2//298/330, and two undated letters sent from Doctor Nâzım to İshak Sükûti, AQSh, 19/106-5//702/1399, and 19/106-5//881/1382.

121. İshak Sükûti to Doctor Nâzım, February 21, 1898, Private Papers of Bahaeddin Şakir.

122. "Cevab-ı Umumî," *Osmanlı*, no. 10, April 15, 1898, 3.

123. Diran Kelekyan's letter dated [July 1, 1898], BBA-YEE, 15/74-26-c/74/15.

124. "Hakka Taaddi," *Hakk-ı Sarih*, no. 3, August 9, 1900, 4.

125. "Zât-ı Şâhâne'ye Açık Mektub," *Kanun-i Esasî*, no. 24 [January 6, 1898], 1.

126. "Tashih," *Kanun-i Esasî* 2, no. 2 [January 17, 1898], 1.

127. BBA-BEO/Serasker Reft, 257-6/65, 25 [March 16, 1898], 162 [April 10, 1898], BBA-BEO/Mısır Hidiviyet-i Celilesinin Tezâkir Defteri (62), 1036-68/8, 1068-160 [March 16, 1898], 805-17 [April 10, 1898].

128. Salih Cemal İshak Sükûti, Cairo, February 28, [1]898, AQSh, 19/106-7//586/1975.

129. Salih Cemal to İshak Sükûti, undated [1898], AQSh, 19/106-7//85/1974.

130. AQSh, 19/106-7//586/1975.

131. Pertev Tahsin to İshak Sükûti, October 28, [18]98, AQSh, 19/106-6//280/1765.

132. Pertev Tahsin to İshak Sükûti, December 27, 1898, AQSh, 19/106-6//280/1765.

133. Salih Cemal to İshak Sükûti, October 17, [18]98, AQSh, 19/106-6//297/1766.

134. "Bismillâhirrahmanirrahim," *Osmanlı (2)*, no. 3, January 1, 1898, 1.

135. "Ağyara İ'tizâr Eşrara İnzâr," *Kanun-i Esasî*, no. 76 [January 5, 1899], 1–2.

136. See [Hoca Kadri], "Memalik-i Osmaniye Akvâmına Bir Nazar," *Havatır*, no. 1 [August 17, 1898], 3–4, "Emr-i Hilâfet," *Havatır*, no. 2 [September 1, 1898], 1.

137. Ottoman authorities described the newspaper as "incredibly seditious." BBA-BEO/Hariciye Reft, 185-5/41, 868/88998.

138. It menaced the palace by establishing a large "anarchist society of Armenians and Young Turks." See "Nasihat: 6, Hafiyelere," *Nasihat*, no. 3, July 27, 1898, 3.

139. "Nasihat: 1, Padişaha," *Nasihat*, no. 1, June 29, 1898, 1–3, and "Nasihat: 3, Genc Türklere," ibid., 4.

140. Information concerning his activities was given in an unsigned letter sent to the khedive, dated March 10, 1900, Abbas II Papers, Durham University, F. 39/2. After publishing three issues of his journal he was bought off by the Palace and given directorship of Marmaris Harbor. However since he found his salary insufficient he fled once again to Cyprus and then sojourned in Egypt where he took part in the Young Turk activities. See the spy report dated January 18, 1900, Abbas II Papers, Durham University, F. 26/286.

141. "Inna al-nafs ammāratun bi al-sū'i," *Enîn-i Mazlum*, no. 8, July 12, 1899, 63–64.

142. The developments in the Egyptian branch were depicted in a play written after the Young Turk revolution. The story is accurate but somewhat exaggerated. See Bekir Fahri, *Jönler Mısır'da* (Istanbul, 1326 [1327-1911?]).

143. Burhan Bahaeddin to İshak Sükûti, Nicosia, October 19, [1897], AQSh, 19/106-1//212/495.

144. Burhan Bahaeddin to İshak Sükûti, Nicosia, February 3, [18]98, AQSh, 19/106-1//497/59.

145. Burhan Bahaeddin to İshak Sükûti, April 9, [18]99, AQSh, 19/106-1//205/501.

146. Ahmed Rıfat to İshak Sükûti, Berlin, December 15, [18]98, AQSh, 19/106//40/1.

147. The letter sent by the founder of the branch to İbrahim Temo, dated June 23, 1898, Temo, *İttihad ve Terakki*, 74–76. For more information see "Adana ve Mersin'den Aldığımız Hususî Mektublar," *Osmanlı(2)*, no. 2, December 15, 1897, 7.

148. AQSh, 19/135//111/135.

149. Tahsin Bey to the Commander of Aleppo and Adana [August 23, 1898]/no. 140, *Haleb ve Adana Kumandan Vekâletine Mahsus [Defter]*, BBA-YEE, 36/2470-18/147/XVI.

150. The lists were given in the dispatch from Ali Muhsin to the Chamberlain's office [September 10, 1898]/no. 147. Ibid.

151. Governor Bahri Bey to the Chamberlain's office [October 30, 1898]/no. 160, *Girid Fırka-i Hümayûn Kumandanlığıyla Muhaberat Kaydına Mahsus Defterdir*, BBA-YEE, 36/139-45/139/XVIII.

152. Governor Bahri Bey to the Chamberlain's office [November 17, 1898]/no. 62, ibid.

153. Some of them were later released by the local court, arousing the governor's anger. See Bahri Bey to the Chamberlain's office [February 7, 1899]/no. 31, *Trablusgarb Vilâyet ve Kumandanlığı, Haleb Vilâyet ve Adana Vilâyet, Basra Vilâyet ve Kumandanlığı, Selânik Vilâyeti ile Muhaberata Mahsus Defter*, BBA-YEE, 36/139-42/139/XVIII.

154. Necmeddin Ârif to İshak Süküti, January 1, [18]99, AQSh, 19/106-5/
/168/1696.

155. "Ziya Gökalp'in Muallimi Kim İdi[?]" *İkdam*, October 27, 1924.

156. Abdullah Cevdet, *Bir Hutbe Hemşehrilerime* (Cairo, 1909), 3.

157. Behçet Bey to İshak Süküti, Diyar-ıbekir [July 16, 1897], AQSh, 19/
135//52/231-301.

158. Fahri Bey to İshak Süküti, undated letter, AQSh, 19/106-2//107/766.

159. Enver Behnan Şapolyo, *Ziya Gökalp, İttihadı Terakki ve Meşrutiyet
Tarihi* (Istanbul, 1974), 72.

160. Temo, *İttihad ve Terakki*, 246.

161. For their activities see Governor Halid Bey to the Chamberlain's office
[February 17, 1899]/no. 48, [February 23, 1899]/no. 49, [March 3, 1899]/no.
50, [March 5, 1899]/no. 51, [March 8, 1899]/no. 53, *Gümülcine Mutasarrıfıyla,
Adana, Diyar-ıbekir Vilâyetleri Muhaberat Kaydına Mahsus Defterdir*, BBA-YEE,
36/139-54/139/XVIII.

162. Chamberlain's office to the commander of Diyar-ıbekir [April 18,
1899]/no. 131, *Dördüncü Ordu-yu Hümayun Müşiriyetiyle Muhaberata Mahsus
Defter*, BBA-YEE, 36/2470-4/147/XVI.

163. Governor Halid Bey to the Chamberlain's office [April 1, 1900]/no. 5,
and [February 14, 1901]/no. 10, *[Diyar-ıbekir Vilâyetiyle Muhaberata Mahsus
Defter]*, BBA-YEE, 36/2470-33/147/XVI.

164. Lieutenant Colonel Es'ad Bey to the Chamberlain's office [July 17,
1898]/no. 695, *Memurin-i Müteferrikaya Mahsus Kayd Defteridir*, BBA-YEE,
36/139-84/139/XX.

165. Murad Bey's proposal dated [October 26, 1895], Private Papers of Şevket Bey.

166. Tunalı Hilmi to İshak Süküti, December 3, [1898], AQSh, 19/106-3/
/592/99.

167. Ali Fahri, *Emel Yolunda*, 227–28.

168. Colonel Mustafa to the Chamberlain's office [December 2, 1897]/no.
283, *Memurin-i Müteferrikaya Mahsus Kayd Defteridir*, BBA-YEE, 36/139-84/
139/XX, and K.A. to İshak Süküti, Tripoli of Barbary [May 4, 1898], AQSh, 19/
106-6//569/1785.

169. Lieutenant Colonel Es'ad Bey in Baghdad to the Chamberlain's office
[July 5, 1898]/no. 601, and [July 6, 1898]/no. 603. *Memurin-i Müteferrikaya
Mahsus Kayd Defteridir*, BBA-YEE, 36/139-84/139/XX.

170. Mehmed Kâmil to Colonel Mustafa and Captain Hasan Bey [November
23, 1897]/no. 285, and these officers to the Chamberlain's office [November 25,
1897]/no. 289, ibid.

171. Chamberlain's office to Colonel Mustafa Bey in Tripoli of Barbary
[December 1, 1897]/no. 291, ibid.

172. Abdullah Cevdet, "Hüseyin Tosun'u Gaybettik," *İçtihat*, no. 289, January 15, 1930, 5323.

173. Namık Bey to the Chamberlain's office [August 28, 1898]/no. 23,
*Trablusgarb Vilâyet ve Kumandanlığı, Haleb Vilâyet ve Adana Vilâyet, Basra
Vilâyet ve Kumandanlığı, Selânik Vilâyeti ile Muhaberata Mahsus Defter*, BBA-
YEE, 36/139-42/139/XVIII.

174. Decipher from the Chamberlain's office to the Governorship and Com-
mandership of Tripoli of Barbary [October 29, 1899]/no. 5312-225, *Mabeyn'den
Devâir ve Vilâyetlerle Bâzı Zevata Yazılan Tezkere ve Muharrerat Müsveddelerini
Hâvi Dosya Defteri*, BBA-YEE, 36/398/146/XIV.

175. Kâzım Nami Duru, *Arnavutluk ve Makedonya Hatıralarım* (Istanbul, 1959), 6, 11–12.

176. From Durazzo through Derviş Hima, receipt no. 1150, Fr 58, January 23, [18]97, AQSh, 19//62//109/2.

177. Tunalı Hilmi to İshak Sükûti, January 3, [1898], AQSh, 19/106-3//592/99.

178. "Arnavudluk'dan Mektub-i Mahsus," *Osmanlı*, no. 15, July 1, 1898, 3. On the other hand an anti-Young Turk Albanian organ asserted that "Albanians' loyalty" to the sultan "was an [enormous] obstacle before [the Young Turks]." See "Shqipetaret dhé ana é Turqvé Riñ," *Albania*, vol. C (1899), [Supplement to no. 3], 55.

179. Mehmed Kâmil to the Governor and Commander of Ioánnina [January 23, 1898], *Yanya Vali ve Kumandanlığıyla Muhaberata Mahsus Defterdir*, BBA-YEE, 36/139-84/139/XX.

180. Niyazi Bey in Golos to the Chamberlain's office [March 7, 1898]/no. 413, *Memurin-i Müteferrikaya Mahsus Kayd Defteridir*, BBA-YEE, 36/139-84/139/XX.

181. The acting commander of the Third Army, Hüseyin Fevzi, to the Chamberlain's office [March 27, 1898]/no. 46, and [April 2, 1898]/no. 50, *Üçüncü Ordu-yu Hümayun Müşiriyet-i Celilesiyle Muhaberata Mahsus Defterdir*, BBA-YEE, 36/2470-11/147/XVI, and Major Mehmed Ali in Salonica to the Chamberlain's office [April 2, 1898]/no. 7, *Memurin-i Askeriyeye Mahsus Altıncı Muhaberat Defteridir*, BBA-YEE, 36/139-43/139/XVIII.

182. Âtıf Bey in Salonica to the Chamberlain's office [March 1, 1898]/no. 390, and [August 7, 1898]/no. 778, *Memurin-i Müteferrikaya Mahsus Kayd Defteridir*, BBA-YEE, 36/139-84/139/XX.

183. Âbidin Bey to the Chamberlain's office [December 11, 1898]/no. 76, *Cezaîr-i Bahr-i Sefîd ile Muhaberat Kaydına Mahsusdur*, BBA-YEE, 36/139-46/139/XVIII.

184. The lieutenant governor of Aydın to the Chamberlain's office [April 22, 1898]/no. 449, and [August 3, 1898]/no. 761, *Memurin-i Müteferrikaya Mahsus Kayd Defteridir*, BBA-YEE, 36/139-84/139/XX.

185. The commander of Izmir, Osman Pasha, to the Chamberlain's office [August 20, 1898]/no. 840, ibid.

186. Mehmed Kâmil to Reşid Bey [June 28, 1898]/no. 100, and the latter's response [June 29, 1898]/no. 101, *Beyrut Vilâyetiyle Muhaberata Mahsus Defter*, BBA-YEE, 36/2470-6/147/XVI.

187. BBA-BEO/Hariciye Âmed, 158-5/41, 565 [April 27, 1898], and BBA-BEO/Hariciye Reft, 184-5/40, 219 [May 1, 1898]/83872.

188. İbrahim Temo's letter dated, October 16, [18]98, AQSh, 19/106-3//270/1066.

189. Temo, *İttihad ve Terakki*, 112.

190. Ibid., 116.

191. Ibid., 118–19.

192. [İbrahim Temo], "Kariîn-i Kirâma," *Sada-yı Millet*, no. 1, March 5, 1898, 1.

193. V[asile] M. Kogălniceau, "Osmanlı Milleti Romen Kavmi," *Sada-yı Millet*, no. 1, 2.

194. BBA-BEO/Posta ve Telgraf Nezareti Gelen, 579-17/4, 118 [March 8, 1898], and BBA-BEO/Hariciye Reft, 184-5/40, 1 [March 13, 1898])/81708.

195. BBA-YP, 17 L 1315/no. 1199, BBA-BEO/Hariciye Reft, 184-5/40,

1802 [March 9, 1898]/81622, BBA-BEO/Hariciye Âmed, 157-5/13, 4038 [March 10, 1898].

196. See "Osmanlı ve Kanun-i Esasî Gazeteleri," *Meşveret*, no. 29, 3, "Sada-yi Millet," *Osmanli Supplément Français*, no. 5, 4.

197. Kadri Bey's letter dated [March 14, 1898], AQSh, 19/135//117/783.

198. "Havâdis-i Dahiliye," *Sada-yı Millet*, no. 9, May 1, 1898, 1–2.

199. "Explusarea lui Cadry Bey," *Epoea*, April 23, 1898.

200. BBA-BEO/Hariciye Âmed, 157-5/13, 62 [March 19, 1898]. For the protest of the Geneva center over these developments, see "Les Jeunes Turcs et la Roumanie," *Osmanli Supplément Français*, no. 10, January 5, 1899, 7.

201. "Avane-i Huvvane-i Şehriyarîden Melhameler," *Osmanlı*, no. 21, October 1, 1898, 6.

202. "Havâdis-i Hariciye," *Muvazene*, no. 23 [January 9, 1898], 4.

203. "Mağmumî Bey'e," *Muvazene*, no. 11 [November 17, 1897], 4.

204. "Bulgaristan Havâdisi," *Muvazene*, no. 11, 2, BBA-BEO/Bulgaristan ve Şarkî Rumeli Hülâsa Defteri (43), 942-60/6, 888-244 [May 29, 1898]. A MTZ. (04) DH (1314. 4. 6), BBA-BEO/Mümtaze Kalemi Şarkî Rumeli Evrakı, 39/39 (1314. 6. 18).

205. "Havâdis," *Osmanlı*, no. 5, February 1, 1898, 8, and "Bulgaristan Havâdisi," *Muvazene*, no. 16 [December 22, 1897], 2.

206. "Teşekkür," *Meşveret*, no. 18 September 8, 108 [1896], 6.

207. BBA-BEO/Hariciye Âmed, 157-5/13, 5 [March 13, 1898], BBA-BEO/Hariciye Âmed, 158-5/14, 753 [May 16, 1898].

208. BBA-BEO/Bulgaristan Hülâsası (41), 941-60/5, 3570-1019 [January 9, 1898] A MTZ 04 DH (1315. 8. 16), 854-3325 [December 22, 1897]), A MTZ 04 HR (1315. 7. 29), BBA-BEO/Bulgaristan Komiserliği Reft, 677-24/6, 186-899 [December 22, 1897], BBA-BEO/Bulgaristan Masasının Tezkere Kayd Defteri (73), 959-60/23, 386-1019 [January 9, 1898]).

209. BBA-BEO/Bulgaristan ve Şarkî Rumeli Hülâsa Defteri (43), 942-60/6, 409-1092 [February 7, 1898].

210. BBA-BEO/Dahiliye Giden, 96-3/45, 3101 [January 4, 1898].

211. BBA-BEO/Hariciye Âmed, 157-5/13, 3325 [December 13, 1897]. The central organ criticized Kaptchef and recommended him to pursue Ottomanism instead of separatism. See "Makedonya Komitesi," *Osmanlı*, no. 29, February 1, 1899, 1.

212. See BBA-BEO/Hariciye Âmed, 157-5/13, 2671 [October 14, 1897], BBA-BEO/Bulgaristan Komiserliği Muharrerat Defteri (90), 965-60/29, 770-267 [October 18, 1897].

213. BBA-BEO/Hariciye Âmed, 157-5/13, 1917 [November 6, 1897], 3036 [November 16, 1897], 3159 [November 28, 1897].

214. "Havâdis," *Balkan*, no. 6, May 25, [18]98, 2.

215. A.F., "Ruscuk'da Ahmed Zeki Efendi'ye," *Balkan*, no. 4, May 11, [18]98, 2.

216. *Balkan*, no. 4, 1–2.

217. *Balkan*, no. 4, 1, "Bulgaristan Havâdisi," *Muvazene*, no. 44 [July 8, 1898], 2, Ibrahim Thémo, "La Bulgarisation de L'Albanie," *Albania*, vol. B, no. 4 (July 15–31, 1898), 63–64.

218. BBA-BEO/Bulgaristan Komiserliği Gelen, 672-24/1, 111 [June 21, 1898], 115 [June 23, 1898].

219. BBA-BEO/Bulgaristan ve Şarkî Rumeli Hülâsa Defteri (43), 942-60/

6, 360-1184-1201, A.MTZ. (04) HR (1316. 1. 30), 111/332 [June 27, 1898], A.MTZ 04 DH (1316. 2. 2), 115/333 [June 23, 1898], A.MTZ (04) DH (1316. 2. 4), BBA-BEO/Hariciye Âmed, 158-5/14, 671 [May 10, 1898].

220. İsmail Hakkı Tevfik Okday, *Bulgaristan'da Türk Basını* [Ankara, 1980], 21, 38–39.

221. BBA-BEO/Bulgaristan ve Şarkî Rumeli Hülâsa Defteri (43), 942-60/ 6, 741-286 [December 25, 1898], A.MTZ 04 HR (1316. 8. 26), 742-287 [December 25, 1898], A.MTZ 04 HR (1316. 8. 20),777-3243 [January 11, 1899]), A MTZ 04 HR (1316. 8. 28).

222. "Tebşir ve İbret," *Osmanlı*, no. 29, 7.

223. "Tarafımızdan Açık Mektub," *Osmanlı*, no. 11, May 1, 1898, 3.

224. İshak Sükûti's letter to Tunalı Hilmi dated September 20, 1899 in Kuran, *İnkılâp Tarihimiz ve İttihad ve Terakki*, 128.

225. See Deliormanlı Bir Molla, "Köstence'den," *Osmanlı*, no. 24, November 1, 1898, 8; see also "Ruscuk'dan," *Osmanlı*, no. 6, February 15, 1898, 4.

226. "Ulemamıza, Vaizlerimize Numûne-i İmtisâl," *Osmanlı*, no. 32, March 15, 1899, 2.

227. A copy of İbrahim Temo's letter was sent to the palace enclosed with the letter of Âbidin Bey to the Chamberlain's office [December 18, 1898], *Cezaîr-i Bahr-i Sefîd ile Muhaberat Kaydına Mahsusdur*, BBA-YEE, 36/139-46/ 139/XVIII.

228. "Paris'de Münteşir Cerâid-i Mu'tebereden (La Diplomatie) Gazetesine İstanbul Muhbiri Tarafından Yazılan Mektubun Sureti," *Osmanlı*, no. 9, April 1, 1898, 6–7; Abdullah Cevdet, *Hadd-ı Te'dib*, 39–41.

229. "Teessüf mü Edelim İftihar mı?" *Osmanlı*, no. 24, 2.

230. M. Samim to Şerafeddin Mağmumî, May 27, [1898], AQSh, 19/135/ /226/1.

231. L. Lâli [Mehmed Reşid] to İshak Sükûti, [January 30, 1898], AQSh, 19/106-4//200/1139.

232. BBA-İrade-Hususî, Safer 1316/no. 34-167, and no. 69-308; Deniz Müzesi Arşivi—Mektubî Bölümü, I, 1119/218, July 26, 1898.

233. Lacau to Delcassé, Tripoli of Barbary, July 2, 1898/no. 37, AE-NS-T, 2 (1898), 86; to Schillingsfürst, Tripoli of Barbary, July 4, 1898/no. 204, A. 8359, PAAA, 732/2, Die Jungtürken, 198 (Bd.1-2).

234. "Son Haber," *Osmanlı*, no. 16, June 15, 1898, 8.

235. BBA-İrade-Hususî, Rebiy'ülâhir 1316/no. 24-372.

236. BBA-YSHM, 12 R 1316/no. 635.

237. Archives of the Turkish Embassy in Paris, D. 287.

238. BBA-BEO/Hususî İrade-i Seniye, 378-8/101 [August 21, 1898]/ 88428.

239. Münir Bey to the Chamberlain's office, November 12, [18]99/no. 21, *Paris Sefaret-i Seniyesiyle Muhaberata Mahsus Defterdir*, BBA-YEE, 36/2468/ 141/XII.

240. Abdullah Cevdet's note on behalf of the Geneva center, Archives of the Turkish Embassy in Paris, D. 287. A photo of this document was provided to the Swiss authorities in order to prove that the CUP leaders were blackmailers. Bundesarchiv-Bern, E. 21/14'248.

241. İshak Sükûti's note on behalf of the Geneva center. Private Papers of Salih Münir Pasha. A photo of this document is in Bundesarchiv-Bern, E. 21/ 14'248.

242. See Reşid Bey to İshak Sükûti, 29 [?] [18]98, AQSh, 19/106-6//311/ 1824, and Nuri Ahmed to İshak Sükûti, October 2, 1898, AQSh, 19/106-5// 243/1623.

243. Undated [1898] letter from İbrahim Temo to İshak Sükûti, AQSh, 19/ 31//773/95.

244. Albert Fua to İshak Sükûti, Colombes, October 10, 1898, AQSh, 19/ 106-2//256/373, and Abdullah Cevdet to İshak Sükûti, December 4, [18]98, AQSh, 19/106//181/1.

245. "Merkezin Emriyle Vükelâ-yı Fehâm Hazerâtına," *Osmanlı*, no. 26, December 15, 1898, 1–2.

246. Le Comité Ottoman d'Union et Progrès, *Un horrible assassinat commis sur l'ordre spécial du Sultan Abdul-Hamid II: Assassinat de Midhat Pacha d'après les documents de la Jeune Turquie* (Genève, 1898).

247. Abdullah Cevdet to İshak Sükûti, Paris, December 19, [18]98, AQSh, 19/106//184/2.

248. "Turkey," *Times*, January 28, 1899.

249. "Turkey," *Times*, January 31, 1899.

250. CUP members in the Istanbul prison sent a secret letter to Queen Victoria imploring her humanitarian intervention. (PRO/F.O. 78/4943). Sanderson later asked Salisbury's opinion about helping those prisoners. But the latter simply refused any assistance. See the minutes of Sir Thomas and Lord Salisbury on the letter from Currie to Salisbury, April 3, 1898/no. 207, PRO/F.O. 78/4914.

251. Entzifferung, Bern, March 23, 1899/no. 33. For further applications see Entzifferung, Pera, March 18, 1899/no. 98, and March 24, 1899/no. 110, A. 3222, and A. 3483, PAAA, 732/3, Die Jungtürken, 198 (Bd.1-2).

252. The report presented by the Swiss embassy in Berlin, March 30, 1899 (vertraulich und persönlich), A. 3720, PAAA, 732/3, Die Jungtürken, 198 (Bd.1-2). Additional information was given by a report sent by the German ambassador in Bern to Auswärtiges Amt, Bern, March 30, 1899/no. 34, A. 3808 and zu. A. 3808, PAAA, 732/3, Die Jungtürken, 198 (Bd.1-2).

253. To von Bülow, Entzifferung, Bern, March 23, 1899/no. 32, A. 3247 and to von Bülow, Bern, March 30, 1899/no. 34, A. 3808, PAAA, 732/2, Die Jungtürken, 198 (Bd.1-2).

254. Marschall von Bieberstein to von Bülow, Pera, April 6, 1899/no. 59, A. 4183, and zu. A. 4183, PAAA, 732/3, Die Jungtürken, 198 (Bd.1-2).

255. Note of Political Bureau, Bern, March 27, 1899 (P.P. 252-konfidentiell) and Müller's note dated March [28?], 1899 (P.P.252), Bundesarchiv-Bern, E. 21/ 14'248.

256. Investigation report sent to the Federal Ministry of the Interior, Geneva, April 10, 1899 (P.P.252), Bundesarchiv-Bern, E. 21/14'248.

257. Münir Bey presented his application on April 13, 1899, and the embassy passed on his appeal to the Political Bureau on April 14, 1899/no. 236, Bundesarchiv-Bern, E. 21/14'248,

258. See investigation report dated Bern, April 15, 1899 (P.P.175), and the report enclosed with the translations, Bern, April 24, 1899 (P.P. 175), Bundesarchiv-Bern, E. 21/14'248.

259. Münir Bey's letter, Paris, April 8, 1899, and enclosed photos taken from the documents, Bundesarchiv-Bern, E. 21/14'248.

260. Constans to Delcassé, Pera, March 15, 1899, AE-NS-T, 3 (1899–1901),

23. Constans was accused by the Young Turks of conspiring against them. See Ali Nouri, *Sâye-i Şâhânede: Unter dem Scepter des Sultans* (Berlin, 1905), 174 ff.

261. "Note pour le Ministre, Paris, April, 14, 1899," AE-NS-T, 3 (1899–1901), 117–20.

262. Note "Communiquer à M. Louis Renault, March 2, 1899," AE-NS-T, 3 (1899-1901), 24.

263. Léon Gattegno to İshak Sükûti, Lyon, February 1, 1897, AQSh, 19/106-4//190/1147.

264. Münir Bey's application, Paris, February 26, 1899, the answer given to him by the French Foreign Ministry, March 23, 1899, a report concerning the activities of the two Young Turks, April 14, 1899, a police investigation report, May 3, 1899, and the appeal published by them are in AE-NS-T, 3 (1899-1901), 26, 117–23.

265. Mustafa Réfik, *Ein kleines Sündenregister Abdul Hamid II's* (Geneva, 1899).

266. "İthaf," *Osmanlı*, no. 30, February 15, 1899, 1, "Mustafa Refik Efendi'nin İfade-i Mahsusası," *Osmanlı*, no. 33, April 1, 1899, 5–6.

267. See The Ministry of the Interior to Delcassé, Paris, March 29, 1899, AE-NS-T, 3 (1899–1901), 27, notes prepared in Auswärtiges Amt, Berlin, March 30, 1899, A. 3414, A. 3547 and A. 3548 (Entzifferung), PAAA, 732/3, Die Jungtürken, 198 (Bd.1-2), notes prepared by the Swiss Department of Justice and Police in Geneva, dated March 22 and 23, 1899 (P.P.252). In another note prepared concerning Mustafa Refik Bey dated April 7, 1899 (P.P.252), he was described as a "hervorragenden Führer" of the CUP. Bundesarchiv-Bern, E. 21/14'248. For the displeasure that the Ottoman diplomats expressed because of the book, see Tevfik Pasha to the Chamberlain's office, March 30, [18]99/no. 220, and [April 30, 1899]/no. 229, *Roma, Berlin Sefaret-i Seniyeleriyle Muhaberata Mahsus [Defter]*, BBA-YEE, 36/139-52/139/XVIII.

268. Tevfik Pasha to the Chamberlain's office, March 7, [18]99/no. 213, *Roma,Berlin Sefaret-i Seniyeleriyle Muhaberata Mahsus [Defter]*, BBA-YEE, 36/139-52/139/XVIII, and [Ali] Fahri, *Vambéry Tehlikede* (Geneva, 1316 [1900]), 3–5.

269. Şerif Bey to the Chamberlain's office, February 21, [18]99/no. 79, March 27, [18]99/no. 93, April 29, [18]99/no. 104, June 17, [18]99/no. 139, *Stockholm Sefaret-i Seniyesiyle Muhaberata Mahsus Defterdir*, BBA-YEE, 36/139-44/139/XVIII.

270. A note dated June 5, [18]98, AQSh, 19/135//49/598.

271. Ahmed Rıza," İsrafat," *Osmanlı*, no. 36, May 15, 1899, 1.

272. Ahmed Rıza, "Evham-ı Hümayûn," *Osmanlı*, no. 40, July 15, 1899, 2.

273. "Muahezât ve Teselli," *Osmanlı*, no. 41, June 1, 1899, 1–2.

274. "İhtar-ı Mahsus," *Osmanlı*, no. 35, May 1, 1899, 1.

275. Ahmed Rıza's undated letter (pr. November 15, 1898, Malta), A. 13682, PAAA, 732/3, Die Jungtürken, 198 (Bd.1-2).

276. The best example is "Türkiye ve Almanya," *Osmanlı*, no. 35, May 1, 1899, 1–4.

277. Faïk bey Konitza, "Notes Politiques," *Albania*, vol. C, no. 5 (1899), 94. They further published a note proclaiming the assertions of Dutch press that Ahmed Rıza was also the delegate of the Muslim Albanians, false. See "[İhtar]," *Albania*, vol. C, no. 5 (1899), 96.

278. "İlân," *Osmanlı*, no. 38, June 15, 1899, 1.

279. BBA-BEO/Hariciye Âmed, 159-5/15, 1163 [June 25, 1899]; the draft of the note from Dutch Foreign Ministry to the ambassador in Istanbul, June [?], 1899, Kab.8/28, Algemeen Rijksarchief, Kabinet en Protocol (1871–1940), 60/141.

280. Marschall von Bieberstein to Schillingsfürst, Therapia, May 23, 1899/no. 180 (Entzifferung), A. 6122, PAAA, 732/3, Die Jungtürken, 198 (Bd.1-2).

281. See Ahmed Rıza, "La Haye'den Mektub," *Osmanlı*, no. 39, July 1, 1899, 1–2, and his notes to İshak Sükûti from The Hague, one of which was dated June 15, 111 [1899] two others were undated. See respectively, AQSh, 19/106//810/8, 19/106//242/16, and 19/106//243/17.

282. To Schillingsfürst, The Hague, June 22, 1899/no. 86, A. 7639, PAAA, 732/2, Die Jungtürken, 198 (Bd.1-2); to Delcassé, June 23, 1899, AE-NS-T, 2 (1899-1901), 137–38.

283. The Ottoman delegation required the extradition of Ahmed Rıza and Tscheraz. See the Dutch Cabinet paper dated June 24, 1899/no. 8, *Bescheiden Betreffende de Buitlandse Politek van Nederland 1899–1919*, ed. C. Smit (S-Gravenhage, 1957), 77–78.

284. Ahmed Rıza, "Mémoire," *Mechveret Supplément Français*, no. 79, 1. A Turkish translation was given in *Osmanlı*, no. 38, June 15, 1899, 1. Since Ahmed Rıza and Minas Tscheraz delivered their speeches in French, in which they were proficient, the characterization of U.S. representative White was erroneous. See *Autobiography of Andrew Dickson White* 2 (New York, 1905), 288. However, it has been accepted on face value by some researchers. See, for instance, James Brown Scott, *The Hague Peace Conferences* 1 (Baltimore, 1909), 179.

285. "Gevaarlijke Hervorming," *De Hollandsche Revue* 4 (1899), 726–27.

286. The Ottoman diplomats had been instructed to require the Foreign ministries of the Great Powers to ignore claims by the joint CUP-Armenian delegation. See Tahsin Bey to the Ottoman ambassador in St. Petersburg, May 22, [18]99/no. 132, *Petersburg Sefaret-i Seniyesiyle Muhaberata Mahsus defterdir*, BBA-YEE, 36/139-44/139/XVIII.

287. "L'adhésion de M. van Kol," *Pro Arménia*, no. 6, February 10, 1901, 43–44, "Minas Tchéraz en de Armenische Quaestie," *De Standard*, November 24, 1899. Pierre Anméghian also praise the common action in The Hague. See Pierre Anméghian, *Pour le jubilé du Sultan* (Brussels, 1900), 26–27.

288. O'Conor to Salisbury, Constantinople, June 2, 1899/no. 283, PRO/F.O. 78/4994.

289. According to the CUP circle the Ottoman representative Turhan Pasha had challenged Ahmed Rıza to a duel. See Abdullah Djevdet, "L'assassin se montre partout," *Mechveret Supplément Français*, no. 79, July 1, 1899, 6. For a supportive review of Ahmed Rıza's activities at the conference and his relations with the Ottoman representatives see "al-Aḥrar fī mü'tamar al-salām," *Enîn-i Mazlum*, no. 10, 78–79.

290. "La Jeune-Turquie à La Haye," *Mechveret Supplément Français*, no. 79, 1.

291. See Laarman, Secretary General of the Christelijke Vereeniging voor Jonge Mannen, to Beaufort, Gravenhage, August 25, 1899/no. Kab.4, Algemeen Rijksarchief, Kabinet en Protocol 60 (141), and "De Heer Minaz Tchévaz [sic]," *Het Nieuws van den Haag*, June 6, 1899.

292. See "Haagsche Sprokkelingen," *De Nederlander*, June 5, 1899, "Turksche Involoeden," *De Nederlander*, June 6, 1899, A. H. Swaving, "Een stem uit Indië," *Bijvoegsel van de Java-Bode*, August 29, 1899, "La Conférence de la Paix: Panislamisme," *L'Arménie*, no. 130, August 1, 1899, 1–2.

293. To Beaufort, Constantinople, June 5, 1899/no. 597-220. Algemeen Rijksarchief, Kabinet en Protocol 60 (141).

294. Ahmed Rıza, "La Jeune-Turquie et le gouvernement Hollandais," *Mechveret Supplément Français*, no. 84, October 15, 1899, 2.

295. He also met with the Danish opposition leaders. See BBA-YSHM, 400/34, 14. 5. 1317.

296. Şerif Pasha's letter to Comte Douglas, Stockholm, August 1, 1899, and the draft of Comte Douglas' response, Stockholm, August 2, 1899, Rijksarkivet, Kabinettet för utrikes brevväxlingen, Koncept, 1899, Vol.6, Noter, Turkiets beskickning, 6.

297. See BBA-BEO/Hariciye Âmed, 159-5/15, 1856 [August 24, 1899], "A Christiania," *Mechveret Supplément Français*, no. 81, August 15, 1899, 1–2.

298. Ahmed Rıza, "Christiania'dan Mektub," *Osmanlı*, no. 42, August 15, 1899, 1–2. This was underscored while the Swedish press depicted his mission, "Det ungtyrkiske Parti," *Morgenbladet*, August 4, 1899.

299. Ahmed Rıza's letter to Joseph Reinach, October, 21, 111 [1899], Bibliothèque National (Paris), MSS Occ. Correspondance de Joseph Reinach, XXXVIII, 13556, 69–70.

300. Şerif Bey to the Chamberlain's office, February 23, [18]99, *Stockholm Sefaret-i Seniyesiyle Muhaberata Mahsus Defterdir*, BBA-YEE, 36/139-44/139/XVIII.

301. See BBA-YMGM, 189/82, 1316. 7. 8/ no. 8298, 189/89, 1316. 7. 9/ no. 9334 and 189/116, 1316. 7. 17/no. 9718.

302. Yıldız, April 13, 1899, Archives of the Turkish Embassy in London, Box 339 (8).

303. Coded telegram from Anthopulos Pasha to Tahsin Bey (Jeunes Turcs et agitateurs Arméniens), April 15, 1899, Archives of the Turkish Embassy in London, Box 339 (8).

304. Archives of the Turkish Embassy in London, Box 339(8).

305. "Renseignements fournis sous sa dictée par Dembski (anarchiste)," Archives of the Turkish Embassy in London, Box 339(2).

306. For more information concerning this accident and Dembski's role see Staatsarchiv des Kantons Zürich, Akten über die Anarchisten, P. 239.4 and (PP 32.40/no. 142), J[ohann] Langhard, *Die anarchistische Bewegung in der Schweiz von ihren Anfängen bis zur Gegenwart und internationalen Führer* (Berlin, 1903), 312, 473, idem, *Die politische Polizei der schweizerischen Eidgenossenschaft* (Bern, 1909), 285–86; "The Manufacture of Bombs," *Times*, March 9, and 11, 1899, "Suisse," *Le Temps*, March 11, 1889. It is unclear to which group Dembski belonged. Swiss documents and Langhard claim membership of Dembski in "der russischen terroristischen Partei." Another source, which refers to the anarchist as Alexander Dembinski, asserts anarchist-communist group membership. See Herman Rappaport, *Anarchizm i Anarchiści na ziemiach Polskich do 1914 roku* (Warsaw, 1981), 305.

307. Avetis Nazarbek, "Die armenische Frage und der Sozialismus," *Die*

Neue Zeit 14, no. 2 (1895–1896), 498–505, 666–68. However, he presented the aims of the society as peaceful ones in his book. See *Through the Storm* (London, 1899), xxiii–xxiv.

308. See BBA-HNA- End.M.T, K.808/E.no. 479, and K.810/E.no. 885.

309. Ugo Fedeli, *Giuseppe Ciancabilla* (Cesena, 1965).

310. Max Nettlau, *Geschichte der Anarchie*, Teil 1, *Anarchisten und Syndikalisten* (Vaduz, 1984), 300.

311. Hermia Oliver, *The International Anarchist Movement in Late Victorian London* (London, 1983), 146–47.

312. Nettlau, *Anarchisten und Syndikalisten*, 93, 223, 376.

313. A. Rıfat to İshak Sükûti, October 9, 1899, AQSh, 19/106//44/1.

314. This version was first told by Lardy (see "Jeunes-turcs," *Journal de Genève*, October 1, 1899), then repeated by the Young Turks, "Yıldız Hükûmeti'nin Cenevre'de Haydud Yataklığı," *Osmanlı*, no. 45, October 1, 1899, 1, and "Le Docteur Lardy et le Sultan," *Mechveret Supplément Français*, no. 81, November 15, 1899, 3–4.

315. "Yıldız'ın Ric'at-ı Kahkarîyesi," *Osmanlı*, no. 46, October 15, 1899, 1–4. He further claimed that the CUP center in Geneva was financed by Lardy. See "Folie ou aberration," *Journal de Genève*, September 29, 1899.

316. Resul Bey's letter dated, September 2, 1899, in "Correspondance," *Journal de Genève*, October 3, 1889.

317. For his role in the Albanian movement, see "Note confidentielle" (Brussels, April 20, 1897), enclosed with the letter from Khevenhüller to Goluchowski, Brussels, April 21, 1897/no. 51, HHStA, PA XII 2 Albanien. For the ideas that he propagated see V[isco] Babatashi, "Ç'Eshte per te Bere?" *Albania*, vol. A, no. 2, April 25, 1897, 17–18, "Kombi Shqipetar," *Albania*, vol. B, no. 11, March 31, 1898, 181–82.

318. "Complot contre le Sultan," *Journal de Genève*, October 7, 1899.

319. See interrogation proceeding dated October 6, 1899 (156), Bundesarchiv-Bern, E. 21/14'248.

320. See interrogation proceeding dated, October 6, 1899 (154), Bundesarchiv-Bern, E. 21/14'248.

321. See interrogation proceeding dated October 7, 1899 (157), Bundesarchiv-Bern, E. 21/14'248.

322. See interrogation proceeding dated, October 5, 1899 (155), Bundesarchiv-Bern, E. 21/14'248.

323. His letter dated September 29, [18]99, and his undated note to Commissar Anbert (P.P.150), Bundesarchiv-Bern, E. 21/14'248.

324. See his interrogations dated October 5 and 6, 1899, (158–59) Bundesarchiv-Bern, E. 21/14'248.

325. See "Rapport à Monsieur le President du Dept. de Justice et Police sur le prétendu complot parmi à Genève contre la vie du Sultan," and "Angeblich von Dr. Lardy und den Jung-Türken gegen des Sultan vorbereitene Komplott," Bundesarchiv-Bern, E. 21/14'248.

326. To Schillingsfürst, Bern, October 22, 1899/no. 82, A. 12492, PAAA, 732/3, Die Jungtürken, 198 (Bd.1–2); and to Delcassé, Genève, October 20, 1899, AE-NS-T, 3 (1899–1901), 152–53.

327. "Jeunes Turcs," *Le Genevois*, October 20, 1899.

328. This number is given in E.T., "Une interview," *Tribune de Genève*, March 16, 1898.

329. Abdullah Cevdet to İshak Sükûti, March 24, 1899, AQSh, 19/106//170/188. Identical assertions made in an undated letter exchanged between the two leaders. AQSh, 19/106//855/275.

330. For his explanations concerning his role, see his letter to İshak Sükûti, Paris, March 24, 1899, AQSh, 19/106//902/18.

331. Doctor Burhan Bahaeddin to İshak Sükûti, Paris, April, 18, [18]99, AQSh, 19/106-1//206/502.

332. Abdullah Cevdet to İshak Sükûti, Paris, March 27, 1899, AQSh, 19/106//168/187.

333. Ahmed Rıza to Doctor Nâzım, undated postcard [June 1899], Private Papers of Bahaeddin Şakir.

334. Rahmi Bey to Doctor Nâzım, June 29, 1899, Private Papers of Bahaeddin Şakir.

335. Doctor Nâzım to İshak Sükûti, undated [1899], AQSh, 19/106-5//196/1421.

336. Nâbi Bey to the Chamberlain's office, August 18, [18]99, *Paris Sefaret-i Seniyesiyle Muhaberata Mahsus Defterdir*, BBA-YEE, 36/1468/141/XII.

337. Necmeddin Ârif to İshak Sükûti, Paris, July 28, [18]99, AQSh, 19/106//234/1681.

338. Ahmed Celâleddin Pasha to Kâmil Bey, July [28], [18]99, *Paris'de Feridun Bey, Ahmed Celâleddin Paşa, Roma'da Tahir Paşa ve Ferid Paşa [ile Muhaberata Mahsus Defter]*, BBA-YEE, 36/2328-4/146/XV.

339. Abdullah Cevdet to İshak Sükûti, undated letter [1899], AQSh, 19/106//164/222.

340. Rauf Ahmed to İshak Sükûti, August 7, [18]99, AQSh, 19/106-6//243/1895.

341. Telegram dated August 18, 1899/no. 6177, AQSh, 19/106//26/263.

342. Seraceddin Bey to İshak Sükûti, August 19, 1899, AQSh, 19/129//247/1.

343. Münir Bey to the Chamberlain's office, November 12, [18]99/no. 21, *Paris Sefaretiyle Muhaberata Mahsus Defterdir*, BBA-YEE, 36/2468/141/XII.

344. Undated letter from Halil Muvaffak to İshak Sükûti, AQSh, 19/106-3//858/938.

345. The investigation ended on May 12, 1900, and the warning was given on May 18, 1900. See "Auszug aus dem Protokoll der Sizung des schweizerischen Bundesrates, 18 Mai 1900," (P.P.85), Bundesarchiv-Bern, E. 21/14'250. Since most of the members of the CUP center in this town received posts at the Ottoman embassies and consulates, this warning did not affect them. See "Auszug aus dem Protokoll der Sizung des schweizerischen Bundesrates, 6 September 1904," (P.P.300). Archives de la Justice et Police-Genève, Dossier: Abdullah Djevdet, Beilage: 8.

346. BBA-YMGM, 5 Ra 1318/no. 1808. He had thrown stones at the residence of the Ottoman representative in Vidin and broken the windows. He and his friends were later tried and acquitted by a local Bulgarian court in Vidin. See BBA-BEO/ Mümtaze kalemi Bulgaristan Tasnifi Evrakı II, 66, 20 (1318. 1. 18), BBA-BEO/Bulgaristan ve Şarkî Rumeli'nin Muharrerat Defteri (91)-966-60/30, 578–81 [May 17, 1900]. But during this trial the Ottoman diplomats requested his extradition from Switzerland.

347. Doctor Nâzım to İshak Sükûti, undated [1899], AQSh, 19/106-5//1348/1.

348. BBA-İrade-Hariciye, Cemaziy'ülevvel 1317/no. 14-1145, BBA-YP, 9 C 1317/no. 1026.

349. *Salnâme-i Nezaret-i Hariciye* (Istanbul, 1318 [1900]), 231–32, 234.

350. BBA-BEO/Re'sen İrade-i Seniye, 358-8/76 [October 19, 1899])/ 103306.

351. Chamberlain's office to the foreign ministry, [October 26, 1899], Reşid Sadi's telegram from the Rome embassy, October 30, 1899, *Mabeyn ve Devâir ve Vilâyetlerle Bâzı Zevata Yazılan Tezkere ve Muharrerat Müsveddelerini Havî Dosya Defteri*, II, BBA-YEE, 36/398/146/XIV; Mahmud Nedim, Ottoman ambassador in Vienna, to the foreign ministry, November 24, [18]99/no. 315 and December 1, [18]99/no. 321 Dışişleri Bakanlığı Hazine-i Evrak Arşivi, Tercüme Mütenevvia: D. 29; BBA-YP, 7 C 1317/no. 958, BBA-YMGM, 28 B 1317/no. 1250-5897.

352. Abdullah Cevdet to İshak Sükûti, Vienna, October 23, and November 24, 1899, AQSh, 19/106//198/1, 19/106//228/1.

353. *Reşadiye Cemiyetinin Maksad ve Suret-i Teşekkülünü Müş'ir, Türkçe, İngilizce ve Fransızca Olarak Kaleme Alınan Mevadd-ı Esasiye* (Geneva, 1315 [1899]).

354. *Object and the Standing Orders of the Rechadie Committee* (Geneva, 1899).

355. Mustafa Ragıb to İshak Sükûti, December 18, 1899, and November 30, 1899, AQSh, 19/106-4//158/1278, and 19/106-4//148/1280.

356. To the federal attorney general, September 11, [18]99/no. 487 (P.P.252-166), Bundesarchiv-Bern, E. 21/14'248.

357. The application of the Ottoman consul was quoted in the note of the department of justice and police, October 13, 1899/no. 2311, Bundesarchiv-Bern, E. 21/14'248.

358. To the federal attorney general, October 18, 1899/no. 555 (P.P. 252-242), Bundesarchiv-Bern, E. 21/14'248.

359. Bundesarchiv-Bern, E. 21/14'248.

360. See Abdullah Cevdet's draft entitled "The letter I had written with the intention of sending to Ahmed [Celâleddin] Pasha, however I did not send." AQSh, 19/106//198/1.

361. See Ahmed Tevfik Pasha to the Chamberlain's office, February 10, 1900/no. 144, *Berlin Sefaret-i Seniyesiyle Muhaberata Mahsus Defter*, BBA-YEE, 36/139-51/139/XVIII, Abdullah Cevdet to İshak Sükûti, [Berlin], December 1 and 3, 1900, AQSh, 19/106//189/1, 19/106//201/1.

362. Necmeddin Ârif to İshak Sükûti, September 12, 1899, AQSh, 19/106-5//864/1749. Ahmed Celâleddin Pasha offered Fr 2,500 to those who signed a petition promising not to get involved in "seditious" activities and return to the Empire. See from the justice and police department to the federal attorney general, October 9, 1899/no. 533(P.P.252-242), October 10, 1899/no. 530 (P.P. 252-242), Bundesarchiv-Bern, E. 21/14'248. Also see BBA-YMGM, 24 C 1317/no. 1223-1043.

363. Muhtar Bey's postcard, Marseilles, September 4, 1899, AQSh, 19/106//29/266 and Ferid Bey's undated letter to İshak Sükûti, AQSh, 19/102//282/937.

364. Necmeddin Ârif to İshak Sükûti, October 28, November 11, and November 15, 1899, AQSh, 19/106-5//128/1260, 19/106-5//193/1658, 19/106-5//245/1657.

365. Seraceddin Bey to Nuri Ahmed, Geneva, February 5, [18]98, AQSh, 19/129//52/242.

366. İbrahim Temo to Abdullah Cevdet, January 20, 1899, AQSh, 19/31//23/1, and to İshak Sükûti, May 4, 1900, AQSh, 19/106-3//160/1058.

367. Abdullah Cevdet to İshak Sükûti, Vienna, November 24, 1899, AQSh, 19/106//228/1.

368. D[r] A[bdullah] D[jevdet], "La fortresse de Tripoli," *Osmanli Supplément Français*, no. 13, August 1, 1899, 3–5.

369. Document signed by the prisoners saying that they had been released after the settlement was published in Abdullah Cevdet's journal after his death, in order to prove that he was not an opportunist and had done everything in accordance with the orders of the CUP. See "Suret," *İçtihat*, no. 358, December 1932, 3–5.

370. Undated letter signed "one of the Egyptians," AQSh, 19/135//315/467.

371. Necmeddin Ârif to İshak Sükûti, Paris, August 4, [18]99 and September 18, [18]99, AQSh, 19/106-5//146/1678.

372. Tunalı Hilmi to Ahmed Rıza, Cairo, August 15, [18]99, Private Papers of Ahmed Rıza (1).

373. Tunalı Hilmi to Ahmed Rıza, September 4, [1]899, Private Papers of Ahmed Rıza (1).

374. Nejad Bey's letter to Ahmed Rıza on behalf of the Tripoli of Barbary branch, December 3, [18]99, Private Papers of Ahmed Rıza (1).

375. Doctor Nâzım to İshak Sükûti, undated, AQSh, 19/106-5//916/1390.

376. Doctor Nâzım to İshak Sükûti, undated, AQSh, 19/106-5//1348/1.

377. Tunalı Hilmi to Marshal Cevad Pasha, the commander of the Fifth Army, September 15, [18]99, enclosed with the dispatch sent by the latter to the Chamberlain's office [September 28, 1899]/no. 48, *Suriye Vilâyeti ve Beşinci Ordu-yu Hümayun Müşiriyetiyle Muhaberata Mahsus Defterdir*, BBA-YEE, 36/139-49/139/XVIII.

378. İbrahim Temo to İshak Sükûti, May 4, 1900, AQSh, 19/106-3//160/1058.

379. Kuran, *İnkılâp Tarihimiz ve İttihad ve Terakki*, 132–33.

380. "Congresso di Giovani Turchi a Brindisi," *Il Corriere di Catania*, October 6, 1899.

381. Léon Bey to Tevfik Pasha, October 7, 1899/no. 992-1, Dışişleri Bakanlığı Hazine-i Evrak Arşivi, Siyasî: Box 424.

382. M. de Bunsen to Salisbury, Therapia, October 5, 1899/no. 472 (confidential), PRO/F.O. 78/4995.

383. "Konstantinopel," *Berliner Lokal Anzeiger*, October 25, 1899.

384. To Schillingsfürst, Athens, November 29, 1899/no. 84, A. 14262, PAAA, 732/3, Die Jungtürken, 198 (Bd.1-2); to Goluchowski, Yeniköy, October 18, 1899/no. 48, HHStA, PA XII 172, Türkei Berichte, 1899 VIII–XII.

385. To Goluchowski, Bern, April 26, 1900/no. 29, HHStA, PA XXVII Schweiz Berichte 1900.

386. Detailed information about the lawsuit is given in a letter from Cromer to Lansdowne, April 14, 1902/no. 59 (confidential), PRO/F.O. 78/5226; in the "Note sur l'Imprimerie 'Osmanieh'" prepared by H. Boyle, Cromer Papers, PRO/F.O. 633/11; Gazi Ahmed Muhtar Pasha to the Sublime Porte [April 15, 1902],

BBA-BEO/Mümtaze Kalemi: Mısır, 15/B. S.59, 1320. 1. 6; and the memorandum presented to the khedive concerning the lawsuit, Abbas II Papers, Durham University, F. 29/17. The viewpoint of the newly established branch is given in "Hülâsa-i Muhakeme," *Hak*, no. 2, September 15, 1899, 1, and in "Ma'a al-Lord Cromer," and "Osmanlı İttihad ve Terakki Cemiyeti Mes'elesi," *Enîn-i Mazlum*, no. 9, June 26, 1899, 71–72.

387. More information had been given in two letters sent by Abdullah Cevdet to İshak Sükûti. One of them is undated and the second was written on February 6, 1899. See respectively AQSh, 19/106//855/275, and 19/106//172/1.

388. Salih Cemal to İshak Sükûti, undated, AQSh, 19/106-7//586/1975.

389. "Osmanlı İttihad ve Terakki Cemiyeti Mes'elesi," *Enîn-i Mazlum*, no. 10, July 10, 1899, 80.

390. Bahaeddin Bey to İshak Sükûti, March 22, [1899], AQSh, 19/106//277/1.

391. Tunalı Hilmi summarized his efforts in reorganizing the Egyptian branch in a pamphlet, *al-ma'rûḍ amâma allâh wa al-nâs* (Cairo, 1317 [1899]).

392. In an unsigned letter dated [February 15, 1900] and sent to the khedive, Muḥammad 'Alī Halīm Pasha was described as "the leader of the Young Turks in Egypt." Abbas II Papers, Durham University, F. 39/1. In another letter, dated [January 13, 1900] and presented to the khedive, it was asserted that he was presiding over the Young Turks in Egypt and contributing £ 25 per month. Abbas II Papers, Durham University, F. 26/283. The sultan complained to the khedive about Muḥammad 'Alī Ḥalīm Pasha. See Tahsin Bey to the khedive, [June 27, 1901], Abbas II Papers, Durham University, F. 25/1.

393. A copy of the official circular of the "Temporary and Extraordinary Executive Committee of the CUP Egyptian Branch" sent to the Romania branch, July 7, [18]99/no. 1, AQSh, 19/58//582/12.

394. To the fifth branch [Romania], August 31, 1899/no. 2, AQSh, 19/95//236/7.

395. Osmanlı İttihad ve Terakki Cemiyeti Hey'et-i Cedide-i Fevkâlâdesi, "Şu'be'den," *Hak*, no. 1, August 31, 1899, 3, "İlân," *Hak*, no. 1, 3, "Haqq," *Enîn-i Mazlûm*, no. 14, September 4, 1899, 110.

396. "İlân," *Osmanlı*, no. 44, September 15, 1899, 8.

397. "Maksad-Meslek," *Hak*, no.1, 2.

398. "Şu'beden," *Hak*, no. 3, September 30, 1899, 1.

399. See Ali Fahri to İshak Sükûti, Cairo, August 18, 1900, AQSh, 19/106-2//203/723.

400. Comité Ottoman d'Union et de Progrès, *L'horrible vengeance du Sultan sur un Jeune Turc* (Cairo, 1899).

401. For his flight and participation in the branch see "Tebşir," *Hak*, no. 5, October 5, 1899, 4.

402. For the flights of these people and their participation in the movement, see "Havâdis," *Hak*, no. 1, 4; "El-Karar," *Hak*, no. 2, 2.

403. "Hak Halkın Himmetine Bakar," *Hak*, no. 6, November 23, 1899, 1.

404. Undated letter [1898] from Abdullah Cevdet to İshak Sükûti, AQSh, 19/106//281/282. Also announced in the organ. See "Hediye," *Hak*, no. 31, October 30, 1900, 1.

405. Ali Fahri to İshak Sükûti, Cairo [October 27, 1899], AQSh, 19/106-2//135/748.

406. İshak Sükûti to Tunalı Hilmi, September 20, 1899 in Kuran, *İnkılâp Tarihimiz ve Jön Türkler*, 128.

407. See "İntikam, İntikam," *Hak*, no. 2, 4; "Havâdis," *Hak*, no. 6, 4.

408. Ali Fahri to İshak Sükûti [November 26, 1899], AQSh, 19/106-2// 141//750. See also Ali Fahri, "Ahrar-ı Ümmete Garib Bir Tuzak," *Osmanlı*, no. 45, October 1, 1899, 6–7, "Faruk İmzasıyla Alınan Varakadır," *El-Sultan el-Gazi Abdülhamid Han-ı Sânî*, no. 3 [September 25, 1899], 4.

409. O'Conor to Salisbury, Constantinople, March 30, 1899/no. 159 (confidential), PRO/F.O. 78/4992.

410. O'Conor to Salisbury, Constantinople, April 27, 1899/no. 209, PRO/ F.O. 407/151.

411. Cromer to Salisbury, Cairo, April 17, 1899/no. 73, PRO/F.O. 407/ 151.

412. Cromer to Salisbury, Cairo, December 16, 1899/no. 318 (private), Cromer Papers, Letters to Secretaries of State, PRO/F.O. 633/VI.

413. "Die jungtürkische Partei," *Vossische Zeitung*, April 8, 1899.

414. For a very good example see A[hmed] Ş[uayib], "Ulûm-i Siyasiye ve İctimaiye," *Servet-i Fünûn*, no. 488, July 1900, 311–13. Besides referring to the "self-help" idea continuously, the author claims: "Most of the English people who graduate from college ride a ship and take a tour around the world in order to become a second Cecil Rhodes. The Frenchman who finishes his education and military service, on the other hand, runs after rich and beautiful girls. Here is the difference between the cultures of the two great countries."

415. Siyret Bey's written confession dated [November 28, 1899], BBA-YEE, 19/1428/130/58. More information for the background of the event is in İsmail Hakkı, *Vatan Uğrunda Yahud Yıldız Mahkemesi* (Cairo, 1326 [1908]), 139–48.

416. O'Conor to Salisbury, November 20, 1899/no. 537, PRO/F.O. 78/ 4996.

417. PRO/F.O. 78/4996.

418. Undated letter from Abdullah Cevdet to İshak Sükûti, AQSh, 19/106/ /273/851 and Halil Muvaffak to İshak Sükûti, November 24, 1901, AQSh, 19/ 106-3//901/915.

419. O'Conor to Salisbury, Constantinople, November 29, 1899/no. 543, PRO/F.O. 78/4996, O'Conor's political notes, November 20, 21, 23, 24, 29, 1899, O'Conor Papers, Churchill College, Cambridge, 7/4/4.

420. Tahsin Bey to Anthopulos Pasha, November 29, 1899, Archives of the Turkish Embassy in London, Box 338 (3).

421. Tahsin Bey to Anthopulos Pasha, December 3, 1899, ibid.

422. Coded telegram from Anthopulos Pasha to Tahsin Bey, December 4, 1899, ibid.

423. Wladimir Giesl, *Zwei Jahrzehnte im Nahen Orient* (Berlin, 1927), 311.

424. Marschall von Bieberstein to Schillingsfürst, December 3, 1899/no. 353 (Entzifferung-Geheim), A. 14247, PAAA, 732/3, Die Jungtürken, 198 (Bd.1-2).

425. Calice to Goluchowski, Constantinople, December 7, 1899/no. 56, HHStA, PA XII 172, Türkei Berichte, 1899, VIII–XII.

426. Münster to Schillingsfürst, Paris, February 18, 1900/no. 56, A. 2241, PAAA, 733/1, Die Jungtürken, 198 (Bd.2-3).

427. BBA-BEO/Dahiliye Giden, 98-3/47, 3519 [March 1, 1900].

428. See "İsmail Safa'nın Biyografisi," *Türk Düşüncesi* 1, no. 5 (April 1,

1954), 322–24, Memorandum by Adam Block dated August 19, 1900, O'Conor Papers, 6/1/22.

429. For his extreme pro-British tendencies, see his letter to the sultan dated October 9, 1900, 4–5, BBA-YEE, 15/1251/74/14, and Ali Haydar, *Lâyiha ve İstitrad* (Cairo, 1317 [1901]), 8–9.

430. Calice to Goluchowski, Yeniköy, October 18, 1899/no. 48 (vertaulich), HHStA, PA, XII 172, Türkei Berichte, 1899 VIII–XII.

431. For his flight see Ali Haydar Midhat, *Hâtıralarım 1872–1946* (Istanbul, 1946), 142–54. For offers by the palace see coded telegram from the Chamberlain's office to Vefik Bey in Paris, November 17–18, 1899/no. 5356, *Mabeyn'den Devâir ve Vilâyetlerle Bâzı Zevata Yazılan Tezkere ve Muharrerat Müsveddelerini Havî Dosya Defteri*, BBA-YEE, 36/398/146/XIV; "Şehid-i Mağdur Midhat Paşa Hazretlerinin Mahdumları," *Sancak*, no. 1, November 18, 1899, 6–7.

432. Calice to Goluchowski, Constantinople, November 29, 1899/no. 55, HHStA, PA XII 172, Türkei Berichte, 1899 VIII–XII. Relations between Kemaleddin Efendi and the Young Turks were previously underscored by Sir Philip Currie. See his note dated April 9, [18]94 (122–30), Private Papers of Sir Philip Currie, PRO/F.O. 800/114.

433. "İstanbul'dan," *Osmanlı*, no. 49, December 1, 1899, 6, "Ba'd-el-Tertib," *Sancak*, no. 4, December 9, 1899, 6, "Havâdis," *Sancak*, no. 6, December 23, 1899, 5, A[hmed] R[ıza], "Un nouvelle exploit d'Abdul Hamid," *Mechveret Supplément Français*, no. 87, November 1, 1899, 2–3; "Turkey," *Times*, November 29, 1899, "Nouvelles de l'étranger," *Le Temps*, December 2, 1899.

434. He was a member of the CUP Istanbul branch. See "Muhibban," *Muhibban* 2, no. 4 [April 14, 1911], 130.

435. See "İstanbul'da Tevkifat," *Sancak*, no. 4, 6.

436. "İstanbul'dan," *Osmanlı*, no. 49, 6.

437. Chamberlain's office to the Police ministry [October 24, 1899]/no. 5232, *Mabeyn'den Devâir ve Vilâyetlerle Bâzı Zevata Yazılan Tezkere ve Muharrerat Müsveddelerini Havî Dosya Defteri*, BBA-YEE, 36/398/146/XIV.

438. For the distribution of *Hak* in Izmir its and vicinity, see Mehmed Kâmil to the governor [September 10, 1899]/no. 3, *Aydın Vilâyet-i Celilesiyle Muhaberata Mahsus Defterdir*, BBA-YEE, 36/2470-15/147/XVI; the distribution of *Osmanlı* in Aleppo and the arrest of local CUP members sending articles to it see Ali Muhsin to the Chamberlain's office [September 5, 1899]/no. 79, and [September 27, 1899]/no. 85, *Haleb ve Adana Fevkâlâde Kumandanlığı Vekâletine Mahsus Defter*, BBA-YEE, 39/139/139/XVI. For the distribution of *Hak*, *Osmanlı*, and *Mechveret Supplément Français* in Beirut, see Governor Reşid Bey to the Chamberlain's office, [December 14, 1899]/no. 3, and [December 16, 1899]/no. 5, *Beyrut Vilâyetiyle Muhabereye Mahsus Üçüncü Defterdir*, BBA-YEE, 36/2470-23/147/XVI. For their distribution in the Yemen, see Governor Hüseyin Hilmi to the Chamberlain's office [July 18, 1899]/no. 123, *Yemen Vilâyet ve Kumandanlığı ile Muhabereye Mahsus Defterdir*, BBA- YEE, 36/2470-23/147/XVI.

439. "İntibah," *Osmanlı*, no. 28, January 15, 1899, 5–6.

440. Halil Muvaffak, *Saltanat-ı Seniye'nin Bükreş Sefiri Kâzım Bey'e Mektub* (Geneva, 1315 [1899]), 13–19; "Le Sultan de Roumanie," *Mechveret Supplément Français*, no. 70, January 1, 1899, 7–8.

441. Yunus Bekir Kayseri, "Filibe'den Mektub," *Osmanlı*, no. 39, July 1, 1899, 6–7, Ali Rıza Önder, *Kayseri Basın Tarihi: 1910–1960* (Ankara, 1972), 136.

442. "Islah'ın Mesleği," *Islah*, no. 1 [October 16, 1899], 1.

443. See coded telegram from the Chamberlain's office to the Ottoman commissioner in Bulgaria [October 22, 1896]/no. 5183, [October 26, 1899]/nos. 5261, 5266, and 5274; to the Police ministry [October 7, 1899]/no. 5243; note to the Bulgarian diplomatic agent in Istanbul [October 8, 1899]/no. 5273, *Mabeyn'den Devâir ve Vilâyetlerle Bâzı Zevata Yazılan Tezkere ve Muharrerat Suretlerini Havî Dosya Defteri*, BBA-YEE, 36/398/146/XIV.

444. "Havâdis," *Osmanlı*, no. 48, November 1, 1899, 7.

445. [İhsan Adlî], "Asâr-ı Manzume," *Seyf-i Hakikat*, no. 2 [November 1, 1899], 2.

446. "Les Jeunes Turcs à Athènes," *Mechveret Supplément Français*, no. 99, June 1, 1900, 4.

447. "İhtar," *Osmanlı*, no. 48, November 15, 1899, 7.

448. His note to İshak Sükûti, Marseilles, August 17, 1899, AQSh, 19/106-3//144/969.

449. To von Bülow, Tangier, July 15, 1902/no. 84, A. 11117, and August 15, 1902, A. 12636, PAAA, 733/3, Die Jungtürken, 198 (Bd.4–5).

450. Haydarpaşazâde Ârif to İshak Sükûti, Tunis, March 18, 1899, AQSh, 19/106-1//262/384. See also "Turkiyā al-fatāt fī Tūnis," *al-Ayyām*, no. 190, November 23, 1899, 3.

451. "Le Comité Musulman de la Jeune-Turquie," *Correspondance Oriental* (Gibraltar), November 20, 1901.

452. "El Harem del Sultan Abdul-Hamid II," *El Centinela del Estrecho de Gibraltar*, no. 3, November 24, 1901, 2 ff.

453. To Delcassé, Tunis, February 7, 1900/no. 71, AE-NS-T, 3 (1899–1901), 180–82.

454. "Açık Muhabere," *Osmanlı*, no. 19, September 1, 1898, 6.

455. His letter to the Geneva center of the CUP, Habarovsk, May 7, 1900, AQSh, 19/59//182/13.

456. His unsigned and undated note [June 1900?] to the CUP central committee, AQSh, 19/59//27/250.

457. His undated letter [April 1900?] to the CUP central committee, AQSh, 19/59//176/14.

458. His letter to the administration of *Osmanlı*, Orenburg, May 13, 1900, AQSh, 19/33//30/1.

459. Out of the total donations of £ 163, £ 18 was received from Hâris Feyzullah in 1900. See AQSh, 19/62//232/28. Also there were donation receipts from various Turkic persons such as a ruble from Hüsameddin Seyfullah, dated March 29, 1900/no. 22, AQSh, 19/62//325/16, and a ruble from a certain Süleyman, AQSh, 19/62//208/15.

460. His undated letter to the central committee in Geneva from Yalta, AQSh, 19/106-4//619/1169.

461. "İ'tizâr," *Feryad*, no. 2, December 25, [18]99, 8. For measures against the journal, see BBA-BEO/Mümtaze Kalemi: Kıbrıs, 2/72 (1312. 8. 27).

462. Luras to Sanderson, London, February 27, 1899/no. 1169-99, PRO/F.O. 78/5011, and Smith to Chamberlain, Nicosia, January 3, 1899 (confidential), PRO/F.O. 78/5011, and January 17, 1900 (confidential), PRO/F.O. 78/5074.

463. To Sanderson, London, March 3, 1900/no. 3002, PRO/F.O. 78/5074.

464. Chamberlain to Smith, London, March 9, 1900 (confidential), PRO/F.O. 78/5054.

Chapter 6

1. Tahsin Bey's note to the Paris embassy, May 26, 1900, Türk İnkılâp Tarihi Enstitüsü Arşivi, 82/18164-73(1).

2. For the roles of Abdullah Cevdet and İshak Sükûti in the administration of the CUP after their appointments to government posts, see Nuri Ahmed to İshak Sükûti, Dover, September 14, 1900, AQSh, 19/106-5//1541/7, Âkil Muhtar to İshak Sükûti, Geneva, April 27, 1900, AQSh, 19/106-1//423/346, Abdurrahman Bedirhan to İshak Sükûti, undated, AQSh,19/106//104/1, Abdullah Cevdet to İshak Sükûti, Vienna, October 29, 1900, January 1, 1901, undated five letters see respectively, AQSh, 19/106//243/1, 19/106//240/1, 19/106//286/1, 19/106//280/1, 19/106//288/1, 19/106//296/1, 19/106//291/1; "Pek Büyük Bir Ziya'," *Osmanlı*, no. 103, March 1, 1902, 2, "İshak Sükûti'nin Ölümünün Yıldönümü," *İçtihat*, no. 315, February 15, 1931, 5579.

3. "İhtar," *Osmanlı*, no. 49, December 1, 1899, 1.

4. Ahmed Rıfat to İshak Sükûti, Berlin, February 15, 1900, AQSh, 19/106-1//285/445.

5. "Der Zweck unserer Herausgebung," *Osmanli Deutsche Beilage*, no. 1, January 1900, 1. A translation of this article was published in the central organ. See "Almanca İlâvemizin Dibacesi," *Osmanlı*, no. 54, February 15, 1900, 3.

6. The note entitled "Avis" enclosed with his letter dated January 22, 1900, PAAA, 733/1, Die Jungtürken, 198 (Bd.2-3).

7. Halil Muvaffak to İshak Sükûti, January 23, 1900, AQSh, 19/106-3//256/965: "I have read *Osmanlı*. I found the introduction of *Osmanlı* in German utterly absurd. Many things previously written in *Osmanlı* refute this article. Very well, it was written in German out of necessity. What was the reason for its translation?"

8. Unsigned letter to the Geneva center, Berlin, March 18, 1900, AQSh, 19/106-1//268/421.

9. February 22, 1900/17 von Genf, no. 100, Bundesarchiv-Bern, E. 21/14'250.

10. Refik Nevzad to İshak Sükûti, August 28, [18]99, AQSh, 19/106-6//568/1816.

11. The Ministry of the Interior to Delcassé, December 9, 1899, AE-NS-T, 3 (1899–1901), 172–73.

12. See the notes sent to Constans, Paris, January 23 and 27, 1900, AE-NS-T, 3 (1899-1901), 172–3.

13. The story of the flight is given in Joseph Denais, *La Turquie nouvelle et l'ancien régime* (Paris, 1909), 43 ff.

14. See O. Waternau, "La fuite de Mahmoud-pasha," *Le Soleil du Midi*, December 19, 1899, "Mahmoud Pasha," *Times*, December 22 and 25, 1899.

15. J. F. Malan, "Mahmoud Pasha à Marseille," *Le Petit Provençal*, December 29, 1899, "Mahmoud Pasha," *Times*, January 16, 1900.

16. Marschall von Bieberstein to Schillingsfürst, Pera, December 15, 1899/no. 373, A. 14756, A. 15320, Pera, December 22, 1899/no. 380, December 24, 1899/no. 385, PAAA, 732/3, Die Jungtürken, 198 (Bd.1-2).

17. Marschall von Bieberstein to Auswärtiges Amt, December 27, 1899/no. 392 (telegram), PAAA, Eisenbahnen in der asiatischen Türkei, 152 (Bd. 17); BBA-YEE, 31/322/115/8; O'Conor to Sanderson, Constantinople, December 21,

1899, O'Conor Papers, 4/1/17; and N. Nicolaïdès, "De plus en plus Anglophile," *L'Orient* 12, no. 2, January 13, 1900, 3–4.

18. See Marschall von Bieberstein to Schillingsfürst, Pera, December 26, 1899/no. 390 (Geheim), A. 15276, December 27, 1899/no. 391 (Entzifferung), A. 15285, and a special memorandum prepared for the kaiser, Berlin, December 28, 1899, A. 15275, 15276, 15285 (orig.10837), PAAA, 732/3, Die Jungtürken, 198 (Bd.1-2).

19. This is the ninth of the ten letters that Damad Mahmud Pasha sent to various people and were intercepted by Münir Bey, who presented them to the French authorities on March 3 and 6, 1902 in order to prove that Damad Mahmud Pasha was not pro-French but an extreme pro-British person. This particular letter was countersigned by Sabahaddin and Lûtfullah Beys and dated December 23, 1899. AE-NS-T, 4 (1902–1904), 61–62, 75.

20. See "Deutschland und die Affäre Mahmud Pasha," *Die Post*, December 28, 1899, and "Konstantinopel," *Die Post*, July 19, 1900.

21. See Münir Bey to the Chamberlain's office, December 29, [18]99/no. 46, and December 31, [18]99/no. 48, *Paris Sefaret-i Seniyesiyle Muhaberata Mahsus Defterdir*, BBA-YEE, 36/2468-42/141/XII.

22. See Marschall von Bieberstein to Schillingsfürst, Pera, December 25, 1899/no. 388 (Entzifferung), A. 15242, December 27, 1899/no. 392 (Geheim-Entzifferung), A. 15307, A. 15308, PAAA, 732/3, die Jungtürken, 198 (Bd.1-2); January 1, 1899/no. 2, A.43, PAAA, 733/1, Die Jungtürken, 198 (Bd.2-3). The bargain between Damad Mahmud Pasha and Münir Bey was exaggerated by the press. See "Mahmoud Pasha à Paris," *La Libre Parole*, December 28, 1899.

23. The letter signed Hi, London, January 6, 1900, AE-NS-T, 3 (1899–1901), 162.

24. "Havâdis," *Sancak*, no. 10, January 20, 1900, 7.

25. London, January 11, 1900, AE-NS-T, 3 (1899-1901), 166–67. This viewpoint was shared by German diplomats. See Marschall von Bieberstein to Schillingsfürst, Pera, December 26, 1899, A.15422, PAAA, 732/3, Die Jungtürken, 198 (Bd.1-2).

26. From member number 7348 to the central committee, January 22, 1900, Private Papers of Ahmed Rıza (1).

27. R. Figanî, "Damad-ı Şehriyârî Devletlû Damad Mahmud Paşa Hazretleri'ne," *Osmanlı*, no. 55, March 1, 1900, 3, "Galeyân-ı Umumî," *Osmanlı*, no. 60, May 15, 1900, 3–4, "İstanbul'dan," *Osmanlı*, no. 60, 2.

28. "Cenevre'de Münteşir İnkılâb Gazetesinde Damad Mahmud Paşa Hazretlerine Yazılan Mektubdan," *Emel*, no. 1 [March 24, 1900], 3–4, "Para," *Emel*, no. 7 [May 24, 1900], 1.

29. [Hoca Kadri], "Damad Mahmud Paşa Hazretlerine Ariza-i Mahsusa," *Havatır*, no. 15 [September 8, 1900], 1.

30. "Millet-i Osmaniyenin Tedkikine," *Islahat*, no. 4 [December 14, 1904], 3.

31. Seyfullah Bey, the Ottoman General Consul in Marseilles, to the Chamberlain's office, December 21, [18]99, BBA-YEE, 19/39/143/56.

32. "Lettre de Mahmoud Pasha," *Mechveret Supplément Français*, no. 89, January 1, 1900, 1-2. This letter was also published in the French press. See "Une lettre de Mahmoud Pasha," *L'Aurore*, January 1, 1900. Some parts of this letter were later translated into Turkish in a Cretan journal. See "Bir Sada-yı Teessür," *İstikbâl (3)*, no. 42 [April 8, 1909], 1.

33. Münir Bey to the Chamberlain's office, January 3, 1900, BBA-YEE, 19/39/143/56.

34. Anthopulos Pasha to Tahsin Bey, January 6, 1900, Archives of the Turkish Embassy in London, Box 339 (1), and Anthopulos Pasha to the Chamberlain's office [January 20, 1900], *Londra Sefaret-i Seniyesiyle Muhaberata Mahsus Kayd Defteridir*, BBA-YEE, 36/2468/141-63/XII.

35. O'Conor to Salisbury, Constantinople, December 20, 1899/no. 590, PRO/F.O. 78/4996.

36. The letter was undated and the minutes were dated January 4, 1900, PRO/F.O. 78/5074.

37. Their letter dated January 8, 1900, PRO/F.O. 78/5074.

38. Marschall von Bieberstein's telegrams, Pera, January 1, 1900/no. 1, A. 36, and Pera, February 10, 1900/no. 30, A. 1783, PAAA, 733/1, Die Jungtürken, 198 (Bd.2-3).

39. See To Schillingsfürst, Bern, September 13, 1900/no. 93, A. 15297, PAAA, 733/2, Die Jungtürken, 198 (Bd.3-4).

40. Constans to Delcassé, Pera, January 7, 1900/no. 2, AE- NS-T, 3 (1899–1901), 163.

41. Circulaire-Note Verbale of the Ottoman Foreign Ministry, February 4, 1900, PRO/F.O. 195/2091, AE-NS-T, 3 (1899-1901), 176–78.

42. Damad Mahmud Pasha, "Lettre au Sultan Abdul-Hamid," *Mechveret Supplément Français*, no. 91, February 1, 1900, 1.

43. Maimon's telegram to Mahmud Pasha, Pera, March 19, 1900/no. 34020, AE-NS-T, 3 (1899-1901), 190.

44. He sent a telegram to the sultan denouncing his politics and implied that he refused the offer. Geneva, March 27, 1900/no. 39081, ibid., 193.

45. To Delcassé, Vienna, January 16, 1900, and Gerard to Delcassé, January 18, 1900, ibid., 168–69.

46. See T. L. to the editor of Osmanlı, Istanbul, May 30, 1900, AQSh, 19/135//235/1, and a certain Murad to Nuri Ahmed, June 18, 1900, AQSh, 19/135//172/1.

47. To Schillingsfürst, Bern, February 17, 1900/no. 21 (Geheim), A. 2162, Pera, April 7, 1900/no. 116 (Entzifferung), A. 4243, PAAA, 733/1, Die Jungtürken, 198 (Bd.2-3); and to Goluchowski, Bern, April 12, 1900/no. 26, HHStA, PA, XXVII 47 Schweiz Berichte, 1900.

48. For his arrival in Geneva see the note of the Department of Justice and Police, March 31, 1900/no. 156 (P.P. 17/15), Bundesarchiv-Bern, E. 21/14'250.

49. "Schwager des Sultans," *Berliner Tageblatt*, April 2, 1900.

50. For an example see "Aus der Türkei," *Neue Preussische Zeitung*, February 9, 1900. However, these allegations continued afterward. See "Aus der Türkei," "Ausland," *Der Bund*, August 14, 1900, "Damad Mahmud Pasha's thatsächlich Lage," *Neue Freie Presse*, February 24, 1902.

51. Karatodori Pasha to Tevfik Pasha, Geneva, March 30, 1900, Dışişleri Bakanlığı Hazine-i Evrak Arşivi, Siyasî, D. 178.

52. For his flight see "Havâdis," *Osmanlı*, no. 97, December 1, 1901, 8.

53. "La Jeune Turquie-Fuites et exils," *Journal de Genève*, April 18, 1900.

54. Abdullah Cevdet to İshak Sükûti, April 16, 1900, AQSh, 19/106//218/1.

55. Halil Muvaffak's undated letter, AQSh, 19/106-3//102/892, and his letter to Sükûti, dated June 5, [1900], AQSh, 19/106-3//701/861.

56. İbrahim Temo to İshak Sükûti [February 3, 1900], AQSh, 19/106-3//102/1068.

57. For his flight and participation in the Geneva group see, BBA-YEE, 15/74-18-ç/74/15.

58. Mehmed Lütfi to İshak Sükûti, Folkestone, November 2, 1900, AQSh, 19/106-4//379/1179.

59. See Edhem Ruhi, "İntibah!" *Enîn-i Mazlûm*, no. 17, October 16, 1899, 131–32.

60. Nuri Ahmed to İshak Sükûti, Geneva, March 20, 1900, AQSh, 19/106-5//269/1555.

61. Damad Mahmoud Pacha, "Une Lettre de Mahmoud," *La Suisse*, April 6, 1900.

62. Noury-Ahmed, "La Jeune Turquie," *La Suisse*, April 9, 1900.

63. "Damad Mahmud Paşa Hazretleriyle Mülâkat," *Osmanlı*, no. 57, April 1, 1900, 8.

64. The fifty-seventh issue starts with an article by Damad Mahmud Pasha and continues with his note to the sultan, and an interview that the fugitive brother-in-law gave. On pages 2 and 3 the second letter of Sabahaddin and Lûtfullah Beys to the sultan was published. Comments on this letter and a poem by Damad Mahmud Pasha were published on pages 6 and 7 of this eight-page journal.

65. "1 Beilage zur bericht 26 A-B de dato, Bern 12/IV 1900/no. 26," and to Goluchowski, Bern, August 6, 1900/no. 54 (Geheim), HHStA, PA XXXVII 47 Schweiz Berichte 1900.

66. E. Şehrik to the private secretary of Damad Mahmud Pasha, June 28, 1900, AQSh, 19/61//12/14.

67. See "Türkiye Hakkında Bir İngiliz'in Fikri," *Osmanlı*, no. 52, 3–4, "Anadolu'nun Mukaseme-i İbtidaiyesi ve Alman Dostluğunun İçyüzü," *Osmanlı*, no. 56, March 15, 1900, 1–5.

68. "Havâdis," *Osmanlı*, no. 56, 8.

69. BBA-YSHM, 8 M 1313/no. 71. Also see "Ismail Kamal Bey," *al-Moayyad édition Français*, March 17, 1901.

70. Decipher from Sir Nicholas, Pera, April 21, 1900/no. 32, PRO/F.O. 78/5062.

71. O'Conor to Salisbury, Constantinople, April 25, 1900/no. 146, PRO/F.O. 78/5058.

72. Macgregor to Sanderson, Admiralty, April 26, 1900/no.0558 (confidential), PRO/F.O. 78/5074.

73. See Adam Block's memorandum dated May 1, 1900, enclosed with the letter from O'Conor to Salisbury, Constantinople, May 2, 1900/no. 161. PRO/F.O. 78/5058. Also underscored in the coded telegram of Sir Nicholas R. O'Conor, April 30, 1900/no. 36, PRO/F.O. 78/5062, and in "Turquie," *Le Temps*, May 4, 1900.

74. Three letters dated 'le Samedi Matin,' 'le Mardi Matin,' and 'le 30 Avril 1900 à bord du Salamander' were sent to Sir Nicholas and Adam Block. They are enclosed with the letter from O'Conor to Salisbury, Constantinople, May 2, 1900/no. 161, PRO/F.O. 78/5058.

75. Coded telegram from Sir Nicholas R. O'Conor, April 30, 1900/no. 35, PRO/F.O. 78/5062.

76. Coded telegram from Sir Nicholas R. O'Conor, May 1, 1900/no. 37, PRO/F.O. 78/5062.

77. The telegram sent by the central committee was published in the central organ. See "Havâdis," *Osmanlı*, no. 60, May 15, 1900, 4. Damad Mahmud Pasha's undated [May 1900] letter is in PRO/F.O. 195/2086.

78. Major Morgan's report, Constantinople, May 1, 1900 (Militärbericht nr. 114) A. 5672, Marschall von Bieberstein to Schillingsfürst, Pera, May 3, 1900/ no. 49, A. 5756, PAAA, 733/1, Die Jungtürken, 198 (Bd.2-3).

79. Marschall von Bieberstein to Schillingsfürst, Pera, May 9, 1900/no. 164 (Entzifferung), A. 5856, PAAA, 733/1, Die Jungtürken, 198 (Bd.2-3).

80. See Marschall von Bieberstein to Schillingsfürst, Pera, May 7, 1900/no. 161 (Geheim-Entzifferung), A. 5805, PAAA, 733/1, Die Jungtürken, 198 (Bd.2-3), to Goluchowski, Bern, July 24, 1900/no. 48 (Geheim), HHStA, PA, XXVII 47 Schweiz Berichte 1900.

81. Egerton to Salisbury, Athens, May 4, 1900/no. 81, PRO/F.O. 421/187. However, the Austrians received contradicting information regarding the impact of İsmail Kemal's flight. See Petrović to Goluchowski, Valona, December 11, 1900/no. 41, HHStA, PA, XIV 7, Albanien.

82. February 28, 1900/17 von Genf/no. 142, Bundesarchiv-Bern, E. 21/14'250.

83. This idea was shared by many diplomats. See to Goluchowski, Bern, July 8, 1900/no. 46, HHSta, PA XXVII 47 Schweiz Berichte 1900; to Schillingsfürst, London, July 6, 1900, A. 8887, PAAA, 733/2, Die Jungtürken 198 (Bd. 3-4).

84. A Diplomatist, "The Sultan's Entourage," *Standard*, May 18, 1900.

85. O'Conor to Sanderson, Therapia, July 17, 1900, Vambéry Papers, PRO/F.O. 800–33; O'Conor to Chirol, Therapia, November 5 [1899], O'Conor Papers, 5/3/4.

86. Prince Sebaheddine-Prince Loutfoullah, *Lettre au Sultan Abdul-Hamid II* (Angers, [1900]), [3–4].

87. PRO/F.O. 195/2085.

88. The letter dated June 12, 1900, PRO/F.O. 78/5074.

89. The letter dated June 22, 1900, PRO/F.O. 78/5074.During the period the Istanbul center of the CUP under the dominance of a pro-British group wrote to the British ambassador that "the partisans of reform in Turkey may continue to count on the support of England." See O'Conor to Salisbury, Constantinople, May 25, 1900/no. 186, PRO/F.O. 78/5059.

90. Damad Mahmoud Pacha, *Protestation de S. A. Damad Mahmoud Pacha contre la nouvelle décision prise par le Sultan Abdul Hamid II à l'égard des Turcs résidant à l'étranger*, [London, 1900], [2].

91. Their telegram to the queen, Geneva, July 19, 1900, PRO/F.O. 78/5074.

92. M. de Bunsen to Cromer, Constantinople, November 10, 1900/no. 386 (confidential), PRO/F.O. 78/5061.

93. O'Conor to Salisbury, Constantinople, May 25, 1900/no. 186, PRO/F.O. 78/5059.

94. Letter, Paris, June 6, 1900, and telegram, London, July 7, 1900, PRO/F.O. 78/5074.

95. Cairo, March 16, 1900, PRO/F.O. 195/2085, and Cairo, January 5, 1901, PRO/F.O. 195/2108.

96. His letter from Cairo dated January 18, 1901, PRO/F.O. 78/5141.

97. Chamberlain's office to the Berlin embassy, January 26, 1901/no. 20,

Berlin Sefaret-i Seniyesiyle Muhaberata Mahsus Defterdir, BBA-YEE, 36/139-66/ 139/XVIII.

98. Âsım Bey to Anthopulos Pasha, October 14, 1900, Archives of the Turkish Embassy in London, Box 348 (2).

99. Anthopulos Pasha to Âsım Bey, October 17, 1900, Archives of the Turkish Embassy in London, Box 382 (2).

100. See Butler-Johnstone to Lansdowne, Brussels, July 4, 1901, and Sanderson to Butler-Johnstone, July 17, 1901, PRO/F.O. 78/5142.

101. Ismail Kemal Bey, "The Transvaal Question from the Mussulman Point of View," *The Forthnightly Review* 69 (January 1901), 147–73.

102. See Ismail Kemal, *La question du Transvaal ou rôle civilisateur de l'Angleterre jugé au point de vue Musulman*(Paris, 1901), and idem, *Transvaal Mes'elesi* (Cairo, 1318 [1902]). Summarized in "Un Programme Politique," *Le Progrès*, March 15 and 16, 1901.

103. See "Siyah Bir Rub' Asır," *Osmanlı*, no. 66, August 15, 1900, 4, "Kaiser ve Padişâh," *Osmanlı*, no. 82, April 15, 1901, 6.

104. "Jungtürken," *St. Petersburger Herald*, April 21, 1901.

105. See [Halil Halid], "The Sultan's Gifts," *The Review of the Week*, March 1, 1901, 490.

106. İshak Sükûti opposed the intervention of ulema in politics. See Edhem Ruhi to İshak Sükûti, August 19, 1901, AQSh, 19/106-2//143/683.

107. The best example is "Müslimine Hitab," *Osmanlı*, no. 59, May 1, 1900, 1–2. Republished by a Cairo-based Young Turk organ. See *Emel*, no. 7 [May 24, 1900], 4.

108. Edhem Ruhi to İshak Sükûti, Folkestone, November 7, 1900, AQSh, 19/106-2//617/1.

109. French intelligence report, London, January 11, 1900, AE-NS-T, 3 (1899–1901), 166–67.

110. Undated spy report [1900], *Bazı Hususî İradeleri Havî Defter*, BBA-YEE, 24/11/162/VII.

111. "The Arrests in Turkey," *Standard*, May 10, 1900.

112. Henry Durbec, "Arrivée de Mahmoud Pacha à Marseille," *Le Figaro*, December 21, 1900.

113. "Security and Justice," *Armenia*, no. 92, June 1, 1900, 1.

114. Halil Muvaffak to İshak Sükûti, May 2, 1900, AQSh, 19/106-3//305/ 928.

115. Martos Ferciyan to the CUP central committee, New York, April 16, 1900, AQSh, 19/58//238/4.

116. Tahsin Bey to Anthopulos Pasha, September 14, 1900, Archives of the Turkish Embassy in London, Box 347 (2).

117. The letter of a certain Şehriyan who worked as the spy of the Ottoman embassy in London, dated, September 12, 1900, Archives of the Turkish Embassy in London, Box 347 (2).

118. Damad Mahmoud Pacha, "Lettre ouverte aux Arméniens," *Pro Arménia*, no. 2, November 10, 1900, 3.

119. Hagopian, "Hyphenated Nationalism", 211.

120. See the appeal of the society dated [September 24, 1900], and Anthopulos Pasha to Tahsin Bey, October 17, 1900, Archives of the Turkish Embassy in London, Box 347 (2).

121. See Anthopulos Pasha to Tahsin Bey, June 7, 1901, Archives of the Turkish Embassy in London, Box 347 (2).

122. See his telegrams and letter to the khedive dated, respectively, August 4, 1900, August 6, 1900, and [January 25, 1900], Abbas II Papers, Durham University, F. 25/9–10, 25/8 and 25/6–7.

123. Telegram from Gazi Ahmed Muhtar Pasha to Âsım Bey [October 24, 1900], BBA-BEO/Mısır Fevkâlâde Komiseri Gazi Ahmed Muhtar Paşa'dan Vürûd Eden, 747-36/5. Two financial records provide detailed information on support given to Damad Mahmud Pasha. See Abbas II Papers, Durham University, F. 25/4 and 25/5.

124. See Hüseyin Kâmi, *Nutk-i Siyasî* (Istanbul, 1326 [1908]), 7.

125. Rodd to Salisbury, Cairo, September 15, 1900/no. 99 (telegraphic). The translation of the message was also sent by the former to the latter, Cairo, September 23, 1900/no. 156, PRO/F.O. 407/155.

126. "Minute by the Council of Ministers," which was enclosed with the dispatch from Rodd to Salisbury, Cairo, September 23, 1900/no. 156, PRO/F.O. 407/155.

127. Rodd to Salisbury, Cairo, September 15, 1900/no. 100 (telegraphic), PRO/F.O. 407/155.

128. Rodd to Salisbury, Cairo, September 17, 1900/no. 101 (telegraphic), PRO/F.O. 407/155. The sultan made similar remarks to M. de Bunsen during an audience given to him. See M. de Bunsen to Cromer, Constantinople, November 10, 1900/no. 386, PRO/F.O. 78/5061.

129. Rodd to Salisbury, Cairo, September 22, 1900/no. 103, PRO/F.O. 407/155.

130. Salisbury to Rodd, September 25, 1900/no. 45 (telegraphic), and September 23 [26?], 1900/no. 46 (telegraphic), PRO/F.O. 407/155. This attitude seemed to be shared by Lord Cromer. See to Delcassé, Le Caire, September 25, 1900/no. 173, AE-NS-T, 3 (1899–1901), 209.

131. See O'Conor to Salisbury, Constantinople November 10, 1900/no. 386 (confidential) and November 13, 1900/no. 392 (confidential), PRO/F.O. 78/5061.

132. Adam Block's memorandum enclosed with the letter from O'Conor to Salisbury, Constantinople, November 10, 1900/no. 385, PRO/F.O. 78/5061.

133. To von Bülow, Cairo, October 24, 1900/no. 122, A. 5705, PAAA, 733/1, Die Jungtürken, 198 (Bd.2-3).

134. See to Goluchowski, Cairo, February 28, 1901/no. 16 (streng vertraulich), HHStA, PA XXXI 21, Ägypten Berichte 1901; Cogordan to Delcassé, Cairo, April 9, 1901/no. 50 (très confidentiel), AE-NS-T, 3 (1899–1901), 222–23; "[Damad Mahmud Paşa]," *Havatır*, no. 26 [May 9, 1901], 3; "La question de Damad Pacha," *al-Moayad édition Français*, April 14, 1901.

135. Cromer's telegram to the Foreign Office, April 4, 1901/no. 32 (confidential), PRO/F.O. 195/2108.

136. Cogordan to Delcassé, Cairo, April 22, 1901/no. 56, AE-NS-T, 3 (1899-1901), 237.

137. Coded telegrams from Gazi Ahmed Muhtar Pasha to Âsım Bey [March 27, 1901]/no. 98, and [April 12, 1901]/no. 107, BBA-BEO/Mısır Fevkâlâde Komiseri Gazi Ahmed Muhtar Paşa'dan Vürûd Eden, 747-36/5; Tahsin Bey to

the khedive [August 4, 1901], Abbas II Papers, Durham University, F. 25/2.

138. Necmeddin Ârif to İshak Sükûti, Cairo, April 18, 1901, AQSh, 19/106-5//244/1719.

139. İshak Sükûti to Doctor Nâzım, April 7, 1901, Private Papers of Bahaeddin Şakir; Ali Fahri to İshak Sükûti, August 18, 1900, AQSh, 19/106-2//203/723.

140. Anthopulos Pasha to Tahsin Bey, December 17, 1900, Archives of the Turkish Embassy in London, Box 362 (1).

141. In his memoirs he gave little information about his relations with the central committee and its organ. See *The Memoirs of Ismail Kemal Bey*, 308.

142. See Faïk Bey Konitza, "Ismail Cémal bég Vlora," *Albania*, vol. E, no. 8 (September 10, 1900), 12, Conte Vladany, "Ismail Kemal-bey-Vlora," *Laimtari i Shcypenies* 2, no. 11/18 (1900), 132.

143. Cogordan to Delcassé, Cairo, March 18, 1901/no. 35, AE-NS-T, 3 (1899-1901), 221–22.

144. Reşid Bey to Âsım Bey, April 7, 1901/no. 21, *Roma Sefaret-i Seniyesine Mahsus Muhabere Defteridir*, BBA-YEE, 36/2469/141/XII.

145. "Ismail Kémal Bey," *Pro Arménia*, no. 12, May 10, 1901, 95, F[aï]k Bey Konitza, "L'Albanie et la Grèce," *Albania*, vol. F, no. 6 (June 20, 1901), 95–96.

146. Governor of Beirut to the Chamberlain's office [May 21, 1901]/no. 48, *Beyrut Vilâyetiyle Muhaberata Mahsus Üçüncü Defterdir*, BBA-YEE, 36/139-59/139/XVIII.

147. This was published in dailies. See "Şuûnat," *İkdam*, March 25, 1901.

148. BBA-YP, 16 L 1318/no. 1397, 6 Za 1318/no. 1573, and 28 M 1319/no. 99; O'Conor to Lansdowne, Therapia, June 18, 1901/no. 238, PRO/F.O. 78/5122.

149. Nuri Ahmed to İshak Sükûti, Folkestone, November 30, 1901, AQSh, 19/106-5//70/1467.

150. Edhem Ruhi to İshak Sükûti, Folkestone, September 2, 1901, AQSh, 19/106-2//114/682.

151. The original text is in AQSh, 19/60//639/18-4. For the text published in the central organ see "Protestonâme," *Osmanlı*, no. 67, September 1, 1900, 1.

152. Their letter to the French President, Paris, August 25, 1901, AE-NS-T, 3 (1899-1901), 261–62.

153. Biographical information about him is provided in three sources: Khayr al-Dīn al-Ziriklī, *al-A'lām* 7 (Beirut, 1979), 157–58; 'Umar Riḍā Kaḥḥālah, *Mu'jam al-mū'allifīn* 12 (Damascus, 1960), 139–40, and al-Maghribī, "al-Shaykh Badr al-Dīn al-Ḥasanī," *Majallat al-Majmā' al-Ilmī al-'Arabī* 13, nos. 5–6 (1935), 296–99, and nos. 7–8 (1935), 351–58. However, nowhere is there any mention of this *fatwā*. Ziriklī writes that the CUP leaders asked Ḥasanī during the First World War to be the caliph, which seems very unlikely. He was accused of trying to undermine Ottoman authority in Syria in 1896. See Commins, *Islamic Reform*, 51. There is a spy report presented Münir Bey, dated [May 5, 1900], accusing al-Marrākushī of taking part in a CUP venture with other prominent Arab figures to incite Arabs in Syria, the Yemen, and Tripoli of Barbary against the sultan's regime. See Archives of the Turkish Embassy in Paris, D. 192.

154. Ketebe-ül-fakîr-ül-hakîr müfti-el-mü'minin Esseyid Şeyh Muhammed el-Marakeşî, "İslâma Tebşir," *Osmanlı*, no. 75, January 1, 1901, 1.

155. See "Fetva," *Osmanlı*, no. 58, April 15, 1900, 1, "İstilâm-ı Şer'i," *Osmanlı*, no. 66, August 15, 1900, 1.

156. Note from the central committee to Sir Nicholas R.O'Conor, dated January 10, 1901, PRO/F.O 195/2108.

157. See O'Conor to Lansdowne, Constantinople, January 16, 1901, PRO/F.O. 78/5120. The minutes written by the British statesmen are as follows: "This is the same as the communication recently sent to the Queen. It now appears that it was sent from Folkestone. I do not see that the Home Office can do anything. We had better wait. THS [Sir Thomas Sanderson]", and "This can't do much but it is as well that they should know of this further exhibition of activity at Folkestone. S [Lord Salisbury]".

158. Yaşar Bey to İshak Sükûti, Athens, January 29, 1901, AQSh, 19/106-3//21/1119.

159. Necmeddin Ârif to İshak Sükûti, January 10, 1901, AQSh, 19/106-5//1720/421.

160. "Φόβοι 'Επαναστάσεώς έν Κώνσταντινουπόλει," 'Ακρόπολις, January 14, 1901.

161. İsmail Hakkı to Ahmed Rıza, Candia [February 6, 1901], Private Papers of Ahmed Rıza (1). For another criticism made in a Geneva-based Young Turk journal, see "İlân-ı Hakikat," *Vatan*, no. 2, January 18, 1901, 1–2.

162. "Netice-i Hâl," *Vatan*, no. 3, January 25, 1901, 1–2.

163. A copy of the appeal based on the *fatwā* was enclosed with the dispatch from Anthopulos Pasha to Tahsin Bey, February 23, 1901/no. 5, Archives of the Turkish Embassy in London, Box 361 (3). The *ḥadīth* referred to appears in Al-Muttaqī, *Kanz al-'ummāl* 5, (Hyderabad, 1946–51), 465 (*ḥadīth* # 2577).

164. "Bükreş'de Teessüs Ederek Arnavudluk'da Islahat Maksadını Ta'kib Etmekde Olan (Drita) Nâm Cemiyet Tarafından Damad Mahmud Paşa Hazretlerine Hitaben Yazılmıştır," *Osmanlı*, no. 61, June 1, 1900, 1–2.

165. Scutari branch to the central committee, June 15/28, 1316/1900, AQSh, 19/59//231/18.

166. For the efforts of İsmail Kemal, see Âsım Bey to the Governor of Ioánnina [August 5, 1901]/no. 39, *Yanya [Vilâyetiyle] Muhaberata Mahsus Defter]*, BBA-YEE, 36/2470/147/XVI; a spy report given to the Ottoman ambassador in London, dated May 1, 1901, Archives of the Turkish Embassy in London, Box 362 (1). Berlin embassy to the Chamberlain's office, April 17, 1901/no. 60, and [April 18, 1901]/no. 62, *Berlin Sefaret-i Seniyesiyle Muhaberata Mahsus Kayd Defteridir*, BBA-YEE, 36/139-61/139/XVIII; to von Bülow, Cairo, June 8, 1901/no. 115, A. 9214, PAAA, 733/2, Die Jungtürken, 198 (Bd.3-4).

167. "Jungtürken und albanische Bewegung," *Wiener politische Korrespondenz*, July 25, 1901.

168. For his activities, see Rıf'at Bey to Âsım Bey [December 10, 1901]/no. 181, [December 12, 1901]/no. 182, [December 23, 1901], *Çetine, Stockholm, Brüksel, Washington, Korfu Sefaretlerine Mahsus Muhabere Defteri*, BBA-YEE, 36/139-60/139/XVIII; to Delcassé, Athens, December 12, 1901/no. 14, and Corfu, September 2, 1901/no. 10, AE-NS-T, 3 (1899-1901), 287; to von Bülow, Athens, August 16, 1901/no. 44, A. 12040, PAAA, 732/2, Die Jungtürken, 198 (Bd.3-4).

169. "Reyb-ül-menûn," *Meşrutiyet*, no. 6, April 11, 1901, 4.

170. Stronge to Lansdowne, Athens, August 19, 1901, *A & P* 87 (1903), 91.

171. To von Bülow, Athens, August, 16, 1901/no. 43, A. 12039, PAAA, 732/2, Die Jungtürken, 198 (Bd.3-4).

172. Capreville to Delcassé, Athens, December 28, 1901/no. 114, AE-NS-T, 3 (1899-1901), 265–66.

173. BBA-İrade-Hususî, Şevval 1319/no. 40-781.

174. BBA-YMGM, 14 Ş 1319/no. 34-7227; to Delcassé, Corfu, December 23, 1901/no. 20, AE-NS-T, 3 (1899–1901), 292.

175. See "S.A.Damad Mahmoud Pacha," *Daoul*, no. 2, October 26, 1900, 2. Although his publication annoyed the palace and drew attention within the diplomatic circles, his activities were baseless. See BBA-YMGM, 14 L 1318/no. 1161-7519, 24 M 1319/no. 207-1691; to von Bülow, Rotterdam, May 14, 1901/ no. 1310, A.8167, May 30, 1901/no. 59, A. 8167, June 1, 1901/no. 1456, A. 8333, PAAA, 733/2, Die Jungtürken, 198 (Bd.3-4).

176. He suddenly published an article favoring the Young Turk movement see Alfred Rustem Bey, "La Jeune Turquie," *La Gazette de Lausanne*, May 25, 1901. For the remark made by the French diplomat, Miébaut, see his letter to Delcassé, Bern, May 29, 1901, AE-NS-T, 3 (1899–1901), 239.

177. See his letter to the CUP center in London, dated January 21, 1901, AQSh, 19/93//588/6. See also Nuri Ahmed to İshak Sükûti, January 25, [1]901, AQSh, 19/106-5//59/1539.

178. "İhtar-ı Mühim," *Osmanlı*, no. 68, September 15, 1900, 1.

179. Edhem Ruhi to İshak Sükûti, Geneva, August 14, 1900, AQSh, 19/ 106-2//182/643.

180. Celâleddin Ârif to İshak Sükûti, Geneva, July 26, 1901, AQSh, 19/106-7//166/1901.

181. "Halil Muvaffak Bey'in Londra'daki Hesâbâtı," AQSh, 19/62//103/ 29. Damad Mahmud Pasha also sent small sums irregularly. See Nuri Ahmed to İshak Sükûti, London, May 22, [1]900, June 1, 1900, and Folkestone, November 2, 1900, AQSh, 19/106-5//158/1562, 19/106-5//138/1566, 19/106-5// 407/1559.

182. BBA-BEO/Hariciye Reft, 185-5/41, 1291 [February 4, 1901]/ 121097, 1273 [February 6, 1901]/129896; BBA-İrade-Hususî, Safer 1319/no. 38-104.

183. See two letters from Memduh Pasha to İshak Sükûti, one of them undated and the second one with the date [March 30, 1900], AQSh, 19/106-4/ /2161/1213, and 19/106-4//259/1212. Also see Abdullah Cevdet to İshak Sükûti, May 6, 1900, AQSh, 19/106//251/1.

184. Abdullah Cevdet to İshak Sükûti, Vienna, March 30, 1900, AQSh, 19/ 106//153/22.

185. Ali Kemal's letter dated September 23, 1900, in "Kitab-ı Ahd-i Atik," *İleri*, February 2, 1919.

186. See Nuri Ahmed to İshak Sükûti, Folkestone, March 5, 1901 and March 12, 1901, AQSh, 19/106-5//274/1525, and 19/106-5//190/1521.

187. The CUP headquarters in Folkestone to Todoraki Efendi in London, December 7, [1]900, Archives of the Turkish Embassy in London, Box 361 (2).

188. See Baron de Richtofen's letter to Münir Bey, dated, Geneva, November 26, 1900, published in "L'espionnage turc à Genève," *La Suisse*, May 30, 1902; coded telegram from Anthopulos Pasha to Tahsin Bey, April 21, 1901, Archives of the Turkish Embassy in London, Box 362 (2).

189. Nuri Ahmed to İshak Sükûti, Folkestone, November 22, 1900, and December 26, 1901, AQSh, 19/106-5//59/1539, and 19/106-5//373/1603.

190. For complaints and accusations of "immorality," see Lâli [Mehmed Reşid] to İshak Sükûti, Tripoli of Barbary [April 19, 1901], AQSh, 19/106-4//247/1145, and Mehmed Lütfi to İshak Sükûti, undated [1900?], AQSh, 19/106-4//815/1188.

191. AQSh, 19/60//28/19.

192. Nuri Ahmed to İshak Sükûti, Folkestone, February 4, 1901, AQSh, 19/106-5//304/1538.

193. See Azdî [Mustafa Refik] to İshak Sükûti, Berlin, February 11, 1900, AQSh, 19/106-2//275/471; Ahmed Rıfat to İshak Sükûti, March 20, 1900, AQSh, 19/106-1//272/423; and Mustafa Reşid to İshak Sükûti, Berlin, December 1, 1900, AQSh, 19/106-4//369/1237.

194. See Edhem Ruhi to İshak Sükûti, Folkestone, May 30, 1901, and August 5, 1901, AQSh, 19/106-2//243/695, and 19/106-2//127/691; Halil Muvaffak to İshak Sükûti, undated [1901?], AQSh, 19/106-3//114/891.

195. Rauf Ahmed to İshak Sükûti, Folkestone, May 4, 1901, AQSh, 19/106-6//242/1926.

196. Many of the reports of this detective agency are in the Archives of the Turkish Embassy in London, Box 339 (1).

197. The drafts of Sir Thomas Sanderson's letters to the Home Office, November 8, 1900, PRO/F.O 78/5075, and November 19, 1900, PRO/F.O. 78/5075, and Murdock to Sanderson, November 24, 1900/no. 34143, PRO/F.O. 78/5075.

198. Folkestone Borough Police Chief H. Reeve's letter to the Home Office, December 30, 1900, PRO/F.O. 78/5141, the draft of Sir Thomas Sanderson's memorandum to the Ottoman ambassador, January 14, 1901, PRO/F.O. 78/5140; Edhem Ruhi to İshak Sükûti, January 1, 1901, AQSh, 19/106-2//277/728.

199. Draft of the note sent to M. de Bunsen, January 8, 1901, PRO/F.O. 78/5119.

200. "Ziya'-ı Azîm," *Osmanlı*, no. 77, February 1, 1901, 1. CUP leaders believed that the answer had actually been signed by the king. Nuri Ahmed wrote: "Just now we have received a response to the telegram of condolence which we had sent to the British King. I am impressed by the answer. This telegram is a kind of passport for us, i.e., for the CUP." See his letter to İshak Sükûti, Folkestone, January 25, 1901, AQSh, 19/106-5//22/1540.

201. The draft of the memorandum by Sir Thomas, April 3, 1901, PRO/F.O. 78/5141.

202. The draft of the memorandum by Sir Thomas, April 16, 1901, PRO/F.O. 78/5141.

203. Drafts of Sir Thomas's memoranda dated May 25 and 27, 1901, PRO/F.O. 78/5141.

204. The draft of the memorandum sent by Lord Lansdowne to Anthopulos Pasha, February 20, 1902, PRO/F.O. 78/5209.

205. A confidant of Ahmed Rıza warned him concerning Damad Mahmud Pasha's close relations with the British and required the positivist leader not to take a strong stand against the fugitive, stating that he was constantly denying charges that he was a British agent. See letter, Paris, June 19, 1900 (confidentielle), Private Papers of Ahmed Rıza (2).

206. "L'Intervention des étrangers," *Mechveret Supplément Français*, no. 107, December 1, 1900, 1.

207. Doctor Nâzım to İshak Sükûti, undated [mid-1900], AQSh, 19/106-5//845/1382.

208. Ahmed Rıza's letter to Şerif Bey, dated October 24, 1901, Şerif Paşa, *İttihad ve Terakki'nin Sahtekârlıklarına*, 12–17. He later wrote that he had not only sent money but supported other activities of Ahmed Rıza. See Şerif Paşa, *Mücahede-i Vataniye: Muhalefet-i İttihad ve Terakki Cemiyeti* (Istanbul, 1330 [1912]), 7–9.

209. For these developments, see Ahmed Saib, "İfade-i Mahsusa," *Sancak*, no. 65, October 1, 1906, 1.

210. "Maksad ve Meslek," *Sancak*, no. 1, November 18, 1899, 1. Also see Ali Fahri to İshak Sükûti, Cairo [November 26, 1899], AQSh, 19/106-2//141/750.

211. Ahmed Saib, "Karilerimize İhtar," *Sancak*, no. 25, May 19, 1900, 1.

212. Ahmed Rıza, "Makam-ı Sadarete Açık Mektub," *Sancak*, no. 27, June 1, 1900, 3 ff.

213. "Ahrar-ı Osmaniyeye Üçüncü Mektub," *Sancak*, no. 33, September 15, 1900, 1.

214. "Les Jeunes-Turcs," *Mechveret Supplément Français*, no. 105, 3–4.

215. "Hâl-i Hazırda Ahrar-ı Osmaniye," *Sancak*, no. 53, July 15, 1901, 3.

216. See Rauf Ahmed to İshak Sükûti, Paris, November 13, 1900, AQSh, 19/106-6//371/1904; Necmeddin Ârif to İshak Sükûti, Paris, May 23, 1900, AQSh, 19/106-5//272/1455; Halil Muvaffak to İshak Sükûti, Ferrovia, December 10, 1899, AQSh, 19/106-3//156/543; Edhem Ruhi's unsigned note, Folkestone, January 21, 1901, AQSh, 19/135//303/756; "İttihat ve Terakki!" *Milliyet*, June 3, 1934.

217. Ahmed Saib described the events as follows: "That company's attitude toward me is peculiar. They have not sent me the journal [*Osmanlı*] since I began to publish *Sancak*. They finally sent a copy this week. Abdullah Cevdet has sent two of his books. I did not accept and sent them back. İshak Sükûti is begging me making the late Ârif Bey's son Necmeddin a go-between. He requests that I deny what I wrote about him and not publish anything against *Osmanlı* again. I refused to do these." See Ahmed Saib to Ahmed Rıza, Cairo, October 28, 1900, Private Papers of Ahmed Rıza (1).

218. "(Sancak) Gazetesi Tabi'i Ahmed Saib Efendi'ye," *Osmanlı*, no. 72, November 15, 1900, 8.

219. See Edhem Ruhi, *Mısır'da Sancak Gazetesi Müdiri Ahmed Saib Bey'e* [London, 1900], 10, 14–17.

220. Ahmed Saib, "Enzâr-ı Dikkate," *Sancak*, no. 36, November 1, 1900, 2.

221. Ahmed Saib to Ahmed Rıza, Cairo, October 28, 1900, Private Papers of Ahmed Rıza (1).

222. Rauf Ahmed to İshak Sükûti, Paris, November 4, 1900, AQSh, 19/106-6//399/1905, Mustafa Reşid to İshak Sükûti, November 27, 1900, AQSh, 19/106-4//416/1241.

223. Hüseyin Tosun's undated letter to İshak Sükûti, AQSh, 19/106-3//370/1003.

224. Ahmed Rıza to the khedive, Paris, January 12, 1900, Abbas II Papers, Durham University, F. 26/170.

225. Hüseyin Tosun to İshak Sükûti, February 23, 1901, AQSh, 19/106-3//306/1007.

226. The best examples of İsmail Kemal's approach were Ismail Kemal Bey, "Un appel à l'Europe à la France," *Pro Arménia* 1, no. 24, November 10, 1901, 186–87, and "Lettre au Parliament Français," *Pro Arménia* 2, no. 1, November 25, 1901, 4–5.

227. For Ahmed Saib's criticisms, see "Ahrar-ı Osmaniye ve Avrupa," *Sancak*, no. 25, May 19, 1900, 2.

228. See Cabinet du Ministre, May 25, 1900; Constans's telegram dated June 7, 1900/no. 66, and an urgent note to Waldeck-Rousseau, Paris, June 8, 1900, AE-NS-T, 3 (1899–1901), 197–98, 201–202.

229. The founder of the society was Refik Nevzad, and the other participants were Ahmed Verdanî, Ali Galib, Fevzi Fâzıl, Fuad Nevzad, Galib, Georgos Spinelli, Joseph Hadjès, Salih Fuad, Şemseddin, and Zeki Cemil. See the undated memorandum prepared by the Ottoman embassy in Paris [1901], Archives of the Turkish Embassy in Paris, D. 244.

230. M. Galib to İshak Sükûti, Paris, November 7, 1901, AQSh, 19/106-4//51/1297.

231. Tunalı Hilmi, *Murad*, 38–39.

232. The memorandum prepared by the Department of justice and police, "Jungtürken," Bern, June 9, 1900, Bundesarchiv-Bern, E. 21/14'250.

233. "Geht zum Dossier Mechveret (Jung-Türken) als nr. 2," Bundesarchiv-Bern, E. 21/14'250.

234. Nuri Ahmed to the Swiss President on behalf of the CUP, February 17, 1901, Bundesarchiv-Bern, E. 21/14'251.

235. See Ahmed Celâleddin Pasha to the Chamberlain's office, June 26, [1]900/no. 26, *Paris'de Bulunan Ferik Ahmed Celâleddin Paşa'ya Mahsus Muhabere Defteridir*, BBA-YEE, 36/2328-2/146/XV.

236. Richtofen to Münir Bey, November 26, 1900/no. 1, published in *La Suisse*, May 30, 1902.

237. Richtofen to Diran Kelekyan, July 6, 1900, Türk İnkılâp Tarihi Enstitüsü Arşivi, 82/20097.

238. To Goluchowski, Bern, June 10, 1901/no. 23, HHStA, PA XXVII Schweiz Berichte 1901.

239. Münir Bey to Anthopulos Pasha, Paris, March 14, 1899, and Anthopulos Pasha to Münir Bey, March 15, 1899, Archives of the Turkish Embassy in London, Box 340 (7).

240. See Naim Gergor, *El-Harâb* (Geneva, [1900]), 5 ff.

241. "Mukaddeme," *İnkılâb*, no. 1, January 15, 1900, 1–3.

242. "İntikam İhtilâl İledir," *İnkılâb*, no. 1, 4.

243. For its publication, see Archives d'Etat-Genève-Chancellerie, B. 8, 44, and department of justice and police to the Ministry of the Interior, April 21, 1900/no. 205, Bundesarchiv-Bern, E. 21/14'250.

244. "İzah-ı Maksad," *Darbe*, no. 1, September 15, 1900, 2–3.

245. "Milletin Nazargâh-ı İntibâhına," *Darbe*, no. 1, 9, 16.

246. Nazmi Bey to İshak Sükûti, Geneva, November 24, 1901, AQSh, 19/106-5//73/1344.

247. For its establishment, see Archives d'Etat-Genève-Chancellerie, B. 8, 50, 57.

248. For its publication and distribution, see department of justice and police

to the federal prosecutor, March 23, 1901/no. 88 (P.P. March 24, 1901/no. 130), Bundesarchiv-Bern, E. 21/14'251.

249. Yıldırım, "Köpekler Sürüsün," *İntikam*, no. 28, March 14, 1901, 4. For similar themes see Yıldırım, "Bir Hatve Daha," *İntikam*, no. 22, January 31, 1901, 4: "What shall we accomplish by learning more? What we need is blood, blood! Here is the great news! Now is the time to swim in an ocean of deep red blood." Also see "Ne Vakit Tepeleyeceğiz [?]" *İntikam*, no. 25, February 21, 1901, 4.

250. "İfade-i Mahsusa," *Tokmak*, no. 1, March 1, 1901, 1.

251. "Emirnâme," *İntikam*, no. 1, November 2 [19], 1900, 1. Also see "Yeni Osmanlılar," *İntikam*, no. 29, March 21, 1901, 1–2.

252. "İstanbullulara," *İntikam*, no. 14, January 34, 1901, 4.

253. The undated letter from Romania, AQSh, 19/53//14/187.

254. Halil Muvaffak to İshak Sükûti, October 8, 1901, AQSh, 19/106-3//160/549.

255. Hamid Hüsni, *Ne Yapmalıyız [?]* (Geneva, 1900), 5 ff.

256. See BBA-YP, 9 L 1318/no. 1416.

257. "Ya Muvahhid," *İntikam*, no. 25, 1–2.

258. Hey'et-i Tahririye, "Hürriyet," *İntikam*, no. 1, 2; "İntikam," *İntikam*, no. 2, November 22, 1900, 1–2.

259. "İstanbullular, Taşralılar!" *İntikam*, no. 31, April 4, 1901, 2. The satirical journal published by the society also used similar themes. For instance, in a cartoon in which a tax collector and a peasant are pictured, the following remark is made: "Poor peasants give the morsels in their mouths while they are suffering under the stick of the tax collector." *Tokmak*, no. 3, May 1, 1901, 2.

260. See Archives d'Etat-Genève-Chancellerie, B. 8, 55.

261. "Tevzi'-i Evrak," *İstirdat*, no. 17, October 25, 1901, 3.

262. "Müstahberât," *İstirdat*, no. 7, March 10, 1901, [4].

263. "Otel Métropole İctima'ı ve Bîtaraf Yeni Osmanlılar Cemiyeti," *İntikam*, no. 41, August 2, 1901, 8, and Âkil Muhtar to İshak Sükûti, Geneva, July 19, 1901, AQSh, 19/106-1//157/353.

264. Âkil Muhtar to İshak Sükûti, Geneva, August 20, 1901, AQSh, 19/106-1//359/44.

265. Edhem Ruhi to İshak Sükûti, Folkestone, May 30, 1901, AQSh, 19/106-2//243/695.

266. Edhem Ruhi to İshak Sükûti, Folkestone, December 3, 1900, AQSh, 19/106-2//297/728.

267. See Âkil Muhtar to İshak Sükûti, December 1, 1900, and July 4, 1901, AQSh, 19/106-1//359/44, and 19/106-1//423/346; Ali Fahri to İshak Sükûti, Geneva, March 19, 1901, AQSh, 19/106-2//288/757.

268. Undated note from Âkil Muhtar to İshak Sükûti, AQSh, 19/106-4//1329/4.

269. "Ahmed Rıza Bey," *İstirdat*, no. 3, January 30, 1901, [2–3].

270. See Bundesarchiv-Bern, E. 21/14'259.

271. See Alfred Erich Senn, *The Russian Revolution in Switzerland* (Madison, 1971), 5 ff.

272. Department of justice and police to the federal prosecutor, April 18, 1900/no. 85 (P.P. April 19, 1900/85), and April 19, 1900/no. 184 (P.P. April 19, 1900/181), Bundesarchiv-Bern, E. 21/14'250.

273. See "Genf," *Vossiche Zeitung*, December 29, 1900.

274. For press articles about the event, see "Ein türkische Generalkonsulat,"

Berliner Tageblatt, February 7, 1901, "Schweiz," *Müncher Allgemeine Zeitung,* February 12, 1901.

275. To Goluchowski, Bern, November 22, 1900/no. 72, and November 27, 1900/no. 73, November 29, 1900/no. 75, HHStA, PA XXVII 47 Schweiz Berichte 1900; and Bern, February 9, 1901/no.6, HHStA, PA XXVII 48 Schweiz Berichte 1901.

276. See "Le remplacement de Karathédory," *La Gazette de Lausanne,* December 1, 1900, "La Turquie en Suisse," *La Suisse,* January 19, 1901, "Die türkische Wirtschaft in Genf," *Der Bund,* February 12, 1901, and "Bundesrat," *Nationale Zeitung,* February 13, 1901.

277. "La Turquie en Suisse," *La Gazette de Lausanne,* December 24, 1900, "Das Völkerrecht in der genfer Konsulatsfrage," *Der Bund,* May 9, 1901.

278. See his letter dated May 8, 1901/no. 91, Bundesarchiv-Bern, E. 21/14'259.

279. Bundesarchiv-Bern, E. 21/14'251. His efforts were condemned by the Young Turks. See "Yine Sefir Münir Bey," *Osmanlı,* no. 87, June 1, 1901, 7–8.

280. See to Delcassé, July 6, 1901/no. 58, AE-NS-T, 3 (1899–1901), 255–56.

281. See the investigation report dated May 7, 1901/no. 167 (P.P. May 8, 1901/no. 167 (P.P. May 8, 1901/130), Bundesarchiv-Bern, E. 21/14'251.

282. The Swiss Political Police initially interrogated Hamid Hüsni, Ali Fahri, Ali Galib, Mahir Said, and Hikmet Süleyman on May 6, 1901 (P.P. May 8, 1901/78). On June 21, 1901, Ali Fahri, Hüsni Hamid, and Ali Galib were once again interrogated (interrogation documents ff. 59–62) and Âsaf Nazmi was interrogated twice on June 21 and July 3, 1901 (interrogation documents ff.62 and 78). Bundesarchiv-Bern, E. 21/14'251.

283. For the application written in two languages see Hey'et-i Tahririye, "Âlicenâb ve Misafirperver İsviçrelilere," *İntikam,* no. 35, May 9, 1901, 2, and "A le généreuse hospitalité de la Suisse," *İntikam,* no. 35, 1.

284. See "Les exploits de Munir Bey," *La Gazette de Lausanne,* July 9, 1901.

285. See BBA-İrade-Hususî, Rebiy'ülevvel 1319/no.7-21, BBA-BEO/Hariciye Âmed, 160-5/16 976 [July 20, 1901]/125783; BBA-YSHM, 2 Ra 1319/no. 261 and 9 Ra 1319/no. 295.

286. BBA-YSHM, 21 Ra 1319/no. 340; to von Bülow, Bern, July 6, 1901/no. 53, A. 10120, PAAA, 733/2, Die Jungtürken, 198 (Bd.2-3); to Goluchowski, Bern, July 13, 1901/no. 28, HHStA, PA XXVII 48 Schweiz Berichte 1901.

287. See leading articles in the following dailies: "Die Jungtürken," *Schweizer Handels-Kurier,* July 27, 1901, "Eidgenossenschaft," *Neue Zürcher Zeitung,* July 28, 1901, "Le droit d'asile et les Jeunes-Turcs," *La Nationale Suisse,* July 30, 1901. For the articles criticizing the Ottoman government and Münir Bey, see "Lettre de Turquie," *La Gazette de Lausanne,* July 24, 1901, "Unter dem Halbmond," *Der Bund,* July 24, 1901, "Genf," *Basler Nachrichten,* July 25, 1901, "La Turquie en Suisse," *La Gazette de Lausanne,* July 29, 1901. For the interview given by Ali Fahri, see "Les Jeunes Turcs," *La Gazette de Lausanne,* July 26, 1901.

288. An interesting project proposed by Bahriyeli Rıza in late 1899, was to write a pamphlet on Sheikh Abū al-Hudā al-Ṣayyādī and sell it to the palace to solve the financial crisis. See Bahriyeli Rıza to İshak Sükûti, Cairo, October 27, [18]99, AQSh, 19/106-5//134/1617. An interesting remark regarding the blackmailing efforts of the Young Turks in Egypt was made by Lord Cromer who stated: "The Palace clique at Constantinople instigates the Young Turks, who abound here, to

start a newspaper in Cairo. No one reads it, but if it is sent to Constantinople and frightens the Sultan, he buys it up. When blackmail has thus been levied, the newspaper ceases, and shortly reappears under another name and with slightly changed *dramatis personæ.* Then the process begins again." See Cromer to Salisbury, Cairo, December 16, 1899/ no. 318 (Private), Cromer Papers, Letters to Secretaries of State, PRO/F.O. 633/VI.

289. "Hakka Taaddi," *Hakk-ı Sarih,* no. 3, 1.

290. Edhem Ruhi to İshak Sükûti, Geneva, August 7, 1900, AQSh, 19/106-2//194/640.

291. AQSh, 19/61//742/19-1.

292. "Şu'beden," *Hak,* no. 22, July 15, 1900, 1.

293. A'ḍā' Jam'īyyat Ittiḥād wa al-Taraqqī al-'Uthmānī bi Miṣr, *Bayān,* [1900]. A copy of it is in AQSh, 19/60//366/21. A Turkish translation was given in *Sancak,* no. 29, July 15, 1900, 3. Similar accusations were made in the organ of those who broke off from the branch. See "Hakka Taaddi," *Hakk-ı Sarih,* no. 2, July 25, 1900, 2.

294. "Şu'beden," *Hak,* no. 22, 1.

295. Ali Fahri to Nuri Ahmed, Cairo, May 23, 1900, AQSh, 19/135//169/24; M. Galib to İshak Sükûti, March 12, 1900, AQSh, 19/106-4//283/1319.

296. Necmeddin Ârif to İshak Sükûti, Cairo, June 5 and 21, 1901, AQSh, 19/106-5//183/786, and 19/106-5//186/1734.

297. Hüseyin Tosun to İshak Sükûti, Cairo, November 13, 1901, AQSh, 19/106-3//1010/1901.

298. To Schillingsfürst, Alexandria, September 23, 1900/no. 120, A. 13872, PAAA, 733/2, Die Jungtürken, 198 (Bd.3-4). The activities of Damad Mahmud Pasha and his friends were described as the establishment of a new faction of the Young Turks. See "Turkiyā al-fatāt," *al-Manār* 4, no. 4, April 20, 1901, 160.

299. To Goluchowski, Cairo, February 28, 1901/no. 16 (streng vertaulich), HHStA, PA XXXI 21, Ägypten Berichte 1901.

300. The Chamberlain's office to the Berlin embassy, January 26, 1901/no. 26, *Berlin Sefaret-i Seniyesiyle Muhaberata Mahsus Kayd Defteridir,* BBA-YEE, 36/139-61/139/XVIII. See also an undated spy report of Turhan and Alexandris Pashas in Asaf Tugay, *Saray Dedikoduları ve Bazı Mâruzat* (Istanbul, 1963), 62.

301. M. Galib to İshak Sükûti, December 8, 1900, AQSh, 19/106-4//1329/4.

302. "Esbab-ı Teşekkül," *Hak,* no. 32, 1.

303. "Abdülhamid Han-ı Sânî Hazretlerine Açık Mektub," *Hak,* no. 32, 1.

304. "Abdülhamid Hazretleriyle Hariciye ve Dahiliye Nezaretlerine ve Umum Sefaret-i Ecnebiyeye Takdim Eylediğimiz Muharreratın Suretleridir," *Hak,* no. 37, February 28, 1901, 1–2. A copy of one of these letters bears the date February 11, 1901 and is in PRO/F.O. 195/2108. They attracted very little attention in diplomatic circles. See O'Conor to Lansdowne, Constantinople, March 9, 1901/no. 97, PRO/F.O. 78/5121, to von Bülow, Cairo, February 25, 1901/no. 16, A. 3464, PAAA, 733/2, Die Jungtürken, 198 (Bd.3-4).

305. "Bahriyeli Rıza Bey Tarafından İrad Olunan Nutkun Suretidir," *Hak,* no. 33, December 31, 1900, 1, and "Suikasd," *Hak,* no. 29, November 31, 1900, 1.

306. See "Abdülhamid Hazretlerine İhtar-ı Mahsus," *Hak,* no. 34, January 15, 1901, 1–2.

307. See "Hakka Taaddi," *Hakk-ı Sarih,* no. 3, 4.

308. See "Sancak," *Sancak*, no. 29, 3, "Tekzib," *Sancak*, no. 37, November 15, 1900, 1.

309. See Salih Cemal's letter to the khedive dated October 22, 1901, Abbas II Papers, Durham University, F. 26/288.

310. Celâleddin Ârif to İshak Sükûti, Geneva, July 26, 1901, AQSh, 19/106-7//166/1901-2055.

311. Berlin embassy to the Chamberlain's office [April 3, 1901]/no. 52, *Berlin Sefaretiyle Muhaberata Mahsus Kayd Defteridir*, BBA-YEE, 36/139-61/139/XVIII.

312. See deciphers from Lord Cromer, March 19/20, 1901/no. 22, and March 23, 1901/no. 23, PRO/F.O. 195/2108.

313. See Ahmed Kemal's undated letter to the khedive, Abbas II Papers, Durham University, F. 39/16, and BBA-BEO/Dahiliye Giden, 100-3/49, 442 [April 29, 1901)/123864.

314. See Chapman's letter dated July 6, 1901, Abbas II Papers, Durham University, F. 39/13; Léon Fehmi's memorandum entitled "Résumé des incidents lors de l'imprisonnement au Palace Recetdin." Enclosed with the letter from Cromer to Lansdowne, November 5, 1904/no. 121 (secret), PRO/F.O. 78/5367; Léon Fehmi's two letters, one of which is undated, and the second dated Athens, September 8, 1901, respectively, in Abbas II Papers, Durham University, F. 39/19-20, and 21; to Delcassé, Cairo, July 4, 1901/nos. 18 and 93, AE-NS-T, 3 (1899–1901), 251–54; Earl of Cromer, *Abbas II*, 77–79.

315. See BBA-YP, 18 N 1318/no. 1267.

316. The minutes of this meeting are in the Yıldız Palace Archives. See BBA-YP, 23 Ş 1319/no. 1177.

317. This information was given in a letter sent from Silistireli Hacı İbrahimpaşazâde Hamdi to the CUP through Bahaeddin Şakir, Istanbul [September 14, 1908], Private Papers of Bahaeddin Şakir.

318. O'Conor to Lansdowne, Constantinople, March 9, 1901/no. 97, PRO/F.O. 78/5121.

319. Special imperial order [December 15, 1900]/no. 57, *Bâzı Hususî İradeleri Havî Defter*, BBA-YEE, 24/11/162/VII.

320. See AE-NS-T, 3 (1899–1901), 246–50.

321. "Eshâb-ı Hamiyete Tebşir," *Osmanlı*, no. 82, April 15, 1901, 8.

322. "Havâdis," *Osmanlı*, no. 73, December 1, 1900, 8.

323. See Edhem Ruhi to İshak Sükûti, Folkestone, November 22, 1901, and December 3, 1901, AQSh, 19/106-2//40/669, and 19/106-2//53/671.

324. To Schillingsfürst, Bucharest, March 8, 1900/no. 21, A. 3256, PAAA, 733/1, Die Jungtürken, 198 (Bd.2-3).

325. Ali Kâmi to İshak Sükûti, Cairo, October 15, 1901, and November 15, 1901, AQSh, 19/106/89/1, and 19/106/47/298.

326. "Manastır'dan," *Osmanlı*, no. 83, May 1, 1900, 7.

327. See "Osmanlı İttihad ve Terakki Cemiyeti'nin Bulgaristan Şu'besinden Damad Mahmud Paşa Hazretleri'ne Takdim Olunan Diğer Bir Arizadır," *Osmanlı*, no. 61, June 1, 1900, 1; and "Protestonâme," *Osmanlı*, no. 69, October 1, 1900, 1–2.

328. "Filibe'den," *Osmanlı*, no. 102, February 15, 1902, 7.

329. BBA-BEO/Hariciye Âmed, 159-5/15, 2280 [November 7, 1900].

330. Necmeddin Ârif to İshak Sükûti, January 8, 1901, AQSh, 19/106-5//1729/1049.

331. See "Bulgaristan'dan," *Osmanlı*, no. 90, August 15, 1901, 6, and "Muvazene Gazetesi," *İntikam*, no. 40, July 4, 1901, 4.

332. Its regulations are in AQSh, 19/89//518/13.

333. The spy report of Ali Nâzım, dated [August 6, 1900]/no. 17, *Bâzı Hususî İradeleri Havî Defter*, BBA-YEE, 24/11/162/VII.

334. [September 13, 1900]/no. 59, ibid.

335. "Philipoppel," *Wolff's Telegraphisches Bureau*, no. 1182, March 16, 1901.

336. Ahmed Lûtfullah and Mehmed Sabahaddin, "Umum Osmanlı Vatandaşlarımıza," *Osmanlı*, no. 81, April 1, 1901, 2–5, and *Hak*, no. 38, March 15, 1901, 1–4.

337. "Hanedân-ı Âl-i Osman," *Osmanlı*, no. 81, 1.

338. "Mes'ele-i İctima'," *İntikam*, no. 32, April 11, 1901, 1.

339. See Ali Fahri, *Yeni Osmanlılar Kongresi* (Geneva, 1316 [1900]), idem, *Yine Kongre* (Paris, 1318 [1900]), and Tunalı Hilmi, *Murad*, 149–56.

340. İsmail Hakkı to İshak Sükûti, Cairo, April 15, 1901, AQSh, 19/106-1//252/485.

341. For the expectations of the Armenians, see Pierre Quillard, "La Quinzaine," *Pro Arménia* 1, no. 10, April 10, 1901, 76.

Chapter 7

1. [Colmar] von der Goltz, "Türkische Aussichten," *Asien* 7, no. 12 (September 1908), 157.

2. For the expression of Süleyman Vahid, assistant to the mayor of Adana, see "Matbaamıza Varid Olan Hususî Telgrafnâmeler," *Servet-i Fünûn Tevcihat ve Havâdis Kısmı*, no. 339 [September 9, 1897], 7–8.

3. See Gazi Ahmet Muhtar Paşa to the Sublime Porte [May 5, 1903]/no. 364, BBA-BEO/Mısır Fevkâlâde Komiseri Gazi Ahmed Paşa'dan Vürûd Eden, 747-36/5.

4. See Ayşe Osmanoğlu, *Babam Sultan Abdülhamid* (Istanbul, 1984), 44, 133.

5. Saî [Şerafeddin Mağmumî], "Tohum ve Semereleri," *Meşveret*, no. 6, February 15, 108 [1896], 4.

6. "Acaba Rüesâ mı?" *Muvazene*, no. 26 [March 2, 1898], 2.

7. A congratulatory letter for the twenty-fifth anniversary of the sultan's enthronement was signed by many notables and big landowners. See *Rumeli-i Şarkî Ahali-i Müslimesinin Abdülhamid-i Sânî'ye Gönderdikleri Ariza-i Tebrikiye* IUL, Turkish Manuscripts, no. 9390.

8. Schilcher, *Families in Politics*, 196.

9. "Muhtasaran Tarihçe-i Hayatım," enclosed with the letter from İbrahim Temo to Karl Süssheim, Medgidia, June 25, [1]933, Nachlaβ Süssheim.

10. For his ideas, see his pamphlet *Refutation d'une brochure Grecque par une Valaque Epirote* (Istanbul, 1881), passim.

11. See [Tunalı Hilmi], *Makedonya: Mazi-Hâl-İstikbâl* [Cairo, 1316 [1898]), 14. "Kutzo-Vlaks should form the Macedonian Rumanian element into a branch of the CUP." For the good relations between the CUP and the Aromenis organizations after the Young Turk revolution see Max Demeter Peyfuss, *Die Aromunische Frage: Ihre Entwicklung von den Ursprüngen bis zum Bukarest (1913) und die Haltung Österreich-Ungarns* (Vienna, 1972), 110–11.

12. His approach and that of his father, who served as the Minister of the Interior, were underlined in Bulgarian sources. See *The Bulgarian Question and the Balkan States*, (Sofia, 1919), 197. For his further condemnation by the Bulgarians see Milan G.Markoff, *The Political Lot of the Dobrudja after the Berliner Congress* (Lausanne, 1918), 11 ff. ; A.Ischirkoff, *Les Bulgares en Dobrudja: Aperçu historique et etnographique*, (Bern, 1919), 97. For the ideas of Kogălniceanu see his book, *Dobrogea 1877–1909* (Bucharest, 1910), and V[asile] M. Kogălniceanu, "Osmanlı Milleti, Romen Kavmi," *Sada-yı Millet*, no. 1, 1–2.

13. "Afv-ı Eşkiya," *Sada-yı Millet*, no. 3, March 30, 1898, 2.

14. Among a list of the subscribers to *Osmanlı* and *Meşveret* we come across a coffee house called Berka along side the names of other prominent Bosnian Muslims. Bundesarchiv-Bern, E. 21/14'248.

15. [İshak Sükûti], "Arnavudlar ve Kürdler," *Osmanlı*, no. 51, January 1, 1900, 1. This article was praised in the CUP circle. See undated letter from Ali Sebati to İshak Sükûti, AQSh, 19/106-1//312/724.

16. See Bir Kürd, "Mısır el-Kahire'den," *Osmanlı*, no. 78, February 15, 1901, 8; "İttihad Kuvvetdir," *Hak*, no. 7, December 8, 1899, 3, "Lufta kundre popuivé qe siane Sllave," *Shqipetari*, no. 7, August 24, 1903, 2.

17. "Arnavudluk," *Osmanlı*, no. 31, March 1, 1899, 1.

18. İshak Sükûti prepared his famous article about the Albanians and Kurds for this journal but published it in the official organ. See AQSh, 19/101//691/11-13. For Abdurrahman Bedirhan's requests for articles from İshak Sükûti, see his letter, Cairo, November 14, 1900, AQSh, 19/106//90/1. For Abdullah Cevdet, see [Abdullah Cevdet], "Paris'e Muvasalat," *Kürdistan*, no. 17 [August 27, 1899], 2–3.

19. "Bedirhan Bey," *Kürdistan*, no. 14 [April 19, 1899], 2–4, "Kürdçe Kısım," *Kürdistan*, no. 27 [March 13, 1900], 1–2.

20. See *Akte të Rilindjes Kombëtare Sqiptare, 1878–1912 (Memorandume, vendime, protesta, thirrje)* (Tirana, 1978), 144–45, 156–57, Trank Spirobeg, "A propos d'une note," *Albania*, vol. B, no. 11, March 31, 1898, 187. For another prominent Albanian figure in the Young Turk movement, Derviş Hima, see *Mendimi Politik e Shoqëror i Rilindjes Kombëtare Shqiptare* 1 (Tirana, 1971), 254.

21. "Notes et Documents," *Albania*, vol. A, no. 7, November 15, 1897, 120.

22. See İbrahim Temo to İshak Sükûti, December [6], [18]99, AQSh, 19/106-3//316/1077.

23. "Manastır'dan Bir Sada," *Sada-yı Millet*, no. 5, April 3, 1898, 2.

24. "Devlet-i Osmaniye Neye Muhtacdır [?]" *Sada-yı Millet*, no. 7, April 17, 1898, 1.

25. "Arnavudlar ve Arnavudluk," *Osmanlı*, no. 33, April 1, 1899, 3.

26. For the Albanian claims see Bir Arnavud, "Arnavudluk'dan," *Osmanlı*, no. 75, January 1, 1901, 8. For the article in response and the refusal by the central committee see "Bir Arnavud Mektubuna Cevab," *Osmanlı*, no. 76, January 15, 1901, 8.

27. See Şerafeddin Mağmumî, "Ne İdik, Ne Olduk [?]" *Meşveret*, no. 18, September 8, 108 [1896], 4, and "Bend-i Mahsus," *Girid*, no. 6, April 6, 1897, 1.

28. Although some intermediary groups supported the CUP or the idea of creating a common front with the Turks, the separatist groups refused these invitations. For instance, a Syrian group worked together with the CUP and published a journal in Turkish and Arabic, called *Enîn-i Mazlûm (Moan of the Oppressed)*.

The editor Emin Bey, who was a Catholic Arab from Antioch (see the spy report entitled "Jön Türklerin meşruhatlı esamisi," Abbas II Papers, Durham University, F. 26/281), attacked the separatist Syrian organization called Sūriya al-fatāt and asked them "to join the liberal committee [the CUP], which had remained in its inception for twenty years instead of forming an independent organization." See "Sūriya al-fatāt," *Enîn-i Mazlûm*, no. 6, May 15, 1899, 48. Also see "Ḥizb Sūriya al-fatāt wa ta'thīruhu 'alā al-'uthmāniyya," *Enîn-i Mazlûm*, no. 8, July 12, 1899, 57–58. This person further translated Tunalı Hilmi's *Hutbes* promoting the idea of Ottomanism into Arabic and published them in installments. See "Hutbe: Danışan Dağları Aşdı Danışmayan Düz Ovada Yoldan Şaşdı," *Enîn-i Mazlûm*, no. 12, August 7, 1899, 92 ff. However, the Syrian nationalist organization refused to join the Young Turk movement and undertook an independent action. See "Sūratu al-'ilm: Sūriya al-Fatāt, New York fī 27 Ayār sanat 1899: al-manshūru al-thālith ilā anṣar al-ḥurriya," *Enîn-i Mazlûm*, no. 9, June 26, 1899, 68–69, and "Ra'y al-Ayyām fī Sūriya al-fatāt," *al-Ayyām*, no. 156, July 20, 1899, 1–2. In the case of Albanians, although a group within the *Albania* movement favored a union of Turks and Albanians, it was asking the latter to be Ottomans first. (See Toptanzâde Murad, "Vatandaşlar," *Arnavudluk*, September 1–30, 1898, 1–3, and "Okuyub Anlayana," *Arnavudluk*, July 1, 1898, 1.) However, a stronger group implemented ideas such as the union of all Albanians regardless of their religious affiliations (see "Bashkim, Bashkim!" *Albania*, vol. A, no. 8, December 30, 1897, 121.) or the replacement of Turkish words in the Albanian language with words of Albanian origin (see "Ghuka," *Albania*, vol. B, June 15–30, 1898, 24–25.) thus provoking the irritation of CUP members of Turkish origin. The CUP and its prominent members of Turkish origin were sharply criticized by this second group, who gradually gained control over the Albanian movement. See Faïk Bey Konitza, "Contre les Jeunes-Turcs," *Albania*, vol. A, no. 8, December 30, 1897, 130, "Avis," *Albania*, vol. A, no. 8, 130–31, "L'albanie et les Turcs," *Le Libre Parole*, December 26, 1896, Sh[aban] Demiraj and K[ristaq] Prifti, *Kongresi i Manastirit: Ngjarje me Rëndesi në Lëvizjen Kombëtare Shqiptare* (Tirana, 1978), 52–53.

29. David Kushner, *The Rise of Turkish Nationalism, 1876–1908* (London, 1977), passim.

30. "Suret-i Hatt-ı Hümayûn," *Mizan*, no. 167, March 12, 1896, 2419, and "Türkiya var mı?," *Hak*, no. 35, December 31, 1900, 2.

31. M.A., "Osmanlı İttihadı," *Meşveret*, no. 5, February 1, 108 [1896], 1.

32. "İstanbul'dan Yazıyorlar ki," *Mizan*, no. 183, July 1, 1896, 2551.

33. [Tunalı Hilmi], "Makam-ı Akdes Cenâb-ı Hilâfetpenâhiye," *Osmanlı*, no. 1, 2–3. Similar ideas were constantly exhibited. See "Girid-Yeşil Kitab-Arnavudluk," *Osmanlı*, no. 2, December 15, 1897, 1, and "Matbuat," *Mizan*, no. 181, June 18, 1896, 2536. Similar descriptions may be found in the private letters exchanged among the CUP leaders. One from Ahmed Rıza to Doctor Nâzım dated July 14, [1897], discusses "the national pride of the Turks." Private Papers of Bahaeddin Şakir.

34. See Tunalı Hilmi, *Peşte'de Reşid Efendi İle* ([Geneva], 1317 [1899]), 96, Tunalı Hilmi, *On Birinci Hutbe: Türkiyalılık Osmanlılık; Osmanlılık Türkiyalılıkdır* ([Geneva], 1318 [1901]), passim.

35. Âkil Muhtar to İshak Sükûti, October 2, 1898, AQSh, 19/106-1//2759//335.

36. Undated letter from Halil Muvaffak to İshak Sükûti, AQSh, 19/106-3//128/887.

37. Edhem Ruhi to İshak Süküti, Folkestone, May 13 and 28, 1901, AQSh, 19/106-2//228/700, and 19/106-2//232/698.

38. See "Abdülhamid ve Arnavudlar," *Arnavudluk (2)*, no. 1 (1901), 1–2.

39. "Matbuat-ı Cedide," *Osmanlı*, no. 86, June 15, 1901, 8, and "İsmail Kemal ve Arnavud Kardeşlerimiz," *İntikam*, no. 10, December 20, 1900, 1–2.

40. It was called a "vile journal." See Ali Fahri to İshak Süküti [November 26, 1899], AQSh, 19/106-2//141/750. For denouncements of this journal in the CUP endorsed Egyptian publications see "İttihad," *Enîn-i Mazlûm*, no. 17, October 16, 1899, 134, and "İhtar," *Enîn-i Mazlûm*, no. 18, October 30, 1899, 140.

41. Cemiyet-i İttihadiye-i Çerâkese, "Cemiyet-i İttihadiye-i Çerâkese'nin İlânı Lâzım Gelen Âzâ-yı Hariciye Nizamnâmesi," *İttihad Gazetesi*, no. 1 [October 15, 1899], 6.

42. Tunalı Hilmi wrote a lengthy letter in which he criticized the ideas propagated by this organization and invited its members to join the CUP. This letter was first published in a New York-based Syrian journal in Arabic. See "Ra'y Turkiyā al-fatāt fī Sūriya al-fatāt," *al-Ayyām*, no. 183, October 30, 1899, 1–2 and no. 184, November 2, 1899, 1–2 For the Turkish translation see Tunalı Hilmi, "Azîz Vatandaşlarım," *Enîn-i Mazlûm*, no. 21, November 11, 1899, 162–65. Later this journal supported the efforts of Tunalı Hilmi Bey. See "Ḥilmī Bey wa al-Ayyām," *Enîn-i Mazlûm*, no. 22, November 25, 1899, 171–72. However, the Syrian organization responded unfavorably. See "Naẓra fī sūriya al-fatāt wa turkiyā al-fatāt," *Enîn-i Mazlûm*, no. 22, 173–74.

43. To Schillingsfürst, Cairo, November 20, 1899/no. 135, A. 12645, PAAA, 732/3, Die Jungtürken, 198 (Bd.1-2).

44. Tunalı Hilmi, "Azîz Vatandaşlarım," *Enîn-i Mazlûm*, no. 21, 165.

45. For measures against the Albanian committees, see BBA-BEO/Dahiliye Giden, 97-3/46, 2159 [September 16, 1898])/89628; for measures against the Sūriya al-fatāt, see BBA-BEO/Hariciye Âmed, 159-5/15, 236 [July 2, 1899])/ no. 1248-1078 and a coded dispatch to the province of Syria [May 4, 1894], 669/ 726-55/339, BBA-BEO/Mısır Hidiviyet-i Celilesinin Muharrerat Defteri, 71-1032-68/4; for measures against the Circassian society and its organ established by Mehmed Emin see coded telegram from the Chamberlain's office to Gazi Ahmed Muhtar Pasha [October 13, 1899]/no. 5283, *Mabeyn'den Devâir ve Vilâyetlerle Bâzı Zevata Yazılan Tezkere ve Muharrerat Müsveddelerini Havî Dosya Defteri*, BBA-YEE, 36/398/146/XIV.

46. Ahmed Riza, "Le parlementarisme et la Jeune Turquie II," *L'Orient* 7, no. 36, December 7, 1896, 6.

47. For the criticism of the conservatives, see [Mehmed Ubeydullah], "Kuduz Köpek Cami Duvarına Siyermiş," *Sada*, no. 26/50, May 29, 1897, 1.

48. See "Almanya İmparatoru ve Sultan Hamid," *Osmanlı*, no. 12, May 15, 1898, 4, "Abdülhamid Çıldırmış," *Osmanlı*, no. 22, October 15, 1898, 4, "Anarşist Kim [?]" *Osmanlı*, no. 23, October 29, 1898, 2–3, "İtalya Kralının Katli," *Osmanlı*, no. 66, August 15, 1900, 7.

49. For an article on the nihilist movement, see "Bir Misâl-i İbret: Nihilizm ve Rusya," *Emel*, no. 6 [May 1, 1900], 1–3.

50. Abdullah Cevdet, "Bolşeviklik Hakkında," *İctihad*, no. 143, February 15, 1922, 3005.

51. Abdullah Djevdet, "Désarmement," *Les Temps Nouveaux Supplément Littéraire*, no. 9, June 24–30, 1899, 1.

52. For instance, see Yahya Kemal, *Çocukluğum, Gençliğim*, 102.

53. See Jean Grave, *La société mourante et l'anarchie* (Paris, 1893), 13 ff.; Jean Maitron, *Histoire du mouvement anarchiste en France (1880-1914)* (Paris, 1955), 328.

Chapter 8

1. For a description of the congress, see my "Der Jungtürkenkongress von Paris und seine Ergebnisse," *Die Welt des Islams* 33, no. 1 (1993), 23–65.

2. Ahmed Lûtfullah and Mehmed Sabahaddin, *Umum Osmanlı Vatandaşlarımıza* [Cairo, 1901]. For the French text see *Appel général aux Ottomans* (n.p., [1901]).

3. Pansa to Prinetti, Constantinople, April 3, 1901, R.234/74, *I Documenti Diplomatici Italiani* 5 (3d. ser. 1896–1907 Rome, 1974), 102.

4. "Zur jung-türkischen Bewegung wird uns geschrieben," *Hamburger Nachrichten*, February 1, 1902.

5. To von Bülow, Belgrade, March 3, 1902/no. 47, PAAA, 733/3, Die Jungtürken, 198 (Bd.4-5).

6. See memorandum sent to Chamberlain's office, dated February 10, 1902/no. 28 and entitled "Feuilles Révolutionnaires Publiées par les sujets de l'Empire Ottoman dans le Territoire de la Grande Bretagne," Archives of Turkish Embassy in London, Box 361 (3). In order to prevent the activities of this group and to stop publication of *Osmanlı*, the Ottoman embassy hired a certain Captain Norman. See Tahsin Bey to Anthopulos Pasha, December 4, 1901, Ibid.

7. Hüseyin Tosun to İshak Sükûti, Folkestone, October 7, 1901, AQSh, 19/136-3//120/1023-1901.

8. Nuri Ahmed to İshak Sükûti, Folkestone, October 21, 1901, AQSh, 19/106-5//96/1481.

9. Ali Haydar Midhat to İshak Sükûti, November 1, 1901, AQSh, 19/106-5//158/316.

10. Edhem Ruhi to İshak Sükûti, Folkestone, December 17, 1901, AQSh, 19/60//823-22/6.

11. For the text, see AQSh, 19/60//823-22/6.

12. Doctor Burhan Bahaeddin made this offer while stating that he had contacts with anarchists. See his letter to İshak Sükûti, Istanbul, November 10, 1901, AQSh, 19-106-1//33/521.

13. This was the idea of Bahriyeli Rıza. See his letter to İshak Sükûti, Cairo, January 3, 1902, AQSh, 19/106-2//32/677.

14. Reasons for the failure were discussed in a letter sent from Hüseyin Tosun to İshak Sükûti, December 9, 1901, AQSh, 19/106-2//32/677.

15. BBA-İrade-Hususî, Şevval 1319/no. 34-773.

16. See BBA-YMGM, 24 Za 1319/no. 2183. It is understood from several notes which were sent from the prosecutor of the Istanbul Court of Appeal and from the Criminal Court that Edhem Bey, the second clerk of the Court of First Instance in Milâs, had been accused of "forming a conspiratorial committee and publishing appeals." See "Dersaadet İstinaf Mahkemesi Müdde'i-yi Umumiliğinden," *Ceride-i Mahakim-i Adliye*, no. 38, February 19, 1902, 1, "Ahz ü Girift Emri," *Sabah*, February 20, 1902, "Dersaadet Cinayet Mahkemesinden," *Sabah*, February 23, 1902.

17. Tevfik Pasha to Hariciye, March 29, 1901/no. 74, Archives of the Turkish Embassy in Paris, D. 283.

18. "Dersaadet İstinaf Mahkemesi Müdde'i-yi Umumiliği Memuriyet-i Âliyesinden," *Sabah*, April 25, 1901.

19. Hilmy Tounali, *XI Houtbe (Discours)* (Geneva, 1901), 14–15, 21–22.

20. Tunalı Hilmi, *Onbirinci Hutbeye İlâve 1: Kongre-Cevabları-Cevabımız* (Cairo, 1319 [1901]), 15.

21. Ibid., 14.

22. Ibid., 6–7.

23. Tunalı Hilmi, *Onbirinci Hutbeye İlâve 2: Kongre Nedir, Nasıl Olmalıdır?* (Alexandria, 1319 [1901]), 12.

24. Tunalı Hilmi, *İlâve 1*, 10.

25. Tunalı Hilmi, *İlâve 2*, 8.

26. See BBA-Hariciye Gelen, 160-5/16, no. 73, 2977, 3128, 3211; *BBA-İrade-Hususî*, Zilhicce 1319/ no. 8-872; BBA-YP, 17 Za 1319/no. 1500 and 1527.

27. BBA-İrade-Hususî, Rebiy'ülevvel 1319/no. 7 21.

28. BBA-İrade-Hususî, Safer 1319/no. 38-104.

29. For instance, an imperial order was issued to place Fethi and Mehmed İhsan Beys, who had been working at the governorship's office in Aydın, under close surveillance. See BBA-İrade-Hususî, Şevval 1319/no. 33-872. Later Fethi Bey was exiled to Harput and Mehmed İhsan to Kastamonu. See coded telegram sent by Minister of the Interior Memduh Pasha to the province of Aydın [December 10, 1901], BBA-YEE-Kâmil Paşa Evrakına Ek I, 86/14-1, 1319. 8. 29.

30. BBA-İrade-Hususî, Cemaziy'ülevvel 1319/no. 77-432, and BBA-BEO/Zabtiye Giden, 663-26/14, 68 [December 15, 1901]/133345.

31. For the first information Ottoman intelligence received see Tevfik Pasha to Anthopulos Pasha, October 30, 1901/no. 97-45516, Archives of the Turkish Embassy in London, Box 361 (1).

32. See BBA-YSHM, 18 N 1319/no. 1078, 19 N 1319/no. 1092, 21 N 1319/no. 1103, 23 N 1319/no. 1112, 28 N 1319/no. 1138, 5 L 1319/no. 1158, 10 L 1319/no. 1183, 15 L 1319/no. 1028, 29 L 1319/no. 1293.

33. BBA-YEE, 11/1324/120/5.

34. 7.1.1902, A. 334, PAAA, 733/3, Die Jungtürken, 198 (Bd.4-5).

35. Draft of the letter sent to Sir Nicholas R.O'Conor from Foreign Office, December 31, 1901/no. 296, PRO/F.O. 78/5119.

36. "Résumé du Télégramme Circulaire de Son Excellence Tevfik Pacha à Son Excellence Costaki Anthopulos Pacha en date de Constantinople, Décembre 24, 1901," PRO/F.O. 78/5209.

37. Telegram supplement to the dispatch numbered 373. Paris, January 20, 1902/no. 2, AE-NS-T, 4 (1902-04), 2.

38. BBA-YMGM, 23 N 1319/no. 4717.

39. BBA-İrade-Hususî, Şevval 1319/no. 40-781, BBA-YMGM, 2 L 1319/no. 1964.

40. For the announcements, see "Zübde-i Havâdis," *Sabah*, January 16, 1902; "Dersaadet Cinayet Mahkemesinden," *Ceride-i Mahakim-i Adliye*, no. 28, January 15, 1902, 1, no. 30, January 22, 1902, 1.

41. The full text of the verdict is dated May 2, 1902 and in Archives of Turkish Embassy in Paris, D. 244, BBA-YP, 24 Za 1319/no. 1514. For the announcement in newspapers, see "Dahiliye," and "Ceza-yı İdam," *Sabah*, Feb-

ruary 6, 1902; "Damad Mahmud and His Accomplices," *Levant Herald,* February 9, 1902. For the comments of German diplomats about the significance of the verdict, see Marschall von Bieberstein to von Bülow, Pera, February 6, 1902/no. 31, A. 2302, PAAA, 733/3, Die Jungtürken, 198 (Bd.4-5).

42. BBA-YSHM, 28 Z 1319/no. 1695, 28 Z 1319/no. 1678, BBA-İrade-Hususî, Zilkade 1319/no. 70-946 and 81-958, BBA-İrade-Hususî, Zilhicce 1319/no. 81-1113.

43. BBA-İrade-Hususî, Zilkade 1319/no. 81-958.

44. "Avrupa'da Bâzı Eşhâs-ı Rezile Aleyhlerinde İttihaz Olunan Tedâbir-i Tenkiliye," *Sabah,* January 29, 1902.

45. BBA-İrade-Hususî, Zilhicce 1319/no. 94-1126.

46. See Jean Longuet, "Aux pieds du Grand Assassin: Le gouvernement Grec et Mahmoud Pacha," *La Petite République,* December 24, 1901.

47. For an example of these claims, see "Lettre de Turquie: L'Ambassadeur de Turquie à Paris," *Le Grand Moniteur Universel,* November 1, 1900. See also Ali Şefik, *Ahrar-ı Ümmet'e İmparator'un Yâdigârı* (Paris, 1314 [1898]), 11 ff. [idem], *Padişâh'ı İğfâl Edenler* (Istanbul, 1324 [1908]), 20–22.

48. This time information was given by Ahmed Rıza. See B. G., "Les deux Munir," *L'Aurore,* January 19, 1902.

49. "Takibât-ı Zalimâne," *Osmanlı,* no. 101, February 1, 1902, 4–5.

50. "Mandat d'arrêt contre Mahmoud Pacha," *Pro Arménia* 2, no. 5, January 25, 1902, 55. This journal criticized Munir Bey's efforts. See "S. E. Munir Bey et les Princes Loutfoullah et Sebahaddin," *Pro Arménia* 1, no. 12, May 10, 1901, 95.

51. "Ahrar-ı Osmaniye Kongresi," *Kürdistan,* no. 31 [April 14, 1902], 3.

52. BBA-YMGM, 17 L 1319/no. 7903.

53. Undated police report made in response to Nabi Bey's application dated January 17, 1902, Archives de la Préfecture de Police de Paris (Sabahaddine et Loutfullah)/ no. B. A (1653)-171154.

54. Police report dated January 17, 1902/Cabinet: 17194, ibid.

55. Münir Bey to Delcassé, Paris, January 29, 1902, AE-NS-T, 4, (1902-1904), 8–13.

56. "Note," January 21, 1902/AE-Cabinet du Ministre, ibid., 14.

57. (Waldeck Rousseau/Pr. du Conseil), Paris, January 24, 1902, ibid., 18.

58. For the answer sent to Delcassé, Cairo, February 6, 1902/no. 16, ibid., 24–25.

59. "Note," Paris, February 7, 1902/AE-Cabinet du Ministre, ibid., 26.

60. To Delcassé, Bern, January 29, 1902/no. 4, ibid., 22–24.

61. This event took place on January 24, 1902, at 4 p.m. See the unnumbered police report written on the same day. Archives de la Préfecture de Police de Paris (Sabahaddine et Loutfoullah). Abbreviated information was given by the French press. See "Les Jeunes Turcs," *Les Temps,* January 27, 1902.

62. This information is from a left-wing French journal, in which the text of the alleged conversation was published, based on the account of Sabahaddin Bey. In the text he was presented as "one of the princes." Some phrases attributed to Lépine seem to be especially exaggerated. See "Interdiction du Congrès Libéral Ottoman," *L'Européen* 2, no. 9, February 1, 1902, 3.

63. "Les Jeunes Turcs," *L'Eclair,* January 26, 1902. In this article, too, the information was said to have been given by one of the princes. However, the police report dated January 25, 1902, reveals that it was Prince Sabahaddin who had

visited the editors of the newspapers. Archives de la Préfecture de Police de Paris (Sabahaddin et Loutfullah). Lépine's act was praised by the Ottoman press: "In fact, some of these criminals had gone to Paris because they could not stay in the countries where they had been residing. The Police director of this city, His Excellency M. Lépine, dismissed and expelled the above-mentioned scoundrels, telling them that 'the French government would not allow criminals and conspirators to convene here.'" See "Bâzı Eşhas-ı Şerirenin Fransa'dan Def' ve Teb'idleri," *Sabah*, January 31, 1902. This praise, however, was condemned by left-wing French journals. See "Échos," *L'Européen* 2, no. 10, February 8, 1902, 3.

64. "Paris'de Osmanlı Kongresi," *Osmanlı*, no. 101, February 1, 1901, 7.

65. "Yeni Osmanlılar Kongresi," *İntikam*, no. 50, March 10, 1902, 1.

66. Reşid Sadi to Ahmed Rıza [London], January 30, 1902, Private Papers of Ahmed Rıza (2).

67. "Résume du Télégramme circulaire de Son Excellence Tevfik Pasha à Son Excellence Anthopulos Pacha en date de Constantinople 28 Janvier 1902," PRO/F.O. 78/5209.

68. Anthopulos Pasha to Lansdowne, London, January 30, 1902 (confidentielle), PRO/F.O. 78/5209.

69. Interesting information was given by Sir Nicholas R.O'Conor about how the sultan treated the French ambassador Constans. See O'Conor to Lansdowne, Constantinople, December 26, 1901/no. 451 (confidential), PRO/F.O. 78/5124.

70. Sembat also gave press conferences intending to influence French public opinion on this subject and about Armenian affairs. See "La Conférence de M. Marcel Sembat sur le conflict Franco-Turc et les massacres d'Arménie," *Moniteur Ottoman*, no. 15, October 26, 1901, 2.

71. *Annales de la Chambre des Députés: 7me Législature: Débats Parlementaires* (Session Extraordinaire de 1901), 65.I, I. Partie (October 22–November 26, 1901), (Paris, 1902), 59.

72. *Annales de la Chambre des Députés: 7me Législature: Débats Parlementaires* (Session Extraordinaire de 1901), 65.II, II.Partie, (November 28–December 24, 1901), (Paris, 1902), 1126.

73. He mentioned his efforts later when he wrote articles favoring partition of the Ottoman Empire. See Denys Cochin, "The Ottoman Empire," *The Balkan Review* 3 (February-July 1920), 21–26.

74. *Annales de la Chambre des Députés: 7me Législature: Débats Parlementaires* (Session Ordinaire de 1902), 66.I, I.Partie (January 14- February 18, 1902), (Paris, 1902), 75–80.

75. Two examples are a letter sent to the editor of the newspaper *Standard* on the expulsion of Ottoman spies from France, and complaints about French Police surveillance of Ahmed Rıza and his friends. See, respectively, Ali Haydar Midhat Bey, "The Turkish Secret Police," *Standard*, September 16, 1901, and Youssouf Fehmi, *Les Turcs de Paris: Espionnage et contre police* (Paris, 1908), 26 ff.

76. His letter dated January 13, 1902. Archives de la Préfecture de Police de Paris (Sabahaddine et Loutfullah).

77. Préfecture de Police to Delcassé, January 19, 1902, AE-NS-T, 4 (1902–04), 7. A copy of this letter is in Archives de la Préfecture de Police de Paris (Sabahaddine et Loutfullah). The Préfecture de Police wrote that the incident at the root of Sabahaddin Bey's complaint arose from a visit paid by a political police officer

to his house. The officer questioned the doorman, showing him a picture of Damad Mahmud Pasha and asking whether he had returned to France.

78. Police report dated January 18, 1902, Archives de la Préfecture de Police de Paris (Sabahaddine et Loutfullah).

79. These developments were discussed in the letter of the Préfecture de Police dated January 19, 1902, and in the police report dated January 18, 1902, mentioned above. The last document concerning the activities of Ottoman intelligence agents in the files of the French political police was dated September 16, 1901, and described the activities of a certain Sinapian who followed Ahmed Celâleddin Pasha and the khedive of Egypt during their stay in France. See Archives de la Préfecture de Police de Paris (Ambassade de Turquie-Police Ottomane à Paris), no. B. A (109.700-2). For the discussion in the French parliament concerning Sinapian and other individuals who had been expelled, see "Journalisme Turc," *L'Européen* 2, no. 12, February 22, 1902, 11. Sinapian continued his intelligence activities in Istanbul. See Bapst to Delcassé, Therapia, July 28, 1902/no. 127, AE-NS-T, 4 (1902–04), 115–16, and J[oseph] Fehmi, *Tablettes révolutionnaires d'un Jeune Turc* (Paris, 1903), 35.

80. Sabahaddin and Lûtfullah Beys' letter to Delcassé dated January 27, 1902, AE-NS-T,4 (1902–04), 20–22.

81. Police report dated January 24, 1902, Archives de la Préfecture de Police de Paris (Mahmoud Pacha), B. A (1169)- 139990-9.200.

82. "Paris'de Osmanlı Kongresi," *Osmanlı*, no. 102, February 15, 1902, 5.

83. "Jungtürkischen," *Wiener politische Korrespondenz*, March 11, 1902; and "The Congress of Ottoman Liberals," *Times*, February 11, 1902.

84. The letter written by Sabahaddin and Lûtfullah Beys to the French President dated August 25, 1901, was presented with the visiting card of Denais, AE-NS-T, 3 (1899–1901), 263. This letter and Denais's comments on it were published by the Young Turks for propaganda purposes. See "Protestations de Princes du sang," *Moniteur Ottoman*, no. 12, September 14, 1901, 1–2.

85. An author who later established close relations with Sabahaddin Bey pointed to Clemenceau's role. See Nezahat Nurettin Ege, *Prens Sabahattin: Hayatı ve İlmî Müdafaaları* (Istanbul, 1977), 25–26.

86. "Ahrar-ı Osmaniye Kongresi," *Kürdistan*, no. 31, 3.

87. Télégramme, February 6, 1902/no. 40-4, AE-NS-T, (1902-04), 24.

88. "Congress of the Young Turks," *Times*, February 8, 1902. İsmail Kemal also said that "at the last moment M. Waldeck-Rousseau, President of the Council and Minister of the Interior, withdrew the opposition." See *The Memoirs of Ismail Kemal Bey*, 307.

89. Radolin to von Bülow, Paris, January 27, 1902/no. 64, A. 1571, PAAA, 733/3, Die Jungtürken, 198 (Bd.4-5).

90. See Pierre Sorlin, *Waldeck-Rousseau* (Paris, 1966), 132-33; Ernst Ed. Berger, *Die Große Politik Delcassés: Frankreich's Kampf um die Vorherrschaft in Europa* (Essen, 1939), 53–54.

91. See John Francis Parr, *Théophile Delcassé and the Practice of the Franco-Russian Alliance 1898–1905* (Moret-sur Loing, 1952), 101–12; Pierre Renouvin, *La politique extérieure de Th. Delcassé (1898–1895)* (Paris, 1962), 16–17, Erich Lindow, *Freiherr Marschall von Bieberstein als Botschafter in Konstantinopel* (Danzig, 1934), 71–73.

92. See Paul Reynaud, *Waldeck Rousseau* (Paris, 1913), 219 ff. For the criticisms made against Waldeck-Rousseau by deputies, including Marcel Sembat, see

[Pierre René] Waldeck-Rousseau, *Politique Française et étrangère* (Paris, 1903), 122–27.

93. *Daily Chronicle*, February 14, 1902.

94. Louis Lépine, *Mes souvenirs* (Paris, 1929).

95. See L'Hermite Marcel, *La police de sa majesté Lépine Ier par l'Hermite de Monmartre* (Paris, 1908). For a more sympathetic view, see Ernst Raynaud, *Souvenirs de Police: Au Temps de Félix Faure* (Paris, 1925), 110–23.

96. M. Baudin, chief inspector of police, and M. Frédéric, private secretary of the Paris police director, were awarded the decoration of Osmanî of the fourth degree. The reason given for the decoration was that they were "well-wishers of the Ottoman Government." See, respectively, "Nişan," *Sabah*, July 20, 1902, and September 30, 1902. This decoration was strongly criticized in the left-wing French press. See "Echos," *L'Européen* 2, no. 39, August 30, 1902, 4, and no. 46, October 18, 1902, 3–4.

97. "Osmantsi Azadaganneri Hamazhoghově," *Droshak* 12, no. 2 (122), February 1902, 23.

98. This was demanded by İzzet Bey on the occasion of his visit to the German embassy when he showed, by way of example, an article published in an illustrated Berlin journal. See Marschall von Bieberstein to von Bülow, Pera, March 19, 1902/no. 43, A. 4600, PAAA, 733/3, Die Jungtürken, 198 (Bd.4-5).

99. *The Memoirs of Ismail Kemal Bey*, 306.

100. Ibid.

101. "Notre Banquet-Conférence," *Moniteur Ottoman*, no. 8, July 2, 1901, [3].

102. The letter dated January 1, 1902, and sent by Sabahaddin and Lûtfullah Beys to Ali Fehmi, editor of the journal *Muvazene* in Varna, was published in this organ. See "Ahrar-ı Osmaniye Kongresi ve Cemiyet-i İttihadiye-i Osmaniye," *Muvazene*, no. 224 [March 12, 1902], 1.

103. For the letters sent to Ali Haydar Midhat, see Ali Haydar Midhat, *Hatıralarım*, 165–68.

104. Ali Haydar Midhat to İshak Sükûti, July 14, 1901, AQSh, 19/106-5//158/315.

105. Ahmed Rıza's note dated January 11, 1902, Private Papers of Ahmed Rıza (2).

106. Anthopulos Pasha to Tahsin Bey, June 7, 1901/no. 25, Archives of the Turkish Embassy in London, Box 362 (2). In his application he also claimed that he had never been a Young Turk. However, he provided a different account later. See Doktor Lütfi, *Türkiye Cumhuriyeti ve Siyaset-i Milliye, İktisadiye* (Istanbul, 1340 [1926]), 6–7n.

107. Anthopulos Pasha to Tahsin Bey, June 8, 1901/no. 26, Archives of Turkish Embassy in London, Box 362 (2).

108. Docteur Loutfi, "Lettre au Comité de Rédaction," *Moniteur Ottoman*, no. 13, October 3, 1901, 1.

109. "Gazâ-yı Hürriyet-Hareket-i Mezbûhâne!: İsmail Kemal Bey," and "La justice Hamidienne," *Moniteur Ottoman*, no. 8, June 2, 1901, [2] and [4], and "Comptons sur nous mêmes," *Moniteur Ottoman*, no. 14, October 23, 1901, 2.

110. See his letter dated January 29, 1902 in Kuran, *İnkılâp Tarihimiz ve İttihad ve Terakki*, 184.

111. İsmail Hakkı, *Vatan Uğrunda*, 231–32.

112. See Nuri Ahmed to İshak Sükûti, Geneva, January 24, 1902, AQSh, 19/106-5//243/1623.

113. İshak Sükûti, who was the veiled leader of this group, was prejudiced against Dashnaktsutiun. See Halil Muvaffak to İshak Sükûti, October 16, 1901, AQSh, 19/106-3//63/1027. However, *Droshak* praised the efforts of Sükûti after his death, saying that he was the author of the appeal published in that journal addressing the Kurds in 1900. See "Doktor Ishak Sukuti Beyi Mahĕ," *Droshak* 12, no. 3 (123), March 1902, 47–48.

114. This was also the idea behind the appeals to the Armenians prior to the convention to join forces with the Young Turks. For an excellent example, see "Jeunes Turcs et Arméniens," *La Gazette de Lausanne*, July 18, 1901. For another appeal to the Young Turks, Armenians, and Macedonians to unite against the regime of Abdülhamid II, see Sélim Wékil, *Concentration des volontés patriotiques* (Paris, [1901?]), 3–9.

115. *Ethem Ruhi Balkan Hatıraları-Canlı Tarihler* 6, 28.

116. Hagopian, "Hyphenated Nationalism," 213.

117. "Osmantsi Azadaganneri," *Droshak* 12, no. 2 (122), 23.

118. Hagopian, "Hyphenated Nationalism," 214. Another source asserts that three representatives from Dashnaktsutiun and two from the Verakazmial organizations participated in the convention; however, only Minas Tscheraz received a personal invitation. See "L'Article paru dans les Journaux Révolutionaires Arméniennes: Les Congrès Ottoman," BBA-HNA-End. S.III, K.S.282, D.5.

119. "Teessüf," *Sancak*, no. 49, May 15, 1901, 4.

120. He also asked for the establishment of an Albanian executive committee in Naples. See *Mendimi politik* 1, 225. This translated article published in this book originally appeared in *La Nazione Albanese*.

121. For his activities, see *Akte të Rilindjes Kombëtare Shqiptare*, 142n, and Hasan Kaleshi, "Dr. Ibrahim Temo: Osnivač Mladoturskog Komiteta 'Ujedinjenje i Napredak': Prilog osvetljavanju uloge Albanaca u mladoturskom pokretu," *Prilozi za Orientalnu Filologiju* 22–23 (1972–73), 225–26.

122. Two Albanian leaders became students at the Albanian-Romanian Cultural Institute established by the Drita Society in Bucharest. See Johannes Faensen, *Die albanische Nationalbewegung* (Berlin, 1980), 57–58. Later, in 1900 they published a radical organ called *Independenta Albanie* there. This was a continuation of Hima's journal *L'Indépendance Albanaise*. See Christine B. Körner, *Entwicklung und Konzeption der Presse in Albanien und albanischen Exilpress* (Munich, 1982), 357. Erebera asked the Albanians to form national institutions after the Young Turk revolution. See [Yaşar Sadık Erebera], "Kıymet-i Maarif," *Üsküb*, no. 1 [September 9, 1911], 1.

123. İbrahim Temo, *İttihad ve Terakki*, 158. The Young Turks in the Balkans also sent Sheikh Şevki as their second representative. The claim made by Skendi that Temo participated in the convention is erroneous. See Stavro Skendi, *The Albanian National Awakening* (Princeton, 1967), 336.

124. This claim was also made by Skendi. See ibid.

125. He described himself as a Herzegovinian peasant. See Mehmed Kadri Nâsıh, *Sarâyih*, 36.

126. The Ottoman press described him as a "Bosnian Muslim" (Boşnak taifesinden). See "Zübde-i Havâdis," *Sabah*, January 16, 1902.

127. For instance, Skender Luarasi, *Ismail Qemali: Jeta dhe Vepra* (Tirana, 1962), 47–48 and Kaliopi Naska, *Ismail Qemali në Lëvizjen Kombëtare Shqiptare*

(Tirana, 1987), 47. Luarasi and Naska claimed that all Albanians taking part in the convention supported the "decentralization" idea of Sabahaddin Bey against Ahmed Rıza and his followers. Another author further underscored this claim. See Masar Kodra, "Mladoturskata Revoludziya i Albanskoto Osloboditelno Dvizenje," *Glasnik* 12 (I-1968), 119. However, Sabahaddin Bey did not create his thesis on "decentralization" until 1905.

128. See Alexis Alexandris, *The Greek Minority of Istanbul and Greek-Turkish Relations 1918–1974* (Athens, 1983), 40–41.

129. *The Memoirs of Ismail Kemal Bey*, 298.

130. Adam Block's undated confidential memorandum, enclosed with the letter from O'Conor to Salisbury, Constantinople, May 8, 1900/no. 168, PRO/F.O. 421/187.

131. A. J. Panayotopulos, "Early Relations between the Greeks and the Young Turks," *Balkan Studies* 21 (1980), 88. For the acts of these Greeks in the convention and their later activities, see Ἀλέξης Ἀλεξανδρής, "Οἱ "Ελληνες στήν Ὑπηρεσία τῆς Ὀθωμανικῆς Αὐτοκρατορίας 1850–1922," Δελτίον τῆς Ἱστορικῆς καί Ἐθνολογίκῆς Ἑταιρείας τῆς Ἑλλάδος, 23 (1980), 365–404.

132. See "Γεώργιος Φαρδής," Μεγάλη Ἑλληνική Ἐγκυκλοπαιδεια (1929), 23, 827.

133. Fardis had translated George Jellinek's famous work into French under the title *La déclaration des droits de l'homme et du citoyen: Contribution à l'histoire du droit constitutionnel moderne* (Paris, 1902). However, his own works on constitutional theory were published later. See Ἡ Ἐθνική Κυριαρχία ἐν τῷ Ἑλληνικῶ Συντακτικῶ Δικαίω (Thessaloniki, 1932), Συνταγματικόν Δίκαιον: Πανεπιστημιακαί Παραδόσεις (Thessaloniki, 1947).

134. *Le Congrès des libéraux Ottomans* (Paris, [1902]), 1.

135. See "Jungtürkischer Congreß in Paris," *Neue Freie Presse*, February 11, 1902; "The Congress of Ottoman Liberals," *Times*, February 11, 1902; "Nouvelles du Jour," *Le Temps*, February 14, 1902.

136. Sefer E. Berzeg, *Gurbetteki Kafkasya II* (Ankara, 1987), 12.

137. Naci Kutlay, *İttihat ve Terakki ve Kürtler* (Istanbul, 1991), 84–85.

138. "Le Congrès des libéraux Ottomans," *Pro Arménia* 2, no. 7, February 25, 1902, 53.

139. "Jungtürkischen," *Wiener politische Korrespondenz*, March 11, 1902.

140. "Ahrar-ı Osmaniye Kongresi," *Muvazene*, no. 224, 2.

141. "Osmantsi Azadaganneri," *Droshak* 12, no. 2 (122), 24.

142. The latest list of "leading harmful individuals" prepared by the Ottoman authorities prior to the convention provides an opportunity for comparison. Although some of the Young Turks in this list participated in the meeting, others were not even invited. The list is as follows
(People with an asterisk participated in the convention):

1. Captain Medical Doctor Ahmed Hamdi in Paris.
2. Bedirhanpaşazâde Abdurrahman in London.*
3. Necib Hindiye in London.
4. Nuri Ahmed in London.*
5. Nazmi in London.*
6. Mehmed in Athens.
7. Captain Silistireli Mustafa Hamdi in Vienna.*
8. Former secretary general of Kosovo Province, Hamdi in Paris.

9. Former junior clerk at Foreign Press Department, Nemira Efendi in Paris.*

10. Adjutant Major Medical Doctor İsmail Kemal in Paris.

11. Lieutenant Süleyman in Paris.

12. Hasan Fehmi in London.

13. Naim in Geneva.

14. Former Navy accountant Ali Fahri in Geneva.*

15. Kâzım in Geneva who claims that he is a medical doctor.

16. Halil Muvaffak in Geneva.

17. Âsım in Geneva who claims that he is an infantry officer.

18. Catholic journalist Emin in Geneva.

19. Edhem Ruhi in Geneva.

20. Kâmi in Geneva.

21. İbrahim Edhem [Temo].

22. Deserter Seyfi Salim.

23. Derviş Pasha, the owner of the journal *Zaman* in Cyprus.

24. First clerk of the Ottoman embassy in Washington, Alfred Bey, who is now in London.

25. Ottoman Vice-Consul in London Halil Halid.

The first twenty-three names were in the list enclosed with a memorandum from Tevfik Pasha to Anthopulos Pasha, December 29, 1901/no. 3-40775, and the last two names were in the supplementary list enclosed with the above mentioned document, from Anthopulos Pasha to Tevfik Pasha, May 12, 1901/no. 38-42310. Archives of the Turkish Embassy in London, Box 361(1).

143. [Not]," *Muvazene*, no. 223 [March 5, 1902], 4.

144. "Ahrar-ı Osmaniye Kongresi," *Muvazene*, no. 224, 1.

145. Police reports dated January, 21, 25, and 27, 1902, Archives de la Préfecture de Paris (Sabahaddine et Loutfullah).

146. "Ahrar-ı Osmaniye Kongresi," *Muvazene*, no. 224, 1.

147. Police report dated January 26, 1902, Archives de la Préfecture de Police de Paris (Sabahaddine et Loutfullah).

148. Ibid., Police report dated January, 27, 1902, (Sabahaddine et Loutfullah).

149. "Yeni Osmanlılar Kongresi," *İntikam*, no. 50, 1.

150. These names were taken from the original document signed by all the participants at that gathering. Private Papers of Ahmed Rıza (2).

151. This document was published in two journals, both of which belonged to the "minority" group. There are minor differences between them. See "Ahrar-ı Osmaniye Kongresi ve Netice," *Sancak*, no. 64, March 5, 1902, 1, and "Ahrar-ı Osmaniye Kongresi," *Muvazene*, no. 224, 1. The former published the original document verbatim. The French translation is given in "Compte rendu du Congrès," *Mechveret Supplément Français*, no. 126, February 15, 1902, 2.

152. This is a quotation from the original document. Private Papers of Ahmed Rıza (2). The same text was published in "Compte rendu du Congrès," *Mechveret Supplément Français*, no. 126, 2-3, with some minor changes made at the convention. A Turkish translation of the text is in "Paris'de Osmanlı Hürriyetperverân Kongresi," *Osmanlı*, no. 104, April 16, 1902, 4.

153. The draft of a letter written by Ahmed Rıza, Private Papers of Ahmed Rıza (2).

154. AQSh, 19/60//638/7.

155. Department of justice and police to the Ministry of the Interior, Geneva, January 30, 1902/no. 28 (P.P. January 31, 1902/no. 75) and February 22, 1902/no.61 (P.P. February 23, 1902/no. 75), Bundesarchiv-Bern, E.21/14'258.

156. A good comparison can be made with a letter of İsmail Kemal which he had sent to Delcassé, dated November 14, 1901, AE-NS-T, 3 (1899–1901), 274–77.

157. To Goluchowski, Constantinople, January 27, 1902/no. 6 (vertaulich), and Constantinople, February 22, 1902/no. 11, HHStA, PA, XII 178, Türkei Berichte, 1902 (I–V).

158. "Yeni Osmanlılar Kongresi," *İntikam*, no. 50, 1.

159. Ismail Kemal, "Un appel à L'Europe," *L'Européen* 1, no. 1, December 7, 1901, 9. This letter was originally published by *Le Matin*.

160. "Une lettre d'Ismail Kemal," *Pro Arménia* 1, no. 22, October 10, 1901, 172.

161. Undated draft of the letter sent to İsmail Kemal from Ahmed Ferid, Private Papers of Ahmed Ferid Tek.

162. These are their names: Abdülhalim Memduh, Abdurrahman Bedirhan, Anastase Adossidis, Ahmed Ferid, Ahmed Muhtar, Ahmed Rıza, Ali Fahri, Ali Fehmi, Ali Haydar Midhat, Babanzâde Hikmet Süleyman, Garabet Basmacıyan, Celâleddin Rıza, Çobanyan Efendi, Georges Fardis, Albert Fua, Khalīl Ghānim, Musurus Ghikis, Halil Muvaffak, Hamid Hüsnü, Derviş Hima, Hüseyin Siyret, Hüseyin Tosun, İsmail Hakkı, İsmail Kemal, Hoca Kadri, Kâzım Bey, Çerkes Kemal, Kemal Midhat, Doctor Lütfi, Lûtfullah Bey, Mahir Said, Silistireli Mustafa Hamdi, Doctor Nâzım, Nemira Efendi, Nuri Ahmed, Nüzhet Bey, Re'fet Bey, Refik Nevzad, Sabahaddin Bey, Salih Bey, Konstantinos Sathas, Sisyan Efendi, Sheikh Şevki Celâleddin, Minas Tscheraz, Yaşar Sadık Erebera, Yusuf Akçura, and Zeki Bey. These names are in Münir Bey's letter to Delcassé, Paris, January 20, 1902, AE-NS-T, 4 (1902–1904), 8–13, Paul Fesch, *Constantinople*, 365n, picture published in *Osmanlı*, no. 104, 1, and the issues of this journal and *Droshak*, Ελληνισμός, *İntikam*, *Kürdistan*, *Mechveret Supplément Français*, *Muvazene*, *Pro Arménia*, and *Sancak* giving information about the convention; "Le Congrès des Libéraux Ottomans," *L'Européen* 2, no. 11, February 15, 1902, 8–9.

163. "Paris'de Osmanlı Hürriyetperverân Kongresi," *Osmanlı*, no. 104, 2.

164. Ibid.

165. "Jungtürkischer Kongreβ in Paris," *Neue Freie Presse*, February 11, 1902.

166. "Osmantsi Azadaganneri," *Droshak* 12, no. 2 (122), 24.

167. "Ahrar-ı Osmaniye Kongresi," *Kürdistan*, no. 31, 3–4.

168. "Paris'de Osmanlı Hürriyetperverân Kongresi," *Osmanlı*, no. 104, 2–3.

169. Ibid., 3.

170. "Yeni Osmanlılar Kongresi," *İntikam*, no. 50, 1.

171. "Paris'de Osmanlı Hürriyetperverân Kongresi," *Osmanlı*, no. 104, 3.

172. "Osmantsi Azadaganneri," *Droshak* 12, no. 2 (122), 24.

173. "Ahrar-ı Osmaniye Kongresi ve Netice," *Sancak*, no. 64, 1.

174. "Paris'de Osmanlı Hürriyetperverân Kongresi," *Osmanlı*, no. 104, 4.

175. "Compte rendu du Congrès," *Mechveret Supplément Français*, no. 126, 3; *Les Congrès des libéraux Ottomans*, 4–5. The Turkish translation was given in "Paris'de Osmanlı Hürriyetperverân Kongresi," *Osmanlı*, no. 104, 4. Unfortunately we lack copies of the original French text read by Prince Sabahaddin. Besides this there are minor discrepancies between the French and Turkish texts. As we

shall see, the original French text was amended on the second day in response to discussions.

176. AQSh, 19/60//241/63.
177. "Ahrar-ı Osmaniye Kongresi," *Muvazene*, no. 224, 3.
178. "Yeni Osmanlılar Kongresi," *İntikam*, no. 50, 1–2.
179. Ibid., 2.
180. "Compte rendu du Congrès," *Mechveret Supplément Français*, no. 126, 3.
181. Private Papers of Ahmed Rıza (2).
182. "Yeni Osmanlılar Kongresi," *İntikam*, no. 50, 2.
183. "Ahrar-ı Osmaniye Kongresi," *Kürdistan*, no. 31, 3.
184. Ibid., 4.
185. "Paris'de Osmanlı Hürriyetperverân Kongresi," *Osmanlı*, no. 104, 4.
186. "Ahrar-ı Osmaniye Kongresi," *Muvazene*, no. 224, 3.
187. "Paris'de Osmanlı Hürriyetperverân Kongresi," *Osmanlı*, no. 104, 4.
188. Ibid.
189. Ibid., 5.
190. Ibid., 5–6.
191. "Yeni Osmanlılar Kongresi," *İntikam*, no. 50, 2.
192. "Ahrar-ı Osmaniye Kongresi," *Muvazene*, no. 224, 3.
193. AQSh, 19/60//227/14.
194. Private Papers of Ahmed Rıza (2).
195. İsmail Hakkı, *Cidal Yahud Ma'kes-i Hakikat* (Cairo, 1907), 22–23.
196. Albert Fua, "Les états de service du Comité d'Union et Progrès," *Mècheroutiette*, no. 43 (June 1913), 36. However, it was claimed that Fua himself offered to replace the term "action bienveillante" with "concours moral." See "Compte rendu du Congrès," *Mechveret Supplément Français*, no. 126, 2.
197. Ibid., 3.
198. "Ahrar-ı Osmaniye Kongresi," *Muvazene*, no. 224, 3.
199. Fua, "Les états," *Mècheroutiette*, no. 43, 36. This letter was presented to Lord Derby by Odian Efendi, who was sent to London on a special mission by Midhat Pasha. Lord Derby gave information about this attempt in his letter to Salisbury and Elliot dated January 4, 1877/no. 10, PRO/F.O. 424/37. For Odian Efendi's mission, see Ali Haydar Midhat, *The Life of Midhat Pasha* (London, 1903), 136 ff; Bekir Sıtkı Baykal, "Midhat Paşa'nın Gizli Bir Siyasî Teşebbüsü," *III.Türk Tarih Kongresi: Kongreye Sunulan Tebliğler* (Ankara, 1948), 473–74.
200. "Ahrar-ı Osmaniye Kongresi," *Muvazene*, no. 224, 3.
201. Ibid.
202. "Osmantsi Azadaganneri," *Droshak* 12, no. 2 (122), 24.
203. "Ahrar-ı Osmaniye Kongresi," *Kürdistan*, no. 31, 4.
204. İsmail Hakkı, *Cidal*, 23.
205. "Yeni Osmanlılar Kongresi," *İntikam*, no. 50, 2.
206. Only in Έλληνισμός it was claimed that "seven or eight participants, belonging Ahmed Rıza's group," voted against the supplement. See "Τὸ ἐν Παρισίοις Συνέδριον τῶν Φιλελευθέρων Ὀθωμανῶν," Έλληνισμός 5, no. 2 (February 1902), 127. However, this number seems implausible.
207. As I have mentioned, Ali Fehmi wrote that he had abstained in the vote for the program, the supplement, and for the election of members in the new permanent committee. However, Ahmed Rıza claimed in a letter sent to Ahmed Saib that Ali Fehmi was acting together with the minority. See "Rıza Bey Biraderimizin Yazdığı Mektub da Şudur," *Sancak*, no. 64, 1. Most probably Ali Fehmi's

depiction of his own conduct was colored by his wish to retain support among the Young Turks in Bulgaria by not joining a faction. Another possibility is that he abstained regarding the program and voted against the supplement.

208. The most significant source for these names is "Rıza Bey Biraderimizin," *Sancak*, no. 64, 1.

209. The names were: Siyret, Kâzım, Re'fet, Lütfi, Kemal Midhat, Musurus, Sabahaddin, Lûtfullah, İsmail Hakkı, Sathas, Ali Haydar, Zeki, Salih, Hüseyin Tosun, Derviş Hima, Yaşar, Ahmed Muhtar, Nemira, and Avni Kemal. Private Papers of Bahaeddin Şakir.

210. To von Mérey, Paris, February 15, 1902, HHStA, PA IX 154, Frankreich Varia, 1902.

211. "Yeni Osmanlılar Kongresi," *İntikam*, no. 50, 2.

212. Ibid.

213. "Osmantsi Azadagenleri," *Droshak* 12, no. 2 (122), 24.

214. "Déclaration des délégués Arméniens," *Pro Arménia* 2, no. 7, February 25, 1902, 49. The Turkish translation is given in "Paris'de Osmanlı Hürriyetperverân Kongresi," *Osmanlı*, no. 104, 6.

215. E. K. Sarkisian, *Politika Osmanskogo pravitel'stva v zapadnoi Armenii i derzhavy v poslednei chetverti XIX i nachale XX vv* (Erevan, 1972), 231.

216. *Le Congrès des libéraux Ottomans*, 5. For the Turkish translation of this text see "Paris'de Osmanlı Hürriyetperverân Kongresi," *Osmanlı*, no. 104, 6.

217. Ibid.

218. "Yeni Osmanlılar Kongresi," *İntikam*, no. 50, 2.

219. "Paris'de Osmanlı Hürriyetperverân Kongresi," *Osmanlı*, no. 104, 6.

220. "Yeni Osmanlılar Kongresi," *İntikam*, no. 50, 2.

221. The draft of Ahmed Rıza's speech which he delivered at the convention. Private Papers of Ahmed Rıza (2).

222. "Yeni Osmanlılar Kongresi," *İntikam*, no. 50, 2.

223. Ibid., 3.

224. "Paris'de Osmanlı Hürriyetperverân Kongresi," *Osmanlı*, no. 104, 6.

225. Karl Blind, "The Prorogued Turkish Parliament," *The North American Review* 175, no. 548, (July 1902), 45. Because the Armenian committees perceived that these comments could hurt their cause they sent an explanatory correction to various dailies and journals affirming that although they wanted to have special reforms they also favored the reproclamation of the Ottoman Constitution. See their note dated February 13, 1902, "Échos," *L'Européen* 2, no. 11, February 15, 1902, 3.

226. "Paris'de Osmanlı Hürriyetperverân Kongresi," *Osmanlı*, no. 104, 6. According to Ali Fehmi, İsmail Kemal also told the Armenians that "if you do not want the application and execution of the constitution and the reform and happiness of the Ottoman country, we do not want you at all." See "Ahrar-ı Osmaniye Kongresi," *Muvazene*, no. 224, 3.

227. "Paris'de Osmanlı Hürriyetperverân Kongresi," *Osmanlı*, no. 104, 7.

228. "Ahrar-ı Osmaniye Kongresi," *Kürdistan*, no. 31, 4.

229. "Ahrar-ı Osmaniye Kongresi," *Muvazene*, no. 224, 3.

230. *Le Congrès des libéraux Ottomans*, 6. The Turkish text is given in "Paris'de Osmanlı Hürriyetperverân Kongresi," *Osmanlı*, no. 104, 6.

231. A draft in the papers of Ahmed Rıza entitled "Séance 8 Fév[rier] 1902 M. Ahmed Riza." Private Papers of Ahmed Rıza (2). Ahmed Rıza expressed similar

opinions about the Armenian and Bulgarian committees prior to the Congress. See his undated letter [December 1901] to the editor of *L'Européen*. "Échos," *L'Européen* 1, no. 2, December 14, 1901, 9.

232. "Yeni Osmanlılar Kongresi," *İntikam*, no. 50, 3.

233. "Paris'de Osmanlı Hürriyetperverân Kongresi," *Osmanlı*, no. 104, 7.

234. "Yeni Osmanlılar Kongresi," *İntikam*, no. 50, 3.

235. "Paris'de Osmanlı Hürriyetperverân Kongresi," *Osmanlı*, no. 104, 7.

236. "Ahrar-ı Osmaniye Kongresi," *Muvazene*, no. 224, 3.

237. "Paris'de Osmanlı Hürriyetperverân Kongresi," *Osmanlı*, no. 104, 7.

238. The text is given in two journals. See "Yeni Osmanlılar Kongresi," *İntikam*, no. 50, 3, and "Ahrar-ı Osmaniye Kongresi," *Kürdistan*, no. 31, 4.

239. Blind, "Turkish Parliament," *North American Review*, 45.

240. "Osmantsi Azadaganneri," *Droshak* 12, no. 2 (122), 25.

241. "Paris'de Osmanlı Hürriyetperverân Kongresi," *Osmanlı*, no. 104, 7.

242. "Şuûnat," *İntikam*, no. 50, 4.

243. Pierre Quillard, "Le Congrès des libéraux Ottomans," *Pro Arménia* 2, no. 7, February 25, 1902, 49–50.

244. "P.S.," *Mechveret Supplément Français*, no. 126, 4.

245. This fact was underscored by a Hungarian daily. See BBA-YMGM, 17 Za 1319/no. 226-81.

246. Ahmed Rıza's first efforts to republish this journal continued until 1900. A year later he redoubled his efforts with the financial aid of Şerif Bey, the Ottoman ambassador to Sweden. See Ahmed Rıza's letter to Şerif Pasha, Paris, October 24, 1901, Şerif Paşa, *İttihad ve Terakki'nin Sahtekârlıklarına*, 12; Youssouf Fehmi, *La Révolution Ottomane*, 162. At the time the congress convened, his preparations were complete. See "Rıza Bey Biraderimizin Yazdığı," *Sancak*, no. 64, 1.

247. "Ahrar-ı Osmaniye Kongresi," *Kürdistan*, no. 31, 4.

248. This quote is taken from the translation of an article published in the Varna-based Armenian journal *Iravonk*. The translation is enclosed with the letter from the Ottoman commissioner to Bulgaria to the grand vizier [May 24, 1902]. BBA-BEO/Mümtaze: Bulgaristan Tasnifi Evrakı, A MTZ 04, 77, 75 (1320. 2. 18).

249. Türk İnkılâp Tarihi Enstitüsü Arşivi, 82/18330 (92-2-34).

250. For an example, see Un Diplomate, "Les réformes en Turquie et le Parti Jeune-Turc," *L'Humanité Nouvelle* 1–6, no. 32 (1900), 133–34.

251. "Un appel aux Kurdes," *Pro Arménia* 1, no. 12, May 10, 1901, 92. An Armenian source claims that appeals to the Kurds were distributed by *Droshak* in 1895. (See Louise Nalbandian, *The Armenian Revolutionary Movement: The Development of Armenian Political Parties through the Nineteenth Century* [Los Angeles, 1963], 175, 219.) A Kurdish source, however, claims that the appeals to Kurds were distributed in 1901. Malmısanij, *Yüzyılımızın Başlarında Kürt Milliyetçiliği ve Dr.Abdullah Cevdet* (Uppsala, 1986), 24–25. This claim was also confirmed in, Hagopian, "Hyphenated Nationalism," 204–206. Abdurrahman Bedirhan said after the Young Turk revolution that "they had not failed to publish articles annulling the discord between the Kurds and Armenians." See "Bir Ermeni Kilisesinde Bedirhanpaşazâde Abdurrahman Beyefendi'nin İrad Etdikleri Nutk-i Beliğ," *Serbestî*, February 18, 1909.

252. His letter to the British ambassador in Istanbul dated Geneva, November 13, [18]98. PRO/F.O. 195/2037.

253. Ali Haydar Midhat, *Menfa-yı İhtiyarî Hatıratı* (Geneva, 1905), [iii-iv].

254. *Tezkere-i Ulema: Ulema-yı Arabın Şer'-i Mübîn ve Ahbâr-ı Sahihadan İktiyasları ve Damad Mahmud Paşa'dan Sultan Abdülhamid Han-ı Sânî'ye Mektub* (Cairo, 1316 [1900]), passim.

255. "Ūrubbā wa al-Islam: Ḥadīth ma'a ṣāhib al-Liwā'," *al-Liwā'*, July 22, 1902. For his earlier comments on the Young Turks see "Ein Beitrag zur Ideengeschichte der ägyptischen Nationalbewegung," *Die Welt des Islams* 4, no. 4 (1956), 291. For Kāmil Bey's positive views about Abdülhamid II, see his letter to Juliette Adams, Istanbul, September 21, 1902 in *Awraq, Muṣṭafā Kāmil: al-Mursalāt* (Cairo, 1982), 175–76, and " 'Īd al-julūs al-Sulṭānī," *al-Liwā'*, September 14, 1902. For the comments of the British about this see O'Conor to Salisbury, Therapia, September 22, 1903, PRO/F.O. 78/5269.

256. "Mū'tamar al-aḥrār al-kabīr," *Juhayna*, no. 24, March 20, 1902, 3. For more information about this journal see BBA-BEO/Dahiliye Gelen, 97-3746, 1573 [June 14, 1898], and 1643 [November 2, 1898].

257. See "Ziya-ı Elîm," *Şûra-yı Ümmet*, no. 131, March 15, 1908, 2, Ahmed Rıza, "Mort glorieuse," *Mechveret Supplément Français*, no. 197, 2–3, "Mısır Gazeteleri," *Türk*, no. 128, May 3, 1906, 2. This viewpoint was shared by the Turks living in Russia. See "Mustafa Kâmil Paşa," *Tercüman-ı Ahvâl-i Zaman*, no. 12, February 15, 1908, 2.

258. Joseph Denais, *La vraie Turquie* (Paris, 1905), 11.

259. "Ahrar-ı Osmaniye Kongresi," *Kürdistan*, no. 31, 4.

260. "Les Hommes du Jour: Damad Mahmoud Pacha, Princes Sabahaddine et Loutfoullah," *L'Eclair*, February 19, 1902.

261. "Sebeb-i Teehhür," *Osmanlı*, no. 120, August 15, 1903, 1.

Chapter 9

1. Underscored by Vambéry. See his memorandum entitled *On the Constitutional Movement in Turkey*, which was enclosed with his letter to Sir Charles Hardinge, Vambéry Papers, PRO/F.O. 800–33.

2. Bahaeddin Sâî, *Güldeste*, 47–48. This was also one of the most frequently used themes in CUP propaganda. See "Redd'ül-merdud," *Osmanlı*, no. 12, May 15, 1898, 3; "Abdülhamid'in Peygambere İsyanı," *Osmanlı*, no. 16, July 15, 1898, 6; "Neuzübillâh," *Osmanlı*, no. 17, August 1, 1897, 7, "Lâtife," *Osmanlı*, no. 58, April 15, 1900, 3; "Jübileye Yâdigâr Yahud Utanmayan Kimdir?" *Ümid*, no. 2, September 1, 1900, 2; *Abdülhamid-i Sânî*, AQSh, MS 19/36, 28 ff.

3. [Abdullah Cevdet], *Mahkeme-i Kübra* [Paris, 1895], 20–21.

4. See Ahmed Riza, *Tolérance Musulmane* (Paris, 1897), passim, *Vazife ve Mes'uliyet 1, Mukaddeme, Padişah, Şehzâdeler* (Cairo, 1320 [1902]), 5 ff., Abdullah Cevdet, *Hadd-ı Te'dib*, 65–66; and *Uyanınız! Uyanınız!* (Cairo, 1907), passim.

5. Ahmed Rıza to Fahire Hanım, December 27, 1885, Private Papers of Ahmed Rıza (1).

6. V[ittorio] Alfieri, *İstibdad*, tr. Abdullah Cevdet (Geneva, 1317 [1899]), 115–18n.

7. Ettore Rossi, "Una Traduzione Turca Dell'opera 'Della Tirannide' di V. Alfieri Probabilmente Conosciuta da Al-Kawākibī," *Oriente Moderno* 34, no. 7 (July 1954), 336–37.

8. Abdullah Cevdet to İshak Sükûti, December 21, 1897, AQSh, 19/106//186/1.

9. Ahmed Rıza, *Lâyiha*, 15, "Tabaka-i Bâlâdan," *Osmanlı*, no. 5, February 1, 1898, 8.

10. Abdullah Cevdet, *Uyanınız!*, 32, idem, *Bir Hutbe*, 10.

11. See Abdullah Cevdet, *Hadd-ı Te'dib*, 65–66; "Bir Mükâleme," *Şark ve Garb*, no. 1 (March 1896), 24.

12. Abdullah Djevdet, "Une profession de foi," *İctihad*, no. 6 (May 1905); 89. Also see Abdullah Cevdet, "Mısır'da Necm ül-Terakki ül-İslâmî Medresesi," *İctihad* 2, no. 1 (July 1906), 17.

13. "Tahkikat-ı İlmiye," *İctihad*, no. 1, September 1, 1904, 16. Specialists such as Gustave Le Bon, R. G. Corbet, Martin Hartmann, J. Léger, and D. S. Margoliouth answered the query.

14. "Ḥadīth ma'a Ismā'īl Kamāl Bey," *al-Muqaṭṭam*, March 13, 1901.

15. Ahmed Riza, "L'Islamisme," *La Revue Occidentale* 3, no. 2 (1891), 117–18, idem, "Le cléricalisme Français en Turquie," *Mechveret Supplément Français*, no. 56, May 15, 1898, 2.

16. Ahmed Rıza's response to an inquiry on war and militarism in *L'Humanité Nouvelle* 3 (May 1899), 221.

17. Maurice Ajam, "Un positiviste dans l'Islam: Ahmed Riza," *La Revue Positiviste Internationale* 6, no. 3, April 1, 1909, 276.

18. An unsigned letter sent to Doctor Nâzım, Geneva, June 16, 1896, Private Papers of Bahaeddin Şakir.

19. Hercule Diamandopulo, *Le réveil de la Turquie* (Alexandria, [1908]), 258–59, Abdullah Cevdet, "Profesör Dozy'nin Mütercimi ve İttihad-ı İslâm," in Celâl Nuri, *İttihad-ı İslâm* (Istanbul, 1331 [1913]), 379.

20. Abdullah Cevdet, "Mezheb-i Bahaullah Din-i Ümem," *İctihad*, no. 144, 315–16.

21. The foremost work in this field was Ahmed Rıza's *Tolérance Musulmane*, which was also published in *La Revue Occidentale* 13 (1896), 304–17, and *Mechveret Supplément Français*, no. 27, January 15, 1897, 4 ff. For another striking article allegedly written by "un Chrétien ami de l'Islam," see "L'esprit libéral de l'Islam," *Osmanli Supplément Français*, no. 10, January 5, 1899, 4–6.

22. Abdullah Cevdet, *Fünûn ve Felsefe*, 2d ed. (Cairo, 1906), 22–23.

23. Ibid., 23.

24. Ibid., 30–31.

25. Abdullah Cevdet, *Fünûn ve Felsefe* (the book bears the year of drafting, 1309 [1893], and was published in [Geneva, 1897]), 24–25.

26. "Âsâr-ı Müfide," *Mizan*, no. 14, April 5, 1897, 4, and "Ahmed Rıza Bey," *Hürriyet*, no. 79, August 1, 1897, 2.

27. For instance see *Qānūn*, June 18, 1890, 2.

28. Mustafa Fâzıl, *Paris'den Bir Mektub* (Istanbul, 1326 [1908]), 24.

29. *Mısırlı Mustafa Fâzıl Paşa'nın Paris'den Hakipâ-yı Şâhâneye Takdim Etmiş Olduğu Arizaya Cevaben İzmir Ulemasından Şakir Efendi'nin Tahrir Etmiş Olduğu Mektubdur*, in *Mecmua-yı Muharrerat-ı Siyasiye*, Istanbul Archaeology Museum Manuscripts, no. 338, 1–6.

30. For the Young Turks' "higher teachings" on Islam see Ali Fehmi, *Bulgaristan İslâmları* (Plovdiv, 1901), 3 ff.

31. See Auguste Comte, *Système de politique positive, ou traité de sociologie, instituant la religion de l'humanité* 3 (Paris, 1853), 562, and 4 (Paris, 1854), 505–11.

32. See his letter dated February 4, 1853 in *Auguste Comte: Correspondance générale et confessions* 7 (Paris, 1987), 38–41.

33. "Le Discours de Midhat-Pacha," *Le Courrier de France*, August 29, 1877.

34. See "Nouvelles," *La Revue Occidentale* 16, no. 3, May 1, 1898, 469. In 1906 Ahmed Rıza, along with fourteen other positivists, formed the Société Positiviste Internationale. See "Constitution de la Société Positiviste Internationale," *La Revue Positiviste Internationale* 1, no. 1, July 1, 1906, 5 ff.

35. See Youssouf Fehmi, *Troisième brochure de l'apostolat des chevaliers Positivistes: Considérations sur la Turquie vaincue* (Paris, 1913), 6 ff.

36. See "M. Ahmed Riza," *La Revue Occidentale* 12, no. 3, May 1, 1896, 343–44; J. H. Bridges, "Paragraphs," *The Positivist Review* 4, no. 37, January 1, 1896, 15; "Discours de M. Ahmed Riza," *La Revue Occidentale* 31, no. 6, August 15, 1905, 211, Albert Fua, *Le Comité Union et Progrès contre la Constitution* (Paris, 1909), 74.

37. S. H. Swinny, "The Annual Address," *The Positivist Review* 17, no. 194, February 1, 1909, 26–27; Frédéric Harrison, "La réforme Turque," *La Revue Positiviste Internationale* 4, no. 2, February 15, 1909, 176–78, "Ahmed Riza," *Menschheitsziele* 3 (1909), 98–99.

38. "Les Positivistes et politique internationale," *Mechveret Supplément Français*, no. 19, September 15, 1896, 6.

39. "Discours de M. Ahmed Riza," *La Revue Occidentale* 16, no. 2, March 1, 1898, 228–29.

40. Ahmed Rıza, "The Caliph and His Duties," *Contemporary Review* 70 (August 1896), 209.

41. See "İfade-i Mahsusa," *Osmanlı*, no. 1, 1; Ahmed Rıza, *Mektub*, 4; idem, *Lâyiha*, 28; Câzım, *İttihad* (Geneva, 1900), 9 ff.

42. [Murad], "Biz Neyiz?" *Mizan*, no. 178, May 28, 1896, 2506.

43. Ahmed Rıza, *Vazife ve Mes'uliyet 1*, 10.

44. Ibid., [27].

45. See Ahmed Rıza, *Vazife ve Mes'uliyet 2, Asker* (Cairo, 1323 [1907]), and *3, Kadın* (Paris, 1324 [1908]).

46. Abdullah Djevdet Bey, *De la nécessité d'une école pour les éducateurs sociaux* (Paris, 1900), 23–24.

47. Leopoldo Zea, *Positivism in Mexico* (Austin, 1974), 156–61; Walter N. Breymann, "The *Científicos*: Critics of the Díaz Regime," in *Positivism in Latin America, 1850–1900*, ed. Ralph Lee Woodward Jr. (Lexington, 1971), 87 ff.

48. For examples from the eighteenth and nineteenth centuries, see *Siyaset-i Medeniye Hakkında Risâle* IUL, Turkish Manuscripts, no. 6950, especially, 22 ff., and *Abdülaziz Döneminde Yazılan Bir Risâle* TPL, MR 925, passim.

49. Pierre Laffitte, *The Positive Science of Morals* (London, 1908), 141–42.

50. Leopoldo Zea, *The Latin American Mind* (Norman, 1963), 159–60.

51. See Arturo Ardao, *Espiritualismo y Positivismo en el Uruguay* (Buenos Aires, 1949), 66–67, Ricaurte Soler, *El Positivismo Argentino* (Panama, 1959), 180–81.

52. Giacomo Barzellotti, *The Ethics of Positivism: A Critical Study* (New York, 1878), 278–79.

53. For an interesting example see Malcom Quin, *Memoirs of a Positivist* (London, 1924), 40–42.

54. See J. H. Bridges, "Armenia," *The Positivist Review* 4, no. 38, March 1,

1896, 53–57; Editor [Edward Spencer Beesly], "Russia and Turkey," *The Positivist Review* 4, no. 48, December 1, 1896, 245–50. For Ahmed Rıza's critiques of Great Power politics from a similar viewpoint, see "La politique Française en Orient," *La Grande Revue* 4 (1901), 560–65.

55. "Discours de M. Ahmed Riza," *La Revue Occidentale* 21, no. 6, November 1, 1900, 342.

56. His work *La Crise de l'Orient* was published in *La Revue Positiviste Internationale* in installments beginning with the 1, no. 4 (November 15, 1906) issue of the journal. It was also published as a book in Paris in 1907 by the CUP.

57. Ahmed Riza, *La faillite morale de la politique Occidentale en Orient* (Paris, 1922).

58. Editions Bouslama [1979]. Later it was translated into Turkish (see *Batının Doğu Politikasının Ahlâken İflâsı* [Istanbul, 1982]), and English (see *The Moral Bankruptcy of Western Policy Towards the East*, tr. Adair Mill [Ankara, 1988]). The latter was accomplished by the Turkish Ministry of Culture.

59. Ahmed Rıza first expressed his ideas on the matter in a conference: "Question de la Macédoine," *La Revue Occidentale* 30, no. 4, July 1, 1904, 44–47. Later V. E. Pépin's accusations against the Turks (see "Terre et peuples," *La Revue Occidentale* 32, no. 7, October 1, 1905, 313–15), caused a prolonged debate in which Ahmed Rıza expressed his views. See Ahmed Rıza's letter to the editor, "Correspondance," *La Revue Occidentale* 32, November 15, 1905, 444–45, Pépin's letter to the editor, "Controverse," *La Revue Occidentale* 33, no. 1, January 1906, 109–112, Ahmed Riza, "Controverse," *La Revue Occidentale* 33, no. 2, February 15, 1906, 207–208, "V. E. Pépin, "Controverse," *La Revue Occidentale* 33, no. 3, April 1, 1906, 331–36, Ahmed Rıza, "Controverse," *La Revue Occidentale* 33, no. 4, May 15, 1906, 443–45.

60. Mehmed Murad, "İkiden Hangisi [?]" *Meşveret*, no. 17, August 23, 108 [1896], 1.

61. "Tekzib," *Mizan*, no. 24, June 14, 1897, 3.

62. M[ehmed] Sabahaddin, "Genclerimize Mektub: İntibah-ı Fikrîmiz," *Terakki*, no. [1], 2.

63. See Tunalı Hilmi, *Murad*, 43–139; idem, *Un projet d'organisation de la souveraineté du peuple en Turquie* (Geneva, 1902), passim; and idem, *Ahali Hakimliği, Bir Şart, Bir Dilek* (Geneva, 1320 [1902]), 6–31.

64. See Abdülhalim Memduh, *Mazlum Türklere: Mev'ize* (Paris, 1902), 8; "Esaret," *Şark ve Garb*, no. 2, April 1312 [1896], 50.

65. "Kitab el-İstibdad Kütüphane-i Ahrara Bir Hediye," *Osmanlı*, no. 54, February 15, 1900, 6–7. This was also the idea behind the translation of Alfieri's *Del Principe e Delle Lettere* into Turkish. See Abdullah Cevdet's preface to *Hükümdar ve Edebiyat* (Geneva, 1905).

66. Ahmed Rıza, *Lâyiha*, 24. For the influence of Le Bon in the years following, see idem, *La faillite morale*, 35.

67. Hoca Muhiddin, "Zât-ı Şâhâneye Takdim Kılınan Arizadan Ma'bad," *Kanun-i Esasî*, no. 2, December 28, 1896, 5.

68. "Türkiya'da İhtilâl," *Anadolu*, no. 4, June 7, 1902, 2–3.

69. "Abdülhamid ve İlm-i Ruh," *Osmanlı*, no. 24, April 15, 1899, 5, and "Küstahlık," *Şûra-yı Ümmet*, no. 75, May 30, 1905, 1–2.

70. "Abdülhamid!" *Osmanlı*, no. 90, August 15, 1901, 3.

71. Abdullah Cevdet, "Doktor Gustave Le Bon," *İctihad*, no. 8 (July 1905), 120.

72. *Ruh'ül-akvâm* (Cairo, 1907).

73. For a review and definition of the characteristics of his work see Harry Elmer Barnes, "A Psychological Interpretation of Modern Social Problems and of Contemporary History: A Survey of the Contributions of Gustave Le Bon to Social Psychology," *The American Journal of Psychology* 31, no. 4 (October 1920), 333–35.

74. M., "Mektub," *Meşveret*, no. 26, October 25, 1897, 4, and "Havâdis," *Osmanlı*, no. 37, June 1, 1899, 6.

75. Doctor Nâzım to İshak Sükûti, undated [1900?], AQSh, 19/106-5// 845/1362.

76. Tunalı Hilmi, *Murad*, 104–5.

77. "Niyet ve Maksadımız," *İstikbâl (2)*, no. 1 (1901), 2.

78. See "Esbâb-ı Felâket," *İstikbâl*, no. 27, June 21, 1895, 1–2.

79. Bir Kürd [Abdullah Cevdet], "Bir Muhavere," *Sada-yı Millet*, no. 6, April 10, 1898, 2.

80. "L'Élite," *Mechveret Supplément Français*, no. 52, February 1, 1898, 1, Abdullah Cevdet, *İki Emel* (Cairo, 1316 [1898]), 3, 21.

81. "Abdülhamid ve İlm-i Ruh," *Osmanlı*, no. 24, 5.

82. Abdullah Djevdet Bey, *De la nécessité d'une ecole*, 27–28.

83. "Küstahlık," *Şûra-yı Ümmet*, no. 75, 1–2.

84. See his biography in *Le Journal*, April 12, 1896.

85. Abdullah Djevdet Bey, *De la nécessité d'une école*. It was translated into German; see *Über die Erziehung der Lehrer* (Vienna, 1902).

86. Lâli [Mehmed Reşid] to İshak Sükûti, May 16, 1900, AQSh, 19/106-5//122/692.

87. AQSh, 19/89//518/13.

88. "Açık Muhabere," *Osmanlı*, no. 102, February 15, 1902, 8.

89. See "Padişâh-ı Maarifperver Hazretlerine," *Osmanlı*, no. 46, October 15, 1899, 8, "Mühim Bir İtiraf," *Osmanlı*, no. 64, July 15, 1900, 7–8, and "Maarife Dair," *Şûra-yı Ümmet*, no. 8, July 21, 1902, 2–3.

90. Şerif Mardin, *Continuity and Change in the Ideas of the Young Turks* (Istanbul, 1969), 23.

91. This book was translated into Turkish by Abdullah Cevdet at a relatively late date. See *Terbiye ve Veraset* (Istanbul, 1927).

92. İ[brahim] Edhem Temo, "Tagaddi ve Devam-ı Hayat," *Musavver Cihan*, no. 16 [December 16, 1892], 123.

93. Ahmed Rıza, *Lâyiha*, 17.

94. Mağmumî, *Hakikat-ı Hal*, 4.

95. *Organicisme et société* (Paris, 1896), and *Philosophie des sciences sociales*, 3 vols. (Paris, 1903–1907).

96. J[acques] Novicow, *Harb ve Sözde İyilikleri*, tr. Abdullah Cevdet (Istanbul, 1927), 9.

97. "Kıyam," *Osmanlı*, no. 5, February 1, 1898, 5.

98. "Reşad Efendi İstibdadı Nasıl Muhafaza Edebilir?" *Hak*, no. 39, April 1, 1901, 2.

99. For Le Bon's focus on the race issue see "L'Anthropologie actuelle et l'étude des races," *Revue Scientifique* 28/2, no. 25 (December 17, 1881), 772–82, "Sur la formation d'une race dans les monts Tatras," *Revue Scientifique* 29/3, no. 11 (March 18, 1882), 338–45; "Applications de la psychologie à la classification des races," *Revue Philosophique* 22 (December 1886), 593–619.

100. See *L'évolution juridique dans les diverses races humaines* (Paris, 1891), *L'évolution littéraire dans les diverses races humaines* (Paris, 1894), *L'évolution de l'esclavage dans les diverses races humaines* (Paris, 1897), *L'évolution de l'éducation dans les diverses races humaines* (Paris, 1898).

101. [Ali Kemal], "İngiltere'de Bulunan Paris Muhabirimizden İngiltere Mektubları," *İkdam*, August 28, 1898.

102. Rıza Tevfik, "Abdullah Cevdet Bey," *Nevsâl-i Millî* (Istanbul, 1330 [1914]), 99–100, and Joseph Denais, *La Turquie nouvelle*, 76.

103. Daniel Gasman, *The Scientific Origins of National Socialism* (New York, 1971), 39.

104. Enrico Ferri, *Socialism and Positive Science* (London, 1909), 2 ff.

105. See Darwin's letter to W. Graham, dated July 3, 1881, in *The Letters of Charles Darwin* 1, ed. Francis Darwin (London, 1888), 316.

106. Yusuf Akçura, "Üç Tarz-ı Siyaset," *Türk*, no. 24, April 14, 1904, 1ff.

107. "Spencer'in Japonlara Vasiyetnâmesi," *Türk*, no. 23, April [7], 1904, 4. Spencer's recommendations were also quoted by Ahmed Rıza in his response to criticisms made by European statesmen. See "Réponse de H. Spencer à Berthelot," *Mechveret Supplément Français*, no. 154, July 15, 1904, 6–7. Spencer made his recommendations to Kentaro Kanedo in 1892. See *Life and Letters of Herbert Spencer* 2, ed. David Duncan (London, 1908), 14–18. In 1904 these recommendations became a matter of discussion and criticized by the British press. See "Mr. Herbert Spencer and Japan," *Times*, January 18, 1904.

108. A[bdullah] C[evdet], "Doktor Gustave Le Bon ile Mülâkat," *İctihad*, no. 190, October 15, 1925, 3762.

109. "Me'yus Olmalı Mıyız [?]" *Şûra-yı Ümmet*, no. 62, October 24, 1904, 1.

110. See Ali Muzaffer, "Düyûn Umumiye-i Osmaniye Varidât-ı Muhassese İdaresi Yahud Hükûmet İçinde Hükûmet," *Kanun-i Esasî*, no. 39 [May 30, 1899], 4–5; Ahmed Rıza, "Kuvve-i Bahriyemiz," *Osmanlı*, no. 13, June 1, 1898, 1; "Selânik'den Mektub," *İlâve-i Meşveret*, no. 9, April 1, 108 [1896], 3, "Devlet-i Osmaniye ve Avrupa," *Osmanlı*, no. 5, February 1, 1898, 1.

111. Letters sent from those places outnumbered those sent from within the empire. See AQSh, 19/97.

112. "İttihad-ı İslâm," *Gayret (2)*, no. 148 [May 11, 1898], 1.

113. "Siyasî," *Emniyet*, no. 7 [November 12, 1896], 1.

114. For the so-called Turkish secret defence committee see Cumberbatch to Currie, Angora, January 10, 1895/no. 5. Enclosed with the letter from Currie to Kimberley, Constantinople, January 14, 1895/no. 33 (confidential), PRO/F.O. 78/4607.

115. Blanc to Hanotaux, Canea, August 18, 1895/no. 11, *Documents Diplomatiques: Affaires d'Orient-Affaire de Crète* (Paris, 1897), 17.

116. Le Comité, "Aux nobles consciences," in *Constitution Ottomane promulguée le 7 Zilhidje 1293 (11/23 Decembre 1876)* (Geneva, 1898), [2].

117. [Colmar] von der Goltz, *Millet-i Müsellaha*, tr. M. Tahir (Istanbul, 1301 [1884]). For the admiration of the Ottoman military toward von der Goltz, see "Goltz Paşa ve Fuad Bey'in Mektubu," *Asker* 1, no. 2 [September 14, 1908], 71–74.

118. Le Bon's impact on French military is well examined in Robert N. Nye, *The Origins of Crowd Psychology: Gustave Le Bon and the Crisis of Mass Democracy in the Third Republic* (London, 1975), 123–53.

119. Enver Bey to a German woman with whom he frequently corresponded, Ain al-Mansur, September 2, 1912, Ernst Jäckh Papers, Yale University, MS 466. For Le Bon's impact on the Ottoman military, see İsmail Hakkı Hafız, *Bozgun* (Istanbul, 1334 [1914]), 20–21, 51.

120. Ahmed Rıza, *Vazife ve Mes'uliyet 2.*

Chapter 10

1. "Geht zum Dossier Mechveret (Jung-Türken)," May, 10, 1902 (P.P. 17/66), Bundesarchiv-Bern, E. 21/14'250.

2. Ferid, "İntikadât," *Sebil'ür-Reşad*, no. 283 [February 12, 1914], 358.

3. A similar action took place in France to reconcile positivism with Catholicism. See L. Laberthonnière, *Positivisme et Catholicisme* (Paris, 1911).

4. For an example see Daniel Seelye Gregory, *The Crime of Christendom or the Eastern Question* (New York, 1900), 284–85.

5. [Johann Friedrich von] Schiller, *Guillaume Tell*, tr. Abdullah Cevdet (Cairo, 1314 [1898]). For the implementation of the theme of patriotism, also see R. Figanî, *Elveda' Yahud Fatih-i Hanya Yusuf Paşa'nın Serbâlinde Bir Feryad* (Geneva, 1316 [1898]), passim, and Giridli Bir İslâm, *Bıçak Kemiğe Dayandı* [Geneva, 1898], passim.

6. *The Memoirs of Ismail Kemal Bey*, 11–12.

7. Akçuraoğlu Yusuf, *Türk Yılı 1928* (Istanbul, 1928), 394–95.

8. See Tengku Hasan M. di Tiro, "Indonesian Nationalism: A Western Invention to Contain Islam in the Dutch East Indies," in *The Impact of Nationalism on the Muslim World*, ed. M. Ghayasuddin (London, 1986), 65–67.

9. Ahmed Rıza, *Vazife ve Mes'uliyet 1*, 6.

Selected Bibliography

For the sake of brevity, this selected bibliography omits many materials used in preparing this book and many items cited in endnotes. The archival material has been listed generally. All manuscripts, official publications, and published documents used in preparing this book are given. The works of the Young Turks used, except for their translations of various European books, are also enumerated, although neither this list nor the list of the Young Turk journals given here by any means represents a complete compilation of the Young Turks. Dates of the works are converted into the Gregorian calendar. A list of secondary journals and newspapers is also given. This list does not include the journals and newspapers that provided contemporary articles with related information. No secondary work published either during the Young Turk movement or afterward is mentioned in the bibliography. Full descriptions of the secondary works can be found in the endnotes.

Archives

Albania

Arkivi Qendror Shtetëror (Tirana)

Fondi Dr. I. Temo : 19

Files:

31
33
36

53
57
58
59
60
61
62
89
92
93
95
97
102
103
104
106
106-1
106-2
106-3
106-4
106-5
106-6
106-7
107
127
129
135
136-3
158

Austria

Haus-, Hof- und Staatsarchiv (Vienna)

Akten des k.u.k. Ministeriums des Äußeren 1848–1918 (Politisches Archiv).

    XII 168 (Türkei Berichte 1897 VI–XII)
    XII 2 (Albanien 1897)
    XII 170 (Türkei Berichte 1898 X–XII)
    XXXVIII 406 (Konsulat Saloniki 1898)
    XII 172 (Türkei Berichte 1899 VIII–XII)
    XXXVIII 313 (Konsulate 1899, Smyrna)
    XXVII 47 (Schweiz Berichte 1900)
    XIV 7 (Albanien 1900)
    XII 173 (Türkei Berichte 1900 I–VII)
    XXVII 48 (Schweiz Berichte 1901)
    XXXI 21 (Ägypten Berichte 1901)
    XIV 7 (Albanien 1901)
    XII 178 (Türkei Berichte 1902 I–V)
    IX 154 (Frankreich Varia 1902)

Belgium

Archives Générales du Royaume Belgique (Brussels)

L'Administration Publique-Police des Étrangers: Dossiers Individuels: 619796

France

Archives du Ministère des Affaires Étrangères (Paris)

Correspondance Politique-Turquie:

524
525
526

Correspondance Politique-Politique Intérieure (Syrie-Liban): Dossier Générale 2 (1897)

Nouvelle Série-Turquie:

1 (1897)
2 (1898)
3 (1899–1901)
4 (1902–1904)

Archives de la Préfecture de Police de Paris

Ambassade de Turquie-Police Ottomane à Paris, B. A (109.700-2).
La Colonie Ottomane de Paris, B. A (1653)- 1097003.
Karl Blind, B. A (963)- 58423235 RD.
Mahmoud Pacha, B. A (1169)- 139990-9.200.
Sabaheddin et Loutfullah, B. A (1653)-171154.

Germany

Bayerisches Hauptstaatsarchiv (Munich)

Bayerische Gesandschaft in Berlin, no. 1174 (Politische Versammlungen, 1876–1914).

Bundesarchiv (Koblenz)

NL. 182.

Geheimes Staatsarchiv (Berlin)

III. HA Bl. 2617–2618.

Politisches Archiv des Auswärtigen Amtes der Bundesrepublik Deutschland (Bonn)

Eisenbahnen in der asiatischen Türkei, 152 (Bd. 17)

Die Jungtürken 198
732/3 (Bd. 1–2)
733/1 (Bd. 2–3)
733/2 (Bd. 3–4)

733/3 (Bd. 4–5)

Türkische Militärs 159 (Bd. 2–3)

Israel

Central Archives of the Jewish People (Jerusalem)

Archives Galante RP 112, Dossier 21.

The Netherlands

Algemeen Rijksarchief (The Hague)

Tweede Afdeling: Kabinet en Protocol, 60 (141).

Sweden

Rijksarkivet (Stockholm)

Kabinettet för utrikes brevväxlingen, Koncept, 1899, vol. 6, Noter, Turkiets beskickning.

Switzerland

Archives de la Justice et Police (Geneva)

Dossier: Abdullah Djevdet.

Archives d'Etat-Genève

Chancellerie:
B.7
B.8

Bundesarchiv (Bern)

E. 21/14'248
E. 21/14'249
E. 21/14'249 Bd.1
E. 21/14'249 Bd.2
E. 21/14'249 Bd.4
E. 21/14'250
E. 21/14'251
E. 21/14'258
E. 21/14'259

Staatsarchiv des Kantons Zürich

Akten über die Anarchisten: P 239.4.

Turkey

Archives of the Turkish Embassy in London (London)

Boxes

259 (2)

277 (8)
295 (2)
303 (1)
303 (3)
319 (2)
332 (3)
332 (4)
338 (3)
339 (1)
339 (8)
340 (7)
347 (2)
348 (2)
361 (1)
361 (2)
361 (3)
362 (1)
362 (2)
362 (10)
382 (2)
383 (6)
404 (1)

Archives of the Turkish Embassy in Paris (Paris)

Dossiers

D. 176
D. 192
D. 195
D. 220
D. 237
D. 244
D. 283
D. 287

Archives of the Turkish Embassy in Rome (Rome)

Boxes

50 (1)
50 (2)
51 (1)
52 (1)
71 (3)

Başbakanlık Arşivi (Istanbul)

1. İrade Tasnifi.

İrade-Dahiliye
İrade-Hariciye
İrade-Hususî

2. Bâb-ı Âli Evrak Odası

a. Nezaret ve Devâir:

Adliye Giden
Bulgaristan Hülâsası
Bulgaristan Komiserliği Muharrerat Defteri
Bulgaristan Komiserliği Gelen
Bulgaristan Komiserliği Reft
Bulgaristan Masasının Tezkere Kayd Defteri
Bulgaristan Muharrerat Defteri
Bulgaristan ve Şarkî Rumeli Hülâsa Defteri
Bulgaristan ve Şarkî Rumeli'nin Muharrerat Defteri
Dahiliye Gelen
Dahiliye Giden
Harbiye Gelen
Harbiye Giden (Serasker Reft)
Hariciye Gelen (Âmed)
Hariciye Giden (Reft)
Hidiviyet-i Celile-i Mısriyenin Tahrirat Defteri
Hususî İrade-i Seniye
Mısır Fevkâlâde Komiseri Gazi Ahmed Muhtar Paşa'dan Vürûd Eden
Mısır Hidiviyet-i Celilesinin Muharrerat Defteri
Mısır Hidiviyet-i Celilesinin Tezâkir Defteri
Mısır Hülâsa Defteri
Mısır Komiserliği Âmed
Re'sen İrade-i Seniye
Şehremaneti Giden
Telgraf ve Posta Nezareti Gelen
Telgraf ve Posta Nezareti Giden
Zabtiye Gelen
Zabtiye Giden

b. Vilâyetler Gelen-Giden (2)

Anadolu Telgrafi 903
Arabistan Müteferrikası 211
Arabistan Telgrafi 956
Arabistan Vilâyâtı Giden 235
Devâir-Mühimme (Hariciye) 1347
Devâir Mühimme (Zabtiye) 1345
Haleb Giden 297
Jurnal 3 (Mühimme) 1296
Suriye Gelen 345
Suriye Giden 352

c. Bulgaristan Tasnifi Evrakı I-II
d. Mümtaze Kalemi: Kıbrıs
e. Mümtaze Kalemi: Mısır
f. Mümtaze Kalemi: Şarkî Rumeli Evrakı

3. Yıldız Tasnifi

a. Yıldız Esas Evrakı

Sections:

5

11
14
15
18
19
24
30
31
34
36

b. Yıldız Esas Evrakı-Kâmil Paşa Evrakına Ek I
c. Yıldız Mütenevvî (Günlük) Marûzat
d. Yıldız Perâkende
e. Yıldız Sadaret Hususî Marûzat
f. Yıldız Sadaret Resmî Marûzat

4. Bâb-ı Âsâfî, Mesâil-i Mühimme 129/VIII

5. Tezâkir-i Samiye Dosyaları
398
400
401
402

6. Mahremâne Müsvedât
14
38
68
80
81
82
129

7. HNA (Hariciye Nezareti Arşivi)

End. MT
End. S.III

8. Divan-ı Hümayûn: Muhtelif ve Mütenevvî Defterler: Muharrerât-ı Umumiye:
84

9. Ayniyat Defterleri:

1637/14
1689: Zabtiye

Cerrahpaşa Tıp Fakültesi Tıp Tarihi ve Deontoloji Arşivi (Istanbul)

Dossiers:

Doktor İbrahim Temo (I-1935)
Doktor Şerafeddin Mağmumi

Deniz Müzesi Arşivi (Istanbul)

Sections:

Umumî Evrak
Şûra-yı Bahrî

Dışişleri Bakanlığı Hazine-i Evrak Arşivi (Istanbul)*

Box

Siyasî: 424

Dossiers:

İdarî. 198
Siyasî. 178
Tercüme Mütenevvia: 29

Topkapı Sarayı Arşivi (Istanbul)

E. 1518/1
E. 9321

Türk İnkılâp Tarihi Enstitüsü Arşivi (Ankara)
Files:

1c
82

United Kingdom

Public Record Office (London)

CAB

37/37
37/40
37/42
37/43

F.O.
a. General Correspondence

78/4463
78/4606
78/4611
78/4613
78/4614
78/4618
78/4623
78/4629
78/4646
78/4701
78/4705
78/4706

* This used to be an independent archive and was recently acquired by the Başbakanlık Archives. The recataloging is currently ongoing.

78/4720
78/4723
78/4724
78/4744
78/4797
78/4798
78/4801
78/4804
78/4805
78/4806
78/4840
78/4912
78/4914
78/4943
78/4992
78/4994
78/4995
78/4996
78/5011
78/5058
78/5059
78/5060
78/5061
78/5062
78/5074
78/5075
78/5119
78/5120
78/5121
78/5122
78/5124
78/5126
78/5140
78/5141
78/5142
78/5209
78/5259
78/5367
78/5269
78/5394
371/154

b. Embassy and Consular Archives

195/1332
195/2008
195/2037
195/2085
195/2086
195/2091
195/2108

195/2280
195/2091
226/214

c. Confidential Print

407/151
407/155
407/190
421/152
421/187
424/29
424/37
424/46
424/49
424/55
424/184
424/191
424/222
429/192
Conf. 6853 (1896)

H.O.

Registered Papers

45: 9650-A. 38025 b.
45: 9741-A. 55743.

Private Papers

Young Turks

Private Papers of Abdullah Cevdet (Gül Karlıdağ's private collection-Istanbul).
Private Papers of Ahmed Rıza (1) (The author's private collection).
Private Papers of Ahmed Rıza (2) (Faruk Ilıkhan's private collection-Istanbul).
Private Papers of Ahmed Ferid Tek (The late Emel Esin's private collection-Istanbul).
Private Papers of Bahaeddin Şakir. (The author's private collection).
Private Papers of Şevket Bey (The late Emel Esin's private collection- Istanbul).
Private Papers of Tevfik Nevzad (The late Benâl Nevzad Arıman's private collection-Istanbul).

Other

Abbas II Papers, Durham University.
Nachlaß Fürsten von Bülow, Bundesarchiv (Koblenz, NL. 182)
Cromer Papers, PRO/F.O. 633
Private Papers of Sir Philip Currie, PRO/F.O. 800/14.
Damad Ferid Pasha's Letters, Bibliothèque Nationale (Paris), MS Or. Supplément turc 1445.
Ernst Jäckh Papers, Yale University Sterling Memorial Library, MS. 466.

Kimberley Papers, National Library of Scotland.
Layard Papers, British Library Add. MSS.
O'Conor Papers, Churchill College, Cambridge.
Correspondance de Joseph Reinach, Bibliothèque Nationale (Paris), MS Occ. XXXVIII.
Rosebery Papers, National Library of Scotland.
Ryan Papers, PRO/F.O. 800/240.
Private Papers of Salih Münir Pasha (The author's private collection).
Lord Sanderson's Private Papers, PRO/F.O. 800/1.
Private Papers of Cléanthi Scalieri (Private collection of Constantin Svolopulos-Thessaloniki).
Nachlaß Süssheim, Staatsbibliothek Preussischer Kulturbesitz: Orientabteilung.
Vambéry Papers, PRO/F.O. 800-32 and 33.

Manuscripts

'Abd al-Jamīl, *al-Ẓafar al-Hamīdiyya fī ithbāt al-Khalīfa* Marmara University, İlâhiyat Fakültesi Library MS no. 30.
Abdülaziz Döneminde Yazılan Bir Risâle TPL, M.R. 925.
Abdülhamid-i Sânî Arkivi Qendror, 19/36.
Lâyiha-yi Tatarcıkzâde Abdullah Efendi IUL, Turkish Manuscripts, no. 6930.
Ahmed Azmi Efendi'nin Sefaretnâmesidir IUL, İ.M.K.İ Manuscripts, no. 2491.
Ahmed Salâhi, *Osmanlı ve Avrupa Politikası ve Abdülhamid-i Sânî'nin Siyaseti* IUL, Turkish Manuscripts, no. 9521.
Arab Medeniyeti (translation of the first chapters of Gustave Le Bon's book *La civilisation des Arabes*), IUL, Turkish Manuscripts, no. 9928.
Avrupa Medeniyeti ve Ümranı Hakkında Risâle IUL, Turkish Manuscripts, no. 6623.
Avrupa'dan Düvel-i Muazzamadan Addolunan Fransa ve Rusya ve İngiltere ve Avusturya ve Prusya Devletlerinin ve Sair Zayıf ve Sagir Düvelin Ahvâl ve Keyfiyet-i Mülkiyeleri TPL R. 1615.
Avrupa'ya Dair Tarihce SL, Es'ad Efendi, no. 2963.
Bahaeddin Sâî, *Güldeste-i Hatırat-ı Ahrar ve Eslâf-Refuge [Réfugié] Turc à Paris* Istanbul Hakkı Tarık Us Library, MS D. 38/1.
Beyân-ı Faide-i Cedide Atatürk Library, Muallim Cevdet Manuscripts, K. 51.
1205 Senesinde Sefaretle Prusya'ya Gönderilen Ahmed Azmi Efendi'nin Sefaretnâmesidir İ.M.K.İ Manuscripts, IUL, no. 2491.
Bir Osmanlı Zabiti ile Bir Ecnebî Zabitin Mükâlemesi IUL, Turkish Manuscripts, no. 6623.
Dersaadet'de Mekteb-i Tıbbiye-i Şâhâne Talebesinden Bir Zât Tarafından Diyar-ıbekir'de Akrabasından Bir Zâta Yazub Gönderdiği Mektubdur ki Aynen Bu Mahalle Derc ve Tahrir Olundu [1890], Princeton University, Islamic MS (S. 3), no. 276-II.
Devlet-i Aliyye'nin Ahvâl-i Hâzırasına Dair Risaledir SL Hüsrev Paşa Manuscripts, no. 851.
Devlet-i Aliyye'nin Ahvâl-i Politikasına Dair Bâzı Malûmat TPL, Y. 242.
Devlet-i Aliyye-i Osmaniye'nin Bin Üçyüz Onüç Senesine Mahsus İstatistik-i Umumisidir IUL, Turkish Manuscripts, no. 9184/6.
Ebubekir Ratib Efendi'nin Seyahatnâmesidir IUL, Turkish Manuscripts, no. 6096.

Hikmet, *Terakkiyat-ı Cedide-i Bahriye* IUL, Turkish Manuscripts, no. 4177.

İbrahim Müteferrika, *Usûl ül-Hikem fî Nizâm ül-Âlem* IUL, Turkish Manuscripts, no. 6694.

İcmâl-i Ahvâl-i Âvrupa SL, Es'ad Efendi, no. 2062/1.

İcmâl-i Ahvâl-i Avrupa TPL R. 1648.

İcmâl ül-Sefâin fî Tüccar ül-Âlem SL, Es'ad Efendi, no. 2062/2.

İngiltere Memleketiyle Londra Şehrinin Bâzu Usûl ve Nizamâtını Bildiren Seyahatnâme IUL, Turkish Manuscripts, no. 5085.

İngiltere Seyahatnâmesi IUL Turkish Manuscripts, no. 5083.

'İşknâme TPL, H.263.

İstanbul Valiliğine Gelen Tahrirat-ı Umumiye Suretleri IUL, Turkish Manuscripts, no. 9886.

İzah ül-esrar IUL, Turkish Manuscripts, no. 4832.

Journal du voyage de Mahmoud Raif Efendi en Angleterre écrit par lûy même TPL, III.Ahmet 3707.

Mahmud Şevket Paşa Su-ikasdi İddianâmesi [1913] Manuscript Copy of the court proceedings. The author's private collection.

Mehmed Emin Behic, *Sevanih el-Levâyih* TPL H.370.

Elhac Mustafa Efendi, *Nemçe Sefaretnâmesi* Fatih Millet Library, Trh. MS. no. 844.

Namık Kemal, *Rüya* Princeton University, Islamic MS (S. 3), no. 276-I.

Nemçe Sefaretnâmesi Fatih Millet Library, Trh MS, no. 844.

Nizâm-ı Devlete Dair Risâle IUL, Turkish Manuscripts, no. 2095.

Ömer Subhi bin Edhem, *Yunanistan-ı Kadîm Mader-i Medeniyet Midir?* IUL, Turkish Manuscripts, no. 3225.

Osmanlı İttihad ve Terakki Cemiyeti Merkezi'nin 1906–1907 Senelerinin Muhaberat Kopyası Atatürk Library, Belediye MS O. 30.

Sefaretnâme-i Râsih Efendi IUL, Turkish Manuscripts, no. 3887.

Rıfat Osman, *Hayatım ve Hatıratım*, vol. 1, Cerrahpaşa Medical School Manuscripts, no. 213/69.

Risâle der Beyân-ı Lüzûm-i Temeddün ve İctima'-yı Beni Âdem SL, Halet Efendi Manuscripts, no. 765/13.

Risâle der Beyân-ı Temeddün ve İmaret TPL, R. 2044.

Risâle fî Fazilet ül-İlm ve'l Ulema Istanbul Devlet Library, MS no. 7891/2.

Rumeli-i Şarki Ahali-i Müslimesinin Abdülhamid-i Sânî'ye Gönderdikleri Ariza-i Tebrikiye IUL, Turkish Manuscripts, no. 9390.

Sadr-ıâzâm Mahmud Nedim Paşa'nın Âyine-i Devlete Dair Kitabı Fatih Millet Library, Trh. MS, no. 1022.

Mısırlı Mustafa Fâzıl Paşa'nın Paris'den Hakipâ-yı Şâhâneye Takdim Etmiş Olduğu Arizaya Cevaben İzmir Ulemasından Şakir Efendi'nin Tahrir Etdiği Mektubdur, in *Mecmua-yı Muharrerat-ı Siyasiye* Istanbul Archeology Museum Manuscripts, no. 338.

Sarı Abdullah, *Tedbir en-Neş'eteyn ve Islâh en-Nüshateyn* TPL, E.H. 1359.

——, *Telhis en-Nesayih* TPL, R. 358.

Sefaretnâme-i Vahid Efendi IUL İ.M.K.İ Manuscripts, no. 3040/1.

Siyaset-i Medeniye Hakkında Risâle IUL, Turkish Manuscripts, no. 6950.

Spinoza Mektebine Reddiye TPL, H. 372.

Sual-i Osmani ve Cevab-ı Nasranî TPL, H. 1634.

Sultan Abdülhamid'in Kime Hitaben Yazıldığı Anlaşılamayan Tezkere-i Serzeniş-âmizi IUL, İ.M.K.İ Manuscripts, no. 3310.

Tahrirat Mecmuası IUL, İ.M.K.İ Manuscripts, no. 2522.

Tahrir-i Asker Maddesine Dair Lâyihadır SL Hüsrev Paşa Manuscripts, no. 807-10.

Taife-i Nasaranın Sefer ve Harb ü Darb ve Hıfz-ı Memlekete Müteallik Bâzı Tedbirleridir ki Tercüme Olunub İşbu Safahata Şebt Olundu IUL, Turkish Manuscripts, no. 3984.

Tarihî Notlar TPL, Y.Y. 89.

Tedâbir-i Umûr-i Saltanata Dair Bir Lâyiha IUL, Turkish Manuscripts, no. 6925.

Usûl-i Hendese Atatürk Library, Muallim Cevdet Manuscripts, K. 118.

Zaman-ı Kadimde Umûr-i Âlemin Nizam Üzerine Olub Şimdi İhtilâl Üzerine Olduğunun Hikmet ve Sebeblerini Beyân Zımnında Risâledir IUL, Turkish Manuscripts, no. 6939.

Ziya Paşa'nın Rüyanâmesi IUL, İ.M.K.İ Manuscripts, no. 2461.

Published Documents, Official Publications

A & P (Accounts and Papers-State Papers)
109 (1895)
95 (1896)
110 (1896)
87 (1903)

Akte të Rilindjes Kombëtare Shqiptare, 1878–1912 (Memorandume, vendime, protesta, thirrje) (Tirana, 1978).

Annales de la Chambre des Députés: 7me Législature: Débats Parlementaires 65.I, I. Partie (Session Extraordinaire de 1901) (October 22–November 26, 1901), (Paris, 1902); 65.II, II.Partie (Session Extraordinaire de 1901) (November 28–December 24, 1901), (Paris, 1902); 66.I, I.Partie (Session Ordinaire de 1902) (January 14–February 18, 1902), (Paris, 1902).

Bescheiden Betreffende de Buitlandse politek van Nederland 1889–1919 ed. C. Smit (S-Grevenhage, 1957).

I Documenti Diplomatici Italiani, vol. 5 (3d. ser., 1896–1907) (Rome, 1974).

Documents Diplomatiques: Affaires Arméniennes: Projets de Réformes dans l'Empire Ottoman 1893–1897 (Paris, 1897).

Documents Diplomatiques: Affaires d'Orient: Affaire de Crète (Paris, 1897).

Documents Diplomatiques: Affaires d'Orient: Autonomie Crétoise (Paris, 1898).

Documents Diplomatiques Français (1871–1914), 1 Série, vol. 12 (Paris, 1951)

Düstûr 2nd Ser., vol. 1, 1911.

Die Große Politik der Europäischen Kabinette 1871–1914 10, *Das türkische Problem 1895* (Berlin, 1923). 12/1, *Alte und neue Balkanhändel* (Berlin, 1923).

Hansard's Parliamentary Papers 34 (1895).

Journal Officiel: Sénat: Session ordinaire de 1894 (48e Séance), (49e Séance).

Meclis-i Meb'usan Zabıt Ceridesi 3/8 (1333/1917).

Salnâme-i Nezaret-i Hariciye (Istanbul, 1900).

Works of the Young Turks

Abdülhalim Memduh, *Mazlum Türklere: Mev'ize* (Paris, 1902).

Abdullah Cevdet, *Bir Hutbe Hemşehrilerime* (Cairo, 1909).

———, *Dimağ: Dimağ ile Ruh Arasındaki Münasebât-ı Fenniyeyi Tedkik* (Istanbul, 1890).

———, *Fizyolociya-yı Hıfz-ı Sıhhat-i Dimağ ve Melekât-ı Akliye* (Istanbul, 1894).

———, *Fizyolociya-yı Tefekkür: Mehazımın Esası C[K]raft und Stoff Unvânlı Kitabın Tefekkür Bahsidir* (Istanbul, 1890).

———, *Fünún ve Felsefe* [Geneva, 1897], 2nd and enlarged edition (Cairo, 1906).

———, *Goril* (Ma'muret-el-Azîz, 1893).

———, *Hadd-ı Te'dib: Ahmed Rıza Bey'e Açık Mektub* (Istanbul, 1912).

———, *Hiç* (Istanbul, 1889–90).

———, *İki Emel* (Cairo, 1898).

———, *Mahkeme-i Kübra* (Paris, 1895).

———, *Ma'sumiyet* (Istanbul, 1893).

———, *De la nécessité d'une école pour educateurs sociaux* (Paris, 1900).

———, *Ramazan Bağçesi* (Istanbul, 1890–91).

———, *Türbe-i Ma'sumiyet* (Istanbul, 1890–91).

    (and Hoca Şakir), *Ulema-yı İslâm Enârallahu Berahinehum Taraflarından Verilen Feteva-yı Şerife* (Paris, 1896)

———, *Uyanınız! Uyanınız!* (Cairo, 1907).

Ahmed Rıza, *La crise de l'Orient* (Paris, 1907)

———, *La faillite morale de la politique Occidentale en Orient* (Paris, 1922).

———, *Tolérance Musulmane* (Paris, 1897).

———, *Vatanın Haline ve Maarif-i Umumiyenin Islâhına Dair Sultan Abdülhamid Han-ı Sâní Hazretlerine Takdim Kılınan Altı Lâyihadan Birinci Lâyiha* (London, 1894).

———, *Vatanın Haline ve Maarif-i Umumiyenin Islâhına Dair Sultan Abdülhamid Han-ı Sâní Hazretlerine Takdim Kılınan Lâyihalar Hakkında Sadarete Gönderilen Mektub* (Geneva, 1895).

———, *Vazife ve Mes'uliyet 1, Mukaddeme, Padişâh, Şehzâdeler* (Cairo, 1902), 2, *Asker* (Cairo, 1907), 3,*Kadın* (Cairo, 1908).

Ahmed Saib, *Abdülhamid'in Evâil-i Saltanatı* (Cairo, 1908).

———, *Rehnüma-yı İnkılâb* (Cairo, 1900).

Ali Fahri, *Açık Mektub: Ali Pinhan Bey'e* (Cairo, 1904).

———, *Emel Yolunda* (Istanbul, 1910).

———, *Kandil ve Muhtar Paşa* (Cairo, 1908).

———, *Vambéry Tehlikede* (Geneva, 1900).

———, *Yeni Osmanlılar Kongresi* (Geneva, [1900]).

———, *Yine Kongre* (Paris, 1900).

Ali Fehmi, *Bulgaristan İslâmları* (Plovdiv, 1901).

Ali Haydar Midhat, *Hatıralarım 1872–1946* (Istanbul, 1946)

———, *Lâyiha ve İstitrad* (Cairo, 1901).

———, *Menfa-yı İhtiyarî Hatıratı* (Geneva, 1905).

Ali Kemal, *(Cenevre'de) Neşredilmekde Bulunan Osmanlı Gazetesinin (17) Numerolu ve (1) Ağustos 1898 Tarihli Nüshasında (Darbe-i Hak) Unvânı ile Neşredilmiş Bir Fıkra-i Müfteriyâneye Cevabdır* (Paris, 1898),

———, *Paris Musahabeleri*, vol. 1 (Istanbul, 1912); vol. 2 (Istanbul, 1914).

Ali Nouri, *Sâye-i Şâhânede: Unter dem Scepter des Sultans* (Berlin, 1905).

Ali Şefik, *Ahrar-ı Ümmet'e İmparator'un Yâdigârı* (Paris, 1898).

———, *Padişâh'ı İğfâl Edenler* (Istanbul, 1908).

Azimzâde Hakkı, *Türkiya'da Meclis-i Meb'usan* (Cairo, 1906).

Bir Osmanlı, *Mısır Fevkâlâde Komiseri Devletlû Gazi Ahmed Muhtar Paşa Hazretlerine* (Istanbul, 1906).

Câzım, *İttihad* (Geneva, 1900).

Comité du Parti Constitutionnel Ottoman à Constantinople, *Lettres ouvertes: A la majesté impériale le Sultan Abd-ul-Hamid: Première lettre* (Paris, 1895).

Le Comité Musulman de Constantinople, *Lettre ouverte* [1896].

Comité Ottoman d'Union et Progrès, *Affaires d'Orient: Réponse au 'New York Herald' et à Mahmoud Nedim Bey ambassadeur de Turquie à Vienne* (Paris, 1896).

———, *Constitution Ottomane promulgée le 7 Zilhidje 1293 (11/23 Decembre 1876)* (Geneva, 1898).

———, *Un horrible assassinat commis sur l'ordre spécial du Sultan Abdul-Hamid II: Assassinat de Midhat Pacha d'après les documents de la Jeune Turquie* (Geneva, 1898).

———, *L'horrible vengeance du Sultan sur un Jeune Turc* (Cairo, 1899).

Les Congrès des libéraux Ottomans (Paris, 1902).

Damad Mahmoud Pacha, *Protestation de S. A. Damad Mahmoud Pacha contre la nouvelle décision prise par le Sultan Abdul Hamid II à l'égard des Turcs résidant à l'étranger* (London, 1900).

Edhem Ruhi, *Mısır'da Sancak Gazetesi Müdiri Ahmed Saib Bey'e* [London, 1900].

Ethem Ruhi Balkan Hatıraları-Canlı Tarihler 6 (Istanbul, 1947).

R. Figanî, *Elveda' Yahud Fatih-i Hanya Yusuf Paşa'nın Serbâlinde Bir Feryad* (Geneva, 1898).

Albert Fua, *Le Comité Union et Progrès contre la constitution* (Paris, 1909).

Füzelâ-yı Müderrisinden Bir Zât, *Ulema-yı Din-i İslâma Da'vet-i Şer'iye* ([Cairo], 1896).

Giridli Bir İslâm, *Bıçak Kemiğe Dayandı* [Geneva, 1898].

Halil Halid, *A Diary of a Turk* (London, 1903).

Halil Muvaffak, *Saltanat-ı Seniye'nin Bükreş Sefiri Kâzım Bey'e Mektub* (Geneva, 1899).

Hamid Hüsni, *Ne Yapmalıyız [?]* (Geneva, 1900).

[İbrahim Temo], *Hareket* (Istanbul [Bucharest], 1896).

———, *İttihad ve Terakki Cemiyetinin Teşekkülü ve Hidemati Vataniye ve İnkılâbı Milliye Dair Hatıratım* (Medgidia, 1939).

İmamet ve Hilâfet Risâlesi (Cairo, 1896).

İsmail Hakkı, *Cidal Yahud Ma'kes-i Hakikat* (Cairo, 1907).

———, *Vatan Uğrunda Yahud Yıldız Mahkemesi* (Cairo, 1908).

İsmail Kemal, *The Memoirs of Ismail Kemal Bey*, ed. Somerville Story (London, 1920).

———, *La question du Transvaal ou le rôle civilisateur de l'Angleterre jugé au point de vue Musulman* (Paris, 1901).

———, *Trablusgarb Vali-i Esbakı İsmail Kemal Bey Tarafından Atabe-i Ûlyâ-yı Padişâhî'ye Takdim Olunan Lâyiha Suretidir* (Geneva, 1897).

———, *Transvaal Mes'elesi* (Cairo, 1902).

Mehmed Kadri Nâsıh, *Sarâyih* (Paris, 1910).

Mehmed Murad, *Mücahede-i Milliye: Gurbet ve Avdet Devirleri* (Istanbul, 1908).

———, *Müdafaa Niyetine Bir Tecavüz! : Kırkanbar'a Cevab* (Paris, 1896).

———, *Le Palais de Yildiz et la Sublime Porte le véritable mal d'Orient* (Paris, 1895).

———, *Tatlı Emeller, Acı Hakikatler Yahud Batn-ı Müstakbele Âdâb-ı Siyasiye Talimi* (Istanbul, 1912).

———, *Yıldız Saray-ı Hümayûnu Yahud Şarkın Derd-i Aslisi* (Cairo, 1896).

Leskovikli Mehmed Rauf, *İttihad ve Terakki Cemiyeti Ne İdi?* (Istanbul, 1909).

[Mehmed Reşid], *İnkılâb Niçün ve Nasıl Oldu?* (Cairo, 1909).

Doktor Lütfi, *Türkiye Cumhuriyeti ve Siyaset-i Milliye, İktisadiye* (Istanbul, 1926).

Hoca Muhiddin, *Hürriyet Mücahedeleri Yahud Firak ve Menfa Hatıraları* (Istanbul, 1908).

Mustafa Réfik, *Ein kleines Sündenregister Abdul Hamid II's* (Geneva, 1899).

Naim Gergor, *El-Harâb* (Geneva, [1900]).

Osmanlı İttihad ve Terakki Cemiyeti Nizamnâmesi (n.p., n.d.).

Osmanlı İttihad ve Terakki Cemiyeti Nizamnâmesi-Niẓam jam'iyyat al-ittiḥād wa al-taraqqi al-'uthmāniyya (n.p., n.d.).

Procès contre le Mechveret et la Jeune Turquie (Paris, 1897).

Reşadiye Cemiyeti'nin Maksad ve Suret-i Teşekkülünü Müş'ir, Türkçe, İngilizce ve Fransızca Olarak Kaleme Alınan Mevadd-ı Esasiye (Geneva, 1899).

Rıza Nur, *Tıbbiye Hayatından* (Istanbul, 1909).

M. Sabahaddine-A. Loutfoullah, *Appel général aux Ottomans* (n.p., [1901]).

———, *Lettre au Sultan Abdul-Hamid* (Angers, 1900).

———, *Umum Osmanlı Vatandaşlarımıza* [Cairo, 1901].

Sélim Wékil, *Concentration des volontés patriotiques* (Paris, [1901?]).

Şerafeddin Mağmumî, *Başlangıç* (Istanbul, 1889–90).

———, *Hakikat-ı Hal* (Paris, 1897).

———, *Kamus-i Tıbbî* (Cairo, 1910).

———, *Paris'den Yazdıklarım* (Cairo, 1911).

———, *Seyahat Hatıraları, Anadolu ve Suriye'de* (Cairo, 1909).

———, *Seyahat Hatıraları, Brüksel ve Londra'da* (Cairo, 1908).

———, *Seyahat Hatıraları, Fransa ve İsviçre'de* (Cairo, 1914).

Süleyman Nazif, *Bahriyelilere Mektub* [Paris, 1896?].

———, *Yıkılan Müessese* (Istanbul, 1927).

Şûra-yı Ümmet-Ali Kemal Da'vası (Istanbul, 1909).

Tezkere-i Ulema: Ulema-yı Arabın Şer'-i Mübin ve Ahbâr-ı Sahihadan İktiyasları ve Damad Mahmud Paşa'dan Sultan Abdülhamid Han-ı Sânî'ye Mektub (Cairo, 1900).

Tunalı Hilmi, *Ahali Hakimliği, Bir Şart, Bir Dilek* (Geneva, 1902).

———, *İkinci Hutbe: al-'ulamā warathatu al-anbiyā'* [Geneva, 1896].

———, *Makedonya: Mazi-Hâl-İstikbâl* (Cairo, 1898).

———, *al-ma'rūd amāma allāh wa al-nās* (Cairo, 1899).

———, *Murad* (Geneva, 1899).

———, *Onbirinci Hutbe: Türkiyalılık Osmanlılıkdır; Osmanlılık Türkiyalılıkdır* (Geneva, 1901).

———, *Onbirinci Hutbeye İlâve 1: Kongre-Cevabları-Cevabımız* (Cairo, 1901).

———, *Onbirinci Hutbeye İlâve 2: Kongre Nedir, Nasıl Olmalıdır?* (Alexandria, 1901).

———, *XI Houtbe (Discours)* (Geneva, 1901).

———, *Peşte'de Reşid Efendi İle* ([Geneva], 1899).

———, *Un Projet d'organisation de la souveraineté du peuple en Turquie* (Geneva, 1902).

Vatan Tehlikede! (Paris, 1895).
Vatanperverân Cemiyetine Mahsus Müderrisinden, *Birinci Vaaz* (Istanbul, 1897).
Youssouf Fehmi, *La Révolution Ottomane* (Paris, 1909).
——, *Tablettes révolutionnaires d'un Jeune Turc* (Paris, 1903).
——, *Troisième brochure de l'apostolat des chevaliers Positivistes: Considérations sur la Turquie vaincue* (Paris, 1913).
——, *Les Turcs de Paris: Espionnage et contre police* (Paris, 1908).
Yusuf Akçura, *Türk Yılı 1928* (Istanbul, 1928).

Unpublished Theses

J. Michael Hagopian, "Hyphenated Nationalism: The Spirit of the Revolutionary Movement in Asia Minor and the Caucasus, 1896–1910," Ph.D. diss., Harvard University (1942).
Berna Kazak, "Ömrüm: Ali Kemal'in Hatıratı," Senior Thesis, IUL, no. 7528 (1954).

Young Turk Journals

Anadolu (Cairo)
Balkan (Ruse)
Basiret'üs-Şark (Cairo)
Beberuhi (Geneva)
Cür'et (Geneva)
Darbe (Geneva)
Daoul (Rotterdam)
Dolab (Folkestone)
Emel (Cairo)
Enîn-i Mazlum (Cairo)
Ezan (Geneva)
Feryad (Nicosia)
Gencine-i Hayâl (Geneva)
Girid (Geneva)
Hak (Cairo)
Hakikat (Athens, Geneva)
Hakk-ı Sarih (Cairo)
Havatır (Cairo)
Hayâl (2) (London)
Hidmet (Geneva)
Hürriyet (London)
İctihad (Idjtihad-İçtihat) (Geneva, Cairo, Istanbul)
İnkılâb (Geneva)
İntikam (Geneva)
Islah (Ruse)
Islahat (The Piraeus)
İstikbâl (Naples, London)
İstikbâl (2) (Geneva)
İstirdat (Geneva)

İttihad Gazetesi (Cairo)
Kanun-i Esasî (Cairo)
Kokonoz (Nicosia)
Kürdistan (Cairo, Geneva)
Mizan (Cairo, Geneva, Istanbul)
Mechveret Supplément Français (Paris, Copenhagen)
Meşrutiyet (Geneva)
Meşveret (Paris, Geneva, Brussels)
Moniteur Ottoman (Paris)
Muvazene (Plovdiv, Varna)
Nasihat (Alexandria)
Osmanlı (Geneva, London, Folkestone, Cairo, Geneva)
Osmanli Deutsche Beilage (Geneva)
English Supplement to Osmanli (Geneva)
Osmanli Supplément Français (Geneva)
Osmanlı (2) (Cairo)
Rumeli (Plovdiv)
Sada-yı Millet (Bucharest)
Sancak (Cairo)
Şark ve Garb (Paris)
Seyf-i Hakikat (The Piraeus)
Şûra-yı Ümmet (Cairo, Paris, Istanbul)
Terakki (Paris)
Tokmak (Geneva)
Türk (Cairo)
Ümid (Cairo)
Vatan (1) (Athens)
Vatan (Geneva)
Zaman (Nicosia)

Other Newspapers and Journals*

*Abhandlungen der Philosophisch-Philologischen Klasse der Königlich
Bayerischen Akademie der Wissenschaften*
L'Acacia
L'Agance Libre
'Ακρόπολις
Albania
Annales de l'École Libre des Sciences Politiques
Armenia
L'Arménie
Âsâr-ı Perâkende
Asker
L'Aurore
al-Ayyām (New York)
The Balkan Review
Basler Nachrichten

* In cases where confusion is likely due to a common name or tangentiality, I have provided the place of publishing in parentheses.

Bedreka-i Selâmet
Berliner Lokal Anzeiger
Berliner Tageblatt
Beyan'ül-hak
Bijvoegsel van de Java-Bode
Blackwood's Edinburgh Magazine
Der Bund (Bern)
El Centinela del Estrecho de Gibraltar
Ceride-i Mahakim-i Adliye
Comptes Rendus de l'Académie des Sciences (Paris)
The Contemporary Review
Correspondance Oriental (Gibraltar)
Il Corriere della Sera
Il Corriere di Catania
Il Corriere di Napoli
The Cosmopolis
Le Courrier de France
Le Courrier Européen (Paris)
The Crescent
Dağarcık
Daily Chronicle
Daily Graphic
Daily Mail
Daily News
Daily Telegraph
Dimanches Littéraires
Ḍiyā'al-Khāfiqaīn
Droshak
Eastern Daily Press (Norwich)
L'Eclair
Ἑλληνισμός
Emniyet
Epoea
L'Européen
L'Evénement
Le Figaro
The Fortnightly Review
Frankfurter Zeitung
Gayret (1) (Istanbul)
Gayret (2) (Plovdiv)
La Gazette de Lausanne
Le Genevois
Le Grand Moniteur Universel
Güneş
Hafta
Hamburger Nachrichten
Hayâl (1)
Hazine-i Fünûn
Historische Zeitschrift
De Hollandsche Revue

L'Humanité Nouvelle
Hürriyet (1) (London)
İbret
İkdam
İleri
The Imperial and Asiatic Review
L'Indépendence Belge
L'Intransigeant
İstikbâl (3) (Canea)
L'Italie
La Jeune Turquie (Paris)
Le Journal
Le Journal d'Abou Nadarra
Le Journal des Débats
Journal de Genève
Journal Officiel
Juhayna
La Justice
Kashf al-Niqāb (Paris)
Laimtari i Shcypenies (Rome)
Levant Herald
The Liberal Magazine
La Libre Parole
Living Age
al-Liwā'
The Longman's Magazine
L'Union Républicaine du Havre
Maarif
Malûmat
al-Manār
al-Mashriq
Mècheroutiette (Paris)
Mecmua-yı Ebüzziya
Mecmua-yı Fünûn
Menschheitsziele
Mir'at-ı Álem
Mırsad
al-Moayyad édition Français
Monatschrift der christliche Orient
Le Moniteur Oriental
Moniteur de Rome
Le Moniteur Ottoman
Morgenbladet (Stockholm)
The Morning Advertiser
Morning Post
Muhibban
Müncher Allgemeine Zeitung
al-Muqaṭṭam
Musavver Cihan
La Nationale Suisse

Nationale Zeitung
The Near East
De Nederlander
Neue Freie Presse
Neue Preussische Zeitung
Die Neue Zeit
Neue Zürcher Zeitung
New York Herald (Paris—European Edition)
New York Times
Het Nieuws van den Haag
The Nineteenth Century
The North American Review
La Nouvelle Revue
Ogledalo
Opinione
L'Orient (Paris)
La Paix
The Pall Mall Gazette
La Patrie
Pester Lloyd
Le Petit Provençal
La Petite République
Peyâm-ı Sabah
The Positivist Review
Die Post
The Prespyterian Quarterly and Princeton Review
Pro Arménia
Le Progrès
The Progressive Review
Qānūn (London)
La Rassegna Nationale
La Réforme
Resimli Gazete
The Review of the Week
Revue Bleue
La Revue de France
La Revue de L'Islam
La Revue de Paris
La Revue des Deux Mondes
Revue du Monde Musulman
La Revue Occidentale
La Revue Philosophique
La Revue Positiviste Internationale
La Revue Scientifique
Sabah
Sada (Paris)
Schweizer Handels-Kurier
Sebil'ür Reşad
Il Secolo
Şehbâl

Serbestî
Servet-i Fünûn
Shqipetari (Bucharest)
Σκρίπ
Le Soleil
Le Soleil du Midi
St. Petersburger Herald
The Standard
La Suisse
El-Sultan el-Gazi Abdülhamid Han-ı Sânî (Cairo)
Takvim-i Vekayi'
Tan
Tanin
Tasavvuf
Le Temps
Les Temps Nouveuax
Tercüman-ı Ahvâl-i Zaman (Bağçesaray-Crimea)
Tercüman-ı Hakikat
Tevhid-i Efkâr
The Times
Tribune de Genève
Türk Yurdu
Turkiyyā al-fatāt
La Turquie Contemporaine
La Turquie Libre
Üsküb
Vakit (1)
Vakit
Vekayi'-i Tıbbiye
Volkan
Vossische Zeitung
Die Welt des Islams
Wiener politische Korrespondenz
The World's Work
Yeni Gazete
Yeni Tasvir-i Efkâr
Le Yildiz
Yolların Sesi
Zeitschrift für Psychiatrie

Index